_____

PRESENTED TO

_____

FROM

_____

DATE

THE FAMILY PRAYER BIBLE

ACKNOWLEDGMENTS

A book is never the project of a single author. The influence of godly parents, teachers, and friends, influence the thinking of the author, and hence the book. I want to give credit to all those who have contributed to *The Family Prayer Bible*. Special thanks to Linda Elliott, my editorial assistant who supervised this project from conception to completion and her husband Roger Elliott for his contribution to the manuscript.

Also special thanks to Renee Grooms, my executive assistant, who typed many of these stories, and recognition is given to Debbie Barber and Mary Davis who not only edited, but they "kidsized" the stories.

Sometimes my academic orientation keeps me placing the cookies on the lower shelf. Thanks for the use of the images from James (Jim) Padgett and Sweet Publishing, http://sweetpublishing.com, Hurst, Texas, and Gospel Light Publications, Ventura, California, for the use of the images. Also, appreciation is extended to Sherman Smith and his team from Heritage Builders Publishing, Clovis, California, for all the guidance of this project and the successful delivery of the final printed copy.

CONTENTS

GETTING INTO THE FAMILY PRAYER BIBLE

The Bible was written to illuminate your mind with truth from God. I have written *The Family Prayer Bible* into stories from the Bible for the whole family to read together; but on some occasions you may choose to read it by yourself.

The Family Prayer Bible begins with 12 stories from the Old Testament to give you a background of the life and ministry of Jesus Christ. Then there is a transition from the Old Testament to the New Testament. There you will read stories about events before Jesus was born. Next you will trace the life of Jesus from His birth . . . to His death . . . to the resurrection.

The life of Jesus is told in four books, called the four Gospels: Matthew, Mark, Luke and John. In *The Family Prayer Bible* we follow Jesus' life chronologically, from birth to resurrection choosing the story in the gospel that best tells about Jesus.

Then our story line will follow the establishment of the church in the Book of Acts. We will follow the triumphant growth of the church that fulfills Jesus' last command, i.e., the Great Commission. "Go into all the world and preach the Good News to everyone" (Mark 16:15). Then we will survey the letters (called Epistles or Books) written by the Apostle Paul and others. We end up where the New Testament ends, showing pictures of heaven and where we will spend eternity with God.

A Time to Worship

The Family Prayer Bible includes 52 stories from the book of Psalms, telling how each Psalm was written and something about its message. One Psalm is included every seven days to remind you to praise and worship God. Just like God planned one day—a Sunday—in each week for us to attend church and worship Him, *The Family Prayer Bible* will focus on worship each week.

Family Event

The story for each day ends with four sections for family participation. The first one is *Talk About the Story*. This has questions for parents to guide their youngest to re-tell the story. Having children re-tell the story gets the meaning into their hearts. The message doesn't really settle into their hearts until they tell it in their own words.

Next, there is the verse of the day in the section titled *Scripture*. The application of the story is found in this key verse. It is good to repeat the verse as a group, or let each child repeat it. Then memorize and meditate on its meaning.

The third is *Family Time* where each person can talk about the story and apply the meaning to his/her everyday living. Obviously a younger child will see the simple meaning of that day's story, while the older child will interact at their level of insight.

The fourth includes the essence of a *Prayer for the Day*. This prayer can be prayed by children as they read the words, or the meaning can be summarized by those who understand what that day's story meant to their lives.

549 Principles of Prayer

There is an added bonus for the older reader. There is a superscript or footnote number added at the end of some sentences in the story. That number refers to the back section of *The Family Prayer Bible Coloring Book Supplement Edition* called the *549 Principles of Prayer*.

The *549 Principles of Prayer* in the back of the coloring book supplement explain many conceivable ways to pray. From the Yielding Prayer, to Worship Prayer, to Intercession Prayer, to the Affliction Prayer: these principles hold truths that will transform your prayer life. For example, the number (278) Life's Plan-Prayer (Rom. 12:1), means we receive strength when we know God's plan for our life and we commit ourselves to doing God's personal will. We pray for a full life of usefulness, and then we pray that our children may carry out God's plan for their life (Gen. 25:1-11, 28:12-15; Rom. 12:1). (See Laziness-Corrective Prayer, Life-Defining Prayer).

The *549 Principles of Prayer* in the back of the coloring book supplement also become a resource to teach you more about prayer. If you are in need of specific guidance this tool will help you find many different ways to pray. From the Escaping-Danger Prayer, to Strategy Praying, to Wisdom-Directed Prayer, there is prayer for every situation.

Stretching Your Faith

The stories in *The Family Prayer Bible* include more Bible content than most Bible storybooks for children. Also, it contains many things about the Bible not included in other books for children. There is material for parents yet told in story form for children.

You will find stories telling how each New Testament book was written.

www.thefamilyprayerbible.com

It would be a good exercise for the children to learn the books of the New Testament in order. Perhaps parent and child can repeat them together.

Also, there is background for the geographical, cultural and historical stories that are not found in most other story books. We believe children are smarter today because of television and other influences in their world. So they can grasp more information and get deeper insight into the Bible stories. You—the parent—can guide them into a firm understanding of the Bible.

Together

The purpose of *The Family Prayer Bible* is to bring your family closer together. And what place is closer than when a child and parent both bow before God to read His Word together and pray together. You may never be closer to your child than when you pray to the heavenly Father. Also your child may never feel closer to you than when he/she prays to God in your presence.

The Family Prayer Bible is an adventure waiting for you and your family. May you all enjoy God's Word, learn more than you have ever known, and draw closer to God. Use *The Family Prayer Bible* to reach out and touch God, but more importantly let God touch you.

Written from my home
On top of Liberty Mountain

Elmer Towns
2016

CHAPTER 1

WHAT THE OLD TESTAMENT IS ALL ABOUT

How We Got the Bible

The Bible is a collection of sixty-six books that are recognized as divinely inspired by the Christian church. They are divided into the Old Testament (39 books) and the New Testament (27 books). Collectively these books included law, history, poetry, wisdom, prophecy, narratives, biographies, personal letters, and apocalyptic visions. They introduce us to some of the most amazing people who have ever lived: shepherds, farmers, patriarchs, kings, queens, prophets, priests, evangelists, disciples, teachers, and most of all—the most unique person who ever lived—Jesus of Nazareth.

How We Got the Old Testament

God revealed his Word to ancient Israel over a thousand-year period (ca. 1400–400 B.C.), and then Scribes copied the biblical scrolls and manuscripts for more than a millennium after that. The process by which the Old Testament books came to be recognized as the Word of God, and the history of how these books were preserved and handed down through the generations enhances our confidence in the credibility of the Old Testament as inspired Scripture (2 Tim 3:16).

GOD CREATED EVERYTHING

Scripture: Genesis 1-2:13
Place: The Earth
Time: At the beginning of the world

In the beginning God created the heavens and the earth out of nothing.[93]
    On the first day, God said, "Let there be light," and light suddenly appeared.[450] God called the light day, and the darkness He called night.[500] The light and the dark formed the first day.[364]
    On the second day, God said, "Let there be air in the sky;[311] and He separated the sky to make heaven, then He made water on the earth.[464] This happened on the second day.
    On the third day, God said, "Let all the waters on the earth be gathered together into oceans and let land be dry.[364] God created rivers to carry water to the

seas. And it happened. God called the dry land earth, and God called the waters seas and oceans. And God said, "It was good."

God said, "Let the earth grow grass, bushes, fruit trees, and let each tree produce fruit with seeds that will feed people. And let there be seed in the fruit trees to grow more trees."[170] When it was done, God said, "It was good."[388]

On the fourth day, God said, "Let there be lights in the heaven which are called stars at night. Let them divide the day from the night, then people will be able to tell time by days and years. God made two great lights: the sun to give light in the day, and the moon He made to guide the night.[283] God saw it was good. That was done on the fourth day.

On the fifth day, God said, "Let the waters have a lot of fish and other sea creatures and let the skies have a lot of birds."[170]

God created big fish as well as the small ones to swim in the waters. He also created birds to fly in the sky. He was pleased and told them to reproduce after their kind.[388] That was the fifth day.

On the sixth day, God created animals, including cattle, wild animals and reptiles.[170] He made each one after its kind. When God saw the animals, He said, "It was good."[364]

Then God said, "Let Us make a man who is like Us, and let him control the fish in the oceans, the birds in the sky, and the cattle, beasts, and every reptile on the earth.[43] So God created man like Himself. Then God created a woman. God was pleased with the man and the woman,[46] so He blessed them and said, "Be fruitful and multiply and fill the earth."[179]

On the seventh day God completed His creation of heavens and the earth.[93] He set aside the seventh day for people to rest from their work, to get their strength back, and to enjoy life and the creation He had made. But most of all, God wanted people to worship Him on that day.[541]

Talk About the Story: What did God create on each day? What did God think about the different things He made? What was the last thing God created? What is the purpose of the last day of Creation?

Scripture: "In the beginning God created the heavens and the earth." Genesis 1:1

Family Time: Why do you think God created all things? How can we learn about God through His creation? God has a big plan for His creation; how can I fit into His plan?

Prayer: Father, thank You for the world, the sun and stars that reflect Your power and beauty. Thank You for food to eat, for life on earth, and for the privilege of worshiping You. Amen.

THE BEGINNING OF PEOPLE

Scripture: Genesis 2
Place: The Garden of Eden
Time: At the beginning of the world

God created the earth, sun, moon and stars in six days.[93] He also created all life, including animals, birds, and everything that swims in the sea. Every living thing was created male and female.

All three person of the Godhead were involved in creation. The Father was the architect planning it all. The Son was the Creator-foreman, directing the task (John 1:3) and the Holy Spirit was the breath of God breathing life into every atom and molecule. God is one God in three persons, equally creating everything in the universe.

In God's creation plan, He saved the best for last! As the angels watched in amazement, God knelt on the earth and shaped a man—Adam—from the red clay. The name Adam means red man. God breathed into the nostrils of the man. "Why," one of the angels asked. God hadn't breathed into the animals that way. "What was God doing to the red-clay man?"

God made a man like Himself.[392] The rough red clay turned to skin. The angels couldn't see inside the man, but dirt turned into blood vessels, muscles, and bones. God created a man who would eat to grow and became strong, just as each animal must do.

www.thefamilyprayerbible.com

Slowly the man sat up. He could see the world about him. He stretched and breathed in fresh air. His new emotions enjoyed what he felt. He smelled the early morning grass and with his fingers picked a flower. Adam was perfect in every way. He was made according to God's divine-plan.

The man could understand the things he saw. He could remember the things he did a few minutes ago. He could change his actions accordingly to what he remembered. Adam was created with a mind and was able to learn and grow.

God gave the man a task, "You are placed in this Garden of Eden here between the Euphrates and Tigris Rivers. I want you to till this garden for Me."[179] God said that the whole earth was created for Adam. He and the children born after him were to take care of the earth, and it would take care of them.[47]

God had another task. Adam was to name all the living creatures God had created. That was a giant task but God made it easy for Adam. The name Adam gave each animal was the name it was supposed to have. The mind of Adam was big enough to call each by their name.

As Adam was giving names to each, he noticed that there was always a male and female. For every "poppa" animal, there was a "mama." They were to produce baby animals just like them.

In God's perfection, He created a perfect universe that was self-perpetuating and self-supporting and self-directing. Only a perfect God could do that.

But Adam didn't yet have someone else like him. God said, "It is not good for man to be alone." God put Adam into a deep sleep and took a rib out of his side and closed up the flesh. Then God made a woman out of the rib.[343] When Adam woke up, God brought the woman to him. Adam said, "You are made of the same bone and flesh. She shall be called woman because she was taken out of man."[93]

Talk About the Story: How did God make people? What are some ways people are different from the other things God created? What did God give Adam responsibility for?

Scripture: "I will praise You, for I am fearfully and wonderfully made; marvelous are Your works, and that my soul knows very well." Psalm 139:14

Family Time: What are some wonderful things about each person in our family? What marvelous things might God do in and through our family?

Prayer: Father, we praise You for the way You made each one of us. We know that You are always doing good and amazing things. Please help us to live for You. Please use us for some of the good things You are doing in the world today. Amen.

THE BEGINNING OF SIN

Scripture: Genesis 2:16–17; 31–24
Place: Garden of Eden
Time: At the beginning of the world

The Garden of Eden was full of trees and plants growing good food. In the center of the garden, God added a special tree. God told Adam "You can eat fruit from every tree[177] but do not eat the fruit of the Tree of Knowledge of Good and Evil in the center of the garden. The day you eat it, you will surely die."[108]

Now the serpent was the most cunning of all the animals. The serpent said to Eve, "Is it true that God said you should not eat from every tree in the garden?"

Eve answered, "We can eat fruit from any tree in the garden but the fruit of the tree in the center of the garden we can't eat it, not even touch it, lest we die."[352] Eve added the part about touching; God hadn't said that.

The serpent then lied to Eve, "You shall not surely die! God knows that the day you eat it you will become like God, knowing good and evil."[114]

Eve picked a piece of fruit. She looked at it. It was pleasant to the eyes. It also had an appetizing aroma and it felt good in her hand. "Eating this will make us wise!" she said. She took a bite. Then she handed it to Adam, who was standing next to her. Adam also ate it.

Instantly, they knew they were naked, and they felt ashamed! It was a feeling they had not previously felt. Quickly they made clothing out of large fig leaves to cover their bodies.[217]

That evening they heard the Lord coming to talk with them in the cool of the day. Adam and Eve ran from God and hid among the trees.[479] They knew they

had disobeyed Him.

"Where are you?" God called to them. God knows everything. He knew where they were! God was calling to tell them they were "lost" from Him.

"I heard your voice," Adam answered, "and I was afraid because I was naked."

God answered, "Who told you that you were naked? Have you eaten the fruit of the tree I told you not to eat?"[522]

Adam tried to excuse himself, "The woman You created gave me the fruit, and I ate it."[548]

The Lord said to the woman, "What have you done?"

Eve answered, "The serpent tricked me, and I ate it."[402]

Then God turned to the serpent, "You are cursed for your part; you will slither on your belly for the rest of your life."[341] God knew Satan was behind all of this so He declared, "There will be war between you and the woman's offspring for the rest of your life. You will wound the Seed of the woman, but He will crush your head."[263]

This is the first reference in the Bible to the coming of Jesus Christ, the Son of God. Even though Adam and Eve sinned and would die, God had a plan from the beginning to save His people!

Then God turned to Eve; you will have sorrow in your life. Having children will be painful. And your relationship with your husband will be difficult.[9] He will be the head of the family.

Then God turned to Adam, "Because you listened to your wife and ate the fruit that I told you not to eat, the ground will grow weeds and thorns. You will work hard planting and harvesting.[440] You will sweat to make a living until you are buried in the ground from which you were made.[452]

Adam and Eve had to leave the beautiful Garden of Eden. Life became difficult for them because of their sin.

Talk About the Story: Why did Adam and Eve choose to disobey God? What happened as a result?

Scripture: "For the wages of sin is death, but the gift of God is eternal life in Christ Jesus our Lord." Romans 6:23

Family Time: What was the good news in the middle of the curse on the serpent? How has Jesus destroyed the deception and sin that happened in the Garden of Eden? What does this good news mean for us today?

Prayer: Father, thank You for your plan for salvation from the beginning of time in the Garden of Eden. Thank You that You offer us forgiveness and life, even though we have sinned against You. Amen.

THE BEGINNING OF MURDER

Scripture: Genesis 4
Place: Outside the Garden of Eden
Time: The beginning of the human race

God had sent Adam and Eve out of the Garden of Eden. He put an angel there to keep them out. So they had to make a life in a new different world.[116]

It wasn't long before Eve gave birth to a baby boy. Cain was that first baby boy. He crawled, then walked and soon was running. Like all parents, Adam and Eve had to teach Cain to be honest, to obey and do his chores.[327]

Cain loved to grow vegetables, and he was very good at it![43] Cain surrounded his garden with fruit trees. His garden became the thing he loved most in life.

A second son was born named Abel. Abel was different; he loved animals and loved to feed and take care of them.

As time passed, Adam and Eve had other children. As the children grew up, they formed new families. (Sisters and brothers could marry in the beginning because the genetic structure was perfect before Adam and Eve sinned. Now, brothers and sisters don't have perfect genes, so they don't marry. It creates birth defects.)

Abel wanted to worship God. He loved God and he brought the sacrifice of

his best lamb to God. Rabbinical tradition says God accepted Abel's sacrifice[22] when fire fell from heaven to consume his offering. Cain also wanted to worship God, but he loved his garden. So he brought vegetables to God. But God did not accept Cain's vegetables—this was not the way God had said to worship Him.

Cain got angry at God! What he offered to God was what HE wanted to give, not what God said to give!

God said to Cain, "Why are you so angry? If you'd obeyed Me, you would be happy now!"[58]

Then God told him, "Watch out. Sin is waiting to drag you down." But Cain didn't listen.

Cain and Abel went for a walk. While they walked Abel said, "You must come to God with a lamb. It is His way to forgive our sins."

"No," Cain yelled at his brother, "my vegetables are the best I have! If God won't accept them, then I won't give him ANYTHING!"[114]

They argued, then fought; but at the end, Cain killed his brother.[79] He buried his brother's body.

But soon, God came. He asked Cain, "Where is your brother Abel?"

Cain answered, "I don't know. Do I have to take of my brother, too?!"

God answered, "What have you done? your brother's blood cries to me from the ground! Now you will always wander on the face of the earth."[108] The Lord put a mark on Cain so that no one would kill him.[111]

Cain left. He didn't talk to God again. He built a city called Enoch, the name of his son.[118] His children loved to do wrong. They were stubborn like their father.

The Lord saw the evil in Cain's family growing. God could see that their thoughts and attitudes were getting worse and worse. It was a sad, sad family.[440]

Talk About the Story: What did Cain love best? Why did God accept Abel's sacrifice and not Cain's? Why was Cain angry? What did he do? Could he hide from God?

Scripture: "Behold, I set before you today a blessing and a curse: the blessing, if you obey the commandments of the Lord your God which I command you to-day; and the curse, if you do not obey the commandments of the Lord your God." Deuteronomy 11:26–27

Family Time: What is something that no one in your family likes to do? What is something you are glad to do? When it's hard to obey God, what can we do?

Prayer: Father, none of us likes to obey sometimes. We are all sinners. Thank You for loving us and helping us to obey You. In Jesus' name, Amen.

THE FLOOD DESTROYED

Scripture: Genesis 6-9
Place: The Euphrates River Valley
Time: Several generations after creation of people

After Cain killed Abel,[79] Adam and Eve had another son, Seth. He and his children called on the name of the Lord. There was a son named Enoch who walked so close to God that he went walking with God one day, but didn't come back. God took him to heaven.

The ungodly line of Cain began to intermarry with the children of Seth. Fewer people called on God. Their wickedness grew and grew.

God saw the wickedness of people throughout the known world. God said, "I will destroy all mankind from the face of the earth . . . all people and all animals, and all living things" (Genesis 6:7, *ELT*).[267]

But Noah found favor in God's face.[198] God told Noah about the coming flood to destroy all living things.[267] God commanded, "Build a large boat and cover it with tar. It will be 450 feet long, 75 feet wide, and 50 feet high. Put a window on the top and build three stories in the boat for the animals that will be saved. Bring two animals from every living family, male and female. Take enough food for a year."[388]

www.thefamilyprayerbible.com

Noah and his three sons began building the boat. All the while he preached to everyone telling of the coming judgment of God on the earth with water. It took 120 years to build the boat, all the while the evil people of the world mocked Noah.

Finally the boat was finished. God told Noah, "Come into the boat because I have seen that you and your family walk righteously before Me." God called the animals, and they came two by two, male and female. They were seven days on the boat before they heard the first sound of rain. Then it rained for 40 days and 40 nights. Water also came up from the ground—more water than anyone had ever seen.

Soon the waters covered all the trees, hills and eventually the tallest mountain peaks. Every living thing on the earth died, including people, animals—everything that lived.[549]

After 40 days it stopped raining, and the waters slowly receded. The boat settled on Mount Ararat in Turkey, the headwaters for the Euphrates River.

After 10 months when the earth was dried, God told Noah to leave the ark and take the animals with him.[413] Noah built an altar and sacrificed a burnt offering to the Lord. That pleased the Lord who said, "I will never again destroy the earth with a flood.[191] From now on there will be seasons, spring and harvest, cold and heat, summer and winter, and day and night will not cease."[413]

God sent Noah and his sons into all the world, "Be fruitful, multiply, and fill the earth."[179]

Talk About the Story: Why did God send the flood? Who was saved? Why do you think Noah found favor with God?

Scripture: "But without faith it is impossible to please Him, for he who comes to God must believe that He is, and that He is a rewarder of those who diligently seek Him." Hebrew 11:6

Family Time: Enoch walked with God, and Noah found favor with God. What are some ways we can walk with God today? What does Hebrew 11:6 tell us about pleasing God?

Prayer: Father, we want to please You and walk with You every day. Please help us to have faith in You and to talk with You and learn from Your Word more and more. Amen.

THE TOWER OF BABEL

Scripture: Genesis 11
Place: Euphrates River Valley
Time: A few generations after the flood

After Cain and his family, things got worse and worse on Earth. Finally, God sent a flood to clean the earth of the evil. After the flood, God started again.

Noah, who had built the ark, had sons named Shem, Ham, and Japheth. Everyone now on Earth came from these three men and their wives! At that time everyone spoke the same language and lived near the Euphrates River.

Nimrod, a grandson of Ham, became the natural leader of the people. He was a great hunter. He built many cities, and people began to move into them.

In the middle of one city, the people decided to build an extremely tall tower, called a ziggurat (like a tall pyramid). They wanted to make themselves famous! "Soon, people will come from all over to see this great tower. It will reach to heaven! WE can do this. WE are important!"[424]

The Lord came down to see what these people were doing.

He said, "These people have one language. They think they can do anything they set their minds to do."

These people didn't recognize God, nor worship Him. They were all about themselves and what THEY would do!

The Lord said, "We're going to confuse their language so they can't understand one another."[163]

And so God did! Suddenly, people who were working together couldn't understand each other.

When one worker said, "Hand me a brick," the man beside him heard something entirely different. Perhaps he heard, "You smell like sour milk," or "You walk funny."

There was total confusion! No one could figure out what the other people wanted! And soon, their city was called Babel because the people could only babble to one another.

But more than just changing language, God was creating different cultures of the world. Now, the one language of the world was gone.

The Bible tells how Japheth took his family and headed north into what is called today Europe and Russia. Ham took his family south toward Africa. Shem settled in the area known today as the Middle East and Persia, India, and Asia. Thus, each culture began and grew in its own way.[160] Each person in a culture thought, felt and decided differently from people in other cultures.

God loved each and every one because they were made in His image, and because He created each culture. Every culture, every language, is important to God. As the song says, "Jesus loves the little children of the world."

Talk About the Story: Why did the people of Babel want to build a tower? How many languages were there? What did God do? What culture do you live in?

Scripture: "And He has made from one blood every nation of men to dwell on all the face of the earth, and has determined their preappointed times and the boundaries of their dwellings." Acts 17:26

Family Time: Who is the oldest family member you know? What places did that person live? Where do you now live? Tell stories of how God has taken care of your family.

Prayer: Lord, please help us to love others, no matter what culture they come from. We want to show Your love to every person You made. In Jesus' name, Amen.

PSALM 1

THE ROAD YOU CHOOSE, DETERMINES WHO YOU BECOME

David left his throne to walk northward out of his palace toward the temple. A court servant ran to remind the King he had more people to see that day. David ignored him. Another servant reminded David a big banquet was waiting for him, "Your favorite spicy meat is cooked just the way you desire." Still David continued walking toward the Temple and worshiping God.

David thought about the different things attracting him in life, but he would not be sidetracked. David continued to walk toward the Temple. He wanted to be there for the 4:00 pm prayers.

The book of Psalms beginning with the word "Blessed." It can be translated "Happy." Because David was a man after God's heart, he enjoyed a happy life. He put God first. What a person seeks determines who he becomes in life. Because David enjoyed worshiping the Lord, he was blessed by God.

www.thefamilyprayerbible.com

As he walked, David began to sing a Psalm.

> *"Happy is the person who does not*
> *Listen to the bad advice of rebels against God,*
> *Spend his time doing evil with evil people,*[389]
> *Or join in with the sin of sinners.*
> *But his happiness is in doing what God teaches,*
> *He meditates on Scripture all day and night."*[302]

David was doing what he wanted to do. He had learned that his decision to put God first had led to the throne. Because David was a man after God's own heart, God had chosen him as a young 16-year old boy to be king. David was now older and he also knew his decision to continually worship God, would keep him on the throne. His prayers.

> *"Lord, I want to be like a tree*
> *Planted by living waters.*
> *I want to bear fruit in season*
> *And my leaves keep growing."*[386]

But there was also a negative side to following God. There were scoffers and the ungodly that rebelled against God. God had promised to punish them.

> *"The ungodly are like died husks*
> *That the wind blows away.*
> *They shall be condemned in judgment*
> *And thrown out of the presence of God.*
> *The Lord protects the life of the godly*
> *But the ungodly shall perish."*[410]

David had a new Psalm to sing in God's presence that day.

Talk About the Psalm: What did you learn about the psalm writer in this story? What did you learn about God?

Psalm 1: Read this week's psalm in your Bible together. Choose a verse to read aloud as a prayer.

Prayer: Thank You, God, for the psalm prayers in the Bible. Thank You for teaching us about You and about how to pray. In Jesus' name, Amen.

ABRAHAM, ISAAC, JACOB, JOSEPH

Scripture: Genesis
Place: Ur, Haran, Canaan
Time: 1920 BC–1706 BC

A man called Abram lived in Ur of the Chaldees. God talked to Abram. God said, "Leave your country and your relatives. Take your wife Sarai and go. I will show you a land I will give to you and your children."[58]

Then God made a covenant-promise.[92] He said, "I will make a great nation from you. I will bless you and make you famous.[62] I'll bless those who bless you and curse those who curse you. Everyone on Earth will be blessed because of you!"[387] God also promised to give Abram the land of Canaan.

So Abram obeyed God and a family began. This family became the Hebrews or Jews. Through Abraham, every family on earth has been blessed—because through him came the people whose story is told in the Old Testament, the people of Israel. And from that family, came Jesus Christ, the Savior of the world![539]

Abraham lived in tents. He waited for the place God had for him, and said he was a nomad on Earth.

www.thefamilyprayerbible.com

Abraham is remembered because of his faith. Even in hard times, Abraham trusted God and his faith grew.[151] Although God had promised him a great family, he and Sarai (later Sarah) had no children![459] But Abraham kept on believing. When Sarah was 90 years old, Isaac was finally born![92]

Isaac grew up living in tents. God told Isaac to believe the covenant promise God gave to Abraham, "I will cause your descendants to become as numerous as the stars of the sky, and I will give them all these lands. And through your descendants all the nations of the earth will be blessed" (Genesis 26:4, *NLT*).[47]

Isaac's wife Rebekah gave birth to twins. They called the first Esau. The second was named Jacob ("trickster"). Jacob tricked Esau out of his birthright, and later tricked his father Isaac so he could get Esau's family blessing, too.[521] Esau was ANGRY! So Jacob ran off for 20 years, and tricked his Uncle Laban, too. But finally, God told Jacob it was time to return to Canaan.

On that trip, Jacob wrestled with God all night. God blessed Jacob there, and gave him a new name, "Israel," which means "Prince with God."

Jacob had twelve sons; Joseph was his favorite. The 10 older brothers were jealous and planned to kill Joseph, but instead they sold him as a slave to traders headed for Egypt.

Like Abraham, Joseph trusted God. God gave him such favor that finally the pharaoh himself made Joseph the second ruler of Egypt! Pharaoh asked Joseph to save food, for God had sent a dream to show that a famine was coming. Joseph's work saved many lives, including the lives of his brothers! They came to Egypt for food, but didn't recognize Joseph. Finally, Joseph told his brothers who he was. He said, "You meant this for evil, but God meant it for good!"

All of Joseph's family moved to Egypt and lived there for almost 400 years. Over time, the family grew so LARGE that a new king decided to make them slaves in Egypt. They helped build the pyramids. But God never forgot them. He always took care of them!

Talk About the Story: What is Abraham remembered for? Who was his son? What were the names of the twins? Jacob had many sons. Which one saved his family's lives?

Scripture: "I will sing of the mercies of the Lord forever; with my mouth will I make known Your faithfulness to all generations." Psalm 89:1

Family Time: What do you know about your family history? Of how many generations does your family have records? What is a way God has been faithful to your family?

Prayer: Lord, we see how You have been faithful and kind through many generations. You keep Your promises. You are faithful—and we are thankful! Amen.

MOSES DEFINES A NATION

Scripture: Exodus - Deuteronomy
Place: Egypt and Sinai Peninsula
Time: Circa 1445 BC

The Egyptians tried to get rid of the Jews, but they couldn't. An order came from the king's palace, "Kill all the boy babies born to the Jews."

But that didn't stop them. Jochabed and her husband gave birth to a boy and hid him for three months. When the baby's crying attracted attention, the mother made a basket-boat and waterproofed it with some tar. The basket was set afloat among reeds where Pharaoh's daughter would come to bath.

She saw the basket and sent a servant to fetch it. When the lid was opened, the crying baby captured her heart. She sent for Jochabed to nurse the baby for her with the promise, "I'll pay you a mother's wages."

The princess named the baby Moses, the name means to "draw up," a picture of her drawing Moses from the river. She adopted Moses and raised him in the palace, "Moses mastered the education as Pharaoh's son, and was extraordinarily brilliant—with words and leadership ability" (Acts 7:22, *ELT*).[364]

Later, God called Moses to deliver Israel from slavery in Egypt. God led him to perform 10 miracle-signs. Each amazing miracle demonstrated that the one

www.thefamilyprayerbible.com

true God was far superior to the false gods the Egyptians worshiped.[377]

Finally, the Egyptian pharaoh told Moses to take the Israelites and go. They left quickly!

But later, Pharaoh changed his mind. He sent his soldiers and chariots to attack them at the Red Sea. It looked like Moses and the Israelites were trapped! There were mountains on each side and Pharaoh with 600 chariots and his army was ready to attack from the rear. Moses encouraged the people, "Don't be afraid, stand fast and watch how God will deliver you" (Exodus 14:13, *ELT*).[57]

And God DID deliver them! He made a dry path through the Red Sea! Moses continued to lead the people to Mount Sinai. There, God gave Moses the 10 Commandments. These commandments, or laws, became the foundation of the Jewish civilization, as well as many nations founded on Christian principles.

Many amazing things happened as Moses led the people. God miraculously provided food and water in the wilderness, God led the people to build a tabernacle and learn to worship Him, God even allowed Moses to see part of Himself!

Moses was a great leader and an intelligent person. He wrote the first five books of the Old Testament so that people could know God and follow His ways. Moses not only delivered Israel from slavery, but he also established the foundation of the nation.

Moses died on the top of Mount Nebo overlooking the land God had promised to the Israelites. He was 120 years old and didn't get to enter it; he only saw what God has promised.

Talk About the Story: How did God protect Moses as a baby? What did God use Moses to do when he grew up?

Scripture: "For I know the plans I have for you, declares the LORD, plans for welfare and not for evil, to give you a future and a hope." Jeremiah 29:11 *ESV*

Family Time: God knew Moses from birth, and He knows you, too! What do you think God has planned for your family? What are some ways you can serve Him like Moses did?

Prayer: Father, thank You that You know us and love us. Thank You for wanting to use us to do good things. Help us to live for You. Amen.

DATE ___/___

JOSHUA CONQUERED THE PROMISED LAND

Scripture: Book of Joshua
Place: Promised Land
Time: Circa 1380 BC ff

Moses led Israel as they traveled to the Promised Land. When they got near, 12 spies were sent out to survey the land. They said it was a land filled with milk and honey (Numbers 13:27),[179] but they also had bad news, "The people are fierce; their cities have high thick walls. There were giant warriors . . . but we are grasshoppers" (Numbers 13:31-33, *ELT*).[504]

The people were filled with fear. They refused to trust God to lead them into the Promised Land.

So God promised they would not enter the land. They would have to wander for 40 years in the wilderness until they all those who refused to trust God had died. Even Moses would die!

When the 40 years were up God told Joshua—Moses' second in command—"Moses My servant is dead. Now therefore, arise, go over this Jordan, you and all this people, to the land which I am giving to them" (Joshua 1:2, *NKJV*).[99]

The large city of Jericho was their first obstacle. God told Joshua exactly

www.thefamilyprayerbible.com

what to do. The priests and soldiers walked around the city once each day for six days. On the seventh day they circled the city seven times, then blew their trumpets loudly and all the people shouted. The walls fell down and the soldiers charged, conquering the city.

Joshua led the soldiers to many victories as they obeyed God's instructions. Once, when people from the city of Gibeon made an ill-choice peace pact with Joshua, five other city-nations attacked the Gibeonites. Joshua's soldiers marched all night to deliver the city. As night approached, Israel was winning the battle. Joshua prayed, "Let the sun stand still over Gibeon." So it was until Joshua defeated the five nations (Joshua 10:13, *ELT*).[466]

Eventually, Joshua led the people to take over the whole land, according to all that God had said to Moses. Things were going great!

The people served the Lord all the days of Joshua. But after Joshua and all the elders who had worked with him got old and died, things started to change. The people began ignore God. Then they started to worship false gods![113] The people sinned more and more, forgetting about God and His ways.

When Israel sinned, "The anger of the Lord was hot against Israel. So He delivered them into the hands of the surrounding nations" (Judges 2:14, *ELT*).[57] For the next 400 years various groups of Israel were in servanthood to fierce nations around them.

But every time the people repented and cried out to God, He raised up deliverers (called judges) to rescue them.[109] These people were called judges because they were military leaders and spiritual leaders. They also made decisions about what was right and wrong so the people could live for God.

Again and again, the people sinned, got into trouble, asked God for help, and then be rescued by a new judge God sent. They just kept doing what was right in their own eyes instead of obeying God and living His way.[101]

Talk About the Story: What did Joshua lead the people to do? Why do you think the people obeyed God during Joshua's life? Why did they stop obeying God after Joshua died?

Scripture: "But this is what I commanded them, saying, 'Obey My voice, and I will be your God, and you shall be My people. And walk in all the ways that I have commanded you, that it may be well with you.'" Jeremiah 7:23

Family Time: What are some things that can happen when we choose to ignore and disobey God? Why is choosing to live God's way better for us?

Prayer: Dear God, thank You that You love us so much that You are willing to help us, even when we have done wrong things. Help us to choose to live Your way and obey You every day. Amen.

DAVID, A KING AFTER GOD'S HEART

Scripture: 1 & 2 Samuel, 1 & 2 Kings
Place: Israel
Time: 960 BC–560 BC

Old Samuel was puffing as he climbed the hill to Bethlehem. Years earlier, Saul had been anointed the first king of Israel. Saul was tall and good looking, but his outward appearance didn't matter. God looks on his heart. Saul had disobeyed God and sinned against Him.

The Lord told Samuel, "Saul's time as king is over soon. I am sending you to Bethlehem. Anoint one of Jesse's eight sons as king. I'll show you which son."[152]

When the sons came to Samuel, God rejected the oldest son, and the next, and the next—God said no to seven sons!

"Are there any MORE sons?" old Samuel asked.

"Well, the father replied, "David, the youngest, is out tending the sheep." God chose the youngest, the least important one, who was busy doing his job.[63]

When David came, Samuel anointed him as his brothers watched.[16] The Spirit of the Lord came upon David from that day onward.[167]

Not long after this, David was sent to carry food to his brothers fighting the Philistines. They all were afraid of Goliath, a giant who challenged anyone in

Israel's army to fight him. The winner of that fight would determine which army won. But no one would fight Goliath, not even King Saul.

David was not afraid. He went out to fight him with a slingshot, and five smooth stones.[441] He yelled to Goliath, "You come to me with a sword, . . . I come to you in the name of the Lord of hosts, the God of the armies of Israel!" [192] David ran toward him and let go one stone that hit Goliath in the forehead, knocking him out.[70] Then David drew the giant's own sword and cut off his head.[423]

King Saul became jealous of David. Several times, he tried to kill David! David hid in the desert for 13 years, writing some of his greatest psalms (poems), and establishing himself as the spiritual leader of Israel.

When King Saul died in battle, David became king and led Israel in worshiping the Lord. Many say he was the greatest king of Israel. When Jesus returns to rule the world, it will be like the kingdom of David.

When David died, his son Solomon ruled. It was a time of peace, and he wrote the wisdom books of Proverbs, Ecclesiastes, and Song of Solomon.[59]

Solomon's son, Rehoboam, was not as godly as King David nor as wise as Solomon. Rehoboam didn't listen to wise advice and the kingdom split.

King Jeroboam set up the Northern Kingdom (Israel) in Samaria, and set up his own way of worshiping God. Rehoboam led the south, called Judah.

The two kingdoms of God's people fought for almost 300 years. Each kingdom had many kings during that time. Some never followed God, but there were some good kings.

Because of their idol worship, God allowed the nation of Assyria to destroy the Northern Kingdom in 720 B.C. It was the end of the Northern Kingdom.

Eventually God allowed King Nebuchadnezzar from Babylon to destroy Jerusalem in 586 B.C.

When God's people would not love Him first, and obey Him, they had to leave their homes for 70 years, and the prophets had warned them. But that's not the end of the story—later, God brought them back!

Talk About the Story: Who was the first king of Israel? Who became a hero by stopping Goliath? What was David's son's name? What were the names of the two kingdoms after Solomon?

Scripture: "Choose for yourselves this day whom you will serve . . . . But as for me and my house, we will serve the Lord." Joshua 24:15

Family Time: What are some reasons you love God? What are some reasons to obey Him? Read your lists aloud as a prayer.

Prayer: Lord, You are worthy of our love, our worship and our obedience. Please help us to put You first in everything. Amen.

GOD SENT THE PROPHETS

Scripture: Isaiah through Malachi
Place: Promised Land
Time: 840 BC—430 BC

God used three groups of people to lead His people. First there were kings who led or managed the kingdom. Second were priests who ministered in the Temple and connected people with God by praying for them and offering sacrifices to forgive their sins. The third were the prophets who spoke the Word of God to the people. Sometimes prophets predicted the future. Sometimes prophets spoke boldly against sin and announced how people should live in order to please God. The prophets spoke for God—God gave them messages He wanted His people to hear.

Many consider Isaiah the greatest prophet because of the excellence of his book called Isaiah. He predicted the future accurately because he spoke and wrote by God's Spirit. The Jewish people were looking for a national deliverer like King David who would defeat all her enemies. Isaiah predicted the coming Deliverer would be born by a miracle, "The Lord will give you a miracle, a girl who is a virgin will be pregnant. She will give birth to a Son and His name will be called Immanuel (God with Us)" (Isaiah 7:14).[256]

Isaiah also predicted that the Deliverer would not come to fight military battles, but would win a spiritual struggle by dying for the people's sin. "He *was* wounded for our transgressions, *He was* bruised for our iniquities; the chastisement for our peace *was* upon Him, and by His stripes we are healed.[394] All we like sheep have gone astray; we have turned, every one, to his own way; and the Lord has laid on Him the iniquity of us all" (ISAIAH 53: 5–6).[173]

The prophet, Jeremiah, spoke for God in Jerusalem when it was attacked and surrounded by the Assyrian army. The leaders came to Jeremiah seeking a message of encouragement from God. But Jeremiah boldly announced, "The Babylonians are coming." He announced God would judge the nation with a huge Babylonian invasion. The leaders didn't like what Jeremiah told them. They jailed him in a deep pit. When they opened the pit, Jeremiah thundered again, "The Babylonians are coming."

The prophet Ezekiel described the sins of God's people taking place in the Temple. It was filled with idols to heathen gods, and the people there were doing all kinds of sin. Ezekiel announced God would leave the Temple. Later, when God's Spirit was no longer in the Temple of Jerusalem, He then allowed Babylon to destroy it.

Prophets who wrote long books were called *major prophets*. These were Isaiah, Jeremiah, Ezekiel, and Daniel. Those with short books are called *minor prophets*. Their messages were not less important, they were just shorter.

One of them, Zechariah, predicted exact things about Jesus. He predicted Palm Sunday, "Rejoice greatly . . . your King is coming to you . . . riding on a donkey" (Zechariah 9:9).[256] He predicted Judas betraying Jesus, "So they weighed out for my wages thirty *pieces* of silver." He predicted the scene at the cross, "They shall look upon me whom they have pierced" (Zechariah 12:10, *KJV*).[530] Finally, he predicted the wounds of Jesus, "'What are these wounds in thine hands?' Then he shall answer, 'Those with which I was wounded in the house of my friends'" Zechariah 13:6, *KJV*).

Talk About the Story: What did the prophets do? What was Isaiah known for? What about Jeremiah? What did Zechariah tell about?

Scripture: "I have also spoken by the prophets, And have multiplied visions; I have given symbols through the witness of the prophets." Hosea 12:10

Family Time: Why do you think God used prophets to tell His messages to people? What are some other ways God has given us messages?

Prayer: Father, thank You for the messages You sent through the prophets. I want to learn more about what You have to say. Help me to read and listen to Your Word. Amen.

THE RETURN TO THE PROMISED LAND

Scripture: 2 Chronicles 36:15–23
Place: Babylon, Persia, and the Promised Land
Time: 534 BC

King Nebuchadnezzar from Babylon attacked Judah, the southern kingdom in 586 B.C. God had said that the Jews would be in captivity for 70 years.[267]

After a while, Persia conquered Babylon. So there was a new king in Babylon. It cost money for the government to take care of the Jewish captives, so the new king, Cyrus, decided to send the Jews back to their land. They could farm and do business—and pay him taxes!

Cyrus announced, "The God of the heavens has assigned me to build Him a Temple in Jerusalem.[183] You may go to Jerusalem, and those Jews who stay behind will support you with silver, gold, tools and other offerings."[363]

The Jews who returned to Jerusalem found the walls fallen down and the city burned. But they had learned something while they were captives. They should put God first! So, they built an altar to God where they could offer a sacrifice for their sins.[399] Now they felt they were home! They shouted for joy, so loudly that they could be heard for a long way! Many old priests, who had seen the first Temple, wept loudly for joy.[480] People couldn't tell the shouting from the weeping![290]

The book of Ezra tells that 4,400 Jews came back. Ezra worked hard to teach them God's laws.[449]

Nehemiah, a butler to the king, was sad because he'd heard how the city of Jerusalem was broken down. He fasted and prayed.[161] When the king asked why he was so sad,[112] he asked God to use his answer. Nehemiah told the king that Jerusalem was in ruins and his people, the Jews, were being raided by robbers.[494]

The king sent Nehemiah to go rebuild the walls![23] He gave what he needed to get the job done. When Nehemiah returned to Jerusalem, the people were discouraged. He set the people to build the walls in front of their houses. There were all types of opposition, but God helped His people, so that the wall was finished in only fifty-two days![513]

The book of Esther was written to tell how God looked after His people who didn't return, but stayed in Persia. This is how God protected them:

Esther was an orphan, raised by her cousin Mordecai.[375] She was chosen to be the queen for King Xerxes![364] The prime minister, Haman, hated all of the Jews because they would not bow to him. He especially hated Mordecai, Esther's cousin.

Haman got the king to make a law that on a certain day anyone could kill a Jew and keep their money and houses.[189]

The Jews were terrified! Mordecai told Esther, "You must go to the king and stop this law."[249]

Esther could only see the king when he called for her. So Esther asked, "Fast for me. I will fast also. Then I'll go to the king. If I perish, I perish."

Esther went to the king—and wasn't killed! She invited the king to dinner and asked him to bring Haman.[76]

At dinner, Esther told the king about Haman's plot to kill the Jews. The king had the prime minister hanged, and Esther and Mordecai were able to get the king to make another law that saved the Jews' lives![109] Esther and Mordecai became heroes!

Talk About the Story: Many people returned to Israel. Who taught them? Who led them? What did they rebuild? What did Esther do to save the Jews who stayed in Persia?

Scripture: "The righteous cry out, and the Lord hears, and delivers them out of all their troubles. The Lord is near to those who have a broken heart, and saves such as have a contrite spirit." Psalm 34:17–18

Family Time: What are some times God has helped your family out of troubles? Who is the Lord near to? What does "contrite" mean?

Prayer: Lord God, thank You for always hearing and helping us. We are glad that You are near us and save us when we repent. We love You! Amen.

PSALM 2
THE NEW KING

This Psalm is about David becoming King of Israel. When that happened, surrounding nations got mad, "Why are the nations mad with God because He put David on the throne? Why are the unsaved always angry with God?"

While this Psalm describes David, it is a picture of Jesus who one day will rule all people and all nations.

> "Why are the kings of the nation's saying
> We will not honor the Lord of Heaven;
> Why are secular leaders saying
> We will not do what God wants us to do?"[189]

How does God in heaven react when He sees people fighting Him? God created people that all may glorify Him. When the first couple Adam and Eve sinned, God sent His Son to die for the sins of all people. Now God wants everyone to be saved by His Son. But people reject the Son, what does the Father do? "He that is sitting in the heavens will laugh. God will be stirred to action because of their rebellion.

"God will show them His anger because they reject Him.
He will make them frightened because of their rebellion.[268]
God says, 'I will set up My king over them.'[367]
I will tell him, 'You are my begotten Son.'
One day My Son will rule over all people,
He will punish those who reject Him."[162]

So what does this Psalm tell the people of the world? It shows that now they can have their own way and do what they want to do. The Bible teaches people are influenced by their selfish ways so that they reject God's plan for their life. So what must people do?

"Respect God with awe, and do what He commands,
Remember God has great power to punish.
Kiss the Son so He won't be angry with you
(The word kiss means to love and obey God's Son).
Only those who obey the Son will be happy
He will give them security and peace."[452]

This Psalm helps us understand why some people show their hatred towards God by cursing, criticizing Christians, attacking the church and breaking God's laws of purity. This Psalm also explains when some make fun of you as a Christian. It's not always you they don't like, they may reject the Lord you follow. They don't want anyone telling them what to do, especially God. They may think God is too narrow, or He takes all the fun out of life. But we know better. Those who love Jesus and live for Him are the happiest and He blesses them.

Talk About the Psalm: What did you learn about the psalm writer in this story? What did you learn about God?

Psalm 2: Read this week's psalm in your Bible together. Choose a verse to read aloud as a prayer.

Prayer: Thank You, God, for the psalm prayers in the Bible. Thank You for teaching us about You and about how to pray. In Jesus' name, Amen.

THE 400 SILENT YEARS

Scripture: Intertestament
Place: Promised Land
Time: 430 BC to 4 BC

There was a long time of silence between the Old Testament and the New Testament. For 400 years God did not send a prophet with a message.[424] There were no more Old Testament books with messages from God to the Jews. God didn't speak audibly from heaven . . . only silence. But silence doesn't mean inactivity.

Daniel had predicted there would be four world empires (Daniel 2:31-43). First the Babylonians (Iraq) had destroyed Solomon's original Temple. King Nebuchadnezzar ruled from his capital city of Babylon on the banks of the Euphrates River. This was the first empire to rule the known world.

In 539 B.C. King Cyrus of Persia (Iran) captured the city of Babylon in a one day battle. Then they ruled the civilized world.

The third world empire was ruled by Alexander the Great from Greece. He began to conquer the Medo-Persian Empire. When Alexander reached India, he didn't know about any other kingdoms (China was unknown to him) so he sat down to weep because there were no more empires to conquer.

Alexander died in 323 B.C. and his kingdom was divided into four parts. Four generals began to rule their area. While they lost political influence, the cultural influence of Greece with its Western civilization spread throughout the world.

The fourth world empire was Rome which conquered Jerusalem when Caesar Augustus captured the city in A. D. 70. From then until the time of Jesus, the world and the Holy Land was at peace. There were Jewish terrorists, known as zealots, but they only fought hit and run skirmishes with Roman soldiers.

God was preparing the world for the birth of His Son and the spread of the gospel through the early church. The term *Pax Romania* meant the peace of Rome; there were no major wars when Jesus was born.

The world used Latin, the legal language of the day. They spoke Greek the cultural language, and in Jesus' world, they spoke Aramaic; the language of the people. Jews also spoke Hebrew, their language.

Rome built a highway system that made travel easier. Its postal system facilitated communication.

At the end of the 400 silent years, "when the fulness of the time was come, God sent forth his Son, made of a woman" (Galatians 4:4, *KJV*).[6]

But God was also preparing His people, the Jews. They never got over the punishment of the Babylonian captivity because of their addiction to idolatry. Now the Jews worshiped one God who was spirit. And they separated themselves from outward sins; but they were legalistic to the Law.

As Jews moved all over the Mediterranean world, they built houses of worship called synagogues, a name meaning a place to teach. Synagogues were houses to teach the Jews their heritage. There was one Temple in Jerusalem for sacrifices, but every town with at least 10 families built a synagogue.

The world conditions were ready for God to break the 400 years of silence with a word from heaven. "God spoke to Israel in various times and in various ways in the past, now He was ready to speak through His Son . . . who created the world, who is the brightness of His glory, and who holds all things together" (Hebrews 1:1-3, *ELT*).[93]

Talk About the Story: What are some things in the world that changed when Rome took over? Why do you think God waited to send Jesus?

Scripture: "The Lord had heard my supplication; the Lord will receive my prayer." Psalm 6:9

Family Time: When have you felt like God was not listening to you? What do you think God might have been doing during those quiet times?

Prayer: Father, thank You that You are always working and doing good things, even when we don't see or understand what is happening. Help us to trust you all the time. Amen.

CHAPTER 2

THE GOSPELS ARE ABOUT JESUS

The New Testament begins with four writers telling the story of Jesus. Each tells how Jesus was born of a virgin, lived without sin, and healed many sick by a miracle. He announced the coming kingdom of God where He would rule within the hearts of His followers. The Jewish leaders of His day rejected Jesus' teachings and were threatened by His authority. They plotted to kill Him and planned to use Roman justice to execute Him.

But God, the Father, sent Jesus to die as a substitute for the sins of the world. Because God loved all people, He would take them to heaven when they confessed their sins, and believed in Jesus as their Savior. Jesus died upon a Roman execution's cross, but was raised from the dead on the third day. His new life was given to all who followed Him. The death, burial, and resurrection of Jesus is called the gospel. Therefore these first four books are called The Gospels.

The first is the Gospel of Matthew written by a tax collector. It emphasizes Jewish backgrounds and shows Jesus as a King. The key phrase, "Kingdom of heaven," occurs 32 times.

The second Gospel was written by Mark, a young man who was in the company of those who followed Jesus. He emphasizes the activities and miracles of Jesus and the keyword is immediately that occurs 39 times.

The third Gospel was written by Luke, a Gentile doctor who was a personal physician to the apostle Paul. Luke emphasizes the human aspect of Jesus and the key phrase, Son of Man, occurs 80 times.

The fourth Gospel was written by John the youngest of the 12 disciples, but he wrote when he was almost 100 years old. John was very close to Jesus and was the one who leaned on Jesus at the last supper. John knew the God-like qualities of Jesus and emphasizes His deity. His key word believe, occurs 96 times.

A GIANT FAMILY TREE

Scripture: Old Testament Overview
Place: Israel
Time: From Creation to Jesus' birth

After Adam and Eve disobeyed God in the garden way back at the very beginning of the world, God made an important promise. God promised Eve, "You'll have a descendant who will crush the head of the serpent that caused you to sin" (Genesis 3:15).[263] Many generations later, God promised that the Savior would come through Abraham's family line.

Then God narrowed the promise to the family of Judah, Abraham's great-grandson. God said, "The Delivering-Ruler will ultimately come through Judah, and all nations will obey Him" (Genesis 49:9, 10, *ELT*).[517]

Finally God promised the Deliverer-King would come through David, a descendant of Judah. The prophet Nathan told David, "God has this message for

www.thefamilyprayerbible.com

you. He will establish with you a kingly family line and will establish your throne in Israel."[42]

"When you open the New Testament you read about the family of Jesus called a *Family Tree*.

Our family tree tells our parents and grandparents, and others who have come before us. Paying attention to the people in our family trees gives us information about where we come from.[160]

Jesus had a family tree. But even more than that, Jesus had all the promises that God made about Him from the beginning of time. In Jesus' preaching, He claimed to be the King-Deliverer of Israel and the world. And Jesus' birth record backs this up. It says, "The record of the ancestors of Jesus the Messiah, the son of King David, and of Abraham" (Matthew 1:1, *ELT*).[160]

Most of the time, people skip over the genealogy at the beginning of the New Testament, but it gives authority to Jesus' claims to be the Savior of the world. Jesus was born of a woman (God's promise to Eve), of Jewish heritage (God's promise to Abraham), from the tribe of Judah (God's promise to Jacob), and the line of King David (God's promise to David). Throughout the Old Testament, God guided history—making a family tree—until His own Son, the promised Savior was born.[207]

God predicted the birth of Jesus through Old Testament history. Jesus was like us—born with a past and future. We were born to a specific father and mother. We can't deny our past, nor should we fight it. We must accept who we are, knowing God has a plan for our life,[40] and He will guide us to complete that plan as we yield to His will.[53]

Talk About the Story: Who began Jesus' family tree? Who were some of the people in Jesus' family tree? What promises were made to these people?

Scripture: "God, who at various times and in various ways spoke in time past to the fathers by the prophets, has in these last days spoken to us by *His* Son, whom He has appointed heir of all things, through whom also He made the worlds" (Hebrews 1:1–2).

Family Time: What does our knowledge of Jesus' family tree tells us about Him? What do we know about our family tree? Since God had a plan for Jesus, and He has a plan for our lives; how can we find and do God's will?

Prayer: Father, thank You for predicting the birth of Jesus Christ in the Old Testament. I'm glad You had a plan for Jesus' birth and life. That means You have a plan for my life. I yield myself to Your plan and purpose for my life. Amen.

HOW MATTHEW WROTE HIS GOSPEL

Scripture: The book of Matthew
Place: On the trail with Jesus
Time: Throughout Jesus' life

Matthew was a government tax collector. His job was to make sure each person who lived in or did business in and around the town of Capernaum paid their taxes.

Most people didn't really like tax collectors. The taxes were collected for the Roman government to pay for Roman soldiers and government leaders who usually didn't care anything about what Jewish people thought or needed.

As a tax collector, Matthew had to keep very detailed records. He kept track of who lived in each home, how many fish the fishermen caught and sold, who traveled along the commercial trading route near Capernaum along with anything they had to sell.

Matthew needed to be able to speak and write in Latin, Greek and Aramaic. And Matthew would have grown up studying Hebrew as well. He must have been pretty smart to know all those languages!

Matthew, like all tax collectors, had kind of an ugly way to make a living. The Romans required a certain amount of money to be collected. But they let the tax collectors keep anything extra that they collected. Because of this, people didn't like tax collectors at all! People thought they were all cheaters!

But Jesus asked Matthew to follow Him. And Matthew did! He gave up his profitable job in order to be one of Jesus' disciples.[314]

As Matthew followed Jesus, he kept up his habit of writing things down. Matthew kept a journal of Jesus' miracles, sermons, and activities. He probably wrote his notes in the Hebrew language.

After Jesus returned to heaven, Matthew traveled north and west of Jerusalem to preach about Jesus. When he preached, Matthew would have referred to his Hebrew notes.

A number of years later, Matthew used his notes to carefully write the story

of Jesus in the Greek language so that Jewish people who lived far from Jerusalem and spoke the Greek language could know the truth about Jesus.

Matthew quoted from the Old Testament and included Jewish traditions in many of the stories he told about Jesus. Matthew often called Jesus the Son of David. He used that term to remind people that Jesus is the Messiah, or Christ, the King God had promised to send.

Talk About the Story: Who was Matthew? Where did he pick up the habit of writing? What did He write when following Jesus? Why do you think he wrote his book about Jesus in Greek? What did Matthew want people to know about Jesus?

Scripture: And Simon Peter answered and said, 'You are the Christ, the Son of the living God'" (Matthew 16:16).

Family Time: What did Matthew emphasize about Jesus? How is Jesus the king of our lives? What are some ways we can show that we honor Jesus as our king?

Prayer: Father, thank You for Matthew who wrote about the kingdom of heaven. I want Jesus to be the king of my life and rule my life from within. Amen.

MARK WRITING A GOSPEL

Scripture: The book of Mark
Place: Outside the Promised Land
Time: 65 AD

The tramp of Roman soldiers woke young Mark up. Mark had been sleeping in the Garden of Olives, wrapped in his linen coat. He had followed Jesus and His disciples from their Passover meal to the garden. Mark was sure something would happen that night—and something WAS happening! Mark, jumped up, threw on his linen coat, and ran closer to investigate.

"Hey you!" a soldier thinking the boy was one of Jesus' disciples, tried to grab him. Mark ran to safety in the early morning darkness, leaving his coat in the soldier's grasp.

Mark was afraid that night, but after Jesus died and came back to life again, Mark grew and learned to be a true follower of Jesus.

Just a few years later, Mark joined Paul and Barnabas on their first missionary trip to Cyprus and Turkey. The trip went well for a while, but something went wrong. Mark ended up leaving Paul and Barnabas in the middle of the trip. Paul was NOT happy!

Paul refused to take Mark on the second journey. But Barnabas, Mark's uncle, wanted to give Mark another chance. Paul and Barnabas argued and split up, heading in different directions. Paul took Silas with him to Syria. But Barnabas took Mark and headed to Cyprus.

Eventually, Mark started spending time with the apostle Peter. He probably heard many stories about what Peter did with Jesus.

Several years later, maybe in Rome, Mark wrote down the stories he had learned about Jesus. We can read these stories in the Gospel of Mark.

Mark wanted the Romans to know and understand who Jesus is.[523] Mark didn't spend time or space in his gospel mentioning Old Testament prophecies or Jewish customs like the other gospel writers did. They were not important to the Romans! But Mark did include interpretations of some words so that the Romans would understand.

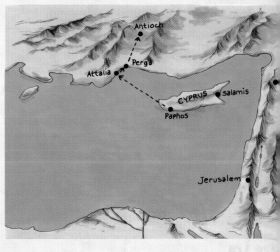

Mark emphasized Jesus as the Servant of God[431] and the Redeemer of people. Mark told about many of Jesus' miracles to show His power and compassion for others.

But Mark also wrote his gospel in a way that is full of action and easy to read. Mark used the words "immediately" or "quickly" many times in his book. The quick pace of the book appealed to the Romans. It is also a fun book for us to read today! It is short and full of action—just like an action movie!

Talk About the Story: Who was Mark? Why do you think he wrote his book about Jesus? What did Mark want people to know about Jesus?

Scripture: "For even the Son of Man did not come to be served, but to serve, and to give His life as a ransom for many" (Mark 10:45).

Family Time: How can we follow Jesus' example in serving others? If you have never read one of the gospels, try reading through the Gospel of Mark together.

Prayer: Jesus, thank You for showing us how to live and for making it possible for us to live forever with You. Please help us to follow Your example in serving others. Amen.

LUKE WRITING A GOSPEL

Scripture: Luke 1:1–3
Place: Caesarea
Time: 58–59 AD

"Luke, I'm so glad you have been here with me on this journey!" Paul said.

Luke and Paul and the others walked down the gangplank from the ship. Finally they were in Rome! Luke looked forward to finding a medical vendor so that he could purchase new medicine. Luke had used up all his supplies during the long journey from Jerusalem.

Dr. Luke cared about his patients. Maybe that is why he volunteered to travel with Paul, even though Paul was being taken as a prisoner to Rome. Luke wanted to make sure that Paul stayed healthy and that all his needs were taken care of.

Luke also wanted to find someone selling papyrus so that he could do some more writing. Luke's promise to Theophilus was on his mind.

Luke had promised to finish writing a full account of Jesus' life, death and resurrection for Theophilus, an important leader back home. Luke had been working on this account for quite a while now, interviewing Jesus' family, His disciples, and others who had met Jesus, and investigating political and historical records from the time of Jesus' birth until His death and resurrection. Luke wanted to make sure all the facts were in order.

As a physician, Luke was used to listening to what people said and carefully considering what was true. This skill had helped him during his research! Now it was time to finish the job. Theophilus and other Greeks needed to know the truth about Jesus. They needed to know and trust Him!

As Luke wrote, he thought about how Jesus called Himself the Son of Man. Yes, Jesus is the Son of God, but He was also a real human person. He got hungry and thirsty like everyone else. He experienced being tired, sad, and angry. He understood people's feelings and temptations because He had been there!

Luke also noticed Jesus' compassion for others. Luke was struck by Jesus' love and compassion.[337] Jesus was the perfect Son of Man. He clearly identified with the suffering of people, and He came to die on the cross to save people and make it possible for them to be made whole.

Since the Greeks loved the arts, beauty and literature, Luke made sure to include the parables (stories) Jesus told. These stories would help people understand what Jesus taught about God's kingdom.[24]

Finally, Luke was ready. Luke wrote these words: "I am writing to you, Theophilus, with the events and speeches of Jesus' life in chronological order, including eyewitness, and written accounts of His life. I am led by the Holy Spirit to write this perfect account so that you will have confidence in the truth you've heard about Jesus Christ" (Luke 1:1-4, *ELT*).[425]

Talk About the Story: Who was Luke? Why did Luke write his book about Jesus? What is the main emphasis about Jesus in this book?

Family Time: Since Luke used his background and talents to serve God by writing a gospel, how can I use my talents to serve the Lord?

Scripture: "For the Son of Man has come to seek and to save that which was lost" (Luke 19:10, *NKJV*).

Prayer: Father, thank You that Jesus was the perfect man who lived without sin. Thank You He died for my sins. Just as Jesus was seeking sinners, so I will pray and be a testimony to my unsaved friends and family. Amen.

DATE ___/___

JOHN WRITES A GOSPEL

Scripture: John 20:31
Place: Ephesus
Time: 90 AD

The apostle John was about 90 years old, but everyone said he was much younger than his age. His memory was keen, and his spry legs could walk the hilly streets of Ephesus. He still preached every week in the building up on a high hill and walked to pray over the sick.

"I'm going to write the life story of Jesus," John told his congregation. John explained more traveling preachers come to Ephesus with a different view of Jesus than he remembered. He complained, "They think Jesus was not fully God." John knew Jesus well. He had been one of Jesus' closest disciples. When Jesus was on the cross, John stood with Jesus' mother Mary. It was there Jesus committed His mother, Mary, to the care of John.[402]

John told his congregation, "I'll begin my book, 'In the beginning was Jesus, the Word of God. He was face to face with God in eternity, and He is God'" (John 16, *ELT*).[192]

The church in Ephesus smiled, they agreed with their pastor. Three other gospels had been written: Matthew emphasized Jesus as King, Mark emphasized Jesus as a Servant, and Luke emphasized Jesus in his humanity calling Him the "Son of Man."

"Everyone will know that Jesus is God when they read His miracles that show He is God."

John loved reading the Old Testament. He knew that "seven" was the number of perfection. God created the world in seven days! So John planned to emphasize this number in his gospel. He would write about seven miracles Jesus did, and seven statements Jesus made about Himself. These were times Jesus said, "I AM."

John featured several personal conversations Jesus had with people. There was Nicodemus, the woman at the well, the man who couldn't walk at the Pool of Bethesda, and the man born bind. Since people were always important to Jesus, John wrote of Jesus' sensitivity to individuals—both men and women.

Since there were people who were telling lies about Jesus, claiming that He wasn't really God, John wrote to make sure that people knew the truth.

John wrote about the Pharisees and their attacks of Jesus and how Jesus answered them. Then he made sure everyone understood the purpose of His work, John wrote, "These events in Jesus' life are written so you will believe that Jesus is the promised Messiah, the Son of God; and when you believe, you will receive eternal life." (John 20:31, *ELT*).[271]

Talk About the Story: Who was John and how old was he when he wrote? Where did he write the gospel of John? What was he doing? Why did he write the gospel of John and what was he trying to prove?

Scripture: "For God so loved the world that He gave His only begotten Son, that whoever believes in Him should not perish but have everlasting life." John 3:16

Family Time: What is the simple message of John? What does the fact that Jesus is God mean to you? Since He is God, will He answer your prayers, and care for you!

Prayer: Father, I love the simplicity of this gospel, and I love Jesus as much as John who knew Jesus intimately. I believe in Jesus and His miracles, just as much as John. Thank You for this easy to understand book. Amen.

PSALM 3
THE MORNING PSALM

Have you ever had a bad dream that scared you? You did not go back to sleep and you heard all of the "creeks" and sounds in the dark night. David had one of those nights. Read what David did. Then you should do the same thing when you cannot sleep at night.

One of David's sons killed another son. Then that son—Absalom—decided to be king and take the kingdom from his father. The crowds rallied to Absalom and he marched on Jerusalem.

David could have stayed behind the protected walls of Jerusalem and fought a battle against Absalom and the rebellious army. But David did not know who in the city was his friend. There were probably enemies in Jerusalem who would take Absalom's side.

David fled from the city with his bodyguards and a small army. The first night out of Jerusalem was difficult. David didn't have his comfortable bed, nor did he have his family nearby. He slept on the hard ground.

But what kept David awake all night? It was not the hard ground or insects, or sleeping next to a fire under the open sky. It was lurking danger. David didn't know how close the approaching army was.

When David went to bed, he complained to God. David knew God had every right to punish him. So he pleads for mercy,

> *"O Lord, don't be mad at me because I sinned;*
> *Don't punish me in Your anger."*

Next David prayed for God to have compassion on him. He asked for God to restore him to the old days when everything was peaceful.[404] So he asked,

> *"Lord, be compassionate to me for I am weak;*
> *Take away my pain and fear.*
> *I am sick over what I have done, and*
> *I am hurting because of Your punishment."*

Then David talked to God because he could not sleep. When David knew God had heard him, he went to sleep. The following morning he awakes in a happy mood. "I woke up in a happy mood."[213]

> *"I laid me down to sleep,*
> *I tossed all night because I was praying.*
> *But in the morning I woke up happy*
> *Because I knew God had heard my prayers."*

Throughout the years Christians have called this "The Morning Psalm." David woke up with confidence and his army destroyed the rebellious army in the coming days.

> *"Wake up God, go out to fight my enemy;*
> *Rescue me from those who would kill me.*
> *Slap all my enemies in the face;*
> *Knock out all their teeth.*
> *I know my victory will come from You,*
> *My Lord, who continually blesses me with favor."*

Talk About the Psalm: What did you learn about the psalm writer in this story? What did you learn about God?

Psalm 3: Read this week's psalm in your Bible together. Choose a verse to read aloud as a prayer.

Prayer: Thank You, God, for the psalm prayers in the Bible. Thank You for teaching us about You and about how to pray. In Jesus' name, Amen.

CHAPTER 3

TOWARD THE BIRTH OF JESUS

The New Testament is the story of Jesus Christ and the Church he established. It begins with his birth and moves through the details of His life and ministry, climaxing with His death and resurrection. From the opening pages of the Gospels, Jesus is depicted as the greatest person who has ever lived. History records many great men and women whose lives have made a deep impact on others; however, the greatest of them does not hold a candle to the blazing brilliance of Jesus.

As the opening pages of the New Testament unfold before us, we walk with Him on the grassy hillsides of Galilee. We sail with Him across the lake and travel with His disciples as they traverse the hills and valleys of Judea. We listen as He teaches, and we watch as He dies for the sins of the world. Then, with amazing wonder, we see Him rise from the dead and commission His disciples to go into all the world proclaiming the "good news."

From Jesus' first coming as a baby in a manger to His triumphal return at His Second Coming, the New Testament is all about Him. Jesus is deity on

foot! He walks among men, but He lives above men. He looks like a ~~man, but~~ He talks like God. He is fully human and yet totally divine.

The New Testament introduces us to the person of Jesus Christ. It connects His claims to the Old Testament messianic prophecies and presents Him as the promised Messiah (Gk. christos). As you study these books, you will come face-to-face with those claims and the beliefs and practices of those who first accepted them. As you read, remember that these books were not only written to their original readers, but they continue to speak to us today as well. Let your reading challenge your mind, stretch your faith, and stir your soul. (Taken from Illustrated Bible Survey, Ed Hindson, and Elmer Towns, Nashville, TN: Broadman & Holman, 2013), 346-347.)

THE FIRST WORD FROM HEAVEN IN 400 YEARS

Scripture: Luke 1:5-22
Place: The Temple in Jerusalem
Time: October, 5 BC

Zechariah looked wishfully off to the distant red mountains. There was a glow in his eyes. He had served God faithfully for many years.[410] After all this time in the priesthood, he finally had been chosen to burn incense and pray in the holy room in the Temple tomorrow!

Zechariah thought about his wife, Elizabeth. *I'll pray for her when I am in the Holy place tomorrow. Even though she is old, she still wishes that she had been able to have children. I want that, too!*

As Zechariah entered the Gate Beautiful into the Temple, he reached out to rub the gold on the gate. Inside he saw the twelve golden stairs, and on a platform the Levitical choir, singing perfectly Psalm 122, "I was glad when they said unto me, 'Let us go into the house of the LORD.'"[183]

Zechariah looked up to the highest point of the Temple, he saw a white robed priest with trumpet in hand. When the sun descended to the perfect spot in the sky—half way between the horizon and full noon—the priest sounded the trumpet. Everyone at the Temple gathered around the golden stairs for evening prayers.[12] Slowly Zechariah began his climb.

The eyes of the crowd watched him disappear between the tall heavy curtains. Zechariah was now in the presence of God.

He bowed his head in prayer. But suddenly Zechariah realized that someone else was in the room. Zechariah looked up to see a young man standing across the room, next to an incense altar. But this was not an ordinary man. Zechariah could see that this was an angel! Zechariah was terrified!

"Fear not," the angel said. "I am sent from God to tell you that your prayers have been heard." Zechariah didn't know what to think![165] "Your wife will have a son and you must call him John," Gabriel said.[376]

"But," the old priest argued, "my wife and I are too old for children."

But Gabriel went on, "Your son will bring you joy and gladness. He will prepare people for the Messiah. When he preaches, many will turn to the Lord."[416]

The old priest shook his head in unbelief. "Can you prove this?" Zechariah sputtered. "How will I know?"

Gabriel frowned. "Because you did not believe the words of God, your speech will be taken from you by God until the words are fulfilled." Then the angel was gone.

The holy place fell quiet. Nothing moved. Silence! Outside the quiet crowd began to wonder. Someone asked, "Where is he?"

The curtains finally rippled. The crowd could see that the priest was finally coming out.

Zechariah stepped out to the top of the stairs, blinking his eyes in the setting sun. The crowd could tell something was wrong. It was time for him to give the benediction. Everyone waited.

"Agh . . ., agh . . ., agh . . .," were the only sounds he could make. Zechariah waved his arms, making signs, trying to explain what had happened.

Another priest stepped up and prayed the benediction,

> *"The Lord bless you and keep you . . .*[37]
> *The Lord make His face shine upon you . . .*
> *And be gracious to you;*[305]
> *The Lord lift up His countenance upon you and give you peace"*
> (Numbers 6:24-26).[347]

Talk About the Story: What did the angel tell Zechariah? How did he respond? What did the angel say would happen because he didn't believe what the angel said? What do you think Zechariah wanted to say at the end of the story?

Scripture: "And they were both righteous before God, walking in all the commandments and ordinances of the Lord blameless." Luke 1:6

Family Time: How does Luke 1:6 describe Zechariah and Elizabeth? Why do you think they had to wait until they were old to have a child? How do you feel when you have to wait for something you really want? What are some good things that can come out of that waiting time?

Prayer: Father, I want to live faithfully for You from my youth till I am as old as Zechariah and Elizabeth. Watch over me and keep me safe. Amen.

BLACK SHEEP IN THE FAMILY TREE

Scripture: Matthew 1:1–17
Place: Promised Land
Time: Written 40 AD or 65 AD

When we read the family tree of Jesus, we find some interesting names! The Jews usually traced their ancestry[160] through the males, not females, yet there are five women listed. And there is a unique, rather scandalous story with each of the women. God used these women to demonstrate His grace, just as He will use you and your failings to demonstrate His grace.[278]

The first woman in the list is Tamar. She ended up in a very complicated situation in which the only solution she could find was to pretend to be a prostitute! As a result, she became pregnant and had twins—the older of the twins was a person God chose to be in the line of Jesus!

www.thefamilyprayerbible.com

The second woman in the list didn't just pretend to be a prostitute. It was what she really was! When the people of Israel were getting ready to fight the city of Jericho at the end of 40 years of wilderness wanderings, Joshua sent spies to find out about the city. The spies hid out at the house of Rahab, a prostitute. She protected the spies because she had become a believer in the Lord God of Israel.[450] Maybe she ended up marrying one of the spies!

The third woman's name was Ruth. She was a Moabite woman, a foreigner from a culture of idol worshipers. Ruth married an Israelite man, but he and his father and brother died, leaving Ruth, her mother-in-law, Naomi, in Moab with no one to help them. When Ruth's mother-in-law returned to Bethlehem, Ruth chose to go with her and to follow the one true God. Ruth ended up marrying Boaz, a man who loved and honored God. Ruth became the great-grandmother of King David.

The fourth woman in the list was Bathsheba. King David wanted her for himself, even though she was already married. King David got her pregnant, and then he got her husband killed! David married her, but the baby died. Later Bathsheba had another baby. His name was Solomon, the next king, and another person in the line of Jesus.

Then we come to the fifth woman—Mary, the mother of Jesus, the Son of God. Mary wasn't yet married when she became pregnant with Jesus. Her friends and family probably thought she had done wrong things.

God could have created the complete human body of Jesus in heaven and dropped Him in the lap of a human mother on earth. But God chose to use people in a family line, people who did wrong things, people who were not liked or respected, people who had trouble and heartbreak, people God loved and cared for.

Jesus is God's love-gift to people who are sinners. God says, "I love you. I will die for your sins. I will forgive you when you believe in me and repent of your sins. I will use you if you will yield yourselves to Me."[295]

Talk About the Story: What do the women listed in Jesus' family tree have in common? How are they different?

Scripture: "But when the fullness of the time had come, God sent forth His Son, born of a woman, born under the law, to redeem those who were under the law, that we might receive the adoption as sons" (Galatians 4:4-5).

Family Time: Why do you think God included flawed people in Jesus' family tree? What does this say about God's love for sinners? What can we do about our failures and flaws?

Prayer: Lord, thank You for loving imperfect people. I am not perfect, either! Please forgive my sin and help me to live for You. In Jesus' name. Amen.

HIS NAME IS JOHN

Scripture: Luke 1:57–80
Place: Abia, a town for priests
Time: July, 4 AD

Zechariah sat with friends on the bench in front of his white stone house. He could hear the moans of Elizabeth inside the house. The midwife whispered words of encouragement to Elizabeth. Elizabeth was having a baby and it hurt.

"Lord, help Elizabeth through this delivery!"[248] was all old Zechariah could pray. Then Zechariah heard the unmistakable sound of new life: "Wa-a-ah!" Zechariah jumped up. His friends cheered.

"THE BABY'S BORN," a young boy cupped his hands to yell down the street for everyone in the village to hear.

Neighbors immediately left what they were doing and came running. Everyone was eager to find out if it was a boy or girl.

"It's a boy," the midwife came out the door, wiping her hands on her apron. She glanced up at Zechariah's worried face. "He's a healthy boy. And Elizabeth is healthy as well."

The gathering crowd in Zechariah's yard cheered. One man reached out to shake the new father's hand. Another slapped him on the back. Zechariah still could not say a word, but everyone could see how happy and excited he was.

Zechariah waved and nodded his thanks to the neighbors and the midwife as he hurried to Elizabeth's side. He couldn't wait to see his newborn son!

Eight days later, the house and yard crowded with friends, family and neighbors. It was the day of the baby's circumcision and introduction to the community. Zechariah and Elizabeth proudly brought the baby out for everyone to see.

"Wa-a-ah! Wa-a-ah! Wa-a-ah!" the bawling baby got everyone's attention. His puffy red cheeks and wide mouth told everyone the baby would be a loud preacher. Elizabeth held him tightly in her arms.

As the baby quieted, an uncle called out, "Call the baby Zechariah." It was the custom to name the firstborn son after his father. "Yes, Zechariah!" the relatives agreed, "Call the baby Zechariah after his father." Everyone in the crowd wanted that name.

Elizabeth spoke up. "No, his name is John."

"What? You don't have ANY relatives with that name! Why would you choose the name John?" They looked at Zechariah and motioned for him to let them know what he thought the baby should be called.

Zechariah motioned for a writing tablet. One of his friends handed a tablet to him. The boisterous group grew silent. They pressed around Zechariah. Everyone wanted to see what he was writing. Zechariah wrote in large bold letters so no one could miss what he was writing.

"HIS NAME IS JOHN."[397]

Suddenly, Zechariah could speak! "Glory to the Lord God of Israel, for He has visited and redeemed His people!"[367] Zechariah went on to tell everyone what the angel had told him about John.

Talk About the Story: What did Elizabeth say the baby's name was? Why did people want to name the baby something different? What happened as soon as Zechariah wrote that the baby's name was John?

Scripture: "Glory to the Lord God of Israel, for He has visited and redeemed His people." Luke 1:68

Family Time: Why did Zechariah praise God as soon as he could speak again? What are some reasons we have for praising God?

Prayer: Father, Thank You for Your gift of salvation through Jesus. Help me speak the words of Scripture just as Zechariah spoke what the angel told him. Amen.

DREAMING GREAT DREAMS IN AN UNLIKELY TOWN

Scripture: Luke 1:27
Place: Nazareth
Time: Spring, April, 4 BC

Mary always smiled, but today she had a worried look as she walked toward the synagogue in Nazareth with her mother. A warm spring had come to the hill country in Galilee, and the sun was grinning its warmth. This should have been the happiest day of her life because Joseph was announcing their marriage this morning in the synagogue. Mary asked, "Suppose the Rabbis say no?"

"They will approve," the wise mother assured her anxious daughter. The mother had talked to the wives of the elders to make sure there were no surprises.

Mary and her mother climbed the outside stairs to the synagogue balcony where women and children sat. Mary placed herself where she could see the elders' response when Joseph approached them.

"They must give approval to Joseph," Mary whispered to her mother. "I have prayed they'll say yes."[152]

The people in the community said Mary was the most godly young woman in the synagogue. The community match-maker described Mary, "She's as good as she is beautiful." When she caught Joseph's eye, the old grandmothers approved. They thought Joseph was a fine catch for her and a godly young man too.

Joseph rose from his synagogue back seat—because he was an unmarried male—he walked toward the elders. Everyone in the synagogue knew what he was requesting. Nazareth was a small village, where everyone knew everyone and kept up on the news of others. Joseph handed the parchment to the ruling elder. He didn't even read it; he turned to the others and nodded.

Normally, the elders frowned when giving disapproval of a marriage. But for Joseph, their wrinkled old eyes twinkled. Then their gray beards nodded up and down in approval. Joseph and Mary were to be married a year from now.

THAT EVENING

Mary ran to the fig tree to pray to God.[506] Not only did she love Joseph, but she loved God. She sat under the branches of the fig tree to pray for future happiness.[213] She covered her dark hair with her father's prayer shawl. Mary had seen her father retreat to the fig tree often, the traditional Jewish place for meditation on God.[302] Mary thought to herself, "*Under the fig tree,*" she reasoned, "*I'll be out of the wind. I'll be able to pray in private.*"

Mary had dreams; she wanted her marriage to be the best of any marriages. She wanted to be a good wife, a good mother, a holy woman of God. She couldn't be happier.

We will not argue, Mary told herself. *We will be forever in love.*

With a smile she parted the fig branches with her hands to search the blue early evening sky for a star. And Mary bowed her head in prayer.

Talk About the Story: Why do you think Mary and Joseph had to ask for permission to get married? What did you learn about life in Nazareth from this story?

Scripture: "But you, when you pray, go into your room, and when you have shut your door, pray to your Father who is in the secret place, and your Father who sees in secret will reward you openly." Matthew 6:6

Family Time: We know from the Bible that Mary loved and trusted God. What habits do you think she had that helped her in her relationship with God? What are some things we can do to spend more time with God in our lives?

Prayer: Father, help each one of us to find private places and times to pray to You. We want to grow in our love for You. Amen.

MARY, CHOSEN OF GOD

Scripture: Luke 1:26–38
Place: Bethlehem
Time: Spring, April, 4 BC

After finishing her chores for the morning, Mary ran to her favorite hiding spot under the fig tree. It was cool and quiet there, the perfect place to pray. Suddenly, her body quivered. She felt the presence of somebody else under the tree. Turning around she saw a stranger.

"Greetings, highly favored one, the Lord is with you!" he said with a gentle smile. Mary could see that this was not an ordinary man—he was an angel![14] The angel continued, "Blessed are you among women!"[47]

Mary was very troubled by this greeting. *What does he mean? Why would he greet me this way? I'm no different from any other young woman!*

"Don't be afraid, Mary. You have found favor with God,"[377] "You are to have a child,"[376] Gabriel said to young Mary. "When He is born, you shall call His name JESUS."[316]

Mary thought to herself about the name JESUS. She had often thought about a son and had thought of many names, but never the name JESUS. Then she began to think in Hebrew, the language of the fathers. In Hebrew the name Jesus meant Joshua— Jehovah Saves.

There were hundreds of little boys running around Galilee who were named Jesus. It was one of the favorite names of young mothers. A little boy named Jesus would remind them of Joshua who conquered the Promise Land, who defeated Israel's enemies, who divided the land among the twelve tribes. Joshua was a good Hebrew name, but the people spoke Greek, they would call Him Jesus.

www.thefamilyprayerbible.com

Gabriel interrupted her thinking. "Jesus will be called the Son of the Highest, and the Lord God shall give to your Son the throne of His father, David."[147]

The Deliverer, Mary thought. She repeated it again softly, "My Son will be the Messiah."

"But," Mary questioned, "I am not yet married."

"Joseph is not to be the father," the angel told Mary. A puzzled look came over her face. Gabriel knew she would have questions, so he explained,

"The Holy Spirit shall come upon you, and the power of the Highest shall overshadow you, and the holy child born to you shall be called the Son of God."

Mary was suddenly filled with worry. *What would her family think? And, what about Joseph? If they don't believe me, they will think I have done something wrong. Joseph may not want to marry me at all!* She loved him so much! Her dream was to marry Joseph. She wanted to have Joseph's child. But more than anything else, Mary wanted to obey God.

The angel must have sensed her struggle, he encouraged her, "With God nothing is impossible."[466]

Gabriel knew Mary was struggling with the startling news about having a child apart from Joseph. The angel knew Mary needed some reassurance.[156] He told Mary, "Your cousin Elizabeth is too old to have children," Gabriel explained, "but she has conceived and will have a son."[200]

Mary knew what she would do. She would decide to do what she always had done. She bowed her head. "Behold, I am the maidservant of the Lord," she said. "Let it be to me according to your word."[279]

Mary looked up. Gabriel was not there. Quickly she stepped to the opening, parting the leaves, but she did not see him leaving down the path. She quickly ran to the other side of the fig tree, he was nowhere to be seen. As she returned to the house, Mary looked to God in heaven. "Lord," she whispered under her breath, "I will be Your handmaiden!"[327]

Talk About the Story: What did the angel tell Mary? How did Mary respond to the angel's news? Why do you think she was willing to obey God, even though others might not understand?

Scripture: "Then Mary said, "Behold, the maidservant of the Lord! Let it be to me according to your word." And the angel departed from her" (Luke 1:38).

Family Time: What can we learn from Mary's response to the angel? When might it be hard to obey God? What are some good ways to respond when we are worried about what might happen if we choose to obey God?

Prayer: Father, may I always do Your will, just as Mary obeyed You. Give me faith to believe You and obey You. Amen.

THE BABE LEAPED IN HER WOMB

Scripture: Luke 1:39–56
Place: A Village near Jerusalem
Time: July, 4 BC

Mary walked up the hilly path toward the village where her relatives lived, about 60 miles from home. Mary jumped from one rock to another.

"Oh," she balanced herself. "I am not as quick on my feet as I was before I got pregnant." Within her body was a human being, put there by God. She bounced across the rocks just a little heavier than before.

"I'll stay with Aunt Elizabeth for a while,"[118] she was concerned what the people in her community would say. She was pregnant and not yet married. Before long everyone would see the telltale signs.

Mary asked directions to the home of Elizabeth and Zacharias. He was a priest who had recently returned from active service in Jerusalem. Someone pointed out they lived in a white stone dwelling at the end of the road.

Mary stood for a moment in front of the open door. The angel Gabriel told her to come see Elizabeth but she felt strange walking in on relatives unannounced. Gabriel said Elizabeth was pregnant when she was too old for children.

Mary walked into the room, she didn't knock. An elderly woman sat looking out the back door.

"Hello, Elizabeth. It's me, Mary, from Nazareth."

"Oh . . ., Oh . . ., Oh . . .," Elizabeth cried out in surprise. She reached for her midsection because of the sudden jolt. Then with a smile she announced, "My babe just jumped in my womb." Elizabeth explained. "My baby jumped like never before."[167]

The baby in the womb of Elizabeth was John the Baptist. It was his task to announce Jesus to the world. The baby John jumped for joy when Jesus entered the room in the womb of Mary. As only God can work out the details, the unborn baby John knew that the unborn Messiah was present.

"Blessed are you among women,"[47] Elizabeth knew what was happening and said to the young woman, "and blessed is the fruit of your womb."[147]

Elizabeth looked old and tired. She sat most of the time, friends wanted her to stay in bed, but Elizabeth wouldn't surrender to the bed. Elizabeth was not used to carrying a baby; she was far beyond the age of having a child. Even though her pregnancy was wearisome, and the dark lines of her face showed it, Elizabeth's happy smile showed her contentment.

Elizabeth asked, "Why has the mother of our Lord come to see me?"[184]

The June sunlight streamed in through the window and door. Even though it was dark in the room, the women were surrounded with light. Mary couldn't give an answer because she didn't know what to say. Then Mary explained to Elizabeth about the angel who told her she would become pregnant with the Son of God. Then Mary said,

"*My soul doth magnify the Lord,*
And my spirit hath rejoiced in God my Savior.[416]
        For he hath regarded the low estate of his
        handmaiden: for, behold, from henceforth all
        generations shall call me blessed."[34]

Elizabeth could see godliness in young Mary's face. They talked until late in the evening, from the joy of marriage begun, to the wisdom of old age, Elizabeth instructed Mary in the ways of perfect love. Zechariah was not home to interrupt them so the ladies talked from one candle to another. The wisdom of elderly Elizabeth was poured into a young eager learner.

Elizabeth asked, "What did the angel tell you to name the baby?"

"Jesus," Mary said softly.

"Jesus is a lovely name," the wrinkled smile on Elizabeth's face closed her eyes in joy. "Our Messiah will be named Jesus, for He will save us from our sins."

Talk About the Story: Why did Mary go to visit Elizabeth? What happened when Mary walked in? What did Elizabeth say about Mary? What did Mary say about God? What do you think Elizabeth taught Mary about marriage and life?

Scripture: "My son, hear the instruction of you father, and do not forsake the law of your mother" (Proverbs 1:8).

Family Time: What are some things you have learned from someone who is older? What are some things we could learn from our grandparents? Aunts and uncles? Other older people in our church? Why do you think that learning from others is important?

Prayer: Father, thank You for allowing an older woman teach many things to Mary. Help me learn from older people who know You and follow You. Help me become wise to live for You. Amen.

PSALM 4
HOW TO SLEEP AT NIGHT

Absalom, David's son, had rejected his father's influence. Absalom killed his brother. Then Absalom began a long campaign to get the people loyal to him and not his father, King David. Finally the day of revolution came. Absalom put together an army to march on Jerusalem. David left the city with his bodyguards and a small army loyal to him.

David led his band of followers across the Jordan and took up defense in the city of Mahanaim. When the army of Absalom finally caught up with David, they were ready to attack. David sent his army out to meet them. But David's army wouldn't let him go fight with them. David was too old and might have been killed in battle. So David stood at the gate to review his troops as they marched out to battle.

While David is waiting for the results of the battle, he wrote Psalm 4. It is a song to be sung when you are scared and don't know what will happen. First, the Bible promises, "The blood of Jesus Christ our Savior has cleansed us from every sin." So pray like David.

*"Lord, You have forgiven my sin
And made me perfect in Your eyes.
You have always answered me when I pray,
Especially when I am in trouble.
Hear me in this trouble;*[189]
Have mercy on me."[304]

Next trust God who works in your heart. Pray like David who trusted God to solve his problem. Take note of this.

*"The Lord will set apart
The redeemed for Himself.
The Lord will listen to me
And will answer me when I pray.*[158]
*Therefore, I will stand before the Holy Lord in reverence
And not sin against Him.
I will lie quietly on my bed in prayer*[235]
As talking with Him at night."[497]

It must have been extremely stressful for David to wait for the results of the battle. He must have been turning in his bed. But that was not the case. When he went to bed, he thought about God and slept. God eventually gave him victory in the battle.

*"Lord, let Your face make me happy;
I will trust in You for victory.*[194]
*You have always given me food to eat,
So I will lie down and sleep.*[212]
I trust you to keep me safe."[413]

Talk About the Psalm: What did you learn about the psalm writer in this story? What did you learn about God?

Psalm 4: Read this week's psalm in your Bible together. Choose a verse to read aloud as a prayer.

Prayer: Thank You, God, for the psalm prayers in the Bible. Thank You for teaching us about You and about how to pray. In Jesus' name, Amen.

JOSEPH

Scripture: Matthew 1:18–25
Place: Nazareth
Time: 4 BC

When Mary went to visit her Aunt Elizabeth near Jerusalem, Joseph missed her. He was in love with her. He thought about her as he worked on the house they would live in together after they were married. He thought about her as he worked hard to earn money to pay for the marriage celebration. He thought about her all the time!

After about three months, Mary returned. She ran straight to Joseph's carpenter shop. But something was wrong! Mary excitedly told him about the angel who came to talk to her.[14] She told him about Elizabeth's greeting. But Joseph could see that Mary was pregnant!

When Mary finished talking, Joseph looked in her eyes sadly and shook his head. He couldn't believe that the baby was the Son of God. That sort of thing just didn't happen! Joseph turned away from her. "Go, Mary. Just go."

Mary realized that he didn't believe her. She sadly walked home and went straight to the fig tree to pray.

Joseph didn't know what to do. He was a good man and did not want Mary to be hurt. His mind was racing. If he went before the elders to explain why he wanted to end the marriage agreement, everyone would know about it. Mary would be in big trouble! She could even be put to death! And if she wasn't killed, no one would ever have anything to do with her again.

Joseph didn't want those things to happen, so he decided to end the agreement privately.[534] Maybe sometime in the future, he would find someone else to marry. Joseph's heart was broken.

That night as he laid in his bed, trying to sleep, Joseph thought about his decision. Joseph fell asleep with tears in his eyes. In his dreams, an angel appeared to him.[128]

The angel said, "Joseph, son of David, don't be afraid to take Mary as your wife, for she conceived a child by the Holy Spirit.[224] She shall bring forth a son and you shall call His name Jesus because He will save His people from their sins."

The angel continued, "This has been done to fulfill what God said through a prophet long ago:

"'Behold, a virgin shall be with child, and bear a Son, and they shall call His name Immanuel,' being interpreted, 'God with Us.'"[393]

The very next morning, Joseph got up with a smile. Joseph loved and trusted God. He was so glad that God sent an angel to confirm the truth about Mary. He had wanted to believe her so much, and now he did![327]

Joseph knew exactly what to do about Mary! Joseph always wanted to obey God, so he went and took Mary home as his wife. Everyone in town thought that they were living as man and wife, and that the baby Mary was pregnant with was Joseph's baby. But Joseph and Mary didn't sleep together until after the baby, the Son of God, was born.

Talk About the Story: Why did Joseph want to end his marriage agreement with Mary? What changed his mind? Why do you think Joseph was willing to obey what the angel said?

Scripture: "And be kind to one another, tenderhearted, forgiving one another, just as God in Christ also forgave you" (Ephesians 4:32).

Family Time: What are some words you could us to describe Joseph? Joseph chose to be kind to Mary before he knew the truth about the baby. When are some times it might be hard to choose to be kind to others today? What are some kind things we can do together as a family this week?

Prayer: Lord, help me to be kind to people as Joseph was to Mary. Also, Lord, thank You for sending Jesus into the world through the Virgin Mary, just as You promised in the Old Testament. Amen.

CHAPTER 4

JESUS IS BORN

Mary was very near the birth of her son when they arrived in the city of Bethlehem. They discovered the city was overcrowded with others who had also come to be counted. Bethlehem was so crowded, the best lodging Joseph could find for his expectant wife was a stable in which livestock was kept.

When Jesus was born, his parent's turned the stable into a nursery. He was wrapped in swaddling clothes and placed in a soft bed of grasses in a manger which was usually used to feed the livestock. Despite the fact that both Joseph and Mary knew the supernatural significance of this birth, it must have seemed a strange way for the Son of God to enter the world. The casual observer of this birth would have seen nothing different beyond the unusual place in which the child was born, but almost a century later, one of that child's future disciples would describe His birth with the words, "And the Word became flesh and dwelt among us" (John 1:14).

While others might not realize what was happening in that Bethlehem

stable, it did not escape heaven's notice. Shortly after the birth of Jesus, an angel appeared to a group of shepherds watching their flocks on the hills outside the city of Bethlehem. As soon as he announced the birth of the Christ child, that angel was accompanied by a multitude of angels praising God.

Sometime later, Jesus was worshiped by a group of eastern rulers known as the Magi. These men may not have been kings themselves, but certainly possessed enough influence to be regarded as king-makers in their society. The appearance of a "star" in the heavens had been interpreted by them as an indication of the birth of the King of the Jews.

When the Magi came to the family, they worshiped Jesus and presented Him with gifts of gold, frankincense and myrrh. Because three gifts were presented, it has been traditionally thought three men were present.

The Magi were not the only ones warned to leave Bethlehem. Once again an angel appeared to Joseph in a dream urging him to take Mary and Jesus to Egypt. Joseph was told Herod would try to destroy the child. Quickly Joseph gathered what was needed and he and his family made their way to Egypt that very night.

JESUS IS BORN IN BETHLEHEM

Scripture: Luke 2:1–14
Place: Bethlehem
Time: December, 4 BC

❝I couldn't have made the trip without the donkey," Mary said, shutting her eyes to constant discomfort.

It had been a long slow journey from Nazareth to Bethlehem. Mary and Joseph followed shepherd's paths for part of the way, hoping to arrive in Bethlehem as soon as possible. They had to stop often to rest. It is not easy for a woman to travel when she is about to give birth!

Finally, Bethlehem was in sight! But they needed a safe and quiet place to sleep that night.

Both had family roots in Bethlehem. Bethlehem was the home of their parents, and the Roman census had commanded everyone return to their hometown to register for taxes.[364] Bethlehem was also where King David was born. God wanted His Son, Jesus, to be born in a placed called the home of kings because Jesus would be a king.[359]

"Why now?" She moaned. It was winter, the weather was blustery.

"OH!" Mary clutched her midsection, "It's a shooting pain." It meant the baby would come soon.[376]

Joseph was frantic as he banged on the door to every inn, but there was no available room. Bethlehem was swamped with travelers returning home for Rome's census.

"No room in this inn," the gruff man refused to open the door, he just yelled his answer through the crack in the door. "We've got to have a place," Joseph's beard was blown by the evening breeze. "My wife's having labor pains . . . the baby's coming." The innkeeper stepped out, closing the door behind him. A pain hit and Mary moaned, "Oh!"

The innkeeper recognized legitimate pain. His wife had a multitude of children. "There—" he pointed to the stable. "You'll be out of the evening chill . . . you'll find plenty of straw. You can deliver your baby in there."

The stable leaned against a giant rock wall. A warm orange glow from a lantern inside invited them into the stable.

"There's a cave in the rock where you'll be out of the breeze," the innkeeper explained.

Mary found some fresh clean hay to lie on. Joseph found the swathes of clean white cloth Mary had packed to wrap the baby and keep him warm.[219]

Two hours later, a healthy baby boy was born. The baby waved His outstretched arms, breathed air into His lungs, and cried. Because all newborns cry, the baby let out a bawl.

"Don't cry, Jesus," Mary reached for her son. "There," she kissed His cheek. Baby Jesus nestled into her loving arms. Mary was the first to call the name *JESUS*.

Joseph heard the name JESUS and smiled in support. They both remembered what the angel Gabriel had said, "You shall call His name Jesus, for He shall save His people from their sins."[385]

The baby slept in Mary's arms; she tenderly stroked His brow and kissed His forehead . . . and the world would be forever changed.

Talk About the Story: Why did Joseph and Mary go to Bethlehem instead of staying home when the baby was about to be born? Why did they have to stay in a stable? What did they name the baby? Why did they choose that name?

Scripture: "In this the love of God was manifested toward us, that God has sent His only begotten Son into the world, that we might live through Him" (1 John 4:9).

Family Time: What are some reasons we celebrate the birth of Jesus? Why did God send Jesus to be born? How has the world been changed forever as a result of Jesus' birth?

Prayer: Father, thank You for sending Jesus into the world. I have received Him into my heart just as Mary and Joseph received Him into this world. Amen.

SHEPHERDS LEARN ABOUT THE LAMB OF GOD

Scripture: Luke 2:8–14
Place: Bethlehem
Time: December, 4 BC

A fire on the hillside burned low as a group of shepherds drew closer to the flames. It was cold that night, and they had to stay outside all night long to watch and care for the many sheep in the field outside of Bethlehem.

"Where is some more fuel for the fire?" One of the older shepherds asked as he looked at the younger shepherds. The youngest shepherd remembered that wood for the fire was his responsibility.

"Sorry!" He scurried off to find more wood.

The shepherds were camped outside the town of Bethlehem, just like they did every year around this time. Many of the sheep they cared for would be used as sacrifices at the Temple in Jerusalem, not far from there. The sheep were the best of the best, and they had the best shepherds in the area to care for them!

Sometimes, wild animals tried to steal a young lamb. Other times, a robber might try to take a pregnant ewe so that he could sell her lamb later.

But on most nights, nothing happened at all. The sheep slept and the shepherds told each other stories their fathers and grandfathers had told them. The younger shepherds loved to hear the stories, especially the stories about Israel's most famous shepherd, the shepherd who became King David!

But tonight, the older shepherds were deep in thought. Maybe it was just too cold tonight.

As the young shepherd returned with more wood for the fire, he stopped in surprise. Something was happening that they did not expect! A sparkling light[26] blinded the shepherds. They covered their heads and hid their faces.[164] They were terrified!

"Don't be afraid," a voice came from the other side of the light.

"What is it?" the young shepherd asked.

An older shepherd answered. "Only heaven can be this bright."

The shepherds slowly began to drop their arms. They squinted into the light.

"Wow!" the younger shepherd whispered.. "I've never seen anything like THIS!"

The blanket of light was not filled with stars, but angels.

"Don't be afraid," the voice behind the light repeated itself. "I have come to give you good tidings of great joy to everyone."[213]

"The shepherds exchanged glances, wondering what good news the angels had. Was it money? Houses? What?"

"Your Savior was born tonight in Bethlehem," the voice instructed. "You will find Him wrapped in swaths of cloths, sleeping in a feeding trough."

Suddenly, the sky was filled with angels. The angels all cried out, "GLORY TO GOD IN THE HIGHEST, AND ON EARTH PEACE TO ALL PEOPLE."[191] Then they were gone.

The shepherds stood together in awe. "Did that really just happen?" one asked.

Another shepherd smiled. "Oh, yes, it did. And we need to go and find that baby.

"LET'S GO!" the younger shepherd leaped to his feet, waving his arms for everyone to get up. "LET'S GO NOW!"[195]

Talk About the Story: What were the shepherds doing? What did the angel tell them? Why do you think the angel told the shepherds about the Savior's birth?

Scripture: "Glory to God in the highest, and on earth peace, good will toward men." Luke 2:14 *NKJV*

Family Time: How did Jesus birth bring peace and good will to people all over the world? What are some things we can say and do to praise God for sending Jesus?

Prayer: Father, I will come worship Jesus when I hear the Christmas story because He came into the world for me. I want to give my best for Jesus. Amen.

SHEPHERDS WORSHIP THE BABY JESUS

Scripture: Luke 2:15–20
Place: Bethlehem
Time: December, 4 BC

Mary and Joseph slept on the straw. It had been a long tiring journey. Baby Jesus was sleeping in the feed trough. Joseph's mind was active; he couldn't sleep soundly. In his sub-conscious he heard noises outside the stable.

"THERE'S SOMEONE OUTSIDE," Joseph awoke. Creeping to the stable door he tried to be silent, but the door resisted, "Skeeeeek . . . ."

Mary awoke, but the baby slept.

"Who's there?" Joseph spoke into the dark courtyard. In the darkness he saw a dozen faces, not the faces of thieves coming to steal from him, but worshipful faces.

"We're shepherds," the voice of the older shepherd replied. "Was there a baby born here tonight?"

"Yes."

"We must see Him," he begged, "the baby is from God."[195] The other shepherds nodded their agreement for they all heard the angels and they all saw the light.

The shepherds had brought a lamp. They set the wick of the lantern to give more light. The orange light was held high, then Joseph saw them; clearly the yard was filled with shepherds. Joseph opened the stable door wider, "Skeeeeek."

"Mary," he whispered her name so he wouldn't awaken Baby Jesus. "Some shepherds want to see Jesus."[538]

The lamp was held to Mary's soft face. She was lovelier than ever before in her life. Giving birth is among the greatest accomplishments in life, making Mary happy and satisfied. She had obeyed God and called her son Jesus, but the Father in heaven called Him the Son of the Highest.[327]

When the light reflected in the baby's face, the shepherds quickly dropped on their knees with their faces to the ground—worshiping. Just one look at the baby did it, they were struck silent. After all, they had been blinded with heaven's glory, they heard the angel. Now all they could do was worship the baby.[367]

Several silent minutes passed. The shepherds worshiped motionless on the ground. Mary and Joseph didn't know how to respond. Then the shepherds looked up to the baby and repeated the song of the angels,

Glory to God in the Highest,
And in earth,
Peace and goodwill to men.[191]

Mary saw their eyes . . . crying eyes surrounded by dirty faces and scruffy beards. Their faces were blackened by the soot of campfires, their faces dirty by perspiration that absorbed the dust blown from open fields. Mary thought to herself, *"THESE ARE ADORING EYES."*[530]

"I don't understand . . .," Joseph broke the silence.

The chief shepherd told about the events in the darkened field, how a sparkling angel appeared to them in a blanket of light.[26] He told how they looked into the light of heaven and heard angels sing. Then the older shepherd told Joseph what the angel said to them,[15] "You will find a baby wrapped in strips of cloth, sleeping in an animal feed trough."[213]

"That's Him," the proud Joseph pointed to Jesus.

"The angel called Him our Savior," none of the shepherds doubted. Now their faces were warmed by the sight of the baby. They looked at the baby with believing eyes.

A young shepherd with sparkling eyes stood up. "We have to tell others!"

The other shepherds broke into wide smiles. "Yes! Let's wake up this sleepy town! The Savior is here. God has sent Him for us all!"[191]

Mary and Joseph laughed. "Yes, spread the good news! He is here!"

With a last, adoring look at Jesus, the shepherds turned and ran into the night. "Wake up! We have amazing news to tell!"

Talk About the Story: Why do you think the shepherds wanted to worship Jesus? What do you think you would have done if you had been there that night? What did the shepherds do after they saw Jesus?

Scripture: "Make a joyful shout to God, all the earth! Sing out the honor of His name; make His praise glorious." Psalm 66:1–2 *NKJV*

Family Time: What are some ways that we worship God for sending Jesus? What can we do differently during Christmastime this year to focus on worshiping Jesus more?

Prayer: Father, I worship You just as the shepherds because You came into the world to be our Savior. Amen.

THE BABY JESUS IS DEDICATED

Scripture: Luke 2:25–35
Place: Jerusalem
Time: 40 days after Jesus' birth

The young couple walked slowly into the Temple courtyard. They were obeying God to dedicate their newborn son in God's house.[389]

"I hope we don't have to wait too long," Joseph tried to see if there was a long line, where babies were dedicated and mothers offered sacrifices for purification.

Joseph walked a few feet in front of Mary, searching where businessmen were selling birds to be sacrificed in the Temple. Joseph couldn't afford a lamb.

According to the law the poor could offer a turtledove or two young pigeons. Joseph spotted cages holding turtledoves and pigeons. Joseph went to bargain for the cheapest turtledoves while Mary waited, shielding the face of her young baby from the sun. Soon Joseph returned with turtledoves, and they walked toward the line of people waiting to dedicate their babies.

"STOP!" They heard a commanding voice. "STOP! I MUST SEE THAT CHILD," a strong aged voice yelled behind them. The courtyard was bubbling with conversation, laughter, and the braying of animals. Few people paid attention to the man calling to them.

Turning, Mary and Joseph saw an elderly man with outstretched arms beckoning to them.

"PLEASE, I must see the child." He was not dressed as a priest in white robes. His robe was gray. He held out friendly arms to them. The wrinkles on his face, and tossed gray hair reminded them of a kindly grandfather. They smiled back and walked over to the man. He announced, "I have been waiting to see this child for years."[526]

Mary and Joseph looked at each other. Was this another one of those unusual circumstances?

Elderly Simeon explained, "This morning the Spirit told me to come to the Temple today. The Spirit told me that I would see the Messiah today."

"Today," he whispered, "my wait is over!"

Years ago God had told Simeon he would not die until he had seen the Messiah who would save Israel.[224]

"Let me have the child," Simeon reached out with both arms. Mary looked at Joseph, and he nodded. She handed the child to Simeon.

Taking Jesus in his ancient hands, he lifted Him toward God, just as the priest would dedicate a baby to God. Simeon lifted the baby up to God, saying, "Behold this child is come for the rising again of many people in Israel,"[283] Simeon's raspy voice was bold; "this child is a sign for us all."

Then looking at Mary, Simeon said an unusual thing, "The sword shall pierce your soul because of this child."[470]

Mary wondered what he meant.

Old Simeon then held baby Jesus tightly and bowed his head in obvious prayer. Simeon thanked God that his life's task had been realized.[278]

Tears trickled from the corners of Simeon's eyes, then disappeared into the heavy wrinkles of his face. Old Simeon looked deeply into the eyes of the baby. He smiled, and his joy brought more tears.

Simeon handed the small baby back to his father. Joseph cuddled the baby in his arms, pulling the swaths of clothes around His kicking legs.

"Now your servant can depart in peace," Simeon said. "Now my eyes have seen our salvation,"[416] he smiled. "This child shall be a light unto the Gentiles and a glory to Israel."[283]

Talk About the Story: Why did Mary and Joseph take Jesus to the Temple? What did Simeon say about Jesus?

Scripture: "My eyes have seen Your salvation which You have prepared before the face of all peoples." Luke 2:30–31

Family Time: What was the salvation that Simeon talked about? How did Jesus bring salvation? Now that we know that God sent Jesus to die for our sins and bring us salvation, what are some ways that we can respond to God's love for us?

Prayer: Father, thank You for showing us Your love by sending Jesus. Thank You for bringing us salvation through Jesus. Amen.

SOME WISE MEN

Scripture: Matthew 2:1–8
Place: From the East to Jerusalem
Time: After Jesus' birth

Agroup of men wearing gold-trimmed turbans bent over the old open scrolls. Lamplight flickered around them. The men talked in hushed whispers as they studied the writing, pointing at one passage and then another.

"Look at this," one said. He read aloud, "There will come a star out of Jacob" (Numbers 24:17). They knew this meant that the Messiah, the promised King of the Jews, would be announced by a star.[264]

They hurried out to the open balcony to look at the stars, pointing to one bright spot in the night sky. "This is the sign. It must be. There is no other explanation! This is an announcement from the one true God," another of the men said.

They went back to the scrolls again and read more of the writing. "Yes, there is not mistake. The long awaited King of the Jews has been born!"

"We must go. The heavens declare His glory. We must go and worship Him." The men all agreed. They sent for a servant. "Make things ready. We must follow this star to see the newborn King!"

The servant hurried out to make arrangements. The trip would take a very long time! They would have to travel over 800 miles. They would need lots of food and water and money and protection! Camels would be the best animals to

take. They could carry large amounts of cargo, and they were not too uncomfortable for riding. As he gathered the other servants to make arrangements, the
wealthy wise men discussed what they should bring as gifts for the newborn king.

"Gold, of course," said one of the men.

"And frankincense. It is right for this king."

"And myrrh. Yes, these gifts are fit for the King of the Jews. We will offer
these to Him."

Months later, the large caravan arrived in the Jewish capitol city. "Surely the
King of the Jews is here. There is the palace. Let's go and worship Him!"

As the wise men arrived, they asked, "Where is the Child that is born King of
the Jews? We have seen His star in the East, and have come to worship Him."[541]

The people didn't know how to answer these rich and powerful looking men.
The current king of the Jews was King Herod. And he was NOT a nice man! He
had been appointed king by the Roman emperor, and he was afraid of anyone
trying to take his place. History tells us that he had already killed several family
members to keep them from trying to take his place, and his servants knew he
would kill again if anyone threatened his place!

Soon everyone in Jerusalem was talking about these strange visitors and the
things they said. And it wasn't long before King Herod heard about them as well!

"Get the priests and scribes here NOW" King Herod bellowed.

When they arrived, breathless and extremely nervous, demanded to hear
what the scriptures say about the Deliverer to be born.[70]

They said, "In Bethlehem of Judea, as it is written in Scripture. Out of Bethlehem—one of the smallest cities—out of you shall come the Messiah that shall
rule God's people."[249]

Herod sent them away as he planned and plotted. Then Herod called for the
wise men. In a very different kind of voice, gently and kindly, Herod told them
what the priests and scribes had said. "When you find Him, please come back and
tell me where He is. I also want to go and worship Him."[231]

Talk About the Story: Why did the wise men decide to travel to worship Jesus?
How did they learn about Him?

Scripture: "They received the word with all readiness, and searched the Scriptures daily to find out whether these things were so." Acts 17:11

Family Time: What have you already learned about Jesus? What questions do
you have about Him? What can you do to learn more about Him?

Prayer: Lord, I will search the Bible to find out more about Jesus, just as the wise
men say the Scriptures to find about His birth. And I, too, will come and worship
the Baby Jesus, just as the wise men went a long distance to worship Him. Amen.

PSALM 8
THE GREATNESS OF GOD

David sat on a small hill, his sheep sleeping in the grassy pasture nearby. Nighttime was David's favorite time to pray. When he saw the moon and twinkling stars, he automatically worshiped God who created them. Tonight the moon appeared to be brighter than usual; its milky surface astonished him. David reached for his harp and sang to God. "I marvel at the night sky, I know all the stars were placed there by Your hand, You also put the moon there."

David thought of the first line of the new Psalm he was writing. He sang, "O Lord, my LORD, Your majesty floods my heart." The Excellency of God's name exceeds the glory of the heavens. He repeated "O Lord, My LORD."[188]

When David meditated on the greatness of the created world, and the magnificence of God, he was overwhelmed with his own human limitation. He sang, "What are we but created humans, we can only think about our God. We are created lower than angels and we are created lower than God. We are nothing but a creation made from the clay of the ground."

Then David remembered his role to care for sheep and protect them from danger. He sang, "We are created lower than God, but the LORD has crowned us

with glory and honor." Just as God created the moon, stars and the entire universe, David realized his responsibility for flocks, birds, wild animals, and all living creature. All he could do in response was worship God.

> "LORD, You are our God
> How excellent is Your greatnes.[188]
> I look into Your hand made sky
> And praise You for Your glory and power.
> You created the moon, stars and put them in place.
> Who am I to even worship Your greatness.
> You created us with human bodies,
> You think about us and You care about us.
> You have created us lower than Yourself,
> Yet You gave us the awesome privilege
> Of being responsible for all Your creation, for
> Flocks, wild animals, birds and creeping things.
> Your world reflects Your glory and greatness."

Talk About the Psalm: What did you learn about the psalm writer in this story? What did you learn about God?

Psalm 8: Read this week's psalm in your Bible together. Choose a verse to read aloud as a prayer.

Prayer: Thank You, God, for the psalm prayers in the Bible. Thank You for teaching us about You and about how to pray. In Jesus' name, Amen.

DATE ___/___

HEROD'S PLOT

Scripture: Matthew 2:1–8
Place: Herod's palace
Time: After Jesus' birth

King Herod stood in his opulent throne room with the wise men from the East.[264] Herod had sent his servants and all the priests and scribes away. Herod did not like the news the priests had brought. They quoted from the Scriptures:

> But you, Bethlehem, in the land
>   of Judah,
> Are not the least among the rulers
>   of Judah;
> For out of you shall come a Ruler
> Who will shepherd My people Israel.[249]
>   Matthew 2:6

The wise men were delighted! "This is the information we have been looking for!" they exclaimed.[541]

www.thefamilyprayerbible.com

Herod turned away with a grimace. The gold trim on their turbans and cloaks left Herod feeling a little jealous. And the news about a newborn king filled him with dread. *I am the only king of the Jews! How dare there be someone else! A STAR announced Him? He must be stopped!*

But Herod controlled himself and forced a friendly smile. "This is most extraordinary news! When did the star first appear?"[70]

"It was no more than a year ago. We studied and searched the ancient writings for a while before we understood the sign. But now we are delighted to be so close!" one of the wise men said.

Another said, "Thank you so much for assisting us in knowing where to go next. Your priests and scribes have been very helpful!"

The wealthy, important wise men from the East bowed to Herod in respect and then turned to leave. They were headed to Bethlehem to worship the newborn King of the Jews.

Herod's thoughts swirled. *What were they thinking? No one is going to take my place as king!* Herod felt fear growing in the pit of his stomach, but as he thought about someone else trying to sit on his throne, that fear grew into anger. And the more Herod thought about it, the more his anger grew into full-blown rage!

Herod took a deep breath and smiled. *I was brilliant!* Herod thought. *Those so-called wise men had no idea!* Herod laughed to himself, *I told them to come back and tell me where the child is so that I could go and worship Him, too.*[231] *But I am not interested in worshiping a little child! I'd much rather KILL Him!*

Herod called a trusted soldier to his side. "I have a plan." The soldier listened carefully, nodding his head as the king spoke. Killing a young child is not something most soldiers look forward to doing, but the king must be obeyed.

"When the wise men return, they will tell us exactly where to find the child. It will be easy to get rid of Him!" Herod said.

Talk About the Story: Why was King Herod fearful and angry? Why do you think Herod pretended to be happy about the newborn king? Why did he lie to the wise men? What do you think King Herod's plan was?

Scripture: "An angry man stirs up strife, and a furious man abounds in transgression." Proverbs 29:22

Family Time: When have you seen anger grow into a big problem? When might jealousy lead someone to sin? Why do you think this happens so often? What are some positive things we can do when we start to feel angry or afraid?

Prayer: Father, help us to recognize our anger and deal with it before it grows into sin and trouble for us and the people around us. Help us to stay away from jealousy as well. Amen.

WISE MEN WORSHIP

Scripture: Matthew 2:7–11
Place: Bethlehem
Time: Up to two years after Jesus' birth

Mary laughed as little Jesus played on the rug in their snug little house. Mary finished washing up from the evening meal and lifted Jesus into her arms. She and Joseph looked out the door into the evening. "I'm glad we decided to stay here in Bethlehem."

"Yes, I think the city of David is the right place for Jesus to grow up," Joseph answered.

As the stars began to show in the night sky, Mary sang softly to Jesus and rocked Him in her arms. It was a peaceful night in their home.

But outside, something was happening. On the road to Bethlehem, a large, colorful caravan stopped. Richly dressed men from the East looked up at the stars in the sky.

"There! There it is!" one shouted. The group of men called out in joy! "The star is here!"[541]

One of the men pointed to a house in Bethlehem. "It is pointing there—to that house, that small house on the edge of the town!"

The caravan continued toward the house. Mary and Joseph heard the caravan approach. Along with their neighbors, Mary and Joseph cautiously opened their door and looked toward the east end of Bethlehem.

This was not just another string of merchants and camels. These camels were dromedaries. Camels with two humps were seldom seen in Bethlehem.

Joseph surveyed the riders of the camels, the gold on their turbans was deeper colored than others, the pink shirts of the attendants were not just faded red, the flashing pink was captivating.

A servant from the caravan walked directly to Mary and Joseph's door. He bowed his head in greeting to Joseph "We have come to honor the child born King of the Jews."[264] The phrase *"King of the Jews,"* startled Joseph. The angel Gabriel had said Jesus would sit on the throne of David, but they hadn't told anyone Jesus would be a King.[27]

The servant bowed his head again in oriental fashion. Then Joseph noticed his milky brown skin was much smoother than people living in Israel. Even the cotton of his tunic was woven differently, smoothly, not like the coarse cotton cloth found around Bethlehem. Then Joseph saw the curled toes on the man's sandals.

"May we visit the young King?" the servant asked. "We have gifts for Him."[184]

Joseph nodded, "Yes."

The servant hurried back to the caravan to speak with his master. His sharp goatee, and slightly slanted eyes told the observers he was from a far distance. He walked to the house followed by two servants carrying a heavy chest. Other richly dressed men followed with their servants carrying other items.

They stood respectfully near the door. "We have come to worship the King of the Jews,"[264] the first spoke in his dialect. "We study the stars," he explained. "The stars tell us God is going to send us a Savior."

Then the wise men turned the conversation to the purpose of their trip. "Bring the gifts!" First, the men presented the chest. It was full of gold! Then there were gifts of frankincense and myrrh. The men knelt before the young child in Mary's arms. They bowed their faces to the ground and spread their hands in praise.[541]

"Bless the Lord, O my soul," the wise men knew many languages. They prayed in the Hebrew tongue. "Bless the Lord with all that is within me. Bless His holy name."[46]

Talk About the Story: How did the wise men know how to find Jesus? What did the wise men do to worship Jesus?

Scripture: "And when they had come into the house, they saw the young Child with Mary His mother, and fell down and worshiped Him. And when they had opened their treasures, they presented gifts to Him: gold, frankincense, and myrrh" (Matthew 2:11).

Family Time: Why do you think it is wise to worship Jesus? What are some different ways that people today worship Jesus? What can we as a family do to worship Jesus this week?

Prayer: Father, I worship Jesus as did the wise men. I will make Him first in my life. Amen.

PREVENTING HEROD'S PLOT

Scripture: Matthew 2:12
Place: Bethlehem
Time: Up to two years after Jesus' birth

"God's blessing and favor be with you and your family," the wise men said as they bowed and turned to leave Mary and Joseph and the young Jesus. The men were so glad to have seen and worshiped the promised King.

As the wise men walked back to their caravan, they were deep in thought. *This King is not like any other! The stars declare His birth, and yet He is not in a palace. He is born to a poor family in an insignificant town. We must learn more!*

The wise men remembered their conversation with King Herod. He wanted them to return and tell him where the child was so that he could also go and worship.[231] Of course, they would tell him!

www.thefamilyprayerbible.com

While the wise men had been in Joseph's house in Bethlehem, the wise men's servants had been hard at work outside of the town. They unpacked tents, pillows, tables, rugs and other items to set up a luxurious camp for their masters. Other servants prepared food. Even more servants made sure that the camp was secure from any possible thieves.

By the time the wise men returned, the camp was prepared for them. One of the wise men said, "I'm glad we brought the gold for the new King. The parents will be able to use that to provide for and protect their Child."

"Yes, that is good," another said. "I do wonder if our stop in Jerusalem to talk with King Herod might cause trouble for them."

The third wise man said, "I don't know about that. But I do know that God has been good to us. He allowed us to see and understand the sign of the star so that we could come to worship Him. I wouldn't trade this experience for anything!"

The wise men continued discussing the young Jesus late into the night. Finally they retired to their tents to sleep.

Later, as they slept, all three wise men had the SAME dream. In the dream, an angel talked to them. "Do not return to Herod. He wants to kill the Child!"[109]

Each of the wise men awoke suddenly; the message of the dream filled their minds. They jumped up and ran to the others. "I had a dream!" they all said at once. As soon as they realized they had all had the same dream, they called for their servants to prepare to leave.

Sleepy servants scurried around the camp, packing as quietly as possible. Within a short time, everything was ready. The wise men climbed onto their camels and they set out in a new direction.

They returned to Persia, not going through Jerusalem or any of the area controlled by Herod's soldiers. They quickly and quietly went home another way.[109]

Talk About the Story: What did the angel tell the wise men in their dream? How did the wise men respond to the angel's news and instructions?

Scripture: "I made haste and did not delay to keep Your commandments" Psalm 119:60

Family Time: Why do you think it is a good idea to make haste and not delay to obey God's commands? What might result from being slow to obey, even if you intend to obey eventually? What are some things in your life that you are putting off doing, even though you know they are the right things to do?

Prayer: Father, thank You for the story of the wise men obeying the angel's instructions. Please help us to follow their example in obeying You quickly and completely. Amen.

HEROD'S RAGE

Scripture: Matthew 2:16–18
Place: Jerusalem to Bethlehem
Time: Up to two years after Jesus' birth

King Herod called his trusted Roman commander to his side. "Have the wise men from the East returned from Bethlehem yet?"

"No, your majesty. We have been watching the road from Bethlehem constantly. They have not returned."

"What is taking them so long!" screamed the king.

The commander could see that trouble was looming. When Herod was angry, heads would roll—literally! "I will ride out to Bethlehem myself right now to check on them," he replied.

Quickly the commander headed for the stables. He and a small group of soldiers mounted their horses and galloped down the road toward Bethlehem. The six-mile trip took just over an hour. The commander grew more and more concerned as he rode through and around the town. *Where were they? What did they do? What will Herod do when I tell him that they are gone?*

The commander sent soldiers in all directions, riding their horses hard to find the caravan. Two hours later, the soldiers returned to Bethlehem. "It's no use. They are long gone," they said.

It was late at night by the time the commander returned to King Herod with his report. Herod was waiting for him. "What took you so long?! Where are they? Where is the child? Did you kill Him already?"

Finally Herod stopped long enough for the commander to speak. Grimly he said, "The wise men have deceived you, O King. They have gone home a different way. We pursued them, but they have gotten too far away."

Herod was filled with rage! "How dare they! I am the king! The only king!" Then Herod let his rage completely take over. "Get your men together. Go to Bethlehem tonight and kill every male child two years old and younger.[43] Do it now!"

The commander groaned inwardly. *This is evil! But what choice do I have?*

The commander called for his most merciless soldiers. "Herod has given us a job to do," the commander announced. They saddled fresh horses and gathered their weapons. Within the hour, a large group of soldiers were headed back to Bethlehem to follow Herod's horrible directions.[313]

Talk About the Story: Why was Herod angry about the wise men? What did he do because of his anger? What did the Roman commander do? Why did he do that? What do you think he could have done differently?

Scripture: "Be angry and do not sin; do not let the sun go down on your wrath." Ephesians 4:26

Family Time: King Herod chose to do evil things when he was angry because he did not honor God. What can we do when we are angry to avoid hurting others? How can we honor God, even when we are angry? What are some things we can do to honor and obey God when someone tells us to do things that are wrong?

Prayer: Dear God, please help us to honor and obey You, even when we feel angry or when someone else tells us to do things that are wrong. Please be with us and give us wisdom and courage to do what is right. In Jesus' name, Amen.

ESCAPE TO EGYPT

Scripture: Matthew 2:13–18
Place: From Bethlehem to Egypt
Time: Up to two years after Jesus' birth

Mary and Jesus slept peacefully. The little town of Bethlehem slept beneath a silent sky. A dog barked in the distance, then let out a lonesome whimper. Joseph was awakened by an angel.

"Get up . . . danger is coming," the heavenly messenger warned him. "King Herod is coming this way to kill the child." Joseph lay stunned almost afraid to stir. "Hurry," the angel warned.[128]

There was a faint light in the eastern sky when Joseph led Mary, holding young Jesus, out to the donkey. He threw two sacks filled with gold, frankincense and myrrh over the animal. "We'll have money to live in Egypt."[327]

The animal's hoofs clicked on the cobblestones. Feeling his way in the dark shadows, Joseph urgently pulled on the reins, "Hurry . . ." he pleaded.

As they left Bethlehem, they heard the tramp of Roman soldiers coming toward the town. Joseph, Mary and Jesus hid in some bushes. They prayed silently as they waited for the soldiers to pass by.

Breathing a sigh of relief, Joseph and Mary started out on the road again as Jesus slept in Mary's arms. They traveled for days and days! After more than a week of traveling along the road to Egypt, Joseph and Mary felt they were finally safe and began to relax.

One night, as they rested at an oasis, a traveler arrived. He began talking about Roman soldiers killing all the babies in Bethlehem.[43] Joseph and Mary listened as he talked. They knew the reason for that horrible action. And they knew that God had kept them safe! As of yet, Mary and Joseph didn't know all the things that would happen to Jesus, but they were beginning to understand! This terrible event actually fulfilled a prophecy in the Old Testament:[327] "In Ramah there was a voice weeping over their children and Rachel would not be comforted because they were all dead" (Jeremiah 31:15, *ELT*).[313]

EGYPT

Finally, they arrived in Egypt. They were safe from Herod! The land of Egypt is quite different from the land of Israel. Idols were mounted in the buildings to their many gods, and etched on the walls of government buildings were images of Ra, the sun god.

Joseph found work as a carpenter. They found a place to live, and Mary worked to make it a pleasant home. Jesus grew just like all other little boys, learning to talk and walk and imitate His parents.

But Joseph and Mary missed their life at home. They must have longed to see the Temple in Jerusalem again and to worship God there as they used to!

Talk About the Story: How did God protect Mary, Joseph, and Jesus? What do you think it was like to live in a different country so far from home? What do you think Mary and Joseph missed most as they lived in Egypt?

Scripture: "But let all those rejoice who put their trust in You; Let them ever shout for joy, because You defend them; Let those also who love Your name be joyful in You." Psalm 5:11

Family Time: How did God protect Jesus when he was little? What are some ways God can protect you?

Prayer: Father, thank You for protecting Jesus so He could do what You sent Him to do. Protect me so I can do what You want me to do in life. I give myself to do what You want me to do. Amen.

CHAPTER 5

JESUS' CHILDHOOD

Apart from his brief exile in Egypt, there is no indication that Jesus' childhood differed much from that of other children. Joseph and Mary had other children in time and Jesus learned to relate to these and other children in the town. He probably joined other boys his age in the Synagogue School of Nazareth where he would be taught the Scriptures and basic skills such as reading, writing, and arithmetic. "And the Child grew and became strong in spirit, filled with wisdom; and the grace of God was upon Him" (Luke 2:40).

The only further record we have of Jesus' childhood is the account of a visit to Jerusalem during the Passover season when He was twelve years old. His family went to Jerusalem for Passover annually. When Jesus was twelve,

He remained in the city without His parent's knowledge. They began the trip back to Nazareth, thinking He was along. Three days passed before they found Him in the temple. While the teachers with whom He was meeting were impressed by His understanding of the law, His parents had been concerned for His welfare. When they finally found Him, Mary rebuked Him admitting both she and Joseph had been worried about Him. He responded, "Did you not know that I must be about My Father's business?" (Luke 1:49).

GOING HOME TO NAZARETH

Scripture: Matthew 2:19-23
Place: From Egypt to Nazareth
Time: 2 BC to 2 AD

Mary and Joseph settled down in a small Egyptian town. Life was different there! People spoke a different language, ate different foods, and believed in different things. People there worshiped the sun and the river instead of the one true God!

Since everyone wanted to live near the Nile River, houses were built on top of each other. Like many people, Mary and Joseph lived in a small house built on the roof of a larger house. Joseph worked in a carpenter shop making furniture for his customers. Because he could carve decorations from Israel, many people ordered chairs made by Joseph.

As Jesus grew, He learned to speak in more than one language. At home Mary spoke Hebrew, and Jesus learned Hebrew words. Because they lived in an Egyptian trade town, many of the merchants spoke Aramaic. So Jesus learned Aramaic words to talk with other children. The tax collector in town spoke Greek because Greek was the official language of the Roman Empire. Jesus quickly learned Greek words.

Little Jesus grew and grew! But Mary and Joseph longed to return to Israel as soon as it was safe.

One night Joseph awoke. An angel spoke to him, "Take the child and His mother and return to Israel." It was a welcome command![387] The angel continued, "Herod, who wanted to kill the child, is dead."[207]

Early the next day, Joseph and Mary began to prepare for their long trip home. Soon Joseph helped Mary and Joseph on their donkey, jerked on the reins and left Egypt, never to return.[327]

Two days later, while they were resting at an oasis, a traveler came into the oasis, speaking the Hebrew language. Quickly Joseph and Mary made his acquaintance; they wanted to know what was happening in Bethlehem and Jerusalem.

"Archelaus is reigning in the place of his father Herod."

The news about Archelaus disturbed Joseph. He was known to be just as evil as his father!"[207] That night the angel came to tell Joseph,

"There is danger in Jerusalem and Bethlehem! Do not go there. Instead, return to Galilee, to Nazareth. So that scripture will be fulfilled—He shall be called a Nazarene."[327]

"Almost home!" Joseph told his little son who was seeing Galilee for the first time. Joseph pointed up to the rocky top of Mount Carmel as it jutted out into the Mediterranean Sea. Then crossing the plain of Armageddon, they began climbing up the foothills, higher and higher, until they came to a bowl shaped valley encircled by hills. Nazareth is built on the west slope of the bowl.

Joseph and Mary arrived on the outskirts of Nazareth at evening time. Women were still coming to draw water as it was their custom.

Soon the little family was surrounded by eager relatives and friends who welcomed them home.

After the first general excitement of their return home, Mary and Joseph settled in to their house to a regular schedule. They were happy to be back home again, safely among friends and relatives.

When everything settled down, Mary had some time to reflect. She sat near the door looking outside at Jesus playing in the yard, but she was not just thinking about today. Mary kept all those things about Jesus' birth in her heart—she thought about them carefully.[302]

Talk About the Story: Where did Mary and Joseph and Jesus live? Why did they want to go home to Israel? What did the angel tell Joseph to do? Why did they go to Nazareth instead of Jerusalem?

Scripture: "But Mary kept all these things and pondered *them* in her heart" (Luke 2:19).

Family Time: How did Joseph protect Jesus? How did Mary teach Jesus? What kind of parents were they?

Prayer: Father, I thank You for parents who looked after me, just like Joseph and Mary protected Jesus. Bless my parents for the love they showed to me. Help me grow up to love You, just as Jesus loved You. Amen.

PSALM 9
THANK GOD FOR YOUR VICTORIES

The Philistine army occupied one side of the mountain, and Israel's army was located across the valley facing them. Goliath their champion came to the center of the valley to challenge one of God's people to battle. The loser and his army would surrender to the winner. Goliath was 9½ feet tall and covered with armor. His spear was huge and he needed a shield-bearer to carry it for him. He challenged everyone in Israel's army to a fight.

David, the youngest of eight brothers, was ready to fight Goliath. His older brothers made fun of young David and tried to talk him out of it. But David said, "Is there not a cause?" Even King Saul tried to talk David out of fighting Goliath. But David answered, "The Lord who delivered me from the paws of the lion and bear, He will deliver me from this Philistine."

David took his shepherd's staff, his slingshot, and five smooth stones, the same weapons used to kill the lion and bear. Goliath cursed David when he saw him, "Am I a dog that you come to me with sticks?" But David answered, "I come to you in the name of the Lord of Hosts." Then David exercised faith, "This day the Lord will deliver you into my hands."

David ran to meet the giant, slung the stone and struck the Philistine in the forehead. Then before Goliath could regain his senses, David took the giant's sword and cut off his head.

David wrote this triumphant Psalm after the battle. In verses 1–6, David joyfully thanks God for his victory.

"God, thank You from the bottom of my heart,
You have given me a marvelous victory.
The enemy army ran away;
They staggered and were killed.
Because You came to fight for us,
The enemy is beaten and is finished.
You have uprooted them and they are gone."[367]

David gave full credit for his victory to God. He not only acknowledged God, he worshiped God for His goodness.

"Lord, You reign forever,
You see the problems of the world;
And You do what is best for Your people,
You punish the wicked with what they deserve.[269]
You are a shelter for us when we are oppressed;
You protect us when we are attacked.
Those who know Your name trust in You.
Lord, You have not forsaken them."[193]

In the final section of this Psalm David asked God to punish all the enemies who oppose Him. Notice God's enemies are David's enemies.

"Lord, arise up when the enemies defy You;
Don't let them get away with their challenges.
Make them tremble and fear Your name,
Show them their sins and foolishness."

Talk About the Psalm: What did you learn about the psalm writer in this story? What did you learn about God?

Psalm 9: Read this week's psalm in your Bible together. Choose a verse to read aloud as a prayer.

Prayer: Thank You, God, for the psalm prayers in the Bible. Thank You for teaching us about You and about how to pray. In Jesus' name, amen.

DATE ___/___

GROWING UP IN NAZARETH

Scripture: Luke 2:52
Place: Nazareth
Time: Jesus, age 3 or 4

As Jesus grew, Mary had Him memorize the psalms of the Bible. She would say, "Repeat after me," "The Lord is my shepherd . . . ."

Little Jesus would repeat, "The Lord is my shepherd . . . . I shall not want . . . ."

Jesus repeated the words of King David who wrote Psalm 23. Mary said to Jesus, "You must learn everything that King David wrote."

Mary also taught Jesus the Hebrew alphabet. He sat on the floor as Mary prepared the meals. She constantly quizzed Him,

"Say aleph . . ."

"Aleph," Jesus could repeat the first letter perfectly.

"Say beth . . ."

"Beth," Jesus repeated the second letter.

"Say gimel . . ."

"Gimel . . ." Jesus repeated the third letter.

"Now say aleph, beth, gimel . . ."

Even though Jesus was God's own Son, He learned and grew like everyone else.[204] As a young boy Jesus had a natural life, although He was really God in the flesh.[191] He played with his brothers, sisters, and other children and developed social skills. Then He was fed a healthy meal by Mary, and she saw the He had a well-balanced diet so that He would have a strong body. He grew physically.

And Jesus grew also mentally. To teach Jesus to write, Mary spread sand on the table and showed Jesus how to write the first letter of the Hebrew alphabet, aleph. Jesus traced her writing with His finger and practiced until He could easily form the letter. Jesus learned how to write the whole Hebrew alphabet on the kitchen table, using a stylus and sand as his writing pad. He was growing mentally.

And Jesus grew spiritually. Mary sent Joseph down to the pond behind the carpenter job to bring in a pile of reeds. She split the reeds and peeled off the bark. Mary soaked the reeds until they were soft and then arranged the reeds like strips of woven cloth. She let them dry in the sun while the sticky nature of the papyrus glued the reeds together to make a sheet like paper. Then she used a stone to smooth the sheets into paper. Finally it was ready!

Mary said, "Jesus, it is said in the writings of Moses that every king must write out his own copy of Scriptures and keep it at his right hand to administer justice to his people." As stated in the Scripture, "When the King sitteth upon the throne he shall write his own personal copy of the law of God and keep it with him at all times. He shall read it, to learn to fear the Lord God, and teach these principles to his people" (Deut. 17:18, 19).

So Mary instructed Jesus to write, "In the beginning God created the heavens . . ." and thus Jesus began to write a copy of the Scripture, just as the kings in the Old Testament had done.

Talk About the Story: What are some things Jesus learned to do? Why do you think God wanted Jesus to learn and grow like everyone else?

Scripture: "Jesus grew in mental ability and physical strength and was respected by God and men" (Luke 2:52).

Family Time: What are some ways the people in our family have grown? What is something you have learned this week? This year? What are some ways we can grow in favor with God this week?

Prayer: Father, thank You for sending Jesus as a man, just like us. Thank You that He experienced life in the same way that we do and that He lived without ever sinning. Help us to learn and grow to please You more and more. Amen.

DATE ___/___

GOING TO JERUSALEM AT TWELVE

Scripture: Luke 2:41–44
Place: Nazareth
Time: April, 8 AD

"I was glad when they said to me, 'Let us go into the house of the LORD'" (PSALM 122:1).[183]

"Look Mary," Joseph said, "I always get a thrill when I first see the Jerusalem sitting high on Mount Zion."

Mary and Joseph left home five days earlier from Nazareth with their family to visit Jerusalem and the Temple as the Scriptures taught.[210] Camping each evening along the way was fun.

Jesus' skin was tanned olive from playing in the sun. He wore a white tunic, bleached by many washings. Jesus' hair was wind-blown with straw often caught there.

Joseph was proud that His twelve-year-old son would go through the Temple ceremony, becoming "a son of the law" or Bar Mitzvah. The parents had chosen this feast of the Passover to celebrate His Bar Mitzvah in Jerusalem. Jesus had memorized the Law perfectly, line upon line. precept upon precept. A conscientious Jewish boy would have memorized the entire Book of Leviticus by age twelve. Jesus could repeat it perfectly from memory.

Joseph glanced from one son to the other—Jesus, James, Joseph, and the

www.thefamilyprayerbible.com

others. "Come children," Joseph announced, "let us sing the Psalm of ascent." He explained they must sing when entering Jerusalem. "This is the day the Lord hath made," the young family sang together, "let us rejoice in this day and be glad."[213]

The family celebrated the Feast of Passover, seven days of worship and feasting. Besides sacrificing the Pascal lamb, Passover was a family reunion. Each night the family ate with different relatives.

Early the first morning, Jesus shook His sleeping father. "Could I walk down to the Temple and be one of the first to enter for worship?"

Jesus entered the Temple through the Gate Beautiful. Immediately the clamor died away and the sweet peace of the psalms rippled through the Temple area. Not only did Jesus hear singing, but also the music of harps and cymbals. He stood to gaze about the whole Temple. Already the smoke of sacrifices ascended into the sky while priests repeated prayers for worshipers who brought their lambs. Some people were kneeling with their faces toward the altar, others had their heads bowed in prayer, still others stood with worshiping hands outstretched to heaven.

Jesus smiled. This was where He longed to be. He was in the house of His true Father. For the first time He was visiting the Temple. This experience had been a long time coming, and Jesus wanted to remember everything.

The priest in front of Him began repeating the Shema, the creed that all Israelites learned by heart. Jesus' childlike voice blended with the deep words of mature priests, "Hear O Israel, the Lord Our God is One Lord, and we will love the Lord with all our heart, and with all our soul, and with all our might."

Jesus entered wholeheartedly into what He heard, for it was the prayer of His heart. As He they walked past another family, Jesus stopped to listen to a priest give the family a benediction,

"The Lord bless you and keep you, the Lord maketh His face to shine upon you and be gracious unto you, the Lord lift up His countenance upon you, and give you peace."

Talk About the Story: Why did Jesus' family go to Jerusalem? What did Jesus want to do while He was there?

Scripture: "I was glad when they said to me, 'Let us go into the house of the LORD.'" PSALM 122:1

Family Time: How did Jesus' family approach Jerusalem? What can we do to make going to church a more worshipful experience? What are some new ways we can worship God together?

Prayer: Father, I will go to Your house to worship You. Just as Jesus enjoyed going to Your house on the Sabbath, I will enjoy attending Your house on the Lord's Day. Amen.

TEACHING SCHOLARS BEFORE HIS TIME

Scripture: Luke 2:45-52
Place: The Temple in Jerusalem
Time: After Passover, 8 AD

Joseph and Mary's family and friends left Jerusalem to return home to Nazareth. After Passover passed, everything was anti-climactic. Now a long walk home faced them. Today was difficult, one hill after another—up and down. The April sun was especially hot.

The big group of travelers came to a good camping area. "We'll camp over there," Joseph pointed to a grassy spot between an olive tree and a large rock. He told his son James, a few years younger than Jesus, "Find your brother Jesus, and gather some sticks for a fire so we can cook supper."

After a few minutes, James returned to say, "I can't find Jesus."

Mary's heart jumped with a frightening thought, *"Where is my Son?"*

Mary and Joseph quickly began asking the other families they were traveling with about Jesus. But no one had seen Him all day!

"Pack up the tent," Joseph told the younger children. "Jesus must still be in Jerusalem." Within minutes, the family was retracing their steps back to Jerusalem.

www.thefamilyprayerbible.com

The next day Joseph and Mary went from one family home to another, searching for Jesus. He was not in any of their houses, nor had they seen Him.

The parents were frantic.[57] "Could He have left Jerusalem to go visit some other relative?" asked Mary. "Would He have gone home with them and not told us?" Joseph remembered that the last place they had seen Jesus was in the Temple. Together they almost ran toward the Temple. Out of breath, Joseph asked the first priest he met, "Have you seen our son?"

The kindly priest suggested, "There is a child sitting with the teachers of the Law, He's causing quite a commotion!"[147]

Dashing into a courtyard, they saw a group of people. From what they could see, someone was the center of attraction.

Jesus loves to learn, Mary thought. Maybe Jesus had found a fascinating teacher and had forgotten about time. They pushed their way through the crowd. There in the middle they saw Jesus.

He said, "Let me ask this question.

The scholars gathered around Jesus as if they were His students.[470]

From back in the crowd, Mary could not contain herself anymore; she spoke out, "Son, why have You worried us?" Jesus sensed deep concern in her voice. "We have been searching for you for three days."

The crowd of men turned to look at Mary. They had heard the innocent questions of children before, but this boy was different. Jesus' questions were deep, challenging even the wisest of men. Jesus asked questions they couldn't answer. Since the greatness of a mind is measured by the depth of its questions, the teachers recognized they were standing in the presence of someone special.

"Don't you know," Jesus answered, "that I would be in my Father's house? That I would be about my Father's business?"[456]

Talk About the Story: What happened when Mary and Joseph headed home to Nazareth? Why did Jesus stay behind? Why do you think Mary and Joseph were worried?

Scripture: "And He (Jesus) returned home to Nazareth with His parents and was obedient to them" (Luke 2:51, *ELT*).

Family Time: Being in the Temple was important to Jesus, but Mary and Joseph didn't understand. When are some times others didn't understand something good you were doing? How can you be respectful and obedient, even when others don't understand?

Prayer: Father, help us to be respectful and obedient to authority, even when others don't understand us. Help us to honor You. In Jesus' name, Amen.

DATE ___/___

CHAPTER 6

THE INTRODUCTION OF JESUS

The climax of John the Baptist's ministry was when he introduced Jesus to the nation. Jesus appeared desiring to be baptized.

The baptism of Jesus was so unique that as Jesus ascended out of the water, He was anointed by the Holy Spirit as the Spirit of God descended like a dove upon Him (Matt. 3:17). The Father in heaven declared, "This is My beloved Son, in whom I am well pleased."

JOHN THE BAPTIST

Scripture: Luke 3:1-17
Place: Jordan River
Time: Fall, 26 AD

66Did you hear about John the Baptist?" one boy asked.

"The preacher who lives in the wilderness?" his friend responded. "Yes! He is interesting to listen to! He says that we need to get ready for the coming of the Messiah."

"Do you think the Messiah is coming soon?"

"John sure seems to think so! We should go and listen to him! Come on!" The boys ran toward the Jordan River.

John the Baptizer didn't grow up like most kids. When an angel told his father that John would be born, that angel said that John would prepare people for the coming of the Messiah God had promised to send. So John's parents raised him the way the angel had said. He was a Nazarite, a person set apart by God. He never cut his hair or drank wine as a way to show that he was living a different way, totally dedicated to God.

As a young man he went into the wilderness to spend his time praying. He wore a leather garment made of camel's hair. John didn't eat regular food. Instead, he ate only locusts and wild honey. When it was time for his preaching ministry to begin, God's Spirit filled him and told him what to preach.

Many people went out to the Jordan River to hear John preach the Word of God. They wanted to hear more about the Messiah God had promised to send. In the crowd were normal everyday people, but there were also Roman soldiers and tax collectors who were known for cheating others.

John preached to all of them! John told them, "Repent, for the Kingdom of Heaven is at hand! Prepare, for the Messiah is coming. You must get ready for Him by repenting of your sins and bring forth fruits of righteousness."[399]

All kinds of people listened and wanted to change! They asked John to baptize them to show that they repented, or turned away, from the wrong things they had done. The people asked him, "What should we do? How should we live now?"

John told them, "If you have two tunics, give one to someone who has none. And if you have food, share it with people who don't have food."[549]

Then some tax collectors came and asked, "Teacher, what should we do?"

John said, "Collect no more than what is appointed for you."[399]

And some Roman soldiers asked him, "And what should we do?"

John said, "Don't intimidate anyone or falsely accuse people. Be content with your wages."[213]

Day after day, more people came to hear John's preaching and to be baptized. John was doing his job to help people get ready for Jesus to come![524]

Talk About the Story: What did John the Baptizer say? What did he do? Why did he say and do those things? How did people respond to his preaching?

Scripture: "The voice of one crying in the wilderness: 'Prepare the way of the Lord; Make His paths straight.'" Matthew 3:3

Family Time: John was the one sent to prepare people for Jesus' coming. What are some things we can do to prepare to worship and honor Jesus today?

Prayer: Father, thank You for sending John to preach and prepare people to accept Jesus as their Lord and Savior. Help us to be ready to listen to Your Word and obey it like the people in the Bible story did. In Jesus' name, Amen.

DATE ___/___

PUBLIC INAUGURATION AT THE RIVER

Scripture: Matthew 3:13–17
Place: Jordan River
Time: December, 26 AD

Jesus knew it was time to begin His ministry. He walked through the bushes toward the Jordan River. Jesus heard a voice speaking loudly. As He walked out on the riverbank, the voice became clearer. He paused, listening to the familiar voice. It was His cousin, John the Baptizer preaching.

"REPENT," the preacher paused for emphasis. "PREPARE THE WAY OF THE LORD! MAKE STRAIGHT HIS PATH."[111]

Then, at the end of John's sermon, he invited those who repented to wade out into the water to stand with him. John baptized them by dipping them in the water, an outward picture of the cleansing of their sins. This is what John did day after day. But on this day, something different happened.

Jesus splashed through the shallow water to the place where John was standing. Jesus didn't need to introduce Himself—John knew Him.

Jesus said, "I am ready to be baptized."

"No," John shook his head, "I can't do it." John knew that Jesus was far greater than he was. John knew that he wasn't worthy to baptize Jesus. John said, "You should baptize me."[228]

"No, we must do it now," Jesus answered plainly. "I am being baptized to fulfill all that God requires." Jesus indicated that His baptism was in obedience to God's desire.[327]

"You must baptize Me," Jesus explained again, "because this is right."

So John agreed. Jesus submitted to the human expression of baptism. He was dipped into the cool waters of the Jordan River. The crowd on the river bank did not fully understand what they saw. The angels in heaven looking down knew they could never be baptized. The Father in heaven smiled down in approval. His voice thundered,

"THIS IS MY BELOVED SON, IN WHOM I AM WELL PLEASED."[492]

Everyone heard something, but they were not sure what they heard. Some thought it was a thunder clap. But there were no dark clouds of an approaching storm. Others distinctly heard a voice, but they didn't understand the words. But some understood that the voice said, "THIS IS MY BELOVED SON, IN WHOM I AM WELL PLEASED."

Then they saw it . . . silently . . . harmlessly . . . gently, just as a dove lightly rests on the branch of a tree—the Holy Spirit rested on Jesus. It was time for Jesus to begin the job He came to earth to do.

Talk About the Story: What did Jesus want John to do? Why did John not want to baptize Jesus? What happened after Jesus was baptized?

Scripture: "And suddenly a voice *came* from heaven, saying, "This is My beloved Son, in whom I am well pleased." Matthew 3:17

Family Time: What did God say about Jesus? How does knowing this about Jesus make you feel? What are some actions you can take this week because you believe that Jesus is God's Son?

Prayer: Dear God, thank You for sending Jesus, Your own Son. Help us to learn from Him and follow His example in our lives. In Jesus' name, Amen.

JESUS FASTED 40 DAYS

Scripture: Matthew 4:1, 2
Place: The wilderness near Jericho
Time: Winter, 26–27 AD

The walk to the Judean Mountains was a tedious journey. The fast moving dark clouds in the winter sky hovered above the mountains. The raw December wind whipped down the valley from the Sea of Galilee chilling His flesh. Jesus was tired. When Jesus got to the top of each hill, there seemed always to be another hill to climb.

The Spirit of God was leading Jesus to the wilderness.[446] Jesus had left right after His baptism. It was time to be alone with God His Father.

The Spirit did not lead Jesus up the road to Jerusalem. Jesus followed the Spirit toward the rugged mountains.[207] He by-passed Jericho, the winter home of Herod. It would have been a restful place to visit. Jericho had three palaces, swimming pools, a complex for horseracing, athletics, theater and musical shows. The city was lined with homes of the rich from Jerusalem.

When Jesus found a secluded place in the mountains, He prayed. It was the purpose for which He came to the mountains. He came to fast and pray for 40 days.[161]

"Father," Jesus began His intercession, "I will fast forty days. I will seek Your face."

Jesus promised not to eat any food for the next forty days.[161] After all, Moses had fasted on Sinai for forty days before receiving the Ten Commandments. Elijah had fasted at Sinai forty days before "a still, small voice" spoke to him.

Kneeling in prayer, Jesus prayed many of the psalms He had memorized. They were a part of Him.[450] "You do not want animal sacrifices or grain offerings." Jesus knew of His coming sacrifice on the cross so He prayed again from the Book of Psalms, "Lo, I have come to do Your will, O Lord."[533]

The weather turned harsh in February. As Jesus approached the end of His fast a storm rumbled through the valley, cold rain was coming. Jesus shivered in a cave, away from the biting wind and rain. He pulled His cloak tightly to retain His body heat.

He dozed peacefully with white snowflakes swirling up and down the ravine.

The next morning Jesus suddenly awakened. He heard a sound of a bird singing. Morning washed away the night. The high sun peered through the canyon walls.

Jesus smiled." A sunbeam warmed His tired body. Jesus thought, *God is good,* Jesus thanked His heavenly Father for the sun.[93]

Jesus drank plenty of water to prevent dehydration, but He didn't eat any food for all 40 day. He just continued in prayer and fellowship with God.

Talk About the Story: Why did Jesus go into the wilderness? What did Jesus do during the 40 days? What did He eat? Who was with Him?

Scripture: "Jesus said to them, "My food is to do the will of Him who sent Me, and to finish His work. John 4:34

Family Time: Food is very important to us! But for Jesus, obeying God was much more important! What are some things that are more important to you than food? How can you show that you value your relationship with God more than other things this week?

Prayer: Father, I thank You that Jesus fasted and prayed to get ready for His earthly ministry. I also want to value and honor You. Help me to spend time in prayer and to live in ways that show honor to You. Amen.

PSALM 11
A PSALM OF SEPARATION

After David killed Goliath, he was taken into King Saul's court. David was not yet 20 years old. Yet, he was thrown in with a bunch of warriors who were hard, and ruthless. They were older men who had tasted blood in battle. Their loyalty was to King Saul, not a new young man who just joined the ranks.

This was a time of testing for David. He and his fellow warriors were a definite minority. The nation of Israel was not ruled by law and order, rather everyone did what they wanted. The Philistines seemed to invade God's people at will to plunder and steal what they wanted. On several occasions King Saul was reluctant to meet them in a battle.

The soldiers of Saul seemed to have no heart for God. They were loyal to Saul, and suspicious of David. On two occasions during a festival meal, Saul threw his spear at David to kill him, pinning his clothes to the wall. David prayed,

> "I put my trust in the Lord,
> How can anyone dare tell me
> Run away to the mountains;

> *Evil men everywhere have their bow ready.*
> *They aim arrows at those who live godly.*[110]
> *When law and order collapse,*
> *What can the righteous do?"*

David pulled away from the ungodly soldiers to spend time with his men. It is what God's people have always done. We Christians can't have fellowship with the wicked things done by unsaved people. God has always gathered His people into a community for fellowship and strength. In the New Testament it will be called a church; sometimes it is called a Christian family. There we can worship God together and fellowship with people like ourselves. David prayed,

> *"The Lord still sits in His Holy Temple;*
> *He controls things from heaven.*
> *He sees everything that happens here on earth,*
> *He gives everyone a chance*
> *To see who will do right and who will be wicked."*[364]

The men with David got strength from David their leader. David got his strength from the Lord. Those men stayed with David during all the 13 years King Saul chased David and tried to kill him. That small group of friends later helped David take over the throne and rule Israel. What happened to Saul and his soldiers?

> *"God will pour fire and brimstone*
> *On those who hate God or reject Him.*[235]
> *But God is good to those who love His goodness,*
> *They will see God's face and live with Him."*[367]

This is a Psalm to encourage God's people when they are in the minority. The *King James Version* of the Bible asks, "If the foundations be destroyed, what can the righteous do?" (Psalm 11:3). The answer is very simple—godly people will have to leave ungodly places and ungodly people. They will have to fellowship with those who fellowship with God.

Talk About the Psalm: What did you learn about the psalm writer in this story? What did you learn about God?

Psalm 11: Read this week's psalm in your Bible together. Choose a verse to read aloud as a prayer.

Prayer: Thank You, God, for the psalm prayers in the Bible. Thank You for teaching us about You and about how to pray. In Jesus' name, Amen.

DATE ___/___

TEMPTING THE UNTEMPTABLE

Scripture: Mathew 4:3-11
Place: The mountain wilderness near Jericho
Time: December, January 26–27, AD

For 40 days Jesus did not eat any food.[161] He drank water found in the natural springs and streams in the mountains. After forty days, Satan came to Jesus to tempt Him, He said, "If you are the Son of God, change these stones into loaves of bread."[454] Satan laughed to himself, "Then you'll have something to eat." Jesus WAS very hungry!

The stones looked like bread. He remembered the small loaves of bread His mother cooked in the oven. He remembered the aroma of baking bread, carefully basted with butter. Jesus was tempted because He was hungry, and He was tempted because He could do it—He could turn the stones to bread.

"No," Jesus answered Satan. He quoted scripture, "Man shall not live by bread alone." In quoting the scriptures, Jesus demonstrated how to gain strength

www.thefamilyprayerbible.com

from the Word of God.[535] So He told Satan, "Man shall not live by bread alone, but by every Word that comes from the mouth of God."

Satan had thought that maybe Jesus would succumb to His hunger. But Jesus had a higher purpose.

So Satan tried a different attack. He took Jesus up to the pinnacle of the Temple in Jerusalem. They could look down on everyone. Satan challenged Jesus, "Since You are the Son of God," Satan reasoned, "throw Yourself down!"

He added, "The Scriptures say that God orders His angels to protect You. They will catch You to keep You from striking Your foot on a stone."[428]

Jesus wanted people to believe in Him, but He didn't want it Satan's way. Jesus was not tempted to get the applause of people by an evil-inspired miracle.

Jesus again quoted Scriptures, "No one must tempt the Lord our God."[429]

But Satan was not finished tempting Jesus. He took Jesus to the top of a very high mountain. Somehow they could see all the nations of the world. Satan said, "Look, You can see all the people of the earth from this mountain." Satan reminded Jesus, "I am the ruler of this world and these are my people." "If you bow down to me,"[479] Satan propositioned, "I will give all these people to you."

Jesus had come to rescue all these people. He wanted to love them and care for them. This was a big temptation! Satan offered to give the people to Jesus without Jesus having to go through all the things He would suffer on the cross.

"Get behind Me, Satan," Jesus answered with firm resolution. "The Scriptures demand we worship God, and Him only are we to worship."[541]

As quietly as Satan came, he left. Jesus had experienced victory over Satan. Jesus knew one day the world would be His, but His path was through self-denial, obedience, and through the suffering of the cross. One day the people of the world would worship Jesus, every knee would bow to Him, and every tongue would confess His name.

Talk About the Story: Why did Satan begin tempting Jesus with food? How did Jesus answer each of Satan's temptations?

Scripture: "For we do not have a High Priest who cannot sympathize with our weaknesses, but was in all *points* tempted as *we are, yet* without sin." Hebrews 4:15

Family Time: What did Jesus quote to help Him stand against temptation? Notice Satan tempted Jesus in three areas: (1) food, the lust of the flesh; (2) things, the lust of the eyes; and (3) power, the pride of life (1 John 2:16).

Prayer: Father, thank You that Jesus successfully turned down Satan's temptation by quoting the Scriptures. I will memorize Scripture so I can stand against temptation. Make me strong and faithful to You. Amen.

WHY ARE YOU BAPTIZING?

Scripture: Mark 1:7–8; John 1:19-28
Place: Jordan River
Time: Winter, 26 AD

As John preached and baptized, more and more people heard about him and came from the surrounding towns and villages to hear his preaching. Finally even the religious leaders in Jerusalem began to pay attention.

"Who is this John baptizing people at the Jordan?[279] Why is he doing this?" the religious leaders debated.

"We must go and see for ourselves," they decided. So they headed out.

The group of men from Jerusalem approached the crowd listening to John. They were not smiling. They huddled together, not sitting. They whispered, then pointed at the preacher in anger. Finally, one of them interrupted John's sermon, yelling out in hostility, "Who are you?" he wanted to stop John from preaching.

These men were unmistakably scribes and Pharisees. They called themselves keepers of the Law. Their tapestry robes looked awkward on a riverbank. The religious men looked hot in the afternoon sun. Sweat trickled into their immaculate beards, half hiding the scowls on their faces.

"I am the voice of one crying in the wilderness,"[399] John answered.

"Are you the Deliverer?" another questioned.

"No!"

"Are you Elijah or one of the prophets?" the persistent voice continued asking.

"I am the voice of one crying in the wilderness to prepare for Messiah."[111]

John called the Pharisees and other religious leaders "a generation of snakes." He said, "You must flee from the wrath of God or you will be judged by Him."[268]

"We have been sent to find out who you are," an older priest spoke with a strong, but condemning voice. "Tell us who you are so we can answer the leaders in Jerusalem who sent us."

"I am a man sent from God whose name is John." The preacher continued, "I am sent as a witness to the Light," John paused to explain himself. "Messiah shall bring light to every man born in the world."

The religious leaders put their heads together, dissecting the answer they just heard. By the scowl on their faces and the violent shaking of their heads, everyone could see they disapproved of John the Baptizer. One man pointed an accusing finger at John while whispering to the others. Finally, all the men agreed on their next question.

"Then why are you baptizing?"

John answered, "I baptize with water, but the One coming after me—the One I preach about—is so great, I am not even worthy to untie His sandal. He will baptize with the Holy Spirit."[30]

"NO!" they violently shouted at John. Agitated at what John the Baptizer had just said, they shook their heads in disagreement and cast sand in the air, their symbol of a curse on John. Then stalking down the path, the religious leaders left the scene.

Talk About the Story: Why did the religious leaders go to listen to John preach? What did they want to know? What do you think happened right after the events of this story? Why?

Scripture: "I indeed baptized you with water, but He will baptize you with the Holy Spirit." Mark 1:8

Family Time: Why did these religious leaders oppose John the Baptizer? Are there religious leaders today who oppose the work of Christ? What should be our response to them?

Prayer: Father, thank You for raising up John the Baptizer to prepare people for Jesus Christ. May I be like John and prepare my friends to meet Jesus Christ. Amen.

JOHN INTRODUCES JESUS

Scripture: John 1:29–34
Place: Jordan River
Time: Winter, 27 AD

John was still preaching, telling people to prepare for the Messiah, to repent, stop doing what is wrong and start doing what is right. But this afternoon John had *something* else on his mind, rather, *someone* else on his mind. Jesus was in the crowd! Turning again to the multitude, John announced,

"I baptize you with water," he paused for emphasis, "but someone is standing here today who will baptize you with the Holy Spirit."[224]

"Today?" a visitor turned to whisper in his wife's ear, "Is our Deliverer here today?"

Turing to look at Jesus, John announced boldly, "Behold, the Lamb of God Who takes away the sin of the world."

That's all John said in describing Jesus. He called Jesus the Lamb of God. He had not announced that Jesus was the Messiah . . . nor the Christ . . . not even the Anointed One. John had simply called Jesus the Lamb of God. In his heart John knew this was the time for which he had been born. This event was his life's purpose.[278]

www.thefamilyprayerbible.com

"No," a mother thought to herself, "this man can't be the Messiah." She thought the Messiah would be a large, powerful warrior who could defeat Roman soldiers in battle. But Jesus looked like an ordinary man!

Other people in the crowd wondered the same thing. But some wanted to learn more about him.

John continued talking, referring to what he had said about the Messiah before: "This is He of whom I said, 'After me comes a Man who is preferred before me, for He was before me.' I did not know Him; but that He should be revealed to Israel, therefore I came baptizing with water."

John continued, "I saw the Spirit descending from heaven like a dove, and He remained on Him. The One who sent me to baptize with water said to me, 'Upon whom you see the Spirit descending, and remaining on Him, this is He who baptizes with the Holy Spirit.'"

Everyone who had been there the day John baptized Jesus remembered the voice from heaven and the strange-looking decent of the Holy Spirit—but they hadn't known what it really meant!

Then John the apostle made the big, amazing announcement: "I have seen and testified that this is the Son of God!"

Even though Jesus was his cousin, John hadn't understood until the day he baptized Jesus that Jesus was really the Messiah he had been preaching about! John knew Jesus was the Messiah because the Holy Spirit told him so.

John still didn't fully understand his announcement, but he said what God told him to say, "The Lamb of God Who takes away the sin of the world."[544]

Talk About the Story: What are some things John said about Jesus? How did John know that Jesus was the Son of God? Why do you think John called Him the Lamb of God?

Scripture: "Behold! The Lamb of God Who takes away the sin of the world" John 1:29

Family Time: In the Old Testament, lambs were sacrificed to take away people's sin, but needed to be done time and time again! But read what John said about Jesus in John 1:29. How would Jesus take away all our sin and end the sacrificial system once and for all? Accepting Jesus' sacrifice and trusting in His forgiveness allows us to be truly forgiven and become part of God's family forever!

Prayer: Father, thank You that Jesus came to take away our sins and to make it possible for us to live as part of God's family now and forever. Help us to know Jesus and why He came to earth. Help me learn more about Him every day. Amen.

TWO YOUNG MEN FOLLOW JESUS

Scripture: John 1:35-40
Place: Jordan River
Time: January, 27 AD

John and Andrew had grown up together in Bethsaida, a little fishing village near Lake Galilee. Both of them began following John the Baptizer[314] because of his promise that the Deliverer of Israel is coming. The Baptizer preached, "Get ready for His coming." Both young men eagerly anticipated the Jewish Deliverer.

Yesterday, they heard John the Baptizer say about Jesus, "Behold the Lamb of God Who takes away the sin of the world."

And today, as they stood talking with John the Baptizer, Jesus walked past again.[512]

John looked at both of them and smiled. "Look! It is the Lamb of God, who takes away the sin of the world." John the Baptizer was pretty sure that John and Andrew were more interested in following Jesus than following him—and John was telling them to go!

Andrew, a well-mannered young man with big round eyes, could see things in the heart of people most others didn't see. Andrew was good at reading people.

John's thin frame reminded people of a tall, solitary tree. He always stood alone, but loved people. He had a temper so people called him a "Son of Thunder."

Perhaps John was too bashful to approach Jesus by himself, so the two men approached Jesus together,

"Rabbi," young Andrew used the title "Rabbi" with deep reverence. "Rabbi, where are You staying?"

"Come and see!" Jesus responded with a smile. Jesus knew the real purpose they came to talk with Him. He answered, "We'll eat together."

The deep red winter sun touched the Judean Mountains. They settled around a meal of simple roasted lamb and bread. The young men barely ate, they wanted to learn more about Jesus.

"When will Your kingdom deliver us from Rome?" They wanted to know.
"With time."
"How will I recognize Messiah's kingdom?"
"Seek first the rule of God's kingdom in your heart,"[358] Jesus told the two young men carefully listening to all He was saying.

Beginning with the Torah—the first five books of Holy Scripture—and tracing God's plan through the prophets and the historical books, Jesus taught them that the Messiah must come first to conquer the hearts of worshipers, later Messiah would come to rule the earth.

All day, Andrew and John listened to Jesus and learned from Him. It was the beginning of the most amazing time in their lives!

Talk About the Story: What did Andrew and John learn about Jesus? What did John the Baptizer tell them? What did they ask Jesus? What did Jesus tell them?

Scripture: "Also we have come to believe and know that You are the Christ, the Son of the living God." John 6:69

Family Time: John and Andrew's first meeting with Jesus was just the start of them coming to know Jesus. When did you begin your relationship with Christ? How have you grown to know and love Him more and more?

Prayer: Father, help me to know Jesus and why He came to earth. Help me learn more about Him every day. Amen.

CHAPTER 7

THE BEGINNING OF HIS MINISTRY

From the very beginning, the most effective means of spreading the gospel has involved people who know Jesus telling others about Jesus. God has given everyone a sphere of influence and we should all use our influence to persuade others to follow Jesus. Some believers like John the Baptist have a large sphere of influence and could be used by God to attract many to personal salvation in Christ. Others can be a faithful witness to members of our own family like Andrew, or we could witness to friends, neighbors or associates, like Philip.

JESUS PRAYED BEFORE EVERYTHING

Scripture: Luke 3:21
Place: The Jordan River
Time: Winter, 27 AD

When Jesus came to the Jordan River to be baptized,[30] there was a large crowd watching John the Baptizer. The preacher had several things to say. At first John did not want to baptize Jesus, "I need to be baptized by You. Why are you coming to me to be baptized?" (Matthew 3:14, *ELT*).[228] Yet, Jesus insisted and was baptized in the Jordan River.

But there's one thing about the baptism of Jesus almost everyone misses. The Bible declares, "Jesus also was baptized; and while He prayed, the heaven was opened" (Luke 3:21).[224] Right before God spoke from heaven about Jesus, calling Him the Son of God in whom God the Father was well pleased,[492] Jesus was praying! Now, Jesus prayed long before He was baptized. As a matter of fact, Jesus spent His life in prayer.

• Jesus preached many great sermons, but He prayed first.

• Jesus healed many sick people, but He prayed first.

• Jesus cast out demons, but He prayed first.

• Jesus spent entire nights praying instead of sleeping!

Remember, prayer is talking to God. Also, prayer is an important part of a relationship with God. Of course, Jesus had an ongoing relationship with His heavenly Father, and talked with Him constantly.

Just as you cannot live without air to breathe, so you cannot live spiritually without breathing prayers to your heavenly Father. If you take prayer away from the believer, they will die spiritually. We do a lot of things that help us spiritually. Such as give money to God, attend church, but nothing is as important as praying! When you stop praying, you stop living with God and for God.

The Psalmist said, "I give myself unto prayer" (Psalm 109:4).[379] If you give yourself to sports, you are defined by baseball, or tennis. People come to know you as a sports person. If you give yourself to doing fun things, you are defined by the fun you have. That's what people think of when they see you! If you give yourself to making money, you are defined by your successful experience, and others know you by the money you make. But if you give yourself to prayer, you are defined by your relationship to God. And that is what people will see in you.

Robert Murray M'Cheyne said, "A man is what he is on his knees before God, and nothing more." Prayer is the most important part of us!

The problem is that we are weakest in the things where Christ was the strongest, i.e., today many churches are known for their preaching, teaching, or ministry to the poor. But a church should be known for its prayer. Didn't Jesus say, "My house shall be called a house of prayer" (Matthew 21:13).[182]

Talk About the Story: When are some times that Jesus prayed during His life on earth? Why do you think Jesus chose to pray so often?

Scripture: "I give myself unto prayer." Psalm 109:4

Family Time: When are some times that you have prayed to God? Why do you think prayer is a good idea? How can you give yourself to prayer?

Prayer: Father, thank You that You want us to pray to You. Help us to remember to talk to you often throughout the day and to plan special times to talk to You alone. In Jesus' name, Amen.

ANDREW AND JOHN BRING THEIR BROTHERS TO JESUS

Scripture: John 1:41-42
Place: Jordan River
Time: Winter, 26 AD

The next morning Andrew and John were gone. They did not tell anyone where they were going; they just left. They had a mission! They were off to speak to their brothers. Andrew and John both knew that their older brothers wanted to know about the Messiah as much as they did. And they didn't want to keep their wonderful discovery of Jesus to themselves any longer!

Andrew found his brother Simon by his fishing boat. "Simon! You have to come and see!"[58]

Simon grunted, "I could have used your help with the fish last night."

"I know, and I'm sorry. But we have found the Messiah![444] You have to come and meet Him!" Andrew responded.

Simon's eyebrows went up. *The Messiah? Oh, yes! I want to meet Him!*

Later that morning Andrew came walking swiftly down the road, bringing his brother with him. When he got within hearing distance, he waved, then yelled, "Look who I got," his eyes crinkled with excitement.[358] "I told my brother Simon that You are the Messiah."[358]

Peter had a muscular chest, was several years older than Andrew, and was nothing like his brother. Andrew was quiet and preferred to talk to people one at a time. Simon was loud; he yelled at the fishermen in the boat what to do.

"Are you Messiah?" was the first question Simon blurted out before even being introduced to Jesus. Simon was a blunt man; his head was as hard as his job of fishing on the Sea of Galilee.

"Your name will no longer be Simon," Jesus told the older brother when first meeting him. "Your name will be Peter," Jesus explained, "you will be as firm as a rock."

Meanwhile, John was having a conversation with his brother James that was very similar to the conversation Simon and Andrew had. James was as eager to meet the Messiah as Simon had been.

Soon John returned to Jesus with his older brother James. James was a fisherman, just like the rest of them.

Talk About the Story: What did Andrew and John do after they met Jesus and became convinced that Jesus was the Messiah? How did Simon and James respond to the news about Jesus?

Scripture: "But grow in the grace and knowledge of our Lord and Savior Jesus Christ. To Him be the glory both now and forever. Amen." 2 Peter 3:18

Family Time: Andrew. John, Simon, and James learned about Jesus and got to know Him. What are some ways that we can get to know Jesus more? What can you say to tell others about Jesus?

Prayer: Father, thank You for my family. Help us to tell people in our family and others about You just like Andrew and John did. Help us be positive influences on them. In Jesus' name, Amen.

PSALM 13
A PRAYER FOR PATIENCE

David was hunted in the barren Judean hills by Saul. After David killed the giant Goliath most would think Saul would appreciate David for getting rid of Israel's enemy. But no, the girls sang, "Saul has slain his thousands, and David his ten thousand" (1 Samuel 18:7). Jealousy got the best of Saul and twice he hurled a spear at him in the dining room. But he missed. Then Saul said he would kill David and sent his army to do it. For 13 years David was chased by Saul's army.

Toward the end of the 13 years David was getting tired and discouraged. He cried out to God in the Psalm,

> *"Lord, how long will you forget about me;*
> *Will you let this go on forever?*
> *How long will You look the other way*

www.thefamilyprayerbible.com

> When I desperately need You to help me?[1]
> How long will I have to hide out;
> Daily I am worried to death?
> How long will my enemy have the upper hand?
> Answer me O Lord."

Notice David said four times, "How long?" This has the ring of desperation. David was getting impatient. This may be the situation of some who have continual pain or constant struggle with an incurable disease, or even famine where they don't have enough food. So, they must pray what David prayed.

> "O Lord, I need an answer.
> Let me know what to expect
> Lest I die before I get an answer.[219]
> O Lord, don't let my enemy get his way,
> Don't let him gloat over my pain,
> And don't let him defeat me."

Sometimes God allows us to suffer so we will be better and stronger. David became a stronger child of God because he had to trust in God more than if he grew into manhood tending sheep on his father's farm. Hard times brought out David's toughness to fight evil. But hardness also softened his heart to God. Note the faith David learned. It is seen in the way he ends this Psalm.

> "From now on I will always trust in the Lord,
> I will rejoice in His salvation for me.
> I will sing to the Lord in all situations
> Because He has always given me good things."[439]

This Psalm is for people who have prolonged suffering. It would be sung during illnesses that seem to linger, or a famine where people had little to eat. These people can sit with David on one of the hills of Judaea to sing with him the prayer for patience.

Talk About the Psalm: What did you learn about the psalm writer in this story? What did you learn about God?

Psalm 13: Read this week's psalm in your Bible together. Choose a verse to read aloud as a prayer.

Prayer: Thank You, God, for the psalm prayers in the Bible. Thank You for teaching us about You and about how to pray. In Jesus' name, Amen.

DATE ___/___

PHILIP FOLLOWS JESUS

Scripture: John 1:43–44
Place: Tiberius and Cana
Time: December, 26 AD

Yesterday, Andrew and John had brought their brothers to meet Jesus. The brothers decided to follow Jesus, too.[537] They left the Jordan River where John was baptizing people and walked north toward Galilee. They had to go through Tiberius a Roman city on the western shore of the Sea of Galilee.

Tiberius was famous for its warm mineral springs. King Herod made his winter home there, and it became a Gentile city within Jewish Palestine. Its protective walls stretched from the mountains out into the sea. They had to walk through Tiberius.

Soldiers were standing guard, casually observing the travelers entering the city. Jesus entered the city gate, paying no attention to the soldiers.

As they walked through the city, John heard someone call his name. He recognized the voice. It was Philip, a childhood friend from Bethsaida.

"Where have you been?" Philip asked John, the way one friend might ask a buddy.

John explained that he was following John the Baptizer until he met Jesus.

www.thefamilyprayerbible.com

"Maybe the Messiah will come today."

John wanted to tell Philip that Jesus was the Messiah, but did not know how to put it into words. So John said, "The Messiah is here!"

"Here?"

"Yes."

"Where?"

John pointed to Jesus; explaining, "John the Baptizer said that He is the Lamb of God, the very One who will deliver Israel." Then John paused,

"Jesus will capture the hearts of people, before he captures cities."

John explained that the kingdom of Jesus would reign in the hearts of people when they believed in Him.

"Do you believe in Him?" Philip asked.

"Yes."[58]

At that moment Jesus stepped over to where the two friends were talking, and Philip looked knowingly at Him. Some men need all their questions answered before they will do anything, and other men need to be coaxed into action. But Philip was a simple straightforward man. He believed what his friend John said about Jesus and he trusted him. Jesus knew Philip was ready, so he said, "Come, follow Me."[327]

Philip left Tiberius with the disciples to follow Jesus. It had only been two days since Jesus was baptized; already five disciples were following Him. The five friends who grew up in the poor fishing village of Bethsaida were now reunited together around a deep-seated yearning for the kingdom of God and for the Deliverer of the Jews to come.

All five young men had gone to the synagogue school in Bethsaida and now looked for Messiah. They remembered what they said to one another at the end of each Sabbath's class, "If not today, maybe tomorrow."[529]

Talk About the Story: Who did John and the others meet in Tiberius? Why do you think Philip chose to follow Jesus? What did John tell Philip about Jesus? What did Philip do?

Scripture: "And this is His commandment: that we should believe on the name of His Son Jesus Christ and love one another, as He gave us commandment." 1 John 3:23

Family Time: What do you believe about Jesus? How did you come to believe in Jesus? Who told you about Him? Who can you tell about Jesus?

Prayer: Father, thank You for all types of people who follow Jesus. May I be as quick to follow Jesus as was Philip. Amen.

NATHANIEL FOLLOWS JESUS

Scripture: John 1:45-51
Place: Outside Cana
Time: Winter, 26 AD

Five men followed Jesus up the Valley of the Doves toward Nazareth.[314] Each had a dream of God's kingdom. Each had a lot to learn about Jesus, the Messiah.

As they neared Nazareth, Philip left Andrew, Peter, John, and James.[496] He walked to Cana, the next town on the road. Philip had chosen to follow Jesus. Now he had to share the good news with Nathaniel,[147] his friend who lived outside Cana.

"Philip saw Nathaniel's large, white flat-roofed house on the top of a hill. "Nathaniel!" he yelled into the front door, but no one answered. Philip was a persevering man, so he checked the barn, but Nathaniel was not there. Philip finally found his friend reading a copy of the Scriptures under the fig tree.

"We have found the Messiah,[444] the One Moses predicted would come, the One the prophets described!"

"Who is this Messiah?"[147] Nathaniel asked.

"Jesus of Nazareth."

A scowl crossed Nathaniel's forehead. He had read the Torah and knew Israel's leaders came from Judah, not Galilee.

"Can anything good come out of Galilee?"[504] Nathaniel asked. It was not a question of unbelief, nor did he reject Jesus. It's just that he was a careful student of Jewish history.[496] What Nathaniel didn't know was that Jesus was from the tribe of Judah, even though he grew up in Nazareth.

"Come and see for yourself,"[504] Philip answered.

The two left Nathaniel's house in Cana to walk to Nazareth. The six-mile journey took between two to three hours. When Jesus saw Nathaniel coming, before Philip or Nathaniel could say anything, Jesus announced, "Nathaniel you are a sincere seeker." Then Jesus explained, "You are an Israelite in whom is no guile."[496]

"How do you know me?" Nathaniel answered. "You haven't talked to me, you haven't asked me a question."[259]

"I saw you under the fig tree when Philip was searching for you,"[259] Jesus explained.

Nathaniel looked at Jesus for a moment. Then he knew. Nathaniel knew that he was standing in the presence of someone special.

"Rabbi," was the first thing he uttered. "You are the Son of God, you are the King of Israel."[147]

Jesus looked into Nathaniel's eyes, "You are impressed that I know what you were doing under the fig tree, but in the future you'll see even greater things."[34]

"I'm ready to follow You," Nathaniel said.

Talk About the Story: What was Nathaniel doing when Philip found him? What did Jesus say when Nathaniel came to meet Him? What did Nathanial say to Jesus when he met the Master?

Scripture: "Nathanael answered and said to Him, 'Rabbi, You are the Son of God! You are the King of Israel!'" John 1:49

Family Time: Nathaniel was ready to follow Jesus because Jesus knew all about him. What about Jesus makes you want to follow Him as your Lord and Savior?

Prayer: Father, thank You for opening Your arms to young people and old people, rich people and poor people. Thank You for inviting me to follow You. Amen.

ATTENDING A FAMILY WEDDING FEAST

Scripture: John 2:1-5
Place: Cana
Time: Winter, 27 AD

As they steadily climbed the Galilean hills, the winter breeze off the Sea of Galilee at their backs pushed them up the slopes. Jesus and six disciples were climbing upward toward the village of Cana.

They were ready for some hot food and a warm room. They were all looking forward to the wedding they had been invited to attend in Cana.[299]

Weddings were a big deal! There would be feasting and dancing and talking and laughing for several days! Peter turned his ear to the wind and announced, "I hear the wedding music already!" Peter loved happy crowds and he loved good food. Cana was a nice town with paved cobblestone streets.

"JESUS!" they heard the greetings of an elderly woman's voice. Jesus saw his mother waving to Him from the yard of a house. She was placing a mixing bowl on the food preparation table.

Jesus exchanged greetings as if he hadn't seen his mother in a long time. Soon Jesus and His disciples were enjoying the wedding with the others.

Levi, an elderly man was the master of ceremonies at the feast. He was short and skinny.

Levi's job was to make everyone comfortable and happy. They entered the winter-darkened room. The candles on the table lit the food, but not the faces of the guests. The early winter evening was quickly fading. Happy talk filled the room.

"Bring Jesus a plate of food," Mary instructed the servants to look after Jesus and his friends. Quickly, warm bread appeared before them, and a large bowl of lamb stew. Jesus broke off a morsel of bread to dip into the lamb stew. He passed the loaf to the disciple next to Him who followed His example. At the head of the table Levi was telling stories, stories about everyone at the table.

But Mary and some of the other women continued helping with the food and drink for the feast. They talked and laughed as they worked. It was a fun job!

But after a while, Mary was interrupted by a whispered voice that was full of worry, "We are out of wine!" Mary knew what to do! Mary came behind Jesus and whispered into His ear, "There's no more wine."[390]

Again, Mary's thoughts went back to the beginning. She remembered the amazing events surrounding the birth of her son; she couldn't forget the angel's announcement or the shepherds who came to the stable. She would never forget the wise men who brought gifts. Mary knew that Jesus could solve the problem that day.

Jesus knew the thoughts of her heart. He answered her, "My hour is not yet come."

Mary smiled at Jesus as she turned to the servants. She was confident in His ability and confident that He cared about this embarrassing situation. "Whatever Jesus says for you to do," Mary gave the servants an order, "do it!"[431]

Talk About the Story: Why was Mary concerned when the wine ran out? Why did she ask Jesus for help?

Scripture: "Casting all your cares upon Him, for He cares for you." 1 Peter 5:7

Family Time: What are some things that worry you? What embarrassing situations do you need help with? Why do you think Jesus cares about things that seem small and unimportant to others?

Prayer: Father, thank You for telling us that Jesus cared about people's worries and embarrassing situations. When I face problems in my daily life, I will take them to Jesus. Thank You for helping me with small issues in my life. Amen.

DATE ___/___

MIRACULOUS WINE

Scripture: John 2:6-12
Place: Cana
Time: Winter, 26 AD

Jesus and six disciples visited Cana where they were invited to a wedding.[299] While there, the wine ran out.[390] Mary, Jesus' mother, asked Him to do something.

Jesus walked to the back of the house. The servants wondered where Jesus was going. They watched. Then He saw six large water pots. Each pot held 20 to 30 gallons of water. These held water that was used for washing, not for drinking.

Jesus said to the servants, "Fill each one with water up to the very top," Jesus put a finger on the lip of the pots, "make sure they are filled up to the rim."

The servants nodded their heads, then obeyed.[431] Jesus continued His instructions, "Draw some out and take it to the master of ceremonies." Jesus' disciples watched and listened in wonder. The servants blinked, there was anxiety in their eyes. If they brought water when the master wanted wine, they were afraid of what he would say and do! The servants would lose their jobs!

www.thefamilyprayerbible.com

But they obeyed. Quickly they filled the larger water pots, each pot to the brim. Then the bravest servant dipped a cup into the water to fill it. He carefully carried the cup to the master of the wedding ceremony. He stood quietly nearby waiting to hear in the master would fire him, or if he should call the other servants to distribute the water.

The master took a drink. "Ah-h-h-h-h," he rolled his happy eyes back, then explained, "that's good." He took a second, deep gulp, a longer draught than the first, and then said again, "Ah-h-h-h-h."

Then a scowl crossed his face. He stared unbelievingly into his cup. The servant panicked. It was the groom's job to provide wine, was it unacceptable? He held his breath. The master turned to the groom and asked, "Why have you hidden the best wine until now?"

The groom shrugged his shoulders, not knowing how to answer.

"This wine is the very best we've had all day."

The other servants were waiting and watching, just out of sight. They all breathed a deep breath of relief. Jesus' disciples eyes grew wide. They knew something that none of the crowd knew. They knew what the master drank came from the water pots. However, it was the best wine they served during the entire wedding feast.

Quickly, the servants filled everyone's glasses so that everyone could enjoy the wine. The wedding feast went on and on. No one was embarrassed for running out of food or wine, no one had to go without, and everyone had a great time as they celebrated the joyful wedding.

As Mary had done on many other occasions, she pondered these things in her heart.

Talk About the Story: What happened at the wedding? Why do you think running out of wine would be a bad thing? Why do you think Jesus chose to help, even though He told Mary that it wasn't yet His time?

Scripture: "He has made His wonderful works to be remembered; The LORD is gracious and full of compassion. Psalm 111:4

Family Time: What are some things you trust Jesus to do? What are some situations in which it is harder to trust Jesus? Why? How does knowing that Jesus is full of compassion for you help you to trust Him more?

Prayer: Father, thank You that Jesus is concerned about my happiness. I will bring my problems to Him in prayer. Thank you for Your gracious compassion toward me. Amen.

CLEANSING THE TEMPLE

Scripture: John 2:13-25
Place: The Temple in Jerusalem
Time: April, 27 AD

Jesus and His disciples went to the Temple in Jerusalem,[210] just as every Jewish male was required to attend Passover each year.

As Jesus and His disciples approached the gate, a ram bolted out of the door, being chased by a young teenage boy. The crowd laughed at the clumsy boy.

Inside the Temple courtyard, the place that was designed for non-Jews to come and pray, there were loud arguing voices.

Jesus and the disciples expected to hear the voices of people singing the Psalms of Israel, and to see small groups of priests and worshipers talking and praying together. But rather than seeing reverence, they saw a tumultuous crowd laughing, jostling, and haggling. The courtyard was crowded with salesmen and traders. People were buying things from businessmen. Tables stacked high with merchandise were everywhere. Dealers were negotiating with worshipers to change their foreign coins into Hebrew coins, charging far more than they needed.[440] It felt like a bazaar full of cheating vendors, not a Temple.

Worshipers were being pulled in every direction by the clamor of businessmen. Jesus and the twelve stood on slightly elevated stairs, surveying the unruly mob.

Jesus quietly picked up three short ropes from the ground, weaving the cords together, leaving the three ends flayed.

He stood to yell loudly, "DO NOT MAKE MY FATHER'S HOUSE A PLACE FOR SELLING THINGS!"

All around the courtyard, people stopped and turned to look. Jesus continued, "THIS IS A HOUSE OF PRAYER."

Stepping over to a table, Jesus turned it over. The sound of coins spilling

everywhere across the cobblestones sobered the crowd. Jesus went to a line of tables, turning over each one of them. No one challenged Him.[360] Jesus continued turning over one table after another, coins bouncing among the cobblestones.

Jesus took His small cord whip in hand, driving salespeople and their animals out of the Temple courtyard. Cages crashed to the ground, turtle-doves and pigeons fluttered in freedom.

The disciples stood shocked. They had never seen this side of Jesus' personality. But they remembered something they had learned from the Scriptures: "Zeal for Your house has eaten Me up." Jesus was full of zeal for God's house!

Talk About the Story: What wrong things were happening at the Temple? Why was Jesus angry about this? What was the Temple supposed to be for?

Scripture: "Zeal for Your house has eaten Me up." John 2:17

Family Time: What are some things that we do that might displease Jesus? What can we do about those things? How can we be zealous to help others worship God?

Prayer: Father, I love to go to Your house to pray and worship You. Show me how my attitudes and actions at church can help and encourage others to also worship You. Amen.

WHY JESUS CLEANSED THE TEMPLE

Scripture: John 2:13-23
Place: The Temple in Jerusalem
Time: April, 27 AD

Suddenly most of the crowd was gone. The animals were gone. The courtyard was finally quiet, although overturned tables littered the area. Cages were smashed and the pens holding the animals were broken.

The people who remained looked at Jesus in wonder. Many of them agreed that the Temple courtyard should be a place of prayer, not a place for buying and selling things. But who was this man with all this authority? They knew that the religious leaders had allowed the merchants to set up in the courtyard.

The priests had been shocked into stillness. No one had dared to do anything about the marketplace before. Some of them wondered, *Did the high priest have a change of heart about the marketplace? Did he send this man?*

Others recognized that Jesus had a different kind of authority. They didn't want to question Him at all. They wanted to learn more about Him!

Still others knew that Jesus didn't get His directions from the high priest at all! They wanted to know why He thought He could make this change! After all, the fees the businessmen paid to be able to set up in the Temple courtyard helped to pay for things!.

Slowly priests began appearing as though they came from nowhere. One by one they appeared through small doors and from behind columns. They whispered among themselves. One of the priests, who seemed to be the leader, finally walked over to Jesus. "By what authority do You cleanse the Temple?"[504]

Jesus turned to look at him.

"The priests are the keepers of the Temple," another priest said. At this point the other priests nodded their heads in approval.

"What right do You have to do this?" the first priest again asked Jesus.

Jesus didn't answer the priest's question. Jesus knew he wasn't ready to accept the truth about who Jesus is. So Jesus just gave him a clue. "If you destroy this Temple," Jesus said in answer, "I will raise it up in three days."[405]

"It has taken forty-six years for Herod to build this Temple," the priest mockingly answered Jesus, "it has taken a long time to build and You think You can rebuild it in three days?"[421]

But when Jesus said, "Destroy this Temple," He did not mean the physical Temple of stones and mortar.[405] Jesus was calling His body a Temple. He knew the priests would plot against Him and have Him killed.[259] But Jesus also knew on the third day He would rise from the dead. That's what Jesus meant when He said, "He would rebuild the Temple in three days."

Talk About the Story: What did people in the Temple courtyard think about Jesus kicking the merchants out? What do you think you would have done if you had been there that day?

Scripture: "Be angry, and do not sin": do not let the sun go down on your wrath." Ephesians 4:26

Family Time: When have you felt angry about something that was wrong? What did you do about it? Talk about good ways to respond when wrong things are happening.

Prayer: Father, I thank You for the emotions that we have. Help us to use our anger for good. Help us to do what is right when we see things that are wrong so that we can help to change things and help others to know and love You. Amen.

PSALM 14
A PSALM ABOUT SELFISH PEOPLE

Saul wanted to kill David, so David and his men were hiding in the wilderness. While there David protected the area's farmers from wolves, bears, and thieves who would try to steal from the farmers. When harvest came, David asked the farmers for some food because he protected them.

A man named Nabal refused to give David anything. The name Nabal means "fool" in Hebrew. When faced with his stinginess, Nabal had a heart attack. A few days later he died. His miserly attitude led to his death. He really was a fool! Nabal allowed his sin to control all of his life. David calls Nabal a fool when he sings this Psalm:

www.thefamilyprayerbible.com

"The fool has said in his heart,
There is no God, and I am not responsible to Him.
The problem is sin, all people have an evil nature,
And no one would do good if left to themselves.[504]
The Lord looks down from heaven to see all hearts,
He is searching to see if anyone will live for Him,
To love Him with all their hearts,
And their neighbor as themselves.
But everyone has turned from God to their own way,
No one naturally does good apart from God.
Don't the unsaved understand their obligation to God,
They are selfish with others because of their selfish nature.
They never ask God how to live."[497]

God wants us to worship Him, but He also wants us to not be selfish. A selfish person thinks he or she is the most important person in the world. That leads people to deny the existence of God. The Bible describes him or her by saying, "The fool has said in his heart there is no God." So the answer is found in what the Psalmist sings.

"Throw yourself into the arms of the Lord,
Then be happy knowing God has received you.
Sing praises to God with all your heart,
Because He is good to those who trust Him."

When people who reject or deny God see the way God works in your life, then they will begin to believe.

Talk About the Psalm: What did you learn about the psalm writer in this story? What did you learn about God?

Psalm 14: Read this week's psalm in your Bible together. Choose a verse to read aloud as a prayer.

Prayer: Thank You, God, for the psalm prayers in the Bible. Thank You for teaching us about You and about how to pray. In Jesus' name, Amen.

A NIGHT INTERVIEW WITH A LEADER

Scripture: John 3:1-3
Place: Jerusalem at night
Time: Spring, 27 AD

A cool breeze rustled the palm branches at the edge of the flat-roofed house. April was hot in the daytime but chilly at night. The moon was so bright that the people could read the Scriptures by its light. It was a perfect canopy for the evening discussion. During Passover in Jerusalem Jews gathered for evening banquets and discussions.

But this night was different. Just one man, a well-dressed man slipped through the shadows toward the house where Jesus was staying. He knocked softly on the door and asked for a private audience with Jesus.

Jesus smiled and invited the man to climb to the cool, quiet roof with Him. There they would be able to talk privately.

The man's name was Nicodemus. He was well known in Jerusalem. He was one of the religious leaders, a Pharisee, and an important and intelligent person.

Nicodemus knew that many of the other Pharisees were not very happy with Jesus at that point. Jesus had driven the merchants out of the Temple courtyard. The religious leaders made money off of those merchants!

Also, Jesus was a different sort of preacher and people were starting to pay attention to Him. This made the religious leaders nervous! Would Jesus start a revolt against Rome? Would He change the way they were used to living? Would He cause trouble?

Nicodemus began the discussion with a respectful compliment, "Rabbi, we know You are a teacher come from God. No one can do the things You have been doing unless God is with Him."[192] Nicodemus' eyes were soft and friendly.

Jesus could see that Nicodemus was sincere. He didn't want to build himself up like many of the other Pharisees. Nicodemus wanted to know the truth. He wanted to know and understand God's Kingdom.

Jesus waited for a few seconds then spoke about the most important thing in every person's life, "Except a person is born again, they cannot enter the kingdom of heaven."[318]

Jesus told Nicodemus that He had not come to set up a political kingdom on earth, or to lead a revolution to overthrow Rome. Rather His kingdom would rule men from the heart. Jesus wanted people to be changed inwardly by being born again. Jesus jumped over the pleasantries, and went straight to the issues.

"Unless one is born again, he cannot see the kingdom of God" (John 3:3).

Talk About the Story: Why did Nicodemus meet with Jesus at night? What was on Nicodemus' mind when he talked to Jesus? What was on Jesus' mind? Why did Jesus talk about being born again?

Scripture: "Jesus answered and said to him, "Most assuredly, I say to you, unless one is born again, he cannot see the kingdom of God." John 3:3

Family Time: What does it mean to be born again? Read these verses and talk about them: John 1:12–13; 1 Peter 1:23; Colossians 2:6.

Prayer: Father, thank You that Jesus emphasized important things to everyone, even important people. I want Jesus to change me from the inside out. I want to be born again. I believe in Jesus. Amen.

DATE ___/___

QUESTIONS ABOUT BEING BORN AGAIN

Scripture: John 3:1-16
Place: Jerusalem at night
Time: Spring, Passover, 27 AD

Jesus and Nicodemus met at night during Passover in the spring of that year. Nicodemus began the conversation by complimenting Jesus on His miracles.[192] Jesus explained His main message,

"Except a person is born again, they cannot see the kingdom of heaven."[318]

Nicodemus understood the idea of "kingdom," he was born a Jew; therefore he was part of the kingdom of Israel. But Jesus was talking about being more than being born a Jew. Or being a part of Israel's kingdom. Jesus talked about a second birth. Obviously, the first birth is physical, when a man is born a Jew. But Jesus talked about a second birth to enter heaven. So Nicodemus asked,

"How can a man be born when he is old?" Nicodemus saw the logical impossibility. "How can a man enter a second time into his mother's womb to be born a second time?"[127]

"Except a man is born of water and of the Spirit . . .," Jesus paused and then repeated, "except a man is born of water and of the Spirit, he cannot enter into the kingdom of God."[259]

With this statement Jesus said a person needs two births to enter into His kingdom. The first birth is physical, when the water sac is broken as the baby is born. That birth comes by water. The second birth is of the Spirit . . . God's Spirit.[353]

The logic of Jesus was so simple. Who could miss it? Who could not accept it?

"When a man is born with a fleshly body . . .," Jesus explained, "that man is flesh, like the parents who gave him birth." Nicodemus understood the simplicity of Jesus' logic because the most profound things in life are simple to understand. Then Jesus explained,

"The man born of the Spirit . . .," Jesus explained, "that man is spiritual." Jesus looked into the eyes of Nicodemus. "Don't be surprised that I tell you to be born again."[118]

Up until now Jesus described the kingdom in abstract terms. Now He applied it to Nicodemus. Jesus told him, "You must be born again."

A gentle evening breeze swept up the street and over the flat-topped house.

Jesus explained, "Being born again is like the blowing of the wind . . .," Jesus used the breeze to illustrate the new birth. "When the wind blows, no one can see the wind; the wind blows where it wants to, but you can feel its results."[506]

"How will the new birth happen?"[545] Nicodemus asked.

Jesus walked to the wall and pointed out people on the street below. People were still walking, returning home from work or an evening meal. Everywhere they looked, there were people.

Then Jesus gave Nicodemus a lesson from the Master Teacher . . . a sermon from the Master Preacher.

For God has so loved every person in the world, that He has sent His Son to be the Savior of the world, and that everyone who believes in God's Son will not die spiritually, but will have everlasting life (John 3:16).

And as many as receive God's Son, enter God's family and become God's children. They that believe on God's Son are born again, not a physical birth, nor a Jewish birth but are born unto God's kingdom" (John 1:12).

Talk About the Story: Where were Jesus and Nicodemus? What did Jesus tell Nicodemus about going to heaven? What does it mean to be born of flesh? What does it mean to be born of the Spirit? Why did the Father send Jesus into the world? What must a person do to go to heaven?

Scripture: "For God so loved the world that He gave His only begotten Son, that whoever believes in Him should not perish but have everlasting life" (John 3:16).

Family Time: Just because anyone is religious like Nicodemus, does not mean they are going to heaven when they die. How can we become a child of the heavenly Father? What must we do to go to heaven when we die? Who does God love? Who does God want to come live with Him in heaven?

Prayer: Father, I believe Jesus came to earth to save people from their sins. Forgive me of my sins; I accept Jesus into my heart. I want to go be with Him in heaven when I die. Thank You for saving me. Amen.

JESUS MEETS A WOMAN AT JACOB'S WELL

Scripture: John 4:1–11
Place: Jacob's well in Samaria
Time: One week after Passover, April, 27 AD

Jesus and His disciples were walking back to Galilee after spending time in Jerusalem. It was a long trip, but the shortest route was one that most Jews refused to take! The most direct route went right through Samaria. And Jews and Samaritans did NOT like each other! But Jesus wasn't like most Jews. He and His disciples headed straight into Samaria.

This spring day was hot, so they decided to rest near the town of Sychar. Jesus sat down to rest at Jacob's Well. Jesus was tired and the small olive trees surrounding the well offered some shade.

The disciples headed to the town to get something to eat. Jesus was resting in the shade when He heard the squeak of a bucket against its leather handle.

It was about noon—the hottest time of the day. Normally, women went to the well first thing in the morning, when the weather was cool and comfortable and the long walk back to town with heavy water jars was easier. But here was a woman coming to the well alone in the noonday heat! Maybe she didn't want to spend time with the other women. Or maybe they didn't want to spend time with her!

Jesus greeted her kindly, then asked, "Could you give me something to drink?"

The woman looked up in surprise. "How can a Jewish man ask a drink of a Samaritan woman?" she asked

"If you knew who I was, and what I could give to you," Jesus said to the woman, "you would ask water from Me." Jesus said to the woman, "If you drink My living water, you'll never thirst again."

The woman began to lower her bucket into the well. The rope hummed as it slid over the wall until they heard, "Splash."

"You can't give me water," she said. "The well is deep and You don't have a rope or a bucket!"

Jesus meant spiritual water, not physical water. Jesus said, "My water will give you everlasting life."[65]

"Go call your husband,"[399] Jesus said to the woman.

"I don't have a husband."[81]

"You are telling the truth," Jesus said to her, "you have had five husbands, and the man you are now living with is not your husband."[499]

Jesus shocked her. She knew that He was right, but He had never met her. She realized He must be a man of God because He knew secret things about her.[544]

The woman wanted to change the subject! "The Samaritans worship in Mount Gerrizim," she noted; "but the Jews say we should worship in Jerusalem."[540]

Jesus knew she didn't really need to have religious questions answered. She needed to know the truth about Him.

"Woman, the hour is coming when we will not worship in Mount Gerrizim nor Jerusalem,[544] but true seekers will worship the Father in Spirit and in truth."[502]

The woman was beginning to understand that Jesus might be the Messiah. So she said, "When Messiah comes, He will tell us all things."[167]

"I am the Messiah," Jesus said.[450]

Talk About the Story: Where did the story take place? Why was the woman startled when Jesus asked her a question? What was Jesus offering the woman? What do you think happened next?

Scripture: "He who believes in Me, as the Scripture has said, out of his heart will flow rivers of living water." John 7:38

Family Time: When Jesus talked about living water, He was using a word picture to describe the Holy Spirit. How is God's Spirit refreshing and life giving like clean cold water is? How have you experienced God's Spirit helping and comforting you?

Prayer: Father, thank You that You care about every person. Thank You for sending Your Spirit to be with us and in us at all times. In Jesus' name, Amen.

JESUS OFFERS SALVATION TO A WOMAN

Scripture: John 4:5–45
Place: Jacob's Well in Samaria
Time: One week after Passover, 27 AD

Jesus and the Samaritan woman talked for a while. The woman was amazed that Jesus knew so much about her. So when Jesus told her, "I am the Messiah," the woman was ready to believe! She turned and ran toward town, leaving her bucket and rope.

The disciples passed her on the road. They wondered what the hurry was—and why Jesus had been talking to her. But they quickly picked up her bucket and use the rope to get water from the well for all of them to drink. Then they offered the food they had bought to Jesus.

Jesus shook His head and said, "I have food that you don't know about."

The disciples looked confused as they wondered who brought Jesus food while they were gone. They did not understand that Jesus was describing spiritual food.

So Jesus said plainly, "My food is to do the will of My Father that sent Me."

Jesus pointed to the grain fields. "Lift up your eyes and look on the fields. They are ready to harvest."

The disciples looked; and coming down the road from the city were people, dozens of people walking quickly toward them. Jesus looked at them and said, "The field is white unto harvest, but the workers are few."[145]

The woman had gone back to the city talking to everyone she knew, "Come see a man who told me everything I ever did. Could He be the Messiah?"[444] She ran from one group of men to another. To each group she said the same thing.

Upon hearing about the man who knew the secrets of the heart, the Samaritans hurried toward the well. They wanted to meet Jesus for themselves. They listened carefully to what Jesus was teaching. Then they pleaded with Him to stay longer and teach them more. After two days, many believed in Jesus, that He was the Christ.[72]

They said, "Now we believe You are the Messiah, not because of what the woman said, but we have heard for ourselves, and we believe that You are the Messiah, the Savior of the world."[416]

Talk About the Story: How was the woman convinced that Jesus is the Messiah? What did she do after she learned who Jesus is? How did the disciples respond? How did the people of the city respond?

Scripture: "But the hour is coming, and now is, when the true worshipers will worship the Father in spirit and truth; for the Father is seeking such to worship Him" John 4:23

Family Time: Why do you think the people of the woman's town were ready to worship Jesus as the Messiah? What are some things we can do to help others be ready to worship Jesus as their Savior?

Prayer: Father, I believe Jesus is the Savior of all people who will believe in Him. Help me to tell others about Jesus just as the woman told the people in her town. Amen.

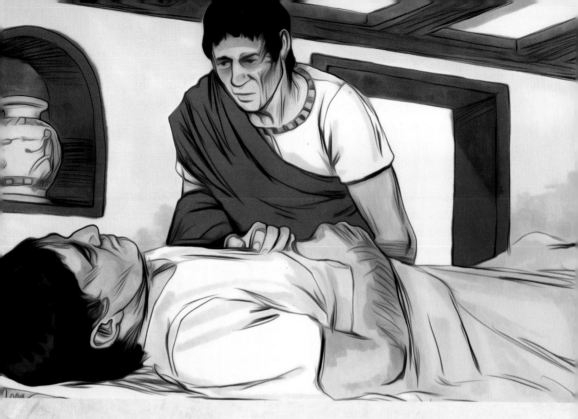

HEALING THE COURT OFFICER'S SON

Scripture: John 4:46–54
Place: Cana
Time: Summer, 27 AD

Jesus and His disciples continued on their journey back toward Galilee. They arrived in Cana, the same village where Jesus had changed water into wine a few months before. Jesus and His disciples sat together talking in the city market area. Nathaniel had just returned from visiting his family in Cana. Now they were casually talking and enjoying the day. Suddenly they saw a dignified man hurrying up the street. They could tell by his dress that he was a nobleman.

The man had been searching for Jesus. His son was so sick[214] he thought the little boy would die. The father began early that morning to walk the twenty-five miles into the hill country to Cana, looking for Jesus. He kept saying to himself, *If He will come and touch my son, Jesus can heal him!*

The nobleman had heard the stories of miracles from the people returning from Jerusalem. He had heard how Jesus cleansed the Temple, but more importantly, how the multitudes flocking to Jesus were healed.

The man thought that if he could have an audience with Jesus, He might be willing to heal his son. When he finally saw Jesus, he ran to bow at His feet to beg for his son's healing, "Come down to Capernaum! My son is at death's door."[435]

Jesus knew that most of the people in Cana didn't really believe He was the Messiah. They were just eager to see miracles and signs! So Jesus responded, "Do you have to see signs and miracles to believe in Me?"[127]

"Please," the man continued to beg. "Please come down to Capernaum to heal my child before he dies."[350]

"Go back home," Jesus told the man. "Your son is healed!"[151]

The man got up off the ground. He heard Jesus' pronouncement that his son was well. Since the man believed Jesus had authority, he was ready to trust Jesus.[151]

"Thank you for healing my son."[470]

The encounter had only taken a few minutes, the man turned to go back down the street, heading out of the village to home. He would not reach Capernaum that night, but would have to find lodging along the way. The following day, he continued winding his way down the hills toward Capernaum. Then he saw a familiar sight, one of his servants was coming up the road to meet him.

"YOUR SON IS WELL!" The servant yelled before he got to him. "Yesterday the fever broke, your son sat up to ask for water. I immediately came to find you. He's healed!"[473]

The man was stunned at the news. He didn't know what to say; this was exactly what he wanted. He wanted Jesus to heal his son. After a moment, he asked, "What time yesterday was my son healed?"

"1:00 pm."

The nobleman no longer required signs and miracles, he believed in Jesus. That was the very time Jesus had told him that his son was well. He believed that Jesus was more than a miracle worker, he believed that Jesus was the Messiah of Israel. He believed that Jesus was the Savior from sins. When he returned home, his whole house believed with him.[24]

Talk About the Story: What did the nobleman believe about Jesus? What was Jesus' response to him? How did the man find out his son was healed?

Scripture: "Ask, and it will be given to you; seek, and you will find; knock, and it will be opened to you." Matthew 7:7

Family Time: How did the father approach Jesus? What does that say about our approach to God? When did the father believe? What was the result of the miracle?

Prayer: Father, I thank You that we can come to you with all our needs and concerns. Thank You that you always hear our prayers and that You answer in the very best ways. Amen.

CONFRONTATION IN NAZARETH

Scripture: Luke 4:16–30
Place: Nazareth
Time: Spring, 27 AD

Jesus visited Nazareth, His hometown. On the Sabbath day, Jesus went to the Synagogue as it was His habit.[210]

The crowd was much larger than usual. Everyone in town had heard about the things Jesus had done and said in Jerusalem and other places. They wanted to hear Jesus speak, now that He was establishing a reputation as a traveling Rabbi. After all, Jesus grew up there!

Visiting Rabbis were usually asked to read from the Scriptures as part of the Synagogue worship.[425]

The leader of the Synagogue handed the large scroll of Isaiah to Jesus. Then Jesus stood to read,

"The spirit of the Lord is upon Me[167] because He has anointed Me to preach the gospel to the poor;[145] He has sent Me to heal the broken hearted and to preach deliverance to the captives, to give sight to the blind, and to set at liberty them that are in bondage, and to preach the acceptable year of our Lord" (Luke 4:18, 19).[416]

Then Jesus stopped and rolled the scroll back up. After handing the scroll to the minister, Jesus sat down.

Every eye in the room was looking at Jesus. They were waiting for the aftersermon, the *pethichah*, which would have been the explanation to His reading. But all Jesus said was, "Today is this Scripture fulfilled."[425] The people smiled in approval. *This is Joseph's son*, they thought.

But Jesus knew that most of the people in Nazareth would not believe in Him. So Jesus went on to say, "Many of you want Me to do miracles here as I have done at Capernaum and at Jerusalem. But no prophet is accepted in his own hometown!"

Jesus continued with an illustration, "There were many lepers in Israel when

the prophet Elisha cleansed Naaman the Syrian. Elisha couldn't cleanse lepers in Israel because of their unbelief."

Now instead of being impressed, the people were angry! "I cannot do miracles in My hometown of Nazareth because of your unbelief. You do not believe that I am who I claim to be."[504]

The congregation had heard enough. They erupted in holy indignation because Jesus had claimed to be their Messiah and He refused to do miracles.

They grabbed Jesus and pushed Him out of the town and all the way to the high cliff on the western edge of town. They wanted to push Him off the cliff to kill Him! But Jesus simply turned and walked away from the angry crowd. They were not able to hurt Him at all

Talk About the Story: Why was Jesus invited to take part in the Sabbath services? What did Jesus say about the Scripture He read? Why did the people get mad at Jesus? What did they try to do to Him? How did Jesus escape?

Scripture: "Believe on the Lord Jesus Christ, and you will be saved, you and your household." Acts 16:31

Family Time: The people of Nazareth refused to believe in Jesus. What is the good news that comes from believing in Jesus? How can we show God's love to people who refuse to believe in Jesus today?

Prayer: Father, thank You that You help us to believe in You today. Help us know how to respond to people who refuse to believe in Jesus today. Amen.

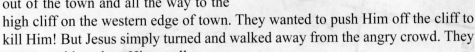

PSALM 16

DAVID'S PRIVATE THOUGHTS ABOUT DEATH

David had been in a terrible battle. One warrior almost got the best of David, almost killing him. But a soldier of David's came to his rescue. After the battle was over, David went alone on a hill to think about his narrow escape from death. He wanted to thank God for deliverance and for the friend who helped him.

"Lord, keep me safe in battle and in life;
I depend on You to protect my life.[298]
I tell everyone You are my God and my master,
Every good thing I have comes from you.[363]
Your godly people are my friends,
I depend upon them and need them constantly.
Those who worship other gods have no assurance,
I will never be a part of sacrifices to them,
Nor will the names of other gods be on my lips. "[113]

As David meditated on the Lord, he again realized God had given him every good thing he had. David praised God for his family, his training, and all the good things in his life. He thanked God for them in the Psalm.

"Lord, You are my first and only passion in life,
Thank you for making me Your choice.[362]
Thank you for bringing me into your family,
And giving me a godly inheritance.[207]
You guide my decisions every day
You confirm to me Your guidance every night.
Lord, I have set You as my guide in life,
Because You are at my right hand, I will not be afraid in battle, or
upset. "[377]

David also knew that God not only protected him in battle, but although he didn't know when he would die, he only knew he would go to live with God in death.

> *"Lord, my heart is happy about life,*
>   *I know when I die and my body is laid in the grave*[397]
> *You will not leave my soul in hell,*
>   *Neither will You let my body see corruption.*[405]
> *You will guide me on the path to eternal life,*
>   *I will enjoy blessedness at Your right hand*
>   *And have pleasure forever more."*[177]

While these words of Psalm 16 apply to David, this also is a picture of the resurrection of Jesus. When Peter was preaching on the day of Pentecost, he quoted the Psalm, then he said,

> *"Men and brethren, let me speak freely to you of the patriarch David, that he is both dead and buried, and his tomb is with us to this day. Therefore, being a prophet, and knowing that God had sworn with an oath to him that of the fruit of his body, according to the flesh, He would raise up the Christ to sit on His throne, he, foreseeing this, spoke concerning the resurrection of the Christ, that His soul was not left in Hades, nor did His flesh see corruption"* (Acts 2:29–31, NKJV).

David believed God would raise him up so he could live with God for eternity. The confidence of David can be ours.

Talk About the Psalm: What did you learn about the psalm writer in this story? What did you learn about God?

Psalm 16: Read this week's psalm in your Bible together. Choose a verse to read aloud as a prayer.

Prayer: Thank You, God, for the psalm prayers in the Bible. Thank You for teaching us about You and about how to pray. In Jesus' name, Amen.

FISHING FOR WHAT?

Scripture: Mark 1:16–20
Place: Sea of Galilee
Time: Spring, 27 AD

A spring storm had rumbled over the Sea of Galilee. Waves had pounded the shore. And even though they had fished all night, the fishermen had not caught anything yet—and the sun was rising. The early morning mist began to evaporate as the sun peeked over the cliffs. Peter looked in the smooth water to see a perfect image of his face and beard.

Fishermen usually caught their fish at night, and slept after the sun got high. But Andrew, Peter's brother, jumped into the boat to help him.

"Let's just cast near the shore," Peter said to Andrew.

"What do you think about Jesus?" Peter asked between the tosses of the net. They had followed Jesus before He left them to go pray in the mountains.[77] But now, they hadn't seen Jesus a couple of months! Since Jesus had left them, the warm rains had turned brown fields into green grass.

Peter said, "Jesus is more than a good teacher.

"Yes, He IS," Andrew said. He turned water into wine at that wedding!"

"He could be our Messiah!" Peter said thoughtfully. "But where IS He? Was it really a miracle?" asked Peter.

"You drank the wine," Andrew laughed. "You tell me!"

Jesus was not the kind of Messiah the brothers had expected. They thought a Messiah might lead an army. But Jesus came to capture people's hearts!

James and John were also nearby, in their boat with their father Zebedee, mending their nets. James had listened carefully to what people said about Jesus, but didn't talk about it much. His brother John, however, was more hot-headed. He'd talked about Jesus to anyone who'd listen, gladly giving his opinions!

While the two groups talked and thought about Jesus, little did they know that Jesus was walking toward them! As Jesus walked toward them, He stepped out onto a rock showing above the water. Then He called to them, "Come!" He beckoned and said, "Follow Me. I will make you fishers of people."[314]

Peter immediately dropped his side of the net! He sloshed through the water toward Jesus. He didn't look back to see what Andrew would do. Peter had made his decision. He would follow Jesus!

Andrew followed his brother, sloshing toward Jesus, too! Like two men rowing a boat together, the brothers moved together to follow Jesus, leaving ripples in the water.

"Come," Jesus called out to James and John. He beckoned to them, as well. The brothers stood and dropped the nets they were mending in the early morning sun.

"Come," Jesus said to the sons of Zebedee. "Come! Follow Me. Learn from Me! I will make you fishers of men." The two brothers hugged their father and turned to follow Jesus. They had also made life-changing choices.

As young John laid aside the nets, he knew he would not return to fishing. He'd followed John the Baptist earlier, but now, he was eager to follow Jesus, the One John had called, "The Lamb of God, who takes away the sin of the world." John didn't know what it would mean to follow Jesus—but he knew his life would be changed![75]

Talk About the Story: What were the names of the four fishermen? What did they talk about? What did Jesus say to them? What did the fishermen do when Jesus called them?

Scripture: "Follow Me, and I will make you fishers of men." Matthew 4:19

Family Time: What were the disciples doing when Jesus called them? What do you think Jesus mean by becoming fishers of men? How does Jesus call people today to follow Him? What's a way we can follow Jesus?

Prayer: Jesus, I want to follow You, as the disciples did. I want to help others follow You, too. Thank You for loving us and calling us! In Your name, Amen.

CHAPTER 8

FIRST YEAR OF MINISTRY

What a morning! Jesus had been asked to teach the lesson at the synagogue, but no one could have anticipated what actually happened. As was becoming the custom, the crowds thronged Him; even the synagogue itself was packed. The message was not what made the great impression that day. It was the interruption! Usually, people were polite and endured the lesson, even if they disagreed with the teacher or thought the message was particularly boring. But that morning, a demon possessed man showed for the service. Suddenly without warning he started calling Jesus "the Holy One of God" (Mark 1:24).

Jesus' response was most unusual; He told the man to be quiet, it was as

though He didn't want him telling some secret. And when He spoke, Jesus spoke beyond the man and talked directly to the demon. The demon came out of the man. As Jesus and His disciples left the synagogue that day, various groups were saying. "What is this? What new doctrine is this? For with authority He commands even the unclean spirits, and they obey him" (Mark 1:27).

Obviously Jesus of Nazareth was going to be discussed. He was the most popular man of the region and news of the events that morning was sure to spread quickly. This first complete year of ministry meant Jesus' reputation was growing and His ministry was gaining acceptance.

A DEVIL IN GOD'S HOUSE

Scripture: Mark 1:21-31
Place: Capernaum
Time: Spring, 27 AD

Jesus was walking through Capernaum with Peter, Andrew, James, and John. It was the Sabbath, the day of rest and worship.

In Capernaum, everyone went to the synagogue on the Sabbath day.[455] The synagogue was the place where people gathered to worship, study and pray to God.

Jesus and His four disciples pulled their prayer shawls over their heads as they entered, just as all the other men did. This was the way they showed respect for God when they entered the synagogue.[455] The men sat on the first floor, and the women sat in the balcony.

Everyone joined in singing the Psalms and prayers. After reading from the Torah, the five books of Moses, the leader invited Jesus to read from the scroll of the prophet Isaiah.[456]

Jesus read in a clear voice, and began to teach the people what the words meant. But suddenly, ANOTHER voice cried out, a kind of strangled scream. Right here in the synagogue, a man had an evil spirit inside him that was making all of the noise!

www.thefamilyprayerbible.com

The shrieking shocked everyone. The elders jerked their heads to stare. Some people moved away from the man the noise was coming from.

Then, from deep within the man came a voice like an echo from a dark cave. The man began shaking violently.[53] The voice snarled, "Let us alone, Jesus of Nazareth! I know who You are. You have come to destroy us. YOU are the Holy One of God!"[259]

The demon had called Jesus a name that meant "Possessor of Heaven and Earth."

"HE'S DEMON POSSESSED," one worshiper shouted. A person possessed by an evil spirit was not new to these people. Some had seen this before. The spirit entering the person seemed to paralyze "body and mind."[53]

Jesus stood looking at the man with the demon. He said, "QUIET!"

Everyone became quiet. But Jesus was not speaking to them. He was speaking to the evil spirit!

"DO NOT SPEAK ANY MORE," Jesus commanded the spirit.

Jesus had come to destroy the works of the devil, but He did not come to destroy or harm this man. Jesus was concerned about what the demon had done to him.

"COME OUT OF HIM!" Jesus commanded.

Suddenly, the man slumped in his seat. Jesus had commanded the demon to go, and it was GONE!

Because Jesus has power and authority, the evil spirit had to obey Jesus and leave.[109] No one doubted that the demonic voice they had heard was NOT going to speak through that man again!

The people were amazed. They had already been surprised by Jesus' teaching: He spoke with authority! Now He had cast an evil spirit out of a man. They couldn't doubt what they had seen and heard!

"What power Jesus has!" one said. "Even evil spirits obey Him." Everyone was amazed at Jesus and glorified God.[188]

Talk About the Story: Who was with Jesus when He went into the synagogue? What interrupted Jesus' reading and teaching? What did Jesus do? Why was Jesus not afraid? How did Jesus send the demon away?

Scripture: "With authority He commands even the unclean spirits, and they obey Him." Mark 1:27

Family Time: Who can command even evil spirits? What else can Jesus do? What can we ask Jesus to help do? Can Jesus protect us from evil?

Prayer: Father, thank You that Jesus is stronger than anything or anyone! We ask You to protect us and are glad you love us. In Jesus' name, Amen.

HEALING PETER'S MOTHER-IN-LAW

Scripture: Mark 1:29–31
Place: Capernaum
Time: Spring, 27 AD

Jesus walked with Peter, Andrew, James and John toward Peter's house. They strolled up the main street that stretched to the front steps of the synagogue from the dock on the lake.

Peter's wife said as they came in at the front door, "My mother is sick. Be careful, Jesus. I don't want You to fall ill with this terrible fever she has!"

But Jesus was never afraid of sickness.

"Where is she?" Jesus asked.

Peter's wife shot him a look. If Jesus was the Messiah, then there was no reason not to let Him see the sick woman!

They led Jesus into the room where she lay. A folded wet cloth lay over her forehead to cool the high fever. A bowl of water sat next to the bed for keeping the cloth wet.

www.thefamilyprayerbible.com

Jesus tenderly bent over the woman. Taking her hand, Jesus spoke in a voice that was soft but commanding: "Fever! Leave."²¹⁴ It was a simple command from Jesus. He spoke to the fever and it left! The older woman opened her eyes and looked up at Jesus. She began to smile as Jesus helped her sit up.

"My fever's gone!" Peter's mother-in-law said with a laugh. She threw back the covers and got to her feet. "My headache's gone. I am WELL!"²¹
Peter introduced his mother-in-law to Jesus saying, "This is Jesus! He's the One I've been telling you about. He is the One who changed water into wine at that wedding a few months ago. And today in the synagogue, He sent an evil spirit out of a man! And now, He has made you well. He can do anything!"³⁵³

Peter's mother-in-law patted Jesus on the shoulder saying, "Then I must show You how much I appreciate Your help!"

The older woman went to the kitchen. She wanted to do all she could to help her daughter feed Jesus and His friends—because she felt better than she had EVER felt! She wanted to show Jesus her love and thanks by serving Him and His disciples.³⁶⁴

Dinner was a joyful, perfect ending to a VERY exciting Sabbath! Peter loved food, and lots of it! His wife always prepared the best for him and the guests he brought home. But it was her mother's help that was her cooking secret! Her mother had taught her to cook, and the two women cooking together—mother and daughter—turned an average meal into a feast! Jesus and His friends enjoyed the love and honor the women showed. Jesus knew how glad they were for Him to be with them as the guest of honor.

Peter clanked his spoon on a cup to get attention. He said, "If Jesus had not healed my mother-in-law—who is an outstanding cook—then we would not be eating this wonderful meal. He not only made her well, but by healing her, He made this meal possible. Thank you, Jesus!" Everyone cheered their approval! ²¹³

Talk About the Story: Who was sick? What did Jesus do? What did Peter's mother-in-law do after Jesus healed her?

Scripture: "Serve the Lord with gladness; come before His presence with singing." Psalm 100:2

Family Time: What are some ways Jesus and His friends honored God on the Lord's Day? What are reasons we want to serve and honor God? What is a song of praise your family knows? Sing it!

Prayer: Jesus, we are glad that You can help sick family members. Please help our sick family members. Thank You for people who serve us each day, and thank You that we can serve You with gladness! In Your name, Amen.

HEALING ALL WHO CAME

Scripture: Mark 1:32–34
Place: Capernaum
Time: Spring, 27 AD

What a day this had been—and it was not over yet! Even though Jesus and His friends had finished dinner, and the sun was setting, there was still more to be done!

You see, this Sabbath day had started out with Jesus going to the synagogue with His four disciples: Peter, Andrew, James, and John. There, Jesus cast a demon out of a man.[114] Now, freeing a man from an evil spirit would have been enough excitement for one day, but there was more!

Jesus returned to Peter's house to rest and have dinner. But Peter's mother-in-law had a fever, so He healed her.[214] Soon, the news spread everywhere that Jesus could do miracles. He could heal people![466]

So even though it was getting close to dark, people were bringing their sick friends and relatives to where Jesus was! They came from everywhere, hoping they'd be able to see Jesus and be healed by Him.

The crowd waited quietly at Peter's front door as Jesus and His friends finished eating. There were sick fathers being carried on mats by their wives and children. There were hurting widows being helped by their daughters and sons. There were children who could not walk, and grandparents who were carried on a chair by their young, strong grandsons. People were bringing loved ones who were sad and people who were facing death but didn't want to die.[99] And all of them were moving toward the door as best they could!

By the time Jesus came out, the red glow of sunset was fading. Two stars could be seen high above the trees.

Stretched down one side of the street to the marketplace, He could see the pallets of sick people. Jesus began to walk between the mats and pallets. His voice was quiet; no one dared speak louder than Jesus.[437]

He stopped at each pallet, listening, nodding and smiling. Sometimes He touched the sick person where it hurt or lay his hand on the person's head. He prayed over each one. Jesus went from one to the next, and then to the next.

It must have looked like a PARTY, for as soon as Jesus prayed over each person, EVERY person He prayed for, every person He touched, was HEALED! And they didn't just feel better; no, they felt the BEST they had felt in their whole lives! They had been made completely well by Jesus!

Some people who knew about Jesus thought He would try to gather soldiers to fight the Romans. But sick people were the ones who came to Jesus! They were fighters, but they had been fighting to stay alive! And now, they had met Jesus. And they ALL were completely WELL!

Jesus was showing the people what God His Father is like. He is a healer, not a revolutionary.[435]

Talk About the Story: What happened at Peter's house? What did people do when they heard that Jesus can heal? How many did Jesus heal? Why did Jesus heal people?

Scripture: "Jesus said to him, 'I am the way, the truth, and the life. No one comes to the Father except through Me. If you had known Me, you would have known My Father also; and from now on you know Him and have seen Him.'" John 14:6–7

Family Time: How was Jesus kind to Peter's mother-in-law? Why do sick people come to Jesus? What are some things Jesus' actions show us about God the Father?

Prayer: Father, thank You for sending Jesus to show us who You are. Please help us to obey You the way Jesus did. In Jesus' name, Amen.

DATE ___/___

JESUS PRAYS

Scripture: Mark 1:35–39
Place: Capernaum
Time: Spring, 27 AD

Jesus' friends Peter, Andrew, James, and John collapsed onto their sleeping mats. They had been busy all day—and it was supposed to be the Sabbath, the day of rest! They were very tired. Peter slept as soundly as a rock. That matched the nickname Jesus gave him—Rock!

But before anyone else was awake in Peter's house, Jesus woke. He got up and pulled on His cloak. He left the house, silently shutting the door behind Him. The roosters of Capernaum had not even announced the new day yet—it was still fully dark! Jesus' footsteps were quiet as He walked outside of the town to find a place to pray to His heavenly Father.[168]

As the sun began to come up, James and John came to Peter's house. It would be their first day of "weekday work duty." They wanted to be there on time!

www.thefamilyprayerbible.com

"Where's Jesus?" John asked as soon as the door was opened. "We're ready!"

A sparkling sun broke over the cliffs to the east and across the Lake of Galilee.

"Jesus is not here," Peter announced. "I've looked all through the house, and He's not here."

The disciples all left Peter's house and spread out in Capernaum. It wasn't very big, so this wasn't hard to do! Peter walked through the marketplace where a few merchants had already set up their stalls. Out of town, in a field, Peter saw a trail through the grass, as if someone had walked away from the town.

Peter followed the trail through the grass. There in a clump of trees growing among some rocks, he saw Jesus praying, with His hands spread toward heaven. "Jesus!" Peter called. "We've been looking everywhere for You!"

Jesus smiled at His friends as they approached, and motioned to them to sit down. He told them how much He needed to be alone with His heavenly Father. Praying and listening to God was what gave Him spiritual strength.[443]

"Everybody in Capernaum is ready to follow You," Peter announced. "Let's go back to Capernaum to get them!"

Peter wanted to go back to Capernaum where people and crowds rallied around Jesus last evening. Perhaps Peter thought Jesus would tell everyone that He is the King.

But Jesus said, "No, first let's go to the other villages around Galilee; they must hear the message of the kingdom of God."

Jesus turned to point to a village sitting high on a far mountain. "I must preach the gospel in these villages. That's one of the reasons I was sent."[520]

Talk About the Story: Why did Jesus leave the house early in the morning? Where did Jesus go? Why? What did Jesus want to do next?

Scripture: "Call to Me, and I will answer you, and show you great and mighty things, which you do not know." Jeremiah 33:3

Family Time: Jesus spent time with God His Father in prayer. This gave Him strength to do what God wanted Him to do. What are some things we can do so that we have strength to obey God?

Prayer: Father, thank You for giving Jesus strength when He spent time with You. Please help us to spend time with You, praying and listening for what You want us to do in Your Word. In Jesus' name, Amen.

A LEPER HEALED

Scripture: Mark 1:40–45
Place: Galilee
Time: Spring, 27 AD

The disciples and Jesus were winding their way up a mountain city that could be seen from Capernaum. Suddenly they heard shouts, "UNCLEAN! KEEP AWAY!"

This was the warning people with leprosy were required to call out. Leprosy was a terrible disease because there was no cure for it. Leprosy is now called Hanson's Disease and can be treated, but in Jesus' day, people with leprosy had to stay outside of cities and away from other people all the time.

Then they saw the man who was yelling the warning. His clothes were filthy, his hair disheveled, His face and arms were covered with sores.

When he saw Jesus, he cried with a loud voice, what he was required to yell when approaching anyone, "UNCLEAN! UNCLEAN!"

www.thefamilyprayerbible.com

But the man didn't move away like people with leprosy usually did when they saw others. He stood still for a moment, Then he knelt down and said to Jesus, "If You are willing, You can make me clean."[214]

This man was asking for something that had been done only twice in the Old Testament! Only Miriam and Naaman were supernaturally healed. The man with leprosy had heard the things Jesus had said and done, and was convinced that Jesus could make him well.

Jesus reached out His hand and touched the man. Jesus said, "I AM willing. Be clean."

Immediately the leprosy was gone! The man's skin looked healthy. All the sores were gone!

Then Jesus said, "Do not tell anyone what has happened to you, but go show yourself to the priest, then offer sacrifice to God for cleansing, required by Moses."[480]

All the disciples knew the words of Moses well. When a person had a rash that appeared to be the first stages of leprosy, that person would be quarantined by the priest. If the rash disappeared, the priest announced that the person had been cleansed. So sending the man to the priest would make it possible for him to get permission to return home and get back to normal life.

But the man did not follow all of Jesus' instructions—he was too excited! He ran into the town, telling everyone he met what Jesus had done for him![478]

Talk About the Story: What is leprosy? What did the man with leprosy do when he saw Jesus? How did Jesus respond? Why didn't the man follow all of Jesus' instructions?

Scripture: "But You, O Lord, are a God full of compassion, and gracious, Long-suffering and abundant in mercy and truth." Psalm 86:15

Family Time: Jesus had compassion for the man with leprosy. Who are some people today that you think Jesus has compassion for? Why? What are some ways that we can show His compassion to others this week?

Prayer: Father, thank You for Jesus' love for people who have been hurt or rejected by others. Help us to extend His love and compassion to others as well. In Jesus' name, Amen.

PSALM 19

THE HEAVENS REVEAL GOD

David lay on the dewy wet grass studying the night sky. The sky was clear—not a cloud anywhere to be seen. He was trying to count the stars. He had never seen so many at one time! He thought, *Only a great God could create so many stars!*

Young David began a song, "The heavens reveal God's magnificent glory, and the sky is evidence of His handwork." He strummed his harp to the new song he was singing in worship to God.

Then David sang, "Every new day the heavens reveal God's ancient work. Every night continually shows the beauty of His creation."[93] David loved to sing about the miracles he saw in God's creation.

David had gone to sleep early last evening, now it was almost time for the sun to come up. He could see the Eastern sky begin to brighten. He asked, "Where is the sun when I can't see it?" Then he imagined it rested in a house, like people sleeping in his town of Bethlehem. He sang,

"God has made a home for the sun, every morning it comes triumphantly out of the front door like a man expecting to get married. It bursts its rays in brilliance like an athlete excited to run a race."

Then David waved his hand from the Eastern horizon to the other end of the heaven where the sun sat in the West. The young shepherd sang, "The sun begins its daily trip from one side of heaven, and runs its course until it finishes each evening in the West."

When the sun arose over the Eastern hills, nothing could hide its rays from warming David's face. He smiled as its friendly light chased away the chill of the night. Again David sang, "Nothing can hide from the heat of the sun, it scorches the sand, melts the ice, and warms our hearts."

To end his song, David sang, "May these words I think in my heart, and may my thought about Your creation be pleasing to You my God. I offer my reflection in worship to You."[60]

Talk About the Psalm: What did you learn about the psalm writer in this story? What did you learn about God?

Psalm 19: Read this week's psalm in your Bible together. Choose a verse to read aloud as a prayer.

Prayer: Thank You, God, for the psalm prayers in the Bible. Thank You for teaching us about You and about how to pray. In Jesus' name, Amen.

GETTING A FRIEND TO JESUS

Scripture: Mark 2:1–12
Place: Capernaum
Time: Late summer, 27 AD

Autumn was coming on in Galilee. There were a few early snows, and white snowcaps showed high on the mountains. In bad weather people stayed indoors. Fewer came out to meet Jesus as He traveled to Capernaum. The weather was one reason Jesus came out of the mountains and came "home" to Capernaum, by Lake Galilee.

Meanwhile, the Jewish leaders in Jerusalem had sent spies to Capernaum. They wanted them to report back whatever Jesus said, and did. If they could, they wanted to trick Jesus into saying something that would get Him in trouble with the leaders.[114]

Early one morning, the room filled and overflowed where Jesus was teaching.[346]

A rabbi or teacher came asking, "May I come in to listen to Jesus?" Along with him came visiting rabbis—the spies from Jerusalem.

Four friends were also trying to get in. They were carrying a mat which held their friend who could not walk. They'd come from a nearby town, each man carrying a corner of their friend's mat. Each friend deeply believed that Jesus could heal their friend whose legs did not work.

"We have a sick man who needs to see Jesus," they called, setting down their friend for a moment. But the crowd wouldn't move or let them through.[31]

So they went to the back door, but they couldn't get in because of the crowd.

They had to do something! They carried their friend up to the roof.

Then, they began to dig and pull at the straw and wood and mud of the roof to make an opening! When the opening was big enough, they tied ropes to the corners of the mat and let their friend DOWN through the roof, DOWN through the air, RIGHT to the feet of Jesus!

Jesus must have laughed out loud! These friends were NOT going to be stopped!

"Cheer up!" Jesus said to the man on the mat. "Your sins have been forgiven."[173]

Jesus looked up and smiled at the four friends looking down through the hole they'd made, eager to see what Jesus would do! He marveled at their faith.[353]

But the rabbis were thinking, "WAIT! Only GOD can forgive sins, right?"[12] They all wondered the same thing, but no one spoke.

They also thought, *"WHY is Jesus speaking as if He is GOD?"*[504]

Jesus knew what the rabbis and religious "spies" were thinking! He knew they did not want to listen to Him and what He taught.[129]

Jesus looked at them—and replied to their thoughts!

"So that you may know that the Son of Man has power on earth to forgive sins," Jesus then turned to the man on the mat. He said to him, "I say to you, get up! Take up your mat and go home."[359]

Suddenly, the man's feet and legs were STRONG. He stood up, and did a little happy dance, jumping around in joy! He rolled up his mat and called for his rooftop friends!

What a happy, dancing, laughing group of FIVE friends went home that day! The four friends had believed Jesus could hear their friend—and He DID!

Talk About the Story: Where was Jesus? Who were the spies sent to trick Jesus? What did Jesus say first, that the man was healed or that he was forgiven?

Scripture: "When Jesus saw their faith, He said to the paralytic, "Son, your sins are forgiven you." Mark 2:5

Family Time: Why do you think these men brought their friend to Jesus? What are ways we can help the people we love get to Jesus and know Him?

Prayer: Father, we believe in Jesus. He can do anything! Thank You that we can trust Him, pray and help the people we love to love Jesus, too. In His name, Amen.

THE CALL OF MATTHEW

Scripture: Mark 2:13–22
Place: Near Capernaum
Time: Summer, 27 AD

The road from Damascus to Egypt ran past the wall of Capernaum. Because it was the road where traders and merchants traveled, a booth was there to collect taxes from them.

The chief tax collector sat at the table, entering numbers into his book. He kept track of how much tax was collected, from whom. A number of other workers did the inspections to decide the taxes. If travelers thought the taxes were too high, first they argued with the assistants. Then they appealed to the official tax collector. He was the only decision maker. Roman soldiers made sure the taxes were collected. Besides the taxes to Rome, each tax collector took in more for himself, too.

Everything was taxed: grain, wine, cloth, produce. Matthew also collected a toll-tax for each person 12 years old and over. Besides that, Matthew collected tax on anything else he wanted to tax.

People did not like tax collectors. Rabbis excommunicated a tax collector's whole family.

Matthew watched from his tax booth as sick people were carried to Jesus, and then walked, danced and ran as they returned.[214]

One day, Matthew looked up to see Jesus at his table. Jesus paused, but not to pay taxes. He said, "Follow Me."[75]

Matthew got up. He closed his ledger and shut his money box. He followed Jesus! Now, Matthew's entire past—his sins, his greed, his separation from fellow Jews—was over. He became Jesus' disciple.

That evening Jesus ate at Matthew's house. His disciples and some Jews who worked for Matthew joined them.[361]

After the meal was over, Jesus began talking with Matthew and the others about the kingdom of God. Visitors from town squeezed into the room to hear the table talk, too. But there were also the religious spies and those who hated Jesus as well. One said to Philip, "How can your Master eat and drink with tax collectors and sinners?"[145]

Jesus heard this and answered, "Healthy people do not need a doctor, but those that are sick need the doctor. I did not come to call the righteous to repent, I came to call sinners."[256]

The followers of John the Baptist had also come to town. When they heard that Jesus was feasting at Matthew's house, they were disturbed. They ate simply and often fasted to God, not eating so they could pray. They were horrified that Jesus was feasting. And He was eating in the home of a tax collector! A disciple of John's said, "We fast often. So do the Pharisees. But look at Jesus—He's feasting." Jesus was eating and enjoying Himself.

Jesus heard the whispered complaint. He said to the crowd at the banquet, "When people go to a wedding, they eat. As long as the bridegroom is with them, they feast. But when the bridegroom is gone, then they will fast.[265] They will fast until He is about to come back."[161]

Instead of rules and laws, Jesus gave people the power and ability to obey God. This was new and wonderful!

Talk About the Story: What was Matthew's job? Why did people hate him? Who complained at the banquet at Matthew's house? What did Jesus say about the complaint?

Scripture "Those who are well have no need of a physician, but those who are sick. I did not come to call the righteous, but sinners, to repentance."[490] Mark 2:17
Family Time When has your family had a feast? What did you celebrate? Talk about reasons you can celebrate Jesus tonight as you eat together.

Prayer: Jesus, thank You for inviting all kinds of people to follow You—even me! I'm glad to follow You! In your name, Amen.

CHOOSING THE TWELVE

Scripture: Mark 3:13–19; Luke 6:12–19
Place: A Mountain West of the Sea of Galilee
Time: Summer, 27 AD

Crowds of people were following Jesus as He taught and healed in the towns around the Sea of Galilee—so many people that Jesus could hardly walk!

By this time, more than 70 disciples were following Jesus, staying with Him most of the time. But Jesus needed a small group of men He could teach and guide and get them ready to do the same kind of work Jesus did.

Jesus could then send these men out to teach and heal the way He was doing. He would give these His own authority.[27] They would be called apostles, or "sent ones." There would be only 12, just as there were 12 tribes of Israel.

Thinking about these things, Jesus climbed a steep hill, looking for a quiet place. He prayed and spent time with God His Father often, but He especially wanted to understand which 12 men God wanted—because these 12 would carry Jesus' good news everywhere![314]

Jesus found a quiet ravine near the top of the mountain. This would be a good place to spend the night. But Jesus wouldn't sleep. No, Jesus prayed all night long, talking to His Father and listening, too. Jesus knelt in that quiet place and prayed "Father, Thy will be done . . . ."[443]

Only after the sun peeked over the mountain did He came down.

Of course, a crowd was waiting for Jesus! Jesus said, "Today I will choose 12

men to be apostles. I will send them in My name. They will stay with Me, learn from Me, pray with Me and help Me."

"Later on," Jesus explained, "they will preach the good news and will have the power to do miracles in My name."

Jesus began to point to one man, then to another.

"Simon," Jesus nodded to the big fisherman, "called Peter. His nickname means 'Rock.'"

Then Jesus pointed to James, a quiet man, strong and always first to cast a net or pull the oars. He was not afraid of work. Then Jesus pointed to James's brother John. Young, probably still a teen, John was eager to learn from Jesus.

Next, Jesus nodded to Andrew. These men had been the first four He had asked to follow Him. In fact, Andrew was the first one Jesus called. Andrew was Peter's brother, quick to notice people's needs. He had already brought people to meet Jesus![296]

"Philip, you too," Jesus said. Philip stepped forward, ready to do anything for Jesus. Philip was good at keeping things in order.

Jesus appointed three other apostles to work with Philip: Nathaniel, his friend Matthew the tax collector and Thomas, who was a twin. They would help Philip handle people and take care of details.

"James! You'll be the ninth disciple, yes, you, the shorter James." There were several followers named James, so to keep them straight, they called this one James the Less.

Thaddeus was chosen to work with James the Less, and so was Simon the Zealot, a man who'd once fought against the Romans.

These eleven were all from Galilee. But for the twelfth apostle, Jesus chose a man from near Jerusalem, Judas Iscariot.[29] Jesus chose him to be the twelfth apostle.[287]

So now Jesus had 12 men who would live with Him, learn from Him and follow Him in everything!

Talk About the Story: What did Jesus do before He chose His apostles? What did the apostles do? How would they help Jesus?

Scripture: "He (Jesus) went out to the mountain to pray, and continued all night in prayer to God." Luke 6:12

Family Time: Why do you think Jesus spent time with God before He chose His apostles? When have you made a big decision? How did God help you? What are decisions to pray about today?

Prayer: Father, please help us to ask You first about everything. Thank You that you love us and promise to give us wisdom. In Jesus' name, Amen.

CHAPTER 9

THE TWELVE DISCIPLES

Fellowship with Jesus was an integral part of what it meant to be one of Jesus' disciples. The two primary reasons Jesus chose twelve disciples were "that they might be with Him and that He might send them out to preach" (Mark 3:14). A disciple was one who first spent time with Jesus celebrating a close and intimate relationship with God. Only then was a disciple involved in a ministry of communicating what he had learned to others.

After a night of prayer, Jesus chose twelve very different kinds of men to follow Him as His disciples. Each of them had their own unique gifts and abilities to contribute to help shape the overall character of the group. During

the time they spent with Jesus, they would become the focus of His attention. None of them were perfect and some were less perfect than others. They were not chosen because of who they were as much as who they would become. Much of Jesus' earthly ministry was wrapped up in training the twelve. When it was over, one of them would betray Him. The other eleven would change the world.

PETER, BOLD AND BEFUDDLED

Special Section: The Disciples
Overview of Peter in the Gospels

Jesus had a special ministry of helping each of the 12 disciples grow into the person God wanted him to be. Peter's brother, Andrew, was the first to follow Christ, then he brought his older brother to Jesus. The first thing Jesus said may be the most important thing about Peter, "You are Simon, son of Jonah, but you will be called Cephas, which means a stone" (John 1:42).[58] Someone could have laughed because Peter was more like shifting sand than like a firm rock.

Peter was impulsive. That means he acted first and thought about it second. The next time Jesus met Peter when walking on the beach, He said, "Follow Me."[259] Peter dropped his nets to follow Jesus. During a storm, Jesus walked on the waters to the disciples. Peter stepped off the boat to walk on water.[112] When the soldiers came to arrest Jesus in the garden, it was Peter who cut off a man's ear to defend Jesus.[164] When the disciples fished all night without a single fish, Jesus yelled to them over the waters. Peter jumped in and swam to talk with Jesus.[393] Peter was always quick to act.

Peter also was quick to speak. He said things at the wrong time and got into trouble.

When Jesus told him he was going to Jerusalem to be killed but would rise again, Peter answered without thinking. "This will never happen to You" (Matthew 16:22).[504] Jesus rebuked him saying, "Get behind Me, Satan" (Matthew 16:23).[220] At the last supper Jesus said the disciples couldn't follow where He was going (to death) but Peter said, "Why cannot I follow You, I will lay down my life for You?" (John 13:37).[29]

After Jesus' arrest, the other disciples ran off to hide. But Peter followed, but a distance away. That shows his love. Yet when a simple servant girl asked if he was a follower of Jesus, he denied knowing Jesus, and he even cursed.

So Peter is a rare combination of courage and cowardice. He was extremely confident, yet inwardly unstable. Peter is like many of us. We are both strong and weak. We bring praise to Jesus, but we are the blame for the problems we get ourselves into.

But Jesus changed Peter from the inside out, making him a strong preacher, teacher, and leader. When the Holy Spirit came at Pentecost, and the city was filled with people from all over the world, it was Peter who preached and explained the good news about Jesus to all the people.[145] And Peter led the early church in Jerusalem to grow, by preaching and doing miracles.

When God wanted the church to reach out to others, He gave instructions to Peter and sent him to a Gentile named Cornelius.[207]

Peter became what he now tells us to do. In the last thing he wrote and preached he said, "Rather, you must grow in the grace and knowledge of our Lord and Savior, Jesus Christ" (2 Peter 3:18).[449]

Talk About the Story: How did Peter grow and change during his time with Jesus? What are some ways you have grown spiritually in the past year?

Scripture: "Grow in the grace and knowledge of our Lord and Savior, Jesus Christ." 2 Peter 3:18

Family Time: What are some things we can do to grow in grace and knowledge of our Lord and Savior, Jesus Christ? How can we encourage each other to grow more like Christ?

Prayer: Dear Lord, help us to spend time with You and to grow closer to You every day. Please change us and help us to become more like You. Amen.

ANDREW WHO BROUGHT PEOPLE TO JESUS

Special Section: The Disciples
Overview of Andrew in the Gospels

Andrew was born in Bethesda, a village of poor fisherman, but prosperity came to the fishing family and they moved to Capernaum. This was a walled city that was a desirable place of refuge. His father's name was Jonah, the Hebrew name, but was called John, the Greek name.

"Father," young Andrew asked, "can I leave the business to you and Simon to go follow John the Baptist?"

Because the father was successful he felt the business would continue with his hard working brother, Simon.

John the Baptist was a tough outdoors man with simple virtues, eating locust and honey. He shunned social life living in the desert, and he practiced holiness.

John was preaching the coming kingdom of God and baptized in water all who repented to wait for the Messiah King. Andrew thought John the Baptist might be right, so he followed the preacher to find answers for his life.

One day while preaching, John pointed to a 30 year-old man in the crowd and announced, "Look! The Lamb of God who takes away the sin of the world" (John 1:29).

The next day Andrew and his friend, John—also a fisherman's son—went to talk to Jesus in the late afternoon. The young men had lots of questions, but Jesus answered them all.

The next day Andrew went to find his brother, Simon. He told him, "We've found the Messiah, who is the Christ."[444] Andrew brought his brother to Jesus[58] who said, "I will no longer call you Simon (name means listener), but you shall be called Cephas (means a rock). Hence the name Peter.

But Peter was not the only person Andrew brought to Jesus. When Jesus was preaching to a crowd of 5,000, they were hungry.[170] So Andrew found a boy with 5 small fishes, and two pieces of bread. Jesus miraculously fed the crowd.[388]

On another occasion in the Temple in Jerusalem, some Greeks were trying to find Jesus but couldn't. Andrew always knew where Jesus was. He brought them to Jesus.

Could you be an Andrew who brings people to Jesus? It seems so simple that anyone could do it. Why don't you do it?

Talk About the Story: Who are some people Andrew brought to Jesus? Why do you think Andrew was so eager to introduce others to Jesus?

Scripture: "And He said to them, "Go into all the world and preach the gospel to every creature." Mark 16:15

Family Time: Who are some people you can tell about Jesus? What are some things you can do to help others know and follow Jesus like Andrew did?

Prayer: Father, thank You for Andrew's example of being willing to tell others about You. Please help us to also share the good news of Your salvation. In Jesus' name, Amen.

JOHN, THE ONE JESUS LOVED

Special Section: The Disciples
Overview of John in the Gospels

John was probably the youngest of the 12 disciples. He left home to be a disciple of John the Baptist, a rugged outdoors prophet and preacher. One day changed everything for John, the young visionary. The old Baptist announced, "Look, there is the Lamb of God who takes away the sin of the world" (John 1:29). John immediately followed Jesus and spent the evening hours with him. The next day he could declare, "We have found the Messiah who is the Christ" (John 1:41).[444]

John was among the first (with his buddy Andrew) to believe Jesus. He also was the first to the empty tomb on that first Easter Sunday morning. He hesitated outside the tomb. But brash Peter ran right in. John followed and examined the empty grave clothes. He saw and believed" (John 20:8).[506]

It is said that John was "the disciple whom Jesus loved"[478] (John 12:23;

19:26; 20:2; 21:7; 21:20). He wrote among his last letters, "From the very first day, we were there, taking it all in—we heard it with our own ears, saw it with our own eyes, verified it with our own hands. The Word of Life appeared right before our eyes; we saw it happen!" (1 John 1:1-2, *The Message*).[192]

But John wasn't always the perfect disciple. He had to learn from his mistakes and grow, just as you must learn and grow. Once he was intolerant, "Teacher, we saw someone using your name to cast out devils, and we told him to stop because he wasn't in our group" (Mark 9:38),[109] like some today who think their church is the only one.

On another occasion, John's mother—perhaps inspired by him—went to ask Jesus if her sons, John and James, could sit on His right and left hand in the kingdom (Mark 10:35).[547] Have you ever felt you were closer to Jesus than anyone else?

But at the cross, when all the other disciples ran to hide, John stood with Mary, Jesus' mother. Jesus said to John, "Behold your mother" (John 19:27). What did he do? "From that hour he took her into his own home" (John 19:27).[402]

Jesus' mother lived with John in Jerusalem. Later they moved to Ephesus when John's influence spread out over all the churches. Jesus' family was important to him, so was his own. John's older brother, James, was the first to die a martyr's death (Acts 12:2).[197] John was the last of the disciples to die. All the other disciples were put to death for their faith in Jesus. Only John died naturally of old age.

Talk About the Story: How would you describe John's relationship with Jesus? What are some good things John did? What are some not so good things he did?

Scripture: "And we have seen and testify that the Father has sent the Son as Savior of the world." 1 John 4:14

Family Time: John followed Jesus because he knew Him and loved Him. And he told many people about Jesus? Why do you follow Jesus? What can you tell others about Him?

Prayer: Father, help us to love You as John loved You. We want to tell others about You and help them to know You. Amen.

PSALM 22

THE PSALM OF THE CROSS

This Psalm by David is very unusual. It is the words of David when he was being tortured. But there is no recorded occasion when this torture might have happened. God used these words to predict the words of Jesus spoken hundreds of years before our Savior was tortured on the cross. This is another proof for the supernatural nature of the Bible. As a result you can trust the Bible's message.

When Jesus was on the cross the soldiers gambled over his clothes (Matthew 27:35).[96] David predicts, "They divided my garments among themselves and threw dice for my clothing" (Psalm 22:18).

www.thefamilyprayerbible.com

Next Jesus was nailed to the cross (John 19:18). So David describes what it's like to hang on the cross. "All my bones are out of joint, my strength has dried up like sunbaked clay. My tongue sticks to the roof of my mouth, they have pierced my hands and my feet" (Psalm 22:14–16, *NLT*).[341]

On the cross Jesus was mocked and ridiculed (Mark 15:31–32). David predicts, "Everyone who sees me mocks me. They sneer and shake their heads. Is this the one who relies on the Lord?' Then let the Lord save him" (Psalm 22:7-8, *NLT*).

David introduced the Psalm with the most important statement Jesus made from the cross, "My God, My God, why has Thou forsaken Me?" (Mark 15:34).

David repeats the same words Jesus cried when He became sin for the world. The Father couldn't look on sin, so the Father looked away when Jesus endured punishment for our sins.

We read the conclusion of Psalm 22 in the *King James Bible*, "He hath done this" (Psalm 22:31). This reading suggests the author of the Psalm actually did this. But actually the Hebrew is translated, "It is finished" (John 19:30),[100] the words Jesus said at the end of His cross suffering.

What was finished? Several things: Jesus' physical life and suffering were over. But also, the ceremony of offering lambs for a sacrifice of their sins was over. Jesus was the "Lamb of God who takes away the sin of the world" (John 1:29). It also means Jesus did it all; we don't have to do anything to get saved. Jesus has finished the task of salvation. All we have to do is believe on Him" (Acts 16:31).[263] Jesus had finished His work on the cross and wraps it up. He has done all that needs to be done for you to be saved. "It is finished!"

Talk About the Psalm: What did you learn about the psalm writer in this story? What did you learn about God?

Psalm 22: Read this week's psalm in your Bible together. Choose a verse to read aloud as a prayer.

Prayer: Thank You, God, for the psalm prayers in the Bible. Thank You for teaching us about You and about how to pray. In Jesus' name, amen.

JAMES, THE QUIET ONE

Special Section: The Disciples
Overview of James in the Gospels

When Jesus called James to follow Him, he was a fisherman in the family business. His father Zebedee lived in Capernaum, a well-to-do town on the northwest edge of Lake Galilee. History tells us the father was so industrious that he had a fleet of camels delivering fresh fish to Jerusalem 75 miles away.

James worked harder than all the others who fished for his father. He was seen pulling boats to shore, and pulling in heavy nets.

James and his brother John had a nickname—Jesus called them the Sons of Thunder. But not much is recorded about the things James did or said. James was probably more quiet than the others, but He was very close to Jesus! Peter, James, and John were always right by Jesus' side. It seems that Jesus talked with them more and invited them to see more of His miracles than any of the other disciples.

www.thefamilyprayerbible.com

One day John came running to James, "We have found the Messiah, the one who will restore the kingdom of Israel!" James was not that interested in politics or fighting Romans.

"Why should I follow this Messiah?" James asked.

"He is Jesus of Nazareth who fulfills the scriptures that predict the Son of David who will rule the earth."

When young John explained to James the personal redemption that Jesus offered, the older brother wanted to know more. "He found his own brother, and he brought him to Jesus" (John 1:42).

Maybe James didn't talk much, but when he did speak, people listened to him and respected him as a close disciple of Jesus.

After Jesus returned to heaven, the Jewish leaders thought they could stop Christianity if one of the lead disciples of Jesus were eliminated. They chose one of the four disciples who had been closest to Jesus. James was arrested and, "Herod stretched out his hand . . . . He cut off James' head" (Acts 12:1-2).[149, 349] James was the first martyr, the first to die for his faith, among the disciples.

James will have a special place in heaven. Jesus promised, "You who have followed Me . . . shall sit upon twelve thrones" (Matthew 19:28). Also the 12 disciples will have their names engraved in walls of the New Jerusalem. "The wall of the city had 12 foundations, and in them the names of the apostles" (Revelation 21:14).[215]

Talk About the Story: Why do you think James chose to follow Jesus? What was he known for? Why was he killed?

Scripture: "Then He said to them, "Follow Me, and I will make you fishers of men." Matthew 4:19

Family Time: Of all the disciples, James had the shortest time to follow Jesus and be a fisher of men. But Jesus valued James as one of His closest disciples. Why do you think Jesus chose James? What about you? Why do you think Jesus wants you to follow Him?

Prayer: Dear Lord, thank You for loving us and choosing us to follow You. Help us to be faithful to you, no matter what happens in our lives. Amen.

PHILIP, THE DISCIPLE WHO WAS ABOUT PEOPLE

Special Section: The Disciples
Overview of Philip in the Gospels

It's unusual that this Jewish man had a Gentile name. Philip's name may say something about his outlook on life. He might be the most secular (non-religious) of the 12 disciples. There was a King Philip of Idumea, a nearby kingdom that included some land of David's kingdom in the Old Testament. He was called Philip, the Tetrarch, who ruled 10 years before Philip the disciple was born.

When walking near the walled city of Tiberius, (a secular Roman city), Jesus located Philip and invited him, "Come, follow Me" (John 1:43). The young liberal Philip decided to follow Jesus when he saw four other young men following Jesus: Andrew, Peter, James, and John. Jesus must have given them days of instruction for Philip went looking for a friend that had similar

www.thefamilyprayerbible.com

views as his—Nathaniel, also called Bartholomew. Philip told him, "We have found the very person Moses and the prophets wrote about. His name is Jesus, the son of Joseph" (John 1:44, 45).[147]

Philip cared about people's needs. Jesus asked Philip where they could get food to feed the 5,000 hungry people. When the Greeks were searching for Jesus at the Temple in Jerusalem, Philip was their first contact.

Philip was analytical and could solve problems. When faced with the impossible task of feeding 5,000 people he answered, "Two hundred pieces of silver wouldn't be enough to buy bread for each person to get a piece" (John 6:7, *The Message*).[127] When the Greeks couldn't find Jesus, Philip knew the answer, "Ask Andrew" because Andrew always knew. Philip searched out Andrew, and together they took the Greeks to Jesus" (John 12:22).[426]

In the Upper Room, Jesus told His disciples He was going back to His home (John 13:31-35).[257] Peter asked where that would be (destination).[261] Thomas asked the way (directions) but analytical Philip asked, "Show us the Father in heaven" (content).

Jesus had many disciples; each one had a special talent who could be used of God. Jesus chose 12 disciples, each with strength different from the others. Philip's strength was people. He was interested in people, knew them, and helped them all find their way to Jesus. Are you a person like Philip who's interested in people? If so, don't try to make other people like yourself, make them like Jesus.

Talk About the Story: What was Philip good at? How did he use his strengths to serve Jesus?

Scripture: "For we are His workmanship, created in Christ Jesus for good works, which God prepared beforehand that we should walk in them." Ephesians 2:10

Family Time: What are some things you are good at doing? What are some ways you can use your strengths to serve Jesus and help others learn about Him?

Prayer: Father, help us to see and to do the good things You have created for us to do. Help us to be obedient to You in everything that we do. In Jesus' name, Amen.

DATE ___/___

NATHANIEL/BARTHOLOMEW, THE DISCIPLE WITH BLUEBLOOD

Special Section: The Disciples
Overview of Nathaniel in the Gospels

Bartholomew was also known by the name Nathaniel. He lived up in the mountains of central Galilee. He did not grow up on the seashore of Lake Galilee like many fishermen who followed Jesus. But he didn't live all the way up in the mountains near Nazareth where Jesus was born. He grew up in a large villa in the high plains country.

The name Bartholomew means "son of Tolmay," and came from the royal family line of the pharaohs of Egypt.

Bartholomew was also known by the Hebrew name Nathan or Nathaniel. When he preached, he was prophetic and authoritative like the Old Testament prophet Nathan. When King David sinned, no one could say a word against the king. But Nathan did, he pointed his finger in David's face and said, "You are the man" (2 Samuel 12:7).[440]

After Jesus' death and resurrection, Nathaniel traveled far and wide to tell others about Jesus. Tradition says that he traveled as far away as India. When Nathaniel was sent out, tradition says Nathaniel had long black hair, fiery eyes, a white robe with purple embroidery and he attacked demons with fierce determination. Tradition also says that he was skinned alive and crucified in Albania because of his faith in Jesus.

Look at how Bartholomew came to Jesus. He was praying under a fig tree. The fig tree was the traditional place where Jewish men went to pray. His friend, Philip, had just started following Jesus. He wanted Bartholomew to also believe in Jesus. Philip looked until he found Bartholomew praying under the fig tree.[259]

Philip announced, "We've found the One Moses wrote of in the Law, the One preached by the prophets. It's Jesus, Joseph's son, the One from Nazareth!" Nathaniel said, "You've got to be kidding" (John 1:45-46, *The Message*).[147] He was not ready to believe in Jesus.

Philip brought him to Jesus. Then Jesus did something that convinced Bartholomew Jesus was the real deal. Jesus said, "When Philip was searching for you, I saw you under the fig tree" (John 1:48). Jesus wasn't there. But Jesus is God, and He knows all things, He knew how they met.

Bartholomew answered the Lord, "Rabbi, You are the Son of God, You are the King of Israel" (John 1:49).[147] Jesus answered, "You've become a believer simply because I saw you one day sitting under the fig tree. You haven't seen anything yet! Before this is over you're going to see heaven open and God's angels descending on the Son of Man, and ascending again" (John 1:50-51, *The Message*).[34]

Jesus chooses all kinds of people to follow Him. Why has the Lord chosen you? He wants you to give Him what you have—rich or poor, a struggling student or a genius. Give Jesus what you have and He'll bless you and use you.

Talk About the Story: What was different about Nathaniel? Why did he believe in Jesus? What did Jesus say to him?

Scripture: "Now you are the body of Christ, and members individually." 1 Corinthians 12:27

Family Time: What are some things that make you different from others? Why do you think Jesus loves to use different kinds of people? How can different kinds of people help each other?

Prayer: Dear Lord, thank You for making each person unique. Help us to respect others and see the ways You want to use us to help others know and love You. Amen.

MATTHEW, THE DISCIPLE ABOUT MONEY

Special Section: The Disciples
Overview of Matthew in the Gospels

Each disciple was different from the others, and each disciple brought a unique talent to Jesus, and could be used according to his strength. Matthew's life was all about money. When he chose to work for the Romans as a tax collector, he also chose to be alienated from his Jewish family, and even the Jewish practice of faith. To some, life is always about money—always.

The Jews of Jesus' day were divided in religious groups. They were Pharisees, Sadducees, and really liberal Jews were called Herodians. But Matthew was called a Portitores, a publican; one who associated with the ruling Romans, or worked for them. Matthew collected taxes for Rome. This was a job where you first became an apprentice, then you assisted in keeping records. Most didn't earn the title tax collector until they spent a long time learning the job. Matthew was at least 40 years old and was probably the oldest disciple. Also, the longer you

stayed on the job, the more money you accumulated. Matthew was probably the wealthiest of all the 12 disciples.

Matthew might have been the best educated of the 12 disciples, too. To be a tax collector, one had to know several languages to converse with all the different people who needed to pay taxes. Matthew probably knew Latin—the government language, Hebrew—the Jewish language, Greek—the classical language, and Aramaic—the trade language.

And Matthew was used to keeping records. So it was only natural for Matthew to write down what Jesus was saying as he followed Jesus from one healing to another, or from one sermon to another. Apparently he wrote these down in Hebrew. He ended up writing the life story of Jesus in Hebrew. The early church is filled with information that when Matthew began ministering, he spoke from a book about Jesus in Hebrew. As he changed his ministry from Jews to Gentiles, he translated or re-wrote it into the Gospel of Matthew. He was probably the first to write a gospel about Jesus, therefore his is the first book in the New Testament.

He calls himself Matthew in Matthew 10:3, but Luke writes, "Jesus approached a tax table of "publican named Levi." He was from the tribe of Levi, and should have been a priest in the Temple. But he chose money. When Jesus walked by his tax table, "And saw a man named Levi at his work collecting taxes." Jesus said, "Come along with Me."[314] And he did—walking away from everything (including his money) and followed Jesus (Luke 6:27, 28, *The Message*).

He gave a dinner for his friends—publicans, sinners and disreputable people—at his home. Jesus told them about His spiritual kingdom. Jesus was criticized for being with the wrong crowd, so the Lord said, "Here is a simple rule of thumb for behavior: Ask yourself what you want people to do for you; then grab the initiative and do it for them! If you only love the lovable, do you expect a pat on the back?" (Luke 6:31–32,[292] *The Message*).

Talk About the Story: Who was Matthew? What are some things he did? Why do you think he wrote a book about Jesus?

Scripture: "And just as you want men to do to you, you also do to them likewise." Luke 6:31

Family Time: Matthew was from a group that people didn't like. Why do you think Jesus wanted Matthew to be one of His followers? Who are some people we avoid today? What might Jesus do instead?

Prayer: Father, thank You that You love all kinds of people, especially people others tend to avoid or dislike. Help us to see each person as You see them and to show Your love each day. Amen.

JUDAS, ALSO KNOWN AS THADDEUS AND JUDE

Special Section: The Disciples
Overview of Judas (not Iscariot) in the Gospels

There were two disciples named Judas. The infamous first was Judas Iscariot, the one who betrayed Jesus. An early historian called the second Judas Trionius, which means "three names." Judas (not Iscariot) started following Jesus early in His earthly ministry, but we don't know why or when. Maybe the fact not much is known about his later deeds, suggest not much is significant about his first encounter with Jesus.

Judas was the kind of guy who faded into the woodwork. When someone came seeking Judas, he was the popular treasurer of the 12 that everyone knew. The only thing that stood out in the second Judas was his full head of white hair. His later name, Lebbeus, was a picture of Mt. Hermon the tallest mountain n the Holy

Land that was covered with snow year round.

The Greek name, Judas, was first the Hebrew name Judah, one of the 12 sons of Jacob and the 12 tribes of Israel. It meant praise. It was one of the most popular names for children in Israel. Judah was the strongest of the 12 tribes.

But after Judas' betrayal of Jesus, the name became pretty unpopular! So what did the second Judas do? He adopted the name Thaddeus. That is what he was called during the 40 days of prayer in the Upper Room (Acts 1:13).[119]

The name came from Theodore, an Aramaic name for Tad, meaning that which is "dear" or "beloved." Tradition tells he was one of the first apostles to leave Jerusalem; he went to Syria, Arabia, Mesopotamia, and Armenia, where he was martyred.

There's only one incident in Judas' life that's mentioned in the Bible. At the last supper, "Judas (not Iscariot) asked, 'Lord, how can You reveal Yourself to us, and not to the world'" (John 14:22).[390] Jesus answered, "All who love Me will do what I say. My father will love him, and We will make our home in him" (John 14:23).[3]

Later in life, Thaddeus wasn't ministering to Jews and those who knew about Judas Iscariot. He wrote the next to last book in the New Testament, using his Latin name Jude.

Talk About the Story: Why did Judas have so many different names? What did Judas do?

Scripture: "A good name is better than precious ointment, And the day of death than the day of one's birth." Ecclesiastes 7:1

Family Time: Judas may have wanted to hide his name because of what another Judas did. When are some times we might want to hide our name or something else about us? Why? How did Judas serve Jesus, even though he had the same name as someone who had betrayed Jesus? How did Judas show that he was more than his name?

Prayer: Father, thank You that You can take even embarrassing things and use them for good. Help us to trust and obey You our whole lives. Amen.

JAMES THE LESS

Special Section: The Disciples
Overview of James the Less in the Gospels

Little is known about James the Less, one of the 12 apostles that followed Jesus. There were at least 70 disciples who followed Jesus at one time. Out of them Jesus chose 12 apostles to be close to Him and serve Him. James the Less was among that group. There were two apostles called James. The best known is James, the son of Zebedee, brother to John the Beloved apostle. Some will call this James "the silent" because the Bible doesn't quote anything he ever said. He was quick to do physical work, and was large and muscular. He was also called "James the Great" because of his physical size.

The other is James the son of Alphaeus. He was perhaps shorter and smaller in stature than his friends. Maybe he picked up the nickname, "James the Less."

www.thefamilyprayerbible.com

Tradition tells us that James the Less made an early choice to be a Nazarite, meaning he committed his life to be set apart for God.[430]

As a Nazarite he never drank strong drink, cut his hair, or ate meat, except the Pascal lamb at Passover.

Tradition also tells us that later in life, the knees of James the Less were calloused from long periods of time spent kneeling in prayer.[210]

Jesus immediately called six disciples (John 1:38-51): Peter, Andrew, John, James, Philip, and Nathaniel). James the Less is not mentioned until the end of Jesus' first year of ministry. Maybe James joined the disciples later during that year.

James the Less may have had a drawn face because of his austere lifestyle. Some early church writers said Jesus had the same facial features and that they looked very similar. When Judas Iscariot told the soldiers who went with him to the Garden of Gethsemane to betray Christ, he said, "Whomever I should kiss, that is He" (Mark 14:44). Judas probably didn't want the soldiers to arrest James the Less instead of Jesus.

Jesus chose all types of followers. Some like James the Less were intensely spiritual, intent in knowing God.[190] Simon the Zealot was a freedom fighter who lived with a gang that raided Roman garrison intent on driving them out of the Holy land. An aged Matthew was a governmental tax collector intent on making money. Jesus loved and valued them all!

Talk About the Story: Each disciple came from a different background, and each brought a different talent to be used by Jesus. What is your background and what talents will you give to Jesus?

Scripture: "Then he said to the crowd, 'If any of you wants to be My follower, you must turn from your selfish ways, take up your cross daily, and follow Me.'" Luke 9:23, NLT

Family Time: What are some things you need to turn away from in order to follow Jesus? What difficulties might come from making these changes to follow Him?

Prayer: Father, please help us to love and follow You. We want to stop doing things that get in the way of knowing and obeying You. In Jesus' name, Amen.

DATE ___/___

PSALM 23
THE LORD IS MY SHEPHERD

David was watching his sheep standing in the hot sun. When they stopped eating, he knew they needed cool shade and some refreshing water. Young David led his sheep down the hill to the shade of a spreading Bay tree. Some of his sheep lay in the soft grass; others drank from the bubbling stream. While the sheep were settling down, David thought, *The Lord is my Shepherd; He leads me—just like I led my sheep. The Lord gives me rest, just as I led my sheep to rest under this Bay tree.*[73]

What does the Lord do for me? David thought. *He restores my soul.* David never forgot about that day.

Many years later when he was a king in his throne room, David wrote this song, "The Lord leads me in the right paths."[307] The king concluded, not steep paths that are difficult, or dangerous paths where his sheep could get hurt.

Then David remembered all the battles where he had to kill or be killed. He wrote, "The Lord leads me through the scary shadows in death's valley."[387] He was glad God led him through the dangerous places, and didn't leave him there.

The Lord gave me a staff to fight off wolves and bears. The Lord gave me a shepherd's crook to lift sheep out of holes and troubles.

The part David liked most of all, "The Lord has a table filled with enjoyable food to make me strong."[388] The Lord filled his favorite cup to the brim with his favorite drink. David knew God loved him and gave him a good life, full of goodness and mercy.

David thought about the house where his father slept each night. But David slept with the sheep on the hard ground where bugs would bite and sticky grass would scratch. So David ended his song, "And I will live in the house of the Lord forever."[215]

Talk About the Psalm: What did you learn about the psalm writer in this story? What did you learn about God?

Psalm 23: Read this week's psalm in your Bible together. Choose a verse to read aloud as a prayer.

Prayer: Thank You, God, for the psalm prayers in the Bible. Thank You for teaching us about You and about how to pray. In Jesus' name, Amen.

THOMAS, WHEN IT'S HARD TO BELIEVE

Special Section: The Disciples
Overview of Thomas in the Gospels

The disciple Thomas was also called "Didymus," which means twin. He must have had a twin brother or sister, but we know nothing about his twin.

When Thomas first came on the scene, he showed that he was extremely courageous. Jesus told the disciples that He was going to Bethany near Jerusalem where the religious leaders had tried to kill Him not long before.[75]

Thomas immediately spoke up to the other disciples: "Let's go also, and die with Jesus" (John 11:16).

At the Last Supper Jesus told the disciples He would leave them. Jesus ex-

plained He's going to His Father in heaven, and He will come back to get them so they can be there with Him. Jesus said, "Where I go, you know, and the way you know" (John 14:1-3).[416]

Then Thomas asked a practical question, voicing what all the others were thinking: "We have no idea where You are going, and how can we know the way?" (John 14:5).[126]

Jesus replied by saying, "I am the way, the truth, and the life!"[415]

After dying on the cross and coming back to life again, Jesus appeared to 10 disciples in the Upper Room on Easter Sunday night. The disciples were glad when they saw the Lord (John 20:20).[397] But Thomas was not there.

When the others told him that Jesus was alive, Thomas said, "Unless I put my finger in the nail holes, I will not believe" (John 20:25).[478] Thomas could not accept the good news.

The following Sunday evening, Jesus came into the room through locked doors and ignored everyone except Thomas. "Take your hand and stick it into My side. Don't doubt any longer. Believe!" (John 20:28).[403] To that invitation, Thomas gave the greatest statement of faith in Scripture: he fell to his knees and declared, "My Lord, and my God!" (John 20:28).[192]

Then Jesus said, "You believe because you have seen My wounds. Blessed are those who believe Me without seeing Me?" (John 20:29).[34]

Talk About the Story: What was Thomas willing to do when people were threatening to kill Jesus? What was he not willing to do after he had seen Jesus die on the cross? What did he say to Jesus when he finally saw Him again?

Scripture: "These are written that you may believe that Jesus is the Christ, the Son of God, and that believing you may have life in His name." John 20:31

Family Time: Why did Thomas have a hard time believing that Jesus was alive? What are some things that are hard for you to believe about Jesus?

Prayer: Dear Jesus, help us to believe and trust in You. Thank You that we can talk to You about our doubts. Thank You that You are patient and loving toward us. Amen.

SIMON THE ZEALOT

Special Section: The Disciples
Overview of Simon the Zealot in the Gospels

Simon was called "the Zealot." In those days, Zealots were revolutionaries who wanted to restore Jewish rule in Israel. They wanted the Romans to be defeated!

So with violent attacks on Roman outposts and the assassination of Roman officials, they had been known to resort to violence and bloodshed.

We don't know how involved Simon was with the Zealots, but he would have

www.thefamilyprayerbible.com

agreed with their ideas. He believed in the re-establishment of the Jewish kingdom. Maybe that's why he wanted to follow Jesus, the Messiah. But he probably didn't become a disciple when Jesus first called for followers. He is not mentioned among the 12 disciples until the end of Jesus' first year of ministry.

Perhaps when Jesus preached the Sermon on the Mount, Simon decided to shift his loyalty from following violence to following Jesus' ideals of peace and righteousness. In that sermon Jesus said, "Seek the Kingdom of God above all else, and live righteously, and he will give you everything you need" (Matt. 6:33, *NLT*).[75] And what did Jesus want His followers to do? "Not everyone who calls out to me, 'Lord! Lord!' will enter the Kingdom of Heaven. Only those who actually do the will of my Father in heaven will enter" (Matt. 7:21, *NLT*).[159]

We don't know when Simon the Zealot fully understood Jesus' idea of the kingdom. But a later statement by Jesus would demand that a Zealot give up violence and bloodshed. "But to you who are willing to listen, I say, love your enemies! Do good to those who hate you.[195] Bless those who curse you.[47] Pray for those who hurt you. If someone slaps you on one cheek, offer the other cheek also. If someone demands your coat, offer your shirt also" (Luke 6:27–29, *NLT*).[330]

Jesus called followers from all kinds of backgrounds. Can you imagine Matthew a tax collector who worked for the government, praying with Simon the Zealot, a revolutionist who wanted to overthrow the government? Jesus could imagine it, so He did it while living on this earth. Today He still does it by calling people together to pray, people with different racial, political, and business backgrounds.[193]

Talk About the Story: How would you describe Simon? How was he different from the other disciples? Why do you think Jesus wanted Simon to be one of His disciples?

Scripture: "But to you who are willing to listen, I say, love your enemies! Do good to those who hate you." Luke 6:27

Family Time: Why do you think loving enemies might have been hard for Simon? When is it hard for people today to love and do good to people who hate us?

Prayer: Father, forgive us for avoiding people who hate us or for hating them in return. Help us to love and do good to people who don't like us. Amen.

JUDAS ISCARIOT, THE DEVIL IN DISCIPLE'S CLOTHING

Special Section: The Disciples
Overview of Judas Iscariot in the Gospels

If the devil wanted to destroy Jesus, how would he do it? He tried tempting Jesus in the wilderness after Jesus was weak from fasting for 40 days. But that didn't work. But what about an unfaithful disciple? Judas Iscariot was so good at deceiving people that the other disciples trusted him with all their money!

Judas Iscariot came from a small town a few miles from Jerusalem. No one knows when Judas began following Jesus, but it might have been when Jesus first visited Jerusalem for Passover after he officially began His ministry. Maybe Judas was there when Jesus cleansed the Temple. Or maybe he heard Jesus preaching or saw Him do some miracles.

Jesus knew what Judas would do, but He allowed him to be part of His closest group. Jesus said, "Did I not choose you, the twelve, and one of you is a devil?" (John 6:70).[113]

Judas' true nature began to show about a week before Jesus died. When Mary anointed Jesus' feet with expensive perfume, Judas said, "That perfume was worth a years' wages. It should have been sold and the money given to the poor!" But really, Judas was a thief and since he was in charge of the disciples' money, he often stole some for himself (John 12:5–6).[440]

At the last supper, Jesus announced, "One of you will betray Me" (Matthew 26:17–30).[455] The disciples were shocked, each responding, "Lord, is it I?" None of them suspected Judas at all! But if you had been watching that night, you might have caught the difference. Eleven asked, "Lord, is it I?" using the term Lord and showing their love and reverence for Him. But Judas answered differently, "Master, is it I?"[208]

Finally, Jesus brought the charade to an end. He told Judas, "Do quickly what you are going to do" (John 13:28, *ELT*).[114] Judas left the supper and went to complete his deal with the religious leaders.

Judas waited until Jesus and the other disciples had gone out to the place they usually went to pray. Then he led the soldiers there and told them, "Arrest the man I kiss."

When Judas realized Jesus was crucified, he was filled with remorse! He took the 30 pieces of silver back to the Jewish leaders in the Temple. They refused to take it back, so he threw it on the Temple floor. The priests bought a field with the money to bury the homeless. Judas then hanged himself and died.[99]

Even though Judas rebelled against God by betraying Jesus, God used Judas' actions to bring about salvation for all who would believe and trust in Jesus.

Talk About the Story: Why do you think Judas Iscariot chose to follow Jesus at first? What do you think led him to betray Jesus? What did he do when he recognized his sin? What could he have done instead?

Scripture: "If we confess our sins, He is faithful and just to forgive us our sins and to cleanse us from all unrighteousness." 1 John 1:9

Family Time: When have you done something wrong and regretted it? Remember that God loves you and will forgive you! What sins do you want to confess? Talk to God about them now.

Prayer: Father, thank You for sending Jesus to make the way for our sins to be forgiven. Please help us to confess our sins quickly and return to You whenever we do wrong things. In Jesus' name, Amen.

CHAPTER 10

THE SECOND YEAR OF MINISTRY

The second year of ministry is known as His year of popularity because the crowds heard Him gladly. They came to learn from Jesus, be healed by Him, and to determine if He was the Messiah for whom they waited.

Jesus has large crowds, yet He always takes time to minister to the individual. Because Jesus is God, He knows all things and knows what is in the heart of each person. So Jesus walks past the multitude at the pool of Bethesda to help one crippled man with no hope of healing. Yet He preaches the Sermon on the Mount. Some feel this is His best sermon.

HEALING AT THE POOL OF BETHESDA

Scripture: John 5:1–9
Place: Pool of Bethesda, one block from the Temple
Time: Passover, April, 28 AD

Jesus went up to the Passover as He did every year. He wanted to worship His heavenly Father in the Temple.

There was an extra-large crowd at the pool of Bethesda blocking the way to the Temple. Usually only 20 or 30 people were waiting to be healed when the water was stirred. But now the crowd was extra large because of Passover. Each person there believed that the first one into the pool after the water began to move would be healed.[159]

www.thefamilyprayerbible.com

The pool of Bethesda was surrounded by beautiful marble columns that reached into the sky. The columns flanked the five porches. What was designed as a resting spot in the middle of Jerusalem had been occupied by the sick[435] and oppressed because news of a miracle that occurred there had spread far and wide. Some people called it the "house of mercy" because that is what Bethesda meant.

One man had waited day by day for 38 years, each time disappointed when he couldn't get into the pool first. He could not walk, so he sat and waited for a miracle.

The shadow of Jesus fell across the man, but he did not look up. Jesus knew his story, so Jesus asked, "Do you want to be healed?"[259]

The man slowly lifted his head toward Jesus, "Sir, I don't have anyone to help me into the pool when the water is stirred. When I am crawling toward the water, someone else always gets in before me."[240]

Jesus turned to look around at the other sick people. None of them seemed to realize that the Healer was standing in their midst. They didn't know He could heal them. Then Jesus commanded the lame man,

"Rise, take up your mat and walk."[214]

Instantly, the lame man felt life in his legs. He felt something he hadn't felt for 38 years.

Immediately, he pulled himself up, and found himself rising as anyone with normal legs. He stood! No one around him noticed. He had been told to rise, take up his mat, and walk; so he instantly obeyed.[327]

He bent over and began rolling his mat, just as each night he had rolled up another hopeless day. But this time was different. He threw the mat on his shoulders, and began walking.[110] He obeyed what Jesus told him to do.

Talk About the Story: Where was the pool of Bethesda? What did people at the pool expect to happen? What did Jesus ask one man? What was his response? What did he do when Jesus told him to get up?

Scripture: "Jesus said to him, 'Rise, take up your bed and walk.'" John 5:8

Family Time: Why do you think Jesus didn't heal all of the people in the crowd? Why do you think some people get healed today and some don't? What are some good things that can result from an illness or disability?

Prayer: Father, thank You for caring about our health. Please help us get well when we are sick, but more than that, help us to grow in knowing and loving You. In Jesus' name, Amen.

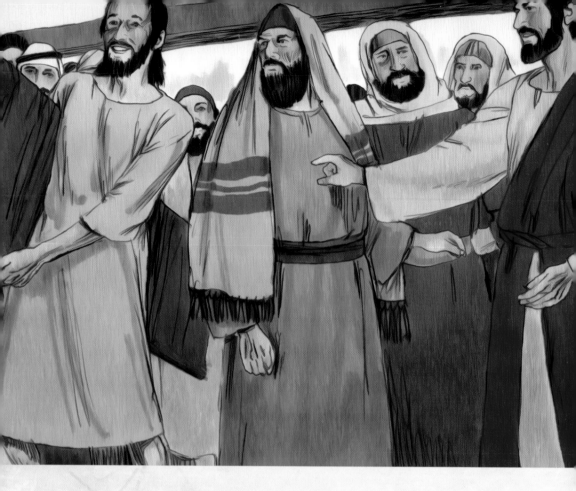

JESUS ENCOURAGES THE HEALED MAN

Scripture: John 5:10–14
Place: Pool of Bethesda, near the Temple
Time: Passover, April, 28 AD

The man who had been crippled walked excitedly into the crowd holding his rolled up mat, doing exactly what Jesus had told him to do! *What an amazing day! After 38 years, I can finally walk! This feels great! Hmm. I wonder who that was who made me well.*

Two Jewish leaders were standing near the entrance to the Temple. They spotted a man carrying his bed, something they did NOT allow on the Sabbath day.[504]

"THIS IS THE SABBATH DAY!" they yelled at him. "It is not lawful for you to carry your bed on the Sabbath!"

The man who was healed explained, "The Healer told me to pick up my mat and walk."[214]

www.thefamilyprayerbible.com

"That doesn't matter! You must not break the Sabbath."

"Why this is a wonderful thing," the man explained. "I have not been able to walk for 38 years. Today a man healed me and told me to pick up my mat and walk."[327]

"What's His name?" the first questioner demanded an answer.

"I didn't ask His name," the man responded.[506]

The man shrugged his shoulders, smiled at the religious leaders, set down his mat in a corner and walked away. It was only a short distance from the pool of Bethesda to the Beautiful Gate of the Temple. The man headed straight into the Temple.

The healed man stood with the crowd waiting for the call to prayer. Then he heard the trumpeter sounding the call to worship. He worshiped with the Psalmist,[541]

"Bless the Lord, O my soul; and all that is within me, bless His holy name! Bless the Lord, O my soul, and forget not all His benefits: Who forgives all your iniquities, Who heals all your diseases" (Psalm 103:1-3).

He wanted to tell God, "Thank You for healing me."

Suddenly, Jesus was there. "God has heard your prayers," Jesus said to him.

The healed man recognized Jesus. Jesus said to him, "Do not sin again, lest something worse happens to you."[147]

The healed man must have seen his own sinful heart as he looked down. Then he looked at Jesus again. He knew Jesus' words were true. It was time to do what is right and obey God!

Talk About the Story: Where did this miracle take place? What did Jesus tell the man to do? Why was the healed man criticized? Where did Jesus tell find the healed man? What did Jesus tell him to do?

Scripture: "Bless the Lord, O my soul; and all that is within me, bless His holy name! Bless the Lord, O my soul, and forget not all His benefits: who forgives all your iniquities, who heals all your diseases." Psalm 103:1–3

Family Time: The man in our story had a great reason to praise God! What are some reasons you have for doing what Psalm 103:1–3 says?

Prayer: Father, thank You for all the good things in my life. Thank You for forgiving our sins and loving us. Help us to trust You and praise You every day. Amen.

CRITICISM OF JESUS' MIRACLE

Scripture: John 5:15-24
Place: The Pool of Bethesda, Jerusalem
Time: Passover, April, 28 AD

After Jesus healed a man at the Pool of Bethesda, some of the religious leaders were not happy! They didn't really care whether or not a man was made well. They cared about whether or not people followed their rules! And that man had carried his mat on the Sabbath—something Jesus told him to do![147]

They followed the man Jesus had made well. They demanded, "Did Jesus heal you?"

The healed man nodded yes. "Did Jesus tell you to pick up your bed and walk?"[349]

"Yes."

Immediately the priests stormed through the crowds after Jesus. To them it was imperative to catch Jesus and confront Him because He had broken their rule. Catching up to Him before He left the Temple, they demanded from Jesus, "Did You tell the lame man to break the Sabbath?"

www.thefamilyprayerbible.com

Then Jesus smiled. And in that smile, He told them what they wanted to know. Even before Jesus could say anything else, they demanded, "WHY?"

"My Father in heaven has been working until now, and I have been working." Jesus said.[195]

The leaders were full of anger at His response! Not only did Jesus break one of their rules, He also was claiming to be just like the heavenly Father.[504]

Jesus didn't worry about their anger. He said,

> *"The Son can do nothing but what the Father tells Him to do,*
> *the Father loves the Son and has showed Him all things to do,*
> *and the Father will do even greater works than these through*
> *the Son"* (John 5:30, *ELT*).[192]

Jesus paused, and looked from face to face, noting the anger and rejection in their eyes. Then He finished,

> *"If you hear My words and believe on Him who sent Me, you*
> *will not only have everlasting life, but you will never be punished*
> *in Hell, you can pass immediately from spiritual death into spir-*
> *itual life"* (John 5:24, *ELT*).

The religious leaders left and put their heads together to discuss what they had just heard. Jesus had called God His Father, using a unique Greek word "My." It meant Jesus considered Himself just like God. They decided: Jesus must die!

Talk About the Story: What was the main concern of the religious leaders? Why were they angry with Jesus? What did Jesus tell them about the heavenly Father? Why did they want to kill Jesus?

Scripture: "Most assuredly, I say to you, he who hears My word and believes in Him who sent Me has everlasting life, and shall not come into judgment, but has passed from death into life." John 5:24

Family Time: The religious leaders refused to believe in Jesus. Who are some people who refuse to believe in Jesus today? Why do you think they choose to not believe?

Prayer: Father, please help the people who choose to not believe in You. Help them to come to know and love You as we do. Help us to show Your love in everything we do. In Jesus' name, Amen.

PSALM 24
A SONG OF FINAL VICTORY

The rebellion against King David was over. His troops finally defeated the people of his own kingdom who rebelled against him. The most amazing fact was that the rebellion was led by David's own son, Absalom. Finally Absalom was killed which ended the rebellion.

When word of Absalom's death reached David, he wept bitterly, "O Absalom, Absalom, my son Absalom" (2 Samuel 19:4).[341]

David was driven out of the city by Absalom, who would have killed him. So what does David plan to do when he enters the city as victor? Punish the people who took Absalom's side in the rebellion? No! David focused his attention on God. He was more concerned with his relationship to God then with his relationship to Absalom and his son's followers. He sang in this moment of victory.

"The earth belongs to the Lord
Everything in it is owned by Him,
Including all the people who live there.

www.thefamilyprayerbible.com

He pushed the oceans back into place
  And established dry land where we would live.[392]
Who can ascend up this mountain of the Lord?
  Who can stand in God's holy Temple?[377]
Only those who have clean hands and a pure heart,
  Only those who do not lie and are not dishonest.[389]
That person will receive good things from God
  Because the Lord has planted righteousness in his heart.[483]
The ones who stand before God
  Must worship Him and seek His face."

David returned to Jerusalem to worship God. God was the most important thing in his hour of victory. The people honored him and received him gladly. David was a man of God who ruled his people with mercy and forgiveness. He sang a Psalm that King Jesus also will sing triumphantly when he returns to rule the world.

"Lift up your gates, O ancient city of Jerusalem,
  Your king of glory shall come in.
Lift up you heads and rejoice,
  Who is the king of glory entering your gates?
He is the Lord, strong and mighty in power;
  He is the Lord who has won the battle."[74]

This picture of David entering Jerusalem is a glimpse of Jesus coming to rule over all people. The people created by God should have obeyed Him and served Him. But they rebelled against God, beginning with Adam and Eve in the Garden of Eden. David is a picture of a broken hearted father rejected by his son. God the Father loves the world, but is broken hearted because His creation has spurned His love to give themselves to sinful pleasures and prideful purposes. This is a picture of God taking up full rule over His children in the coming 1000 years of peace on the earth.

Talk About the Psalm: What did you learn about the psalm writer in this story? What did you learn about God?

Psalm 24: Read this week's psalm in your Bible together. Choose a verse to read aloud as a prayer.

Prayer: Thank You, God, for the psalm prayers in the Bible. Thank You for teaching us about You and about how to pray. In Jesus' name, Amen.

PICKING GRAIN ON THE SABBATH

Scripture: Matthew 12:1–8; Mark 2:23–28
Place: On the Trip from Jerusalem to Galilee
Time: Shortly after Passover, 28 AD

The road from Jerusalem was lined with pilgrims returning from the Passover. Unknown to the disciples, a handful of Pharisees were following Jesus to spy on Him. They knew that Jesus claimed to be God. Spies were following to catch Jesus in any sin or inconsistency so that they could discredit Him or get Him into trouble.[334]

Jesus and His disciples followed a worn path leading along a rocky wall that separated the fields of two farmers.

"Look! This grain is already ripe," one disciple pointed to ripe wheat.

As boys they learned to strip kernels of wheat off a stalk, rub them briskly in their hand, then blow away the chaff. The wheat berries that were left were delicious! And they were full of nutrients as well.

"Pick only in the corners," Philip instructed the others. "Do not pull the farmer's standing grain." The Old Testament allowed the poor to pick grain in the corners of their field.

When the Pharisees saw the disciples picking grain, they immediately yelled,

"THIS IS THE SABBATH DAY," then motioned to Jesus. "YOU'VE BROKEN THE SABBATH DAY."[374]

Uh, oh! They had been caught in the act of picking grain on the Sabbath day. A disciple answered, "The Rabbis taught us to pick only three heads of grain. We're not stealing."

But the Pharisees were not concerned about stealing. They argued, "It is not lawful to work on the Sabbath day."

Jesus sadly shook His head. He said, "Don't you know what the Scriptures said about David when he was hungry? David went into the house of God when Abiathar was High Priest, David ate the showbread when it was not lawful for him to eat it, then he gave it to his followers" (Mark 2:26, *ELT*).

Then Jesus asked the Pharisees another question, "What about the law that requires the priest to work on the Sabbath day?" Jesus asked, "Aren't they breaking the Sabbath when they work at the Temple on the Sabbath?" Jesus quoted Hosea the Prophet who said, "I would have mercy and not sacrifice."[277]

Jesus pointed out that grace and mercy were more important than legalistically keeping the outer Law.

Jesus said, "God didn't make the Sabbath day for man to legalistically keep it, rather God gave the Sabbath day to man so that he might rest and worship God."

The next thing Jesus said infuriated the Pharisees. He said, "The Son of Man is Lord of the Sabbath."[188]

In Jerusalem the Jews had planned to kill Jesus because He claimed to be God. This was another statement by Jesus that only hardened their hearts against Jesus. He claimed to be the Lord of the Sabbath.

Talk About the Story: Since there were no stores to buy food, what did the disciples do for food? Why were the Pharisees upset with Jesus' disciples? How did Jesus answer their criticism?

Scripture: "The Sabbath was made to serve man, not for man to keep its law" (Mark 2:27).

Family Time: How is taking one day a week to rest and worship God good for people? What are some different ways that we can rest and worship God every week?

Prayer: Father, thank You that Jesus always did the right thing, even though His critics accused Him of breaking the Law. I will keep the Lord's Day in a reverent way; I will worship You and serve You on Sunday. Amen.

JESUS HEALS IN THE SYNAGOGUE ON A SABBATH

Scripture: Mark 3:1–12
Place: The Synagogue in Capernaum
Time: A Few Weeks after Passover, Spring, 28 AD

The next Sabbath day, according to His custom, Jesus went into the Synagogue. As people gathered for worship, a middle-aged man approached the Synagogue, his hand dangling useless at his side.[435] Knowing Jesus' habit of healing people, the Pharisees watched the man enter the Synagogue.

The man intentionally hid his damaged hand under his robe, not wanting to draw attention to himself, nor to his withered hand.

Jesus took the seat of visiting rabbis near the front of the Synagogue. The Pharisees glanced from Jesus to the man with the withered hand and back. Because their minds were pre-occupied, they heard nothing from the Word of God.

Of course, Jesus knew that the Pharisees were looking for a reason to confront Him, but Jesus wasn't worried about that![5] Jesus cared much more about caring for people than avoiding trouble.

He looked at the man with the withered hand and asked him to stand up. Everyone in the Synagogue held their breath, waiting to see what Jesus would do. The man nervously stepped onto the pavement at the center of the meetinghouse. Now all eyes focused on the hand that dangled from under his tunic. They knew Jesus was a healer; they wanted to observe a miracle.

Jesus turned to the Pharisees. Jesus asked, "Do you think it is lawful to do good on the Sabbath day, or to do evil?"

Jesus waited for the Jews to answer the question. Silence! Their eyes dropped into their laps. If they were to say, "A good act is lawful," Jesus would then

heal the man's hand as a good work. They couldn't say it was unlawful to do good, so they said nothing.[255] Jesus asked a second question, "Do you think it is good to save a life or to kill on the Sabbath day?"

Again, they refused to answer the question. Jesus was angry at their hardness of heart. He knew they were not concerned about the Law as a matter of obedience to God. So Jesus said to the man, "Stretch out your hand."[214]

The man looked up at Jesus. Rather than looking away, he received assurance from the eyes of Jesus. First, he nodded his head, then he released his fist to flex the fingers, holding out the hand for all to see. He smiled as he pointed with a finger and then clapped and then flexed the fingers again.

The whole congregation gasped. Then they praised God for the miraculous healing.[214] But "the Pharisees went out and plotted against Him, how they might destroy Him."[260]

Talk About the Story: Who was looking for reasons to accuse Jesus? Where did Jesus go on the Sabbath? What did Jesus do, even though He knew people wanted to accuse Him of breaking their rules? Why did He do that?

Scripture: "Therefore, as we have opportunity, let us do good to all, especially to those who are of the household of faith." Galatians 6:10

Family Time: When have you had an opportunity to do something good for another person? When might doing something good be hard or embarrassing? Why?

Prayer: Father, help me to choose to help others, even when the people around me don't understand or want to do good as well. Help me to remember to show Jesus' love to others every day. Amen.

THE SERMON ON THE MOUNT (PART 1)

Scripture: Matthew 5:1-12
Place: On a hill outside Tiberias
Time: Summer, 28 AD

The soft morning broke over the hills around Tiberias, Jesus left the Roman highway to begin climbing up into the hills. He pointed to the top of a small hill, "Up there."

Of course, Jesus always attracted a crowd (Matthew 8:1). A multitude scurried after Jesus, trying to stay close enough to hear all He said and to see all He did.

Arriving at the top, they had a vantage point from which they could see the Sea of Galilee. At the top of the hill—actually a flat top area—Jesus sat on a rock, His disciples clustered around Him (Matthew 5:1). The rest of the people found places nearby.

Jesus had promised He would tell the disciples about the kingdom of heaven. He told them they would learn about the kingdom He was going to establish. However, more than a sermon, it was their training class; they were going to learn how to follow Jesus and how they could bring His kingdom to earth.[495]

The nation of Israel was established with the Ten Commandments, and the original kingdom of Israel attempted to live by these laws. Jesus described a new kingdom, with a different kind of rule. Jesus began talking about His kingdom by describing ten beatitudes that gave life. This message is called *The Sermon on the Mount.*

Jesus taught,

"Blessed are you who trust only in the Father for salvation, for you belong to the kingdom.[42]

Blessed are you who mourn over your sins, for you shall be comforted.[44]

Blessed are the humble who don't seek their selfish ways, for you shall inherit the earth.[61]

Blessed are you who hunger and thirst after righteousness, for you shall be filled.[65]

Blessed are you who give mercy to others, for you shall receive mercy.[305]

Blessed are you who seek a pure heart, for you shall see God.[389]

Blessed are you who make peace between warring factions, for you shall be called the children of God.[347]

Blessed are you when you are persecuted for doing right things, for yours is the kingdom of heaven.[349]

Blessed are you when men shall hate you, persecute you, and lie about you because you follow Me, remember they also lied about the prophets.[405]

Blessed are you that rejoice and are exceeding glad about everything that I give, for you have a great reward in heaven" (Matthew 5:1-12).[409]

Jesus told them the kingdom of God primarily was about internal attitudes. It would deal with their heart attitude.

"You must obey God's Law from the heart. The Law says do not murder, 'I say do not get angry or even think about killing.'[268] *The Law says do not commit adultery, 'I say do not even think about it in your heart.' If you bring your sacrifice to the altar, and then remember a sin in your heart toward a person, go make peace with them before you sacrifice to God'"* (Matthew 5:21–24).[255]

Talk About the Story: Where was Jesus when He preached the *Sermon on the Mount*? How did Jesus describe the Kingdom of God??
Scripture: "And so it was, when Jesus had ended these sayings, that the people were astonished at His teaching, for He taught them as one having authority, and not as the scribes." Matthew 7:28–29

Family Time: What is the main emphasis of Jesus' kingdom of heaven? Name some people you know that are described by the things Jesus said in His sermon. What is one way you want to grow in the attitudes Jesus talked about?

Prayer: Father, I want to live as part of Your kingdom. Thank You for making it possible for me to be part of Your family. Thank You for blessing me in Your kingdom. In Jesus' name, Amen.

THE SERMON ON THE MOUNT (PART 2)

Scripture: Matthew 6:33—7:12
Place: On a hill outside Tiberias
Time: Summer, 28 AD

Many of the people in the crowd following Jesus wanted one thing: they wanted to get rid of the Romans! When Jesus talked about the Kingdom of God, they thought He was talking about the nation of Israel. They hoped that Jesus would lead an uprising to defeat the Romans and become the King of the Jews, leading them to victory over all their enemies. But Jesus wanted them to know about a different kind of kingdom.

Jesus taught the people that God's Kingdom starts inside of them. He said,

"But you should first seek in your heart the kingdom of God and do the right things God requires of you . . . then all of the physical things of life will be added to you" (Matthew 6:33, *ELT*).[75]

www.thefamilyprayerbible.com

Many of the people listening didn't understand the spiritual aspects of the kingdom. The kingdom of Heaven that Jesus told about was not about getting the rewards of battle; it was about God and letting the heavenly Father take care of you.

"Do not take thought about your life, what you are going to eat, what you are going to drink, nor take thought about your body, about what you will put on. Life is more than food and your body is more than clothes.[380]

Look at the birds in the sky, they do not sow, neither do they reap; nor do they reap like farmers but they have all the food that they need.[388]

Your Heavenly Father feeds the birds of the sky, and He will take care of you. None of you can add one inch to your stature by just thinking about it. So, look at the lilies of the field and how they grow, they do not toil, neither do they spin. All the glory of Solomon's great kingdom is not likened unto one of these flowers.

If God can clothe the field with grass, how much more can He take care of you. You must have faith in your heavenly Father. The Gentiles are all seeking an outward kingdom, and your Father knows that you want outward things such as food, drink and raiment; do not think about tomorrow for tomorrow will take care of itself" (Matthew 6:25-34, *ELT*).[187]

People struggled with the things Jesus was saying. They wanted God's soldiers to conquer Israel's enemies, but Jesus was saying that God wanted to conquer soldiers. They wanted to extend the kingdom by force; Jesus was saying the kingdom of God comes from within. It was not an external kingdom, but an internal kingdom. Jesus was more concerned about inner life than outer life.

Talk About the Story: What did many people hope Jesus would do? Why? What was different about Jesus' kingdom and the kingdom of the Romans and the Jews?

Scripture: "For the law was given through Moses, *but* grace and truth came through Jesus Christ" (John 1:17).

Family Time: How does the heavenly Father take care of us? According to John 1:17, what good things have come through Jesus? Why are you glad that God gives us grace through Jesus?

Prayer: Father, thank You for a kingdom of grace and forgiveness. I will always try to live for You and obey Your will. When I fail, forgive me as I will forgive others. Amen.

ASK AND YOU SHALL RECEIVE

Scripture: Matthew 6:5–15; 7:7–12
Place: On a hill outside Tiberias
Time: Summer, 28 AD

Then Jesus talked about prayer. How should the followers of Jesus pray to the heavenly Father? Jesus told them,

"*Don't pray on the street corner with loud prayers, repeating vain repetition. Hypocrites do this to be seen of men, but they have their reward.*[231] *When you pray, go secretly into your closet where your Heavenly Father sees your heart, then He will reward you openly*" (Matthew 6:5-6, *ELT*).[364]

Jesus explained that once in the presence of the Father, they should use the following principles when they pray,

"*Our Father Who is in heaven, may Your name be holy.*[223]
May Your kingdom come.[549]

www.thefamilyprayerbible.com

May Your will be done on earth as Your will is done in heaven.[74]
Give us each day our daily bread that gives us strength, and stamina.[388]
Forgive us our sins as we forgive those who sin against us.[173]
Do not lead us into temptation that will destroy us.[476]
But deliver us from the evil one.[387]
For Thine is the kingdom, and the power, and the glory forever. Amen" (Matthew 6:9-13, *ELT*).[541]

After Jesus explained HOW to pray, He told them WHY they can trust God to hear and answer their prayers. Jesus said,

"Ask, and it will be given to you; seek, and you will find; knock, and it will be opened to you. For everyone who asks receives, and he who seeks finds, and to him who knocks it will be opened."[87]

Jesus then gave an example about why we can always trust God to answer in the very best way. "God is your heavenly Father. Think about how you lead your own children. If your child asks for bread, will give you a stone? Or if he asks for a fish, will you give him a serpent? Of course not!"

Jesus went on to say, "If you know how to give good gifts to your children, how much more will your Father who is in heaven give good things to those who ask Him!"

All the parents in the crowd knew what Jesus said was true. They knew that even though they did wrong things and sometimes were upset with their children, they always made sure their children had what they needed. They worked hard to give good things to their children, and they would never purposefully harm their children. And they knew that God's love was much greater than their love. They could really depend on God!

Talk About the Story: What did Jesus say to do when we pray? What did Jesus say God would do when we ask Him for the things we need?

Scripture: "Ask, and it will be given to you; seek, and you will find; knock, and it will be opened to you." Matthew 7:7

Family Time: What are some things that you need? How do you think God might answer your prayers?

Prayer: Father, thank You for listening to us and caring about us when we pray. Help us to trust in You and to talk to You often. In Jesus' name, Amen.

A WISE MAN'S HOUSE

Scripture: Matthew 7:24–28
Place: On a hill outside Tiberias
Time: Summer, 28 AD

Jesus looked around at the crowd listening to His teaching. He loved and cared about each person there. So He wrapped up His sermon by saying,

"Therefore whoever hears these sayings of Mine, and does them, I will liken him to a wise man who built his house on the rock:[327] *and the rain descended, the floods came, and the winds blew and beat on that house; and it did not fall, for it was founded on the rock."*[460]

Everyone knew that building a house on a rock was hard work. But it was worth the effort! When the rains came in that area, houses that weren't carefully built on strong foundations often were swept away in a flood of rain and mud. Everyone had seen it happen before—and NO ONE wanted that to happen to them!
Jesus continued,

"But everyone who hears these sayings of Mine, and does not do them, will be like a foolish man who built his house on the sand:[171] *and the rain descended, the floods came, and the winds blew and beat on that house; and it fell. And great was its fall."*[268]

Oh, yes! thought the people in the crowd. Some of them remembered a family whose home washed away and were killed. Others thought about a lazy builder who narrowly escaped being injured when part of his house collapsed in a recent storm.

But what did Jesus mean? How was listening to Jesus' words and doing what He says being wise? The people thought about all they heard.

Everyone was astonished at Jesus' teaching. He spoke with so much authority. He didn't try to prove Himself like the scribes and Pharisees did, quoting other teachers who quoted even other teachers. Jesus just spoke the truth clearly.

Those who were willing to believe and listen could see that everything He said was right and true. They knew they were listening to the true Messiah, the One sent by God for the salvation of the world![470]

Talk About the Story: What example of being wise or foolish did Jesus give? Why do you think it is wise to listen to what Jesus says and to obey Him?

Scripture: "I made haste, and did not delay to keep Your commandments." Psalm 119:60

Family Time: Building our lives on Jesus' words is wise! What are some ways we can build our lives on Jesus' words? When can we quickly obey Jesus this week?

Prayer: Dear Jesus, thank You for your Word, the Bible. Please help us to study it and to make it the foundation for our lives. Help us to obey You quickly every day. Amen.

PSALM 26
WHEN SOMEONE LIES ABOUT YOU

Has anyone ever told a lie about you? And that lie would not only embarrass you, but also get you in trouble? David wrote Psalm 26 because he thought there were lies going around that he planned the murder of Ishbosheth, the rival king who was fighting David.

David had been chased in the wilderness by King Saul's army for 13 years. Then Saul was killed in battle. Half of Saul's kingdom (2 tribes) turned to David for leadership. The other 10 tribes made Ishbosheth, Saul's son their king. Then the army of David fought the army of Ishbosheth.

Two of Ishbosheth's army leaders sneaked into his house and killed him and cut off his head. They brought the head to David thinking they would get a reward. But David had them executed for murder. That should have settled any rumor that David was responsible for Ishbosheth's murder. But apparently not. David prayed.

"Lord, I declare my innocence to You;
        I am honest in all my dealings.[497]
Put me on trial about this rumor;
        Cross examine me about the truth.[495]
I put my trust in Your unfailing love
        And I live according to Your truth.[499]
I don't want to be associated with liars
        And I won't have anything to do with hypocrites."

After David proclaimed his innocence, he went into the house of God to offer sacrifices. He then sang the next section of Psalms 26 that describes his worship.

"I am washing my hands to declare my innocence;
        I am coming to Your altar, O Lord.[389]
I am singing thanksgiving to You,
        Telling of Your great miracles on earth.[366]
I love to come to Your sanctuary, O Lord,
        Because it is where Your glorious presence dwells."[254]

After Ishbosheth's murder, David became king over all 12 tribes. He finally united the nation. David knew he needed to be honest and trustworthy. David knew the key to being a good king was his relationship with God. When David reached out to God in worship, God reached out to him in protection and blessing.

Talk About the Psalm: What did you learn about the psalm writer in this story? What did you learn about God?

Psalm 26: Read this week's psalm in your Bible together. Choose a verse to read aloud as a prayer.

Prayer: Thank You, God, for the psalm prayers in the Bible. Thank You for teaching us about You and about how to pray. In Jesus' name, Amen.

FAITH OF THE ROMAN OFFICER

Scripture: Matthew 8:5–13; Luke 7:1–10
Place: Capernaum
Time: Summer, 28 AD

After the Sermon on the Mount, Jesus and His disciples headed to Capernaum. It was like going home! When they arrived, they were met by some of the elders from the town. They had an important message. "Please Jesus," they said, "there is a Roman centurion here who is a good person. He helped us to build our synagogue. He is asking for Your help. He wants You to heal his servant who is very sick."[112]

This Roman centurion must have had heard of Jesus and the miracles He had done. Jesus agreed to go with the elders to the centurion's house. But as they started walking, some other friends of the centurion came running to them.

"The centurion has sent us to say,

www.thefamilyprayerbible.com

Lord, do not trouble Yourself; for I am not worthy that You should enter under my roof.[228] Therefore I did not even think myself worthy to come to You. But say the word, and my servant will be healed.[158] For I also am a man placed under authority, having soldiers under me. And I say to one, 'Go,' and he goes; and to another, 'Come,' and he comes; and to my servant, 'Do this,' and he does it" (Luke 7:6–8).[327]

Jesus stopped, impressed with what He had just heard. He was more than impressed, Jesus was astonished! Here was a man who had true faith in Him! Jesus turned to the elders and others in the crowd. "I have not seen such faith as this man has displayed in all of Israel![156] And let Me tell you a new thing—Gentiles with great faith like this man will be gathered from every far corner of the earth and will enjoy a mighty banquet together with the great patriarchs Abraham, Isaac, and Jacob in God's Kingdom."[74]

The centurion's friends returned to the house to find that the servant who had been sick was completely well.[423]

Talk About the Story: What town was Jesus returning to in the beginning of this story? Based on other clues in the story, what is a "centurion"? Why was Jesus impressed with the centurion? What did the centurion understand about Jesus?

Scripture: "For in it the righteousness of God is revealed from faith to faith; as it is written, "The just shall live by faith."' Romans 1:17

Family Time: Who do you know of with lots of faith in Jesus? How does that person's faith show? What do you think living by faith in Jesus means? What are actions that demonstrate faith in Jesus?

Prayer: Father, thank You for the Bible that teaches us how to live by faith. We want to trust You more and more. Please help us to grow in our faith as we get to know You more every day. In Jesus' name, Amen.

THE WIDOW'S SON IS ALIVE AGAIN

Scripture: Luke 7:11–17
Place: Village of Nain
Time: Summer, 28 AD

Jesus and His disciples walked to many different places. One day, they walked toward the tiny town of Nain. As they approached the town, they saw a large crowd walking out of the town toward them. Some people were crying, others walked silently, but everyone was very sad.

In the middle of the crowd, several men carried an open coffin with a young man laying dead inside. His mother was the only person walking right next to the coffin. She was his only relative. She was a widow, and her only son was now dead.[99] This left her completely alone.

Jesus looked at the woman and understood her pain. She was left with no one

www.thefamilyprayerbible.com

to take care of her in her old age. She was obviously sad, but she was also probably afraid about what would happen to her. Jesus was filled with compassion for her. "Do not weep," Jesus said."

The widow looked up in surprise. Other people looked surprised as well. *It was right to cry at funerals! Why shouldn't she cry?*

But Jesus ignored the people. He walked straight up to the coffin. The men carrying the coffin stopped in their tracks as Jesus reached out and touched the coffin. *Who is this man? What is he doing?* the coffin-carriers thought to themselves, as they stood there. Then Jesus said, "Young man, I say now, get up!"[214]

Instantly, the once dead young man got up and started to move, he even started talking and joking and laughing! Jesus helped him out of the coffin and back to his mother.[147]

Her tears and sorrow were gone! She was no longer completely alone. What a wonderful day!

At the sight of this miracle, the great crowd surrounding Jesus was struck with awe and fear. This caused them to praise God. They said "God has visited us today, in fact, He is right here in our midst!" Because of this great miracle, news about Jesus spread throughout the area.[358]

Talk About the Story: What was the village called where the widow lived? Why do you think Jesus was filled with compassion when He saw the woman? When Jesus raised the widow's son, how did the crowd respond?

Scripture: "But thanks be to God, who gives us the victory through our Lord Jesus Christ." 1 Corinthians 15:57

Family Time: What does this story show us about God and His goodness towards us? How does God give us victory in the midst of really hard times? Believing in Jesus makes us part of God's family. And when we are part of God's family, we live forever with Him!

Prayer: Father, thank You for saving us and giving us the hope of eternal life with You. Jesus, You are the Resurrection and the Life—You have made us new creations and now help us to live for Your glory! Amen.

QUESTIONS FROM JOHN THE BAPTIZER

Scripture: Luke 7:18-35
Place: Machaerus, Southeast of the Dead Sea
Time: Winter, 28 AD

John the Baptizer was arrested by Herod Antipus and imprisoned in Machaerus,[349] a fortress high up in the barren rocky mountains on the southeast shore of the Dead Sea. Herod Antipus had arrested John because John had said that Herod should not have married his brother's wife. This made his wife, Herodias, very angry!

So John sat locked up in the fortress of Machaerus. It stood 3,800 feet above the salt water of the Dead Sea. From high up in Machaerus prison, John the Baptizer looked out to see the world. Looking across the Dead Sea, he saw Hebron; off to the right he saw the hill tops of Jerusalem. Looking due north he saw the

Jordan River, where he preached repentance and told the world, "Behold! the Lamb of God who takes away the sin of the world" (John 1:29).

In this wretched prison, John the Baptizer had many questions. Was the kingdom that he announced really at hand? Was Jesus really the Messiah?[127]

So John the Baptizer sent a message to Jesus, "Are you He that is coming, or should we look for another?"[204]

Locked up in the prison, the bold Baptizer began to second guess himself. Doubts began to crawl into the heart of the Baptizer suggesting that he had made a mistake in identifying Jesus as the Messiah.

Perhaps John the Baptizer wanted more outward results. Perhaps he wanted more hell fire and brimstone in the sermons of Jesus.

"Do we wait for another Messiah?"[390]

The disciples of John the Baptizer caught up with Jesus and asked, "Are you really sent from God?"

Jesus instructed the messengers to go tell John the Baptizer what they saw; the blind received their sight, the lame walked, the lepers are cleansed, the deaf hear, the dead are raised, and the gospel is preached to the poor.[145]

Jesus understood why John had questions. He wanted to make sure that no one rejected John because of his doubts. Jesus said, "John the Baptizer is the greatest man to ever be born of woman!"[358]

The apostle Peter was struck by that. *Why would Jesus say that John the Baptizer was the greatest man to have ever lived? What about Moses the lawgiver, Abraham the friend of God, and David the man after God's own heart?*

Jesus knew what he was thinking. Jesus asked the question that really answered the question in the disciples' minds, "Did the people go out into the wilderness to see a reed shaken with the wind?" Yes, John was more than a prophet. He was the one God ordained to announce the coming of the Messiah!

Talk About the Story: What questions did John have about Jesus? Why do you think he started to have doubts about Jesus when he was in prison? What message did Jesus send to John? How do you think Jesus' message encouraged John?

Scripture: "Blessed *be* the God and Father of our Lord Jesus Christ, the Father of mercies and God of all comfort." 2 Corinthians 1:3

Family Time: Why do you think Jesus took time to send an encouraging message to John? When have you needed some encouragement to continue trusting in God? How could you encourage someone else this week?

Prayer: Father, thank You for giving us what we need to trust in You. Help us to remember to follow Jesus' example in encouraging others to trust in You. Amen.

THE WOMAN WHO LOVED MUCH

Scripture: Luke 7:36–60
Place: Simon's house
Time: Winter, 28 AD

One evening, Simon, one of the Pharisees, invited Jesus to his house for dinner.[388] Simon also invited his friends. It was the custom to greet a guest with a kiss on the cheek, to provide a servant to wash the guest's feet, and to anoint the guest's head with oil. But Simon didn't do any of these things. Maybe he didn't think of Jesus as his friend!

As Simon and his guests ate, a woman carrying an expensive jar of perfume[16] quietly entered the room. She went straight to Jesus, and her eyes filled with tears as she fell at His feet.

I have no water to wash His feet with. She thought. As a swift answer to this lack of water, her eyes flooded with more tears that poured out, drop by drop, onto the feet of Jesus. She wiped each tear with her long hair. Hands shaking, she broke open the jar and poured out the expensive perfume all over Jesus's feet.

She continued to weep. *This man is more than a prophet. This is the Messiah! I know that He forgives me of my sins. All I am, all I have, I give to Him now.*

In Simon's mind though, very different thoughts were circling around about Jesus and His relationship to this woman. *This is disgusting!* He thought. *Surely if this man were a prophet, he'd know just how sinful this woman is and how shameful she is acting towards him now!*[421]

Oh, but Jesus knew what they were thinking, and He answered Simon's secret thoughts out loud.[90] "Simon, let me tell you a story. There was a man who loaned money to two others—to one he loaned 50 pieces of silver and to the other he loaned 500. Neither of the men could repay him, so in his kindness, the man cancelled both debts.[173] In response to this, which one do you think loved the man the most?"

Simon replied sheepishly, "Well of course the man who had the bigger debt."

"Exactly," Jesus replied. Now Jesus turned away from Simon and looked at the woman kneeling at His feet, anointing and washing him still. "When I first entered your house, you did nothing to welcome me as a friend would. But this woman here has gone above and beyond—she has washed my feet with her own tears, wiped them with the very hair[198] on her head, lavishly poured perfume to anoint Me, and all the while she does not stop kissing My feet. She does this because she knows who I truly am!"

Jesus continued on, "And because of her love towards Me, her sins will be wiped clean. But someone who thinks there is little for them to be forgiven of will love little—since they are so convinced they are better than others. Speaking tenderly now to the woman, Jesus said, "Your sins have been washed away and you are forgiven.[173] Take great comfort, daughter, and go in peace."[347]

At this, the Jewish leaders around the table thought in disbelief. *Is he crazy? Who does this Jesus think he is? God alone can forgive sins!*[504] So, whereas the Pharisees watching this scene unfold grew more and more filled with hate and self-righteousness, the woman who cried out to Jesus and worshiped Him in her great need was restored and showered in forgiveness.

Talk About the Story: Who invited Jesus to his house? What did the woman do for Jesus? Why?

Scripture: "We love because He first loved us." 1 John 4:19

Family Time: How should we respond to God's love for us? How does God's forgiveness and love towards us change how we love and forgive others?

Prayer: Father, thank You that You loved us before we ever knew or cared about You. Thank You for forgiving us. Please help us to show Your love and forgiveness to others. In Jesus' name, Amen!

CHAPTER 11

A LONG TYPICAL DAY OF MINISTRY

The first account of activity on this second tour of Galilee is a record of what has been called "The Long Day," because of all the activity described that happened in this one day. Some feel this day is minutely detailed to tell the reader how busy most of Jesus' days were. The long day of ministry is recorded in greatest detail by Mark. It begins with Jesus in a home again in conflict with the Scribes and Pharisees and concludes with Jesus healing a woman with an issue of blood and raising the dead.

This busy day was probably typical of how busy Jesus was in His three and a half years of ministry. As Jesus became increasingly more popular, there were more demands on His time. The long day began as He attracted the attention of those opposed to his ministry. Later His own family (Mark 3:31) came apparently hoping to take Him home and out of the public spotlight for a while.

JESUS' TRUE FAMILY

Scripture: Mark 3:20–35; Luke 8:19–21
Place: Galilee
Time: The Long Day, Summer 28 AD

Crowds of people followed Jesus everywhere He went. There were so many people eager to be with Him that Jesus and His disciples rarely had time to sit down and eat a meal![388] When Jesus' mother and brothers heard about this, they thought Jesus was out of His mind! He needed someone to take care of Him!

So Jesus' mother Mary and His brothers came to see Him. They waited outside and asked His disciples to have Jesus come speak with them. Knowing that family was important, the group of people around Jesus kept encouraging Him to go outside to meet with them.[58]

Now, Jesus loved his earthly family—but He wanted to show His disciples, as well as the rest of people around Him, something even more important: Being in His family meant more than being related to someone by birth.

www.thefamilyprayerbible.com

So Jesus spoke to those around Him, "But who is My mother? And who is My brother? See, all you around Me, you are My family. For anyone who does God's will are My true brothers and sisters and mothers."

Jesus was always moving beyond outward appearances, straight to the most important thing. Families are very important! But our relationship with God is forever, so obeying God and being in His family is even more important than the very most important things in our lives. Jesus wanted His disciples and the others who followed Him to understand that obeying God comes first!

And being part of God's family doesn't come from being born into a physical family. We must be born again into God's family. "But as many as receive Him . . . that believe on his name, are born . . . of God" (John 1:12, 13).[416]

When you believe, you choose to follow Him in order to become part of God's family. God's true family isn't based on our ancestry, it is based on faith in Jesus alone![272]

Talk About the Story: Why did Jesus' mother and brothers want to find and talk to Jesus? What did Jesus say qualifies someone to belong to His family?

Scripture: "So you have not received a spirit that makes you fearful slaves. Instead, you received God's Spirit when he adopted you as his own children. Now we call him, "Abba, Father." For his Spirit joins with our spirit to affirm that we are God's children." Romans 8:15–16

Family Time: How do we become part of God's family? What are things we can do to show that we are part of God's family?

Prayer: Father, thank You for making us part of Your family through faith in Jesus. We are glad You have adopted us as Your children! Help us to live for You and to honor You in everything that we do. We want to obey You and show others that we belong to You. In Jesus' name, Amen.

THE PARABLE OF THE SOWER

Scripture: Matthew 13:1-9
Place: On a mountain, near the Sea of Galilee
Time: The Long Day, Summer, 28 AD

Jesus left and went to the shore of the Sea of Galilee. Many people wanted to learn everything they could from Jesus.[285] Jesus got into a boat so that more people could see and hear Him.

"Look," Jesus said, pointing to a farmer sowing seed in his field. He was only one small hill away, but everyone could see him throwing seed on the ground. Jesus said, "Some seeds fall on the path around the field." Jesus explained, "Seeds on the path won't sink into the soil." The crowds saw birds flocking to eat up the seeds on the pathway. That seed was lost.

Next, Jesus pointed at some seeds that had fallen among some nearby rocks. There wasn't much dirt among the rocks. Even when the seeds go a little way into the ground, they won't grow roots. "The seed will spring up quickly and the hot sun will scorch it. That seed will wither and die."

Next Jesus said, "Some seeds fell among weeds and thorns. They grow up quickly to choke the tender seeds and they die."

Then Jesus described seeds falling on good ground—no thorns, or rocks, or hard packed soil. "This good soil received the seeds and it grew producing fruit, some places 30 percent, other places 60 percent, and the best soil produced 100 percent."[179]

Later Jesus explained to His disciples what the story meant. The seed is the Word of God. Jesus explained the hard path is like the heart of people that is hardened to the gospel. They refuse to listen.

The second type of soil was rocky. This is a picture of people who are glad to hear the gospel, but they don't give attention and let it take root in their lives. When hard times come, they forget about the gospel.[401]

The third soil is filled with thorns and weeds. They choke the young growing sprouts. Thorns could be a picture of worldly possessions or other things that become more important than following Jesus. These things choke a person's faith so that the growing plant dies.

The good soil is a picture of a person who knows he or she is a sinner and needs God's love and forgiveness. That person receives the gospel, just as good soil receives the seeds which grow into a harvest.

Notice, the seed is the same in all four pictures. Also, the farmer sowing is the same in all four pictures. The only thing that changes is the soil.

Jesus invites His followers to tell others about Him. That way we can sow seeds as well![285]

Talk About the Story: Where was Jesus when He told this story? What was the first soil? Why did it not receive the seeds? What happened? What was the second soil? Why did it not receive the seeds? What happened? Notice the sowing and seeds didn't change. What picture does each soil represent?

Scripture: "You have been born again, not of perishable seed, but of seed that never changes. It is the living Word of God that works in the human heart" (1 Peter 1:23, *ELT*).

Family Time: What are the four types of soil? What does each soil represent? Do we know anyone who represents the different types or soil? How can we be sure that our heart is not influenced by the three rejecting soils?

Prayer: Father, give me boldness to share the gospel with family and friends and give me faith to trust You to work salvation in their hearts. Amen.

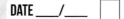

PSALM 27
HIDING IN GOD'S PRESENCE

David was hiding in the hills because King Saul's army was looking to kill him. Saul told his soldiers, "For David shall surely die" (1 Samuel 20:3). David sang, "When evil people want to eat me alive, and my enemy attacks me, they will stumble and fall."[516] David shows his faith in God, "If a mighty army surrounds me, I will not be afraid because I have confidence in God."

David couldn't go to Jerusalem to worship in the Temple. But his enemy can't stop him from worshiping and praising God in the wilderness. He sings, "One thing I ask from the Lord, I want to worship in the house of the Lord for the rest of my life, because my satisfaction and reasons for living is being in God's presence."[416]

David couldn't even go home. He sings, "My parents have thrown me out into the cold. Lord, don't turn your back on me in this dark hour. Keep the door of your presence open to me."[219]

Doeg, one of Saul's military leaders was the one who told the King about David. Apparently he was the man responsible for spreading lies about David. (See I Samuel 22:7-23.)

David sang in this Psalm about his enemies telling lies about him. He sings, "Those liars are out to get me. They spread false rumors about me and threaten to kill me."[516]

Finally, David finds strength and confidence in God. He sings to God, "Now, I will see Your goodness, I will remain loyal to You, I will be faithful to God."[363]

> "The main thing I ask of the Lord
>   Is to enjoy His presence the rest of my life.
> God will protect me when troubles come,
>   He will hide me in His presence.[416]
> God will place me on a high rock
> Where people can't attack me or slander me[387]
> Then I will hold my head up with dignity,
>   Above those who tell lies about me.
> I will come into the presence of God
>   Singing and praising and worshiping the Lord."[266]

Talk About the Psalm: What did you learn about the psalm writer in this story? What did you learn about God?

Psalm 27: Read this week's psalm in your Bible together. Choose a verse to read aloud as a prayer.

Prayer: Thank You, God, for the psalm prayers in the Bible. Thank You for teaching us about You and about how to pray. In Jesus' name, Amen.

JESUS CALMS A STORM

Scripture: Mark 4:35–41
Place: The Sea of Galilee
Time: The Long Day, Summer, 28 AD

After Jesus had told the story of the farmer planting seeds and many other stories, Jesus and His disciples were tired. Jesus said, "Let us go from here to the other side of the lake."

They sailed off with the wind and waves of the sea. The small boat moved easily through the waters at first, but by the time they reached the middle of the lake, huge waves slammed the tiny boat, sweeping it up high and low again.

The disciples, chilled to the bone and filled with fear, looked around for Jesus as the waves got more and more ferocious.[462] What they saw surprised them! There was Jesus sleeping peacefully in the back of the boat! "Rabbi, don't You care that we are about to die out here in this storm?"[347]

Jesus looked at their terrified faces and gently smiled. He stood up and spoke to the wind and waves, "Peace! Calm! Be still once more."[513]

Suddenly, the storm stopped. The sea was quiet and the wind was still, as if there had never been a storm at all!

The disciples stood with their mouths open in shock. What just happened?

www.thefamilyprayerbible.com

Jesus TALKED to the wind and waves and they OBEYED Him! The disciples were filled with fear. *Jesus is much more than a teacher! His power is beyond anything we know!*

Jesus turned back to His disciples. "Why did you fear? Do you still not fully trust Me?"[514]

The disciples didn't know what to answer. They whispered to one another, "Who could this man be? All creation, the winds and waves obey His Word!"[147]

The disciples had seen Jesus do many miracles, but they still didn't understand who Jesus really is—the one and only Son of God. But watching Jesus command the wind and the waves helped them to begin to see the truth.

Though many things still confused them, they were starting to understand—Jesus and God the Father are one and the same![492]

Talk About the Story: What happened in the story that made the disciples so afraid? Where was Jesus sleeping during this? What did the disciples accuse Jesus of? How did Jesus respond?

Scripture: "He calms the storm, So that its waves are still. Then they are glad because they are quiet; So He guides them to their desired haven. Psalm 107:28–30

Family Time: How does Psalm 107 describe God? The disciples would have known these verses. What did the disciples discover about Jesus when He calmed the storm? What are some ways you have come to understand God's love and power in your life?

Prayer: Dear Jesus, You are Lord of all creation. Forgive us when we don't have faith in You. Help us to grow in trusting You. Amen.

DATE ___/___

DEMONS FLEE

Scripture: Matthew 8:28–34
Place: Country of the Gergesenes
Time: The Long Day, Summer 28 AD

The storm had blown them off course. Jesus and His disciples climbed out of their boat in a new spot, the country of the Gergesenes on the other side of the Sea of Galilee, away from Israel.

Suddenly two wild men came toward them out of the tombs on the hillside. The local people knew about these violent, demon-controlled men who lived among the tombs.[114] They had tried to help and control the men, but they couldn't! So they stayed away from the area. But Jesus knew the men were there. And He was not afraid.

The men saw Jesus and yelled out, "Jesus, you are the Son of God, but what are you doing here now? Have you really come to destroy us before the end has come?" The demons knew who Jesus was, the Son of God, but they hated Him and were afraid of Him.

Not too far away, there were pigs grazing up on a cliff. The demons that had been controlling these two men knew that Jesus would make them leave the men alone now. So the demons begged Jesus, "Please send us into that herd of pigs over there!"

Jesus said, "Go now!"[466] And they went. They left the men suddenly and went into the pigs nearby. With nothing but destruction in their minds, they sent the pigs running off the cliff and into the waters beneath them—drowning them all.[268] The people taking care of the pigs ran into town to tell others what had happened.

Townspeople came quickly and were surprised to see the two wild men completely changed. They were no longer scary and wild. They were sitting and listening to Jesus. But the people were afraid. They were afraid of Jesus' power. "Please leave our town," they said.

As Jesus and His disciples turned to leave, one of the two men Jesus healed stopped Jesus. "Please, let me come with You and follow You."

Jesus said, "No, but go and tell your family and friends all that God has done for you."

Talk About the Story: What did the demons call Jesus? After leaving the men, where did the demons go? What did one man ask Jesus to let him do? What did Jesus tell him to do instead?

Scripture: "All that is in heaven and in earth is Yours; Yours is the kingdom, O LORD, And You are exalted as head over all." 1 Chronicles 29:11

Family Time: Why do you think Jesus allowed the demons to go into the pigs? What does this tell us about Jesus' authority? In what ways do you see Jesus using this situation to show others both His power and His love for them?

Prayer: Lord Jesus, We are glad for Your power over everything in this world. We know that You can protect us from every evil thing. Thank You for being with us at all times. Amen.

AN UNSEEN MIRACLE

Scripture: Mark 5:25–34
Place: Capernaum
Time: The Long Day, Summer 28 AD

Awoman was following Jesus, but no one paid attention to her. She was lost in the crowd. When she had heard Jesus had returned to town; she determined to find Him and be healed. The woman had been bleeding for the past 12 years. Because of her bleeding, she couldn't go to worship at the Temple or spend time with her friends. Whenever her family traveled to Jerusalem for festivals, she had to stay home alone.

Life had been miserable! The woman spent all her money on doctors, trying to find a way to stop the bleeding and get well. But nothing worked. The woman had given up hope that she would ever be well again. [214]

But the woman had heard about the things Jesus had done. *Is He the Messiah?* she wondered. *He must be!* She kept thinking, *maybe if I touch Jesus, just the hem of His robe, I'll be made well.* [465]

The crowd following Jesus surged through the street. This was the woman's opportunity. Pushing through the crowd, she came up behind Him. Jesus was wearing His beautiful, white, long tunic, *tsitsith*; even now she hesitated touching it. Then she reached out to the very edge, the corner, the *tallith*; she touched the hem of His garment, thinking in her heart,

"PERHAPS TOUCHING THE HEM WON'T DEFILE HIM."

www.thefamilyprayerbible.com

She believed in Jesus so much that she felt He didn't need to touch her or even pay attention to her. All she had to do was touch Him.

Suddenly, Jesus stopped and looked about. His look of concern captivated everyone. The searching eyes of Jesus surveyed the crowd. Looking to the apostles, He asked, "Who touched Me?"[192]

"Everyone is pressing upon You," Peter, the spokesman, blurted out. "When so many people press upon You, how can You ask who touched You?"

Jesus ignored the question. He continued looking from face to face. Jesus was not simply looking for the person who touched Him; He was looking for the person with faith, looking from one set of anxious eyes to another until He saw her.

The woman was terrified! *Is Jesus angry with me because I touched Him while being unclean?*

But the woman knew that Jesus had healed her instantly. She slowly stepped forward and fell to the ground. Looking down, she said, "I touched You." With a quivering voice, she told Jesus her whole story.

Jesus knew that she had faith in Him. Perhaps Jesus didn't want her to live in shame and fear anymore. In front of that big crowd of people, Jesus kindly said, "Daughter, your faith has made you whole."[156]

The woman looked up at Jesus. He didn't treat her as a worthless person, He stopped to speak to her, even though she hadn't asked Him to take time for her!

She was really finally well! She could go with her family to Jerusalem and worship at the Temple for the next festival. She wouldn't have to stay home alone anymore!

Jesus' power is amazing! He healed the woman without even thinking about it! Jesus smiled back at the woman. "Go in peace," He said, "and be healed of your disease."[241]

Talk About the Story: What was the woman's problem? Why do you think she trusted Jesus to make her well? How did Jesus respond to the woman?

Scripture: "How precious to me are your thoughts, O God! How vast is the sum of them!" (Psalm 139:17)

Family Time: Why did Jesus focus attention on the woman? How do you think the woman felt when she realized that Jesus noticed and cared for her? God notices each of us! What are some things in your life that you want God to notice and care for?

Prayer: Father, I thank You that Jesus didn't overlook an un-named woman. He healed her, even though she was afraid to ask. I know You won't overlook me and my small faith when I reach out to You. Thank You for caring for me. Amen.

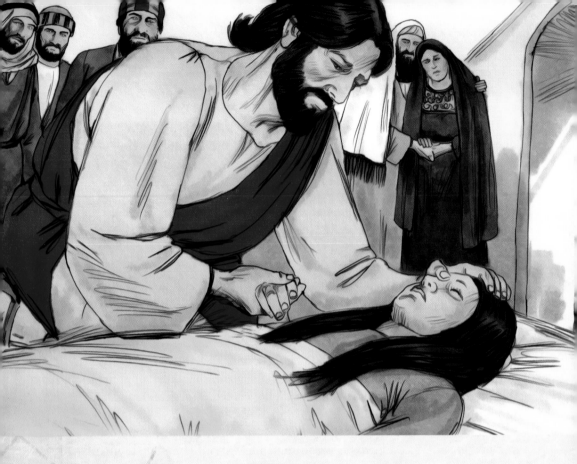

JAIRUS

Scripture: Mark 5:21–24,35–43
Place: Capernaum
Time: The Long Day, Summer, 28 AD

A little while before sunset Jesus and His disciples arrived back in Capernaum. Jairus, one of the Synagogue rulers of Capernaum came running through the street. His dark-green robe was flying behind him as he ran. The garment tied around his head, tilted crazily. Those who saw him knew something was wrong, he yelled,

"My little girl is at the point of death." His red eyes and trembling lips showed his sincerity. "Please, she's my only child."

Jairus pleaded, "Please come lay Your hands on her to heal her."[214]

"I will heal her," Jesus replied, then began walking with Jairus toward Jairus' home. But the crowd slowed them down. Then a woman desperate for healing slowed them down even more.

Soon a servant pushed through the crowd and whispered in Jairus' ear, "Your daughter just died. Don't trouble the Master any further."[504]

www.thefamilyprayerbible.com

This news was too much for Jairus. Jairus could no longer keep his composure no longer.

The crowd heard the anguished cry of Jairus, but Jesus said, "Don't worry. Only trust Me."[466]

Jesus sent the crowd away and took only Peter, James, and John with Him to Jairus' house. As they entered the courtyard of Jairus' home, they heard the mourners wailing for the dead girl.[313]

Jesus looked around at all the commotion and grief. He said, "Why are you making this noise? The girl is not dead, but asleep."

Of course, the people knew the girl had died, so they laughed at Jesus. But Jesus sent them away.

Then Jesus took the girl's parents and His three disciples into the room where they had laid the little girl. Jesus approached the bed where she lay. And taking the girl's hand, He said, "*Talitha Cumi,*[214] which means, "Little girl, get up."

At first her eyes fluttered, then blinked. She rubbed them with both hands, as though rubbing sleep from her eyes. Immediately, she was well! The girl got up and walked across the room. No one knew what to say.[470]

There was no doubt that when Jesus restored her to life, He restored her to the normal functions of a twelve-year-old girl. She said, "I'm hungry."

Her parents stood there, completely shocked at what had happened. Jesus smiled and said, "Give her something to eat."[300] Then He warned them not to say anything about this to others.

Talk About the Story: What did Jairus want Jesus to do? What happened when Jesus got to Jairus' home? Who did Jesus take with Him into the inner room? How did Jesus heal the little girl? What was her reaction?

Scripture: "And her parents were astonished: but He charged them that they should tell no man what was done." Luke 8:56

Family Time: Why do you think Jesus healed some people in private and others in the open? What are some ways that you want Jesus to help you now? How do you think Jesus will help you? Why do you think that?

Prayer: Lord Jesus, You know the things we need. Thank You for caring about us today just as You cared about Jairus and his family. Help us to trust You and depend on You in every situation. Amen.

DAY 116

DATE ___/___

261

HOW JESUS HEALS

Scripture: Matthew 9:27–38
Place: Galilee
Time: Winter, 28 AD

As Jesus walked by, two blind men followed and shouted out to Him, "SON OF DAVID, HAVE MERCY ON US!"[112]

These two blind men continued to follow Jesus all the way home. When Jesus got to the house, He asked them, "Do you believe I can make you well?"[34]

"Yes, Lord."

Jesus touched their eyes to heal them saying, "Because you have faith, you will be healed."[214] Instantly they could see!

Jesus healed many different ways. Sometimes He touched the person, sometimes He spoke. Sometimes He healed because the person had faith for healing. At other times, He was moved with compassion because of their suffering. Now you would think that when Jesus healed a person, that person would do exactly what Jesus commanded. But that was not the case with these two blind men!

www.thefamilyprayerbible.com

Jesus told them not to tell anyone what He had done. But the blind men went everywhere telling what Jesus had done for them.[147]

Jesus left the house, and a man with a demon was brought to Jesus. The man was unable to talk because of the demon. Jesus spoke to cast the demon out of the man, and he began talking. The crowd was so amazed that they began to chant, "Nothing like this has ever happened in Israel!"[264]

The Pharisees had already rejected Jesus so they didn't believe in Him or His miracles. They said nothing about the blind men who were healed, but they started to spread the rumor, "Jesus has made a deal with the devil. He's doing this by the power of the devil."[504]

As Jesus went from town to town, He preached the gospel of the Kingdom.[145] He healed wherever He found the sick, healing people of every kind of disease and illness. Jesus had compassion on the crowds because they seemed confused and helpless. The crowds were like a flock of sheep without a shepherd. He said to His apostles,

"The needy people are like fields ripe to harvest, but there are only a few workers.[199]

Pray the Lord of the harvest that He will send out workers to bring in the harvest"[179] (Matthew 9:37-38, *ELT*).

Talk About the Story: Who are some people Jesus made well? What are some different ways Jesus healed people? Why do you think Jesus cared about people who were sick?

Scripture: "But when He saw the multitudes, He was moved with compassion for them, because they were weary and scattered, like sheep having no shepherd." Matthew 9:36

Family Time: When have you been moved with compassion? What can you do to help people who are weary or lost?

Prayer: Father, thank You for Jesus' compassion toward the people He saw. Help us to have compassion on the people around us. Help us to show Your love to them. Amen.

CHAPTER 12

THE THIRD YEAR OF MINISTRY

The third year of Jesus' ministry could be characterized as a year of opposition. The Scribes and Pharisees were becoming more critical and actually seeking to stop His ministry. During this year of ministry they would plan to kill Him. Herod Antipas was receiving negative reports about Jesus. He withdrew from the crowds more frequently to spend time teaching His disciples.

Sometimes even today people come to Jesus for the wrong reasons. Even some who consider themselves Christians identify with Jesus because they seek a financial or social benefit. They fail to realize the full blessing of a personal relationship with Him. They may belong to a prestigious church for important business contacts, or feel a part of the community. But if they lack personal faith in Christ as Savior, they are missing out on the abundant Christian life and the eternal benefits of heaven. Be sure you are not one who never personally took the step of faith needed to trust Jesus as personal Savior.

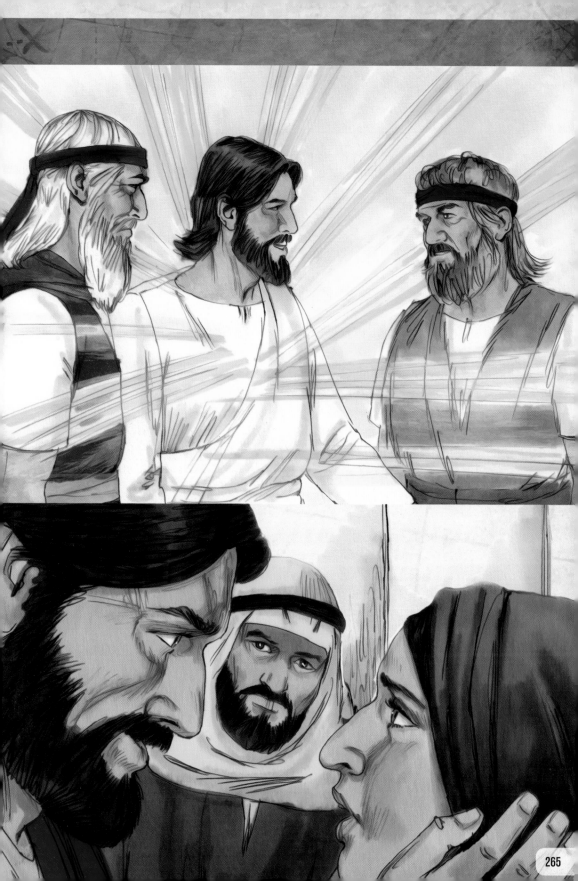

JESUS FEEDS 5,000

Scripture: John 6:1–14
Place: Near Sea of Galilee
Time: April, 29 AD

Jesus and His disciples needed time to rest! No matter where they went, the crowds were always pressing upon them; they didn't even have time to eat properly. So they set off across the Sea of Galilee.

But the roads were filled with pilgrims who were on their way to celebrate the Feast of Passover in Jerusalem. Many people saw where Jesus was heading, so they hurried to the place Jesus' boat was headed. More than 5000 people followed Him!

When Jesus saw the people, He had compassion on them so He began teaching them.[285] Jesus taught all day. He also healed sick people who were there.[301]

Philip was the first to notice the sun was going down. This giant crowd had been out on the hillside all day. They were far from any villages where they could buy food. But the people were so intent on listening to Jesus that they were not thinking about taking care of their physical needs. But Philip realized that this was a problem!

Jesus knew what Philip was thinking, so He asked, "Philip, where can we buy bread to feed these people?"[479]

Being an analytical man, Philip had already counted the crowd. He knew there were about 5,000 men there, plus women and children. So he answered, "Even if we spent half a year's wages, we couldn't buy enough food to feed this large crowd."[127]

Andrew spoke up. "There is a little boy here," he brought the boy up to Jesus. "This boy has five barley loaves and two small fish. But what are they among so many people?"[127]

The boy was ready to share his food with Jesus. His food was wrapped in a cloth. His mother had carefully prepared lunch for him. Jesus smiled at the boy and then turned to the disciples. "Have the people sit down on the grass."

The disciples directed the people to sit in groups of 50. They were not sure where the food was coming from, but when Jesus gave them directions, they obeyed![327]

Jesus took the loaves and prayed, giving thanks to God. Jesus began breaking the bread, dropping the pieces into baskets. He continued until several baskets were filled.

The disciples fanned out into the crowd, holding the baskets for each hungry person to take bread. Miraculously the baskets never became empty! Each hungry listener took as much bread as he or she needed.

The same process was repeated with the fish. Every person ate a satisfying meal provided by Jesus and served by His disciples. After everyone had had plenty to eat, Jesus said, "Gather up the fragments that are left over."

When they had gathered up the fragments, there were twelve baskets left, one for each disciple to enjoy![34]

The people who saw the miracle of the food realized that Jesus really was the Messiah God had promised to send!

Talk About the Story: Why did Jesus ask Philip about food? What was his answer? What was Andrew's solution to the problem? What did Jesus do to the bread and fish?

Scripture: "Then those men, when they had seen the sign that Jesus did, said, 'This is truly the Prophet who is to come into the world.'" John 6:14

Family Time: What would you have thought if you had been there that day? When the people realized that Jesus really was the Messiah, what do you think they did? What are some things you do differently since you realized that Jesus really is the Savior God sent into the world? ?

Prayer: Father, thank You for all the ways You show us who You are. We want to grow in knowing You. In Jesus' name, Amen.

PSALM 29
NATURE SHOUTS "GLORY TO GOD!"

David's sheep were sleeping safely in a cave. He had seen the horizon turn black and the cold east wind stirring the tops of the trees all afternoon. David knew a storm was brewing. Unlike some children who are afraid of lighting and thunder, he looked forward to the display of God's mighty power.

David sat on a ledge overlooking the valley. He was protected from the rain by some overhanging rocks. He was ready for God's show.

Just then lightning struck a hill far away. "Amen God!" he gloried in God's power. Then he heard the rumbling thunder. He waited to see if the ground would shake. This time the lightning was too far away to shake the hills.

Each time the lightning flashed, David could quickly see the whole valley at a glance. Lightning was as bright as the noonday sun, yet only for an instance.

David began singing a Psalm, "God's voice flashes like lightning, and the thunder shows, His mighty power. The voice of God makes the wilderness shake. It twists mighty oaks and strips the tall cedar of its leaves."[367]

David loved watching storms because they reminded him of God's power— greater than any power man can harness. The black winds of a storm reminded him of God's judgment. He can punish anything according to His will. David saw God's glory both in the mighty lightning and in the small blade of grass twisting in the hurricane. Each time a storm sweeps over the area, David traced the power of God and worshiped the Lord for His greatness. Each time the storm passed over and everything became calm, David was reminded of God's sweet closeness.

"Lord, I hear Your voice in the sea's mighty waves,
    I see Your hand in the thundering sea.[362]
Your voice is powerful in the storm,
    Your lightning splits the mighty Cedars,
    Your storm strips them of their leaves.[366]
Your storm skips over the hills like a deer,
    Your hurricanes climb over the tallest ridges,
    Like the mountain goat, nothing is too high for You.[362]
You speak in the strike of each lightning bolt,[193]
    And the power of Your thunder shakes the wilderness.
Everything in nature shouts, 'Glory to God';[192]
    The storms remind us You rule the world."[322]

Talk About the Psalm: What did you learn about the psalm writer in this story? What did you learn about God?

Psalm 29: Read this week's psalm in your Bible together. Choose a verse to read aloud as a prayer.

Prayer: Thank You, God, for the psalm prayers in the Bible. Thank You for teaching us about You and about how to pray. In Jesus' name, Amen.

PETER WALKS ON WATER

Scripture: Matthew 14:22–43; John 6:15–19
Place: Sea of Galilee
Time: April, 29 AD

Jesus had just fed a large group of people—more than 5,000 men, plus women and children.[170] All of those people were so amazed by Jesus' miracles that they were convinced He was the Messiah. "Jesus must be our king!" they said.

More and more people agreed. "Yes! Jesus can heal any disease or injury. And He can make enough food for all of us from one simple lunch! There is no way the Romans can stand against Him!"

Jesus knew what they were thinking. He had not come to earth for a military confrontation with Rome. Jesus knew from the beginning that He would die for the sins of the world.[385] Quickly Jesus directed His disciples toward their boat, then pointing across the sea, Jesus instructed them, "Go to the other side, go to Capernaum."[327]

Just as quickly, Jesus walked between several clusters of men, He then stepped between some rough, sharp rocks. Before anyone realized it, Jesus was gone.[18]

As the sun settled over the western hills of Galilee, Jesus climbed higher into the hills. He wanted to be alone that night; He wanted to pray to the Father.[300]

As Jesus prayed on the mountain, a large storm rolled in, creating torrential rain

and driving wind on the Sea of Galilee. The disciples in their boat struggled to row against the storm,[462] fighting to keep the boat upright. They rowed for hours!

Of course Jesus knew about the storm, and He knew His disciples were out in it—and He knew they were safe because He was always protecting them!

Finally Jesus walked down to the water. But He didn't stop when He got to the water's edge. He kept walking, right on top of the waves. Jesus was going to keep walking all the way to the other side![467]

Suddenly, one of the disciples screamed in terror. "IT'S A GHOST!"[57]

All the disciples looked where the first one pointed, full of fear. They all saw the figure walking on the water. But Peter reached for a rope, steadying himself to peer through the sheets of rain. Then the fisherman yelled back to the men at the oars, "IT'S THE LORD!"[192]

At the same moment, Jesus spoke to them, "It is I, do not be afraid."

Peter moved to the edge of the boat to yell out over the water, "LORD, IF IT IS YOU, LET ME COME TO YOU!"

Jesus replied with only one word to Peter, "Come."[72]

Peter leaped from the boat onto the water. And then he began walking toward Jesus, walking on the water.[112]

Peter kept his eyes on Jesus as he walked. How amazing! He was walking on the water! But suddenly, Peter noticed the large waves swirling around him and became afraid. He began to sink into the water.

Peter quickly cried out in fear, "LORD, SAVE ME!"[109]

Jesus reached out and took Peter by the hand and asked Peter, "Why do you have such little faith?"[127]

Peter and Jesus walked back to the boat. When they entered, Jesus looked out at the raging waves, then commanded them, "Peace, be still."[57]

The disciples looked at Jesus in awe. Then they bowed down to worship Him, saying, "Truly You are the Son of God."[264]

Talk About the Story: Why did Jesus send the disciples away while He went alone to pray? What did the disciples first think? What was Peter's reaction? How did Jesus save Peter? What did Jesus tell him?

Scripture: "Then those who were in the boat came and worshiped Him, saying, 'Truly You are the Son of God.'" Matthew 14:33

Family Time: How did Peter demonstrate his faith in Jesus? Peter's faith was not strong, but Jesus protected him anyway. When are some times you might have a weak faith? How do you think Jesus might help you in those times?

Prayer: Father, I thank You that You know when I am in danger. I know You will be with me and will help me. Give me faith to trust You for help. Amen.

THE SYROPHOENICIAN WOMAN

Scripture: Mark 7:24–30
Place: Northern Galilee, near border of Tyre and Sidon (today's Lebanon)
Time: Spring, 29 AD

Jesus and His disciples left the Sea of Galilee and headed northwest toward the Mediterranean Sea close to the cities of Tyre and Sidon. Most Jews had gone to Jerusalem for the Passover; but they were headed in the opposite direction, seeking solitude.

Jesus and the disciples entered a house, but they did not want anyone to know about it. They were seeking privacy and rest. They needed a quiet time so Jesus could teach His disciples about future events.[443] They planned to rest one night in this distant home, then move on.

"Don't tell anyone I'm here," Jesus instructed.

But word got out about where Jesus was. Soon a woman from Lebanon/Syria came to the house where they were staying. She fell at Jesus' feet, begging Him for help. Through her tears she pleaded, "My little girl is tormented by a demon.[435]

Doing miracles was not Jesus' purpose in coming to earth. But Jesus did perform miracles to demonstrate He was the Messiah sent from God. He came to offer salvation; miracles were only the badge of His authority. But the Gentile

woman didn't care about outward distinctions. She only cared about her possessed daughter. She pleaded, "My daughter is grievously tormented with a demon."[87]

Jesus told the woman, "I am sent to the lost sheep of the house of Israel. I did not come to do miracles for Gentiles."

Completely destitute and desperate, she cried out in anguish, "LORD, HELP ME!"[214] She begged from a broken heart. Jesus answered her with a short parable. He said,

> *"It is not right to take the bread from the children, and cast it to the dogs who are under the table"* (Mark 7:27, *ELT*).[62]

Even though Jews called Gentiles dogs, in this analogy they were like the puppies kept in the house. The woman understood what Jesus was saying, she answered, "Yes, Lord. If there are puppies under the table, then they belong to the Master, and when He breaks bread for the children, some of the crumbs will fall under the table. The puppies eat the crumbs."[43]

Jesus was amazed at her faith. She recognized that the children belong to the Master just as the puppies belong to the Master. In this statement, the woman was asking to be a member of God's family, even though just a puppy. She was putting her trust in Jesus. She had exercised true faith in asking to be a part of the family. Jesus said to her, "Woman, you have great faith."

She no longer was just looking for a miracle for her demonized little girl. She had put her faith in Jesus. He said, "Because of your great faith, it shall be even what you ask."

Jesus said to her, "Go your way. The demon has left your daughter."[214]

Talk About the Story: How did the woman approach Jesus? What did Jesus tell her? How does the picture of "puppies" help explain the story? How did Jesus help the woman?

Scripture: "The LORD lives! Blessed be my Rock! Let God be exalted, The Rock of my salvation! 2 Samuel 22:47

Family Time: How was Jesus the woman's salvation? What did she do to show that she had faith in Jesus? Her daughter was healed, but what was an even greater result?

Prayer: Father, I'm glad You love and accept all people from every nation, even me. I come to You in faith, just as the woman came in faith. Thank You for Your love. Amen.

DEAF AND DUMB MAN

Scripture: Mark 7:31–37
Place: Northern Galilee
Time: Spring, 29 AD

Jesus and His disciples continued on their travels. They left the region of Tyre and Sidon.[443] They walked through the ten cities area called the Decapolis. Then they finally came to the Sea of Galilee. The disciples took a deep breath, breathing in the sea air and familiar scent of fish and lake water at Galilee. It smelled like home!

Soon people saw that Jesus and His disciples had returned. News spread quickly as always! The disciples waited for the rush of the crowds—and it didn't take long at all!

From the nearest village, they saw people coming, leading a man who looked shy and a little scared. The disciples watched to see what Jesus would do.

The man the people brought was deaf, and he could not talk properly. Maybe he had been deaf all his life and had never learned to speak because he couldn't hear others speaking. "Please, Jesus," the people said. "Please put your hand on him to make him well!"[214]

Other people crowded around, excited to see Jesus do another miracle. But Jesus took the man aside, away from the curious crowd. Jesus put His fingers in the man's ears. Then Jesus spat on His finger and touched the man's tongue.

Jesus sighed, maybe thinking about all the people who cared more about seeing miracles than about honoring God or showing love to others. Jesus looked up to heaven said to the man, "Ephphatha." That was the Aramaic word for "Be opened."[27]

Immediately the man was healed! He could hear the people around him, and he could talk so that others could understand him easily! It was another amazing miracle. The man and the people who brought him to Jesus were thrilled!

Jesus said, "Don't tell anyone what happened here today!" But they did not listen to Jesus.[193] They told everyone they met! The people were completely astonished![470] They said to each other, "Jesus has done all things well. He makes both the deaf to hear and the mute to speak. No one else can do the things He does!"[264]

Talk About the Story: What did the people want Jesus to do? Why do you think that wanted Jesus to heal the man? Why did Jesus sigh when He healed the man? Why do you think Jesus didn't want the people to talk about the miracle He did?

Scripture: "In that day the deaf shall hear the words of the book, And the eyes of the blind shall see out of obscurity and out of darkness." Isaiah 29:18

Family Time: Jesus healed people just as the Old Testament said the Messiah would. Because of His miracles, many people believed in Jesus. Why do you believe in Jesus?

Prayer: Father, thank You for sending Jesus to fulfill all the Old Testament prophecies and to show Your love to us. Help us to grow in our belief in You. In Jesus' name, Amen.

I WILL BUILD MY CHURCH

Scripture: Matthew 16:13–19
Place: Caesarea Philippi at the foot of Mt. Hermon
Time: Fall, 29 AD

Jesus and the disciples headed towards Mount Hermon, the perpetual snow-capped peak over 9,000 feet tall that marked the northern boundary of Israel. Jesus wanted to take the disciples away from the crowds of people that had been following them. Mount Hermon was a great place for a retreat!

Jesus and His disciples stopped near Caesarea Philippi. This town was far away from the crowds. Jesus knew His disciples needed time alone with Him so that He could teach them more and get them ready for what was coming soon. Jesus knew that in only six months He would die on the cross. So He asked, "Who do people say that I am?"

The apostles looked from one to another, one answered, "Some say you are John the Baptist." This was impossible because John the Baptist had been killed!

www.thefamilyprayerbible.com

"Some say you are Elijah." That was because some people expected Elijah to come and do miracles before the great Day of the Lord.

"Others say you are Jeremiah who will come to find the Ark of the Covenant to lead the people to defeat Rome."

Jesus expected these answers because people had been saying these things for quite a while. Then He asked, "But you," Jesus was specific. "Who do you say that I am?"[256]

Simon Peter, always the spokesman of the twelve, took center stage, "You are the Messiah, the Son of the Living God."

Jesus didn't respond immediately. He allowed His disciples to think through their answer. The apostles looked at one another, and slowly they nodded their heads in agreement.

"God has helped you, Simon Peter," Jesus said to the disciple, "because my Father in heaven has told you this answer. You did not learn this answer from people."[458]

"Peter, you are a foundation rock, and your words are solid." Jesus added, "On this rock I will build My church."[69]

Jesus used the word *church* in a new way. The disciples recognized the familiar Greek word *church*. They knew the word church was an assembly of politicians or soldiers or people. But Jesus used the word *church* in a new way, an important future way. But they did not immediately understand. Jesus meant the church would be an assembly of God's people.

"Peter, I will build My church upon this rock, and the gates of Hell shall not be able to stand against it." Jesus was still speaking to Peter when He said, "You will have the keys to the kingdom of heaven, and whatever you lock on earth, God in heaven will lock it up. Whatever you open on earth, will also be released in heaven."[145]

Talk About the Story: Where was Jesus when He asked the apostles, "Who am I?" How did some answer? How did Peter answer? What was important about Peter's answer? What is a church? What did Jesus tell Peter he could do?

Scripture: "Simon Peter answered and said, "You are the Christ, the Son of the living God." Matthew 16:16

Family Time: How would you answer Jesus' question to the disciples? Who do YOU say Jesus is? How important is the church to you? Why?

Prayer: Father, thank You for introducing the church to us. I love my church. Thank You for using the church to carry out Your ministry. In Jesus' name, Amen.

FIRST PREDICTION OF DEATH

Scripture: Matthew 16:20–28
Place: Caesarea Philippi at the foot of Mt. Hermon
Time: Fall, 29 AD

Jesus looked sternly at His disciples. First He looked at them as a group, then He looked from man to man and said, "I do not want you to tell anyone what I have just said to you," Jesus explained. "People do not understand now what I will do as Messiah, they do not believe that I am the Son of God."

"There is something else you need to know," Jesus said. "We are going up to Jerusalem where I will suffer at the hands of the Jewish leaders, they will kill Me, but after three days, I will rise again from the dead."[260]

But they did not understand then what He was saying, not because the words did not have meaning, but they were spiritually blinded.

Then Peter blurted out what he was thinking, "ABSOLUTELY NOT!" Peter

www.thefamilyprayerbible.com

pounded one fist into his hand. "LORD, WE WILL NEVER LET THIS HAPPEN TO YOU!"[504]

Peter was argumentative and was known to babble before he thought about his answer. Jesus firmly said,
"Get behind Me, Satan."[220]

Even though Peter wanted to defend and protect Jesus, Jesus called Peter Satan—the enemy!

Peter was stunned at Jesus' abrupt answer. He dropped to the ground, pulling his tunic around him. He felt ashamed of his words, but didn't know what to say.

"If any man will come after Me," Jesus explained to His disciples, "you must put aside any selfish ambition you have for your life, you must take up your cross daily, and follow Me."[428]

Jesus continued, "For whoever desires to save his life will lose it, but whoever loses his life for My sake will find it!" Jesus explained that having everything in the world means nothing if you don't accept His salvation because in the end, He will come back in His glory with all the angels. Then He will reward each according to his works.[524]

The disciples thought about all the things Jesus had said. It was so much to take in! They didn't fully understand, but they wanted to trust Jesus and obey Him.

None of the disciples slept soundly that evening. They had come to the mountain for rest but Jesus' message was heavy. Each one thought about the things Jesus said long into the night.

Talk About the Story: Why did Peter rebuke the Lord telling Him what He couldn't do? Why did Jesus call Peter a "devil"? What else did Jesus tell them?

Scripture: "Then Jesus said to His disciples, 'If anyone desires to come after Me, let him deny himself, and take up his cross, and follow Me.'" Matthew 16:24

Family Time: What are some ways people who follow Jesus deny themselves in order to follow Him? What do you think Jesus meant when He told His disciples to take up their crosses to follow Him? What are some things we can do that show we follow Jesus today?

Prayer: Jesus, I want to follow You like the disciples did. Help me to see ways to follow You and to have the courage to obey You every day. Amen.

THE MOUNT OF TRANSFIGURATION

Scripture: Matthew 17:1–13
Place: On Mt. Hermon
Time: Fall, 29 AD

Six days later Jesus called to Peter, James, and John. He said, "Come with me," He pointed up to the top of Hermon. "Let's go high into the mountain, apart from everyone."[443]

They climbed all that day, going higher toward the snow at the top of Mount Hermon. The surrounding villagers called it *Old Man Mountain* because it always was crowned with snow, as old men are crowned with white hair.

Suddenly a brisk breeze blew a cloud toward them. James and John saw sunbeams dancing in this cloud, sparkling differently than the others. The cloud covered them as a warm blanket, not a damp mist. John looked and saw Jesus as he had never seen Him.

"He's sparkling," John whispered to the other two disciples. Even the clothes of Jesus turned gloriously white, whiter than any freshly washed clothes, whiter than snow, whiter than lamb's wool washed by the strongest soap.[490]

www.thefamilyprayerbible.com

The disciples saw two men talking with Jesus but they couldn't hear what they were saying. Jesus talked with both of them as though they were long, lost friends.

Suddenly Peter realized who the men were. "That's Elijah," said Peter. "And the other one is Moses!"

The three apostles watched in awe. Peter didn't know what to say or think! But he jumped to his feet and yelled out to Jesus,

"We can make three tents! One for You, one for Elijah, and one for Moses!"[390]

It was fortunate for Peter that Jesus didn't have to answer him. No one knows what Jesus was thinking, whether Jesus would have rebuked him or laughed at him. Quickly the sparkling cloud covered the scene. Peter crumpled to the ground.

Then Peter, James, and John heard the commanding voice of God the Father. "This is My beloved Son. Listen to Him!"[492]

Peter wrapped his arms around his head in fear. James and John pulled their shawls over their heads. They also were terrified. For the next few moments nothing moved.[150]

Finally, Peter looked up. Peter didn't see anyone but Jesus. Moses was gone, Elijah was gone, the cloud was gone. Jesus said, "Arise, and don't be afraid."[178] Slowly Peter, James and John arose. As they walked down the mountain together, Jesus told them to tell no one about this until after the resurrection.

Talk About the Story: Who climbed the mountain with Jesus? What happened to Jesus? Who was with Him? What did God the Father say? What did Peter say he wanted to do?

Scripture: "This is My beloved Son, in whom I am well pleased. Hear Him!" Matthew 17:5

Family Time: What does God the Father want us to do, according to Matthew 17:5? Why? What is one thing you have learned from Jesus' teaching that you can obey this week?

Prayer: Father, thank You for glorifying Jesus on the Mount of Transfiguration. I want to glorify Him in my life by obeying His Words. Thank You for Your confirmation that Jesus is the Son of God. I will love Him, serve Him, and obey Him. Amen.

PSALM 30
A PRAYER OF DEDICATION FOR THE ALTAR

The Jews have used this psalm to be read when they dedicated a new synagogue to God. It was first sung by David when he dedicated the threshing floor of Araunah to God.

David had become very proud of his kingdom and what he thought he had built. He commanded his army generals to "number" the men of the nation. This was similar to a nation registering all able-bodied men to be drafted into the army.

God was displeased with David. God had supported David when he was attacked by a larger army. But now David was preparing for war. We don't know who was the enemy. All we know is that David was ambitious in this self-glorifying act.

God told David he was going to be punished for this act.

God offered David three choices of punishment. (1) Seven years of famine, (2) three months of defeat in war, or (3) three days of a nation-sweeping disease. David chose the disease.

Many died and even David himself became sick and almost died. He was led to a hilltop next to Mount Zion. It was Mount Moriah, the place where Abraham had offered Isaac to God.

David bought the place for the altar, even though Araunah tried to donate it. But David realized it was his sin that caused the problem. He confessed, "Surely, I have sinned, and I have done wickedly" (2 Samuel 24:17).[440] David said, "I will not offer burnt offerings to the Lord my God, with that which cost me nothing" (2 Samuel 24:24).[412]

www.thefamilyprayerbible.com

There David built an altar, offered a sacrifice, and begged God for forgiveness.

> *"Oh Lord, my God I cried to You,*
>   *And You healed me of this disease."*[214]
> *For Your anger is but for a moment,*
>   *But Your favor last a lifetime.*
> *Weeping may last a whole night long,*
>   *But joy comes in the morning."*[517]

David confessed his pride for numbering the fighting men as his show of strength.

> *"When I was prosperous, I bragged*
>   *Nothing can stand in my way.*[387]
> *I felt secure in Your favor, O God,*
>   *But You turned away from me and I was shattered.*[164]
> *I cried out to You, O God, for mercy;*[523]
>   *I confessed I could do nothing if I die.*
> *I can't praise You, O Lord, if I am dust;*[543]
>   *I can tell everyone of Your faithfulness.*
> *Hear me, O God, have mercy on me."*[109]

David's sin led him to the top of Mount Moriah to sacrifice to God. It was there David discovered God's presence. It was in that place David planned to build the Temple to God. Today visitors go to the Temple Mount to see the actual Temple Mount where David sacrificed and where the Temple stood.

> *"You have tuned my weeping into a joyful dance;*
>   *You have turned my mourning clothes into happiness*[539]
> *That I might not be silent but sing praises to You.*
>   *I owe all thanksgiving to You, my Lord and God."*[541]

Talk About the Psalm: What did you learn about the psalm writer in this story? What did you learn about God?

Psalm 30: Read this week's psalm in your Bible together. Choose a verse to read aloud as a prayer.

Prayer: Thank You, God, for the psalm prayers in the Bible. Thank You for teaching us about You and about how to pray. In Jesus' name, Amen.

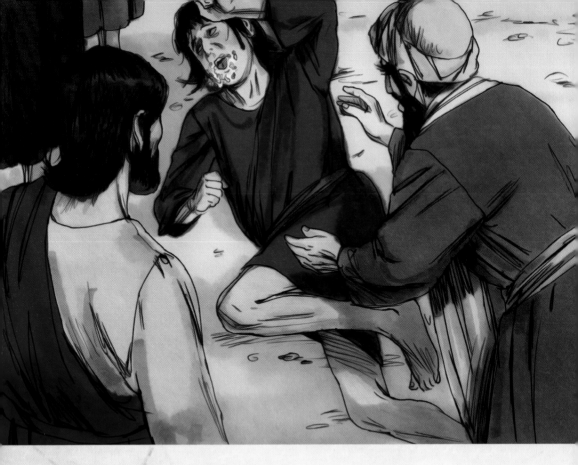

THE POWERLESS DISCIPLES

Scripture: Matthew 17:14-29
Place: Foot of Mt. Hermon
Time: Fall, 29 AD

Jesus descended from the Mount of Transfiguration with His three closest disciples, Peter, James, and John. The other nine disciples were in the small village at the foot of Mount Hermon waiting for Jesus.

As Jesus approached them, a father leading his lunatic son out of the village saw Jesus. He broke out running to Jesus. "Master," he said, "I brought my son to Your disciples, but they couldn't help me. My son cannot speak or hear, and he has a demon.[114] The demon shakes him and throws him into the fire. My boy foams at the mouth and bites everything he sees."[112]

Jesus looked around at the crowd that was gathered around listening to their conversation. Jesus recognized their unbelief.

www.thefamilyprayerbible.com

Jesus said, "This generation doesn't have faith in Me. How long must I be with you before you will learn to trust Me? Bring the boy to Me."[27]

The boy fell on the ground, shaking violently, and then began wallowing in the dirt.[440]

"How long has the boy been doing this?" Jesus asked the father,

"Since he was a child."[435] Then the father asked, "If You can do anything for us, please have compassion on the boy."[348]

Jesus said to the father, "All things are possible to him who believes in Me."[356]

The father knew he didn't have the faith that Jesus described, but without hesitation he cried out, "Lord, I believe in You, but help my unbelief."[340]

Jesus spoke to the demon. "I charge you to come out of him and never enter him again."[53]

The boy shook violently, then fell to the ground as though he were dead.[27] Not a limb moved. To the people standing by, he looked dead.

But Jesus knew better. He reached for the boy's hand, and the young lad began to get up.[359] The boy could hear! Then he began to talk as well! The demon was gone and he was healed.

Later that evening the disciples asked, "Why could we not cast out the demon?"[504]

"Because of your unbelief," Jesus answered. Then He explained, "Verily I said to you, if you have just a little faith, as little as a grain of mustard seed, you could say to this mountain, 'Be removed,' and it will move."[312]

Jesus was saying to them that faith was the source of their power, and their lack of faith was responsible for their lack of power.

On other occasions the apostles had cast out demons and healed the sick, but this time they were not able. Jesus said, "This kind does not go out but by prayer and fasting."[161]

Talk About the Story: Where did the man with the demon possessed boy meet Jesus? Why could the disciples not heal the boy? For what did the father ask?

Scripture: "Assuredly, I say to you, if you have faith as a mustard seed, you will say to this mountain, 'Move from here to there,' and it will move; and nothing will be impossible for you.'" Matthew 17:20

Family Time: How do you think faith grows? What are some things you know about Jesus that helps you to have faith in Him? What has happened in the past that has built up your faith in Jesus?

Prayer: Father, many times I don't have great faith. I pray like the boy's father, "I believe, help my unbelief." Make my faith in You stronger. In Jesus' name, Amen.

PAYING THE TEMPLE TAX

Scripture: Matthew 17:24–27
Place: Capernaum
Time: Fall, 29 AD

It seemed that the Jewish leaders were always trying to find things to accuse Jesus of! Some wondered if He obeyed all of the Sabbath rules, if He answered all the theological questions correctly, even if He and His disciples washed their hands correctly! Sometimes the disciples got tired of all the questions!

After Jesus and the disciples came back to Capernaum, the people who collected the taxes for the Temple approached Peter as he walked alone along the main street in town. "Does your Teacher not pay the Temple tax?" they asked.

Peter responded quickly: "Yes, of course," he said. But then he wondered, *Was that the right answer?*

Peter quickly left and headed back to Jesus and the other disciples. The question about the Temple tax burned in his mind. *What would Jesus have said to those men? I really don't know!*

And when Peter came into the house, Jesus smiled, knowing exactly what Peter was wondering about. Jesus said, "What do you think, Simon Peter? From whom do the kings of the earth take customs or taxes, from their sons or from strangers?"[478]

Peter said to Him, "From strangers." *Uh, oh!* Peter thought. *I think I gave the wrong answer!*

Jesus said to him that meant that since Jesus was the Son of God, He didn't need to pay taxes. "Then the sons are free, aren't they? Nevertheless, lest we offend them, go to the sea, cast in a hook, and take the fish that comes up first."

Peter looked confused. *How would that help? One fish will not sell for enough money to pay the tax!*

Jesus continued with a chuckle, "And when you have opened the fish's mouth, you will find a piece of money; take that and give it to them for My tax and yours."[467]

Peter ran to grab his fishing gear, laughing as he went out to do exactly what Jesus told him. He caught the fish, paid the tax, and satisfied the tax bill.

Talk About the Story: What did the Temple tax collectors want to know? Why do you think Peter was unsure about how to answer them? What did Jesus tell Peter to do? How did Jesus provide money for their needs?

Scripture: "But as many as received Him, to them He gave the right to become children of God, to those who believe in His name." John 1:12

Family Time: Why did Jesus pay the expected tax? Even though we are God's children, why should we follow the rules around us? What good can come from not offending others unnecessarily?

Prayer: Father, thank You for Jesus' example in big things like laying down our lives for You, as well as in little things like not offending people who expect us to meet their expectations. Please help us to be gracious and kind to others in every situation. Amen.

SEVENTY TIMES SEVEN

Scripture: Matthew 18:15–35
Place: Galilee
Time: Fall, 29 AD

Jesus and His disciples stayed in Capernaum and the area of Galilee for a while. Jesus had so much to teach His disciples! It seemed that they were always walking and talking together. And other people were always listening in!

The disciples wanted to learn everything they could from Jesus. One day Peter came to Jesus with a question. "Lord, how often shall my brother sin against me, and I forgive him? Up to seven times?"[173]

Peter knew that Jesus wanted him to show more love and forgiveness than the Pharisees showed. And Peter had learned that forgiving someone three times was good enough. So Peter decided that he should do far more than expected! But Jesus had a surprising answer for Peter!

Jesus said to him, "Not up to seven times, but up to seventy times seven!"[174] That is a LOT of times! Jesus went on to tell a story so that Peter and the others could understand why forgiving others should be a normal part of living in God's kingdom. He said,

"The kingdom of heaven is like a certain king who wanted to settle accounts with his servants. And when he had begun to settle accounts, one was brought to him who owed him ten thousand talents (that is, millions of dollars!). But as he was not able to pay, his master commanded that he be sold, with his wife and

www.thefamilyprayerbible.com

children and all that he had, and that payment be made. The servant therefore fell down before him, saying, 'Master, have patience with me, and I will pay you all.'108 Then the master of that servant was moved with compassion, released him, and forgave him the debt."173

Peter thought about all the sins God had forgiven in his life. Peter whispered a prayer of thanks to God for forgiving him.

"But that servant went out and found one of his fellow servants who owed him a hundred denarii (that is, just a few dollars); and he laid hands on him and took him by the throat, saying, 'Pay me what you owe!' So his fellow servant fell down at his feet and begged him, saying, 'Have patience with me, and I will pay you all.' And he would not, but went and threw him into prison till he should pay the debt."268

Peter thought about the people who sinned against him. Their sins against him were nothing compared what God had forgiven in his life!

"So when his fellow servants saw what had been done, they were very grieved, and came and told their master all that had been done. Then his master, after he had called him, said to him, 'You wicked servant! I forgave you all that debt because you begged me. Should you not also have had compassion on your fellow servant, just as I had pity on you?'304 And his master was angry, and delivered him to the torturers until he should pay all that was due to him."

Jesus finished His story with a warning, "So My heavenly Father also will do to you if you do not forgive your brothers."173

Talk About the Story: What did Peter want to know? What did Jesus teach Peter about forgiveness?

Scripture: "Blessed is he whose transgression is forgiven, whose sin is covered." Psalm 32:1

Family Time: What is the natural result of God's forgiveness in our lives? What happens when we choose to not forgive others? What are some things we can do when it is hard to forgive someone who has hurt us?

Prayer: Father, thank You for Your forgiveness. Help me to remember what You have done to forgive me when I am struggling with forgiving someone else. Please help me to forgive and to love others. In Jesus' name, Amen.

GOING TO THE FEAST OF TABERNACLES

Scripture: John 7:1–14
Place: Trip from Galilee to Jerusalem
Time: October, 29 AD

As the apostles approached Capernaum, a chilly fall wind blew off the Galilean hills. As Jesus and the twelve entered Capernaum, they could see people preparing to go to Jerusalem to celebrate the Feast of Tabernacles and the Day of Atonement.[482]

Jesus dropped by to visit His half-brothers and His mother Mary. After a meal together, Jesus' brothers said, "You should go to the Feast of Tabernacles in Jerusalem. Do Your miracles there. If You want people to know about You, let them see what You can do!"[421]

"No." Jesus' answer was short, kind, but to the point. Then He explained, "My hour is not yet come."[547]

Jesus' brothers didn't yet believe in Him, and they didn't understand what He meant.[504] The disciples knew the phrase; "My hour is not yet come," had deep

    www.thefamilyprayerbible.com

importance. Since timing was everything, Jesus used this phrase when He did not do what people were asking.[90]

The following day the family left for Jerusalem. But Jesus and His disciples remained in Capernaum for the next two days.

Then on the second day Jesus said, "We are going to Jerusalem, but we'll go secretly." They followed shepherd paths through rolling hills. They were always climbing one hill or descending another. The deep blue autumn days were perfect for the journey.

Going through the small out-of-the-way villages of Samaria had its difficulties. The Samaritans had little to do with Jews, most of them hated the Jews, and the racial hatred was returned by the Jews.[334]

Jesus and the disciples stopped at a well outside a small town. James and John went to find a place for them to lodge for the night.

Shortly, John came running down the footpath from the city, James a few steps behind. Anger could be seen in John's face. That's why the disciples had given the brothers a nickname, "*Sons of Thunder.*" John yelled to Jesus, "THEY REFUSE TO RENT US A PLACE TO SLEEP!" The others felt John's anger.[347]

John was smarting from their rebuke. Anger does terrible things to people. John in his youthful anger demanded, "BRING DOWN FIRE OUT OF HEAVEN," He spit out the words, "AND BURN THEM UP!"

But Jesus didn't respond in anger. Jesus looked away from the disciples toward the Samaritan town that just had refused service to Him. "You don't know what you are asking for," Jesus told John. "I didn't come to destroy people, but to save them."

Jesus and the disciples went on to the next village. That night they found a place of lodging and food to eat.[170]

Talk About the Story: What time of year was it? Where was everyone going and why? Why did Jesus go to Jerusalem by a secret path? What happened when the Samaritans refused to rent rooms to Jesus? What was the response of James and John? How did Jesus answer them?

Scripture: "For the Son of Man did not come to destroy men's lives but to save them." Luke 9:56

Family Time: Jesus' brothers did not believe in Him until later. Why do you think they didn't believe? What did Jesus say His reason for coming was? Why might Luke 9:56 be a good thing to remember when you become angry with someone?

Prayer: Father, Give me compassion for people because You love them. Help me control my temper. May I pray for people, rather than criticize them. In Jesus' name, Amen.

DATE ___/___

THE LAST DAY OF THE FEAST OF TABERNACLES

Scripture: John 7:14-53
Place: Jerusalem
Time: Sunday, October, 29 AD

During the Feast of Tabernacles every October, the people of Israel camped outside their houses living in tents or booths. They were celebrating Israel's 40 years wandering in the wilderness when their forefathers lived in tents. The feast lasted for seven days, but on the eighth day—Sunday—was the greatest celebration of all.

Almost immediately after the sun rises, the people leave their booths arrayed in their festival clothing.

Some of the crowd stayed in the Temple to watch the morning sacrifice. Others went to cut down willow branches to make a canopy over the altar in the Temple. Still others followed the priest taking their pitchers down to the pool of Siloam.

Each person carried a branch of a palm, myrtle, or willow tree—sometimes all three tied together.

A chosen priest bearing a golden pitcher on his shoulder walked down toward the pool of Siloam—the only pool in Jerusalem that was fed with living water, a flowing spring.

As soon as the Temple trumpet sounded, hundreds of priests filled their golden pitcher with water from the pool, and began a parade back to the Temple, followed by the crowd. As they walked, they chanted loudly from the Prophet Isaiah,

"With joy shall we draw water out of the wells of salvation. In that day we shall say praise the Lord, call upon His name, declare his works among his people, exalt His name." (Isaiah 12:3, *ELT*)[485]

One priest with a pitcher walked into the Court of the Priests, and was joined by a second priest carrying sweet wine as a drink offering to the Lord. The two priests walked up to the great altar. One priest went to the east end of the altar and poured wine into the appropriate funnel, the other priest poured water into a funnel on the west end.

The people waved their branches toward the altar. A trumpet blasted and the worshipers bowed down. Then there was silence. All the people prayed as the faint sound of pouring water echoed.

Suddenly Jesus stepped out of the crowd and cried out with a loud voice, "IF

ANY MAN THIRST, LET HIM COME UNTO ME AND DRINK!" Jesus was fulfilling Scripture!

There was an instant murmuring among the people. Some were angry that their ceremony was interrupted. Some believed in Jesus. Some were simply curious.

Jesus continued, shouting, "THOSE THAT DRINK OF ME AND BELIEVE IN ME, SHALL HAVE RIVERS OF LIVING WATER FLOWING OUT OF THEIR INNERMOST BEING."[454]

The water just poured into the altar came from the living waters of the Pool of Siloam. Now Jesus was offering Living Water to those who believed in Him—the water of eternal life.

The celebration in the Temple degenerated into disagreements. "This man is the prophet that is going to come to announce the Messiah."[426]

Others disagreed, "No, Jesus is the Messiah."[507]

"No," others disagreed. "The Messiah won't come out of Galilee; He'll come from Bethlehem, David's city."[534]

The priests went running to the Temple guards. "Why did you not arrest Jesus?" they asked."[504]

The Temple guards said, "Well, we have never heard any man speak like this!"[256]

"Are you also deceived?" the leaders answered.[277]

Talk About the Story: What did the priests do at the ceremony? What did Jesus do and say? What was the reaction of the people? Of the priests?

Scripture: "If anyone thirsts, let him come to Me and drink. He who believes in Me, as the Scripture has said, out of his heart will flow rivers of living water." John 7:37–38

Family Time: Why do we need water? How does water make our lives better? How is a relationship with Jesus as important to our lives as water is?

Prayer: Father, I believe Jesus is Your Son, and I have taken Him as my Savior. He satisfies me as water quenches my thirst when I'm thirsty. I will let Your living water flow through me to others. Amen.

A WOMAN CAUGHT IN THE ACT OF ADULTERY

Scripture: John 8:1–12
Place: Temple
Time: Monday after the Feast of Tabernacles

Before the sun came up, Jesus was in the Temple to worship His heavenly Father; the early crowds were drawn to Him. Jesus was sitting on a low wall in the court of the women—an area available to all. People were gathered around, listening to Him teach.[72] Some were sitting at His feet, others were standing in small groups listening to Him. The Pharisees and priests stood at a distance, but today they didn't have their usual scowl of disapproval. Rather, the Pharisees wore a fiendish smile because they had a plan. Then the crowd heard,

"No!" A woman's cry was heard as she was being dragged to Jesus.

Two Pharisees held her by each wrist, dragging her toward Jesus. Panic in her eyes revealed terror. She was thrown onto the pavement in front of Jesus. One of the men announced, "This woman was taken in the act of adultery."[5]

Another Pharisee said, "The Law commands that we stone her." Then with a sneer he questioned, "What do You say?"[268]

Everyone knew the Pharisee was right about what the Law said, and they wondered what Jesus would say. If Jesus was really from God, He must agree with what the Law said. But at the same time, Jesus preached forgiveness, love, and mercy.

Rome had taken from the Jews the authority to execute anyone. Only a Roman court could condemn a person to death. If Jesus said "stone her," He could be in trouble with Rome. The crowd continued to wonder, *"What will Jesus say?"*[130]

Jesus said nothing. He knelt down and scribbled some writing on the ground.[401] The Pharisees persisted, "Moses demands that we stone a person taken in adultery! What is Your verdict?"[176]

Jesus looked up from the ground to look into the face of each Pharisee. "You who are without sin, you cast the first stone."[6]

Then Jesus simply returned to writing in the dirt, ignoring the men.

After a few moments of embarrassment, the Pharisees began to walk away, staring with the oldest in the group, and continuing until they all left.[164]

The woman still knelt on the ground in front of Jesus. Finally Jesus looked at her and asked, "Where are the people who accuse you?"[84]

"They're gone. There's no one left."

"Then if they don't accuse you, I don't accuse you." Jesus said to the woman. "But go and sin no more."[399]

Talk About the Story: Where did the encounter with the woman take place? What did Jesus do? What were the Pharisees' asking? How did Jesus answer?

Scripture: "For God did not send His Son into the world to condemn the world, but that the world through Him might be saved." John 3:17

Family Time: Did Jesus say it was all right to sin? How did Jesus want the woman to live after He forgave her? How should we live? What does Jesus expect of us after He forgives our sin?

Prayer: Father, I'm glad Jesus had compassion on the woman and I'm glad He forgives my sin. Help me see the sin in my life; both sins in actions and sins in attitudes. Forgive all my sin. Amen.

PSALM 37
TRUST IN THE LORD

David sat in his palace listening to some people complain because their life was hard. These complainers were jealous that some evil people were better off than they. Some evil people were riding fine horses, while the complainers walked in dirty streets. Evil people had beautiful homes and servants to wait on them. The complainers lived among the poor and had to do all the chores around the house.

David broke out into a Psalm, "Don't fret over evil people who seem to get all the breaks in life, and don't envy their house, horses, or possessions." David had lived a long time and had seen many things. He knew money or possession didn't bring happiness. He also knew both rich and poor, whether good or evil will eventually die. So David sang, "They will be soon cut down like grass and they will wither and die."

David told his audience about his age and experiences. "I once was young and ambitious, and now I am old and grey. I have never seen the godly begging for a living, nor are his children rebellious. The godly are constantly helping people and giving to them. They get great satisfaction living for others. I have never seen the children of the godly rebelling against God or their parents."

David composed this Psalm in alphabetical order of the Hebrew language. Each verse begins with a letter of the alphabet in order. He instructed, "I wrote this psalm so children would have an easier time memorizing it. Also, I wrote it like Proverbs; each verse has a complete thought in itself.

David concluded, "People will always be perplexed why evil people prosper, and some godly people have so little of this world's goods."

> *"Trust in the Lord and do good, you will live in the Promised Land*
> > *And will always have something to eat.*
> *Delight yourself in God, making Him number one in your life*
> > *And God will hear your prayers and give you your desire.*[426]
> *Commit everything you do to God and trust Him;*
> > *He will take care of you and make all things happen for your good,*
> > *Your righteousness will not fail in the light of judgment.*
> *Rest in the Lord, and wait patiently for Him.*[207]
> > *Don't fret yourself when evil people prosper,*
> > *Nor when they do their evil things.*
> *Quit being angry and serve the Lord joyfully;*
> > *Above all, don't let your bitterness make you sin."*

Talk About the Psalm: What did you learn about the psalm writer in this story? What did you learn about God?

Psalm 37: Read this week's psalm in your Bible together. Choose a verse to read aloud as a prayer.

Prayer: Thank You, God, for the psalm prayers in the Bible. Thank You for teaching us about You and about how to pray. In Jesus' name, Amen.

JESUS ARGUES WITH PHARISEES

Scripture: John 8:31–59
Place: Jerusalem
Time: A few days after the Feast of Tabernacles, 29 AD

"How dare you?" the Pharisees snarled at Jesus. "You are a liar." It was the day after the Feast of Tabernacles was over and the Pharisees were still angry at Jesus' outburst during the feast when he invited people to come drink of Him. They told Jesus He was a sinner who was making outlandish claims.

"None of you can point out any sin I have ever committed," Jesus answered.[34]

A Pharisee yelled at Jesus, "YOU ARE A SAMARITAN DOG!"

Calling anyone a Samaritan was the worst slur imaginable; it was the worst slander against a Jew. The Jewish leaders were angry. They yelled at Jesus, "NOT ONLY ARE YOU A SAMARITAN, BUT YOU HAVE A DEVIL."[139]

"If anyone keeps My words," Jesus answered with a quiet voice, "that man who obeys My words shall never see death."[416]

"Ha!" a Pharisee jeered heartily, throwing both arms into the air, "now we know You are demon possessed!" The crowd of Pharisees laughed heartily. The onlookers withdrew in disbelief. They were worshipers in Jerusalem, and had come to the Temple to talk to God. All they heard were angry voices.

"Abraham rejoiced to see Me," Jesus answered. The Pharisees laughed at what Jesus claimed, "Abraham was glad to see My day!"[264]

"Abraham is dead and so are the prophets," the angry voice of a Pharisee yelled. "This mad man says He has seen Abraham."[504]

Another religious ruler stroked his beard in sarcasm, ridiculing Jesus, "Are You greater than our father Abraham who is dead?" Then lowering his voice, he

www.thefamilyprayerbible.com

asked, "Who do You think You are? God?"[84]

Jesus answered, "Your father Abraham rejoiced when he saw Me and was glad when it happened."[264]

"Ha!" the Jews laughed in Jesus' face. One Jewish leader put his finger to his Temple and ran it in a circle, implying that Jesus was a lunatic. Another Jewish leader answered Jesus, "You are not even 50 years old and You claim to have seen Abraham."[504]

The Jewish leaders looked at one another, then laughed again. Jesus waited until their laughter subsided, then said, "Verily, verily I say to you," Jesus wrapped His tunic about His chest as a Rabbi does when finishing a sermon, then concluded, "before Abraham lived, I Am."[500]

John heard those words before. The descriptive phrase for Yahweh is "I Am." That was a phrase of deity. Jesus called Himself "I Am!" He was claiming to be God!

"BLASPHEMY!!!" one man shouted at Jesus.

"Get stones," another commanded to the crowd. Then he commanded to the other Pharisees, "We must stone this blasphemer."

The Pharisees chanted. "Yes! Stone the blasphemer!"

The clank of stones was heard as they began gathering them into their arms. The atmosphere in the Temple was sharp. The clank of stones echoed off the walls of the Temple. But Jesus walked calmly away from the center of the crowd.[142] He seemed unhurried and undisturbed. The disciples scurried to walk beside Jesus.

The Pharisees stood silent, cuddling their rocks to their bosom. Like soldiers waiting for the command to charge, but no one moved as Jesus walked away from the Temple that day.

Talk About the Story: What was the time of year? Why were the Jewish leaders angry with Jesus?

Scripture: These are written that you may believe that Jesus is the Christ, the Son of God, and that believing you may have life in His name. John 20:31

Family Time: The Pharisees refused to believe that Jesus is the Son of God. Think about people you know who refuse to believe in Jesus. What can you do to help them come to believe in Jesus?

Prayer: Father, I want people to know and believe in Jesus. Please help me to be a good witness for Him. Guide my words and my actions so that they will honor You and bring others to You. In Jesus' name, Amen.

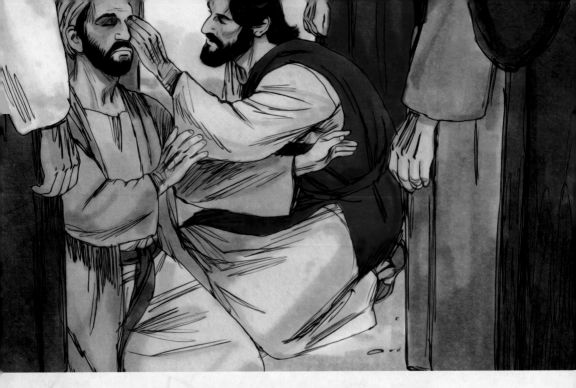

JESUS HEALS A BLIND MAN

Scripture: John 9:1–7
Place: Jerusalem
Time: A few days after the Feast of Tabernacles, 29 AD

Jesus and His disciples walked past a blind man begging at the door into the Temple. The blind man was propped against the stone wall, his vacant eyes stared into space, seeing nothing.

"Master," Philip asked Jesus, "did this man sin or his parents that he was born blind?"[440]

Jesus stopped in front of the blind man, putting out both arms to stop the forward motion of the disciples. Jesus gazed at the blind man, who couldn't see that he was the center of attention. The disciples gathered around Jesus as He spoke, "Neither this man sinned, nor his parents, to cause him to be born blind," Jesus turned to His disciples, making this a teaching moment. "This man was born blind that a miracle of God should be done in him."[188]

The disciples expected a miracle. On several other occasions Jesus had given sight to the blind by touching their eyes, and on another occasion Jesus simply spoke and the blind saw. But Jesus did neither.

Jesus stooped to spit on the ground. Then taking out a bit of clay in the palm of His hands, He began mixing the clay together with His fingers, making a thick paste.

Jesus dipped the tip of His finger into the clay, and reached out to spread the mud on the blind man's eyes.

As Jesus stepped back, His shadow fell across the blind man's face blocking out the glaring sun. Still the blind man did not blink. He couldn't discern the difference between light and darkness.

The Master spoke, "Go wash in the Pool of Siloam." Jesus helped the man up and pointed him in the correct direction. "Wash thoroughly in the clear running water of Siloam."[118]

The Pool of Siloam was all the way down near the outer wall of Jerusalem. It was a long walk, through narrow arches, across shopping bazaars, and down terraced steps. It was a trip the blind man had taken many times. The ragged blind man propped himself on a gnarled walking cane. "Tap, tap, tap," he began tapping his cane on the cobblestones, searching for a passage through the crowds. His steps were unsure on the uneven pavement, yet his feet had direction. He began walking toward Siloam. He knew the way. He knew where he was going. Obeying the directive words of Jesus, he struck a path through the crowd toward the Pool of Siloam.[327]

Near the Pool of Siloam, the steps narrowed and descended steeply. Slowly, step by step, the blind man descended, "Tap, tap, tap, splash, splash," he found the water's edge. Cupping his hands, he splashed clear liquid into his muddied eyes. Then the blind man looked at his reflection in the water. He splashed another handful of water into his face.

He gazed up into the blue skies. "Look!" he said to no one in particular, pointing at the white clouds. Then he stared into the blinding sun and for the first time in his life. He blinked, putting his hands to shield his tender eyes from its piercing rays. He was healed![364]

Talk About the Story: What did Philip ask about the blind man? What did Jesus tell him? Why do you think Jesus used mud to heal the man's eyes?

Scripture: "The Lord opens the eyes of the blind; The Lord raises up those who are bowed down; the Lord loves the righteous." Psalm 146:8

Family Time: Why do you think Jesus didn't instantly heal the man's eyes? When are some times you have had to wait for Jesus' answer to your prayers? What did you learn about God through the time that you waited and obeyed Him?

Prayer: Father, thank You for giving physical sight to the blind man. Also, thank You for giving spiritual sight to me. Help me to understand spiritual things. Help me see Your work in my life. Amen.

HE RETURNED SEEING

Scripture: John 9:7–34
Place: Jerusalem
Time: A few days after the Feast of Tabernacles, 29 AD

The blind man saw for the first time. He saw the Pool of Siloam, the trees, bushes. The blind man walked over to an old man sitting on the stairs. "Shalom," he greeted.

The elderly man stared at the man. "Wait! Aren't you the blind man that sat and begged at the Temple gate?"[275] the man asked. He had seen this man every day for years! He couldn't believe what he saw; the blind man was now seeing.

"No," another man said. "He looks like the blind man, but this isn't him."

The formerly blind man laughed. I AM the man who used to beg there. I WAS blind, but now I see!"[243]

"How were your eyes opened?"[424] another person asked.

"A man called Jesus made clay and put it on my eyes," the blind man answered, "then Jesus told me to come to the Pool of Siloam and wash. When I washed, I could see."[118]

"Come," the men grabbed the man, "We must take you to the priests. They must see this miracle."

They approached the Temple and saw a group of religious leaders standing at the top of the stairs. The man told the priest he had been blind since birth, but now he could see.[478] The religious leaders wanted to know who did this and how. The man explained what happened again.

The leaders. "Surely Jesus didn't do this!"

"GET HIS PARENTS!" one of the Pharisees demanded.

The leaders ignored the man standing there. But he was now seeing for the first time. He looked about the Temple, enjoying the sights he had heard about, but never seen before.

Finally one of the Pharisees said, "I don't believe you were ever blind. You are a LIAR!"[127]

"My parents will tell you I was born blind,"[334] the frustrated man declared.

"If any man is a follower of Christ, we will throw him out of the Temple," one vocal Pharisee pointed to the healed blind man. "We will not allow anyone to worship in the Temple who believes in Jesus."[19]

He thought, *I can see the Temple because of Jesus.* He surveyed the top of the engineering marvel towering 100 feet above him into the air, then thought, *How can I deny the one who made it possible for me to see this?*[188]

A Temple guard brought two old people before them. "Are you parents of this man?" the spokesman pointed to the healed man. "Is this your son?"

Both man and wife nodded approval, they were afraid to speak in front of the threatening religious leaders.[19] Then turning to the parents, the leader snapped, "Was he born blind?"

"Yes," the mother nodded.[478]

"How did he get his sight?"

The parents could have loudly praised God that their son could see. Instead they cowered before angry priests and Pharisees.[19]

"He is a grown man," the father fumbled for an answer, "He is of legal age, ask him."

The formerly blind man could contain himself no longer. "Why here is a wonderful miracle! I was blind but now I see!"

Talk About the Story: How did people respond when they realized that the man who had been born blind could now see? What did the man's parents say when the Pharisees questioned them? What did the man who had been blind say?

Scripture: "I have heard of You by the hearing of the ear, But now my eye sees You." Job 42:5

Family Time: Why did the religious leaders doubt the miracle? Why do people doubt Jesus today? What could you tell someone who says they refuse to believe in Jesus unless they see Him?

Prayer: Father, help me to remember to pray for people who refuse to believe in You. Give me wisdom and compassion as I tell them about You. Amen.

DATE ___/___

GIVE GLORY TO GOD

Scripture: John 9:24–41
Place: Jerusalem
Time: A few days after the Feast of Tabernacles, 29 AD

As the Pharisees argued with each other and with the parents of the man who had been born blind, the man continued to look around the Temple courtyard, drinking in all the amazing sights he had never seen before. But when he heard his parents say, "He is a grown man, ask him," the man turned back to the angry Pharisees.

The formerly blind man could contain himself no longer. "Why here is a wonderful miracle! I was blind but now I see."

The Pharisees answered, "Jesus is a sinner, give God the glory."[188]

"God doesn't hear sinners," the blind man answered. "This is a wonderful miracle—the eyes of the blind are opened. Whether Jesus is a sinner I don't know," the healed man reasoned, "I only know one thing: I was blind, and now I see."[478]

"How did Jesus open your eyes?" the Pharisees continued cross-examining their victim who was growing bolder with each answer.

"How did this Jesus give you sight?"

"I already told you," the healed man answered. "He put clay on my eyes, I washed, and now I see."

Becoming exasperated at their nit picking, he challenged them. "Do you want me to tell you about the miracle again so you can become the disciples of Jesus?"[478]

"We are Moses' disciples,"[424] the Pharisees said, showing disdain for the simple healed man. "You are Jesus' disciples. We know that God spoke to Moses, but this fellow Jesus, we don't know who speaks to Him. We don't know where He is coming from."[424]

"If Jesus were not from God," the blind man would not shut up, "He could not do miracles. He could not heal me."[466]

"OUT!" the leader yelled, pointing to the gate. "GET OUT! YOU CANNOT RETURN."

It seemed all of Jerusalem heard about the confrontation between the blind man and the religious leaders. The worshipers told everyone about the miracle of the blind man and that the leaders had excommunicated him from the Temple.[349] The people were perplexed.

Jesus found the blind man to ask him, "Do you believe in the Son of God?"[479]

Jesus called Himself, Son of God, a title of deity. Jesus was saying He was God.

"Who is He," the blind man asked, "that I might believe on Him?"[190]

"I am He,"[377] Jesus looked deep into the eyes He had healed. The eyes were no longer blinded, but they saw the One talking to him. He saw Jesus and said, "I believe," and worshiped Jesus.[211]

Talk About the Story: How did the blind man respond to the religious leaders? What did mean to be thrown out of the Temple? When Jesus found the healed man, what did He say and what did He do?

Scripture: "Then he said, 'Lord, I believe!' And he worshiped Him." John 9:38

Family Time: Why did the religious leaders doubt the miracle? Why do people doubt Jesus today? What testimony did the healed man give about Jesus? What can we tell the world about Jesus?

Prayer: Father, thank You for healing for the blind man. Help me to see the good things that You do in my life and to praise You for them. Help me to tell others about You. In Jesus' name, Amen.

MARY SAT AT JESUS' FEET

Scripture: Luke 10:38-42
Place: Bethany
Time: October, 29 AD

Jesus and His disciples had been to Bethany, a suburb of Jerusalem, several times. Martha, her sister Mary, and her brother Lazarus lived there. They often invited Jesus and His disciples to stay with them.[72]

As part of the celebration of the Feast of Tabernacles, the courtyard in the back of their house was covered with vines. It was a place for fellowship, conversation, and banquets.

Jesus sat under the leafy booth in the backyard, enjoying the autumn afternoon as He taught His disciples and others who gathered there.

In preparation for the evening banquet, Martha was moving back and forth on her busy errands, again and again passing Jesus as He sat teaching about how to live in the spiritual kingdom of God. Instead of helping Martha, Mary sat in rapt attention listening to Jesus.[285]

To honor Jesus, Martha was preparing the banquet, while Mary honored Him by learning what He taught, sitting at His feet. She honored Him by forgetting everything else that was going on in the backyard. She was so absorbed in what He had to say, that she forgot what was going on around her. New light had illumined her world, and the light had given fresh life that was growing in her soul.

Time after time, Martha passed Mary, she was doing what was necessary to prepare the meal. After many trips past them, Martha could contain her irritation no longer, she said,

"Lord," she addressed Jesus, not her sister, "do you not care that my sister has left me to prepare the meal by myself?"[547]

Even though Martha spoke to Jesus, she was complaining about Mary. Martha was not complaining about Jesus occupying her sister's attention, it's just that Martha was a perfectionist who feels that *doing* things for God is more important than *being* something for God. Martha asked,

"Tell her to help me!"

This reproof of Martha came from a sister who was more concerned about things, than about people. Jesus is concerned about both, but His priority is people first. Jesus repeated her name twice, "Martha, Martha, you are very concerned about things."[325]

In Jesus' statement to Martha, He did not say that looking after things was wrong, He repeated her name twice to tell you that she was important to Him; as was Mary. Then Jesus said,

"Mary has chosen the more important thing to do." Jesus wanted Martha to put things into perspective, "The most necessary thing is to learn how to live in the kingdom of God."

Then to make sure that Martha understood the eternal implication, Jesus said, "What Mary has learned shall not be taken away from her."[381] Then Jesus noted, "The basic necessities of life such as eating, drinking and sleeping are only temporary; for when you do them once; you must continually do them, but if you put the kingdom of God first, you learn something that will never be taken from you."

Talk About the Story: What was Martha doing? Did Mary enjoy what she was doing? What good things did Jesus say to Martha, but how did He correct her? What good things did Jesus say to Mary?

Scripture: "Therefore do not worry, saying, 'What shall we eat?' or 'What shall we drink?' or 'What shall we wear?' But seek first the kingdom of God and His righteousness, and all these things shall be added to you." Matthew 6:31,33

Family Time: What are some things that are easy to worry about instead of focusing on Jesus? What can we do to remember that our relationship with Jesus is even more important that the things we worry about?

Prayer: Lord, teach me to know and do the important things in life—the things that build my relationship with You. I want to sit at Jesus' feet and learn from Him. Amen.

THE GOOD SAMARITAN

Scripture: Luke 10:25-37
Place: Perea
Time: Winter, 30 AD

As Jesus traveled across the Jordan River in Perea, crowds came out to hear Jesus speak. Standing on the edge of the crowd was a lawyer. He was an expert in Jewish law who wanted to *test* the visiting rabbi from Nazareth.[479] The lawyer felt that if he could win a debate with Jesus, his fame and reputation would grow.

The lawyer interrupted Jesus with a question, "Master, what must I do to inherit eternal life?"[281]

Jesus knew the lawyer was not seeking salvation, but rather wanting to debate the fine points of the Law. Jesus put the question back to him, "What is written in the Law? How do you read the Scriptures?"[3]

The lawyer gave an excellent response to Jesus' question. He answered, *"You shall love the Lord your God with all your heart, with all your soul, and with all your mind. And you shall love your neighbor as you love yourself.*[291]

"Your answer is correct," Jesus answered, then added, "if you keep these commandments, you shall have eternal life."

The lawyer could see that his planned debate wasn't going anywhere, so he asked another question. "But who is my neighbor?"[547]

Jesus answered with a parable.

"A certain man walked down the lonely road from Jerusalem to Jericho, thieves attacked him, stripped him of his clothes, beat him severely, leaving him half dead.[1]

By chance, a priest came from Jerusalem came down that same road, and when he saw the battered man in the middle of the road, he passed by on the other side. Also a Levite came down that road. When he saw the beaten body, he, too, passed by on the other side of the road.[424]

By chance, a Samaritan—one the Jews considered a heathen—saw him lying beside the road. He had compassion on him. The Samaritan went to him, bound up his wounds, poured his supply of oil and wine on the wounds, then set the man on his own donkey, and took him to an inn.

That night the Samaritan took care of the wounded man, and on the next day when he left, gave two dinari—the amount of wages for two laborers for a day— and paid the innkeeper to take care of him. He said, 'If more is required, I will repay you when I return'" (Luke 10:25–35, *ELT*).

As Jesus finished His story, He looked into the lawyer's eyes and asked, "Which of these men was a neighbor to him that was beaten by thieves?"[431]

The lawyer was on the spot. The truth was in the story. The lawyer could not say the Jewish leaders were neighbors, for they passed by the needy man. But the lawyer could not even bring himself to say the word *Samaritan*. So the lawyer answered, "The man that showed mercy."[304] The lawyer knew that any other answer would be an obviously lie.

Then Jesus said, "Go and do the same thing."[327]

Talk About the Story: Who challenged Jesus to a debate? What did he ask? How did Jesus answer? What is a parable? What did the Jews think of a Samaritan? Who didn't help the wounded man? What did the Samaritan do? How was he a neighbor?

Scripture: "You shall love the LORD your God with all your heart, with all your soul, with all your strength, and with all your mind, and your neighbor as yourself." Luke 10:27

Family Time: What were the qualities of the good Samaritan? How can we be "good Samaritans"?

Prayer: Father, give me a helping heart like the Samaritan. May I see people in need and be a neighbor to them. Amen.

PSALM 42

REMEMBER GOD WHEN YOU ARE DISCOURAGED

A priest was walking towards Jerusalem. It had been a long time since he had worshiped the Lord in the Temple. He was discouraged because it had been such a long time since he had sacrificed to God.

He was from the Korah family, a line of priests who had been very close to God and those who worshiped Him.

Suddenly he heard the bark of a wild dog or wolf chasing an animal. Quickly a young white tail deer ran out of some bushes, then stopped long enough to drink from a flowing creek. Almost immediately the deer regained his strength, and then darted off to escape his pursuer.

The priest began to compose a song, "As the deer must drink from a creek to regain his strength, so I must drink from the living God to renew spiritual renewal."

The priest walked faster, wanting to get to God's presence as quickly as possible. He added a stanza, "Will I make it to drink from God's presence, can I hold on?"[485]

The priest remembered people mocking him. "Where is your God? Why doesn't He help you?" He sang another stanza, "When can I stand in God's presence to worship Him?"[426]

The priest began to cry as he sang, "I remember how I used to walk into the Temple, leading a happy throng of worshipers. We sang for joy and gave thanks to God."

Then the priest realized God was everywhere. He sang, "I can hear You in the roaring sea and in the surging floods of water." Then he thanked God "for pouring His unfailing love upon him."

The priest sang the song God gave him, trusting God to help him overcome his enemies.

"As The young deer being chased will thirst for water,
    So my soul longs for your presence, O Lord.[485]
I thirst for You, O God.
    When will You let me stand again in Your presence?
Day and night I have cried for You,
    While my enemies jeer, "Where is Your God?"
I remember when I used to come to You,
    Now it breaks my heart that I can't come into Your house.[426]
Because I remember coming to You with a crowd of worshippers,
    I was singing and giving You thanks;
    I was praising You with other worshippers.
"Now I am discouraged in my soul,
    I am cut off from Your house.[20]
Yet, in the future I will return to Your presence;
    I will come again to Your house to praise You.
Now I am depressed because I can't drink from Your fountains,
    Because I remember You sent us water from Mt. Hermon;
Where the head waters of the Jordan begins,
    And from Mizpah where Your presence first dwelt in the land.[485]
"I hear the waves roaring in the sea,
    And I want You to refresh me again.
So I must drink daily from Your love to me,
    I must worship You each night with songs and prayer.
Even when I can't come close to You in the temple,
    I feel lost in the darkness.
And my enemies laugh at my commitment to You,
    They taunt me saying, "Where is Your God?"
When I am discouraged in my soul
    And my Spirit is sad,
I will worship You in my heart;
    Because You strengthen my confidence,
    You are my Lord, and my God. Amen.[463]

Talk About the Psalm: What did you learn about the psalm writer in this story? What did you learn about God?

Psalm 42: Read this week's psalm in your Bible together. Choose a verse to read aloud as a prayer.

Prayer: Thank You, God, for the psalm prayers in the Bible. Thank You for teaching us about You and about how to pray. In Jesus' name, Amen.

JESUS TEACHES HOW TO PRAY

Scripture: Luke 11:5–13
Place: Perea
Time: Early one morning in winter, 30 AD 90 AD

Jesus had prayed all night while the disciples watched and protected Him. The next morning they asked Jesus to teach them how to pray. He taught them the Lord's Prayer.

The Jews were not intimate with God in prayer. In the Old Testament they went to God as Creator and Ruler of the universe. He was powerful and located far away in heaven.

They also went to God as their sovereign king who ruled, much like they went to their king who ruled from Jerusalem. They bowed in reverence and pleaded or begged for the things they wanted.

They knew they were sinners. The Jews lived under Old Testament law that was very exacting and restrictive. They spilt the blood of a lamb to get forgiveness.

www.thefamilyprayerbible.com

They came in a specific way, at a particular place (the Temple) and at designated times (the feast days, and on a regular schedule).[385]

But Jesus was going to teach them a new and better way to pray. They would have a new relationship with God. He would be their Father and they were to come to Him as children. Jesus taught them the heavenly Father was concerned about their daily needs, so they should pray about them.

To illustrate their new relationship, Jesus told a story of a desperate man with an urgent need.

"Which of you shall have a friend, and go to him at midnight and say to him, 'Friend, lend me three loaves; for a friend of mine has come to me on his journey, and I have nothing to set before him'; and he will answer from within and say, 'Do not trouble me; the door is now shut, and my children are with me in bed; I cannot rise and give to you'?[123] I say to you, though he will not rise and give to him because he is his friend, yet because of his persistence he will rise and give him as many as he needs.

Jesus explains that persistence in prayer is actually an expression of faith.[350] Because you know your neighbor has food, you persistently beg and as a result, you get your necessities. The heavenly Father is not callous like a neighbor. He cares for us, so we should continue in faith to ask for what we need, knowing that God cares for us and has the power to help us.[34]

After this story, Jesus taught, "Ask what you need and you'll get it. Go seeking from the Father what you need and you'll find it. Keep knocking on God's door and He will open to you to give you what you seek."[87]

Since our heavenly Father is good and He loves us, we should ask what we need and He will give it to us."[383]

Talk About the Story: What is the setting of the story about begging for food from a neighbor? Why did the neighbor finally get some food? What can we learn about persistence in prayer? What is our new relationship with God?

Scripture: "So I say to you, ask, and it will be given to you; seek, and you will find; knock, and it will be opened to you." Luke 11:9

Family Time: What is something that you keep praying about? How can you remember to have faith that God hears your prayers and will answer in the very best way?

Prayer: Father, forgive me when I pray with the wrong attitude or without believing that You will answer. Help me to remember that You are my loving heavenly Father and I am Your child. Teach me to pray more. Amen.

JESUS TEACHES THE LORD'S PRAYER AGAIN

Scripture: Luke 11:1-4
Place: Perea
Time: Winter, 30 AD

The winter's night was cold and some disciples were wrapped in their tunics, sleeping close to the fire. One disciple remarked, "How can Jesus pray all night?" Jesus had been interceding to His heavenly Father since the evening meal was finished.

Jesus prayed all night; fellowship with the heavenly Father was more enjoyable than sleeping or relaxing near the fire. When the first streaks of dawn lit the sky, Jesus came to the fire. One of the disciples asked, "Lord, teach us to pray, just as John the Baptizer taught his disciples!"

Two years ago Jesus had taught them the Lord's Prayer.[288] He included that prayer in the Sermon on the Mount near the Sea of Galilee. So Jesus explained again the Lord's Prayer. "It has seven petitions, and when a person prays each of these petitions, he's prayed about everything they need from the heavenly Father."

Jesus didn't instruct them to begin with, "Lord, God, or Almighty Master." He instructed them to talk to God as a child talks to an earthly father. "God is your heavenly Father who loves you more than an earthly Father, so begin '*Our*

Father, who is in heaven, hallowed be Your name!"[2]

The first petition involves worship. Just as the angels continually praise God saying, "Holy, holy, holy," so it's the task of God's children to worship Him. The word *hallow* means, "Holy." Begin the Lord's Prayer praying, "Holy be Your name."

The second petition is a request for the Father to rule on earth as He rules in heaven. So pray, *"Your kingdom come on earth as your kingdom rules in heaven."*[74] After all, we should be more concerned with what God does on earth than what we do as His children.

The third petition deals with the personal plan and decision of His followers. Each should want the Father's direction in their lives. Therefore they should direct their personal life by praying, *"Your will be done in my life on earth, the way Your will is carried out in heaven."*[278]

The fourth petition is, *"Give me bread for today because I need bread every day."*[170] The word *bread* stands for all of our daily needs—strength, wisdom, money, or stamina to not give up. We should pray each day for what we need every day.

The fifth petition is for God to forgive our sins. He does this based on the cross, because "The blood of Jesus Christ God's Son cleanses us from all sin" (1 John 1:7). The proof that we are sincere in our prayer for forgiveness[173] is when we forgive those who sin against us.[174]

The sixth petition is for victory over temptation.[476] Because the Lord leads us as He leads all sheep, then we pray for Him to lead us away from the unique temptations that will trip us up.

The seventh petition is for protection from the evil one. There are demons and a devil who want to destroy us, so we should daily ask God to protect us.[387]

The Lord's Prayer ends with, *"For thine is the kingdom, the power, and the glory."* That means God's kingdom rules and is powerful. God's ability to give us what we request is powerful, and God should get all the credit for the things He does in our life.[74]

Talk About the Story: What had Jesus been doing all night? What did the disciples ask Jesus? What are the seven petitions of the Lord's Prayer?

Scripture: "Lord, teach us to pray." Luke 11:1

Family Time: What can we learn about prayer from the way Jesus prayed?

Prayer: Father, may Your name be holy in my life. May Your kingdom come through my life. May Your will be done for my life. Give me bread-strength for today. Forgive my sins as I forgive those who sin against me. Don't lead me into overwhelming temptation. Protect me from the evil one. May Your reign prevail, Your ability accomplish what I ask, and You get all the credit. Amen."

DATE ___/___

JESUS CELEBRATED HANUKKAH

Scripture: John 10:22–42
Place: The Temple in Jerusalem
Time: December, 29 AD

Only two months had passed since the religious leaders in Jerusalem had picked up stones to throw at Jesus and try to kill Him. Returning to Jerusalem at this time was dangerous! But Jesus returned anyway to attend the feast celebrating the dedication of the Temple that lasted for eight days.

Today this feast is called Hanukkah. This feast began when the Temple services were restored by Judas Maccabaeus in the time between the end of the Old Testament and the beginning of the New Testament. At that time, there was only enough oil to keep one sacred candle on the menorah burning for one day. However, by a miracle the oil kept the candle burning eight days. Because of this, the Jews celebrated for eight days.

On the first day of the feast, Jesus walked through the Beautiful Gate into the Temple. The people crowded around Him. A spokesman of the people asked, "How long will You keep us in suspense? Tell us plainly if You are the Messiah."[511] They had seen His miracles and heard His sermons—they should have known that He was the Messiah!

Jesus said,

"I told you plainly that I was the Messiah, but you would not believe it.[24] If you don't believe what I said, believe Me because of the miracles that I do in My Father's name."

Then Jesus explained why people didn't understand His sayings, explaining, "You are not My sheep, therefore you do not believe Me, nor do you understand Me."[504]

www.thefamilyprayerbible.com

Jesus had said that He was the shepherd of the sheep. Building on that analogy, Jesus explained why some do not understand what He is saying.

"My sheep hear My voice, and they follow Me. I shall give them eternal life, and they shall never perish.[217]

My Father, which gave them to Me, is greater than anyone; and no one can pluck My sheep out of My Father's hands."[192]

Then Jesus said, "I and My Father are One."[492]

"BLASPHEMY!" a priest yelled.

Jesus had been saying all along that His work was really the work of the Father, so it only follows that Jesus would claim that He and the Father are One. The crowd did not miss His meaning. They took up stones, with the intention of stoning Him.

Lifting His hands, Jesus spoke in a quiet voice. They quieted, wanting to hear what He said. Jesus asked, "I have healed many people and done the good works of My Father. For which of these miracles do you stone Me?"[220]

"FOR BLASPHEMY!" a young priest yelled at Him.

"If I am not doing miracles, don't believe Me. But if I do miracles—believe the miracles—then you will know that the Father is in Me, and I am in the Father."[72]

The crowd exploded with anger. One man yelled, "DRAG HIM OUT TO THE VALLEY OF HINNON!" He incited the crowd, "LET'S STONE HIM THERE!"

Jesus simply turned His back to the crowd and began walking away. Jesus did not look back, nor was He afraid that they would try to harm Him because it was not yet His hour. He walked slowly out the gate, into the streets, and disappeared through the crowd.[217]

Talk About the Story: What did the people ask Jesus? What did He respond? Why did they try to stone Jesus? How did Jesus escape?

Scripture: "I and My Father are one." John 10:30

Family Time: Why did most people not fully know who Jesus was? Why do people reject Jesus today? How can we know more about Jesus?

Prayer: Father, thank You for protecting Jesus during His lifetime. The people didn't understand His miracles because they were spiritually blinded. Take away any spiritual blindness and help me fully understand who Jesus is and what He does. Amen.

CHAPTER 13

THE PEREAN MINISTRY

Jesus had been involved in public ministry for three years. During His final year of ministry, He intensified His public ministry, particularly in the southern parts which had been most resistant to His teaching. He would soon return to Jerusalem for His final Passover, then determine the fate of the nation.

Much of this time was spent in Perea, the other side of the Jordan River. This area was farther away from Jerusalem and the center of the Jewish nation. It is here Jesus spent some of His last "free time" in ministry before heading to Jerusalem where He would die for the sins of the world.

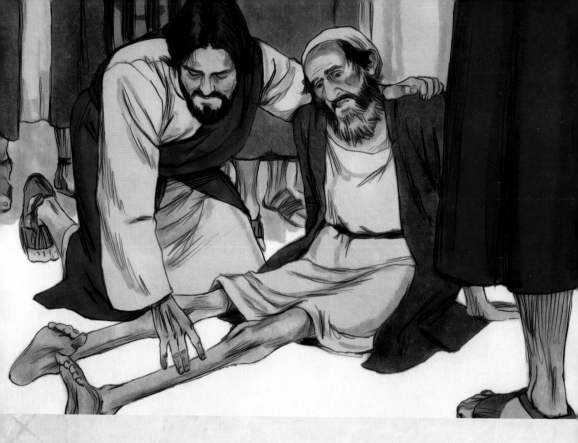

PARABLES ABOUT OUR HEART

Scripture: Luke 14:1–14
Place: Home of a Chief Pharisee
Time: Winter, 30 AD

Jesus sat down for a banquet in the Chief Pharisees' house on the Sabbath day. A man with swollen arms and legs came into the room and stood on the other side of the table, directly across from Jesus. It was impossible for Jesus not to see the man. Jesus saw his uncomfortable swelling. Everyone in the room saw what was about to happen.[435] Jesus asked the question, "Does the Law permit Me to heal on the Sabbath day?"

The Pharisees wouldn't say anything. They wanted to keep the Law, which means that they would not work on the Sabbath day. Yet the crowd would approve if Jesus healed a needy man on the Sabbath.

Jesus healed the man and told him to go his way.[214] Returning to the Pharisees, He asked a question,

"Which of you do not work on the Sabbath day? If you have a donkey that falls into a ditch, do you not immediately get him out on the Sabbath day?" (Luke 14:3, 5, ELT).[76]

www.thefamilyprayerbible.com

The teachers of the Law wouldn't answer Jesus.[214]

Then Jesus watched the religious leaders jockeying for the best seats at the banquet. They wanted to sit as close to the front as possible. Jesus knew it was all about pride or ego. Then Jesus gave the following parable:

"When you go to a wedding banquet, don't choose the best seat because someone more important than you may arrive. That person may be given your seat. You would have to take a lower seat and be embarrassed.[76]

When you go to a wedding feast, sit in the lowest seat.[228] *Perhaps your host will come and ask you to take a higher seat; then you will be honored in the presence of the wedding party.*[288]

Whoever exalts himself shall be humbled; and he that humbles himself shall be exalted" (Luke 14:8-11, *ELT*).

Then Jesus turned to the host of the banquet. Jesus wanted him to know that opening up his banquet feast to all was a picture of God opening up heaven to all who would come to eat.

Jesus told another parable,

"When you put on a special banquet, don't call your family, friends, or neighbors and specifically don't call your rich neighbors thinking that they in turn will invite you to their banquet meal.[547]

Instead, invite the poor, lame, and blind. If you feed those who cannot pay you back, your Father will reward you in the resurrection of the just" (Luke 14:12-14, *ELT*).[145]

Talk About the Story: Who came in to the Pharisee's home? What did Jesus do for the man even though it was the Sabbath? What stories did Jesus tell when he saw the guests at the Pharisee's house trying to get the best seats? What did Jesus want the people to understand?

Scripture: "For whoever exalts himself will be humbled, and he who humbles himself will be exalted." Luke 14:11

Family Time: The Pharisees cared about looking important and making others follow their rules. What does Jesus care about instead? What are some ways to act humbly instead of exalting yourself?

Prayer: Father, I'm glad Jesus knows what we really think in our hearts. We want to obey You from the heart and honor You in every way possible. Amen.

GOD'S PARABLE ABOUT AN INVITATION

Scripture: Luke 14:15–24
Place: Perea, home of a chief Pharisee
Time: Winter, 30 AD

One of the students at the banquet given by the chief Pharisee tried to impress everyone. He jumped to his feet and announced to all, "Blessed is the one that will eat bread in the kingdom of God."[213]

But Jesus knew he was just trying to look important. Jesus told another parable to teach about who belongs in the kingdom of God. Jesus said,

"A rich man made a great supper and sent his servants out to invite many to the supper. The servant said, 'Come because the food is on the table.'[416]
But his friends did not come, but rather made excuses.[140] One person said

that he had bought a piece of ground that he had to inspect. Another had just purchased a yoke of oxen that he had to test, and a third said that he had just gotten married and had to go on a honeymoon.[238]

When the servant told the owner that his friends were not coming, the master got angry and said,

'Go quickly into the streets and lanes; and bring in the poor, the sick, the lame, and the blind.'[72]

The servant did exactly as the man had commanded him, then said, 'We still have room at the table.'

The man told his servant to go into the highways and hedges and invite everyone to come in, so that his house would be filled"[68] (Luke 14:16-23, *ELT*).

After Jesus finished the parable, the Pharisees didn't know what to think of Him. Just to make sure that they didn't miss the point, Jesus told them that being born a Jew was not enough to enter heaven.[316]

"Those who were originally called to the wedding will never come to the table. These are the children of Israel who reject the call of the Father through His Son" (Luke 14:24, *ELT*).

Then Jesus explained His invitation was as wide as the human race. Any could go to heaven if they heard His invitation and responded.[483]

"If any man will come after Me, he must deny himself; take up his cross; and follow Me. He cannot be My disciple if he does not yield his life to Me" (Luke 9:23, *ELT*).[75]

Talk About the Story: What parable does Jesus tell? Who was invited to the banquet? Who refused to come to the banquet? Who was then invited?
Scripture: "For the grace of God that brings salvation has appeared to all men." Titus 2:1

Family Time: Who are the people God has invited to be part of His kingdom? How do we accept God's invitation? What must we do to follow Jesus? What are the hard things about following Jesus? What are the rewards?

Prayer: Lord, thank You for inviting me to be part of Your kingdom. Please use me to help others come as well. In Jesus' name, Amen.

JESUS TELLS ABOUT LOST THINGS

Scripture: Luke 15:1–10
Place: Perea
Time: Winter, 30 AD

As Jesus walked among the multitude, the sinners and outcasts crowded around Him. For the first time they heard that God loved them and welcomed them into His kingdom. The heavenly Father wanted them to have eternal life. The Rabbis had taught that God would not accept them until they repented of every broken law and begin to keep the Law. But Jesus told them that the Father accepted them, forgave them now, not only when they kept the Law perfectly.

As Jesus was talking with the outcasts in the streets, the Pharisees criticized Jesus loudly—so loudly that He could hear it.

"This man has been eating and drinking with sinners and those who rebel against God (Luke 15:2)."[292]

Jesus heard their accusation, so did all of the people standing with Him. He had given a parable inside of the house. Now standing in the streets, Jesus gave another parable,

"If any of you had a hundred sheep, and one of them was lost; would you not leave the ninety and nine and go look for the one that was lost in the wilderness?[145] *When you found the one that was lost, you would put it on your shoulder.*[397]

You would come home rejoicing that you had found the lost sheep.

You would call your friends and neighbors and ask them to rejoice with you because you had found your lost sheep" (Luke 15:4-6, *FPB*).[396]

Then to make sure that the Pharisees heard what He was saying, Jesus told them,

"There is more joy in heaven when one of these sinners repents and comes to the Father than over ninety and nine just people who feel they do not have to repent" (Luke 15:7, *ELT*).

Jesus was not finished telling stories! He wanted the people to understand that He came looking for the needy and offering help to those that could not help themselves. So Jesus told another story,

"A woman had ten pieces of silver that she had received as a wedding gift. One piece was lost in the house. It fell into a crack and was covered in dust.

When she lost the one piece of silver, she lit a candle and swept the house diligently until she found the one piece.[145]

Then she called her friends and neighbors telling them how happy she was that she had found the piece. She asked them to rejoice with her" (Luke 15:8–10, *ELT*).[397]

Note that the coin was lost at home, where the sheep was lost in the wilderness. Those closest to our home can be lost as well as those who are lost in the wilderness of this world.

Jesus finished His stories by telling the people that the Father who loves all will rejoice when one repents and is found.[397]

Talk About the Story: How were the two stories Jesus told alike? How were they different? What did Jesus want people to learn about God through His stories? What was her reaction?

Scripture: "God in heaven rejoices in the presence of the angels over one sinner who repents." Luke 15:10, *ELT*

Family Time: Who is happy when sinners repent? Why do you think God wants each lost person to be found?

Prayer: Father, thank You for wanting each of us to be part of Your family. I will rejoice with You when my family and friends begin following Jesus. Amen.

PSALM 44
WHEN REMEMBERING THE GOOD OLD DAYS

God's people have always thought about the good old days, times when people were more spiritual and God seemed to be working more than He is at present. That was true of Israel during the Babylonian captivity.

Because God's people lost their love for God, they began living like the ungodly nations around them. They lost their desire to go to the Temple for worship and they didn't give as much to God. They let sin creep into their lives. Finally, they began worshiping the idols and gods of the heathen around them. God punished them. Nebuchadnezzar destroyed Jerusalem, burned the Temple, and took all the contents of the Temple to Babylon. Then Nebuchadnezzar took all the inhabitants captive to Babylon.

Psalm 44 is a cry of God's people when they remembered the days when God was active among them. The captives in Babylon prayed,

> *"Lord, we've heard all our lives,*
> *Our fathers told us about Your great work,*
> *And their fathers told them what You did.*
> *How you destroyed all the godless people,[192]*
> *And You gave the Promised Land to our ancestors.[517]*
> *It was not our father's mighty sword,*
> *It was Your miracles that gave them the land."[493]*

www.thefamilyprayerbible.com

Their fathers trusted God for a great victory. By faith and obedience to the Lord they experienced great victories that brought great glory to Him. But the captives sang about their current situation.

> *"Now we are tossed aside in dishonor;*
> *Our armies no longer have any victory.*
> *We were beaten in battle*
> *And our enemies have plundered our homes.*[1]
> *We have been butchered like cattle,*
> *We have been scattered among the nations."*

Those in captivity tell God about their miserable conditions as slaves to the heathen. Yet in their slavery, they have not forgotten God.

> *"Lord, even though You punished our fathers for their sins,*
> *We have not forgotten Your name.*
> *Our hearts have not departed from Your ways,*[205]
> *Yet we are suffering every day.*
> *We have been faithful to You;*
> *We do not deserve all this suffering."*[216]

The people in captivity began praying for revival. They wanted God to do for them what He did many generations ago. That is the prayer that many Christian families should make.

> *"Lord, wake up and help us in our problems,*
> *Do not turn Your back on Your people.*
> *We need You to work in Your people,*
> *To revive us to do Your work again.*[175]
> *Do not ignore our suffering and depression.*
> *We humbly ask for Your grace and power.*
> *Come revive us with Your power and presence,*
> *We need Your love!"*[484]

Talk About the Psalm: What did you learn about the psalm writer in this story? What did you learn about God?

Psalm 44: Read this week's psalm in your Bible together. Choose a verse to read aloud as a prayer.

Prayer: Thank You, God, for the psalm prayers in the Bible. Thank You for teaching us about You and about how to pray. In Jesus' name, amen.

THE PRODIGAL SON

Scripture: Luke 15:11-32
Place: Perea
Time: Winter, 30 AD

Jesus often taught through parables, stories with deeper meanings. Some Pharisees had been criticizing Jesus for eating with sinners and outcasts. So Jesus told this story.

"A certain man had two sons. The younger of them demanded his portion of his inheritance, 'I want it right now, not when I get older.' The father gave him his share.

The younger son went into a different country[29] and spent all he had on his friends and pleasure.[171] Then a famine hit the country.

When the son ran out of money, he went to his friends, but they would not take care of him.[57] He found a job slopping pigs. He became so hungry he ate the garbage that he was feeding the pigs. That brought him to his senses.[440]

He realized that his father had many hired servants who had three meals a day,[229] and here he was starving. He said, 'I will arise and go to my father and

beg him to hire me saying, "I have sinned against you and heaven. May I become one of your hired servants?" '[449]

As he was coming to his father's house, his father saw him a long way off,[292] had compassion on him, ran and kissed him, and embraced him warmly.[361] The son said, 'I don't deserve to be called your son; give me a job as a servant in your house.'

The father told his servants to quickly put a robe on him, a ring on his finger, and shoes on his feet.[270] Then the father commanded the fattest calf be barbequed.[397] 'Let's celebrate the return of my son,' saying, 'My son was dead but is alive again; he was lost but now is found.'[293]

The older brother was working faithfully in the field. He heard the festivities and was furious that the father gave a banquet for the younger son who had squandered his money.

The older brother would not go into the banquet; therefore, the father came to him[90] and said, 'All these years you have had everything.' The older son said to the father, 'I have obeyed your commandments.[327] I have never grieved you, but as soon as my brother comes home, you give him a feast.'

The father explained, 'We should be glad. For your brother was dead, and is now alive; was lost, and is now found'" (Luke 15:11-32, ELT).[396]

The prodigal son is a picture of these outcasts who were coming to Jesus. The older son who criticized the returning prodigal is a picture of scribes and Pharisees. The father of the two sons is a picture of the heart of God the Father for seeking and finding lost sinners.

Jesus wanted His listeners to understand that no one, no matter how good they are, deserves the Father's love. He loves because He has chosen to! And He rejoices whenever any of His children return to Him.

Talk About the Story: Why did Jesus tell this parable? What did the prodigal son do that was wrong? What did he do right? How did the Father react? How did the older brother react?

Scripture: "For the wages of sin *is* death, but the gift of God *is* eternal life in Christ Jesus our Lord." Romans 6:23

Family Time: What can we learn about our heavenly Father from this parable? What can we learn about ourselves?

Prayer: Father, thank You for forgiving all sins of all people. Thank You for receiving big sinners and for receiving people like me. I rejoice with You and all people who repent and turn to You. Amen.

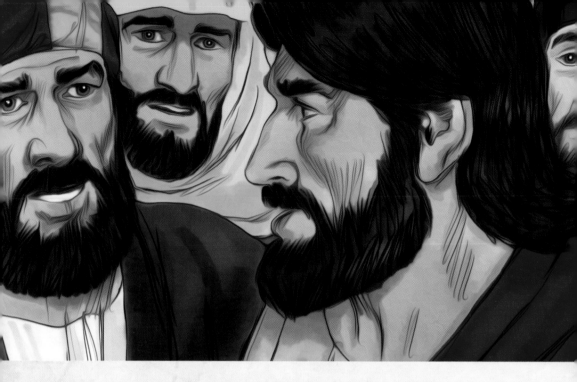

NEWS OF LAZARUS' DEATH

Scripture: John 11:1–27
Place: East Bank of Jordan
Time: January, 30 AD

Flames crackled from the small fire of dead vines and pinecones. Jesus and the twelve huddled around a small flame for warmth; January, 30 AD was especially bitter. They had been up in the high ground of the Moab hills for what seemed like a long time, although they had been there only a few weeks.

"Someone's coming," a disciple announced. The messenger was arriving from Bethany, a hard two day's walk from Jerusalem. Jesus immediately recognized the servant of Mary and Martha; His dear friends who lived outside Jerusalem.[292]

"Lazarus is sick," the servant anxiously spoke to Jesus in low tones. "Mary and Martha want you to come immediately."

"Lazarus is not sick to death," Jesus told the servant. "Lazarus is sick for the glory of God," Jesus added.[188]

"What shall I tell Mary and Martha?" the servant inquired.

"Tell them that God will be glorified through this," Jesus answered.

During the next two days Jesus did not discuss Lazarus' sickness with the twelve.[107] He explained to His disciples that it was necessary for Him to go to Jerusalem,[118] to suffer at the hands of the authorities, be crucified, and on the third day rise again. Even as Jesus explained what would happen, the disciples didn't understand what He meant.

Two mornings later, Jesus said, "We are going to Bethany."

"Not now," the disciples argued. They reminded Jesus that just recently the Jews had tried to kill Him!

But Jesus simply told the twelve, "There are twelve hours of daylight in which to walk. If we walk in the light, we won't stumble."[283]

The twelve pulled their tunics tightly around themselves to keep warm. Jesus felt they needed further explanation about events that were to unfold. He explained, "Lazarus is sleeping." Then He said, "We are going to Bethany so I can wake him out of his sleep."[405]

One of the disciples said, "If Lazarus is sleeping, perhaps it will help him get well."[506]

But that is not the kind of sleeping Jesus was talking about. "Lazarus is dead,"[99] Jesus plainly said.

The disciples were stunned. They had seen Jesus calm the storm, heal a leper, and give sight to the blind. But Jesus had not tried to heal Lazarus!

"I am glad for your sakes I was not there to heal him," Jesus explained. "If I would have healed him, you would have thought this just another miracle."[259]

Jesus and the disciples walked up from the Jordan River, into the mountains of Judea toward Jerusalem. As they drew closer, they sent a message ahead of them to tell Mary and Martha that Jesus was coming.

Shortly, Martha came running down the path toward Jesus. Her solemn face revealed she had shed many tears. She ran to Jesus, fell at His feet and without even greeting Him, blurted out, "Lord, if you had been here, my brother would not have died!"[504]

Martha didn't understand the good thing that Jesus was about to do. She didn't know that her sorrow would not last long at all! Martha was about to learn that she could trust Jesus' love for her even when things seem completely hopeless!

Talk About the Story: Why did the disciples not want Jesus to go to Jerusalem? Who were Mary and Martha? What did Jesus say about time? What did Jesus say after two days?

Scripture: "'For my thoughts are not your thoughts, neither are your ways my ways,' declares the Lord." Isaiah 55:8

Family Time: Jesus knew what would happen, but didn't tell His disciples. God has a plan for our life, but we don't always know about of time what is going to happen. How can we trust God when we don't understand what He is doing?

Prayer: Lord, thank You that You know all things. Help me to follow You and trust You even when difficult things happen. Amen.

HEALING LAZARUS

Scripture: John 11:18-44
Place: Bethany
Time: January, 29 AD

Jesus had the power to keep Lazarus from dying, but He did not do it. Martha knew He had the power to keep Lazarus from dying, but Jesus did not come to heal him, nor did Jesus heal Lazarus from a long distance away.[107]

Martha looked up at Jesus, "Even though You were not here to heal Lazarus," she said, "God will give You whatever You ask."[400]

"Your brother will arise again," Jesus responded.[405]

Martha misunderstood what Jesus meant. "I know my brother shall rise in the future Resurrection Day."[126]

"I am the Resurrection and the Life, those who believe in Me, though they die, yet shall they live.[405] Whosoever believes in Me, shall never die." Then looking at Martha, Jesus asked, "Do you believe this?"[504]

Martha answered, "I believe that You are the Christ, the Son of God, the Promised Messiah for whom we looked."[34]

With hope rising in her heart, Martha ran off to tell her sister Mary that Jesus had arrived. But Jesus waited there on the path.

As soon as Mary heard Martha's whispered message, she jumped up and came hurrying down the path toward Jesus.[72] The professional mourners followed her because they thought she was going to the grave to weep.[313]

When she reached Jesus, Mary said, "If You had been here, my brother would not have died."

Jesus saw her deep sorrow. He felt the sorrow as well. But Jesus simply asked, "Where is the body?"[259]

Mary led the way into a narrow valley filled with limestone caves. Many of these caves had been fashioned into tombs. As Jesus approached the tomb of Lazarus, He stopped and wept.[293]

Someone in the crowd saw His tears and said, "Behold how Jesus loved Lazarus!"[296]

Then out of the crowd came an unknown voice, "This man opened the eyes of the blind. Why didn't He stop Lazarus from dying?"[504]

Jesus was filled with sorrow as He said, "Take away the stone."

But the body stinks!" Martha protested. "He's been in the grave four days!"[479] All the mourners were thinking the same thing!

But Jesus said, "If you would believe, you would see the glory of God."[188]

So Martha agreed. Several young men worked together to move the stone blocking the tomb entrance. Just as Martha had predicted, the strong stench of rotting flesh seeped out of the cave. Looking through the dark shadows where death held the body, they saw the body, wrapped in white sheets that had been anointed with oil.

Then in front of all of them, Jesus lifted His face to heaven and prayed, "Father, I thank You that You have always heard My prayer."[257] Then with a loud voice Jesus commanded, "LAZARUS, COME FORTH!"[493]

At Jesus' words, the body that had been carried lovingly into the cave and carefully placed on a rocky ledge, came out of the cave.

"Take the grave clothes off him," Jesus commanded. Quickly, several young men ran to Lazarus, unwrapping the cloths that had been wound about his body.

Talk About the Story: What did Mary and Martha say about Jesus not coming before Lazarus died? Why did Jesus weep? How did Jesus raise the dead? What do you think happened next?

Scripture: "Hear my prayer, O LORD, Give ear to my supplications! In Your faithfulness answer me, *and* in Your righteousness." Psalm 143:1

Family Time: How can knowing the truth of this story help us trust Jesus more than we do? What are some important prayer requests you are waiting for God to answer?

Prayer: Father, thank You that Jesus raised Lazarus from the dead. Help us to trust You when it seems that You are taking too long to give us what we need. We know that You are good and that You do all things well. Amen.

DATE ___/___

MANY RESPONSES TO JESUS

Scripture: John 11:45–57
Place: Jerusalem
Time: Winter, 30 AD

Jesus raised Lazarus from the dead. What a spectacular miracle! Can you imagine how the crowd responded and what they thought? They all knew that Lazarus had been dead for four days. They knew his body had been anointed for burial, wrapped in grave clothes, and placed in a tomb. They knew the tomb was sealed.

Then they heard the words of Jesus to unseal and open the tomb. They heard Jesus shout, "COME FORTH!" Then they saw with their own eyes Lazarus come out of the grave.[281]

"Therefore many of the Jews who had come to visit Mary, and had seen what Jesus did, believed in him.[405] *But some of them went to the Pharisees and told them what Jesus had done"* (John 11:45, 46, *ELT*).[504]

Many believed in their heart that Jesus raised Lazarus from the dead. They believed Jesus could do this because He is God's one and only Son. They chose to follow Jesus.

Some saw that Jesus had raised a man from the dead but didn't become His disciples.

Still others refused to believe that Jesus was really from God, perhaps thinking He raised the dead by some other power; or perhaps it was a charade. There are skeptics like those today who try to explain away the miracles of the Bible. They reject Jesus, the Miracle-Worker, so Jesus cannot do in their life the miracles of salvation.[189]

After Jesus raised Lazarus from the dead, the crowd dispersed to tell their story, each in their own way. Some who saw it hurried to Jerusalem to warn the Sanhedrin and the High Priest, "Jesus is a threat! He'll get all the Jews to follow Him."[334]

The priests were not worried primarily about losing their jobs, or even losing the crowds. They had a pragmatic worry, one of the priests suggested, "Jesus will whip the crowd into a frenzy to attack the Roman soldiers; we will all perish in a fight with Rome."

That was it! They were really afraid of losing everything. Caiaphas, the High Priest reminded the priests of a well-known Jewish proverb, "It is better that one man should die, than the whole nation perish." *Yes*, they all thought, *it is better for Jesus to die than allow the Romans to slaughter multitudes of His fanatical followers*.[478] Caiaphas was justifying a judicial murder. He was suggesting they get rid of Jesus. They wouldn't actually kill Jesus; they would get Rome to execute Jesus for them. Jesus should be eliminated by Roman justice.[139]

Caiaphas didn't know that he was part of God's plan for Jesus. God planned that Jesus would die for the nation as a substitute for the sins of the world. Caiaphas simply wanted to plot Jesus' death as a way to handle an immediate crisis.

Talk About the Story: Did everyone believe who saw the miracle of Jesus raising Lazarus from the dead? How did God use Caiaphas in His plan for salvation?

Scripture: "It is expedient for us that one man should die for the people, and not that the whole nation should perish." John 11:50

Family Time: According to what God intended, what was the result of what Caiaphas said in John 11:50? How did Jesus' death bring our salvation? The religious leaders rejected Jesus. What can we do to demonstrate God's love to people who reject Jesus?

Prayer: Father, thank You that Jesus died for the whole world, and for me. I pray for people who only know about Jesus, but haven't asked Jesus to come in their heart. I pray they will be saved. Amen.

CHAPTER 14

HEADING TO JERUSALEM

The Jerusalem area posed a danger to Jesus. Although He was aware He would die in Jerusalem, He was concerned about God's timing in His life and knew His hour had not yet come (cf. John 2:4; 12:23). "Therefore Jesus no longer walked openly among the Jews, but went from there into the country near the wilderness, to a city called Ephraim, and there remained with His disciples" (John 11:54). Ephraim was located in what was known in earlier days as the "hill country," and situated high in the mountains.

After a brief stay in Ephraim, Jesus began His final journey to Jerusalem. The most direct route to that city was south, but Jesus still had much to do. In each of the regions He visited on His way to Jerusalem, He found people in need and took time to address their concerns and heal their suffering. Jesus passed through the city of Jericho, apparently for the first and last time during His years of public ministry. Even in that city a couple of individuals found salvation in Jesus.

TEN MEN WITH LEPROSY HEALED

Scripture: Luke 17:11–37
Place: Ephraim, on the border between Samaria and Israel
Time: Winter, 30 AD

While people in Jerusalem were buzzing over Lazarus' resurrection, Jesus and His disciples headed north through the hill country, staying for a while in the city of Ephraim, on the border between Samaria and Galilee. Ephraim is surrounded by green hills and rolling pastures, separated by broken rock walls. Tall Mount Gilboa is within sight.

Leaving Ephraim, a large crowd followed Jesus from village to village—some followed only a short way—others were permanent followers of Jesus. In each village, Jesus healed the sick and taught them the Word of God.[435]

Up ahead, ten men with leprosy living in small temporary shacks outside the village were waiting for Jesus. When they saw Him coming, the ten men began yelling from afar, "JESUS! MASTER! HAVE MERCY ON US."[304]

The men with leprosy came to the edge of the road, holding their hands out, continually begging, "Have mercy on us." In strictest compliance with Jewish law, the men remained outside the village and they remained far from Jesus. Without touching them, or even commanding them to be healed, Jesus said, "Go show yourselves to the priest and be healed."[327]

On one occasion Jesus had done the unthinkable, He touched a man with leprosy to heal him. On another occasion, Jesus healed a man by commanding the leprosy to be cleaned.[214] But Jesus didn't do either for these ten men with leprosy. Jesus told them to go to the priests to be healed.[327] The Jewish Law required a person with leprosy who was healed to be observed by a priest for ten days; then the priest would pronounce to the village that the person was in fact healed. Only then, could they re-enter society.

The ten men obeyed, turning to begin their journey to find a priest. They began walking before they actually experienced healing. As they began their journey, new life flooded through their bodies, healing spread over their skin and the leprous sores began to disappear.

Full of joy and excitement, nine men with leprosy quickened their steps to find a priest. The one Samaritan among the ten turned back and ran to Jesus.[363]

He fell at Jesus' feet, "GLORY TO GOD!"[482]

With his face to the ground, his tears splashed on the ground. The disease on his skin was gone. He no longer had to remain cut off from the village and his family. He was healed both physically and spiritually.

Jesus asked, "Were there not ten men with leprosy cleansed?" Jesus looked down the road but didn't see the others returning; then said, "Where are the nine?"[238]

Jesus told the man what a priest would have said, "Rise, go your way. Your faith has healed you."[188]

Talk About the Story: Where was Jesus when He healed the 10 men with leprosy? What did they expect of Jesus? Jesus healed in different ways, how did He heal the 10 men? What did only one of them do? How did the story end?

Scripture: "And He said to him, 'Arise, go your way. Your faith has made you well.'" Luke 17:19

Family Time: The Samaritan man with leprosy was thankful for Jesus' healing. What are some things you are most thankful for? What can you do to give glory to God for the good things He has done for you?

Prayer: Father, I thank You for the compassion of Jesus that healed the men with leprosy, and that one came back to express gratitude. I am grateful for all You have done for me. Like the one man who returned, I glorify You for saving me, blessing me, and guiding my life. Amen.

CHILDREN SURROUND JESUS

Scripture: Mark 10:13–16
Place: Perea, East of the Jordan River
Time: Winter, 30 AD

The winter of AD 30 swept into Israel from the eastern mountains. Even the eastern road was empty of caravans. Jesus and the twelve passed through the bare villages un-noticed, they enjoyed their solitude. Up ahead was a little village off the beaten path, nestled among white rocks on the top of the hill.[443]

Jesus stopped to rest in the shade of a sycamore tree. Shortly a crowd was heard laughing and shouting, "JESUS! JESUS!" children came running down a mountain path shouting His name.

The children discovered He was there. Maybe they recognized His disciples. Whatever the reason, Jesus was glad to receive the children.[296]

"Blessed are you," Jesus placed His hands on the heads of the children, then looking into heaven He prayed for them.

"Touch my child," a mother pleaded. She had followed her children, wanting Jesus to bless her child.[43]

"Mine, too!"

The disciples were irritated at the children and parents. They began pulling them away, telling the parents to take their children and go away. "BACK UP CHILDREN!" Peter yelled at them. "GET BACK," he sternly ordered.

"Stop!" Jesus ordered. "Don't forbid children to come to Me, for the way they love Me is how all people should come to Me."[90]

The children calmed down because Jesus was no longer talking to them. Jesus talked to the adults standing there. Jesus waved His hands at the children and said, "I want everyone to come to Me, like these children come to Me," Jesus explained. "Children come openly, expectantly, happily. They want Me to bless them. If a person doesn't receive the kingdom of God as little children, "Jesus explained, "that person shall in no wise enter God's presence."[416]

This was a good opportunity to explain the spiritual nature of His ministry. Jesus said, "My kingdom will be a happy place.[213] I have not come to fight, kill and drive people away, as some want Me to drive Rome from our land. I have come to rule from within; I want to sit on the throne of the hearts of people. This is not the time for Me to sit on a king's throne in Jerusalem."[18]

Jesus explained, "The kingdom is within you, and when I enter your life, I will influence life around you through My followers."

Again Jesus pointed to the children. "Everyone must become like these little children. Children are trusting, they laugh and sing. My followers will be like that. Children want to learn, that's the way you'll be as you follow Me."[204]

Then Jesus began—one after another—to pick up children and bless each one. The children were obedient, waiting their turn. Jesus reminded everyone that the word "blessed" meant "happy." When a person was blessed, value was added to their life. They had a new purpose to live for God.[279]

Talk About the Story: How did the children receive Jesus? Who tried to hold back the children? What was Jesus' response to children? How did Jesus describe His kingdom?

Scripture: "Let the little children come to Me, and do not forbid them; for of such is the kingdom of God. Assuredly, I say to you, whoever does not receive the kingdom of God as a little child will by no means enter it." Mark 10:14–15

Family Time: What do children like to do? How do parents make children happy? How does the heavenly Father make us happy? How can you trust God like a little child trusts his parents?

Prayer: Father, I come to You simply as a child. I love You because You are my Father, and I thank You for taking care of me in so many ways. Amen.

PSALM 46
GOD, OUR REFUGE

The Israelites were scared to death. The Egyptian army had 600 chariots and were ready to attack from behind. They were still mad over the 10 plagues God used to punish their nation. Israel was hemmed in. There were steep mountains on both sides, and the Red Sea in front of them. When everything was lost, Moses lifted the rod and the waters began to part. God used a mighty wind to push back the waters. Then a way appeared on the bottom of the sea, dry land. Moses pointed again with his rod and Israel walked across to safety.

When all Israel was safe, the waters returned to drown the Egyptian army. God's people were safe at last.

Moses sat down to write the Psalm of gratitude for deliverance. Later it was a Psalm sung each year on the anniversary of the day Israel crossed the Red Sea.

But it was not a congregational song. The Sons of Korah (a choir known for intimacy with God) was chosen to sing it to God. The word Alameth suggests a high pitch, meaning it was sung in a high key or sung by tenors.

Moses gave thanks for deliverance.

"God, You are our refuge and protection;
You always come to our rescue when danger threatens.[377]
We will not be afraid when earthquakes come,
Nor when mountains fall into the sea;
When the roaring waters threaten to drown us,
Nor when the ground under us shakes.[57]
God, You have rivers of water that give life to the city.
That's where Your holy sanctuary is located.[377]
Lord, You live in the middle of Your holy city
And You send us help, early in the morning."[104]

All night long the winds blew the water of the Red Sea back. In the morning light, everyone saw the way through the sea to the other side. It is here Moses thanked God, "You sent us help, early in the morning." This Psalm also mentions "the heathen raging," which is a reference to the Egyptian army.

"The heathen rage and curse in their chaos,
Their army is being crushed by God's punishment.
God's voice thunders, and the earth shakes.
The Lord's army fights for us;
He will defeat our enemies and give victory."[393]

A few days before the Red Sea, all Israel celebrated the first Passover. This is a picture of Jesus' death on the cross. Three days later, Israel was delivered from death. They walked through the sea—certain death—to the other side. Therefore this Psalm was read on the day Jesus rose from the dead. It is a picture of Jesus' deliverance over death.

Talk About the Psalm: What did you learn about the psalm writer in this story? What did you learn about God?

Psalm 46: Read this week's psalm in your Bible together. Choose a verse to read aloud as a prayer.

Prayer: Thank You, God, for the psalm prayers in the Bible. Thank You for teaching us about You and about how to pray. In Jesus' name, Amen.

THE RICH YOUNG RULER

Scripture: Luke 18:18–30
Place: Perea, east of the Jordan River
Time: Winter, 30 AD

As Jesus talked with others, a young man approached. "Good Master," he said, "what must I do to inherit eternal life?"[416]

Jesus could see that this young man was not trying to start an argument or make himself look important. He really wanted to know the truth.

"Why do you call Me good?" Jesus asked. "There is only one good person that is God."[60]

The man's robe was elegant and expensive. Clearly this young man was very rich. "You know the commandments God has given." Jesus said. "You must not commit adultery, kill, or steal."

"I have never done any of these."

"And don't forget the other commandments to honor your father and mother, not defraud others, and keep all the Law."[425]

"All these things I have observed since I was a child," the rich young man answered.[327]

www.thefamilyprayerbible.com

Jesus silently stared at him for a moment. Jesus knew the man's heart. He knew what was keeping the man from putting God first in his life. "There is one thing you lack," Jesus said.

"Tell me," the young man pleaded. "Quickly, tell me what I must do?"

"Go sell everything that you have." Jesus waited for a moment to let His commandment sink in, "and give the money away to poor people, then come and follow me."[412]

The young man was stunned. He looked down to the ground and didn't answer. The rich young man had accumulated much in property and wealth. His wealth had become more important to him than God.[428]

The young man shook his head. He wrestled with the decision of whether to follow Jesus or to continue following the path of money. Then with a sudden move, the young man turned and walked away.[75]

Jesus watched sadly as the young man walked away. Then Jesus called to the twelve, "It is difficult for people who have money to enter the kingdom of God."[310]

People who value money have a hard time trusting God and putting Him first in their lives. Jesus said, "It is easier for a camel to squeeze through a needle's eye than a rich man to get into heaven."[399]

"Who then can be saved?" Peter blurted out his thoughts.[416]

"Anyone can be saved," Jesus said. "Things that are impossible with men are always possible with God."[356]

"We have given everything up to follow You!"[428] Peter exclaimed.

Jesus smiled at him. "When a person gives up homes, parents, friends, family and even money for the kingdom of God, they shall receive multiple dividends in the next life."

Talk About the Story: What did the rich young man want to know? What did Jesus tell him to do? How did he respond?

Scripture: "But He said, "The things which are impossible with men are possible with God." Luke 18:27

Family Time: What are some things that people tend to think are more important than following Jesus? What about you? What would Jesus say is getting in the way of your relationship with Him? What change can you make this week to put Jesus first in your life?

Prayer: Father, I want You to be most important in my life. I want to live for You. Please help me to see the things that get in the way of my relationship with You. Help me to make changes that will honor You. Amen.

WHO'S NUMBER ONE?

Scripture: Matthew 20:20–28
Place: Perea, east of the Jordan River
Time: Winter, 30 AD

As they were preparing to go up into Jerusalem, Jesus wanted to prepare His disciples for what was soon going to happen. So He pulled them aside and said,

"*Behold, we are going up to Jerusalem, and the Son of Man will be betrayed to the chief priests and to the scribes; and they will condemn Him to death, and deliver Him to the Gentiles to mock and to scourge and to crucify. And the third day He will rise again.*"[260]

This was the third time Jesus had explained this to His disciples, but He knew they still didn't understand completely. He knew they would be frightened and confused when He died on the cross. But Jesus was patient with them and continued to help them understand.

As they continued their journey, the mother of James and John came to Jesus and worshiped Him. Then she said she wanted to Jesus to do something for her.[21]

"What is it?" Jesus answered.

"Grant that these two sons of mine may sit, one on Your right hand and the other on the left, in Your kingdom."[23]

Jesus answered her, "You don't know what you are asking for." Then Jesus turned to James and John, who were with her. "Are you able to drink the cup of suffering that I shall drink, and are you willing to die as I am willing to die?"

Both James and John answered, "We are able to do that."[349]

Jesus knew that they still did not understand what they were saying. But He also knew all that the future held for them. So Jesus said to them, "You shall drink of My cup and you shall be baptized with My death, but I can't give you the right to sit on the right or left hand. It shall be the choice of My Father in heaven."[465]

The other ten disciples heard it and they were angry with James and John.[84] They thought James and John were trying to be more important than they were.

Jesus answered them and said, "In an earthly kingdom men fight over greatness and honor,[27] but it shall not be among you that follow Me. Whoever wants to be the greatest among you, let him be the servant of the others."[428]

Then Jesus gave Himself as an example, "Even so the Son of Man did not come to have people minister to Him, but to minister and give His life a ransom for many."[260]

Talk About the Story: What did Jesus tell His disciples about for the third time? What did James and John want Jesus to do for them? Why? What did Jesus tell them?

Scripture: "The Son of Man did not come to be served, but to serve, and to give His life a ransom for many." Matthew 20:28

Family Time: What example of leadership did Jesus give us? How can you serve others this week?

Prayer: Lord, keep me from being proud and always wanting first place in everything I do. Teach me to be humble as Jesus was humble, and teach me to follow Him as I should do. Amen.

TWO BLIND MEN

Scripture: Matthew 20:29–34; Luke 18:35–43
Place: Jericho
Time: March, 30 AD

Jesus and His disciples crossed the Jordan River and headed for the outskirts of Jericho. Jericho was a lush green island in an otherwise dry sandy valley.

Herod had built a palace there, and a large amphitheater to entertain the people. And he had planted splendid gardens surrounded by tall, stately royal palms. It was beautiful!

The rich gathered in this oasis for winter holidays. Health fanatics came for healing in the hot springs. Businessmen came seeking their fortune. Roman soldiers were stationed there to keep order. Actually, there were two Jerichos; the new Jericho was made up of new homes and palaces. It is where most people lived. The old Jericho was a large pile of rubble, the old fortress that had been destroyed on several occasions. Only the poor and outcasts lived there.[218]

Jesus left the new city and headed to the old section of town. As Jesus left the lush, green pastures of new Jericho, there at the gate was a blind man named Bartimaeus.[435] Each day Bartimaeus came to the gate along with another friend to beg. Being on the main Roman highway, it was an ideal place to make a living; at least an ideal place for a blind man.[388]

Bartimaeus heard the tramp of many people coming. Bartimaeus knew that this great crowd was excited and he could tell by the pitched fervency of their voices that they were escorting some great individual.

"Who's there?" blind Bartimaeus asked vaguely, not knowing who would answer. "Who's coming with the crowd?"

"Jesus," was the only answer he got.

Bartimaeus had heard the stories about the lepers being healed, about the lame walking. He began to cry, "Jesus, Son of David! Have mercy on me!"[263]

As Bartimaeus began to cry, the blind man next to him joined in, their voices barely heard above the pitched fever of the crowd, "Jesus, Son of David! Have mercy on us!"[258]

The crowd following Jesus tried to quiet them. Some yelled at them to "SHUT UP!" But the blind men yelled even louder until Jesus heard them.

Jesus stopped and said, "Bring the men to me." They quickly left their coats and came to Jesus. When they got to Jesus, He asked, "What do you want Me to do for you?"[52]

Bartimaeus, the spokesman, asked, "Will You heal our eyes so we can see?"[214]

Jesus loved them and respected their boldness to yell out for healing. He touched their eyes. They received their sight[53] and both began immediately to follow Jesus.

Talk About the Story: Who called out to Jesus? What did they want from Jesus? What did they do? What was Jesus' response? How did He heal them?

Scripture: "And he cried out, saying, 'Jesus, Son of David, have mercy on me!'" Luke 18:38

Family Time: When are some times you have needed mercy from God? How does Jesus' response to the blind men encourage you?

Prayer: Father, thank You for being merciful to us in forgiving us and giving us what we need. Thank You for loving us. In Jesus' name, Amen.

ZACCHAEUS

Scripture: Luke 19:1–10
Place: Jericho
Time: Early spring, 30 AD

As Jesus entered Jericho, a great crowd gathered around Him. Word about Jesus passed from mouth to mouth, and so the people hung on the walls to look down upon Jesus, others lined the highway two and three deep on both sides of the street. The narrow streets of Jericho were lined on each side with walls, walls to protect gardens, flowers, plants and luscious fruit. Sycamore trees graced the edge of the highway, reaching their covering branches over the streets to give shade.

People were curious about Jesus; a few were sincerely seeking salvation. Mothers held their children high above the crowd just to catch a glimpse of Jesus; some wanted their children to touch Jesus. A wall of onlookers were waiting for Jesus, in back of them was a solid wall of stone.

Zacchaeus came out of his tax office, he wanted to see Jesus. He was curious about this Rabbi who preached about the kingdom of God. Zacchaeus couldn't see Jesus because there were so many people in front of him wanting to see Him. He couldn't see over the crowd so he ran to find a clearing to see Jesus, but there were no openings.[31]

www.thefamilyprayerbible.com

For a man who was very rich, he could buy anything; but he couldn't find a place to see Jesus. And to make the situation worse, Zacchaeus was very short.

If Zacchaeus had only been curious, he might have returned to his tax office. But, there was a flicker of faith burning in the candle of his life. He thought, *I must see Jesus!*

Seeing a sycamore tree down the road, he quickly ran ahead and climbed its branches to look out over the crowd.[76]

Jesus walked down the garden road smiling at people, talking with them. As He walked underneath the sycamore tree where Zacchaeus had climbed, Jesus stopped. His searching eyes saw more than others. He saw more than a short tax collector sitting in a tree, He saw a heart hanging onto faith.

"Zacchaeus," Jesus knew his name because Jesus knew everything, "come down from your tree," Jesus instructed him.

Zacchaeus, was suddenly self-conscious. Everyone was looking at him. For a short man always striving to be someone, this was the first time people looked up to him. Jesus announced, "Today I am going to eat at your house."[72]

There was tremendous excitement in Zacchaeus' household when he brought Jesus and the disciples home for the evening meal. In contrast, Others in town were upset. They angrily said, "Jesus has gone to eat in the house of a notorious sinner!"

But meeting Jesus made Zacchaeus a different person. He announced, "From now on I will give half of my money to the poor, and if I have overcharged any-one for their taxes, I will give them back four times as much."[399]

Sometimes the sudden shock of meeting Jesus will change a life, so Zacchae-us the sinner became Zacchaeus the forgiven; Zacchaeus the thief became the generous giver of gifts. Jesus said to Zacchaeus, "This day salvation has come to your house." Then turning to the crowd, Jesus announced, "For the Son of Man is come to seek and save those who are lost."[415]

Talk About the Story: Describe the city of Jericho. Why would a short man climb a tree to see Jesus? What did Jesus say to Zacchaeus? What did Zacchaeus say about his money?

Scripture: "For the Son of Man has come to seek and to save that which was lost." Luke 19:10

Family Time: What does Jesus care about more than people acting like good people? Why?

Prayer: Father, thank You that Jesus loved all types of people and that He knows what's in the heart of people. Thank You that Jesus saw me, loved me, and called me to follow Him. Amen.

A PARABLE ABOUT FAITHFULNESS FOR MONEY

Scripture: Luke 19:12-27
Place: Zacchaeus' home in Jericho
Time: Early spring, 30 AD

Jesus had gone to the home of Zacchaeus for a meal. It was there Zacchaeus repented of his greed for money. The Pharisees criticized Jesus for going to Zacchaeus' home. Also many people thought that Jesus was going to Jerusalem to become king right away. In response Jesus used Zacchaeus as an occasion for a parable:

"A certain nobleman went into a far country to receive for himself a kingdom and to return.[74] *So he called ten of his servants, delivered to them ten minas (ten thousand dollars), and said to them, 'Do business till I come.'*[154] *But his citizens*

hated him, and sent a delegation after him, saying, 'We will not have this man to reign over us.'

"And so it was that when he returned, having received the kingdom, he then commanded these servants, to whom he had given the money, to be called to him, that he might know how much every man had gained by trading. Then came the first, saying, 'Master, your mina has earned ten minas.' And he said to him, 'Well done, good servant; because you were faithful in a very little, have authority over ten cities.' [27] And the second came, saying, 'Master, your mina has earned five minas.' Likewise he said to him, 'You also be over five cities.' [409]

"Then another came, saying, 'Master, here is your mina, which I have kept put away in a handkerchief. For I feared you, because you are an austere man. [275] You collect what you did not deposit, and reap what you did not sow.' And he said to him, 'Out of your own mouth I will judge you, you wicked servant. You knew that I was an austere man, collecting what I did not deposit and reaping what I did not sow. Why then did you not put my money in the bank, that at my coming I might have collected it with interest?' [76]

"And he said to those who stood by, 'Take the mina from him, and give it to him who has ten minas.' (But they said to him, 'Master, he has ten minas.') 'For I say to you, that to everyone who has will be given; and from him who does not have, even what he has will be taken away from him. But bring here those enemies of mine, who did not want me to reign over them, and slay them before me.'"

Jesus said that everyone who is faithful with the talents that God has given him will receive more. But those who won't use the talents or money he has, God will take them from him." [154]

Talk About the Story: Where did Jesus tell the parable? What was the occasion? What did Jesus want people to learn from this parable?

Scripture: "To those who use well what they are given, even more will be given. But from those who do nothing, even what little they have will be taken away." Luke 19:26

Family Time: What are some things you have learned about living for Jesus? What are some things that you have? These are all things God has given you. How can you use the things you know about Jesus to help others? How can you use the belongings you have to help others?

Prayer: Father, thank You for all the things I have, and thank You for everything that I have learned in life. I give all my things to You. Use them for Your glory. Thank You for everything I have learned; I give all my talent and knowledge to You. Use me for Your glory. Amen.

CHAPTER 15

THE SEVEN "I AM'S"

Our devotions for the next week will cover seven unique statements Jesus made about Himself. These all were spoken in the last year of Jesus' life, and they appear only in the Gospel of John. These seven statements are good Bible verses to learn.

I AM the Bread of Life – John 6:35
I AM the Light of the World – John 8:12
I AM the Door – John 10:9
I AM the Good Shepherd – John 10:11
I AM the Resurrection and the Life – John 11:25
I AM the Way, the Truth, and the Life – John 14:6
I AM the True Vine – John 15:1

I AM Who I AM – John 18:4

The number seven suggests perfection or completion. This means Jesus described Himself in a complete way. But then Jesus used an eighth description of Himself. When the soldiers arresting Him asked for His identity, Jesus said, "I AM." This Greek phrase, "ego εἰμί, suggests Jesus was identifying Himself with the Lord God of the Old Testament. When Moses prayed before the burning bush, he asked the Lord what was His name. God answered, "I AM Who I AM" (Exodus 3:14). So when Jesus used the seven I AMs, He was identifying Himself as the Lord of the Old Testament.

I AM THE BREAD OF LIFE

Scripture: John 6:22–36
Place: Mountain near the Sea of Galilee
Time: Before Passover, 29 AD

Just yesterday Jesus fed 5,000 men—plus women and children—with five loaves of bread and a few fish. The crowd wanted to make Jesus their king! But Jesus knew it wasn't His time, so He left and went off to pray.[18]

The crowd searched for Jesus on the hillside and then back in town. Finally, they found Him. "Jesus," they asked, "when did You get here?"[547] They knew He had stayed behind on the other side of the lake!

But Jesus simply answered, "You come looking for Me because your stomachs are filled."[547] Jesus still knew the thoughts of the crowd, so He told them, "Don't spend your valuable time seeking bread to eat; spend your energy searching for eternal life that I, the Son of Man, can give you."[281]

Then the crowd realized where the bread came from, so they asked, "How can we do the works that You do?"[195]

www.thefamilyprayerbible.com

Jesus answered them, "The work of God is believing on the One the Father has sent into the world."[34]

Yesterday the crowd had eaten the bread that was provided by a miracle. They had also seen Jesus heal people. But someone in the crowd said "Do another miracle for us so we can see Your works and believe in You."[79]

Another person in the crowd said, "Our Jewish ancestors ate bread that Moses gave them while journeying through the wilderness."[547]

Jesus answered, "Moses didn't give them bread, the Father in heaven fed them.[363] The true bread of God comes down from heaven to give life to the world."

The crowd was still thinking of physical bread to feed their bodies. So they asked, "Give us that bread so we can eat it every day."[34]

Jesus answered simply, "I am the Bread of Life, those who come to Me believing will never be hungry, and those who drink of Me will never be thirsty."[65]

But Jesus still knew what they were thinking because He told them, "You have seen Me and the works I do, yet you still do not believe in Me."[127]

Jesus used a metaphor when He called Himself *bread*. A metaphor is a rich word picture that gives truth in a picture. Jesus told them, "Physical strength and life you get from bread is a picture of spiritual life and strength you get from Me."[281]

Bread is probably the food most people share in common. Bread is the staple for most all people in all cultures, of all time. So Jesus is the Savior of the world, and He offers salvation to all people, of all cultures, for all time.[416]

God gave us physical hunger so that we will eat and get strength for our everyday life. But God also gave us spiritual hunger. We all want to know things like why we are alive and what we should do with our lives. The answers to our spiritual questions are found in a relationship with God.

Every time we eat physical food, we should thank God for the food that gives us strength and ask God to guide our life.[463]

Talk About the Story: What metaphor did Jesus use to describe Himself? What does bread do for us? How is Jesus like bread?

Scripture: "And Jesus said to them, 'I am the bread of life. He who comes to Me shall never hunger, and he who believes in Me shall never thirst.'" John 6:35

Family Time: What did Jesus mean when He called Himself, "I am the bread of life"? How does your relationship with Jesus give you strength in your life?

Prayer: Father, thank You for the food I eat each day. Please help the people in the world you do not have enough to eat. Thank You for Jesus, my spiritual bread. Make me strong in heart and character. May I serve You many way Amen.

PSALM 47
SONG FOR A CELEBRATION

This psalm was written by David after he brought the Ark of the Covenant into Jerusalem. It was a congregational psalm sung by the congregation, led by the sons of Korah who were a choir of singers. The people lined the road for miles just to get a look at the Ark. It was the box where God sat—it was called the mercy seat. When the people saw the Ark going into Jerusalem, they knew God's special presence was entering the city. Notice they sang,

"God has gone up to Jerusalem
Surrounded by the shouts of His worshipers.
The Lord enters with blaring trumpets;[290]
Sing praises loudly to God, sing praises.
Sing praises to our King, sing praises."[439]

In the above verse 6, the words "sing praises" are repeated four times. But it is not two words in Hebrew, it is one command. The sons of Korah were singing a command in one word, "YELL LOUDLY PRAISES!"

Every 20 feet the Ark stopped so the priest could sacrifice to God. They wanted the blood sacrifice to cover their ministry going up to Jerusalem. David went before the Ark dressed in priestly garb to dance mightily before God. There were trumpets blaring, different choirs singing and at times the people sang to God. It was a happy celebration.

> *"Join in everyone; clap your hands joyfully.*
>> *Shout praises to God from the bottom of your heart.*[542]
> *He is King over all the earth;*[93]
>> *All people will one day bow to Him.*
> *One day He will rule all nations.*
>> *He sent the sons of Jacob to the Promised Land*
>> *That will be the possession of His people."*[182]

This psalm was also sung when David crowned his son Solomon as the king to follow him. Today, many congregations around the world sing this psalm on Ascension Sunday. That's the day Jesus returned to heaven in His bodily form. Therefore we can sing,

> *"One day the rulers of the world will gather*
>> *With the children of Absolom to recognize their King.*[21]
> *The kings of the earth are powerful,*
>> *But our Lord soars above them all, He is the King."*[406]

Talk About the Psalm: What did you learn about the psalm writer in this story? What did you learn about God?

Psalm 47: Read this week's psalm in your Bible together. Choose a verse to read aloud as a prayer.

Prayer: Thank You, God, for the psalm prayers in the Bible. Thank You for teaching us about You and about how to pray. In Jesus' name, Amen.

I AM THE LIGHT OF THE WORLD

Scripture: John 8:12
Place: In the Temple
Time: Early Monday morning after the Feast of Tabernacles

Jesus finished talking to the woman caught in the very act of adultery. The religious leaders tried to trap Jesus, but couldn't. Jesus said to her, "Neither do I condemn you; go and sin no more" (John 8:11). Jesus shined the light of God's solution on the sin of the woman and the religious leaders. He announced, "I am the light of the world" (John 8:12).[283]

Why did Jesus say "I am the light" at that time? Perhaps Jesus was saying He was God's light to the religious leaders blinded by their hatred of Jesus.[374] Perhaps Jesus was saying He was the light of salvation to the woman's adultery. About that time the brilliant sun just broke over the hills surrounding Jerusalem.

Perhaps the Temple keepers had just lit the lights inside the Temple.

Jesus didn't say He was *a* light among all the heathen religions. Jesus didn't say He was the light for *some*, or He was the light for just you. No! Jesus said He was light for the world—for every person in the world, down to the least worthy.[166]

Do you realize light is absolutely necessary for existence? All animals and plant life absolutely depend on life-giving energy from the sun. Without light, plants die. Animals and humans eat plants that give energy. Plants also produce oxygen that is needed to breathe. If plants don't have light, our life-cycle collapses. Just as it is impossible to have physical life without light, it is impossible to have spiritual life without Jesus.

If you were in a dark room, what would you do? You would turn on a light. You wouldn't try to clean the room first. That wouldn't produce light. Worrying about it wouldn't produce light. No, you would turn on the light. When we have Jesus the Light at the center of our life, He guides us to clean up clean up our lives and overcome worry.[207]

Jesus said earlier in His ministry, "You are light to a darkened world" (Matthew 5:14, *ELT*).[283] Since we are followers of Jesus, we should shine His light into darkness. Since Jesus lives in our heart,[227] we should shine for Him everywhere we go, and in everything we do.

Yes, we must shine for Jesus in our family and in our church. But you don't need a flashlight in a room that is lit with bright ceiling lights. We need to shine for Jesus among our friends and fellow workers who don't know Him. There are many dark places in our world, so we must shine for Him everywhere.[527]

Talk About the Story: Why did Jesus refer to Himself as light? Why is light absolutely necessary? How does light give life to our physical world? How do we light up a dark room? How can we let Jesus' light shine in our world?

Scripture: "The Lord *is* my light and my salvation; Whom shall I fear? The Lord *is* the strength of my life; Of whom shall I be afraid?" Psalm 27:1

Family Time: How is Jesus our light? How can Jesus shine through us?

Prayer: Father, thank You for helping me understand the Scriptures and thank You for showing me how to live for You. I will be Your light to my family and friends so they can see Jesus and follow Him. Amen.

I AM THE DOOR OF LIFE

Scripture: John 10:7–9
Place: In the Temple
Time: October, 29 AD

Jesus had been talking to the religious leaders in the Temple at Jerusalem. They had just cast the blind man out of the Temple. That meant he no longer had access to the religious life of Israel. The blind man was out and the Jewish leaders were in. But honestly, who determined whether someone is welcomed in, or is excluded? Jesus not only directs people to the door of life, Jesus IS the door to eternal life.[203]

Jesus said, "I am the door of the sheepfold."[416] Everyone listening to Jesus knew what He meant. They had all seen a sheepfold, or enclosure for sheep. It usually had a high rock wall to keep predators out and the sheep in. Usually, there was an opening about three to five feet wide. After the sheep entered the sheepfold each evening, the shepherd slept in the opening. The shepherd was the gate.

www.thefamilyprayerbible.com

The sheep knew they were safe as long as the shepherd was their door. Wolves came to eat the sheep, and robbers came to steal the sheep. The shepherd was their protection.

Sometimes several sheep owners would hire a shepherd to protect the sheep at night. Jesus described him, "A hireling—one who does not own the sheep, sees the wolf coming and leaves the sheep and flees and the wolf catches the sheep" (John 10:12).[164]

Jesus was referring to the religious leaders who only served God for money. They could be religious leaders of Jesus' day or today. And the robbers referred to anyone who tries to take people away from following God.

Jesus protects us with His presence. Just as the shepherd lies in the door-way to protect his sheep, so Jesus said, "I lay down my life for the sheep" (John 10:15).[2] Jesus meant He died on the cross for our sins.

Notice what Jesus, the Door, does for us in life. When He is our door, we "go in and out and find pasture" (John 10:9).[203] That means Jesus the Shepherd protects us each day as we work or go to school.

There is another blessing by having Jesus guard the door to our life. "I have come that they may have life, and that they may have it more abundantly" (John 10:10).[72] What is abundant life? It means we are happy because we have a purpose in life. We are satisfied, not worrying or being stressed out over every little thing that disrupts our life.[347]

Talk About the Story: To whom did Jesus tell the illustration of being the door to the sheep? What is a sheepfold like? How is Jesus like a door?

Scriptures: "I am the door. If anyone enters by Me, he will be saved, and will go in and out and find pasture." John 10:9

Family Time: How does thinking of Jesus as your secure and safe door give you courage? What good things come from trusting Jesus as Your Savior?

Prayer: Father, thank You that Jesus is the door to eternal life. I am happy in the presence of Jesus who watches over me. Amen.

I AM THE GOOD SHEPHERD

Scripture: John 10:11–18
Place: In the Temple
Time: Monday, after the Feast of Tabernacle

Jesus had a heated argument with the Jewish leaders after He told the woman caught in adultery, "Go and sin no more."[399] Then Jesus told them, "I am the light of the world." He even said they were blind (John 9:41).[208]

As Jesus left the Temple He put clay on the eyes of a blind man and told him to go wash in the Pool of Siloam. He was healed. When the healed man argued with the religious leaders, they banished him from the Temple. Jesus knew they were wrong to shut him out of the Temple, so He said, "I am the door of the sheepfold." It was a picture of entrance into eternal life, which was greater than entrance into the Temple.[416]

Next, Jesus followed up with an illustration, "I am the good shepherd."[67] Those who heard Jesus probably related it to Psalm 23, "The Lord is my shepherd; I shall not want" (Psalm 23:1).

When Jesus called His people *sheep*, it was not complimentary. Sheep are dumb and get lost easily. They have poor eyesight and will stray into dangerously deep water, or stray off a cliff. Most animals can be trained, but not sheep.

When Jesus said, "I am the good shepherd" (John 10:11), He was describing how He cares for us. A good shepherd knows the sheep intimately, and many times he knows what they would do before they did it.

The shepherd gives a name to each sheep. That way the shepherd could "call his own sheep by name" (John 10:3).[362] They recognize and respond to the shepherd's voice. "The sheep hear his voice" (John 10:3). They know not the voice of a stranger" (John 10:5).

When Jesus looks at people—including you and me—He really knows us. He knows our weaknesses, our flaws, and our desires to know Him and serve Him. Jesus says, "I know My sheep and I am known by My own" (John 10:14).[3]

Jesus, the good shepherd, leads His sheep, but they don't always follow Him. They may walk away and get hurt. They might be cut with thorns, and covered with briars and burrs.

Just because you are a sheep that belongs to Jesus, doesn't mean you won't have difficult times. We have the shepherd's promise, "Yea though I walk through the valley of the shadow of death, I will fear no evil; for you are with Me" (Psalm 23:4).[387] Our Shepherd will not keep us from problems, but He will always be with us.

Notice the Shepherd is called *good*. He's good to us, and He does what is good for us. He will lead us where we need to go, not where we always want to go. Also, He will give us the good things we need. Sometimes the good God gives us means we will have less money or other things that people think are important. But the Shepherd, who knows us, will always give to us what is best for us.[203]

Talk About the Story: Where was Jesus when He said, "I am the good shepherd"? To whom was He speaking? What are the characteristics of sheep? What are the characteristics of the good Shepherd?

Scripture: "I am the good shepherd. The good shepherd lays down his life for the sheep." John 10:11

Family Time: How are we like sheep? How is Jesus like a good shepherd? How can we follow Jesus, our Shepherd?

Prayer: Father, I love Jesus who is my Shepherd. Thank You that He takes care of me. I will follow Him and serve Him. Even when I walk through the dark shadows of danger, I will not fear because I trust Jesus, my Shepherd. Amen.

I AM THE WAY

Scripture: John 14:1–6
Place: The Upper Room
Time: Thursday night April 3, AD

Judas Iscariot had quietly left the upper room, on his way to lead the religious leaders and soldiers to arrest Jesus later that night.

But now, Jesus began to talk to the other eleven disciples in the upper room. "Where I am going you cannot follow Me," Jesus said.[268]

Peter answered that he would follow Jesus anywhere, even die for Jesus' sake, but Jesus gently told Peter that Peter would deny Him three times before the rooster crowed the next morning.[114]

Then Jesus told His friends, "I am going to prepare a place for you: I want you to be where I am."[215]

Thomas was puzzled. "Lord, we do not know WHERE You are going! How can we know the way there?"[126]

Jesus gave His sixth, "I Am" statement. He said, "I am the way, the truth, and the life. No one comes to the Father, except through Me."[415]

The word *way* in the Greek is the word *hodos*, which is a road. Jesus used the word here to mean He is the road to heaven.

Jesus said He is the only way to heaven. Many other religions claim to be a way to heaven, but Jesus said He is the only way. Jesus didn't want people to be more religious. Instead, He was trying to help people OUT of religion. He wanted people to be in a living relationship with Him. That comes by knowing we can't help ourselves and believing in Jesus!

Jesus died on the cross—which is the reason He came to Earth. God the Father would not have allowed His Son to suffer a horrible death on the cross for our sins if there was another way to get us to heaven![316]

Some people think they can be saved by their good deeds. They might think all their good deeds will outweigh their evil deeds when they appear before God. But the Bible teaches that it is by God's kindness or grace we are saved through faith in Jesus. It is God's gift to us, not because of anything we do—not even good works.[157]

Jesus was not picking an argument with any religion; Jesus knew He is the only way for anyone to be saved. So He said, "I am the way, the truth, and the life. No one comes to the Father except through me."[72]

Talk About the Story: Who left the upper room? What did Peter say? Where was Jesus going? What did Thomas ask? How did Jesus answer?
Scripture: "I am the way, the truth, and the life, no one comes to the Father except through me." John 14:6

Family Time: Some people think there are many ways to heaven. What did Jesus say about other ways to heaven? Who is someone you can humbly tell about Jesus? Who is someone you can pray for?

Prayer: Father, thank You that Jesus has died for me and will take me to be with Him when I die if I believe in Him. Thank You that You love my unsaved family and friends. Help them to know Jesus. Amen.

I AM THE VINE

Scripture: John 15:1–5
Place: Walking to Gethsemane
Time: Thursday night, April 6, 30 AD

With Jesus going away, it was more important than ever that the disciples know how to stay close to Him—even if they couldn't see Him! Jesus told a parable, a short story that teaches a lesson, to help them understand what He meant.

"I am the true grapevine," Jesus said, "and My Father is the gardener." The disciples remembered the vineyards, fields of grapes, they'd passed on walks with Jesus through the hills near Jerusalem.

"The gardener cuts off branches that don't grow fruit," Jesus continued. "And He prunes branches that do grow fruit, trimming them down and cleaning them up. Then they'll grow even MORE fruit.[418] Like those branches, you've been pruned," Jesus explained. "The things I've taught and told you, My word, has cleaned you."[389]

Jesus' words, found in the Bible today, pruned and cleaned them. A clean branch is healthy, not covered in bugs or dirt that keep fruit from growing. So a healthy branch would grow LOTS of fruit.

"Remain close to Me, joined to Me,[297] just as I'm joined to you," Jesus continued. "A branch can't produce fruit if it's not joined to the vine,[179] the source of its nourishment. In the same way, you can't live fruitful lives unless you stay close to Me."[327]

A branch without a vine that makes it grow is just a stick! It'll NEVER produce fruit, the disciples realized.

"I'm the vine. YOU are the branches," Jesus said.

His words confirmed what the disciples had started to suspect. *Jesus is our source of nourishment, the vine, the One we cling to who helps us, the branches, grow.*

"If you stay close to Me, joined to Me like a branch to a vine, you will grow much fruit,"[180] Jesus said. The disciples imagined all they would do, remembering Jesus' promise that they'd do even bigger things on earth than He had done!

"Far from Me, without Me, you can do nothing,"[29] Jesus cautioned. Without faith in Jesus, the disciples would be just like those sticks, unable to grow any fruit, unable to do anything.

But if we stay close to Jesus, fruit will naturally grow! Imagine all the fruit— the miracles, the crowds of people that will know God as we do! the disciples marveled. *God, the gardener, will smile SO BIG when He sees how well the branches He cares for have grown fruit for Him!*

Talk About the Story: In the story Jesus told, who was the vine? The gardener? The branches? What kind of branches produce fruit? What kind don't? What would clean the branches to help them grow more fruit?

Scripture: "I can do all things through Christ who strengthens me." Philippians 4:13

Family Time: What are ways you can stay close to Jesus? When you're close to Jesus, what kind of "fruit" might you produce? How do you think God feels when you stay close to Jesus and produce fruit for Him?

Prayer: Dear Lord, You wanted the disciples to stay close to You so that they would live fruitful lives—helping others know You and living in ways that please You. Help us remain close to You, reading your Word and praying to You, so that we produce much fruit for Your glory. In Jesus' name, Amen.

I AM THE RESURRECTION

Scripture: John 11:1–44
Place: Bethany
Time: January, 29 AD

Mary and Martha lived in Bethany with their brother, Lazarus. When Jesus came through their valley, he stayed in their home.[72] When Lazarus fell deathly ill, the sisters sent Jesus a message that Lazarus was sick.[435]

Jesus didn't go immediately, but said, "This sickness is not unto death, but for the glory of God that the Son of God may be glorified through it" (John 11:4).[188]

Sometimes God doesn't answer our request immediately, but He waits. Always, God has a reason for waiting![107]

Jesus told Martha, "I am the resurrection and the life. He who believes in Me, though he may die, he shall live" (John 11:25).[405]

Notice, both life and resurrection is in a person. It's in Jesus. He is the power of all life in the universe, including resurrection life—that's life after death that lasts forever with God.

Martha was confused. She said, "I know he (Lazarus) will rise again in the resurrection at the last day" (John 11:24).[126] Martha was thinking about the future, but Jesus was talking about something bigger than just the future.

Jesus came to give us life now AND forever. And Jesus was using Lazarus to show everyone that He really did have power over life and death.[405]

Notice the two meanings of die. "I am the resurrection and the life, those believing in Me may die physically, yet they live in God's presence. Everyone who believes in Me and lives for Me will  never die spiritually" (John 11:25-26, FPB).[34]

The child of God may die at the end of his/her life on this earth. That's physical death where the heart stops beating, the lungs don't breathe, the mind shuts down and the soul leaves the body. If Jesus doesn't return for us, we will all die. But there's a second death in this verse, "Shall never die." That's spiritual life. We will live forever with God through faith in Jesus.[405]

This is the fifth time Jesus used the phrase, "I Am" to describe what He does for believers. "When you die, I am there with you to take you to heaven. I will be there for your future life with the Father in heaven. No matter where you are, I am there for you."[517]

Talk About the Story: Why did Mary and Martha send for Jesus? What did Jesus do? Why did Jesus wait before going to Bethany? What did Jesus say about Himself? What did Jesus mean about the word, "die"? When will Jesus be our resurrection?

Scripture: "Jesus said to her, 'I am the resurrection and the life. He who believes in Me, though he may die, he shall live.'" John 11:25

Family Time: What are the two types of death mentioned by Jesus? What did Jesus mean when He used the present tense, "I Am"? What assurance can we have that there is life after we die?

Prayer: Father, I know that Jesus died to forgive my sins, and He came back to life to give me new life. I believe in the resurrection of the dead, and know You will raise me to live with You in heaven. Amen.

PSALM 51

WHAT TO DO AFTER YOU HAVE SINNED GREATLY

This is a horrible story. One night King David saw a woman named Bathsheba taking a bath on a nearby rooftop. He sent for her and slept with her. Later she sent word to David that she was pregnant and he was the father.

David tried to cover up what he had done, but his plans didn't work, so he sent her soldier husband into battle, instructing the commanding officer to position him where he would be killed.

When the husband was dead, David married Bathsheba. God was very displeased with what David had done. Bathsheba had the baby but it was deathly sick. The prophet Nathan told David, "Because of what you have done, your child will die" (2 Samuel 12:14, *NLT*).

David realized he had sinned against God. He repented with agonizing prayers. Then he wrote Psalm 51, "What to do after you have sinned greatly." In verses 1–4 he seeks forgiveness.

> "Be merciful to me because of Your unfailing love,
>   Blot out my sin because of Your compassion.[305]
> Cleanse me from my sin,
>   Blot out the stain of my disobedience.[399]
> I recognize my shameful disobedience,
>   I can't get my sin out of my mind.
> I sinned against You and You alone.
>   You called my action evil
> You are right and I am wrong,
>   I deserve any punishment You give me."[440]

After David pleaded for forgiveness, he turned his thoughts to restoration. David knew he had sinned; now he wanted to get back into fellowship with God.

> "I have been a sinner since birth,
>   I was conceived with a sin nature;
> You demand truthfulness from the heart
>   So You can teach me to live for You.[451]
> Purify me from my sins so I will be clean,

> *Wash away my sin so I will be white as snow.*[173]
> *You have broken me, I want my joy back;*
> *   I need peace and happiness.*
> *Create a clean heart within me, O God,*
> *   Put the right spirit within me.*[71]
> *Don't send me away from Your presence;*
> *   Don't take the Holy Spirit from me.*
> *Give me back the joy of Your salvation;*
> *   Give me a strong spirit to serve You.*"[167]

When David was restored, he was concerned about usefulness. He wanted to serve the Lord again. He wanted God to use him. So he promised to live godly and serve God with a yielded spirit.

> *"Then I will tell sinners about salvation,*
> *   They will turn to You with repentance.*[458]
> *Take away my guilt of sin*
> *   So I can tell others about Your forgiveness.*
> *   I bring You the sacrifice of a broken heart,*
> *   You accept those broken people who repent."*

Finally, David prayed for his kingdom. He wanted God to bless Jerusalem and the nation.

> *"Show Your love to the nation of Israel*
> *   And help rebuild the walls of Jerusalem.*
> *Please accept the sacrifice I bring to You*
> *   And my offerings of thanksgiving on the altar."*

Talk About the Psalm: What did you learn about the psalm writer in this story? What did you learn about God?

Psalm 51: Read this week's psalm in your Bible together. Choose a verse to read aloud as a prayer.

Prayer: Thank You, God, for the psalm prayers in the Bible. Thank You for teaching us about You and about how to pray. In Jesus' name, Amen.

CHAPTER 16

THE LAST WEEK

Passover fell on April 6, in A.D. 30, but by the end of March the city of Jerusalem was already filling up as Jews from all parts of the world. Although the feast was intended as a time to reflect back to God's deliverance of the nation from Egypt, many came to the city for this feast were asking, "What do you think," they wondered, "that He will not come to the feast?" (John 11:56). By now, it had become obvious to just about everybody that Jesus was opposed by the religious establishment. "Both the chief priests and the Pharisees had given a command, that if anyone knew where He was, he should report it, that they might seize Him" (John 11:57).

As Jesus began His final week of public ministry on earth, the people celebrated His coming and witnessed great demonstrations of His messianic power. But the crowds that chanted, "Hosanna to the Son of David! Blessed is He who comes in the name of the Lord!" (Matt. 21:9) on Sunday were the same crowds who early Friday morning cried out, "Away with Him, away with Him! Crucify Him!" (John 19:15). Their worship of Christ on Sunday lacked commitment to Him and turned to opposition by Friday.

MARY ANOINTS JESUS

Scripture: John 12:1–8
Place: Bethany
Time: Saturday night, March 31, 30 AD

Jesus and His disciples were nearly to Jerusalem. But they stopped to stay with Martha, Mary and Lazarus, who lived in Bethany.[72] Mary had sat at Jesus' feet to learn from Him.[285] Jesus had raised Lazarus from the dead not long before this! They had MANY reasons to show their love for Jesus. So Martha gave a big feast for Jesus.[405]

Many people came to the feast, to see Jesus but also to see Lazarus—they had heard about Jesus raising him from the dead! They wanted to see Lazarus, too![72]

Mary was so thankful for Jesus' love and help to her family. She wondered, *What can I do to show love and honor to Jesus?*

After dinner, she went to find her most precious possession. There, hidden in her trunk—was a bottle of very expensive perfumed oil. It had been given to her many years before. She had kept it safe, being careful not to break the seal lest it lose its fragrance. She had not even opened this oil to anoint her dear brother

Lazarus when he died—that's how precious it was to her! She had always thought she might save this perfumed oil for her wedding—or for just the right time.[295]

Now, Mary knew the right time had come. Jesus was the MOST important person EVER. It only made sense to give Him this expensive oil, and give it ALL to Him.

Sometimes, at a king's banquet, the guest of honor was anointed with perfumed oils, usually at the beginning of the banquet. The fragrance set the scene for the feast.[354]

It's all I have. So it will have to do, Mary thought. Entering the room, she held the bottle close to her heart, hoping no one would ask what she was doing. She knelt behind Jesus and broke the seal on the flask. The fragrance flowed out like a desert rain rolling down a canyon. The aroma filled every corner of the room. Before anyone noticed, she had poured some onto Jesus' head. Then every conversation stopped. Every nose sniffed deeply and every eye turned to watch her honor Jesus and humbly worship her King and Lord.[16]

She then turned the bottle toward His feet and poured out the rest of the fragrance, tipping the jar until the last drop fell onto Jesus' feet. Before it could flow down onto the cushions, she wiped His feet with her own hair. Now the scent would cling to her for a long time, reminding her of Jesus and of her love for Him.

Judas was upset.[29] He kept the money for the disciples and said, "This expensive ointment could have been sold and the money given to the poor."

But Judas didn't care about poor people. He had been stealing money given to Jesus and wanted more.

"This is wasteful," Judas growled.[440]

Jesus said, "Hush. You will always have the poor with you, but you won't have Me very long.[256] She has done a beautiful thing for Me. She has prepared Me for burial. And wherever this story is told, she will be remembered for her act of love."[544]

Talk About the Story: What are some reasons Mary loved Jesus? What did Mary do to honor Jesus? Why did Judas complain? What would you have given Jesus if you had been there?

Scripture: "Worthy is the Lamb who was slain to receive power and riches and wisdom, and strength and honor and glory and blessing!" Revelation 5:12

Family Time: In this verse, everyone in heaven is praising Jesus. What is Jesus worthy to receive? What is a way you can honor Jesus and show your love for Him?

Prayer: Lord, thank You for Mary. She loved Jesus so much that she gave Him the most precious thing she had. I love Jesus, too. I want to give Him the most precious thing I have: my heart. Amen.

FINDING THE DONKEY

Scripture: Matthew 21:1-11; John 12:12-19
Place: Road from Bethany to Jerusalem
Time: Sunday, April 2, 30 AD

In the middle of the morning, Jesus and the disciples left Bethany where Mary, Martha and Lazarus lived. The village is on the far side of the hill known as the Mount of Olives. Jesus and His disciples began climbing to the top of the Mount of Olives.

They soon came to the path that led to Bethphage—a small village known for its figs. It wasn't far from the main highway to Jerusalem.

Jesus pointed toward Bethphage. He told Peter and John, "Go into that village.[117] You'll find a small donkey tied near the side of the road."[327]

The disciples' eyes grew wide. They knew the words of the prophet—that the King would ride into Jerusalem on a young donkey. Was THIS the day? Would Jesus ride in to become king of Israel?

Jesus went on, "No one has ever sat upon this donkey. He is not broken, but I will ride him into Jerusalem."

www.thefamilyprayerbible.com

Peter and John looked at each other. A young wild donkey was impossible to ride; but they also knew that Jesus had stopped the wind, walked on water and cast out demons. Of course He ruled the animals, too!

Jesus told them exactly what to do. "When you loose the donkey, the owners may ask what you are doing untying that donkey. Tell them the Lord has need of the donkey, and they will let you take him."[74]

Bethphage wasn't far. And Peter and John entered the town, they saw a young donkey tied next to its mother. Peter and John untied the donkey to lead it away.[327] The owners of the donkey asked, "What are you doing?"

"The Lord needs the donkey," they said. "We think He is going to ride triumphantly into Jerusalem," Peter explained. The owners understood the great honor of providing a ride for Jesus, the One who everyone said was a prophet and who many said was the MESSIAH! Maybe on THIS day, He would become the KING!

Leading the donkey back to Jesus, Peter and John took off their outer cloaks and draped them over the animal, making a place for Jesus to sit on its back.[147] It was a short walk up to top of Olivet, and then they began to go down the valley.

As they were approaching Jerusalem, the disciples began singing! This was a tradition which dated back many, many years. When people would come to Jerusalem for one of the feasts, there were psalms that everyone sang on the way. They were called the Hallel (praise and thanksgiving) psalms. Jesus' friends sang,

"Open to Me the gates of righteousness:
I will go into them
I will praise the Lord."[538]

Soon, more people joined in the singing! Their voices grew louder and more people joined in the songs as everyone walked toward Jerusalem.

"This is the day the Lord hath made," they sang. "We will rejoice in it and be glad."

Talk About the Story: Where did Jesus tell His friends to find an animal to ride? How was this a miracle? What music was sung? Who was singing?

Scripture: "Rejoice greatly, O daughter of Zion! Shout, O daughter of Jerusalem! Behold, your King is coming to you; He is just and having salvation, Lowly and riding on a donkey, A colt, the foal of a donkey." Zechariah 9:9

Family Time: What things are said about Jesus in this verse? What is He called? What does the verse tell people to do? Today, sing a song together to rejoice! Make up a family shout to praise Jesus!

Prayer: Lord Jesus, we are glad that You did everything God sent You to do. Help us to be like the donkey, willing to go where You want to go. Amen.

PALM SUNDAY

Scripture: John 12:12–18; Luke 19:36–38
Place: Road from Bethany to Jerusalem
Time: Sunday, April 2, 30 AD

Passover is a week every year when God's people celebrate and remember how God freed them from being slaves in Egypt. Sunday is the first day of the celebration. People eat and stroll, visiting family and friends.[110]

During one Passover, pilgrims flocked to Jerusalem from all over the world. Most of them heard that Jesus might be the Messiah. They'd heard that He was in Jerusalem, and they wanted to see Him. Most of them had dreams of a king who would lead an army to drive the Romans out. Could Jesus be that king? Would He enter Jerusalem the way the prophet said their Messiah-King would come?[529] They did not know. They also did not know that King Jesus would not come as a conquering king. Instead, He would come as a spiritual king. He would rule and reign over their hearts and lives.

Early Sunday morning, a little crowd left Jerusalem to walk to Bethany. They were fired up with enthusiasm! They'd heard Jesus was in Bethany, and they wanted to see Him! They knew Jesus was a prophet, and they hoped He might be the Messiah. But the Law said they could not walk that far on Saturday, the Sabbath. So they'd waited until Sunday morning.[327]

As this crowd came towards Bethany on that bright Sunday morning, another crowd marched down the road toward Jerusalem. Jesus rode ahead of them, on the little donkey they'd brought. They swept over the ridge and got their first view of Jerusalem. They saw the beautiful gardens—terrace upon terrace—that bloomed up the side of the hill. The walls of Jerusalem sparkled white and dazzling in the sun. Huge towers protected its gates. Inside, Jerusalem was known as a city of palaces—all those who were rich wanted to have a palace in God's Eternal City![33]

Excitement passed from person to person. The crowd with Jesus shouted as they came over the ridge and saw the city. Enthusiasm leaped as a fire from heart to heart. The crowd loudly sang the Hallel psalms, the songs always sung on the way to Jerusalem. Sometimes they sang together like a choir, other times they sang alone or in little groups as they neared the City of David.[439]

At some point, the crowd coming TOWARD Jesus met the crowd coming WITH Jesus! Shouts of joy arose! And suddenly, people were running to lay their coats on the road. They were running to cut palm branches and lay them in the road, too. Jesus and His donkey began to ride over a beautiful carpet of colors—for this is the way that people welcomed a KING![188]

The people waved branches and sang one of the ancient Hallel psalms: "'Blessed is He who comes in the name of the Lord!' Hosanna in the highest! Peace in heaven and glory on the earth!"

Soon everyone in the crowd was shouting, "HOSANNA!" which means, "SAVE NOW!"[416]

When they cried, "Hosanna!" we don't know whether they were asking for salvation from sin or whether they were asking for freedom from Rome. But the shout rolled down the valley and up the hill to the city. It did not stop![87]

"HOSANNA!"

Talk About the Story: What did people celebrate at Passover? What song did they sing on the way to Jerusalem? How did the people welcome a king?

Scripture: "Blessed is he who comes in the name of the LORD! We have blessed you from the house of the LORD." PSALM 118:26

Family Time: What do you think "blessed" means? Look it up! Then see if you can think of three ways your family can bless the Lord.

Prayer: Lord Jesus, You are worthy of everyone's praise! We welcome You as our King and want You to be in charge of our lives. Amen.

PALM SUNDAY: INTO JERUSALEM

Scripture: John 12:17–19; Luke 19:37–44
Place: Into Jerusalem
Time: Sunday, April 2, 30 AD

A number of Pharisees had come with the crowd from Jerusalem—because they wanted to spy on Jesus. Caught up in the surge of the cheering, singing crowd, they were distressed.

One Pharisee turned to another to say, "See? Everyone in the whole world has gone after Him!"

"We must do something to stop Him," the second Pharisee agreed.

They shook their heads. These religious men who hated Jesus were shocked to see the how people freely showed love and honor to Jesus as Messiah and King![188] The fact that the people of Israel were honoring Jesus made them wild with anger and jealousy!

But amid the excited welcome, as Jesus came halfway down the hill toward the brook Kidron, something happened that many in the crowd never saw nor heard.

Jesus knew that a terrible future was coming to Jerusalem. He saw a vision of destruction, of the enemy camped around the city, tearing down its walls, destroying the Temple so that not one stone would be left on another.

Jesus wept over the city, saying, "You don't know the things that are going to happen to you . . . this is a day of rejoicing . . . but the days will come when the enemies will trample your walls, not leaving one stone on another—because you rejected the Son of Man."[268] (The "Son of Man" is another name for Jesus.)

Jesus finished speaking and rode the donkey on down toward Jerusalem. Everyone wanted to welcome the King! He was coming just as The Old Testament prophet, Zachariah, had predicted, riding a donkey and having salvation!

Another Pharisee couldn't stand the sound of the people's praise a minute more! So he ran out to Jesus on the donkey and with some agitation in his voice, said, "Master! Tell Your disciples to quiet down!"

Jesus looked the man in the eye and said, "If I should tell My disciples to be quiet . . ." Jesus gestured toward the great stone walls, "these very stones would immediately cry out in praise."[367]

Jesus rode the donkey[327] on through the gate of the city and into the narrow streets. The whole city was now abuzz with the story of Jesus! Pilgrims who had come from the far corners of the earth were eager to know, "Who is this Man?"

Others answered, "This is Jesus, the prophet from Nazareth, a town in Galilee." And maybe they added, "Many say He is the Messiah! The King of Israel! Could it be that our king comes to us?"

Jesus rode on, all the way into Temple courts. The religious leaders didn't like Him, but there He was—and everyone was praising Him!

In a few days, some of this crowd would shout for Jesus to die. But today the tramp of their feet and the shout of their voices would not be silenced.

Talk About the Story: What did many people hope Jesus would do? What were the people singing? What did the Pharisees say about Jesus? What future did Jesus see for the city? What did the Pharisees say to Jesus? What did Jesus say?

Scripture: "And when He had come into Jerusalem, all the city was moved, saying, 'Who is this?' So the multitudes said, 'This is Jesus, the prophet from Nazareth of Galilee'" Matthew 21:10, 11

Family Time: What do you think it sounded like in Jerusalem as Jesus rode through? Describe it! How can we show that Jesus is the King of our lives today?

Prayer: Jesus, please help us to praise You always, not just when it is easy. You are our King. Amen.

CURSING THE FIG TREE

Scripture: Mark 11:12-19; Matthew 21:12-17
Place: Outside Jerusalem
Time: Monday, April 3, 30 AD

Early Monday morning, Jesus and His apostles left Bethany. They were on their way to Jerusalem, so they walked up to the top of the Mount of Olives, then began heading down toward Jerusalem.

There by the roadside in front of them was one solitary fig tree, growing through a crack in the rocky ground. The tree grew on the Bethphage side of the road; Bethphage meant "house of figs."

Of all the places in Israel, Bethphage was famous for its figs. It grew the best figs and often, the earliest figs of the season. The warm spring breezes blew up from the Geba Valley toward Jerusalem, warming Bethphage at the top of the valley. As a result, the fig trees in Bethphage blossomed earlier. Many said that these fig trees had sweeter fruit than any other place in Israel. Back in Jesus' hometown, figs wouldn't be ripe for another two weeks or more. But here at

Bethphage, the figs were ready.

The humanity of Jesus peeked through His divinity. He was hungry.[229] Walking to the tree, he pushed back the leaves to find a fig. Back in Jesus' hometown, the figs were blue-black, but these trees produced a red colored fig, known as a sweet sugar fig.

Jesus looked left and right. He looked up and down. There was not a fig to be seen anywhere on that tree! He thought, *Nothing here but leaves!*

He was about to do something that people might expect a prophet to do. In Old Testament times, God often told a prophet to do something that seemed strange to others. They would do it to get people's attention so that they could tell the people a message God wanted the people to know. Jesus was going to use this fig tree to be a picture of what had happened in Israel.

On the fig tree, there were no figs, no fruit. And in Israel, there was a lot of religious activity, but there was no spiritual fruit. People were not growing in friendship with God; they spent their time busy fussing over religious things they were told they needed to do.

Jesus stepped back from the fig tree.

He quietly said to it, "Let no fruit grow on you from now on, forever."[268]

Throughout the Old Testament Israel had been compared to a fruitful fig tree. The fruit of doing right was what showed off God's glory to the people around them who did not know God. So when Jesus came to Israel, He was looking for that kind of spiritual fruit. But instead, He found a lot of religion and "nothing but leaves."[192]

What Jesus said to that empty tree was a word picture about Israel. He had come to Israel and found no fruit.

The disciples were astonished. They did not yet see how the empty religion of Israel was like the empty tree.

Talk About the Story: Where did Jesus spend the night? What did He do when the fig tree didn't have fruit? What did Israel not have?

Scripture: "But the fruit of the Spirit is love, joy, peace, longsuffering, kindness, goodness, faithfulness, gentleness, self-control. Against such there is no law." Galatians 5:22-23

Family Time: What are some things people will see in us, if we know God through Jesus, and have His Spirit in us? What does it look like to show gentleness? Longsuffering or patience?

Prayer: Father, we want to be like a healthy fig tree. We want to have the fruit of Your Spirit showing in our lives. Please help us to listen to You and obey You, so that we can grow good fruit! Amen.

JESUS CLEANSES THE TEMPLE

Scripture: Mark 11:12-19; Matthew 21:12-17
Place: Temple
Time: Monday, April 3, 30 AD

Monday morning broke over Bethany, a soft new spring day. Jesus' friends were excited that Jesus had been welcomed like a king the day before! Now, the disciples felt that this week, Jesus would become king—they thought it might be the best week of their lives!

As they entered the Temple courtyard, Jesus saw the same things He had seen three years before. Nothing had changed. People were busy buying, not praying. The place was filled with people selling large animals for large sins, and small turtledoves for small sins.[440]

As He walked through the Temple courtyard, Jesus saw more merchants. These were taking Roman coins from the worshipers, and giving them Hebrew coins in return. No Jew was allowed to bring an image of Caesar into the Temple. So moneychangers traded them for the kind of coins they could use to worship Jehovah—but it cost people a big fee. There was nothing wrong with changing Roman money into Hebrew money—but the unfair fee was cheating and stealing from the worshipers.[246]

Jesus knew that Caiaphas the High Priest, and Annas his father-in-law also

www.thefamilyprayerbible.com

made money on every exchange. The High Priest gave the merchants permission to do their business in the Temple. And he got a part of all the sales. Caiaphas and Annas took so much money, it made the merchants charge even more!

Jesus went into action. Just as He had done three years before, He turned over the tables of the money-changers[389] and spilled out their coins. He pointed to the gate and shouted, "OUT! THIS IS A HOUSE OF PRAYER! DO NOT MAKE MY FATHER'S HOUSE A DEN OF THIEVES!"

The merchants began to run for the exits. Levites who should have kept the Temple pure, disappeared through little doors. No one challenged Jesus, no one asked Him why He was doing this, and no one stopped Him. Everyone knew about this cheating. They were all ashamed.

Next Jesus strode to the animal pens.[27] He tore down the barriers. Sheep, goats, and cattle began running in all directions. He opened the cages holding the small birds, and they fluttered and flapped their way toward freedom in the sky.

Jesus looked around at those who stood watching, their mouths open in surprise! Jesus told them, "The Scriptures say to respect the House of God! God said His house shall be called the House of Prayer for everyone,[182] but you have turned it into a robbers' hideout!"[51]

Within minutes, the porches were clear, the animals were gone, the birds had flown. Silence. At last, there was peace in the Temple of God. It was finally quiet enough to pray!

But in the quiet, the shuffle of slow feet was heard across the Temple's stone floors. First one came, then another: the blind, lame, and sick began coming out to Jesus. They came quietly, reverently, and expectantly. They could hear Jesus softly say, "Be healed . . ."[214] as He prayed and lay His hands on each and every sick one. He healed them all.

Healing people, not cheating people, was a right way to use God's Temple! Praying and healing, not lying and stealing, was what pleased God!

Talk About the Story: Why was Jesus upset? What had changed? Why did people have to pay to get different money? What did Jesus say about God's Temple?

Scripture: "Even them I will bring to My holy mountain, and make them joyful in My house of prayer. . . for My house shall be called a house of prayer for all nations." Isaiah 56:7

Family Time: Is it easy or hard to pray to God when it is loud and busy? Why? What is a way we show our love for God when we are at church? When we pray at home?

Prayer: Lord, we want to honor You by the words we say and the way we pray. Thank You for loving us and showing us how to do that. In Jesus' name, Amen.

PSALM 55
A PSALM FOR THE DISCOURAGED

David got word his son, Absalom, had gathered an army and was coming to take his throne. A messenger told David, "The hearts of the men of Israel are with Absalom" (2 Samuel 15:13). David had to run for his life. David fled the city, going down the mountain. It is then that Shimei began cursing David and throwing stones at him. It is then David sang,

"Oh Lord, please listen to my prayer;
   Don't hide from me because I need You.
Come near to hear my prayers;
   I need you more than any other time in my life.
My enemies are shouting curses at me;

They laugh and heap guilt on me.[387]
My heart is pounding and I am scared;[99]
    My knees are trembling and I don't know where to turn.
I wish I had the wings of a dove;
    I would fly away from all my troubles."

David was a brokenhearted father. He bore the shame of a son who hated him. This was perhaps the darkest hour of his life. David left his throne, his palace, and his home. He had nothing but his friends around him. He prayed before going to sleep that night. Perhaps David's friends wondered if he would sleep well on the ground, knowing his son was sleeping in his bed, in the palace. David meets God in prayer,

"I will call upon God for help;
    He has always saved me in the past.
I will pray morning, noon, and night;
    He will listen to my problems and do something.
I have fought many battles in my life;
    God has always rescued me and given me victory."[24]

David met the Lord the first night he slept on the ground. Because the Lord encouraged him, he arose with optimism.

"Lord, I cast my burdens on You;
    I know You will see me through these problems."

Over the next few days David developed a strategy to fight the enemy. He was too old to go into battle. Those loyal to him won the battle.

Talk About the Psalm: What did you learn about the psalm writer in this story? What did you learn about God?

Psalm 55: Read this week's psalm in your Bible together. Choose a verse to read aloud as a prayer.

Prayer: Thank You, God, for the psalm prayers in the Bible. Thank You for teaching us about You and about how to pray. In Jesus' name, Amen.

DATE ___/___

CHILDREN IN THE TEMPLE

Scripture: Matthew 21:14-17
Place: The Temple, Jerusalem
Time: Monday, April 3

Jesus looked around, breathing heavily. In the Temple courts, coins were spilled, a few animals still roamed, confused. The animals had been penned up to become sacrifices. But now they were set free! The people had disappeared, running to hide when Jesus began to shout that it was WRONG to turn God's House into a marketplace, crowding out people who wanted to worship and then CHEATING them, besides!

So now, there was silence, except for a few bleating animals.

And once all of that mess was cleared away, there was space for something else!

First, the sick people came, those who hadn't been able to get close to Jesus before. They began to come through the quiet, empty Temple court, with hearts full of faith. Reverently, they came. And Jesus began to greet each one, pray for each one, heal each one.[72]

But then, there was room for someone else. There was finally room for the CHILDREN! Around the people waiting for Jesus to heal them, and the dancing, happy people who'd already BEEN healed, came children! First the silence was broken by the voice of one child, just one child solitary voice, "Hosanna, to the Son of David!"

But then, other children joined in, waving branches as they had done on the road to Jerusalem. They sang and danced and waved their branched to welcome Jesus into the Temple! They declared who Jesus is, even if they did not know it. There, in God's Temple, Jesus was finally being welcomed! Instead of angry leaders who wished they could keep Jesus OUT, the children and sick people were GLAD to see Jesus IN the Temple. You see, the Temple did not belong to the leaders. It belonged to God and to His Son and Spirit!

And so, the children sang. And as they sang, still more children joined them. Finally there was a loud children's choir! They joyfully sang over and over, "Hosanna! Hosanna to the Son of David."[61]

Of course, the leaders did NOT like this. They understood that the children were welcoming Jesus into the Temple. They could SEE that the sick people were joyfully joining in the praises! And THEY wanted the Temple to belong to THEM, no matter what religious words they said about God!

They gave Jesus dirty looks. They scowled. But the children kept on singing!

Finally, they could not stand it any longer![16]

They said to Jesus, "Don't You hear what these children are saying?"

Jesus said to them, "Yes I DO hear! Have you ever read the words in the Psalm, 'Out of the mouth of children and babies God has made praises be perfectly sung'? They are fulfilling the words of Scripture."

Jesus looked around, smiling. He could see that His work was done here, and it was time to go. He called His disciples from dancing with the children and the formerly sick people, and they left the Temple grounds, walking toward Bethany, where they would stay with Mary, Martha and Lazarus.

Talk About the Story: Who came when there was finally room for them? What did the children sing? Why do you think they called Jesus the Son of David? Ask mom or dad to tell who David was. Why were the leaders angry? What did Jesus tell them?

Scripture: "O Lord, our Lord, how excellent is Your name in all the earth, who have set Your glory above the heavens! Out of the mouth of babes and nursing infants You have ordained strength, because of Your enemies, that You may silence the enemy and the avenger." Psalm 8:1–2

Family Time: Why do you think Jesus is glad to hear kids praise Him? What are some words of praise you know? Some songs of praise you know? List them. Then say and sing them!

Prayer: Dear Lord Jesus, we praise You and thank You for loving us. We are glad to praise You because You loved us first and you loved us best! Amen.

A LESSON IN FAITH

Scripture: Mark 11:12–14, 22–25
Place: Walking to Jerusalem
Time: Tuesday, Passover Week, April 4, 30 AD

As the light dawned on Tuesday morning, Jesus and His disciples left the home where they had stayed with Martha, Mary, and their brother Lazarus. They started down the road to Jerusalem where Jesus would teach in the Temple.

As they got closer to the fig tree Jesus had cursed the day before, Thomas ran up to it. He crumpled its leaves in his hands. They were dry as if the tree had been dead for weeks. The limbs were shriveled.

Soon the others came to look. The tree was dead, right down to the roots. Even though Jesus had said the tree would not bear fruit again, they didn't expect THIS to happen![470]

www.thefamilyprayerbible.com

Jesus used the tree to teach His friends.

"Have faith in God." Jesus said. "If you have faith in God, He will help you with all His power. But many people act as if God doesn't exist. You must believe that He exists and will do what He wants to do for you."[156]

Jesus told His disciples that by faith they could overcome the things that were keeping them from doing God's will. He pointed to the Mount of Olives and reminded them, "If you say to this mountain, 'Be moved to the sea,' it will happen."[157]

Jesus explained that faith is what moves God to action. So they had to say to their problems or obstacles, "Be removed" and it would be as good as done.

In the Old Testament this had happened many times. When Moses and the Israelites were about to be captured by the Egyptians, he said, "Stand still, and see the salvation of the LORD!"

When Elisha was surrounded by enemies, he told his servant, "Do not fear. Those who are with us are more than those who are with them." Then he asked God to open the eyes of his servant to see "the mountain was full of horses and chariots of fire around Elisha" (2 Kings 6:17).[178]

Jesus explained, "You must believe it will happen and have no doubt in your heart" (Mark 11:23, *NLT*). The disciples knew they wanted God's help, but they also knew they had doubts in their hearts.[127] Jesus added, "I tell you, you can pray for anything, and if you believe you've received it, it will be yours" (Mark 11:24, *NLT*).

First, they had to believe that God COULD do something. Second was to act on their faith by saying what they wanted from God. Third, they needed to ask in prayer for what they wanted. Fourth, they had to forgive everyone else.

Jesus finished, "I tell you, you can pray for anything, and if you believe that you've received it, it will be yours" (Mark 11:25, *NLT*).[34]

Talk About the Story: How do you think the disciples felt about the withered tree? What did Jesus teach them about using the tree? Is having God's help like being a superhero? What do we need to believe about God?

Scripture: "And whenever you stand praying, if you have anything against anyone, forgive him, that your Father in heaven may also forgive you your trespasses." Mark 11:24

Family Time: Why do we need to forgive? Who are people we need to forgive? What do we know about God when things seem to be against us?

Prayer: Father, we have weak faith. Please help us to believe Your promises. We want You to help us overcome the hard things in our lives. Thank You that You can help us. In Jesus' name, Amen.

BY WHO'S AUTHORITY?

Scripture: Matthew 21:23–42
Place: Temple, Jerusalem
Time: Early Tuesday morning, April 4

Jesus came up the Roman road toward the Golden Gate of the Temple. It was early on the Tuesday of the week Jesus died. A crowd followed Him into Solomon's Porch, where rabbis often taught. Before Jesus even began, people rushed for seats so they could hear.[285]

The priests watched the crowd and grew angry. They were jealous—EVERY-ONE seemed to love Jesus! But they wanted people to listen to THEM, not Him! So they wanted to trap Jesus, make Him look foolish.

From among the priests, someone shouted, "WHO GAVE YOU AUTHORITY TO TEACH?"

Jesus looked over the crowd at the priests standing in the rear.

He answered, "I will ask you one question. If you can answer Me, I will tell you who gave Me the authority to teach."[27]

Now the priests loved this kind of arguing and questioning. It made them look smart!

"Who sent John the Baptizer to baptize?" Jesus asked. "Was John's authority from heaven . . . or men?"[30]

The priests knew that Jesus' question was a good one. If they said that John got his authority from heaven, Jesus would then ask why didn't the priests listen to John. On the other hand, if the priests denied that John got his authority from heaven, the people would turn against them—everyone knew John the Baptizer was loved by everyone.[28] No matter what they answered, the priests would lose. So they answered, "We cannot tell."

"Then I will not tell you where I get My authority, either."

Jesus turned to the crowd and told this parable: A man had two sons. He asked the first son to go work in his vineyard. [23]

The first son shook his head and said, "No, I won't." But later, he changed his mind. He worked in the vineyard. The man also asked his second son to work in the vineyard.

She second son said, "Sure!" But he never left the house. He never went out to the vineyard and got to work!

Jesus asked, "Which son did what the father asked?"

The priests looked at each other. They knew why Jesus was telling the story. He was saying that people—even people the priests thought were really BAD— had turned from their sin. They had changed their mind, like the first son. They would go first into the kingdom of God.[34] THIS made the priests even MORE angry! Jesus was saying that bad people like tax collectors would go into the kingdom of God before them—because the priests were like the second son. They SAID lots of things about God. They talked a lot about obeying, but they would not turn away from their hate and jealousy. They refused to obey their Heavenly Father, who told them to love and forgive.[127]

Talk About the Story: Where was Jesus teaching? Who was listening to Jesus? Why did the priests try to embarrass Jesus? What question did Jesus ask the priests? Which of the two sons in the story obeyed the father? Which one did not?

Scripture: "Not everyone who says to Me, 'Lord, Lord,' shall enter the kingdom of heaven, but he who does the will of My Father in heaven." Matthew 7:21

Family Time: Is it easier to talk about God's will or to do God's will? Why do you think so? What does doing God's will show about what you believe? What is something you can do today to show your faith in God?

Prayer: Father, thank You for sending Jesus to Earth. We want to obey You and honor him. In His name, Amen.

THE PARABLE OF THE VINEYARD

Scripture: Matthew 21:33–46
Place: The Temple, Jerusalem
Time: Monday, April

The crowd of listeners in the Temple still sat around Jesus, listening to His every word—and snickering at the priests just a little. The priests were still growling at each other in the back of the crowd. They were already angry that Jesus had said SINNERS would enter the kingdom of God before THEM. They were PRIESTS in God's TEMPLE! Certainly, THEY were the BEST men anywhere! How dare Jesus question them, when they were clearly VERY important and VERY righteous!

But Jesus had more to say to these angry men who were so sure of their own rightness. He told another parable, or story that made His point.

This is Jesus' story:

A man owned a piece of land. He planted a vineyard there. He put a fence around it, dug a winepress in it and built a tower to protect it. Then he rented the vineyard to some men who said they would take care of it.[195] Then he went away to live.

Now when it was time for the harvest, the owner sent his servants to his vineyard. He wanted his servants to bring back some fruit.[180] But the renters did NOT want to share anything, not even with the owner! No, they grabbed his servants, beat one, killed one, and stoned another.[100]

So later, the owner sent other servants, more than the first. Maybe the renters would act differently this time. But no. Those renters did horrible things to these servants, too, just as bad if not worse than the first time!

Then last of all, the owner sent his son to them. He said, "Surely, they will respect my son."

But when the renters saw the son, they said to each other, "Look! He's the heir. He will inherit this vineyard. So if we kill him, we can take his inheritance for ourselves. The vineyard will be OURS!" So they took the son, threw him out of the vineyard and killed him.[260]

Jesus looked straight at the priests. He asked, "So. When the owner of the vineyard comes, what do you think HE will he do to those renters?"

They said to Him, "He will destroy those wicked men miserably,[268] and lease his vineyard to other renters who will do what is right and give him the fruit they should."[100]

Jesus just smiled as the priests began to realize what Jesus had just said, and what THEY had just said! Oh, the priests were steaming mad now! They knew EXACTLY what Jesus' story was about. His story was calling THEM the evil renters. Religious leaders had killed the prophets God had sent to them. He was saying that THEY would be so evil that they would be willing to KILL the SON of the OWNER. Jesus was saying that He knew they wanted to kill Him. They just stood there clenching their fists!

Jesus said to them, "Have you read this Scripture?"

'The stone which the builders rejected has become the chief cornerstone.[147] This was the Lord's doing, and it is marvelous in our eyes.'[734]

"So let Me be clear. The kingdom of God will be taken from you. It will be given to people who will bear the fruits of it. Anyone who falls on this Cornerstone will be broken; but if the Cornerstone falls on anyone, it will grind that soul to powder."[268]

The religious leaders were SO ANGRY! But even they knew that the crowd around Jesus believed He was a prophet. So they were afraid to arrest Him right then.[164] Jesus got up and left, probably knowing that they were arguing over whether or not to call the Temple guards to arrest Him. He knew it was not His time yet. They would have to wait a few more days.

Talk About the Story: Who owned the vineyard? What did the renters do to the servants? What did the owner say about the son? What happened to the son? Who did Jesus say the religious leaders were like?

Scripture: "But seek first the kingdom of God and His righteousness, and all these things shall be added to you." Matthew 6:33

Family Time: We don't want to be like those renters! What are some ways we can seek God first? What does Jesus promise happens when we put God first in our lives?

Prayer: Lord Jesus, we want to obey You first. We want to please You first. We want to be people who show the fruit of Your kingdom and Your Spirit. Amen.

IMAGE ON A COIN

Scripture: Matthew 22:15–46
Place: The Temple
Time: Tuesday, April 4, 30 AD

Later Tuesday morning Jesus left the crowd, walking through the Temple. Three groups of religious leaders followed Him. The three groups hated each other, but they hated Jesus even more! So they were working together.[189]

One group was the Herodians. They were loyal to King Herod and they didn't mind the Romans so much.

Another group was the Sadducees They did not believe in angels or miracles or he resurrection of people who died.

The last group was called the Pharisees. They worked hard to obey all 613 commands given by Moses. They had already asked the question about authority.

Now the Herodians tried a tricky question: "Master, we know that You teach the Word of God truthfully,[231] and You don't care if anyone disagrees with You." They asked, "Is it lawful to pay taxes to Caesar?"[479]

Jesus knew their trick. If He said DON'T pay taxes, they would report Him to Rome and have Him arrested. If Jesus said PAY taxes, then He would make people mad who didn't like Rome.

Jesus asked for a coin.

Now a "good" Jew would never bring a Roman coin into the Temple. It carried a picture of Caesar. That was considered an idol! It would be wrong. But a Herodian had a coin.

Jesus watched as the man held the coin between His thumb and forefinger. Jesus asked, "Whose picture is on this coin?"[476]

"Caesar's," the man answered. "Everyone knows Caesar's picture is on the coin."

Jesus smiled and said, "Give to Caesar whatever things are Caesar's. Give to God whatever things are God's."[310]

The crowd was amazed at Jesus' answer. What belonged to Caesar bore Caesar's image! Of course! And who bore God's image? People! So Jesus was saying for people to give themselves to God and let Caesar have his money! Jesus had stopped the Herodians.[382]

Now some Sadducees stepped up. They asked a long, complicated question about brothers who marry the same woman and then die.

They went on and on, and finally asked, "Whose wife would this woman be in the resurrection?"[405]

"You don't know the Scriptures," Jesus answered. He knew Sadducees did not even BELIEVE in the resurrection!

> "In the resurrection there is no marrying. People in heaven will be like the angels of God. "

Then the Pharisees had a question. They asked, "Of all the laws, which is the most important?"[476]

Jesus said to him, 'Love the Lord, Your God, with all your heart, with all your soul, with all your mind.'[292] This is the greatest commandment." Then Jesus answered, "And the second commandment is just as important: 'Love your neighbor as yourself.'"[291]

Talk About the Story: What did Jesus say about the tax question? What did Jesus say is the most important command? Which one is just as important?

Scripture: "Love the LORD YOUR GOD WITH ALL YOUR HEART, WITH ALL YOUR SOUL, AND WITH ALL YOUR MIND . . . . LOVE YOUR NEIGHBOR AS YOURSELF." MATTHEW 22:37, 39

Family Time: How can someone tell they love God with all their heart, soul, and mind? What do you think it looks like and sounds like to love another person as much as you love yourself? What's a way you can show love to God today? How can you show love to your neighbor?

Prayer: Father, thank You for Jesus' wisdom. Thank You that You promise wisdom to us, too. Amen.

JESUS' QUESTION

Scripture: Matthew 22:41–46
Place: The Temple
Time: Tuesday April 4, 30 AD

Jesus had spent most of the day in the Temple again. The children had welcomed Him in the day before, but on THIS day, the leaders PRETENDED to welcome Him. They flattered Jesus, tried to soften Him up, hoping Jesus might say something that they might use against Him!

The leaders very much wanted to arrest Jesus and have Him killed. But they did not know how they could do it, because the people all loved Jesus and believed He was sent from God!

So the day had worn on, with rulers asking Jesus lots of questions, trying to trip Him up. But instead, Jesus' wisdom had stopped THEM. He had won every debate with them and answered every question.[382]

But before the leaders could leave, JESUS had a question that HE wanted to ask THEM! After all, they were the religious leaders of the Jewish people. They tried hard to make everyone believe that they were the wisest and holiest men in Israel! So of course, they would have the answer to even the hardest questions!

Jesus stopped them as they began to leave. He called out to them as they turned to go, "But what do you think about the MESSIAH? From whose family will He be born?"[192]

AH! They KNEW the answer to THAT question! They crossed their arms confidently, and cocked their heads.

"Messiah will be the son of King David. He will be a man who is a descendant of David's kingly line. The prophets say so!"

Jesus smiled. Then He asked, "Then how could God's Spirit cause King David to say, "The Lord said to my Lord, 'Sit at My right until I make your enemies into a footstool for you.'?[105] If King David called the Messiah his Lord, then how can the Messiah be the son or descendant of King David?"

The leaders harrumphed. They stroked their beards. They tried to look wise. They had NO IDEA how to answer this. Indeed, King David had written just that! And they all believed that God had inspired the words. So this was something GOD HAD SAID.

That meant David called the coming Messiah (Jesus!) his LORD. He had used the same word as the word for God, in the same sentence! The words he wrote are about God the Father telling Jesus to sit at His right hand (the place of honor) until God the Father makes an end of all of Jesus' enemies. Jesus had not yet died and risen, but after He went back to heaven, the Bible tells us that He DOES sit at God the Father's right, just as David described it!

So Jesus was telling these leaders that if what David said was true, then Messiah is GREATER than even King David. The Messiah is just the same as God Himself!

And nearly everyone in Israel believed Jesus was the Messiah. So if they believed these words, they'd have to agree that Jesus is the Messiah and the Son of God. THAT was not something they wanted to do!

So they didn't say a WORD. Jesus smiled at them as they left, muttering and harrumphing. And from then on, they did not ask Jesus ANY more questions![476]

Talk About the Story: Why did the leaders ask Jesus so many questions? What did Jesus ask them? Who wrote this prophecy? What does it show?

Scripture: "The Lord said to my Lord, 'Sit at My right hand, until I make Your enemies Your footstool.'" Psalm 110:1

Family Time: We think of the Psalms as songs, but this song told of a day yet to come. Where is Jesus now? Who is He with?

Prayer: Lord Jesus, we see how wise You are. Please help us to be wise when people ask us questions. Help us to remember we can always ask You to help us. In Your name, Amen.

PSALM 59
WHEN YOU ARE CURSED

David should have been the hero to all Israel. He killed Goliath. With the Philistine leader dead, the Philistines ran away. The young women sang, "Saul has killed his thousands, David has killed his ten thousands." But King Saul was too jealous to recognize David.

Once Saul threw his spear at David in the dining hall, but missed. David escaped. Then Saul sent soldiers to David's house to watch the house and kill him. David was married to Michal, Saul's daughter. She warned David and let David down through a window to escape. The soldiers came to the door for David; she sent them away saying he was sick.

Saul sent the soldiers back with the instructions to bring David in the bed to him. Michal stuffed the bed to look like David was sleeping and put goat's hair to look like David's head (1 Samuel 19:10-18).

David began his prayer about this situation asking God to save him. He told about his problems. People were waiting to kill him, yet he knew he was innocent. David didn't attack those who came against him, he pleaded his case to God.

> "O God, protect me from my enemies;
>   Save me from those who come to destroy me.
> Protect me from those who would murder me;[387]
>   They are only criminals who do evil.
> They are waiting for me in the shadows;
>   Those powerful soldiers lurk for me.
>   They are prepared to kill me, but I am innocent;
>   I have not broken the law."

David asked God to help him and defend him against his enemies. He called on God to come to his aid.

> "Lord, come see what they are doing to me,
>   You are the Lord God of the fighting angels.
> Come and punish their evil plans,
>   Don't let them off easy."[268]

David returned to his complaint. He described what the evil men were doing and what they wanted to do to him.

> "They come back to spy on me at sun down;
>> They sneak around the city looking for me.
> They yell cusses at me, and then they curse God;
>> They think no one hears their curses.
> But the Lord hears everything,
>> And He hears what is said by the heathen nations;
> So I wait on You my God to help me."[105]

Then David prayed about the soldiers waiting to arrest him or kill him. David reminded God they were cursing Him. So David knew God could punish them.

> "Don't kill them; they need to learn a lesson.
>> Let them suffer because of their sin; bring them down.
> They are angry with their curses,
>> So show Your anger against them.
> Let them find out that You rule all people,
>> And let the other evil men know it too."[248]

At the end of the psalm, David examined his heart. He opened up his voice to sing this psalm to God.

> "But as for me, I sing of Your power,
>> I will sing out loud Your mercy tomorrow morning,
> You planned a safe place for me to hide;
>> You defend me when I can't defend myself.[362]
> You are a strong God who defends me,
>> I will always count on Your help."[439]

Talk About the Psalm: What did you learn about the psalm writer in this story? What did you learn about God?

Psalm 59: Read this week's psalm in your Bible together. Choose a verse to read aloud as a prayer.

Prayer: Thank You, God, for the psalm prayers in the Bible. Thank You for teaching us about You and about how to pray. In Jesus' name, Amen.

THE WIDOW'S MITE

Scripture: Luke 21:1-4
Place: The Temple Treasury
Time: Tuesday, April 4, AD 30

Jesus sat with His friends near the treasury in the Temple. This was the place where there was a large gold covered chest into which offerings were received.[310] The large brass funnel at the top of the box sounded like a chime as coins clanged into the chest. Of course, the BIGGEST amounts of money poured into the chest sounded loudest! Everyone stopped to notice the giver who made so much noise!

A rich man slowly poured a bag of coins into the horn with a clatter . . . clang . . . zing . . . ping . . . bing! He was giving an immense offering, and wanted everyone to notice his impressive large offering.

And then some poorer people came by. They didn't have as much as the rich,

but they still wanted to impress everyone with how much money they were giving to God. They tossed their coins, one at a time, so that every coin made a ting . . . ping . . .bing!

Then Jesus saw a woman, a widow in black. She quietly crept toward the offering box. She looked both ways to make sure no one was watching her, but she didn't need to worry. No one saw her, no one cared. No one paid much attention to poor widows.

She had in her hands *two perutahs*—the smallest coins minted by Israel. Her two coins made up one *guadrans,* which made up a ninety-sixth part of a denar. THAT was only as much as a slave made in a day. She didn't have much to give.[412] But it was all she had.

She dropped the two small coins into the treasury. There was just the tiniest tink . . . tink. No one noticed, except Jesus. He said to His disciples,

"I tell you the truth: this poor widow has given more[428] in the offering than all the rich who gave large amounts of money to impress others." Compared to the rich, this woman gave much more of her wealth to God.[412]

Of course, Jesus' friends were confused! WHAT? They had heard a LOT of money being put into the treasury! And it had NOT come from that widow!

Then Jesus said, "The rich people gave SOME of their money, but they still have a lot left. And you see, this poor woman gave all that she had."

God notices how much you gave up to give to Him. God knows how much money you have left. And God knows WHY you gave.

The widow had given God everything. She had put God first. She was trusting God to take care of her. And those who put God first can trust God to take care of them!

The widow did not know that Jesus was watching. But she did know that God would take care of her. And God used the story of what she did to be greater than any big gifts given that day. Her story would be read and heard for years to come, all over the world. She gave all she had, and millions would know about her gift!

Talk About the Story: Who gave the most coins? Who did Jesus say gave the most? Why? How did she show she put God first?

Scripture: "But seek first the kingdom of God and His righteousness, and all these things shall be added to you." Matthew 6:33

Family Time: What are ways we can look for and ask for God's rule in our lives? What do you think it means to seek His righteousness? Look up the word, then talk about it!

Prayer: Lord, help us never be afraid to give our money to You. We want to obey You first, and give to You first, knowing You will take care of us. Amen.

GREEKS SEEK JESUS

Scripture: John 12:20–24
Place: The Temple and Mount of Olives
Time: Late Tuesday Afternoon, April 4, 30 AD

As the sun dipped towards the horizon, the last thing Jesus would do in the Temple unfolded. A group of Greeks in the Temple were searching for Jesus; they wanted to see Him.[541] Jesus spent His time in the Temple with the sick and children the day before. Today, Jesus spent time arguing with the Jewish leaders.

The Greeks felt unworthy of Jesus' time, so they waited until the day was almost over. Now they thought Jesus might have some time. The Greeks knew that Philip the apostle was in charge of details, for he was always checking where Jesus was and what He was doing. The Greeks asked Philip for an appointment with Jesus. They asked,

"Sir, we would see Jesus . . . ."[426]

Philip had lost track of Jesus for a moment, so he asked Andrew—Peter's younger brother—where to find Jesus.[314] No matter where Jesus was, Andrew always knew where to locate the Master. Greeks couldn't leave the Gentile part of the Temple, so Philip and Andrew brought Jesus out to them.

When Jesus met them, His reaction surprised everyone!

Instead of greeting them and inviting them to sit with Him, Jesus announced, "The time is come for the Son of Man to be glorified."[188]

WHAT? Philip and Andrew looked at each other, confused. Did Jesus mean the Temple gate would close soon? The crowd was beginning to leave, the sun was going down.

Jesus' friends didn't know it, but this day in Jesus' life would be His last public ministry before His death and resurrection. Little did they know that the last public audience Jesus would give was not to the Jews, but to Gentiles, people from outside of Israel. They would be the ones who would eventually carry His message around the world.

After Jesus said, "The hour is come," He said to the Gentiles, "Most assuredly, I say to you, unless a grain of wheat falls into the ground and dies, it remains alone; but if it dies, it produces much grain." (John 12:24).[415]

Traditionally Gentiles could only enter into the Court of the Gentiles. They had sent to see Jesus because they could not come to Him. They could not enter the Temple area. They were Greeks by birth. But their pure desire to see Christ gave evidence of their hearts. To them Jesus was more than Israel's Messiah, Jesus was more than the Son of David; they wanted to know Him as Jesus the Savior—their Savior and the Savior of the world.[419]

The giant Golden Gate to the Temple clanged as it shut. The Temple was closed to the Messiah now. But before long, He would prove that He is Lord of all.

Talk About the Story: Who wanted to see Jesus? If you plant a seed, does a plant come up right away? What happens after it seems to be dead a while? How is that like Jesus' dying and then living again?

Scripture: "I say to you, unless a grain of wheat falls into the ground and dies, it remains alone; but if it dies, it produces much grain." John 12:24

Family Time: Andrew and Philip brought people to Jesus. How could you bring people to Jesus?

Prayer: Jesus, help us to notice people who need to come to You. Help us to show them the way! Amen.

SERVANTS GIVEN MONEY TO GROW

Scripture: Matthew 25:14–30
Place: Near Jerusalem
Time: Wednesday, April 5, AD 30

Jesus and His friends were walking out toward the Mount of Olives. Jesus had a lot to tell His friends before He died. You see, they thought they knew JUST how the Kingdom of God would come. They thought that when Jesus entered Jerusalem, He would get rid of the Romans and rule over the Jews like King David had done.

But this kingdom was going to be different. So Jesus told them a parable to help them know how they should act while they waited for the Kingdom of God. This is Jesus' story:

A rich man was about to go on a long trip. But before he left, he called his servants to talk with him. He gave each servant a large amount of money. To one man, he gave five piles of money. To another, he gave two piles of money. To a third man, he gave one pile of money. He did not give everyone the same amount, because he knew what they were good at. So he gave them what he knew would be best for each of them.

He told each of them, "Use this money to make more. Use it wisely until I get back."[431]

The master left. The man who'd gotten five piles of money went right to work. He bought sheep and sold cattle. He worked until his five piles of money became TEN!

The man who had two piles went to work, too. He made things and sold things. He turned his two piles of money into FOUR!

But the man who had been given one pile didn't use it AT ALL. Instead, he dug a hole and BURIED the money! He didn't want to risk anything to make his master more money.

One day, the rich man returned from his long trip. Of course, he wanted to know what his servants had done with the money he had given them!

The first servant told his master, "I invested the five piles of money and now I have ten to give to you."[117]

The rich man said, "Well done! You're a good and faithful servant. Because you have been faithful in this little thing, I will put you in charge of much more."

The next servant said he had used his two piles of money to make two more. He had four to give his master. And the master said the same thing! The master was glad to see that he did something with the money!

The third servant came saying, "Lord, here is the one pile of money you gave me. I saved it. You might have punished me for losing it, so I buried it in the ground."[275]

The rich man said, "I will judge you by your own words. Yes, I don't want you to lose my money. So why didn't you at least give my money to the bank? You could easily have done that! I could have made some interest from it."

Then the rich man said, "Take what this lazy servant has. Give it to the man who has ten. Everyone who has been faithful in serving me will be given more. [409] And everyone who not been faithful will have everything taken from him."[275]

Talk About the Story: Who worked to make more? What reward did these two have? Why did the third servant not trust the master enough to obey?

Scripture: "His lord said to him, 'Well done, good and faithful servant; you have been faithful over a few things, I will make you ruler over many things. Enter into the joy of your lord.'" Matthew 25:23

Family Time: What gifts has God given you? What is a way you can use your gifts wisely today to obey God?

Prayer: Lord, while we wait for You to return, help us to trust You, obey You and be glad to see You when You return! Amen.

A DAY OF ANTICIPATION

Scripture: Matthew 26:1–5; Mark
14:1–2; Luke 22:1–6
Place: Near Jerusalem
Time: Wednesday, April 5, AD 30

Jesus had been talking about the future with His disciples. They were a little shaken by the things Jesus was saying. But Jesus wanted them to be ready for hard times that were going to come later.

You see, Jesus' friends thought that soon, Jesus would be crowned King of Israel. They thought He would get the Romans out of the country. The Romans were the empire that was in charge of Israel, and most of the people did NOT like that!

But Jesus knew the truth. He knew that He was not going to become a king in the way His friends expected. No, He knew that soon, He would be arrested, tried and killed on a cross. But Jesus was willing to do this. It was the main reason Jesus came to Earth!

So Jesus told His friends, "As you know, Passover is in two days. That's when the Son of Man will be handed over to the leaders. Then He will be crucified."[260]

Jesus' friends looked at each other. They wondered, *What is Jesus talking about? It's true that the leaders don't like Him, but the people all LOVE Jesus! How could He even think of such a thing?*

We are a lot like that! Sometimes, we spend more time thinking of reasons something can't be true than we do paying attention to the truth!

Jesus' friends whispered. "How could this be? I thought Jesus was going to become our King!"

"I don't know. If HE dies, it's all over!"

But of course, Jesus knew the truth. He knew that the chief priests and the leaders were gathering in the palace of Caiaphas, the high priest that year. They were coming together to think of a way to arrest Jesus! They wanted to arrest Him and KILL Him.[165] But because so MANY people loved Jesus, they were sure they could not do it during Passover. Many more people had come for the holiday. And since Jesus had just made Lazarus alive after four days of being dead, EVERYONE was going to Bethany to see Lazarus! In fact, some leaders wanted to kill Lazarus, too!

You see, the leaders had ONE GOAL: to stay in power. They wanted to continue to be in charge! So they did NOT want to start a riot. If there was any kind of riot or trouble, then the Romans would send in more army troops. The Jewish leaders might lose their power and position. No matter what, THEY wanted to stay in charge! So they wanted to kill Jesus before anyone noticed what they were doing.

But Jesus knew. He knew that His friend Judas Iscariot would soon offer to help these leaders arrest Him without people seeing it.[139]

Jesus' friends worried. But Jesus knew God was working His plan to take away the sin of the world. By Jesus' one great act of love, sin would be paid for, once and for all. The leaders might think they could kill Jesus, but they could not stop God from raising Jesus back to life again!

Talk About the Story: Why did Jesus' friends worry? What did the leaders want to do? Why did they not want people to know what they were doing? What did Jesus know?

Scripture: "He said, 'Behold, I have come to do Your will, O God'. . . . we have been sanctified through the offering of the body of Jesus Christ once for all." Hebrews 10:9–10

Family Time: Jesus came to do God's will. Tell about a time when obeying God was hard. What happened? What did Jesus do by obeying God?

Prayer: Lord, we are glad that You obeyed God the Father and died and rose again. Help us to obey, too! Amen.

DATE ___/___

NEGOTIATING 30 PIECES OF SILVER

Scripture: Matthew 26:14-16, Luke 22:3-6
Place: Temple
Time: Wednesday, April 6, 30 AD

Judas Iscariot stood waiting in line. He smoothed the wrinkles of his tunic and stroked his beard. Judas was not waiting to make a sacrifice for his sin, although he was waiting in that line. He had a secret mission.[238]

Judas had grown unhappy with Jesus. Judas wanted to be leader, but he had the treasurer's job. Although Judas was trusted with money, he had been stealing some money for his own personal use. Judas decided he should be paid extra for counting money, paying bills, and dealing with merchants.

So unhappy Judas made a plan to betray Jesus, to get Jesus arrested by the Jewish leaders without his being seen.

And Judas knew that Jesus could do miracles. So couldn't He just escape from them like He had done before?

When Judas' turn came, he whispered to the Levite, "I am one of Jesus' disciples." He looked both ways to make sure no one heard him. "I must talk to your leaders."

The Levite whisked Judas through a small door into a room where Levites got ready for their duties. After the Jewish leaders were certain that Judas was one of Jesus' followers, Judas announced to them,   "I can help you capture Jesus."[139]

The group nodded to one another. This was the moment they'd waited for.

Judas explained, "Jesus will celebrate the Passover meal on Thursday evening. After the meal Jesus is likely to pray in the Garden of Gethsemane. It will be late at night. No one will be out. And . . . I can lead you to Him."

Judas knew the Jewish leaders wanted to arrest Jesus quietly, away from people. Nearly everyone believed Jesus was a prophet or the Messiah!

The leader asked, "How can we help you get ready?"

Judas had an answer. Thirty pieces of silver was the price of a slave. To him, 30 pieces was the right amount for Jesus.

He said to the leaders, "I'll need 30 pieces of silver . . . this money will be given to the poor . . . doing the work of God . . . ."[101]

Judas lied. The money was for himself. When he mentioned 30 pieces of silver, his voice did not drop, he didn't flinch. This was a business deal.

The leaders talked a moment. Was it legal to pay money to capture an enemy? They weren't sure they could trust Judas, but what else could they do? They answered, "We'll do it . . . ."[10]

A young man left the room and brought back a tied leather sack of coins. He tried to hand it to the leader, but the leader wouldn't touch money paid for a person's life. He nodded toward the table, and the bag of coins thudded down with a jangling noise.

"We are glad to give to the poor. Here are 30 pieces of silver . . . may your mission be successful," said the leader.

Judas grabbed the bag and stuffed it into his tunic. He strode out of the Temple, trying to act as if he had not just betrayed his Lord for a slave's price.[438]

Talk About the Story: Who was Judas Iscariot? What position did he hold among the apostles? What lie did he tell the leaders?

Scripture: "And from that time he sought opportunity to betray him." Matthew 26:16

Family Time: What does it mean to betray a person? What are ways we betray or break a person's trust? What helps us to be honest and to not destroy people's trust in us?

Prayer: Father, the devil is the father of lies. Help us to tell the truth at all times and be honest in all we do. Amen.

THE UPPER ROOM

Scripture: Matthew 26:17–19, Mark
14:12–16; Luke 22:7–13
Place: An upper room in Jerusalem
Time: Thursday, April 6, AD 30

It was Thursday of Passover week. Jesus and His friends were walking back to Jerusalem. Jesus said to Peter and John, "Go ahead of us into the city and prepare a place for us to celebrate the Passover feast."[207]

Passover was a lot like Thanksgiving for us. People visited their relatives and usually ate with their families.[300] Everyone who could get to Jerusalem came for Passover. God's law said that everyone who could travel should come and celebrate!

And WHY did people celebrate Passover? Way back in ancient times, Israel's family moved to the country of Egypt. God had sent Joseph ahead to become a ruler there. This way, God saved them from starving when there was no food.

But years went by. The family of Israel grew! The Egyptians made them slaves. For years, they did all the hardest work in Egypt. But finally, they cried out to God to help them be freed from slavery!

God sent Moses to tell the Egyptian pharaoh to let Israel go! But the pharaoh would not. So God sent all kinds of troubles to Egypt. But God protected His

www.thefamilyprayerbible.com

people from most of them. To protect them from a trouble of death that was coming, God told each family to kill a perfect lamb. This lamb's blood was to be painted on the doorposts of their house. That way, the angel of death would "pass over" them. They would be safe. The lamb was to be eaten with bread that had no yeast, for there would not be time to let bread rise—God was going to get them out of Egypt that very night. And GOD DID! So God told them to celebrate how He had saved them from slavery in Egypt. Passover was that celebration.[166]

And know this about the Passover lamb, who died to protect each family from death: After Jesus was baptized, John the Bapitzer called Him "the LAMB of GOD, who takes away the sin of the world!" Jesus was God's own Passover lamb. He would die to take the punishment for sin so that everyone could be protected from sin's punishment!

Passover was a VERY big feast! It wasn't likely that there was ANY place to make a holiday dinner. So it seemed like Jesus had asked His friends to do something impossible!

Peter and John replied, "Where shall we find a place, as late as it is?"

Jesus said, "When you enter Jerusalem, you'll see a man carrying a jar of water."

Usually, a man did not bring water from the well. That was considered a woman's job. So it wouldn't be hard to spot this man.

"Follow the man to the house where he goes. Then ask if they have a room where the Teacher can eat the Passover meal with His disciples.[118] They will show you a large upper room already set with tables and seats. Prepare that room for the Passover.[207]

So Peter and John went on ahead, through the gate of the city, looking toward the well. Just as Jesus said, they saw a man with a tall water jar set up on his shoulder. He led them to the house. And when they asked, of COURSE the people showed them the room, just as Jesus said. So they set up the room for a Passover feast!

When Jesus tells us what to do, we can be sure that He has the details worked out. All we need to do is to obey![327]

Talk About the Story: Why did the Jewish people celebrate Passover? What did John call Jesus?

Scripture: "You are My friends if you do whatever I command you." John 14:14

Family Time: What are three things Jesus commands or tells us to do? What's way you can obey each of those commands?

Prayer: Jesus, You show us that when You have a job for us, we can trust You to work it out. Thank you for helping us to obey! Amen.

PSALM 71
GROWING OLD GOD'S WAY

Two families in a church treated their grandfather differently. In the caring family, "Gramps" still lives in his own house after his wife died. They eat with Gramps every Sunday and his daughter phones each day to check on him. One of the children drops by to do some of the house cleaning chores. Gramps comes over once a week for dinner, and he does some maintenance jobs around the house for them. They gather for big meals on holidays and he takes at least one of the vacations with the family.

Another family puts their grandfather in a nursing home in another city. They seldom visit, but try to phone once or twice a week. They don't have their grandfather visit too often, thinking he would rather spend time with his older friends in the nursing home.

Psalm 71 is about growing old. In some families, the elderly are honored, while other families seem to want the elderly out of the way. We must be careful that we don't become so self-consumed and so busy, and so wrapped up in our own world that we forget about our elderly family members.[160]

Psalm 71 tells us all to prepare for old age for we will all be there eventually. What you will be when you are old is what you are becoming now. If you are not living for God now, you probably won't later; unless God does a miracle. If you are negative and grumpy now, you will not be positive and cheerful later. If you don't worship God now, you will not do it when you are old.

Psalm 71 shows the life of an old man facing problems. He still has people who criticize him but he is still a joyful man who puts his trust in God.

"My God, rescue me from the clutches of the wicked;
You alone are my hope and life.
I've trusted You from my earliest childhood;
You alone have been with me from birth.
So, I am not surprised that I still trust You;
You have been with me throughout life."[387]

The positive habits developed in youth will keep you going in old age. Those good habits will keep you happy and productive in your old age.

> *"My life is an example to all who see me*
> > *That You have been my protection and strength.*
> *That is why I never stop praising You;*[478]
> > *I will declare Your faithfulness all day long.*
> *Don't leave me when my strength gets weaker;*
> > *Don't set me on the shelf with nothing to do."*

Psalm 71 makes a strong point. "God's way to grow old is to walk with Him while you are young." You can handle your problems well as an older person if you solve your problem with God as you grow up.

> *"O God, You taught me how to live from my childhood;*
> > *Now I constantly tell of Your power in my life.*[478]
> *Now that I am older and greyer,*
> > *Stay as close to me as You did in my youth.*
> *Let me tell the next generation of Your ability to strengthen;*
> > *They need to know Your mighty miracles."*[279]

Talk About the Psalm: What did you learn about the psalm writer in this story? What did you learn about God?

Psalm 71: Read this week's psalm in your Bible together. Choose a verse to read aloud as a prayer.

Prayer: Thank You, God, for the psalm prayers in the Bible. Thank You for teaching us about You and about how to pray. In Jesus' name, Amen.

THE LAST SUPPER

Scripture: Matthew 26:20–25; Mark
14:17–21; Luke 22:14–16
Place: An upper room in Jerusalem
Time: Thursday, April 6, sundown

Peter and John finished preparing. This upper room was ready for the Passover dinner, and food would be on its way soon from downstairs. They grinned at each other.

But as the other ten disciples arrived, a tense feeling came with them. On the way, they'd been talking about who was the most important among them. After all, if Jesus was going to be the KING, they ALL wanted who would be the second in command. Instead of being brothers, they all wanted to be first.

Besides this, James and John's mother had recently come to Jesus and asked that her two sons be on His left and right when He ruled. He was kind to her, but she clearly did not know what she was asking. Like the rest, she was expecting a human kingdom, with Jesus as the human king! When the others heard about this, they were angry. So talk of being first was on their minds.

"Who'll get the seat of honor at our Passover supper?" one asked as he climbed the steps toward the narrow door that led into the banquet room.[228]

www.thefamilyprayerbible.com

"Not you," another said. "If you aspire to sit next to Jesus, that proves you don't deserve it." The others laughed nervously.

Not far from the door sat an empty bowl, a pitcher of water and a towel. It was rude to enter a home without washing your feet. But there was no servant to do the dirty job. And as important as they all felt, they certainly were NOT going to do it! So they slipped off their sandals, walked past the washbasin and came into the banquet hall with dirty feet.

"Sit here," Jesus said to Judas, pointing to His left. "I will honor you this evening." Judas' smile broke through his neatly trimmed beard. That made sense. Jesus had appointed him treasurer; he seemed to have done that well.

"Sit on my right," Jesus said to John, who had helped prepare the room. "It is the seat of friendship."[293]

Other disciples glanced at one another. Ever since John's mother had asked Jesus to let her two sons sit to His right and left in the kingdom, the others had been quietly angry.

"Just because her husband died and left her money doesn't mean she can get anything she wants for her two sons . . . ." complained one.

"John's too young to be honored so," another muttered.

But Jesus invited John to sit on His right. Later, He would talk about how being youngest and being a servant are the places of the greatest honor.

"Sit! Wherever you like," Jesus gestured to the rest and they jostled each other to get those seats closest to Jesus.

With their grumbling hearts and their dirty feet, these men were not ready for the Passover meal on the outside OR on the inside!

But Jesus loved them. And He was now about to show them all just how deep and strong His love is. He began with taking care of the outside. He rose to get the bowl and the towel to wash their feet.

Talk About the Story: What had James and John's mother asked Jesus? How did this make the other disciples feel? What did they talk about on the way to the meal? What kind of king did they expect Jesus to be?

Scripture: "He who is greatest among you, let him be as the younger, and he who governs as he who serves." Luke 22:26

Family Time: How is a great or important person usually different from a younger person? Who does Jesus say we should be like? What are ways we can serve Him and others?

Prayer: Lord Jesus, it is not in our nature to want to serve others. Thank You that we can trust You to help us do that. In Your name, Amen.

WASHING THEIR FEET

Scripture: Matthew 26:21–30, John 13:11–12
Place: The Upper Room in Western Jerusalem
Time: Early Thursday Evening, April 6, 30 AD

Here at the Passover dinner, everyone had finally found places at the table, grumbling to themselves, *I should have a better place.*

Some were even still arguing in whispers about the seat of honor. They could smell the food coming up.

But Jesus had seen the attitudes and the actions of His loved friends. And His feet were dirty, too! So when Jesus got up and walked over to the pitcher and basin, everyone knew what He would do.

Jesus took off His outer coat. He laid aside His best tunic. He wrapped the servant's towel around his waist and poured water into the basin that everyone else had walked past. Jesus was going to do the job they would not do.[208]

As Jesus carried the basin toward the table, each disciple glanced down, not embarrassed. They didn't know what to say.

"No!" each one wanted to say.

But who could correct Jesus? He was the Master, their Leader, their Example. In silent shame, they watched and waited.[431]

www.thefamilyprayerbible.com

"Me first," all turned to watch. "Wash mine first. I have the honored seat," Judas said, "so I want my feet washed first."

Jesus knelt before Judas and placed his feet in the basin . . . and washed them . . . and dried them . . . . From His knees, Jesus looked up into Judas' eyes. But Jesus saw deeper into his soul. Jesus was looking for repentance, but He saw stubborn sin.

It would be hard for anyone to wash the feet of someone who was about to betray them, but Jesus washed Judas' feet—not just because they were dirty, but because Jesus is the friend of sinners. Jesus washed the feet of the one who would harm Him most.[139]

Then Jesus came to Peter, who had been thinking of how HE was too good to do the servant's job! Now JESUS was doing it.

Peter said, "Lord, don't wash my feet."

Jesus answered, "You don't know what I am doing. You will understand later."[390]

Peter then answered, "No! You'll never wash my feet."

Jesus responded, "If I don't wash you, you have no part with Me."

So Peter said, "Then don't wash my feet only, but my hands and head, too."[75]

Jesus chuckled. He said, "Those who have taken a bath are clean all over. They need only to wash their feet that get dirty walking in this world."

Then Jesus paused. He said, "But not all of you are clean,"[208] because He knew what Judas had already chosen to do.

When Jesus finished, He put His tunic on and they began to pass the food.

He said, "You call me Master, and Lord, and that is true; I am both Master and Lord.[346] If I your Lord and Master washed your feet, then you should wash one another's feet.[261] Follow My example and treat each other the way I have treated you."

In washing their feet, Jesus gave His friends a picture of how He had chosen to set aside His glory in heaven, and take on human flesh. He came into the world to be a servant.[256]

Talk About the Story: What did Jesus show His friends by washing their feet? What was Peter's response? How did Jesus say they should act?

Scripture: "If anyone desires to be first, he shall be last of all and servant of all." Matthew 9:35

Family Time: When do we like to be first? Last? What are ways to put others first?

Prayer: Father, please give us a humble spirit. We want to be like Jesus. Amen.

DATE ___/___

JUDAS' LAST CHANCE

Scripture: John 13:13–30
Place: Upper Room
Time: Thursday Evening, April 6, 30 AD

After Jesus had washed his friends' feet, He put back on His tunic, sat down with them and began to talk about what He had done. But Jesus did not talk long about washing their feet.

He changed to a more dangerous topic. The apostles had no idea of the drama that was happening in front of them. But Jesus knew. And Jesus wanted Judas to know that his betrayal was not a secret from Him.[139]

While washing their feet, Jesus told them all, "You are clean . . . but not everyone . . . one of you is not clean."

Jesus wanted Judas to realize that He knew. Jesus also wanted to give Judas an opportunity to confess and repent.[399] That's why He had said, "Not all of you are clean."[450] The others did not know what Jesus meant.

But then Jesus said plainly, "One of you will betray Me."[139]

The disciples were shocked! Several shook their heads and denied it; but at the same time, they asked, "Lord, is it I?"[23]

Sitting next to Jesus in the place of honor was Judas. He tilted his head but didn't show any emotion. He stroked his chin, then whispered to Jesus, "Teacher, is it I?"

The 30 pieces of silver were tied to his waist. The question slipped easily off his tongue. Jesus noted that the others called Him "Lord." It was the title He had just used talking about Himself. But Judas used a lesser title . . . Jesus was only a teacher to Judas. Only Judas asked, "Teacher, is it I?" Jesus turned quietly to whisper back, "You said it."[255]

The apostles glanced back and forth, wondering what was in the heart of the one beside him. Peter motioned across the table to young John to ask who the betrayer was. John sitting on the right of Jesus, leaned over close and whispered, "Lord . . ., who will betray You?"

Jesus did not answer immediately. He waited until everyone was paying attention. Perhaps Jesus still held hope that Judas would repent. So Jesus announced to the whole group, "I will give the bread dipped in the bowl to the one who betrays Me."

There was a large bowl of lamb stew served at the Passover meal. The master of ceremonies—usually the father—dipped bread into the lamb stew, then handed the dripping bread to the guest of honor. Judas was the guest of honor, so he got the lamb stew first.[29] Jesus broke off a small morsel of bread, formed a small cup in the bread with His fingers, then scooped up the lamb stew and handed it to Judas. Handing the bread to Judas was the normal thing to do—no one thought Jesus was telling them Judas would betray Him! But Judas knew!

Jesus broke off more pieces of bread. Dipping each one into the stew, He gave it to each of the other disciples. But Jesus' act was a loud, clear message to Judas.[440]   Judas instinctively reached down to touch the 30 pieces of silver tied in his sash. Like a hangman's noose, the sash was squeezing life from Judas. He wouldn't repent. While the others didn't know what was going on, Jesus and Judas[506] both knew.

Talk About the Story: What did Jesus say about who would betray Him? Why do you think Judas called Jesus "Teacher" instead of "Master"? What did Jesus hand to Judas, and then to each disciple?

Scripture: "Even my own familiar friend in whom I trusted, who ate my bread, has lifted up his heel against me." Psalm 41:9

Family Time Who was Jesus' friend, trusted with the money? Describe what you think it means to lift up your heel against someone. (Think of a donkey's kick!)

Prayer: Jesus, we want to be Your true friends. Thank You for helping us when it is hard to be Your friend. Amen.

JUDAS WENT OUT

Scripture: John 13:23–30
Place: The Upper Room
Time: Thursday night April 3, AD

Judas Iscariot grew more and more tense as supper went on. His friends around him laughed and talked and smiled, but Judas' smile had turned to a grimace. The money in the bag inside his belt felt like it was burning a hole right through his heart but he did not care. His mind was made up. .

During the meal, Jesus had made it clear to Judas that Jesus knew EXACTLY what Judas was going to do. He could not hide his heart from Jesus.

Over time, Judas had hardened his heart; finally, he turned his back on God. It began small, as sin often does. He carried the money bag, and began stealing from the money that belonged to all of them.

Maybe Judas decided they owed him extra money for his hard work. Maybe he was jealous of the others. Or maybe he really wanted power—and could not get power through his political friends, so he thought he could get power with Jesus. If Jesus was the next king of Israel, imagine the important position the treasurer might have later!

Whatever wound of Judas's that the devil infected, somewhere Judas decided

www.thefamilyprayerbible.com

that he did not have to obey God's rule: "Do not steal."

Judas had finally gone to the religious leaders to plot how they could secretly arrest Jesus. They gave him the money, he took the job, and he surrendered his soul to Satan.[114] If there had been any flicker of light in Judas' life, it was snuffed out now.

Near the end of supper, Judas was so tense he thought he would explode. Finally, Jesus had looked Judas in the eye and said to him, "What you have to do, do quickly."

Judas rose and snatched up the treasury bag of money—the money that belonged to all of them. He clutched it tightly as a person squeezes the life out of a bird. Without looking back, he slipped to the doorway and then went quietly down the stairs.

One disciple said, "Where's Judas going?" He noticed Judas took the money bag.

Another answered, "He's going to give to the poor. It's almost time for "*Chagigah.*"[388]

The *Chagigah* was the late sacrifice on Passover. The Great Temple gates were opened at midnight to begin early preparation for the offering of the *Chagigah*, a required festival sacrifice. Because many gave extra money to the poor at this time there were poor people thronged outside the Great Temple gates. The others assumed Judas was going to give money to the people at the gate.

Judas stepped out into the darkness with the disciples' money bag clutched to his chest and 30 pieces of silver weighing down his belt. There was no turning back. He would lead the soldiers to arrest Jesus.

Young John watched Judas leave. John went out to close the door he left open at the bottom of the stairs. He looked outside for a trace of light; there was none. Outside, the dark was inky black.[440]

Talk About the Story: What wrong did Judas before he betrayed Jesus? When we do wrong, we all make excuses. What might Judas' excuses have been? What did Jesus know about Judas?

Scripture: "The Son of Man indeed goes just as it is written of Him, but woe to that man by whom the Son of Man is betrayed! It would have been good for that man if he had never been born." Mark 14:21

Family Time: Who is the Son of Man? What does it mean to be betrayed? What habits can we develop that help us be people who do not betray or break people's trust?

Prayer: Lord Jesus, this story is sad. We see how You even love Judas. Thank You for loving us even when we hurt You. Amen.

THE BROKEN BODY AND CUP

Scripture: Matthew 26:26–30; Luke 22:14–20
Place: Jerusalem
Time: Thursday night April 3, AD

❝I've been looking forward to eating this meal with you—" Jesus said to His disciples sitting around the table.[77] Maybe they smiled, hearing these kind words.[388]

"—before my suffering begins," Jesus finished.

WHAT? Suffering? the disciples began to worry. *But this is a meal of CELEBRATION!*

At the holiday of Passover, Jews ate a special meal to remember all their ancestors had suffered in Egypt, and to remember how God had saved them! It was a meal to celebrate God. During a Passover meal, the host held up each item the guests would eat, describing what each part was supposed to help them remember.

Holding up the bread, the host might say, "We eat this to remember what our ancestors ate when they suffered in Egypt." Or holding up the bone from a roast lamb, the host might explain, "This helps us remember the sacrifice our ancestors made. When God sent a deadly plague in Egypt, they painted lamb's blood over their doorposts, a sign they trusted God. Seeing this, God 'passed over' and saved them!"

www.thefamilyprayerbible.com

So it probably wasn't too surprising when Jesus held up the bread and began to speak. Jesus blessed the bread, thanking God for it.[472] Then Jesus broke off pieces of the bread, one piece for each disciple.

"Take and eat this," Jesus said. "This is my body, which is broken like this bread for you. Every time you eat this, remember Me,"[95]

That's not what we expected Him to say! As the disciples chewed, they realized Jesus was giving a new meaning to their meal.

Then Jesus held up a cup. Jesus thanked God for this, too, before sharing it with His disciples.[300] "All of you, drink," Jesus invited them. "This is my blood. It confirms God's new covenant, His plan and promise to forgive people's sins." Each disciple there drank form the cup.

"My blood is poured out as a sacrifice so that many people's sins can be forgiven," Jesus explained. "Every time you drink this, remember Me." Jesus didn't want His disciples EVER to forget Him or God's promise. People would only be forgiven and saved from their sins if they believed God's promise, and Jesus' sacrifice was a BIG part of that promise. But people could only believe the promise if they REMEMBERED it!

Some people might forget and just eat the bread and drink the cup because everyone else did, thinking this would make God happy and save them. But if they didn't remember WHY they ate and drank, it would be just like any ordinary breakfast, lunch, or dinner! They had to remember what the meal meant, believing that Jesus' sacrifice of His body and blood made a way for people to be forgiven and saved.[416]

After the meal, Jesus began to sing and the disciples joined in, remembering God as they worshiped Him.[439]

Talk About the Story: What did eating the Passover meal help people remember? What did Jesus say when He gave His disciples the bread? What did He say when He gave the wine?

Scripture: "I will take up the cup of salvation, and call upon the name of the Lord." Psalm 116:13

Family Time: What did Jesus want His disciples to remember when they ate the bread and drank the wine? Today people take communion in church to remember and be thankful for Jesus' sacrifice that saves them! How can you show you remember God? How can you thank God for what He has done?

Prayer: Dear Lord, thank You for Jesus' sacrifice that makes a way for us to be forgiven for the wrong things we do and be close to God. Help us always remember what Jesus did for us. We praise You for making a way. In Jesus name, Amen.

PETER'S BOAST

Scripture: John 13:36–38
Place: Jerusalem
Time: Thursday night April 3, AD

Dinner was done, but Jesus still had more to tell His disciples. "Dear children," He said, speaking kind words like a loving father. "I won't be with you much longer. You'll search for Me, but you can't come where I'm going."

Not follow Jesus? But we left everything—our friends, our jobs, our homes—to follow Him. We've been following Him for three years! What does He mean we can't come now? Jesus' words left them stunned.

Jesus continued, "So, I'm giving you a new command to follow: Love each other, in the same way I have loved you. When people see the way you show love, they'll know you are My disciples. They'll see Me in you."[296]

"Lord, where are You going?" Peter asked, still thinking about the first (and most shocking) thing Jesus had said.

Jesus knew Peter was asking because he wanted to go with Jesus, to keep following Him. "You can't come with Me there now, but later you will follow Me,"[261] Jesus answered.

"But Lord, why can't I follow You now?" Peter asked. *Why do I have to wait?* he wondered, feeling frustrated and confused. "I'm ready to DIE for You!" Peter blurted out.

www.thefamilyprayerbible.com

Jesus listened patiently. "Do you really think you would do that, Peter? Die for Me?" Jesus questioned Peter's boast. Peter was passionate—and quick to act, or at least quick to promise to act!

Doesn't Jesus trust me? Peter questioned, his own confidence perhaps starting to fade. *Why does He doubt my commitment to Him?* Full of courage in the moment, Peter had felt fearless, ready to go anywhere with Jesus, even if it meant risking his life! But Jesus understood Peter didn't have any idea what he was promising. How could Peter really know what it would be like to die?[99]

Jesus shared the sad truth: "Peter, before the rooster crows tomorrow morning, you will deny THREE times that you even know Me."[29]

WHAT? How humiliating! Peter couldn't believe it. *I'm willing to DIE for Him, but all Jesus thinks I'll actually do is LIE? I'd die, not lie!*

Even though Jesus' followers didn't always understand what Jesus said or did, they had been learning to trust Him. When Jesus said someone would be healed, they were! Jesus' words were powerful and they ALWAYS proved true. But Peter didn't want these words about him to come true!

Maybe Jesus admired Peter's passion, but He knew what was really in Peter's heart, even if Peter himself didn't know! Jesus knew the truth: Peter had spoken too quickly, feeling and speaking instead of THINKING and speaking. Maybe he'd meant well, but he'd made a promise he simply couldn't keep.

Talk About the Story: What did Jesus say that shocked the disciples? What questions did Peter ask Jesus about it? What did Peter boast about to Jesus? How did Jesus react to Peter's boast?

Scripture: "Do you see a man hasty in his words? There is more hope for a fool than for him." Proverbs 29:20

Family Time: Peter promised he'd die for Jesus, but Jesus said Peter would actually do what? How do you think Jesus' words made Peter feel about his boast? About himself? Peter spoke quickly, without really thinking about his boast. When is a time you or someone you know spoke too quickly, making a promise that wasn't kept? When the promise wasn't kept, how did this make you and others feel?

Prayer: Dear Lord, Peter loved You so much he wanted to follow You no matter what. But Peter boasted without really thinking, making a promise he could never keep. When we make promises we can't keep, we hurt others and ourselves. Help us remember to think before we make promises. In Jesus' name, Amen.

PSALM 72
PRAYER FOR THE NEW RULER

Solomon had just become king over all Israel. He called himself, "The son of the king." He sacrificed to God as his father David had done. Then God appeared to Solomon and said, "Ask what I shall give you?" (1 Kings 3:5).[128] Solomon asked for wisdom confessing, "I am like a little child." Specifically, "Give me an understanding mind so that I can govern Your people well and know the difference between right and wrong."[534]

God was pleased that Solomon didn't ask for riches, honor, or long life. So God promised, "I will give you a wise and understanding mind such as one no else has ever had or will ever have."[239] Notice what Solomon prayed in Psalm 72,

> *"O God, give understanding to your king;*
> *Help this king's son make wise decisions.*
> *Help him judge his people in the right way;*

> *Let all the poor be treated fairly.*[416]
> *May our farms give prosperity to all*
>   *And may our fields be fruitful and plenty.*[74]
> *May I the king do what is right;*
>   *Help me protect the poor who can't defend themselves,*
> *May I rescue children in need."*

But Solomon didn't ask for riches, honor or long life, God said He would also give these things to him.

One of the first tough decisions to face Solomon was an argument between two women. The women had babies only three days apart. As they were sleeping with their babies, one woman rolled on to her baby in the night and it died. She then took the other woman's baby. The next morning both women claimed the living baby and both denied the dead baby was hers. They argued their case before Solomon.

He said, "Take a sword and cut the live baby in half, and give each woman a half."

The real mother said, "No," she was horrified her baby would be killed.

The woman who stole the baby said, "Go ahead and cut the baby in half." She didn't show the heart of a real mother. Solomon then gave the baby to the real mother.

"Word of the king's decision spread quickly through all Israel and the people realized the great wisdom God had given him to render decisions with justice (1 Kings 3:28). Solomon continued to pray for a peaceful reign with prosperity for his people.

> *"May the king's rule be refreshing like spring rain on the grass*
>   *Like showers that bring life to the earth.*
> *May godly people prosper during the king's rule;*
>   *May people have plenty.*[74]
> *As long as the moon shines,*
>   *May the king rule from sea to sea,*
> *From the Euphrates River to the ends of the earth."*[46]

Talk About the Psalm: What did you learn about the psalm writer in this story? What did you learn about God?

Psalm 72: Read this week's psalm in your Bible together. Choose a verse to read aloud as a prayer.

Prayer: Thank You, God, for the psalm prayers in the Bible. Thank You for teaching us about You and about how to pray. In Jesus' name, amen.

LOTS OF QUESTIONS

Scripture: John 14
Place: Jerusalem
Time: Thursday night April 3, AD

Jesus is going AWAY—without us? the disciples worried about Jesus leaving and the other things He had told them would happen soon.

"Don't let your hearts feel troubled,"[414] Jesus said. "Believe in God. Believe in Me."[497] Jesus knew their worries, and He wanted them to know that trusting God would help them not feel so troubled.

"I'm going to prepare a place for you, where you can join Me,"[215] Jesus said. "You know the way there." Jesus wasn't abandoning the disciples, and He said He had a good reason for going!

"But Lord, we don't know WHERE You're going," said Thomas, one of the disciples. "How can we know the way?"[126]

"I am the way, and the truth, and the life," Jesus answered. "The only way to the Father is through Me."[415]

Is that where He's going then? To His Father? the disciples wondered.

"If you really knew Me, you would know My Father, too. And actually, you do know Him! You've seen Him!"[271] Jesus added.

If we did see Him, let's see Him again, to be sure who Jesus means, Philip, another disciple, probably thought. "Lord, show us the Father," he said. "Then we'll be content."[2]

"Philip, I've been with you all this time, but you still don't know who I am?"[271] Jesus asked. "When you see Me, you see the Father![492] I do and say what the

Father does and says THROUGH Me. Don't you believe what you see, that I'm in the Father and He's in Me?"

"Believe!" Jesus encouraged them. "Anyone who believes in Me will do even BIGGER things than I've done."[34] The disciples remembered Jesus' miracles—all the people He'd healed and helped.

How can we possibly do more than THAT? they wondered.

"Pray for anything in My name,[23] and I'll do it, giving the Father glory,"[188] Jesus said. Jesus wanted His followers to pray using His name to show they trusted Him to control the outcome.[316] Jesus might not always answer prayers in the way people expected, but He would answer in the way that would give God glory, in the way that would show God to the people.

"And if you love Me, do what I've told you," Jesus added. "Those who obey Me love Me. And My Father will love them! I'll show each person who loves me who I am!"[327] Jesus added.

Showing people God, to help people know Him, was very important to Jesus. It's why He came to earth, and it's even why He was now going away. "When I go away," Jesus explained, "My Father will send the Helper, the Holy Spirit, to be with you and remind you of what I've told you and help you understand even more!"[224]

And that's not all Jesus was leaving them with! "I'm leaving you with a gift," Jesus said. "You can't buy or get this gift from anyone else. Only I can give it—PEACE, for your mind and heart. So, don't be troubled or afraid."[257] Again Jesus reminded the disciples not to worry. Jesus would help them know God. Knowing God would help them trust Him more. Then, no matter what, they could feel peace![347]

Talk About the Story: Why do you think the disciples felt troubled and worried? What questions did they ask? Jesus told His disciples to pray how? What would God do when they prayed that way?

Scripture: "Let not your heart be troubled; you believe in God, believe also in Me." John 14:1

Family Time: What instruction did Jesus repeat to His disciples? What was Jesus leaving with His disciples to help them trust Him and not be afraid? God wants us to trust Him and feel peace. When are times you feel worried? When you're worried, what might help you remember to trust God?

Prayer: Father, the disciples worried because they didn't understand why or where You were going away. But You helped them know how to pray to You and trust You, and You gave them peace! When we start to worry, help us believe You are in control and remember we can trust You. Amen.

NEW LOVE, NEW HOPE, NEW PEACE

Scripture: John 15:9—16:33
Place: Walking to Gethsemane
Time: Thursday night, April 6, 30 AD

Jesus' friends yawned. They were feeling tired and overwhelmed. It had been a long day. They had SO MUCH to think about! But Jesus knew He would be leaving them very soon. So He wanted to tell them everything they needed to understand.

"You know," Jesus said, "I'm telling you all this so that you might be as happy as I am! Love each other the way that I have loved you.[291] The greatest love on Earth is for a man to lay down his life for his friends.[145] Love each other like that. You are my friends. So I've told you all that the Father has told Me."

Jesus went on, "I'm telling you these things so that when hard times come, you won't be afraid. People are going to chase you and want to kill you. They'll think they are pleasing God. Remember that I told you this. Don't forget, don't worry."[387]

The disciples shook their heads, hoping to settle all of this down into their brains! They didn't want to forget anything. But HOW could they remember it all?

Jesus smiled at His dear friends. He loved them so. He told them, "I am going back to My Father who sent Me." Jesus had said that before. It made His disciples want to scream in panic! *NO! WAIT! DON'T GO!*[116]

"But," Jesus added, "leaving you is the BEST THING I can do for you— because then, the Holy Spirit will come! And that will be even BETTER than having Me here with you. It will be like having Me with no human limits! He will help people see where they are wrong. He will show them truth. He will help them know the Father."[219]

"I have much more to tell you, but you can't understand it yet. So let Me tell you something happy! God's Holy Spirit will guide you into the truth. He will tell you everything you have heard from Me and will help you remember everything I said."[383]

Oh, good! The disciples thought. *We could never remember all of this on our own!* They began to realize that when the Holy Spirit came, they would have everything they had with Jesus, and more! Now they felt a little more hopeful![455]

"Remember, God loves you because you love Me and believe He sent Me," Jesus added. "Soon, you all will run away from Me, but that's OK. I won't be alone. God My Father will be with me."

"I've told you all this so you will have peace. There's always trouble here in the world. But cheer up! I have overcome the world!" Jesus would be with them by His Holy Spirit and He would give them hope, fill them with God's love and bring them peace!

Talk About the Story: What did Jesus tell His friends about love? Who did Jesus say He would send? What would give them hope? Why can Jesus' friends have peace in this world, even when things are hard?

Scripture: "These things I have spoken to you, that in Me you may have peace. In the world you will have tribulation; but be of good cheer, I have overcome the world." John 16:33

Family Time: Where can we find peace? Find and read the definition for the word "tribulation." Why can we be cheerful even in hard times?

Prayer: Lord Jesus, we are glad that the Holy Spirit helps us know about You. Thank You that we can choose to trust You, so we have peace and hope. You are good! Amen.

JESUS' PRAYER FOR ALL WHO FOLLOW HIM

Scripture: John 17
Place: Jerusalem
Time: Thursday night April 3, AD

It feels like we'll never run out of things to learn from Him! the disciples thought as they listened to Jesus during supper and after. But now Jesus wasn't looking at them. *Is that all?* they wondered. Jesus looked up to heaven. He focused His attention on God and started to pray.

"Father, it's time," Jesus began. "Give Me, your Son, glory so I can give it back to You."[188] Jesus knew everything He was about to experience would be talked about for thousands of years—and more! But Jesus didn't want the fame for Himself. He wanted people to KNOW God through Him.

"To know You, the one true God, and to know Me, Your Son, is the only way people can have eternal life—living again, even after dying!"[281] Jesus said.

"I've shown My followers what You are like, and I've taught them this message You gave Me to share," Jesus continued. "They believe it and believe You sent Me."[451]

Jesus knew He was going to suffer soon, but even then He didn't pray just for Himself. "I'm praying for those You've put in My care,"[536] Jesus said. "Protect them, Father, by the power You have. I protected them while I was with them. I

taught them many things so they would be filled with My joy.[327]

"I'm going away and they are staying here, in this world," Jesus continued. "This world isn't an easy place to live. The people here hate My followers who believe in Me and are like Me." Perhaps Jesus thought of the angry religious leaders and even the people from His hometown who rejected Him. Since people hated Jesus so much, Jesus knew His followers, who loved Him and lived to be like Him, would face trouble from these people, too.

So Jesus asked God for help. "I'm not asking You to take them out of this world," He prayed, "but to keep them safe from My enemy.[258] Make them holy. Teach them the truth." Jesus understood that knowing the truth, God's Word, would keep His followers safe. God's Word, the Bible, calls Jesus' enemy, the devil, a liar (see John 8:44), so knowing the truth would help the disciples not believe the lies Jesus' enemy tells to keep people from believing God.

"I'm praying not only for My followers here now but for ANYONE who will EVER believe in Me."[248] Jesus prayed for people not even born yet—for people today!

"Help them be united, just as You, Father, and I are united. Let them be one with us. Then the whole world will see how much You love them, as much as You love Me."[185]

God's family, made of everyone who would believe in Jesus, would be HUGE! But with lots of brothers and sisters, there might be differences, even fights! So Jesus prayed that instead these believers would be like one big, loving family. Then the world would see His family's love, God's love.[293] This would help even MORE people know what God is like and believe in Him.

Talk About the Story: Why did Jesus pray for glory? Who did Jesus ask God to help? Jesus asked God to protect His followers how? Knowing what would help them?

Scripture: "Let each of you look out not only for his own interests, but also for the interests of others." Philippians 2:4

Family Time: Knowing He was about to suffer, Jesus could have prayed only for Himself. But He prayed for all who would ever believe in Him—including us! Who could you pray for? How could you ask God to help them?

Prayer: Dear Lord, Jesus trusted You so much that even when He faced a hard time, He remembered to pray for others. When we experience challenges, help us trust You are taking care of us. Help us pray not only for ourselves but for others, too. Amen.

PRAYING IN GETHSEMANE

Scripture: Luke 22:39–46; Mark 14:32–42
Place: Outside of Jerusalem
Time: Early Friday morning, April 7, 30 AD

Quickly the eleven disciples followed Jesus from their supper table to the city walls of Jerusalem, and into the dark valley beyond. They slowed only as they climbed the hills surrounding the Mount of Olives.[73] They arrived at Gethsemane, a place where people crushed olives to make oil. Jesus often came here to pray.

This nighttime hike, after such a long day—after MANY long days journeying with Jesus—left them exhausted! "Sit here while I pray,"[357] Jesus said, letting them rest. He motioned to Peter, and the two brothers, James and John. "Come with Me," He said, leading them into the shadowy grove of olive trees.

"My heart is breaking from sadness," Jesus told them. "Keep watch and pray." Then Jesus left them, too, walking only as far as you could toss a stone.

Jesus had taught His followers to find a private place to pray, to focus on God (see Matthew 6:6). And that's what Jesus did now. Once He'd spent all night praying in a private place like this (see Luke 6:12). But He knew He didn't have much time now. Soon He'd be betrayed, handed over to His enemies who wanted to kill Him.

After a few more steps, Jesus fell to the ground. As He thought of the troubling things to come, His sadness felt like a heavy weight upon Him. Kneeling, Jesus prayed, "Abba, Father, I know everything is possible for You." Jesus called God "Abba," a word like "daddy" or "papa," showing how close He felt to God.

"Please take this cup of suffering away from Me,"[465] Jesus asked. Jesus knew punishment was coming. He hadn't done anything wrong, but God planned for Jesus to step in and take the punishment for people who had done wrong. Jesus called this punishment a "cup of suffering" because it was like a bitter drink He'd have to swallow.

A kid who's sick might have to drink medicine that tastes disgusting! "Don't make me drink it!" the kid begs. But the dad knows the kid will only get better by drinking it. In the same way, Jesus asked His Father not to make Him "drink," or suffer people's punishment.

"But do what You want, not what I want," Jesus said. He prayed for what He wanted but trusted His Father knew what was best. Just as the sick kid could only get better by trusting his dad and drinking the medicine, people could only get better, could only be forgiven if Jesus followed His Father's plan.

Even though God didn't answer Jesus' prayer in the way Jesus wanted, God still cared for Jesus. He heard Jesus' prayer. Suddenly, an angel appeared to strengthen Jesus![14]

After, Jesus prayed even HARDER.[54] Feeling so distressed, He began sweating drops of blood to the ground. Two more times Jesus prayed, sharing His feelings with God and asking God to take away the suffering. But each time, Jesus didn't tell God what to do. Instead, Jesus asked for what God wanted, and to do what was best in the end. And God answered in the way that was best for ALL people, to save them.

Talk About the Story: Where did Jesus pray? What special word did Jesus call God, His Father? What does this show about Jesus' feelings for God?

Scripture: "There are many plans in a man's heart, nevertheless the Lord's counsel—that will stand." Proverbs 19:21

Family Time: Jesus prayed for what He wanted but trusted God's way is best. When have you prayed for something God answered in a different way? Why was God's answer to Jesus' prayer better than what Jesus asked for?

Prayer: Dear Father, Jesus is right: You are able to do anything. And You always do what's best. Even when we don't get exactly what we pray for, help us trust You will answer in a better way. Amen.

COULD YOU NOT WATCH?

Scripture: Matthew 26
Place: Jerusalem
Time: Early Friday morning, April 7, 30 AD

"Get up. It's time. Look, here comes the man who is betraying Me," Jesus said.

Peter, James, and John followed Jesus' gaze through the trees. Sure enough, there was Judas, one of the twelve disciples! He'd left after supper, but the disciple didn't know where he'd gone.

"Greetings, Rabbi!" Judas kissed Jesus on the cheek, like family. Suddenly, an angry mob circled around Jesus, carrying torches to light their way in the darkness and swords and heavy clubs. The kiss was just a sign Judas used to show the crowd which man was Jesus. As the crowd began to pull Jesus away, the disciples rushed to defend Him—one pulled out His sword to fight!

"Do you think I couldn't ask My Father for help?" Jesus asked. "All this is happening as God planned." The disciples ran away after that, maybe scared the crowd would take them, too.

But after awhile, maybe they began to regret that. *Oh, if we'd only done what He'd told us!* Peter, James, and John thought back to that night, earlier when Jesus had wanted to pray.

"Keep watch and pray," He had instructed. But they were so sad and so sleepy that they hadn't watched OR prayed!

The first time Jesus went to pray, maybe each man assumed the other would keep watch, so it would be OK for him to rest, just a little.

"You're sleeping?" Jesus asked, having returned

"Huuuuuuh?" slowly the three disciples awoke.

"Could you men not keep watch for an hour?"[332] Jesus asked, looking at Peter.[525]

Is that all it's been? It felt like no time had passed!

"Watch and pray so that you won't give in to temptation," Jesus instructed. "The spirit is willing and wants to do right, but the body is weak."[340] Just before, Jesus had been praying about HIS own temptation. He didn't want to face the suffering to come that was part of God's plan. But still, Jesus' spirit wanted to do what God wanted.[549] After Jesus prayed, God sent an angel to strengthen Him for what was to come. So Jesus spoke from experience! Praying would strengthen them, helping them not give in to temptations.

How humiliating! Peter thought as Jesus walked away to pray again. *I'll pray NOW. But first, I'll just close ONE eye,* maybe he reasoned. Soon they all were fast asleep. ZZZZZZZ.

When Jesus returned a second time, the disciples woke up. Jesus didn't say anything and left to pray more. [29]

I've let Him down again . . . This time I'll REALLY watch and pray! each man determined.

But not before long, Jesus found them just as He had before—ASLEEP!

"Are you still sleeping?" He questioned.

Maybe they thought of all the ways they would stay awake NEXT time. But that's when Judas arrived. *Sure, we rested, but how much stronger might we have been if we'd prayed for strength, like Jesus?* they wondered now.

Talk About the Story: What did Jesus tell His disciples to do while He prayed? When Jesus returned, He found them doing what? How do you think this made the disciples feel? Jesus feel?

Scripture: "But God is faithful, who will not allow you to be tempted beyond what you are able, but with the temptation will also make the way of escape, that you may be able to bear it" 1 Corinthians 10:13

Family Time: Why did Jesus tell the disciples to pray? They didn't have to pretend to be strong! God knew their weaknesses and would help them when they asked. When are times you feel tempted and weak? You can tell God how you really feel and ask for help! Then what might happen?

Prayer: Dear Lord, the disciples slept, even though Jesus told them how to be strong and not give in to temptations! When we feel tempted, help us remember to pray to You. Thank You for promising to help us stay strong! Amen.

I AM WHO I AM

Scripture: John 18:1–9
Place: Garden of Gethsemane
Time: Early Friday morning, April 7, 30 AD

In the last few months of Jesus' ministry, He had called Himself seven different things. These were word pictures He had used: "I AM the Bread of Life . . . I AM the Light . . . I AM the Door . . . I AM the Good Shepherd . . . I AM the Resurrection and the Life . . . I AM the Way, the Truth and the Life; I AM the Vine." Since seven is the number of completion, these seven word pictures give us a good view of who He is.

But on the night Jesus was arrested, He showed He is the Son of God by saying, "I AM."

Jesus went to the Garden of Gethsemane with His friends to pray. He'd often gone there to pray.[73] We know that Jesus prayed so intently that the perspiration on His forehead actually contained blood. This happens when people are under tremendous stress.

www.thefamilyprayerbible.com

While Jesus prayed, Judas led armed soldiers to the garden because He knew Jesus was there.

Jesus met them asking, "Who are you seeking?"[259] They answered, "Jesus of Nazareth!" That was His name and home address.

Jesus answered, "I AM . . . ."

The traditional Bible translation reads, "I am *He*" with the "He" in italics because it is not in the original language. Jesus simply said, "I AM," with no descriptive word.[466]

Suddenly, the guards fell to the ground backward, as if they'd been knocked back by His words![26]

Perhaps Jesus briefly unveiled His glory so they fell backwards, as a person would fall down backwards by the explosion of gasoline on fire.

Perhaps the soldiers fell backwards because the words Jesus used, *ego emi,* i.e., I AM, were so powerful. When Moses was on his face before the burning bush he asked, "Who are You, LORD?"

God answered, "I AM WHO I AM"[60] (Exodus 3:14). Jesus' words to the soldiers is the same name that God gave to Moses. Jesus could have been declaring, "I AM GOD" by His answer.

When the soldiers got up, Jesus asked them a second time, "Who are you looking for?" They gave the same answer, name and home address: Jesus of Nazareth.

At this point Jesus said, "I have told you I am the man; let these go,"[387] pointing to His sleepy but terrified friends. Jesus protected His disciples by keeping the soldiers from arresting them. Jesus showed His divine insight; He knew He would die the next day for the sins of the world (John 18:9).[385]

Talk About the Story: How many times did Jesus use the special word picture of Himself, "I AM"? What are the seven pictures? When and where did Jesus use the last "I AM"? How did the soldiers respond when Jesus said, "I AM"? What did Jesus mean?

Scripture: "Now when He said to them, 'I am He,' they drew back and fell to the ground" John 18:6

Family Time: How do Jesus' "I AMs" help us know more about Him? How do they show Jesus is God? Which is your favorite "I AM"? Why?

Prayer: Father, thank You that Jesus is bread for strength, light for guidance, and the door for entrance to heaven. Thank You that Jesus is my shepherd, my hope for resurrection, my way to heaven, and my vine that gives me life. Amen.

PSALM 84
BEING IN GOD'S HOUSE

The priest from the Korah family brought his young son into the Temple. The Korah priests were known for their love of Temple choirs that worshiped the Lord. They were especially known for their holiness and devotion to God. The priest was telling his son about his job. Fathers like to tell their sons about the place where they work.

"Look up there," the son pointed to a nook in the Temple ceiling. The boy saw a bird's nest near the Holy of Holies where God lived. The Lord's presence sat on the Ark of the Covenant, something like the sparrow sitting on its nest.

"Why don't you get rid of the nest?" The boy asked.

The father explained it was a sparrow's nest, and that sparrows made their nests in the spring. "Just like our family comes to the Temple for Passover, so the birds come to be close to God. Then he explained, "Both mother and father sparrows make their nest out of twigs, branches, leaves, and brittle things they find on the ground. Then they cover the inside of the nest with soft grass and feathers. They begin laying their eggs – usually 4 eggs – in the spring.

"Why do they make their nest in the Temple?"

The father smiled, "Maybe they want their young – hatched in 12 days – to be near God. Just like I bring you to the Temple so you will be near God."

Again the son asked, "Why don't you tear down the nest?"

The father answered, "We take them down in the fall when the sparrows have finished producing their young birds. The young usually fly out of the nest about 2 weeks after they have been hatched. Then the parents will hatch another brood of young birds. When the sparrows are through for the year someone from the Temple will take away the old nest."

The next day the priest went alone in the Temple to worship God. When he saw the sparrow's nest, he began singing a Psalm of praise.

> "Lord I love Thy Temple, Your dwelling place.[377]
> I love to enter Your courts with praise.
> With my whole body and soul I joyfully worship You.
> Even the sparrows find peace in Your presence,
> It is here they build a home and raise their young.
> They want to be near Your altars.
> One day in Your house is better than a 1000 days elsewhere,
> I would rather be a simple door keeper here,
> Than live in a beautiful home of the wicked.[254]
> Lord you create a sun and shield for life and protection
> You will not withhold good things from Your children."[44]

Talk About the Psalm: What did you learn about the psalm writer in this story? What did you learn about God?

Psalm 84: Read this week's psalm in your Bible together. Choose a verse to read aloud as a prayer.

Prayer: Thank You, God, for the psalm prayers in the Bible. Thank You for teaching us about You and about how to pray. In Jesus' name, Amen.

BEFORE ANNAS AND CAIAPHAS

Scripture: Mark 14:53–65; Luke 22:66–71; John
18:12–14,19–24
Place: Jerusalem
Time: Early Friday morning, April 7, 30 AD

"To Annas's house!" a soldier shouted, yanking on the ropes tied around Jesus. They marched through the dark back to Jerusalem.

Annas wasn't officially in power, but he had special connections. His son-in-law, Caiaphas, was high priest over ALL the religious leaders. LEGALLY, Jesus should have been taken to Caiaphas.

"Who are your followers?" Annas asked Jesus. "What did you teach them?"

"I didn't teach secretly," Jesus answered. "I taught openly at the Temple and synagogues.[259] Ask the people who heard Me what I said." LEGALLY, Jesus could ask for witnesses.

But a guard slapped Jesus. "How dare You speak to him like that?!"[465]

Calmly Jesus replied, "If I said anything wrong, then tell Me what was wrong. But if I've said the truth, why are you hitting Me?"

"Send Him to Caiaphas!" Annas commanded. The guards pulled Jesus away. Maybe Annas was frustrated; despite his power, Annas couldn't get the answers he wanted.

Most people were still sleeping at this early hour, but Caiaphas had gathered a BIG council: elders, religious teachers, and priests. LEGALLY, Jesus should have been sent there during the day.

Caiaphas's job was to find witnesses for a fair trial. But Caiaphas didn't care about being fair. *Jesus threatens our power,* the council feared. *We'll get rid of Him—we'll kill Him! But we can't, LEGALLY, unless we prove He's done something wrong.*

LEGALLY, Jesus could only be "guilty" if at least two witnesses proved it. But Jesus hadn't done anything wrong!

So the witness will have to LIE, the council realized. But all the witnesses told different stories. *We can't use them! We just need TWO to lie the same way.*

At last two told the same lie,[440] which sounded like truth: "We heard Jesus say He'd destroy the Temple, and in three days build another!"[405, 84]

"Well, aren't You going to say something?" Caiaphas questioned Jesus. But Jesus said nothing.[436] He didn't defend Himself. Those witnesses had twisted a truth into a terrible lie (see John 2:19).

Caiaphas stood up. Feeling big and powerful, he began to bully Jesus. "I command You in God's name, tell us, are You the Messiah, the Son of God?"[189]

"I am," Jesus answered. "And you will see the Son of Man seated at the right hand of God, coming on the clouds of heaven!"[135]

Boiling with anger, Caiaphas grabbed at the closest thing—the robe he wore—and tore it! RIP!

"How insulting!" he screamed. "Why do we need more witnesses? You've all heard Him disrespect God!"

I can't believe He'd lie, claiming power like God's! Caiaphas thought. But what about Caiaphas's lies, and the lying witnesses? They didn't understand Jesus had told the truth.

"Guilty!" they accused Him. "He deserves to die!" They spit at Him. They blindfolded Him, hitting Him and mocking Him.

Everything was unfair. But still Jesus didn't defend Himself. He trusted God's promise, the truth Jesus had shared: Soon He'd sit next to God, an even more powerful judge. God would be on His side, and Jesus trusted Him to make everything right.

Talk About the Story: Who was Annas? Who was Caiaphas? Why was Jesus taken to these men? What did they do?

Scripture: "In God I have put my trust; I will not be afraid. What can man do to me?" Psalm 56:11

Family Time: What unfair things happened to Jesus? How did Jesus react? Jesus could have defended Himself, but He cared more about what God thought than what people thought. When people are unfair, how can you react? How might remembering God's on your side help you?

Prayer: Dear Lord, when people Jesus treated unfairly, He could have fought back. But He trusted You to defend Him. When others are unfair to us, help us remember You will help when we ask and trust You. Amen.

PETER DENIES HIS LORD

Scripture: Matthew 26:57–58,69–75; Luke
22:54–62; John 18:15–18,25–27
Place: Jerusalem
Time: Early Friday morning, April 7, 30 AD

Peter hid in the shadows as he ran through the dark, keeping his distance from the soldiers leading Jesus away. *Where are they taking Him?* he wondered. They'd left one house, and now they were on the move again.

The crowd marched through a door in a wall—and the door shut! *Oh no!* The cold air of the early morning chilled Peter to the bone. *What will happen to Jesus now?* Peter worried.

Suddenly, the door opened just an inch. "Aren't you one of Jesus' disciples, too?" a servant girl asked.

"No, I'm not,"[159] Peter lied, stepping forward.

I'm not about to give myself away as one of Jesus' followers! This is Caiaphas's house—the high priest! What might happen to me then? John, another follower of Jesus, had already gotten through this door. He'd asked the girl to let Peter in, too. Maybe she suspected they'd come together.

In the courtyard, servants and soldiers huddled around a fire, trying to keep warm. Feeling numb from the cold, Peter shuffled up to them, seeking a place

www.thefamilyprayerbible.com

to warm his hands, too. He just wanted to be part of the crowd, to hide and keep warm. That felt safest.

Peter gazed into the flames, thinking over the events of that night, worrying about what was to come. Feeling uneasy, he looked up. Peter sensed someone watching him. Another servant girl was staring right at him!

"You were with Jesus," she said. Everyone around the fire looked up at Peter then.

"I don't know what you're talking about,"[29] Peter said, denying he ever knew Jesus or had ever followed Him. He slipped away from the fire then, not wanting to be seen in its light, even if he was cold. But an hour later, Peter was back to warm up. He exchanged a few, short words with those standing there.

"Surely, you were with Jesus! We can tell from you're accent you're from Galilee like Him!" someone said.

"Yes, didn't I see you in the garden, when we arrested Him?" a man added, squinting his eyes to get a better look at Peter's face.

"No. No! NO!" Peter answered. He began to curse and swear. Jesus would NEVER talk like that. *Maybe if I don't sound like a follower of Jesus, they'll leave me alone!*

Immediately a rooster crowed.[440] Peter looked up at the sound, and through the crowd, Jesus locked eyes with him. Jesus' words to Peter from earlier that night flooded his mind: "Before the rooster crows, you will deny Me three times" (Matthew 26:34).[476]

Peter left the fire, walking far away. The cold didn't matter. The pain he felt now, realizing he'd rejected Jesus, hurt far worse than frostbitten fingers. *I AM a follower of Jesus, but I was too scared what would happen if people knew.* Peter cried, disappointed in himself and feeling embarrassed. *Jesus knew I'd fail Him . . . and I did.*

Talk About the Story: Why did Peter follow after the guards taking Jesus away? Where did they take Jesus? What did Peter do there?

Scripture: "We speak, not as pleasing men, but God who tests our hearts." 1 Thessalonians 2:4

Family Time: Why do you think Peter followed behind Jesus? Why do you think Peter lied about knowing Jesus? Peter worried what others might think if they knew he followed Jesus. When are times you've felt afraid to tell people you follow Jesus? How do you feel when you hide it? How do you think God feels?

Prayer: Dear Lord, Peter lied about following You because he feared what people might do or think if they knew about it. Help us follow You fearlessly, never ashamed or afraid to tell others about You. In Jesus' name, Amen.

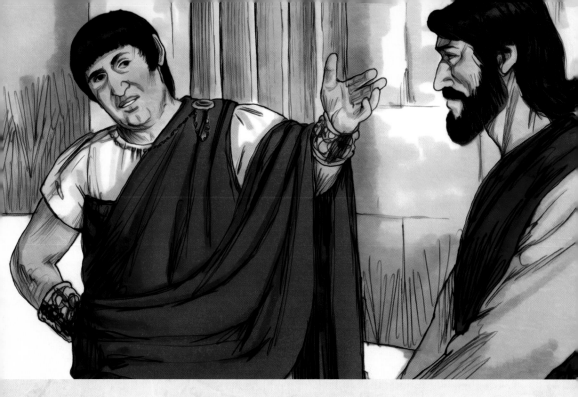

JESUS BEFORE PILATE

Scripture: Luke 23:1–7; John 18:28–38
Place: Jerusalem
Time: Friday morning, April 7, 30 AD

As the sun began to rise, a crowd marched out of Caiaphas's house. "Send Jesus to Pilate!"[5] At Caiaphas's command, the guards began pushing and shoving Jesus ahead of them. Caiaphas watched as he trailed behind the crowd. *Yes, we'll kill Jesus,* he thought over their plan, *but we'll get someone ELSE to do it.*

Even though as high priest Caiaphas had a lot of power, there was someone who had more. Pontius Pilate was the Roman governor in charge of all Judea. And he had come to Jerusalem for the special Passover feast days. He didn't care about celebrating—it was a Jewish holiday. But with so many Jews in town to celebrate, people might get unruly, and he wanted to be close by, to keep control.

At the entrance to the palace Pilate used as his headquarters in Jerusalem, the crowd stopped short. "We can't go in there!" the religious leaders objected. "We have to stay good, keep our consciences clean, so that we can be a part of our religious ceremonies this week. Going into a place like that—where criminals are judged—will make us dirty. We won't be able to celebrate!"

What's all that commotion outside? Pilate grumbled, walking outside. Seeing

Jesus bound with ropes, Pilate addressed the crowd: "What are your charges against this man?"[382]

"He tells people not to pay their taxes, and He calls Himself a king![374] He's a criminal! That's why we brought him to you," they shouted.

"Well, why don't you judge Him then?" Pilate shouted back.

"No, YOU do it. Only Romans are allowed to put criminals to death," they replied.[231]

Pilate sighed. "Bring Him in," he commanded his soldiers.

Well, He certainly doesn't LOOK like a king, Pilate thought to himself, as Jesus was brought before him. *But He doesn't look like a dangerous criminal either.*

"Are you REALLY the king of the Jews?" Pilate asked Jesus.

"My kingdom is not of this world.[74] If it were, my followers would stop this from happening," Jesus answered.

"So you ARE a king then." *He said He has a kingdom, after all,* Pilate reasoned.

"What you say is the truth," Jesus replied. "All who love the truth know that what I say is the truth."[499]

"What is truth?" Pilate said, turning away from Jesus with a shrug of his shoulders. *We're not getting anywhere! Some "criminal." All He does is talk!* Pilate may have thought, feeling annoyed that the religious leaders had wasted his time.

Pilate left Jesus; going back to the religious leaders he said, "I can't find anything wrong with Him,"[518] Pilate addressed them.

"Oh, but He IS a criminal!" He caused riots by the things He said and taught in Jerusalem and Galilee—"

"Galilee?" Pilate asked, a note of fear rising in his voice. "Send Him to Herod then. He's the ruler over Galilee!" *Let someone else judge Him.* Pilate thought. *I don't want to be responsible for this mess.* So Jesus was sent away—again.

Talk About the Story: Who was Pilate? Who sent Jesus to Him? Why? What did Pilate ask Jesus?

Scripture: "Learn to do good; seek justice." Isaiah 1:17

Family Time: What did the religious leaders want Pilate to do? What did Pilate want Herod to do? The religious leaders decided to do something wrong—to kill Jesus. No one would stand up for the right thing; they just told someone else to kill Jesus. When are times you had to choose between doing right or wrong? What helps you do or stand up for the right thing?

Prayer: Dear Lord, the religious leaders planned something bad, and nobody, not even the governor, stopped them. When we are faced with a decision between right and wrong, help us stand up for the right thing, as You would. Amen.

PILATE'S DECISION

Scripture: Matthew 27:15–26; Luke 23:13–25;
John 19:1–16
Place: Jerusalem
Time: Friday morning, April 7, 30 AD

So much for Herod dealing with this problem, Pilate thought. He'd sent Jesus away to Herod, and Herod had sent Jesus back. The crowd of religious leaders and other Jews waited to hear what Pilate would do now.

"Alright," Pilate addressed them. "You claimed Jesus is some terrible criminal. But I examined Him. Herod did too. And we both found Him NOT guilty. So I'll punish Him and let Him go." Pilate sent Jesus away to the guards, who whipped Him. They put a purple robe on Him, and a crown made out of thorny twigs, dressing Him up to make fun of Him for claiming to be king.

"Look! Here He is!" Pilate presented Jesus to the crowd when the guards brought Him back.

Seeing this, the crowd began to yell. "KILL HIM! Set Barabbas free instead!" At the Passover celebration it was custom for the governor to set one prisoner free—anyone the crowd wished—like a gift from the governor to the people. Pilate probably planned for this person to be Jesus. Barabbas was in prison for starting a riot—and in the process He had murdered someone!

"Who should I set free?" Pilate asked the crowd. "Jesus, the King of the Jews, or Barabbas?"

At that moment, a messenger arrived from Pilate's wife with a message for him: "Don't harm that innocent Man! I had a troubling nightmare about Him!"[465]

Pilate hesitated, surprised by his wife's news. *I know He's innocent,* Pilate thought. *They're just envious because people would rather follow Jesus than them.*

"Who do you want me to set free?" Pilate asked again, maybe hoping the people would change their minds.

"Barabbas!" they shouted.

"But what should I do with Jesus?" Pilate asked. He would only set one prisoner free, and he wanted it to be Jesus, the innocent man.

"Kill Him on a cross! Crucify Him!"[96] the crowd cried louder.

"But why? What did He do wrong?" Pilate questioned.

"He called Himself the Son of God, so by our law He should DIE!" the crowd roared even louder.

Son of God? This made Pilate nervous. He went inside and questioned Jesus. "Where are You from?" he asked.

Jesus didn't answer.

"Don't You realize I have the power to KILL You?" Pilate demanded, growing frustrated.

"Only God gives people power," Jesus replied.

Pilate tried even harder to get the crowd to set Jesus free then.

"If you don't kill this man—a 'king'—you'll be an enemy to the REAL king, Caesar!" the crowd threatened. Pilate feared they'd start a riot if he didn't give in.

So dipping his hands in a bowl of water, Pilate addressed them: "See this? MY hands are clean. I won't be caught 'red-handed,' responsible for killing this innocent man."[352]

"We'll take the blame!"[268] the people shouted.

So Pilate gave them what they wanted. Jesus would be killed.

Talk About the Story: Who did Pilate want to set free? Who did the crowd want to set free? What did Pilate's wife dream?

Scripture: "The fear of man brings a snare, but whoever trusts in the Lord shall be safe." Proverbs 29:25

Family Time: Why did Pilate wash his hands? Who do you think was responsible for killing Jesus? How might things have ended differently if Pilate hadn't feared the crowd's threats? When was a time that being afraid affected a choice you had to make?

Prayer: Lord, Pilate could have believed the truth about Jesus—that He is Your Son—but his fear kept him from making the right choice. When we have important decisions to make, help us not be ruled by our fears. Help us make the right choice as we trust You. In Jesus name, Amen.

DATE ___/___

TO THE CROSS

Scripture: Luke 23:26–32;
John 19:17–29
Place: Jerusalem to Golgotha
Time: Friday morning, April 7, 30 AD

A pitiful parade of people was leaving the city. First came a centurion with a hammer swinging from his belt. He was followed by four soldiers who were experts at crucifixion. They always made sure the victims carried their own heavy, wooden crosses. Now they shouted at Jesus to pick up His cross. But after the beating, Jesus was too weak to carry His load. He continually fell.

"Up!" one of the soldiers cried over and over, lashing at Jesus each time.

Behind the soldiers and Jesus came two thieves who carried their crosses, too. They were all going to a nearby hill. It was called Golgotha—Calvary in Greek— which means the Place of the Skull: the cliff on one side looks like a skull, with eye and nose holes and a mouth.[260]

Following close behind this sad parade was John, the only one of Jesus' friends who hadn't run away.

A wooden sign was placed around Jesus' neck; it would be nailed to the top of the cross before they put Jesus up to die. On the sign Pilate had written, "JESUS OF NAZARETH, THE KING OF THE JEWS."[192] The Jews didn't like that one bit, but Pilate didn't care what they thought.

After Jesus had fallen again, the soldiers looked around for someone strong.

"You!" shouted a soldier, pointing to a man in the crowd. Simon was coming into the city to celebrate Passover. He was from the land of Cyrene, and his dark-green robe and red tunic stood out in the crowd.[256]

"YOU! Pick up that cross. Follow us."

So Simon, the big man from Cyrene, hefted the cross onto his shoulder. We don't know if Simon knew who Jesus was then, but we are sure he did later. In fact, his sons Rufus and Alexander were well known in the early church! Simon walked steadily, hating this horrible, murderous Roman custom—and it disrespected Passover, too. But he carried the cross for Jesus to the place called Golgotha.

There, the cross was laid down and Jesus was stretched out on the timbers. Ropes tied His hands and feet to the cross. Then a Roman soldier took a black iron spike, placed it in the palm of Jesus' right hand, and with one mighty swing of his hammer, drove the spike into the wood.

The soldiers barely noticed. They had crucified many men for Rome.

The soldier put a spike through Jesus' other hand, then did the same to the feet.

A hole almost two feet deep had been chiseled out of the limestone. With Jesus nailed to the cross, the soldiers put their huge shoulders to the cross and lifted it until it was nearly upright. Then one of them kicked the base so that the cross dropped into the hole, THUMP.

Jesus squeezed His eyes shut. His body shook with pain, but He said nothing.

Then He lifted His eyes to Heaven and prayed, "Father, forgive them. They don't know what they are doing."[238]

It was now nine o'clock in the morning.

Talk About the Story: Why did Jesus not carry His own cross part of the way? Who carried it for him? Why was this man in town? Who were his sons?

Scripture: "By this we know love, because He laid down His life for us." 1 John 3:16

Family Time: Why did Jesus die on the cross? Could Jesus have stopped the men who crucified Him? What did Jesus show us about love?

Prayer: Jesus, we can never thank You enough for Your love. Thank You for dying to take the penalty for our sin. We love You. Amen.

CHAPTER 17

THE SEVEN SAYINGS FROM THE CROSS

People who are being executed commonly utter defiant and blasphemous statements. Their last words reflect their heart. If they curse the jailer, the government or God, it shows the kind of life they lived. But that was not the case with Jesus as He hung on the cross. Jesus spoke from His cross seven times. These seven sayings reflect His divine-human nature and His commitment to accomplishing the salvation of God.

In His first statement from the cross, Jesus prayed a prayer of forgiveness: "Father, forgive them, for they do not know what they do" (Luke 23:34). In the midst of His intense pain and suffering, Jesus paused to pray for those who were the cause of that suffering. In this prayer, He revealed God's immense love for sinners (cf. Rom. 5:8).

Jesus' next statement was one of acceptance. Initially, the thieves who were crucified with Jesus ridiculed Him. Then one of the men realized he was spiritually

condemned. When this thief asked to be remembered by Jesus, He responded, "Assuredly, I say to you, today you will be with Me in Paradise" (Luke 23:43).

Jesus' third statement from the cross recognized Jesus' responsibility to care for His mother. Looking at His mother He said, "Woman, behold your son!" (John 19:26). Then to John He said, "Behold your mother!" (John 19:27).

Jesus' fourth statement from the cross reveals the extent of His anguish over His separation from God as He became the sin-bearer of the world. His words were preserved in their original language, "Eli, Eli, lama sabachthani?" which means "My God, My God, why have You forsaken Me?" (Matt. 27:46).

Jesus' fifth statement from the cross reflected the nature of the physical suffering He was enduring on the cross. When Jesus cried out "I thirst" (John 19:28), it demonstrated He was not exempt from the physical suffering.

Jesus' sixth statement, "It is finished!" (John 19:30), was a cry of victory. Jesus' final statement from the cross was a benediction, "Father, into Your hands I commit My spirit" (Luke 23:46). When He had accomplished all He was meant to accomplish in life, Jesus committed Himself to God in death.

FATHER, FORGIVE THEM

Scripture: Luke 23:34
Place: Jerusalem
Time: Friday, April 7, 30 AD

Jesus shut His eyes as His body shook with pain, but He said nothing. It was nine o'clock in the morning—early but it felt like such a long and never ending, painful day. Jesus lifted His eyes to Heaven in prayer. "Father, forgive them, for they know not what they do."[173]

Jesus didn't say exactly which people He wanted God to forgive. But He didn't need to say. God knew. God knew about every person who had a role in Jesus being killed on that cross. Maybe Jesus was praying for Judas, the disciple who betrayed Him into the hands of the angry, jealous priests. Maybe Jesus was praying for those priests, Caiaphas and the other religious leaders who unfairly accused Him of crimes He never committed. Maybe Jesus included in this prayer the witnesses who lied about Him, too, saying He was guilty and deserving of death. And maybe Jesus was praying for Pilate, the Roman governor who knew Jesus was innocent but sentenced Him to die, fearing what might happen to him if he didn't.[325]

Even now, still others continued to hurt Jesus, treating Him cruelly. Maybe

Jesus was praying for them, too. A crowd watched as Jesus hung on the cross, painfully dying. It was getting harder for Jesus to breathe because of the throbbing, aching, unbearable pain that coursed through every nerve of His muscles and flesh. The weight of His own body like a load pulled Him down.

"He saved others," the religious leaders watching in the crowd laughed. "If He really IS the Messiah, God's Chosen One, let Him save Himself!"[238] When Jesus had taught and healed people earlier, His power and popularity had made these religious leaders scared and jealous. With more people listening to and following Jesus, they didn't feel as powerful as they had when those people only listened to THEM. They smiled smugly, enjoying seeing Jesus look so weak and helpless now.[424]

Closer to the cross, soldiers were gambling on the dusty ground with lots, a game like rolling dice, to win Jesus' clothing. They couldn't care less that Jesus, God's own Son, was dying before them. They just tried to pass the time as they waited for Him to die.

Even as He died, Jesus wasn't thinking about Himself, how much His wounds hurt or how depressed He felt because of the wrong things these people were doing and had done. He was thinking about others—these same people who were mean and cruel to Him—and He prayed for them![337]

Jesus didn't call them guilty, as they'd called Him; He recognized they didn't understand just how wrong they were. Instead, Jesus prayed to God, trusting Him to judge. And Jesus asked God to judge with mercy, to show them kindness that they didn't deserve, because that's how much Jesus loved them.[304]

Talk About the Story: Who watched as Jesus died? What did they say to Jesus? What did the soldiers do? How do you think this made Jesus feel?

Scripture: "Love your enemies, bless those who curse you, do good to those who hate you, and pray for those who spitefully use you and persecute you." Matthew 5:44

Family Time: When others treat us unfairly or are mean to us, we might want to be mean back. How did Jesus respond to those who were mean to Him? What did Jesus pray? What does Jesus' reaction tell you about how He feels about people, even those who do wrong?

Prayer: Father, thank You for your mercy. Even when people were unfair to Jesus and didn't love Him, He showed them kindness and love. He prayed for those who hurt Him, asking You to forgive them. We're sorry we don't always act in ways that show love to You. Thank You for forgiving us because of Jesus. In His name, Amen.

DATE ___/___

PSALM 90

MOSES' PSALM ABOUT DYING IN THE WILDERNESS

God brought Israel out of Egyptian bondage through ten miraculous plagues. Israel walked through the Red Sea on dry land. In the wilderness God supplied manna to feed them daily. When they were thirsty, God poured water from the rock. But at Kadesh–Barnea Israel turned their backs on God and rebelled at His leadership. God punished their sin. They would wander in the Sinai desert for 40 years until everyone over 20 years old died.

Moses sat at the table at the door of his tent. The cloud of God's presence did not lift off the Tabernacle that morning. So Israel would remain where they were camped. A report of those who died the previous day and night was brought to Moses. He wept as he looked over the names. Some were friends, others he did not know. It was hard on Moses knowing all his friends would die. He picked up a quill and wrote:

"Lord, You have been our home
Through all the generations of Israel.
You are God before mountains were formed,
Before the earth was born, and before the world was created.[188]
You designed for people to return back to dust when they are buried,
Even as You created men out of dust.
A 1000 years on Your calendar, is just like yesterday.
Our life comes and goes like a watch in the night."

Moses was sorry that Israel sinned and that those Jews who came out of Egypt wouldn't go into the Promised Land. He worshipped the Lord with this Psalm:

"You destroyed every Israelite because You were angry.
Your punishment makes us afraid of You.
You put our sins in public view,
We could not hide our secret sins.
Now our days lead toward our deaths.
Our life and death is a tale already told.
Teach us to make the days we have left count,
We will live to be approximately 70 years old.
Some will live to be 80, but with trouble and pain
Then we fly away in death to You."[207]

Moses knew he also would die in the desert. He had lived for God and been used by God. Now he was looking forward to living in eternity with God.

"Lord, give us Your unfailing love each morning,
Make us happy with the years we have left.[46]
Show us the works You do so we can glorify You,
And tell our children of Your wonderful ways.[458]
Let Your beauty be seen in our life and service,
Establish the work of our hands that You do through us.[176]
Yes, establish the work at our hands."

Talk About the Psalm: What did you learn about the psalm writer in this story? What did you learn about God?

Psalm 90: Read this week's psalm in your Bible together. Choose a verse to read aloud as a prayer.

Prayer: Thank You, God, for the psalm prayers in the Bible. Thank You for teaching us about You and about how to pray. In Jesus' name, Amen.

TODAY YOU WILL BE WITH ME IN PARADISE

Scripture: Luke 23:32–43
Place: Jerusalem
Time: Friday, April 7, 30 AD

"Save yourself! Come down from Your cross so we can see and believe,"[424] the religious leaders continued to taunt Jesus as they watched Him die.

Crowds of people passed by Jesus' cross on their way into and out of Jerusalem. The Roman soldiers wanted every visitor to see how criminals were punished so that people would be too scared to do anything wrong. But these people didn't show any fear—or respect. They shouted insults at Jesus, too. "Yeah, why don't you climb down from Your cross?" they jeered. "If you REALLY are the Son of God, save yourself!"[238]

Jesus wasn't the only man nailed to a cross that day. Two criminals, men who'd been caught stealing, were dying on crosses right next to Him, one on His right and one on His left. But even as they died, with some of their last breaths, they struggled against the pain to talk and mocked Jesus![99]

"So, you're the Messiah, the Son of God, are you?" one criminal asked. "Prove it! Save yourself—and us, too!"[231]

The crowd erupted in laughter. Maybe the man liked the attention the crowd gave him now as they listened to his jokes.

The other criminal opened his mouth to speak. But instead of insulting Jesus, he told the first criminal who'd spoken to stop. "Don't you fear God? Don't you have any respect for Him?" he asked. "We deserve to die for the wrong things we did. But not Him. He hasn't done anything wrong."[163]

The two criminals knew they'd spend their last hours alive in pain, suffering as they died for the wrong things they'd done. There was nothing to look forward to, no happy ending in sight. Without any hope of the pain going away, would it really matter if they started being good now?

The second criminal turned his bruised and bloody face the other way. "Jesus," he said, "remember me when You enter Your kingdom."[304]

This man had hope. To Jesus' ears, this man's words were like a prayer. He didn't doubt Jesus. He prayed believing Jesus really is King, the Son of God He claimed to be. He believed Jesus COULD save him, and believing this gave him hope. Even though the criminal knew he soon would die, with Jesus' help, this wouldn't have to be the sad, painful, depressing end it seemed to be.

After hearing so many hurtful words shouted at Him, these words kindly and humbly spoken probably sounded sweet to Jesus. Even as He suffered, Jesus spoke words to encourage the man who was sorry and believed. Jesus helped Him keep hoping! "Assuredly, I say to you," Jesus promised, "today you will be with Me in paradise."[215]

Jesus and the criminal suffered together now. But soon, that very day, Jesus would be in Heaven, where there is no more suffering. And because this criminal was sorry and believed Jesus, he would be there, too! Jesus made a way for him to come, and this gave him hope.

Talk About the Story: Who insulted Jesus as He died on the cross? What did they say?

Scripture: "Whoever calls on the name of the Lord shall be saved." Romans 10:13

Family Time: Why do you think one criminal stopped insulting Jesus? What did he know about Jesus that gave him hope? What things do you know about Jesus that give you hope when you face hard times?

Prayer: Dear Lord, sometimes our situations feel hopeless and we feel stuck in our sins. The criminals next to Jesus were stuck, dying to pay for what they did. But one criminal believed You could save Him, and when he asked, Jesus promised He would! Thank You for promising to forgive and save everyone who believes and asks You. We hope in You. Amen.

WOMAN, BEHOLD YOUR SON!

Scripture: John 19:26–27
Place: Jerusalem
Time: Friday, April 7, 30 AD

Up high on the cross, Jesus looked into the eyes of those below, the crowd that laughed at Him, hurt Him, and watched Him suffer. But some in the crowd were just there to watch. Although most of Jesus' disciples had run away, afraid and now hiding, a group of women who'd followed Jesus stood nearby His cross.

One pair of eyes looking up at Jesus was perhaps more familiar to Him than all the rest. Jesus had looked into these eyes for many years Himself—first as a baby, small and helpless; then as a boy, growing more independent; and finally as a man, who cared for the one who had cared for Him. Mary, Jesus' mother was there. And watching Jesus suffer pain in His body made her suffer pain in her heart.[295]

Mary treasured many memories about Jesus. She remembered holding Him, a little baby wrapped snugly in cloths, in her arms. She remembered fearing she'd

lost Him once as a boy—until she found Him at the Temple where He was always so eager to be! She'd also treasured words others had told her about Jesus, like the angel Gabriel who said Jesus would be called the Son of God (see Luke 1:35).[224] And the shepherds who'd come to see Jesus at His birth, saying He'd been born to be the Savior! (See Luke 2:11).

Perhaps all these memories flashed through Mary's mind as she looked up at Jesus. She'd cared for her child, trying to protect Him, but she felt so helpless now. Mary couldn't do anything to stop what was happening, but maybe she understood it was God's plan. Those messages people had given about Jesus were starting to make sense now.

When Jesus was just a baby, Simeon, a man at the Temple, had blessed Jesus and told Mary her little baby would become a great man![47] But Simeon shared some hard news, too. "God has sent Him," Simeon said, "but many won't accept Him. And the things that will happen to Him will make you so sad, the pain will be like a sword cutting your heart." (See Luke 2:34–35). Mary felt this pain now.

But then Jesus spoke. "Dear woman," He said, "this is your son."[59] John, the only disciple who hadn't run away, was standing next to Mary.

"Here is your mother,"[402] Jesus said to John.

Jesus wanted John to be like a son to Mary now. John hadn't run away from Jesus, and Jesus trusted John wouldn't run away from Mary. He would always be there to help her and take care of her, just as a son should—just as Jesus would have if God's plan hadn't been for Jesus to go away.

After this, Jesus was ready to die. He cared so much for others that even as Jesus died, He wasn't thinking about Himself. Jesus thought about what others needed, especially those close to Him.[296] From then on, John took Mary into his home, and they lived together like family because Jesus had brought them together.

Talk About the Story: Who in Jesus' family watched Him dying? How do you think this person felt while watching this happen? Which disciple watched?

Scripture: "This is love, not that we loved God, but that He loved us and sent His Son. . . . If God so loved us, we also ought to love one another." 1 John 4:10–11

Family Time: Why do you think Jesus told John to be Mary's son? When we follow Jesus, we are His family—with everyone else who follows Him! How can you care for people in God's family, showing love to them?

Prayer: Dear Lord, Jesus wanted John and Mary to be like family, to show Your love to each other and care for each other. Help us love and help our family, all who follow You. Amen.

JESUS' PRAYER FOR ALL WHO FOLLOW HIM

Scripture: Matthew 27:46-50
Place: Jerusalem
Time: Friday, April 7, 30 AD

For three hours, the scorching sun glared down upon Jesus, stinging His skin, making Him sweat. But at noon, usually the hottest hour of the day, the sun stopped shining. For three hours darkness black as a starless night covered the land.[96]

People turned their eyes from the cross to the sky. *Did we cause this? Will the sun ever reappear?* some probably wondered. *What will happen next?* Complete darkness seemed like a bad sign! *How will we tell the time with no day, only night? How will we eat with no sunlight to make our plants grow? How will we LIVE?* Worries like these overwhelmed their minds.[165]

But then at three o'clock the darkness disappeared! At that moment, Jesus cried in a loud voice, "*Eli, Eli,* My God, My God, why have You forsaken Me?" Perhaps Jesus realized God, who controls everything, had allowed the darkness to fall. Jesus knew God had also taken the darkness away. But He hadn't taken Jesus' suffering away. Jesus felt abandoned.[175]

www.thefamilyprayerbible.com

"He's calling Elijah!" some in the crowd assumed, misunderstanding that Jesus said "Eli" as a word for God, not a shortened name for "Elijah," a prophet from many years ago.

Maybe He's just thirsty, another thought, running to fetch Jesus a drink.[485] He returned carrying a sponge dripping sour wine on a stick. He held it up to Jesus' lips so He could suck the sponge and drink, but the crowd shouted, "Wait!"

"Let's see if Elijah comes!" They looked around eagerly, searching for Elijah. They'd heard the Scriptures tell how God did amazing miracles through Elijah—like making fire fall from heaven and rain pour down when Elijah prayed! Anxiously they waited to see what would happen.[325]

Perhaps Jesus waited, too. He waited for God to answer His cry, but no answer came. Even though Jesus was dying a painful death, He didn't cry out, "My God, My God, why don't You stop My pain?" Instead, He asked why God had abandoned Him. Worse than any physical suffering was feeling as if God, Jesus' Heavenly Father, was ignoring Him and didn't love or care about Him anymore.[293]

God loved Jesus, but He hated people's sins. These sins separated people from God. As Jesus died on the cross, He took all the guilt for these sins on HIMSELF. So God turned away from Jesus. He didn't answer His Son's cries.[440]

But God had planned for Jesus to experience this pain, to suffer and die taking the punishment for these sins as if He had done them. Jesus knew how angry God was about these sins—He FELT it. But because Jesus felt it, people who believe in Him and are sorry for their sins NEVER have to feel it. God forgives them and they are not separated from Him anymore! He will never abandon them.[1]

Talk About the Story: What happened to the sun as Jesus was dying? What question did Jesus cry out to God? What did the people watching think Jesus was saying?

Scripture: "He was wounded for our transgressions . . . and by His stripes we are healed." Isaiah 53:5

Family Time: How do you think Jesus felt when God didn't save Him? God's plan was for Jesus to suffer and die so that people wouldn't have to when they ask for forgiveness and believe. How does knowing Jesus took your punishment make you feel? How can you thank Jesus for what He did for you?

Prayer: Father, thank You that Jesus took the punishment for our sins so we never have to. We can be close to You because of what Jesus did. Thank You for forgiving us and promising never to abandon us. In Jesus' name, Amen.

I THIRST

Scripture: John 19:28–29
Place: Jerusalem
Time: Friday, April 7, 30 AD

For three hours Jesus hung on the cross, suffering through every sensation of His body dying—pain, weakness, thirst. The closer He got to death, the more water His body lost and the thirstier He became. Sweat glistened on his skin; blood seeped from his wounded hands, back, and feet; maybe tears also fell from His eyes.

"I'm thirsty,"[260] Jesus said. He hadn't drunk anything in at least three hours, probably much longer, not since the night before when He'd last eaten with His disciples.[485]

A pitcher of sour wine, a drink bitter like vinegar, sat on the ground near the cross. Could Jesus see it from the corner of His eye? Maybe seeing it reminded Him of how He'd once compared dying on the cross to a bitter "cup" of suffering He'd rather not drink (see Matthew 26:39).[549]

www.thefamilyprayerbible.com

Hours earlier, before Jesus was nailed to the cross, some watching had offered him wine mixed with myrrh to drink, like a medicine that would numb the pain He'd feel dying. But Jesus refused to drink it (see Mark 15:23). Jesus understood God expected Him to feel ALL of the pain, not to numb any of it. This pain was a result of people's sins, and Jesus was willing to suffer through it all for them to be forgiven.[385]

Jesus knew an end to His thirst would soon come, more satisfying than any cool, refreshing drink—and much better than that hard-to-swallow, warm and sour wine. Soon He would die. He didn't need the drink, but He needed people to KNOW He was thirsty. His words were not a request, but a sign, to help people understand who He was.

Many years before, David had written a psalm, like a song, telling about some things the Messiah would suffer as He died. Even before Jesus was born, people read and listened to this psalm found in the Scriptures, and they waited for the things the psalm talked about to happen. When they all happened, then they would know who really was the Messiah, God's Son sent to save people.[416]

Watching Jesus' sweat drip to the ground, perhaps some remembered how the psalm said the Messiah's life would seem to pour out of Him, disappearing like water soaking into dry, dusty ground. When Jesus said He was thirsty, maybe this brought to mind the picture the psalm describes, of the Messiah's tongue being so dry as He dies that it sticks to the roof of His mouth[341] (see Psalm 22:14–15).

Jesus wasn't asking for a drink just to quench His thirst. He asked for a drink because people EXPECTED the Messiah to be thirsty. By saying He was thirsty, Jesus would completely fulfill the things David had written about the Messiah. People could know Jesus was the Messiah, the Savior God promised to send, who took the punishment for people's sins.[526]

Talk About the Story: What one need did Jesus show He had as He died? What was Jesus offered to drink?

Scripture: "For all the promises of God in Him are Yes." 2 Corinthians 1:20

Family Time: Why do you think Jesus said aloud that He was thirsty? Jesus met every expectation ever written down about the Messiah. What kind of expectations do people have about you? When you meet these expectations, how do you think people feel about you? Because Jesus met the expectations written about Him, this helps people trust Him.

Prayer: Dear Lord, thank You that Jesus fulfilled every prediction about the Messiah. Help us remember we can trust Him to save us because we know He is the One You sent. Amen.

IT IS FINISHED

Scripture: John 19:28–30
Place: Jerusalem
Time: Friday, April 7, 30 AD

After Jesus announced His thirst, the soldiers surrounding the cross looked around for the little pitcher of sour wine they'd brought. A cup couldn't be handed to Jesus on the cross—His hands had been nailed to the wooden frame.

"Use my sponge," one said, dipping it in the dark, bitter liquid.

"Here, put it on this," another said, grabbing the branch of a hyssop plant to use like a skewer. He stabbed the dripping sponge with the stick.

Even if the Roman soldiers didn't know it, the hyssop plant, a bush blooming with purple and blue flowers, would have been important to Jesus and the Jews. It reminded them of the very first Passover, the holiday being celebrated during the same time Jesus died. At Passover, Jews remembered how God had saved their ancestors when they lived far away, many years ago, under the harsh rule of Egypt and its pharaoh. At that time, God sent a deadly plague to punish the Egyptians for the wrong things they were doing to the Jews. But God had a plan to save the Jews, His people.[278]

www.thefamilyprayerbible.com

God told them to use bunches of hyssop plants like paintbrushes, splattering the blood of a sacrificed lamb over the doors of their homes (see Exodus 12:22). The blood would signal to God that the people who lived in the house trusted Him. He would save them, making the plague "pass over" their houses and not harm them!

As the soldiers raised the hyssop branch to Jesus' lips, Jesus knew He was like that sacrificial lamb, whose blood saved people. Jesus had been bleeding and dying, taking the punishment for people's sins even though He was innocent like that Passover lamb. Because Jesus took the punishment people deserve for their sins, God would forgive them, "passing over" their sins when they believed Jesus died for them.[385]

The sponge touched Jesus' lips, and He tasted it, taking no more than a sip. He wasn't drinking to take away His thirst but to fulfill the things written in the Scriptures about the Messiah, the Savior God would send. Perhaps to Jesus, who knew God's Word better than anyone, the predictions written down about the Messiah were like a to-do list. When every checkbox next to every prediction was checked, people could trust Jesus was the Messiah. One by one, Jesus had met these expectations, and as He tasted the sour wine, the to-do list was complete.[38]

"It is finished!" Jesus said.

That sip of sour wine had wet Jesus' throat just enough to help Him speak a few last words. And He shouted them! Like a champion who wins, Jesus shouted His victory! He'd been determined to experience everything God had planned. He hadn't given up—He'd won, making a way for people to experience this victory, too, and be saved from their sins.[513]

Talk About the Story: What did the soldiers use to give Jesus a drink on the cross? What do you think the hyssop branch reminded Jesus of? At the first Passover, how was the hyssop branch used? How was Jesus like the Passover lamb?

Scripture: "He has appeared to put away sin by the sacrifice of Himself." Hebrews 9:26

Family Time: What did Jesus say after He had drunk? What do you think Jesus finished? How do you think your life would be different if Jesus hadn't finished this? Because Jesus finished God's plan completely, sacrificing His life to pay for people's sins, people who trust Him can be forgiven and saved!

Prayer: Dear Lord, thank You that Jesus didn't give up but finished what You asked Him to do. Because Jesus sacrificed His life for us, You can "pass over" our sins and forgive us. Thank You for planning a way to save us. Amen.

INTO YOUR HANDS

Scripture: Luke 23:44–49
Place: Jerusalem
Time: Friday, April 7, 30 AD

Are they still watching? What time is it anyway? a guard at the Temple wondered when the priests would return. They'd gone to watch Jesus die. It was dark now—but not late. Three hours ago, around noon, the sun had stopped shining! The guard went to check the sky—*RIP!*[188]

What's THAT? He turned and watched as the curtain hiding the inner sanctuary, a special room of the Temple, tore in half, from top to bottom.[488]

What do I DO? the guard worried. *If the priests return and think I tore the curtain, I'll be in BIG trouble. But it seemed to tear all by itself . . .* The guard had been taught that only the holiest of priests could go into the place the curtain covered. That's where the high priest met with God to ask Him to forgive people's sins. The curtain separated people who were sinful from God who was holy. But now that separator had been torn in two!

Moments earlier at the cross, a murmur had swept through the crowd. The sun had started shining again! "Look!" someone shouted, pointing at Jesus. "Is He trying to say something?" All eyes turned from the sky to the cross.

Using His very last breaths, Jesus cried out: "Father, into Your hands I commit My Spirit!" Then Jesus bowed His head and died.[130]

Suddenly, rocks started to crack and the earth began to quake! Tombs, where people's bodies were placed when they died, opened up. Later, the people who had died came out—alive—and headed to Jerusalem to visit people there. Something incredible was happening: death wasn't powerful enough to keep them in their graves anymore![405]

At the cross, the Roman soldiers trembled with fear at everything that had happened. "This Man was innocent!" the officer in charge declared. Looking up at Jesus' body on the cross, he began to praise God.[538]

He'd seen many people die on crosses. A person would usually struggle during his last moments alive, gasping for one more breath of air. But Jesus hadn't died like that. He'd used His last breaths to speak and then calmly and peacefully He bowed His head and died. *It's as if He chose WHEN to die, as if He had power to control death!* the soldier marveled.

"Jesus really WAS the Son of God!" other soldiers joined in, their voices quivering in fear. Perhaps they worried what this all could mean—especially now that Jesus was dead. *We helped kill Him.*

But Jesus had released His spirit, giving up His life. No one took it from Him. Jesus followed God's plan to die for people's sins, and He showed He had power over death and these sins. When people believed in what Jesus did for them, their sins wouldn't have power to separate them from God anymore![109]

Talk About the Story: As Jesus died, what things happened at the Temple? In the sky? On the ground?

Scripture: "I am convinced that nothing can ever separate us from God's love. Neither death nor life. . . . No power in the sky above or in the earth below—indeed, nothing in all creation will ever be able to separate us from the love of God that is revealed in Christ Jesus our Lord." Romans 8:38–39

Family Time: What was different about the way Jesus died? What did the soldiers think about Jesus after He died? Jesus is powerful! Because Jesus took the punishment for people's sins, our sins don't have to separate us from God anymore!

Prayer: Dear Lord, Jesus showed His power, following Your plan and choosing when to die on the cross. We're thankful Jesus' power frees us from sin. Thank You that we don't have to be separated from You anymore. Amen.

PSALM 91
STAY CLOSE TO THE CLOUD IN THE CENTER

Moses was walking on the edge of the camp. There were 660,000 men, plus wives and children in the wilderness. They had been delivered from slavery in Egypt by 10 miraculous plagues on the Egyptians. Then God pushed back the Red Sea for them to safely cross on dry ground. He fed them daily with manna (bread) from the sky, and miraculously brought water from a rock.

From the edge of the camp, Moses could see its center. He knew exactly where it was. The cloud of God's presence rose into the air from the Tabernacle in the center of the camp. Moses traced that plume of smoke into the sky as far as he could see. It wasn't normal smoke from a big fire; it was the glory cloud of God that sat on the Ark of the Covenant in the Tabernacle.

Those families who lived on the edge of the camp had to have extra protection from predators in the night that might kill their flocks, or thieves might sneak in to steal from them. These who lived further in were protected by neighbors who shielded them from the threatening wilderness.

Moses was old and too feeble to fight off predators or thieves. He was glad he lived in the center of the camp. He pitched his tent next to the Tabernacle. He lived right under the cloud.

As Moses thought about where people lived and worked, he began writing a Psalm,

> "Those who trust in the protection of the Most High,
>   Pitch their tents under the shadow of the glory cloud.
> I will let everyone know about my place of safety.
>   The Lord is my protection, I will trust in Him."[254]

Moses thought about those who didn't want to live too close to the Tabernacle. Maybe they wanted to do things that were not approved by God. Maybe they had hidden sins. He continued singing Psalm 91.

> "Do not be afraid of wolves at night,
>   Nor of flying arrows from attacking Nomads.
> Also, don't be afraid of disease that spreads at night,
>   Nor any disaster that happens in broad daylight."[217]

Moses knew that the secret of a happy long life was to live pure lives, stay away from sin, and obey all things God required. Again he sang,

> *"If you let the Lord protect you,*
> > *And you make the Most High your refuge,*
> *No evil will capture you and destroy you.*
> > *The Lord will send His angels there*
> *To protect you no matter where you live.*[109]
> > *The Most High will stomp on snakes and other threats,*
> *He will defeat lions before they attack you."*

Moses understood a snake could be an actual serpent, or it could stand for Satan, who is also called a serpent. God can protect you from the dangers of crime or spiritual temptations. He sang,

> *"The Lord will rescue those who love Him,*
> > *Those who live close to the shadow of the Shekinah cloud.*[292]
> *God protects those who seek His presence*
> > *And live close to Him.*
> *God promises, when they call to Me,*
> > *I will answer and be with them.*
> *I will be with them in trouble,*
> > *And rescue them from dangers physical or spiritual.*
> *I will give them a long life on earth,*
> > *And give them eternal salvation with Me in glory."*[413]

Talk About the Psalm: What did you learn about the psalm writer in this story? What did you learn about God?

Psalm 91: Read this week's psalm in your Bible together. Choose a verse to read aloud as a prayer.

Prayer: Thank You, God, for the psalm prayers in the Bible. Thank You for teaching us about You and about how to pray. In Jesus' name, Amen.

SOLDIERS PIERCE JESUS' SIDE

Scripture: John 19:31–37
Place: Jerusalem
Time: Friday, April 7, 30 AD

"This isn't good," one Jewish leader mentioned to another. They stood on a hill looking at the crosses in the distance.

"You're right. It's almost the Sabbath, a holy day, and they're STILL hanging there," the other sighed.

The Jews, who believed people were made in God's image to be like Him, had rules about respecting bodies—even if those bodies belonged to people being punished, like Jesus and the two thieves hanging next to Him on crosses. One rule said a body couldn't be left out overnight. It had to be buried (see Deuteronomy 21:22–23).[277]

"Let's see if the governor will do something about it," the first man suggested, turning in the direction of Pilate's headquarters.

"Please, sir," they pleaded. "Command your soldiers to break the men's legs. This will make the criminals die faster. Then we can bury them and get on with our Sabbath, as usual."

"Fine," Pilate agreed, sending his soldiers out. It didn't matter to him when the men died. He wanted to keep the Jews happy so they wouldn't cause any more trouble.

Carrying clubs, the Roman soldiers climbed the hill where Jesus and the thieves had been crucified. CRACK! One of the men crucified next to Jesus cried out in pain as the soldiers struck him, breaking his legs. Another loud crack and another painful cry soon followed as the soldiers broke the other criminal's legs. *One more to go . . .* the head soldier thought, turning to face Jesus.

He lifted his club in the air, ready to strike again, but suddenly lowered it. "Oh," he said, looking up. *He's already dead?* the soldier couldn't believe how quickly Jesus had died. He didn't realize Jesus had power to decide when to die.[358]

I guess we don't need to speed things up since He's already dead. The soldier began to walk away then, but another soldier rushed up. Lifting up his spear, he stabbed Jesus in the side! Water and blood gushed out onto the ground.

Humph. I guess He really IS dead. This soldier hesitated, but then he left, too.

The soldiers didn't know it, but this all happened as God had planned. Scriptures written long before told what would happen to the Messiah, the One God would send to save people. One Scripture, talking about the Messiah's bones, said, "not one of them is broken" (Psalm 34:20). And they weren't!

Jesus was like the Passover lamb, the animal the Jews killed to give as a sacrifice every year so God would "pass over" them, forgiving their sins. No bones of the Passover lamb were ever supposed to be broken (see Exodus 12:46). The lamb was perfect. Jesus was perfect, like this lamb.[412]

And that big wound the soldier put in Jesus' side made another Scripture come true—showing Jesus perfectly fulfilled God's plan. This Scripture said people would "look on the one they pierced" (see Zechariah 12:10). One day, people would realize Jesus was the One these Scriptures talked about, and this would help them believe Jesus really was the Savior they'd been waiting for.[526]

Talk About the Story: Why did the Jews want to break Jesus' legs? Why was it important to bury bodies before the Sabbath?

Scripture: "Those things which God foretold by the mouth of all His prophets, that the Christ would suffer, He has thus fulfilled." Acts 3:18

Family Time: Why didn't the soldiers break Jesus' legs? Why do you think one soldier stabbed Jesus? The soldiers didn't know it, but they were part of God's plan to help people in the future believe! How does it make you feel to know God's plan was perfect? How might this help you trust God?

Prayer: Dear Lord, thank You for Your Word and Jesus' perfect life. They match up! This helps us know Jesus is the One You sent to save us. Thank You for helping us believe. Amen.

DATE ___/___

CHAPTER 18

JESUS' BURIAL AND RESSURECTION FROM THE DEAD

Apparently none of Jesus' followers anticipated a resurrection of Jesus despite Jesus' constant prediction that he would rise again (cf. John 2:20; Matt. 16:21; 26:61). The eleven disciples were despondent and had assumed the Cross had marked the end of that special relationship they had experienced with Jesus. Even the group of women who left early that morning to go to Jesus' tomb did not expect to witness a resurrected Savior, but to finish treating a dead corpse. What they discovered when they got there was so unexpected even they themselves did not understand what was taking place at first.

Just as the disciples struggled to come to faith in the resurrection of Jesus, so must each individual come to believe today. Some respond to Jesus with faith quickly like John, but others are like Peter who apparently did not come to faith in the resurrected Jesus until several people told him and he had a personal encounter with Jesus. All who came to faith in the Resurrection found in it a cause for celebration. Even today, the resurrection of Jesus remains a cause for celebration on the Lord's Day.

JOSEPH AND NICODEMUS BURY JESUS

Scripture: Luke 23:5—56; John 19:38–42
Place: Jerusalem
Time: Friday, April 7, 30 AD

Most people had left, beating their chests as they walked to show their sadness. But some of Jesus' followers lingered near the cross.

We can't just leave Him there, Joseph, a wealthy and well-known religious leader thought, looking at Jesus' body on the cross.

Joseph was also a follower of Jesus—although secretly. He feared what other religious leaders, who hated Jesus, might do if they knew he believed. Joseph had been waiting for God's kingdom to come, so when Jesus taught about how to enter God's kingdom, Joseph was ready to believe. While the other religious leaders had agreed to kill Jesus, Joseph had disagreed. *I couldn't stop them. But maybe I can do something now.*[518]

Joseph glanced up, noticing the sun wasn't far from setting. *I don't have much time!* If Jesus' body were to be buried, it had to be done before night.

Quickly he went to the headquarters of the Roman governor, Pilate, inside Jerusalem. Joseph knew he was about to do something risky. If the other religious leaders heard about this, they'd know Joseph followed Jesus! But Joseph's love for Jesus was greater than his fears.

"Sir, please, you must let me have Jesus' body," Joseph spoke boldly to Pilate.

www.thefamilyprayerbible.com

"It's almost the Sabbath—and our Passover holiday! Jesus' body must be respected." The Jews followed God's command to rest on the Sabbath, a holy day people were supposed to spend worshiping and honoring God. They couldn't work on the Sabbath, not even cook food to eat! Everything had to be done early, on the Preparation Day.[327]

"You mean Jesus is already dead?" Pilate couldn't believe it. He called the Roman officer who'd been watching at the cross.

"Yes, sir. He's dead," the officer confirmed.

Pilate pondered this a moment, surprised at how quickly Jesus died. "Fine. Take Him," Pilate gave Joseph permission.

Joseph hurried to the cross. Along his way, Nicodemus, another Jewish leader who'd secretly followed Jesus, joined him.

This Preparation Day was different from any they'd experienced. They spent it preparing Jesus' body for burial. Joseph brought an expensive, clean linen sheet. Nicodemus brought seventy-five pounds of myrrh and aloes, costly spices. As gently as they could, they took Jesus' body down from the cross.[163]

In a garden nearby was a tomb Joseph had paid lots of money to have carved out of solid rock. He expected his own body would rest there when he died. But Joseph gave up his special tomb for Jesus.

At the tomb, the men carefully wrapped Jesus' body in the sheet with the spices, like a mummy. Rolling a heavy stone across the tomb's entrance, they sealed Jesus' body inside and left.[355]

From afar, Mary Magdalene and other women who'd followed Jesus watched. Maybe not knowing the men had treated Jesus' body for burial inside, the women ran to buy spices to honor Jesus' body, too. These followers all wanted to give Jesus the best they had.[354]

Talk About the Story: Who secretly followed Jesus? Why do you think they kept it a secret?

Scripture: "Lay up for yourselves treasures in heaven, where neither moth nor rust destroys. . . . For where your treasure is, there your heart will be also." Matthew 6:20–21

Family Time: What did Joseph give for Jesus' burial? Nicodemus? What did the women plan to do? These followers believed Jesus was the Messiah, God's gift to save people. They gave to God in return, showing honor and love to Jesus. How can you show God you're thankful for the gift of salvation He gives?

Prayer: Dear Lord, thank You for the gift of salvation through Your Son Jesus. He gave His life for us—more than we could ever give. We give You our love and praise. Amen.

A GUARD AT THE TOMB

Scripture: Matthew 27:62–66
Place: Jerusalem
Time: Saturday, April 8, 30 AD

The streets of Jerusalem were quieter the next day. It was the Sabbath, a holy day of the week when Jews rested from their daily work and worshiped God. But a group of priests weren't inside resting. They were on their way to see Pilate, the Roman governor. "Even with Jesus dead and buried, our problems aren't over," one of the priests announced his worries to the group along the way.

"What do you want?" Pilate asked the priests as they appeared in his courts. *Shouldn't they be busy worshiping on their Sabbath?* Pilate may have wondered.

"Sir, we've been thinking. We remember that liar Jesus, when He was still alive, said, 'After three days I will rise from the dead.'"[405]

"And?" Pilate raised an eyebrow.

"We ask that you put guards around His tomb, to watch it closely, till the third day. Otherwise, Jesus' followers might come in the night, while everyone's sleeping, and steal His body! They'll lie to everyone, saying, 'Jesus is alive!' That lie will be even worse for us than the lies Jesus himself told!"[189]

Still the priests didn't understand that Jesus had told the truth. They refused to believe that He really was God's Son, sent to be the Savior.

As Pilate considered their request, perhaps the priests' minds raced with worries. *If people think Jesus is alive again, they might believe He really IS God's Son. People will blame US for killing Him! They won't trust us anymore, and they'll stop giving us the Temple—money. We'll lose ALL our power and authority!*[505]

Pilate gave his instructions: "Take guards and seal the tomb as best you can."

Quickly and eagerly the priests departed, following behind the guards to the tomb.

Maybe now they'll leave me alone. Pilate maybe thought as he watched them leave.

"Make sure that stone is REALLY tight over the entrance!" the head guard commanded the soldiers at the tomb. They rolled the heavy stone into a large groove, making it extra hard to move, and with a huge glob of wax, they sealed the tomb shut. "Stand there, there, and there!" the head guard ordered the soldiers where to keep watch.

Ha! NOBODY is going to get in! the priests thought smugly as they watched, never thinking who might get OUT. So caught up in their fears and worries about what they might lose, they never stopped to think about what they might gain if they believed Jesus really was the Savior and that He told the truth. Soon they'd be in for a BIG surprise.[415]

Talk About the Story: Who did the priests visit on the Sabbath? What did they ask him? What did the priests worry might happen if guards didn't watch Jesus' tomb?

Scripture: "For what profit is it to a man if he gains the whole world, and loses his own soul? Or what will a man give in exchange for his soul?" Matthew 16:26

Family Time: What did the priests fear they might lose if people believed Jesus? The priests missed out on knowing the truth about Jesus. They were too caught up worrying about what they might have to give up—money and power—to realize what they'd gain—life forever with Jesus! What things would be hard for you to give up? What things does Jesus give that are even better?

Prayer: Dear Lord, the priests didn't understand the gift Jesus had to give them—life forever with You. They cared too much about the things they had in this world. We're thankful for everything You give us. But please help us care most of all about Your greatest gift, Jesus. In His name, Amen.

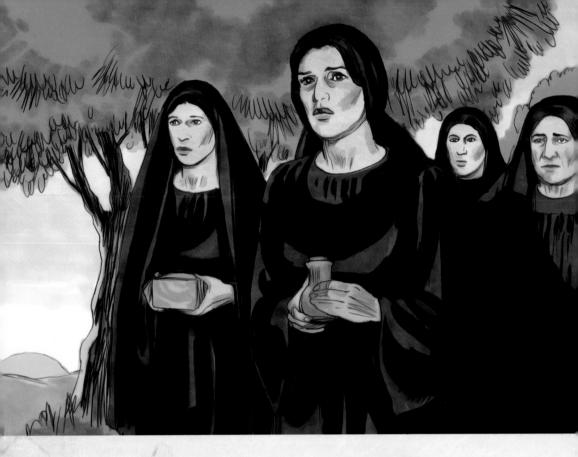

THE STONE ROLLED AWAY

Scripture: Matthew 28:1–4
Place: Jerusalem
Time: Sunday, April 9, 30 AD

It was still dark when some women awoke early on Sunday morning. So much had happened recently, and maybe they were still tired, but they knew in their heart they had something important to do. They got up, grabbed some expensive spices, and hurried to meet their friends.

The women had shared many wonderful times with Jesus. They had listened to Jesus teach about amazing things, like how people could be saved from their sins when they asked God for forgiveness and believed in Him. These women believed in Jesus and enjoyed being with Him. But those happy times had come to an end.

They remembered, just a few days before, watching from a distance as Jesus suffered and died on His cross. *I know Jesus said this had to happen, that it was all part of God's plan to save people from their sins . . . But it's hard not to cry!*

www.thefamilyprayerbible.com

"Did you bring your spices?" one friend asked.

They nodded.

"Let's go."

The Friday night before, they had bought special spices to use to anoint Jesus' body. Sometimes, people put good-smelling spices on the body of a person who had died to preserve it, like a mummy. Anointing was also a way to show honor, like putting beautiful flowers on someone's grave. These spices were probably expensive. But the women loved Jesus so much that they wanted to give Him the best they could to honor Him.

"OK. We have the spices, but how are we actually going to put them on Jesus' body once we get there?" they wondered.

"You saw just as plainly as I did that huge stone Joseph rolled over the tomb to close it," one woman continued. "If only someone could help us."

"You're right," one of the women said, "but let's just get to the tomb and then see."

The day Jesus died, a rich man named Joseph, who wanted to honor Jesus too, had placed Jesus' body there. Maybe Joseph wanted to make sure Jesus' body would be safe from harm. So Joseph brought Jesus' body to a garden where Joseph owned a brand-new tomb carved out of solid rock.[260] It would be impossible for any person to break inside.

As the women reached the garden, the light of the rising sun revealed they weren't alone.

The guards were gone. Before they got to the tomb, the earth trembled. An angel came down from heaven, rolled aside the giant stone,[188] and sat on it.[15]

His face shone as bright as lightning. His clothes gleamed white like snow. Seeing him, the guards shivered in fear, fainted, and fell to the ground.[165]

Talk About the Story: Why did the women go to Jesus' tomb? What did they expect to find there? What did they see?

Scripture: "For I, the Lord your God, will hold your right hand, saying to you, 'Fear not, I will help you.'" Isaiah 41:13

Family Time: Why did the women want to anoint Jesus' body? What did they worry about? How do you think they felt when the angel rolled away the stone? God sent help! God will help us honor Him, even when we face problems. When are times it's hard to honor God?

Prayer: Father, thank You for rolling away the stone. The women knew they faced a problem. But You sent help! When I face obstacles in my life that seem big like that stone, help me still to honor You. Amen.

THE WOMEN AT THE TOMB

Scripture: Matthew 28:5–6; Mark 16:1–8
Place: Jerusalem
Time: Sunday, April 9, 30 AD

Some women came early to the tomb on Sunday morning. They came to anoint the body of Jesus. When they looked into the tomb, it was empty.

Then they saw an angel. The women raised their hands, shielding their eyes to look at his face shining youthful and bright. His white robes flowed out over the stone he sat on, rolled to the right of the tomb.

"Do not be afraid," the angel said. "I know you are looking for Jesus, who you saw die on the cross."[147] The women's minds flashed back to that painful memory.

"Jesus is not here!" The angel continued, his voice full of joy. "He is risen from the dead, just as He promised would happen."[405]

The women gasped in amazement.

"Remember how He told you?" The angel asked. "When Jesus traveled in

Galilee teaching about God's plan, He said, 'The Son of Man must be delivered into the hands of sinful men, and be crucified, and the third day rise again'" (Luke 24:6–7 *NKJV*).[405]

They remembered the disciples talking a lot about Jesus' promise. They all wondered how Jesus' promise would come true. One time, Jesus used a story to explain. "For as Jonah was three days and three nights in the belly of the great fish, so will the Son of Man be three days and three nights in the heart of the earth," Jesus said (Matthew 12:40 *NKJV*).[206]

Sometimes the people listening to Jesus weren't sure what He meant when he told stories like this. Some people doubted His promise, especially after watching Him die. The women were not sure how it would all work out. Waiting to see wasn't easy, but they still hoped.

"Come! Take a look!" The angel invited the women, waving his hand toward the open tomb. "See where Jesus WAS lying—"[24]

The women approached the tomb, curious to see.

"But you won't find Him here!" The angel said.

The women peered inside. Sure enough, the angel was right: the tomb was empty!

Jesus' promise is starting to make sense, They thought. *If He's not here, then could He really be alive?*

"Even now, Jesus is going ahead of you. So go, too. And hurry!" the angel said. Quickly, the women exited the tomb.

"Tell the disciples—especially Peter—this good news: Jesus isn't dead. He's alive![145] And you will see Him in Galilee, just as He promised."

Seeing the empty tomb—a hint that Jesus' promise was true—left the women speechless. Trembling with fear and joy, they ran quick as they could to Galilee, eager to meet Jesus and to see His promise come true.[213]

Talk About the Story: Where did the angel say Jesus was? What did Jesus promise would happen after He died? What did the women see at the tomb?

Scripture: "Commit your way to the Lord, trust also in Him, and He shall bring it to pass" (Psalm 37:5).

Family Time: What did Jesus promise? How do you think the women felt about this promise when Jesus died? How did they show they trusted God? When are times it's hard to wait and trust God?

Prayer: Father, thank You for keeping Your promises. The women weren't sure how You would keep Your promise to come back to life, but they chose to wait and trust You. Even when I don't understand Your promises completely, help me wait and trust You. Amen.

THREE WOMEN WORSHIP JESUS

Scripture: Matthew 28:9–10
Place: Outside of Jerusalem
Time: Sunday, April 9, 30 BC

The women had seen the angel at the tomb. Now they ran to share the amazing news that the tomb was empty.

What other incredible things might happen next? The women wondered. *We went to the tomb on one mission, and now we're being sent on another!*

Mary, and Salome, another woman who had also gone to the tomb, kicked up clouds of dust behind them as they hurried. Maybe they felt their legs couldn't move fast enough to carry them to the disciples. And then there would be more running—on to Galilee, where the angel said they would meet Jesus!

Someone was standing along the road. It was hard to make out who it was in the dim light of the early morning. The women approached, closer and closer. They could see that the person was a Jewish man.

www.thefamilyprayerbible.com

"Rejoice!" the man said, greeting them.

Why should he be greeting us? It was uncommon for a Jewish man to speak with a woman in public, although he might if he already knew them.

After a few more steps, they realized this wasn't just any Jewish man. *It's Jesus!* All of a sudden, the women fell to the ground at Jesus' feet. Had they tripped? No, the rocky, uneven road hadn't made them stumble. But seeing Jesus—alive, just as He promised He would be—caused them immediately to bow before Him.[541]

People would bow to someone to show reverence or honor. They might bow to a ruler or king to show they believed the king had the right to rule. When the women bowed to Jesus, they showed Him they believed He is King, not just of a country or a special land, but of EVERYTHING.

The women reached out their hands and touched Jesus' feet. Not only could they see Him but they could FEEL Him too. *How great to be in His presence again, to have Jesus right here with me!*[264]

But even though the women showed on the outside how happy they were to see Jesus, Jesus knew that, on the inside, the women felt frightened, too. Kings are powerful, and the women must have felt small before Jesus, their powerful King. He had power over everything, even death!

Jesus showed He is also a kind king. "Do not be afraid,"[163] He said. "Go and tell my disciples, who were like brothers to me, that they should go to Galilee. I will meet them there."[526]

The women obeyed. But this time they left feeling grateful to have SEEN Jesus and to have spent time worshiping Him as King.[538]

Talk About the Story: Who did the women meet after leaving the tomb? What did the women do when they met Jesus? What did Jesus say to the women?

Scripture: "The Lord reigns; let the earth rejoice" (Psalm 97:1).

Family Time: Why do you think Jesus told the women to rejoice? Why did the women worship Jesus? We can thank Jesus for the things that make Him King. What are things you know about God that make you want to praise Him?

Prayer: Father, thank You for being King! The women worshiped You when they believed that You are King, just as You promised. Help us remember reasons to worship You as King. Amen.

PSALM 92
A PSALM FOR THE LORD'S DAY

Mother brought medicine in a glass into the bedroom. Her son Micah was sick with an upset stomach. She handed him the glass. "Here, drink this. It is good for you." But Micah didn't want to drink anything. His stomach was hurting. He answered,

"I don't want to."

Micah didn't realize a momentary displeasure—drinking medicine—could give him long term relief. If he drank it, he would feel better, but more than that, it would take away his pain and do away with the germs in his stomach.

The human race is sick with sin. Not only does sin have immediate pain, sin has a long term consequence of punishment in hell after we die. One of the medicines God gives is the Lord's Day. In the Old Testament it was Saturday, today it is Sunday. God offers rest from the drudgery of work, but he also says, "Here, worship. It is good for you."

Micah didn't like to go to church. He complained, "It's boring and I would rather do something else." Micah only attended church because his parents made him go. What does God say about His day?

"God I come to church to tell You how good You are.
God will bless you when you praise Him wholeheartedly."

When Micah goes to church on Sunday morning he will be obedient to God. That means Micah pleases God. But Micah needs to learn to worship God at other times other than Sunday. He can pray with his family like you are doing now. Micah can praise God several times a day.

"Lord, it is good to tell You I love You
In the morning, at night, all the time."[365]

There are several ways Micah can praise the Lord. He can talk to God in prayers, just like telling your mom "thank you." Also he can listen to recorded praise music. You can join in and sing along, giving praise to God.

> "It is good to tell God what's in your heart
>> With recorded music when you sing during the week,
>> Or, you pray inwardly to the music."[230]

What happens to Micah when he talks to God? He is happy because he is obedient. Sometimes you don't want to do something your parents ask you to do. But after you get it done, how do you feel?

> "Lord, the things You have created makes me happy.
>> I enjoy telling You about Your greatness;
> I am happy finding out who You are."

When Micah worships God at church, or at home, he grows inwardly. So will you. We can look forward to Sunday because it is an opportunity to get closer to God and to grow as a Christian.

> "Those obedient to God will grow like a palm tree;
>> They will develop like healthy trees.
> They will grow because they are planted in God's house,[413]
>> And because they are near the presence of God.
> When they are old, they will continue to grow inwardly;
>> They will always be fresh and green.
> They will show everyone that it is good to worship God
>> And that He is good to those who obey Him."[363]

Talk About the Psalm: What did you learn about the psalm writer in this story? What did you learn about God?

Psalm 92: Read this week's psalm in your Bible together. Choose a verse to read aloud as a prayer.

Prayer: Thank You, God, for the psalm prayers in the Bible. Thank You for teaching us about You and about how to pray. In Jesus' name, Amen.

THE MYSTERY OF THE EMPTY TOMB AND MISSING BODY

Scripture: John 20:1-18
Place: Outside of Jerusalem
Time: Sunday, April 9, 30 BC

But what will the disciples think when we tell them? The women may have wondered as they ran from the tomb. *Will anyone even believe us?* Before the women met Jesus on the road—seeing Him with their very eyes!—they wondered a lot about what they'd seen, and about what they HADN'T seen.

Since we didn't see Jesus' body, perhaps He really is alive, out there somewhere, Mary would hope until other questions crowded into her mind: *But where is He? And if He's not alive, then who took His body?*

It was all such a big mystery! Still, Mary kept running and thought about how to explain it.

The angel had said to be sure to tell the news to Peter, so Mary went to him. When she arrived, she saw John there too. They looked so sad; weeping about what had happened to Jesus.[478] These two disciples had been very close with Jesus, like brothers.

Maybe since they knew Jesus so well, they'll have a clue what's happened, Mary may have hoped.

"They have taken Jesus, the Lord, out of the tomb," Mary told them.

Full of worry and confusion, Peter ran to the tomb, eager to investigate for himself and get to the bottom of all this. John followed.[57]

Perhaps the angel took Him. Or maybe the gardener took Him. Mary reasoned, following behind them. *The tomb is in a garden, after all.* Still, no matter how much she tried to solve the mystery, Mary didn't feel right about her explanations. She felt frustrated and upset, to the point of tears—that is, until she saw Jesus![377]

Mary and Peter and John weren't the only ones who tried to solve these mysteries.

The women visited the other disciples. These men were mourning too.

"What do you mean, 'He is risen'? Where is His body then?" the disciples asked.[506]

"We don't know where they have laid Him," the women answered.

"You are talking nonsense," the men said. "What a silly tale!"

Too bad the angel didn't remind them too. Have they forgotten what Jesus promised? Some of the women may have thought, feeling frustrated the men wouldn't believe.

When Jesus appeared to the women, this helped them believe. They saw Jesus alive, as He promised He would be! But before Jesus came to them, it was all a confusing mystery.

Even today, people question and try to explain exactly how it all happened.[4] It's mysterious—but God's Word, the Bible, gives answers to many of these questions. It doesn't have to be a mystery. God's Word, like Jesus' promise, helps people understand and believe!

Talk About the Story: Before she saw Jesus, where did Mary think He was? Did the disciples believe the women's news? What did the disciples say?

Scripture: "But these are written that you may believe that Jesus is the Christ, the Son of God, and that believing you may have life in His name" (John 30:31).

Family Time: What questions did Jesus' followers ask about the empty tomb? Why do you think the disciples doubted the women's news? What questions do you have about Jesus? Look together in the Bible to find an answer to one of your questions!

Prayer: Father, thank You that when we have questions, You have answers. Some of Your followers didn't believe You or tried to solve the mysteries on their own. When we have doubts, help us remember to ask You. Help us believe Your Word. Amen.

SOLDIERS TELL THE SANHEDRIN

Scripture: Matthew 28:11–15
Place: Jerusalem
Time: Sunday, April 9, 30 BC

"How do we explain THAT?" one guard pointed at the big opening to the tomb—it was supposed to be CLOSED! Other guards crawled around, starting to get up from the ground where they had fainted after the earthquake.

"What happened?" one asked.

"No one is going to believe this!" another said.

"We're trained guards!" another soldier said. "What will the priests—and the governor—do when they see we didn't guard it?"

"Let's go to the priests, before the news gets out."

The guards soon left for Jerusalem, heading to the Temple where they would tell the news to the Sanhedrin, and the chief priests.

These priests followed many religious rules and tried to make everybody follow them, too. They didn't believe Jesus' promise that He would come to life again after His death. They didn't want anyone else to believe it either.[334]

Earlier, the priests had sent the guards to the tomb. "Make sure no one steals Jesus' body," they had instructed. "Otherwise people will start to think He really is alive. Then no one will follow our rules—they'll follow Jesus instead!"

So, when the guards arrived at the Temple gates, the priests looked alarmed. "What are you doing here?" they demanded. "Don't you have a tomb to guard?"

The guards told them everything—the earthquake, the empty tomb. The priests met privately with some elders and other powerful men in the Temple, to figure out what to do.

"If people start to believe that nonsense that Jesus is alive, we'll have a HUGE problem," said one priest. "No one will follow our rules. We'll lose all our power and money."[360]

"Here's what we can do," one priest said. "We'll tell a different story, convincing everyone Jesus didn't come back to life. We'll say His followers stole the body, making it only *look* like Jesus is alive!"

"Can we hire you for another job to do?" the chief priest asked the soldiers, showing them a mountain of coins.[189]

The soldiers' eyes grew big with greed. They thought of all they could buy and all they could do with that money. They would be rich!

"There's no denying Jesus' body is gone," the chief priest said. "People will ask where it is. Jesus' followers will say He's alive. But you will say Jesus' disciples came at night and stole the body while you slept."[374]

"But if the governor thinks we were sleeping, we'll be in even more trouble!" one guard whined.

"Don't worry. If the governor hears, we'll talk to him. We'll make sure you don't get in trouble."

So the guards took the money and told the terrible lie. Maybe it seemed like the easiest thing to do—plus they were getting paid!

But the guards' choice had BIG consequences. The lie spread fast and far. Even today, 2,000 years later, some people still believe the lie, instead of the truth that Jesus is alive and saves them.[416]

Talk About the Story: What lie did the priests tell the guards to say? What did the priests give the guards for lying? What is the result of the lie today?

Scripture: "A true witness delivers souls, but a deceitful witness speaks lies" (Proverbs 14:25).

Family Time: Why did the priests choose to lie? Why did the guards choose to lie? When are times people have to choose between telling the truth or telling a lie? What makes it hard to choose?

Prayer: Father, the priests made a bad choice to lie. They tempted the guards to lie, too. This lie hurts others even today. When we're tempted, help us always choose truth over lies. Amen.

RACING TO THE TOMB

Scripture: John 20:1–10
Place: Jerusalem
Time: Sunday, April 9

A quick, soft knock rattled the door.
Peter and John locked eyes. Their saddened, tearful expressions changed to fearful, worried looks. Could it be those leaders who had arrested and killed Jesus? Had they now come to arrest Jesus' followers too? Peter and John and the other disciples had been hiding, wondering what might happen now.

Hesitantly, Peter walked to the door. "Who is it?" He whispered.

"Mary," a gentle voice responded.

Unbarring the locks, Peter swiftly opened the door, and Mary rushed in.

"They have taken Jesus, the Lord, out of the tomb," Mary said.

Peter and John looked puzzled.

"And we don't know where they have put him!"[478] she added.

www.thefamilyprayerbible.com

Soon Peter was out the door and off to the tomb, running as fast as he could. *What could all this mean?* He wondered, faintly noticing the sound of footsteps behind him. Just as he turned his head to look, John zoomed past him! If the men were racing, John would have won. He arrived at the tomb first, but he stopped right at the edge of the entrance.[164]

John peered in. The linen strips were lying there—messy like an unmade bed. *This doesn't look good*, he may have thought. *Mary's right. Somebody must have taken Jesus' body, leaving real quick, but—*

John looked up as Peter zipped by, straight into the tomb! Left, right, up, down—quickly Peter looked all around the tomb. He saw those same strips of cloth John had seen,[426] but that wasn't all Peter saw. Taking a few steps deeper into the tomb, he noticed another cloth.

That's different, he thought. He recognized the head covering, a special piece of linen the size of a hankie, or maybe a big washcloth, that people put on the face of a body when they buried it.

Wondering why Peter hadn't come out yet, John followed him into the tomb. The sight of the head covering made him stop. Lying opposite the long, messy strips, this little cloth was folded, neat and tidy. *But a thief wouldn't have taken the time or trouble to FOLD that!* John thought to himself. Perhaps it was at this point John knew: Jesus' body wasn't stolen. Jesus was alive![506]

"I don't understand it," Peter said, exiting the tomb.

"I don't either," John replied. But John had seen something at the tomb that was helping him believe, even if he didn't tell Peter just yet.

Is that little cloth a sign, to help us know and believe? John may have wondered. *It's like a fingerprint of God, showing Jesus was there—not some thief! And if Jesus isn't there, somehow, He must be alive!*

Talk About the Story: Who ran to the tomb? Which disciple arrived first? Which disciple went inside first? What did they see inside the tomb?

Scripture: "And you will seek Me and find Me, when you search for Me with all your heart." Jeremiah 29:13

Family Time: What helped the disciples know Jesus' body wasn't stolen? What did John have to do to see the face cloth, like Peter? When you spend time with God, what are ways you can "go all the way" to learn more about Him? He wants to help us know Him more!

Prayer: Father, John and Peter went all the way into the tomb to look for You. You wanted to help them believe. When we do things to learn about You and spend time with You, help us not give up. Help us go all the way! Amen.

MARY'S TEARS

Scripture: John 20:11–18
Place: At the tomb outside of Jerusalem
Time: Later in the morning, Sunday, April 9

They've taken Him, Mary worried, wiping a tear from her eye. *After all those unkind things people said and did to Jesus, why couldn't I anoint His body? Couldn't I do something kind to honor Him?* She may have thought.

But I can't anoint Him if He's not here! Mary stooped down, looking into the tomb. Perhaps she had seen Peter and John go in—or at least come out. They had left so quickly. What did they see?

Jesus wasn't there; no body to be found. Expecting the tomb to be dark, Mary was surprised to clearly see two men! On either end of a stone bench, a shelf built into the rock wall, two angels sat, clothed in white robes.[14] *But that's where Jesus should be,* Mary wept.

"Why are you weeping?"[530] The angels asked.

"Because they've taken Jesus, my Lord, and I don't know where!"[56] Mary replied. Perhaps feeling hopeless, she turned to go, but someone stood there.

It must be the gardener, Mary reasoned. *I'm in a garden, after all.*

He too asked Mary why she was crying. "Who are you looking for?" He added.

Maybe Mary didn't want to keep talking about her tears, but she thought the gardener might know something that could help her.

"If you took Jesus away, tell me where," she said. "Then I'll go to Him."[313] Maybe she was still thinking of the spices and her plan to anoint Jesus. Her mind buzzed busily as she wondered what to do next.

"Mary!" The man said, His voice powerful but familiar, like a friend's.

"Rabboni!"[474] Mary exclaimed. This was no gardener. It was Jesus! Mary called Jesus a word meaning "teacher." Maybe hearing Jesus say her name, hearing His voice, reminded Mary of everything else she had heard Him say, about God's plan to save her and help her.

Mary reached out her hand to hold onto Jesus. She was so relieved to find Him and never wanted to lose Him again.

"Don't cling to Me," Jesus said. "I haven't finished yet what God planned for Me. I have to go up to Heaven, to join My Father."

Mary listened to that familiar voice, perhaps feeling comforted.

"Go to my disciples, who are like brothers to me. Tell them I'm going up to My Father. He's my God. And He's their Father and their God, too!"[259]

So Mary now knew what to do. "I've seen Jesus," she said when she met the disciples. "He knew me and helped me know Him! And here is everything He wants YOU to know, too." Then Mary shared with them all Jesus had said.[478]

Talk About the Story: Why was Mary crying? Who did Mary see inside the tomb? Who did Mary think she saw as she left? Who was this really?

Scripture: "Fear not, for I have redeemed you; I have called you by your name; You are Mine." Isaiah 43:1

Family Time: As Mary left the tomb, what did she ask the man there? What helped Mary recognize Him? Jesus knows your name, and He wants you to know Him and trust Him! What are ways you can get to know God better? How might knowing Jesus better help you?

Prayer: Father, sometimes it's hard to hear You, especially when worries and fears bother us. Mary worried what to do, but You called her by name and comforted her. You know everything—our names and our situations. Help us remember You know us and You know just what to do. Amen.

A WALK-AND-TALK BIBLE STUDY

Scripture: Luke 24:13–35
Place: The road from Jerusalem to Emmaus
Time: Later in the day, Sunday, April 9

❝How disappointing," Cleophas muttered, as he and his wife walked to the village of Emmaus. Other followers of Jesus had stayed in Jerusalem. Maybe the couple wanted to leave all that had happened there behind.

"What could those Scriptures about Him mean—especially now He's dead?" Cleophas's wife asked.

Caught up in conversation, they didn't realize at first, but a stranger had joined them, heading the same direction. They welcomed his company.

"What have you been talking about?" he asked. "Even far away, I could tell how focused you are, and also sad."[166]

Where has he been—living under a rock? Cleophas may have wondered. "You must be the only person in Jerusalem who doesn't know about these things!" He exclaimed.[506]

"What things?" the stranger asked.

"Well, about Jesus, of course!" Cleophas answered. "You know, the Prophet? He did and said amazing things to help people know about God and His plan to save Israel."[72]

"We believed Jesus was the king the Scriptures talked about, the One who would free Israel from those harsh Romans," Cleophas's wife explained.

"But our own religious leaders handed Him over to those Romans to die!"[96] Cleophas said. "And that was three days ago."

"Still," Cleophas's wife reasoned, "Mary and the others said angels at Jesus' tomb told them He's alive—"

"But," Cleophas interrupted, "Peter and John also went. They didn't see Jesus."

The stranger listened patiently. Now he spoke: "How foolish to have no faith! Why are you surprised Jesus suffered these things?" he asked. "You've heard for years what the Scriptures said would have to happen to Jesus. Let me help you understand."[377]

What happened next was like a walk-and-talk Bible study! He explained every word ever written in the Scriptures about Jesus—from Genesis to that very day.

"Jesus IS the King you were waiting for," he explained, tracing Jesus' family back to King David, one of the most famous kings in Scripture.

Those seven miles to Emmaus, a few hours of walking, passed quickly as they listened to this wise man. Nearing the village, Cleophas and his wife slowed down, not wanting to leave this stranger who taught them so much.

"Please, join us," they invited him.

They went inside to share a meal. Just as you might say a prayer before eating, the stranger took the bread and blessed it. He broke it and gave it to them.[300]

Perhaps the stories they knew, of Jesus blessing bread to feed thousands, or of Jesus breaking bread with His disciples before He died, flashed through their minds. Instantly they knew Him.[450] And instantly the man—Jesus—disappeared.

"We must return to Jerusalem, now!" Cleophas led his wife out the door. Knowing they'd seen Jesus,[456] they had to share the news. So back to the disciples they went, to help them understand, too.

Talk About the Story: Where were Cleophas and his wife going? Who joined them? What did they talk about?

Scripture: "For where two or three are gathered together in My name, I am there in the midst of them." Matthew 18:20

Family Time: Why were Cleophas and his wife sad? What did the stranger explain? How did the stranger show them who He was? What did Cleophas and his wife do then?

Prayer: Father, thank You for coming to us. You joined Cleophas and His wife and helped them understand Your Word. When they invited You, You showed them who You are, and they told others about You, too! We invite You to come. Please help us know You and share about You with others. Amen.

BEHIND LOCKED DOORS

Scripture: John 20:19–23; Luke 24:36–49
Place: Jerusalem
Time: At the end of the day, Sunday, April 9

"Did you remember to lock that door after they came in?"³⁷⁷ a disciple whispered to another sitting closest to the door.

The Jews killed Jesus. Will we—Jesus' followers—be next? they may have worried.

They huddled around Cleophas, tilting their heads to hear.

"When He broke bread with us, we KNEW it was JESUS!" Cleophas whispered eagerly, telling what had happened earlier that evening. Just then, Jesus appeared in the very middle of their circle!

"Peace be with you,"³⁹⁷ Jesus greeted them.

A ghost! they thought, trembling in fear. *It looks like Jesus, but we know He died. How could this be anything BUT a ghost?*

"Why are you afraid? Jesus asked. "Why do you doubt that it could really be Me?" He knew every fear they had and every question they were asking, without them saying anything.¹⁶⁵

"Look at My hands and feet," Jesus said, wanting to help them trust Him. "A ghost wouldn't have flesh and bones as I do. Touch and see that it is really Me."[156]

The disciples warily approached Him, inspecting Him carefully. They saw the wounds in His hands, where the nails had gone in, holding Him to the cross. That big gash in His side was there too, where they knew a soldier had pierced Him.

How wonderful to see Him again! But it's too good to be true! Still the disciples feared He was a ghost.

"Do you have any food?" Jesus asked. Maybe watching Him eat would help them believe. A ghost wouldn't be hungry—and with no body, the food would just fall to the floor!

They brought Jesus a piece of fish, and some honeycomb. They watched Jesus chew and swallow, eating just as any living person would.[158] Maybe they didn't quite believe Jesus yet, but they were starting to think He might not be a ghost after all.

"These things had to happen: my suffering, death, and coming alive again, just as the Scriptures said," Jesus explained. "This was God's plan for Me. And just as God had a plan for Me, I have a plan for You."[425]

With their fears starting to fade, the disciples listened closely to Jesus now.

"Peace be with You," Jesus said again. "I am giving you my Holy Spirit so that you will have My power to do My work.[167] You will share about Me with others so that their sins can be forgiven. They will have peace with God, too. They won't have to be afraid, because they can believe in Me."[174]

Perhaps even then the disciples were beginning to believe and experience that peace Jesus was talking about.

"This is part of God's plan and promise," Jesus said. "When You receive My Spirit, I will always be with you. I will help you."[450]

Talk About the Story: Who did the disciples think appeared to them? How did Jesus show them He is alive?

Scripture: "These things I have spoken to you, that in Me you may have peace. In the world you will have tribulation; but be of good cheer, I have overcome the world." John 16:33

Family Time: What words did Jesus say twice to the disciples? What did He promise to give them? How would this gift help them? What's something you're worried about that you can ask God for help with?

Prayer: Father, thank You for giving us peace. You replaced the disciples' fears with Your peace. You gave the gift of Your Spirit so they would have You with them to help them. Please take away our fears and doubts. Help us rely on You. Amen.

PSALM 100
HAPPY WORSHIP

Young Jacob waited for King David to ride his beautiful white horse from the Temple in Jerusalem to his palace. This would be the first time Jacob would ever see personally the King.

"What must I do?" Jared asked. "What shall I say?"

The wise father suggested his son should smile and cheer for the king. The father added, "It will make the king happy to see your happy face."

The father explained that the king had done many wonderful things for his people. "The king protects us from enemy attacks. He leads us with justice and mercy. He makes our lives better."

The crowd began to buzz, the king was coming. Jacob could feel the excitement in the air. Then down the street they saw the prancing white steed, with

King David in the saddle. Young Jared's eyes got bigger. Then he began cheering with everyone else.

For the first time in his life, Jared saw the king, but more importantly, the King saw young Jared shouting for joy. The big white horse paused, and King David made eye contact with the boy, and smiled. That was all Jared needed for a lifetime of memory. The King approved of him.

In the same way, Psalm 100 instructs, "Make a joyful noise unto the Lord."[290] God wants us to rejoice and be glad.

God is not happy when people fuss about attending church or gripe about giving tithes and offerings. So when you come to God, remember, "Worship the Lord with gladness."[541] Our happy attitude makes God happy.

"Come before His presence with singing."[541] Sometimes we sing about God, sometimes we sing to God.

Remember, "We are his people, and the sheep of His pasture." We have every reason to be thankful that we belong to God; so "we enter His gates with thanksgiving."[46] That means we come into His presence with a thankful heart.

So when we are happy, worshiping God, what happens? "The Lord is good to us." Then "His mercy continues throughout our life," and He is always faithful to us, forever and ever."[481]

> *"Lord, I shout with joy to you;*[290]
>> *Everyone from every nation joins me.*
> *I worship as I enter Your presence with singing*
>> *Because You, Lord, are my God.*[541]
> *Lord, You made us and we belong to You;*[290]
>> *We are Your people and the sheep of Your pasture.*
> *Lord, I come into Your gates giving thanks;*
>> *I enter the courts with praise.*
> *I bless Your holy name* [46]
>> *By giving thanks for all you've done for me.*
> *Lord, You are good, Your mercy is everlasting;*
>> *And Your truth endures forever.*[481] *Amen*

Talk About the Psalm: What did you learn about the psalm writer in this story? What did you learn about God?

Psalm 100: Read this week's psalm in your Bible together. Choose a verse to read aloud as a prayer.

Prayer: Thank You, God, for the psalm prayers in the Bible. Thank You for teaching us about You and about how to pray. In Jesus' name, Amen.

CHAPTER 19

FORTY DAYS WITH JESUS

In the week following Easter Sunday, the disciples marveled at the awesome responsibility that was theirs, that of being witnesses of Jesus' resurrection and communicating to others how they could experience the forgiveness of sins. They knew they would soon be returning to Galilee where Jesus had promised to meet them again, but first there were some loose ends to take care of. Thomas had not been with them when they saw Jesus. He was strong-minded, silent, but also skeptical. Thomas was among the first to whom the disciples told that they had seen Jesus.

The disciples may have been surprised at Thomas' reluctance to believe their testimony as they reported to him that they had seen the resurrected Jesus. They may have forgotten how reluctant they also had been to believe the early reports of the women and Mary Magdalene that Sunday morning. Thomas was just as

reluctant to believe, and said, "Unless I see in His hands the print of the nails, and put my finger into the print of the nails, and put my hand into His side, I will not believe" (John 20:25).

Jesus, turning to the doubting disciple, said, "Reach your finger here, and look at My hands; and reach your hand here, and put it into My side. Do not be unbelieving, but believing" (John 20:27). But Thomas did not need to look. Seeing Jesus and hearing Him speak again was enough. He expressed his faith simply with the confession, "My Lord and my God" (John 20:28).

Jesus gave the Great Commission to, "Go into all the world and preach the gospel to every person." Then Jesus left His disciples and returned to heaven. You need to prepare yourself to obey that directive to "make disciples" of every person within your sphere of influence.

JESUS AND THOMAS

Scripture: John 20:22–29
Place: Jerusalem
Time: Sunday, April 16

"Oh, if only you had been here!" one of the disciples groaned.

Thomas, another disciple had just returned.

"You missed it!" said the others. "Jesus appeared right HERE. No lock on that door could keep Him out. He showed us the very holes in His hands where the nails went in, keeping Him on the cross. We saw the big wound where the soldier struck Him with a spear. Seeing all that—and more—we knew it HAD to be Jesus, the Lord."

"Well, I won't believe unless I see the nail marks in His hands and put my finger into them, and see that spear wound in His side and put my hand right into it, too," Thomas replied. "Nope, hearing what you say isn't enough. And seeing isn't either. I won't believe unless I SEE and FEEL."[478]

www.thefamilyprayerbible.com

Maybe the disciples shook their heads at Thomas and his hard heart.

The following Sunday, all the disciples were meeting. Still they were afraid, and still they hid behind their heavily locked doors.

As if that will keep those Jews who killed Jesus out! Thomas may have doubted.

Thomas was right about one thing—those locks wouldn't keep out someone determined to get in, especially when that person was Jesus! All of a sudden, Jesus appeared right before him.

"Peace to you!" Jesus said, greeting the disciples as He had before.

Then, Jesus spoke just to Thomas: "See my hands? Put your finger into the nail marks you see. See my side? Put your hand into the wound there. See and feel. Don't doubt. Believe!"[403]

Jesus hadn't been there when Thomas talked about needing to feel the wounds to believe. But Jesus knew all about Thomas's doubts, and He wanted to help Thomas believe. So Jesus invited Thomas to see and feel, giving Thomas the evidence he said he needed.

"My Lord and my God!"[192] Thomas cried, using names for Jesus that showed he finally believed Jesus was who He claimed to be, the Lord of all.

"Thomas," Jesus said, "you believe now because you have seen Me. But people who believe Me without seeing Me are really blessed."[34]

Who are these people? Thomas may have wondered.

Jesus was talking about US—people who wouldn't be able to see Jesus with their eyes, as the disciples had, but who would choose to believe Him still. These people trust Jesus even when they can't see Him. These people have strong faith![271]

Talk About the Story: Which disciple didn't see Jesus the first time Jesus visited them? What did Thomas say he had to do before he could believe the person the disciples saw was really Jesus?

Scripture: "Blessed are those who have not seen and yet have believed." John 20:29

Family Time: Why do you think Thomas wanted to feel Jesus—not just see Him? What helped Thomas believe Jesus? What might help you believe Jesus? Who did Jesus say are really blessed? We haven't seen Jesus, but if we believe Him, we'll be blessed. We'll show we have strong faith!

Prayer: Dear Lord, thank You for blessing us when we believe You. Thomas doubted You and only agreed to believe if You would show Him the proof he wanted. You are happy when we trust You, and You bless us when we do! Please help us trust and believe You even when we can't see You. Amen.

FISHING

Scripture: John 21:1–8
Place: Sea of Galilee
Time: Sunday, April 23

❝I'm going fishing," Peter announced, standing up to go.

When the disciples had last seen Jesus, He told them He would meet them again in Galilee. So they left Jerusalem and headed north. They'd been waiting since, and still no Jesus. Perhaps He had some other people to visit first.

"We're going with you," a few disciples said, standing up to follow. As Peter headed out the door, Thomas, Nathanael, the brothers James and John, and two other disciples hurried after him.

They piled into their fishing boat and launched out on the Sea of Galilee. All night long they threw out their net and dragged it back in, empty every time!

As the sun started to rise, perhaps Peter thought about the last time this had happened. *If only Jesus were here. The first time I met Him I was fishing all night too—unsuccessfully. But He told me where to row and where to throw the nets.*

And then we caught so many fish our nets were breaking. Peter, James, and John, the three fishermen, had decided to leave their fishing and follow Jesus after that. Jesus had provided for them. This helped them trust and follow Him.

But now, discouraged and disappointed, the men were rowing back to shore when they noticed a man watching from the beach.[48]

"Children, did you catch any fish?" the man called out.[285]

'Children?' the disciples may have questioned. *We're grown-up men!*

"No," the disciples called back. *And we don't need reminding that our fishing has failed, either!* they may have grumbled.

"Throw the nets over the right side. Then you'll find some!"[327] the man instructed.

With nothing to lose, the disciples followed the man's advice. Suddenly the water started sparkling. Shiny scales of many fish reflected the light of the morning sun. Whole schools of fish were swimming into their net!

As most of the men watched the fish pouring in, John watched the man on the shore. "It's the Lord!" John shouted, recognizing the man was Jesus, the same man who had helped them know where to fish before.

When Peter heard this, he wasted no time and believed John's word. Peter put on his tunic and jumped overboard, eagerly swimming to shore to meet Jesus again.[393] The other men stayed in the boat, slowly paddling along as they dragged the weight of this great catch the Lord had provided. He had provided just what they needed—and more than they ever expected.

Maybe that's why He called us "children," the disciples may have thought as they rowed. *He provided for us, just as a good father would.*[388]

Talk About the Story: Who decided to go fishing? Who joined him? How many fish did they catch during the night? What happened when they followed the advice of the man on the shore?

Scripture: "The eyes of all look expectantly to You, and You give them their food in due season. You open Your hand and satisfy the desire of every living thing." Psalm 145:15–16

Family Time: Why do you think Jesus called the disciples "children"? What do you think helped John recognize Jesus? Jesus provided for the disciples' needs! What are ways God has provided for you?

Prayer: Father, thank You for providing for us. The disciples didn't catch any fish at first, but You came to them and helped them know where to fish. You provided even more than they needed! Help us trust You are a good Father who will take care of all our needs. Amen.

BREAKFAST, JESUS, AND THE SEVEN

Scripture: John 21:9–14
Place: By the Sea of Galilee
Time: Sunday, April 23

Drip, drip, drip. Drops of lake water fell from Peter's soaking robes as he stood on the beach, waiting for the other disciples to arrive. He had dived right in to swim to Jesus! Dragging their net full of fish, the others rowed slowly behind. After a whole night on the Sea of Galilee, they were likely dripping wet, too—and cold and hungry. Probably nothing sounded better right that moment than a hearty meal and a big, warm fire.

As their boat hit land, what did they see? Fish sizzled and bread toasted over a fire of coals glowing orange.

"Bring some of the fish you caught," Jesus said to them. Peter immediately got up and dragged the net to land.

The disciples didn't say much. Some didn't say anything. Maybe they were busy concentrating on counting all the fish—153 in all!

The first time Jesus helped us fish, our nets broke, Peter and the other disciples may have remembered. *But this time they didn't break at all.* It seemed like another part of this amazing miracle.[327]

"Come and eat breakfast!"[451] Jesus invited them. They didn't have a table to sit at or fancy plates to use to eat, but Jesus invited them to join Him, like a host who had been waiting for them to arrive so He could serve them.[388]

After coming back to life, Jesus had already appeared to the disciples two times. Some disciples had doubted Him then, and each time Jesus helped them believe Him. He showed them His wounds. He even let Thomas touch them! But this time the disciples didn't dare to doubt Him.[405]

Jesus took the fish off the fire, and He took the warm bread, too. He gave it to the hungry men. Maybe as they ate the disciples remembered the last time Jesus had fed them. At that special meal, the night before Jesus died, Jesus had given them a cup to drink, and He had taken bread and broke it then, too, serving it to them. "Drink and eat this and remember Me," He had said.

Perhaps they remembered now; eating a meal Jesus had made might have felt like picking up where they had left off, before He died. Alive again, Jesus had waited for them to join Him. He waited for them to remember what He had said and what He had done for them. When they remembered, this would help them believe Him.

Jesus was ready for them to come to Him, waiting with a good meal to give them! When the disciples believed and came to Him, He would feed them and take away their hunger. They would eat and be satisfied and enjoy being with Him.

Talk About the Story: What did the disciples see at the shore? What did Jesus invite the disciples to do?

Scripture: "Therefore the Lord will wait, that He may be gracious to you; and therefore He will be exalted, that He may have mercy on you." Isaiah 30:18

Family Time: What helped the disciples not doubt Jesus this time? What did they remember? What memories about things God has done help you believe? Jesus invites us to believe Him! Do you want to accept Jesus' invitation?

Prayer: Father, thank You for welcoming us always. The disciples faced a difficult night, but in the morning Jesus was waiting to feed them a good meal! No matter what hard times we face, may we accept Your invitation to come to You and believe You. Amen.

JESUS AND PETER

Scripture: John 21:15–19
Place: by the Sea of Galilee
Time: Sunday, April 23

Peter ate one more bite of the tasty breakfast Jesus had prepared. Then Jesus spoke to him, "Simon, do you love Me more than they do?"

Why didn't Jesus call me "Peter"? Peter probably wondered. *"Simon" was my name before, but when I started following Jesus, He gave me a new name. "Peter" meant "rock." It was as if Jesus was saying, "Peter's faith in Me is rock solid. I trust him."*

Does Jesus not trust me anymore . . . because of what I did? Peter worried. He remembered his promise to Jesus. *"Even if everyone else deserts you, I won't"* (see Matthew 26:3).

And now He's asking if I love Him more than everyone else does! Peter realized. *How embarrassing!*

"Yes, Lord," Peter simply replied. "You know I love You."

"Then feed My lambs,"[295] Jesus said. Jesus sometimes called His followers sheep and Himself their Good Shepherd because He took care of them.

Jesus asked again, "Simon, do you love Me?"

"Yes, Lord. You know I love You," Peter repeated. *But if He really trusted me, He wouldn't have to ask again,* Peter thought, starting to feel sad.

"Then take care of My sheep," Jesus said.[292]

And then Jesus asked a THIRD time, "Simon, do you love Me?"

Being asked a third time REALLY hurt. Before Jesus died, He predicted Peter would lie three times in one night, saying he didn't even know Jesus. And that's exactly what Peter did.

I know Jesus hasn't forgotten, and I haven't either, Peter probably thought, feeling ashamed.

"Lord, You know everything," Peter said. "You know I love You."[208]

"Feed My sheep," Jesus repeated His command.

Even with all my mistakes, is Jesus giving me a job to do? Peter hoped. *Maybe Jesus has forgiven me!*

Jesus continued, "When you were younger, you had things your way. You wore clothes you chose and went wherever you wanted. But when you're old, here's what will happen: others will stretch your hands out, and others will dress you and take you where you don't want to go."[99]

Will I lose my freedom? Peter may have wondered.

Jesus hinted at what would happen to Peter one day. He wanted to prepare Peter now to help him understand God's plan for him later. This plan would give God glory. Even though it would be hard for Peter, through Peter more people would know about God!

"Follow Me," Jesus said then. Peter remembered Jesus saying these words before, when He called Peter to follow Him the first time.

Even with all my mistakes, Jesus chooses me—again! Peter felt so thankful. *I failed Him, but I still love Him. And He loves and forgives me! He has a plan for my good.*

Talk About the Story: What question did Jesus ask three times? How did Peter answer?

Scripture: "Therefore, if anyone is in Christ, he is a new creation; old things have passed away; behold, all things have become new." 2 Corinthians 5:17

Family Time: How do you think Peter felt when Jesus kept asking the same question? Peter made mistakes, but Jesus gave him a fresh start. When did someone forgive you and give you a second chance? How did this make you feel?

Prayer: Dear Lord, thank You for forgiving us. Peter was ashamed of his mistakes, but You forgave him and planned good, new things for him to do. May we never be too embarrassed to return to You. Thank You for giving us a fresh start when we do. Amen.

WHAT ABOUT JOHN?

Scripture: John 21:20–24
Place: by the Sea of Galilee
Time: Sunday, April 23

Peter focused his eyes on Jesus, pondering those clues Jesus had given about Peter's future. *Yes! I'll follow Him! I'm determined to do what the Lord commanded*, he thought.[537]

A rustling behind them caught Peter's attention. He turned around, taking his eyes off Jesus for just a second to see.

John! Did John hear what Jesus said to ME? Jesus had told Peter, "Follow Me," and now John was following, too! Whenever Jesus was around, John always seemed to be close by. Peter remembered another time John had been so close to the Lord.

At the disciples' last meal together, the night before Jesus died, of all the disciples, John sat closest to Jesus. He sat so close he could even lean on Jesus' shoulder! And he did just that when he whispered to Jesus a very serious question: "Who will betray You? Who will tell the religious leaders, those men who want to kill You, where to find You?" All the disciples wanted to know, but John had been the one to ask—maybe because he was sitting so close.

And even though I jumped in the water to swim to Jesus, JOHN pointed Him out on shore, Peter thought. *Would I have even recognized Jesus without John's help?* Peter realized John was close to Jesus—closer than the best of friends. So Peter was curious what Jesus might tell about John's future.

"What about John, Lord?"251 Peter asked. "What will happen to him?" Maybe Peter wondered if John would suffer hard things in the future, like Jesus predicted Peter would. It might be scary to suffer alone! Would John get to follow Jesus without following in the same, possibly difficult, way Peter would?

"Even if I wanted John to stay alive till I came back to get him, how is that your business?" Jesus asked.91

Is Jesus saying John will NEVER die? Peter's eyes grew big at the thought.

"I have a plan for John, too," Jesus continued, "but you don't need to know about it. Focus on My plan for you. Follow Me."259

Humph. That's not the answer I wanted. What about DETAILS? Peter maybe thought. But Jesus had given Peter the only answer he needed. Jesus didn't want anything to distract Peter from Him or God's plan.

Since Jesus won't tell me how John will die, I guess John won't die at all! Peter reasoned. Maybe Peter shared his opinion with the disciples, because somehow they started to believe this rumor about John, too!

But Jesus never said that! He just said it wasn't any of their business to know. Whenever anyone asked John about the rumor, that's just what he told them: God's job is to know. Their job is to follow Him.

Talk About the Story: Who followed Peter and Jesus? How did Peter find out? How do you think Peter felt when he saw John following?

Scripture: "But let each one examine his own work, and then he will have rejoicing in himself alone, and not in another. For each one shall bear his own load." Galatians 6:4–5

Family Time: What did Peter ask Jesus? What answer did Jesus give? Why do you think Jesus didn't give Peter many details? Worrying about John distracted Peter, making it hard to follow Jesus! What distracts you from following Jesus? What are ways you can focus more on God?

Prayer: Dear Lord, we face many distractions that keep us from You. Worrying about John distracted Peter from You. Help us focus, not on ourselves, and comparing ourselves with others but on You and Your good plan for us. In Jesus' name, Amen.

THE GREAT COMMISSION

Scripture: Mark 16:15–18
Place: In Galilee
Time: Several days later

❝I'm hungry! Pass the bread, please," Peter said.

John grunted with his mouth full as he passed the bread basket down to Peter. All eleven disciples were gathered around the table in a house in Galilee. So much had happened since Jesus came back to life!

"I just can't believe all that we have seen," James muttered.

"Did Jesus really make breakfast for you on the beach?" Matthew asked. "I mean, I know you guys tend to tell the truth, but it is just so hard to believe!"

"I know!" Andrew responded. "I was there. I ate breakfast with Him, but I'm having a hard time believing, too!"[504]

"Did Mary and the other women really see Him at the tomb? Is He really, truly the Son of God?" the disciples kept asking themselves.

www.thefamilyprayerbible.com

Suddenly, Jesus was there in the room with them. His disapproving expression showed all of the disciples immediately that Jesus knew their doubts and their thoughts.

"Why are you still doubting? Look and believe in Me," Jesus said. "Stop doubting what the others have said about Me. You can see for yourselves that I AM who I AM!"[127]

Each of the disciples knew what Jesus said was absolutely true. He had shown them over and over again that He really is the Son of God who came into the world to forgive the sins of all who would believe in Him. And they knew that they each had a responsibility to tell what they knew to everyone they possibly could!

Jesus told them,

"Go into all the world and preach the gospel to every creature. He who believes and is baptized will be saved;[416] but he who does not believe will be condemned. And these signs will follow those who believe: In My name they will cast out demons; they will speak with new tongues; they will take up serpents; and if they drink anything deadly, it will by no means hurt them; they will lay hands on the sick, and they will recover."

The disciples listened to Jesus' instructions carefully. They knew they could completely trust Jesus' promises. They could trust Jesus![497] And now they knew what Jesus wanted them to spend the rest of their lives doing!

Talk About the Story: Why did the disciples still doubt Jesus? What did Jesus do to help them stop doubting? What did Jesus tell them to do?

Scripture: "Go into all the world and preach the gospel to every creature." Mark 16:15

Family Time: What are some things that you know are true about Jesus? What are some ways you can tell others what you know? Who are some people you want to pray for and ask God to help you tell them about Jesus?

Prayer: Father, thank You for giving us the Bible so that we can learn more about Jesus. Help us to be brave like the disciples were and tell others about Jesus and Your love. Amen.

PSALM 101

WHEN YOU GET A BIGGER JOB

Julie was treasurer of her class at school last year. She collected money for feeding the homeless and for their class party. She kept an accurate record each day of all the money that came in. She was very careful to keep the money for the homeless separate from the party money. The class liked her and she was voted president that year. What should be her attitude when she became class president? Could she learn from David?

David spent years getting ready to be king of Israel. First he led Israel's army to defeat the Philistines. He personally defeated Goliath. When jealous King Saul tried to kill David, he stayed faithful to Israel and faithful to God. Eventually Saul was killed in battle, then it came time to make David king.

The inauguration was a splendid event. David was crowned and the people shouted, "God save the King." They supported David.

Then the following day David wrote Psalm 101. It is called a Psalm of enthronement. First David praised God for His goodness. Then David pledged to not let wicked people influence his role. Third, he pledged to appoint good people to help him rule. Let's look at David's first section:

"I sing praises to You my Lord and God,
You are kind to make me king,
You worked out circumstance to put me in office."[439]

Then David turned his attention to his task as king. He pledged to do his best in every way. David had the right attitude that would make him the greatest king in Israel's history. David's attitude is a good example for you when you get promoted to a new job.

"I will be careful in everything I do
       Then no one can say I have ever done wrong.[219]
Lord, come to me each morning to help me rule[418]
       Then I will do no wrong.
I will not let wicked people influence my leadership;
       I will not rely on them to get my job done.
Those with wicked plans will not get near me;[476]
       I will not spend time with them.
I will especially watch out for liars and gossipers;
       They will not influence me."[430]

The last part of this Psalm deals with David's pledge to put good people around him.

"I will look for people who obey the Lord;
       I want those kind of people around me.[188]
I want people around me who can be trusted to do right;
       I will look for honest people on my team,
People that will tell the truth all the time.[267]
       Some others will trust them, but not me.
I will not have lying people around me
       Who cannot be trusted by the public;
They shall not serve with me."[426]

David didn't spend a lot of time praising God in this Psalm. He introduced the Psalm with praise. Then he pledged himself to be a king with people around him who were honest. Then he pledged to get rid of liars and gossipers. We can never praise God any better than when we obey His commandments and do the right things. But also this Psalm says, God is praised when we chose good friends and we don't associate with those who would pull us down.

Talk About the Psalm: What did you learn about the psalm writer in this story? What did you learn about God?

Psalm 101: Read this week's psalm in your Bible together. Choose a verse to read aloud as a prayer.

Prayer: Thank You, God, for the psalm prayers in the Bible. Thank You for teaching us about You and about how to pray. In Jesus' name, Amen.

JESUS AND THE FIVE HUNDRED

Scripture: Matthew 28
Place: Galilee
Time: Sunday, April 23

"We've come so far from Jerusalem—it's been almost three days since we left. Will we REALLY see Jesus there?" one disciple asked another as they walked along.

"Don't you remember Jesus' promise?" another disciple replied. "Look, we're almost to Galilee!" He pointed out a mountain on the horizon. "When we ate our last meal with Jesus, before He died, He said He would live again and meet us here."

"Yes, but…"

"No buts! The angel at the tomb told the women that's where Jesus would meet us.[526] Plus Jesus HIMSELF told the women to remind us, too! We've come all this way because we've chosen to trust Him. Don't doubt now!"

A great chattering of voices greeted the disciples at the mountain. "Why, there must be 500 people here!" one disciple exclaimed.

Suddenly, the commotion seemed to still as all eyes turned to the guest of honor: Jesus! Everyone began worshiping Him.[264] But even while they worshiped, some doubted.[126]

We know Jesus died, so how can He be here? some wondered, confused.

Jesus came closer. Would seeing Him help them believe? "God has given me power over everything in heaven and on earth," Jesus said.[147]

Wow! A king rules over a country, but Jesus is ruler over EVERYTHING! The crowd listened in awe.

"Go then and make disciples of all the nations,"[314] Jesus continued. "Tell people EVERYWHERE about Me." Jesus didn't need help with anything, but He gave everyone there—even those people who still had doubts—a job to do! Jesus wanted more than eleven disciples. He planned to have a whole WORLD of disciples, people who would believe and follow God.

But how do we make disciples? many listening wondered.

Jesus answered, "Baptize people in the name of the Father, the Son, and the Holy Spirit."[30] Getting baptized wouldn't save people. Only believing in God would save people. But getting baptized was a way people could share with others their decision to believe God!

But it wouldn't be enough to believe Jesus once, get baptized, and forget about it. "Teach these new believers to obey everything I've taught you,"[303] Jesus added. Just as kids can't really play a game unless they know the rules, people couldn't follow Jesus well unless they knew what He told them to do. Knowing Jesus' instructions would help believers live well the new life Jesus gives.

Will we be able to do ALL this? some listening doubted.

"Count on this," Jesus promised, "I am with you now, and I always will be." With Jesus' help they certainly could!

Talk About the Story: What did the people do when they saw Jesus? Why do you think some doubted? What doubts do you think they had?

Scripture: "For you are all sons of God through faith in Christ Jesus." Galatians 3:26

Family Time: What job did Jesus give the people? How would they make disciples? Who would be with them to help them? Some who worshiped Jesus doubted, but He still gave them an important job to do! Even when we doubt, God still wants to use us to help others know Him. What's something you know about Jesus that you could share with a friend?

Prayer: Father, help us remember that with Your help, we can share about You with others, even when we doubt or don't understand everything about You. Help us believe and follow You as we help others follow You, too. Amen.

JESUS MEETS WITH HIS BROTHER

Scripture: Mark 3; 1 Corinthians 15:7
Place: Jerusalem
Time: Sunday, May 7

After Jesus came back to life, He was busy! Soon Jesus would join His Father in heaven, but before He left, He had special visits to help people who still doubted Him. Whether His visit would help one person or 500 people believe, Jesus appeared. And Jesus made one very special visit—to His own brother, James.

When Jesus was alive, not everyone in His family liked what He was doing. They had heard that such a large crowd surrounded Jesus as He taught that He couldn't get away for even a moment to eat! "He is out of His mind!" his family said (Mark 3:21).

Maybe Jesus' mother worried about her Son growing tired with all His teaching and healing people. Maybe all the attention Jesus was getting made His brothers feel embarrassed, or even afraid.

The things He does and says are making our religious leaders angry! the brothers probably worried. *What might happen to Jesus—and OUR family—if He continues to question their authority?*[164]

So, Jesus' mother and brothers went to Him. "Look, your family's here," someone in the crowd told Jesus. "They want to speak to you."

"Who are they?" Jesus replied. "My true family—God's family—are people who believe and follow God," Jesus said, pointing to His disciples (see Matthew 12:48–50). Jesus wasn't saying this to be mean to His mom and brothers. He said this to show that even though He loved them, He loved God the most and everyone else should love God most, too.[295]

But as Jesus continued teaching, people grew jealous, especially people from His hometown. "Where did this Man get this wisdom and these mighty works?" they asked. "Is not His mother called Mary? And His brothers James, Joses, Simon, and Judas?" (Matthew 13:54–55). *We grew up with Him!* they thought. *What gives Him the idea He's any better than us?*[424]

Even Jesus' brothers didn't believe Him! "Leave our home," they said. "Go do Your miracles somewhere else if you REALLY want more people to follow You" (see John 7:3–4). They didn't understand that Jesus did miracles to help people believe God—and these people included them!

Then sad news came. They heard their brother had died! Mary, their mother, had seen this happen, so maybe she told them. They hadn't even said good-bye! But then there was good news. People were starting to say some of Jesus' followers had seen Him again—ALIVE![405]

Jesus invited many people to join His family, GOD's family. He invited people in His earthly family, too! Jesus appeared to James, one of His brothers. The Bible doesn't tell what happened when they met, but later James became a leader in the church in Jerusalem! He even wrote a letter that is part of the Bible today. This meeting must have changed James's life. James believed in Jesus and joined God's family, and then he helped others know Jesus, his brother, as the Lord![444]

Talk About the Story: How did Jesus' family feel about Him when He was alive? Who in Jesus' earthly family did Jesus meet after He came to life?

Scripture: "For whoever does the will of God is My brother and My sister and mother." Mark 3:35

Family Time: Why do you think Jesus visited His brother, James? How do you think James felt after meeting Jesus? James believed Jesus and joined God's BIG family. We are ALL part of God's family when we believe Jesus! What does it mean to you to live as a member of God's family?

Prayer: Father, thank You for adopting us into Your family. James was Jesus' family on earth, and by believing in Jesus, he joined Your family forever! Sometimes, we forget how much You love us. Help us remember we belong to Your family and Your love and Your family lasts forever! Amen.

DATE ___/___

CHAPTER 20

THE CHURCH BEGINS

The book of Acts written by Luke is not a survey of the ministry of the all twelve disciples; rather it is about Peter (chapters. 1–12) and Paul (chaps. 13–28). But in another sense it's not really about them; it's about what the Holy Spirit does through them. Thus, it could be titled, "The Acts of the Holy Spirit."

The key word is "witness," used more than thirty times. After the Holy Spirit was poured out on the believers at Pentecost, "those who were scattered went on their way preaching the message of good news" (Acts 8:4). The early Christians were so totally convinced that Jesus died for their sins and rose from the dead that they literally gave their lives to witness to the world what He had done.

In the Old Testament, God's glory dwelt in a tabernacle and later in the temple; but in the New Testament God's Spirit lives in the lives of believers,

and they carry Him into the marketplaces and streets as they witness the power of Christ's resurrection. In the Old Testament the Jews were a separate people from the Gentiles, distinctive by the circumcision in their body, plus their language, religious observances, and dress. In the New Testament believers go to everyone—Jews and Gentiles—witnessing what Jesus Christ can do for them. Their impact on Roman society was so great that it was said of them, "These men who have turned the world upside down have come here too" (17:6). The book of Acts begins with the red-hot enthusiasm of a growing church in its first thirty years, and in these thirty years we see all the strengths and weaknesses that will be characteristic of the body of Christ in the next 2,000 years.

WRITING THE BOOK OF ACTS

Scripture: Acts 1:8
Place: various
Time: 63 AD

At the beginning of the book of Acts, Luke addresses the book to Theophilus. Now, this name means "loved by God." So it could have been addressed to people—we are all loved by God![294]

But the opening of this book sounds like Luke is writing to a person named Theophilus. Based on what we know, the story behind the book of Acts might have gone something like this:

Luke had been writing a LOT as he traveled with Paul. But he'd written all he could write, because he realized that the story of what the Holy Spirit was doing was never going to end! *This book will always be unfinished,* Luke thought.

Luke left Paul, who was now in Rome. He traveled to bring his manuscript to Theophilus, a wealthy rancher who preached to the church that met in his house. The two men embraced as Luke entered the courtyard.

"I've been preaching to my household from the book you brought me," Theophilus said. "It is wonderful to have these accurate accounts of all Jesus did and taught.[24] I can never thank you enough, Doctor!"

Since Luke was a doctor and good at research, Theophilus had earlier asked him to write a complete record of Jesus' from His birth to the ascension.[425] Luke had interviewed many people. He took careful notes. Then he asked the Holy Spirit to guide him so that his writing would be true and right.

When Luke had brought his first book to Theophilus, the rancher had gladly given him 10,000 silver pieces to help with Paul's expenses while he was in prison in Caesarea.[363]

This time, Luke had brought another book! It told the amazing story of what had happened after Jesus went back to heaven and sent God's Holy Spirit![224]

Luke handed Theophilus the manuscript. Theophilus laughed, "I am so glad you've come. I will treasure this book!"

Theophilus had gotten more and more excited about this book ever since he heard Luke was coming. He couldn't wait to read how God's family, the church began in Jerusalem and then grew through glorious miracles and conversions.

"Paul is now a prisoner in Rome," Luke said. "We have rented an apartment for him, but he is chained to a soldier all the time."

There was a twinkle in his eye as Theophilus said, "This is a wonderful chance for me to help my dear friend Paul! How much money do you need?"[170]

They also talked about what to call the book. "What about *The Acts of Jesus?*" mused Luke. Theophilus wasn't sure.

Finally they agreed, "Let's call it *The Acts of the Apostles*! It tells how the apostles carried out Jesus' command to tell everyone about Him."

"Excellent!" said Luke, and wrote the name across the top of the scroll. And so it was called The Book of Acts.

Talk About the Story: Paul was in jail in what two places? Why is Luke's account never finished? What is the story of Acts about?

Scripture: "The apostles (and all other believers) received power when the Holy Spirit came upon them so they could preach the gospel to everyone, beginning at Jerusalem, then Judaea and Samaria, and to the ends of the earth." Acts 1:8, *Family Prayer Bible*

Family Time: Why did Jesus send the Holy Spirit? Where did God's family begin? Is your family's story part of this unfinished book? Tell how you became part of this story!

Prayer: Lord, thank You for inviting us to be a part of the book of Acts! Please help us to obey You and use Your power to tell everyone the good news about Jesus. Amen.

JESUS' NEW KINGDOM

Scripture: Acts 1:1–8
Place: In and around Jerusalem
Time: May, 30 AD

What an exciting time! James and John kept laughing. Thomas couldn't wipe his smile off his face. All of the disciples were thrilled! Jesus had died, but He came back to life again! He really is the Messiah! Many, many people saw Him during the forty days after His resurrection![405]

But Jesus did more than just be seen. He spent a lot of time talking with His friends. IMPORTANT things were going to happen SOON—and Jesus wanted them to know what was going to happen. He had plans for a kingdom that would be different and much BIGGER than anything His friends had ever hoped!

Of course, Jesus' friends still were expecting that Jesus might run the Romans out of Israel and establish Himself as the King of Israel! And now that He had risen from the DEAD, everyone could SEE that He had the power to do this! So they were eager to see how Jesus would make this kingdom happen SOON!

But Jesus had other plans—MUCH bigger plans than running the Romans out of Israel! Jesus' plan was a worldwide plan. He was making a kingdom that

would cover the whole world!

He wanted His friends to understand His plan and be ready for the next step in this kingdom. Because for the next step, Jesus would not even be on EARTH. So His friends would need to understand—because it would take some getting used to!

Jesus talked with His friends often during that forty days. But once He told them, "Stay in Jerusalem. I want you to wait there for the Promise of the Father."

Promise of the Father? What is THAT? they wondered. Jesus explained.

"You've heard about this before. Remember that I told you how John baptized with water, but you shall be baptized with the Holy Spirit?[124] That's going to happen! And it's going to happen not long from now!"

Because Jesus had told them about this earlier, now they began asking Him again about this new kingdom!

"Lord, will You NOW restore the kingdom to Israel?"[74]

Jesus smiled at their excitement. They were eager, but He knew they were thinking about the wrong KIND of kingdom!

He said, "It's not your job to know times or seasons. God the Father has those under His own control. That is HIS business. But here is YOUR business: A time is coming soon—the time you'll receive the Holy Spirit! You shall receive power when the Holy Spirit has come upon you. Then you'll be witnesses about Me in Jerusalem, and then in all Judea and Samaria. And in the Holy Spirit's power, you'll go to the end of the earth."[199]

Jesus' big, worldwide kingdom was about to start! Today, we call it "the church" or "the body of Christ." Jesus did not start a religion. By the power of His Spirit, He was going to rule a kingdom that would cover the whole EARTH—and He wouldn't even have to BE HERE! That's how powerful He is!

Talk About the Story: What do you think Jesus' friends thought He would do? What did Jesus tell them about His plan? Which kingdom would be bigger? How would the Holy Spirit help Jesus' friends?

Scripture: "You shall receive power when the Holy Spirit has come upon you; and you shall be witnesses to Me in Jerusalem, and in all Judea, and Samaria, and to the end of the earth." Acts 1:8

Family Time: What job did Jesus give His disciples? That job is for us as well! What can each one of us say about things Jesus has done for us? Telling our stories is a way to be a witness for Jesus!

Prayer: Dear Jesus, we are so glad that You are alive! Thank You for the Holy Spirit. We want this kind of power in our lives, too. We want to be witnesses about You! In Your name, Amen.

DATE ___/___

JESUS ASCENDS TO HEAVEN

Scripture: Luke 24:49–53; Acts 1:8–11
Place: The Mount of Olives
Time: Sunday, May 14, 30 AD

Jesus and His friends looked down on the city of Jerusalem from the Mount of Olives. They could see the glittering white of the Temple and the busy market place below. What a beautiful city! Turning around, they could see the little village of Bethany where Jesus had raised His friend Lazarus from the dead. So many amazing things had happened recently!

Jesus turned to look at His friends. These people had stayed with Him through scary and amazing times. They had listened to Him and learned from Him. These people following Him were Jesus' secret weapon for changing the whole world—and creating the BIGGEST kingdom the world would ever see!

Jesus said to them, "Remember! My Father's Promise is going to come true. Stay in Jerusalem until the Holy Spirit comes.[359] When this happens, then you'll have power to take the good news about Me from here to Samaria—and from there, to the farthest place on Earth you can think of!"

Thomas thought about the stories he had heard about India and China. Philip thought about Egypt and Ethiopia. Peter thought about the lands north of Rome. The earth was a really big place!

Jesus raised His hands to speak a blessing over them.[47] They all looked up expectantly. This was something rabbis and priests often did as a way of saying goodbye. But as Jesus spoke the blessing, He began to RISE into the sky! Higher and higher He rose, until a cloud hid Him. His friends could NOT see Him anymore!

Jesus' friends stood staring into the sky. *Where was Jesus? What was He going to do NOW?* They had no idea!

Two men appeared in shining white robes—angels! And they must have smiled at these people, all looking up into the sky, craning their necks, trying to get a glimpse of Jesus.

They said, "Galileans! Why are you standing here, staring into the sky? You saw Jesus—He was taken up from you into heaven; you saw it happen! Jesus will come back in the very same way as you saw Him go!"

Matthew's mouth dropped open in surprise. Mary's eyes were wide. Nathaniel looked confused. What did this all mean? They turned to look at each other, as words Jesus had said to them began to come back to their minds.

Slowly each of Jesus' disciples began to smile. Of course! Jesus was going back to heaven! And what good news! He wouldn't stay away forever—no, He was coming back![397]

Now, they weren't sad that Jesus left; no, they were EXCITED! There was a lot that they didn't understand. But they DID understand that Jesus had given them a job to do. And He had promised that somehow, they would receive power to DO this big job![16]

So they walked down the hill, past the garden where Jesus had prayed, and back through the gate into the city. They walked on until they reached the little door that led to the upper room where they had eaten their last meal with Jesus.[538]

They had seen Jesus. They had heard Jesus' words. And now, they were together. So what did they do? They PRAYED![366]

Talk About the Story: What did Jesus say God had promised? What would the Holy Spirit do for them? Where did Jesus go? Did Jesus need to be here to make the biggest Kingdom ever? Why or why not?

Scripture: "You shall receive power when the Holy Spirit has come upon you; and you shall be witnesses to Me in Jerusalem, and in all Judea, and Samaria, and to the end of the earth" (Acts 1:8).

Family Time: What is a way you see God's Spirit at work in your family? In your neighborhood? What is something your family can pray for God's Spirit to help you be brave to do?

Prayer: Lord Jesus, we thank You for keeping Your promise! We are glad that You sent Your Spirit to give us power. We want to be brave and glad to tell others the good news about You! Amen.

DATE ___/___

533

JESUS' FRIENDS OBEY

Scripture: Acts 1:12–15
Place: The Upper Room
Time: May 14 to May 24, 30 AD

There was a big crowd in an upper room in a house in Jerusalem. It was a little hot and stuffy, but everyone was glad to be there together.

This was the upper room where Jesus' disciples had eaten their last meal with Jesus. It may have belonged to one of the women who loved and followed Jesus. It was the place where their Master Jesus had washed their feet. He had shown them such love and care in this place. It was a great place to be!

In the crowd, there were eleven disciples—Matthew, Simon, James the son of Alphaeus as well as Simon the Zealot; Philip and Thomas, Judas who was James' son, Bartholomew, Peter and his brother Andrew, James and his brother John.[119] Besides them, there were a LOT of other people—including some of the women who had loved and followed Jesus. This group included Jesus' mother Mary and Jesus' brothers as well.

They had all been together for days and days! Sometimes they sang songs praising God. Other times they told and retold stories about the things Jesus had said and done. They laughed as they reminded each other about the times they didn't understand what Jesus said.

Peter probably laughed the loudest when he told stories about the times he said and did the wrong things! He could laugh because he knew how much Jesus loved and forgave him.

But most of the time, they prayed![10] They thanked God for the time they had spent with Jesus. They asked God for wisdom and courage. They praised God for His amazing plan for salvation.[226]

They were all together in one place—but it was more than being close to each other. All of them, men and women, old and young, were "of one accord." That means they were all thinking alike. They all wanted the same thing. They wanted for God's Holy Spirit to come and give them the power they needed! They were eager to do the NEXT thing Jesus had told them about—even though they didn't know exactly how that next thing might look!

Remember, these people had traveled with Jesus. They had listened to Jesus and watched Him do amazing things. But they couldn't pick up a Bible to read it. There was no Bible! They might have had Old Testament scrolls, but they did not have God's Word as we know it. And until now, they had Jesus to tell them what to do. But now, Jesus was gone. Until God's Holy Spirit came, all they could do was to obey Jesus![224]

So, they stayed together. They prayed together. They must have retold each other every story they could remember about Jesus, and reminded each other of everything He had said to them. And they stayed right there in that upper room in Jerusalem. Because when it's hard to know what to do next, the BEST thing to do is to obey Jesus![11]

Talk About the Story: What do you think was hard about this time where Jesus' friends waited? What do you think was confusing for them? What do you think might have comforted them?

Scripture: "These all continued with one accord in prayer and supplication, with the women and Mary the mother of Jesus, and with his brothers" (Acts 1:14).

Family Time: When have you had to wait? What made the waiting time harder? What made it easier? What is something you have had to obey that was not easy to obey?

Prayer: Dear Lord, sometimes it is hard for us to wait. Sometimes we want to jump in and change things. Please help us to wait for You. Help us to obey You and then know that You will do the things we need to do! In Jesus' name, Amen.

PSALM 105

SUNG WHEN DAVID BROUGHT THE ARK OF THE COVENANT TO THE TABERNACLE

The Ark of the Covenant had been captured by the Philistines in battle. The army of Israel thought they could win a battle if the Ark was carried before them into war. The problem was Israel put their faith in a piece of furniture—the Ark—they didn't put their faith in God. So God allowed the Philistines to defeat Israel in battle and capture the Ark.

Years later the Philistines sent the Ark back to Israel because God punished them when they used it in their heathen worship. The ark was placed temporarily in the home of Abinadab. During that time, "the Lord blessed Abinadab" (2 Samuel 6:11, *NLT*).[386]

David wanted the Lord's blessing on all Israel, so he brought the Ark to Jerusalem. It was a glorious spectacle that honored God. For that long trip the priest stopped to sacrifice an offering for their sins about every 20 feet. "When those bearing the Ark of the Lord had gone six paces, he (David) sacrificed" (2 Samuel 6:13).[412] Then David "danced before the Lord with all his might, wearing a priestly garment" (2 Samuel 6:14, *NLT*).[266] There were trumpets blaring, and the wall of Jerusalem was filled with cheering observers.

A special new Tabernacle was ready. Then, "They brought the Ark of the Lord and set it in its place inside the special tent they had prepared for it" (2 Samuel 6:17).[365]

On that day David gave the lead musician, Psalm 105 to be sung in celebration. It's called "Song of Thanksgiving to the Lord."

David sang,

> *"Tell God thank you and call on His name,*
> > *Tell everyone about God's wonderful works.*
> *Sing songs to God; make music to glorify Him,*[439]
> > *Tell everyone about God's wonderful works.*
> *Be happy that you are known by His name,*
> > *Everyone who goes into His presence is rejoicing.*
> *Seek the powerful Lord.*
> > *Always go to Him when you need help.*[426]
> *Remember the wonderful things that God has done,*
> > *Remember His miracles He did on the Egyptians.*
> *Abraham was a follower of God, who served the Lord,*
> > *And you are a child of Jacob's faith.*
> *The Lord has remembered His covenant with you,*
> > *He will keep His promise for generations to come."*

Psalm 105 tells the people to exalt the Lord. Then it tells four great reasons from Israel's history to exalt the Lord. First, God looked after Israel as an infant nation. Second, God protected them in Egypt. Third, God brought them out of Egypt. And finally God protected them as they journeyed in the wilderness.

Talk About the Psalm: What did you learn about the psalm writer in this story? What did you learn about God?

Psalm 105: Read this week's psalm in your Bible together. Choose a verse to read aloud as a prayer.

Prayer: Thank You, God, for the psalm prayers in the Bible. Thank You for teaching us about You and about how to pray. In Jesus' name, Amen.

THE TWELFTH APOSTLE

Scripture: Acts 1:14–26
Place: The Upper Room
Time: May 14–24, 30 AD

The crowded room was quiet. Jesus' friends had their heads bowed in prayer. Slowly Peter stood up and cleared his throat. All 120 people in the room looked up. Men and women, old and young, some whom Jesus had healed—and Jesus' mother Mary and His brothers were part of this group.

Peter looked serious, and rather sad. He said, "Family, it is time for us to fulfill the words of the Scripture about Judas Iscariot. Think about this: long years ago, God's Holy Spirit predicted what we should do.[38] We thought Judas was one of us—but even though he took part in this ministry, he took money from evil men. He acted as a guide to the people who arrested Jesus. He betrayed the Lord.

"Now, everyone in Jerusalem has heard about what happened to Judas Iscariot.

www.thefamilyprayerbible.com

He took the money those men gave to him. He bought a field with it. He hanged himself there, and his body fell to earth.[267] It's pretty horrible. But now everyone is calling this place 'the field of blood.'" A few people in the crowd had tears in their eyes.

Peter went on. "It is a sad story, but it's not a surprise—God's Spirit told King David what to write, a long time ago. He wrote in a psalm: 'Let his dwelling place be desolate; let no one live in it. Let someone else take over his work.'"[382]

Peter paused to look around. Then he continued. "So family, it is time to do what the prophecy says. It's time to choose someone to take Judas Iscariot's place. This person should be someone who has been with us since we saw John baptize until the day Jesus was taken up into heaven."[166]

There were two men in the room who everyone knew had been with Jesus from the earliest days: Joseph (or Barsabbas) Justus and Matthias. So they prayed, "Lord, You know the hearts of every person. Please show us which of these two men You have chosen to take part in this work which Judas left by choosing to do wrong and now has gone."[207]

Then they cast lots. Casting lots is a little like choosing a number and then rolling dice to see whose number is the closest. It's a way to choose someone or something.[390] Matthias was chosen. So, from that time on he was considered to be one of the twelve disciples, the men who had been with Jesus and learned from Him for three years.[457]

It's a funny thing, but we never read Matthias' name again in the Bible. We don't know what he did. We never find out how he helped. We don't know if he preached or healed. But he WAS the twelfth disciple! Perhaps he was a quiet man. It's possible that he did a lot of things. We'll find out ALL about what he did when we get to heaven!

Talk About the Story: How many people were staying around the upper room? What happened to Judas Iscariot after he betrayed Jesus? How did God show which man was to be the man to take Judas Iscariot's place?

Scripture: "You, O Lord . . . know the hearts of all" (Acts 1:24).

Family Time: When has someone you know had to make a hard choice? What did they do? Why do we pray before we choose? How does prayer help us to choose what is right? (See James 1:5.)

Prayer: Father, thank You for giving us wisdom when we need to make hard choices. Please help us to remember we can ask You for help and wisdom every time we have a choice to make. In Jesus' name, Amen.

THE HOLY SPIRIT COMES

Scripture: Acts 2:1–4
Place: The Upper Room, Jerusalem
Time: May 28, 30 AD

Mary, the mother of Jesus, and the other Mary stood looking out the window of the crowded upper room. In the streets below, they could see people gathering for Pentecost (a feast 50 days after Passover). More and more people came into Jerusalem from villages and towns all around. Others came from even further away—people from all over the world! Many were coming to offer their first ripe barley to God and celebrate His goodness. The streets were full of people who had come for the festival!

Mary smiled. "Remember how Jesus had said He was like a wheat seed? He said that unless a seed was buried, it would never make any more wheat seeds. It would just sit there alone. In the same way, Jesus was saying that He had to die and be buried so that more wheat, more fruit, would grow!"

The other Mary said, "Yes! This festival celebrates the start of a harvest. I wonder how His harvest will come about."

They didn't realize that Jesus, the "seed" who had died and been buried in the ground for three days, was ALSO about to start His OWN celebration. He was about to bring in the "first fruits" of His worldwide kingdom!

The two women named Mary turned back to the group of men and women gathered in the upper room. The disciples were there, of course. Then there were the other women who had loved, supported and followed Jesus. Other members of Jesus' human family were there, too. People Jesus had healed, people who had followed Him and listened to Him—in all, 120 people were gathered there on that day!

All the people gathered there were there to pray. They were all looking forward to and praying about the same thing. They were all waiting for God's Holy Spirit to come![10] Jesus had said they'd have the power they needed, once the Holy Spirit came. They had NO idea how this would happen. But they knew they could trust what Jesus said. So they'd stayed in Jerusalem, praying.

At around 9 that morning, a sound began to rise. It was a sound like a rushing, huge WIND—but no curtain moved. The sound grew louder, like the sound a fire makes when it the wind takes it and makes it blaze! THEN—small flames appeared in the air. A FLAME settled above the head of every person in the room! No one was burned. But each of them was suddenly FILLED with the Holy Spirit of God![167]

All 120 people began to speak in other languages![145] They didn't even KNOW these languages. The Holy Spirit was giving them POWER to speak languages they had never learned—because He had an amazing plan! All the different languages they were suddenly able to speak were languages of people who had come to Jerusalem for the festival![456]

God was about to ANNOUNCE His WORLDWIDE kingdom. He was about to use these 120 people to tell people from every nation who'd come to Jerusalem ALL about God's great salvation, in their own first language![224]

God's Spirit had come. God's power was being shown! But it wasn't power just to show off. No, God had an amazing plan and He was going to make these people able to turn everything upside down, all over the world!

Talk About the Story: How many people were praying together? What did it sound like when the Holy Spirit came? What did people see? What did they hear? What did they do?

Scripture: "And I will pray the Father, and He will give you another Helper, that He may abide with you forever." John 14:16

Family Time: When has God's Spirit given you or someone you know help or power to obey God or do something that was hard? How do you think praying together might help us as we try to do what God wants us to do?

Prayer: Lord Jesus, thank You for sending Your Spirit to help us. Holy Spirit, we ask You to make us able to do whatever it is that You want for us to do. We want to please You, God! Amen.

THE BIG ANNOUNCEMENT!

Scripture: Acts 2:5–40
Place: Jerusalem
Time: May 28, 30 AD

In the streets of Jerusalem, people stopped their talking and walking, their shopping and their eating. They began to look around. *Where was that sound coming from?*[145]

"It's coming from over there!" one person said.

"Let's find out what it is!" his friend responded. People began to trot. They began to hurry. Nothing could make such a sound except a huge WIND or a big FIRE—but there was no breeze. It couldn't be wind. There was no smoke. It couldn't be fire! People followed the sound and soon, the square near the upper room was crowded with people!

But as people arrived in the square, they heard something ELSE. EVERY-ONE—no matter where the person was from—EVERYONE heard words in their own language![506]

"I can hear these men tell about the wonderful things God has done, in my own heart language!" said one.[224]

"I am hearing the SAME things, but in MY own language!"[456] said another. Jesus' friends now had the power of the Holy Spirit, and they were preaching to all these people in EXACTLY the language each person needed to hear! They were amazed![506]

But a few people laughed. "These people are drunk!"[349] they said. But of course no one believed that, probably not even those who said it. At nine in the morning, it wasn't likely they'd be drunk!

Peter stepped forward with the other disciples of Jesus. "Listen!" he said. "People who live here, all of you, these men aren't drunk! What you are seeing and hearing is EXACTLY what the prophet Joel said would happen, so many years ago!"[358]

God said then, "In the last days, I will pour out My Spirit on everyone.[167] And I will cause miracles through my servants, both men and women. And everyone who calls on the name of the LORD shall be saved!"[416]

"Listen! You people of Israel! You know God proved that Jesus of Nazareth is who He said He is by the many miracles that He did.[260] God planned for you Jews to deliver Jesus to the Roman rulers so that they would murder Him by nailing Him to a cross. He died, but God then released Him from death, and He came back to life again. Death could not keep Jesus in the grave! This is what King David talked about when he wrote, 'God, You will not let Your Holy One decay in the grave. You will give Me back My life.'

"We all know that David is dead and buried in his tomb here in this very city. So he didn't write about himself. He wrote that the Messiah would not be abandoned to the grave, and we here are witnesses to that fact![405] Jesus was raised to new life, is exalted at God's right hand, and NOW, God has poured out His promised Holy Spirit![383] David even wrote these words about Jesus the Messiah where he said, 'the LORD said to my Lord, "Sit at My right hand until I make Your enemies Your footstool."'[147]

Talk About the Story: What would you have thought about the noise if you had been in Jerusalem on that day? Whose words from the Old Testament did Peter say were fulfilled? What do you think was the most important thing Peter said?

Scripture: "For the promise is to you and to your children, and to all who are afar off, as many as the Lord our God will call" (Acts 2:39).

Family Time: The Holy Spirit did great things here. What do you need Him to do in your family? In what situation can your family ask God for help and power this week?

Prayer: Lord Jesus! Thank You that Your Church, your Kingdom, is for people all over the world. Thank You for inviting us to be part of Your kingdom, even though we are so far away from Jerusalem. We love You and we're glad You love us! In Your Name, Amen.

GOD'S FAMILY GROWS!

Scripture: Acts 2:36–41
Place: Jerusalem
Time: May into June, 30 AD

Peter wrapped up the talk he was giving to people from every part of the world. They'd gathered because of the sound of a mighty wind when the Holy Spirit had come. They had stayed because they heard people speaking in their own languages. Now, these people were LISTENING to hear what God had to say to them![203]

"ALL of you! Realize that God the Father has made Jesus, the One you crucified, both Lord and Messiah!" Peter said.

Peter told them to listen to God's promises and warnings, and to choose to follow Jesus as their Savior and Lord.[416]

People stood amazed. Peter's words were true. "What should we DO?" they asked.[202]

"REPENT! Turn around. Ask God to forgive your sins and be baptized in

Jesus' Name. You'll receive the gift of the Holy Spirit, just as we have.[383] This promise is for you, your households, and for those in distant places who will call on the Lord!"[199]

"Yes! I repent of the wrong things I have done!" one person said.

"I didn't believe Jesus at first, but now I see that He is the Son of God! I will follow Him with my whole life!" Another declared.

People throughout the crowd agreed. They wanted to be baptized to show everyone that they now followed Jesus.[30]

Philip and Nathaniel directed people to the Pool of Siloam. Andrew and Matthew led other people to the Pool of Bethesda.

Pretty soon, there were big groups of people waiting to be baptized at each of the pools throughout Jerusalem. The pools were FILLED with people who wanted to follow Jesus! Peter and the others who had followed Jesus from the beginning were busy baptizing people ALL day long!

"Do you believe that Jesus is the one and only Son of God?" Peter asked.

"Yes! I do, and I repent of all my sins and want to follow Him from now on!" the young man Peter was baptizing responded.

Peter dunked the young man under the water. When he came up out of the water, another person took his place.

Person after person chose to repent and follow Jesus. Person after person was baptized to show that they were trusting God to forgive their sins. Person after person was filled with the Holy Spirit. By the end of the day, THREE THOUSAND people had joined God's family!

Each of these people wanted to learn more about how to follow Jesus and how to live for Him. Peter and the other disciples preached and taught and baptized and encouraged people.

What a giant job! What an exciting time!

Talk About the Story: What did Peter tell the people? How did they respond? What did Peter tell them they needed to do in order to be saved? What did the disciples do? How many people became part of God's family that day?

Scripture: "And it shall come to pass that whoever calls on the name of the LORD Shall be saved." Acts 2:21

Family Time: Why do you think so many people were ready to respond to Peter's message? When are some good times we can tell others about who Jesus is and what He has done?

Prayer: Father, thank You for forgiving our sins through Jesus. We believe that Jesus is Your Son and that He died for our sins and came back to life again. We want to follow Him all the days of our lives. Amen..

THE CHURCH'S REPUTATION

Scripture: Acts 2:42–47
Place: Jerusalem
Time: May into June, 30 AD

People all over Jerusalem were talking about Jesus. "He is the Son of God!"
     "Jesus died on a cross, but He came back to life again, just like the Scriptures said He would."
   "Jesus is the One God had promised to send. He is the Savior of the world!"
   "Jesus taught us to love God with all that we are, and to love our neighbor as ourselves."
   "He said that our neighbors are not just the people we like. He said that we need

to love people who are hard to love!"

"He loved us so much that He died for us! So we need to love each other!"

As more and more of these new believers listened, learned and loved each other, of course they told MORE people about Jesus, too! So God's big family was getting even BIGGER! There were more people getting baptized and joining God's family every single day!

The apostles were doing many miracles—so everyone around could SEE that this was the power of God.[406] There was no denying that God was doing AMAZING THINGS! They taught about Jesus in the Temple courtyards, in the streets and in homes every day.

Everyone in Jerusalem was in awe! Even if they were not part of God's family yet, they could SEE and HEAR and KNOW that God's Spirit was there. God's family had favor even from people who didn't know or care about Jesus.

Many people who were part of God's family even sold things they owned— land and houses and other things. They wanted to make sure that EVERYONE would have the things they needed.[333] The people who sold things brought the money they made and gave it to the apostles so that the apostles could share the money with anyone who was in need.

They really, truly shared from their hearts. God's love and power was changing the way they thought, even about things they would NEVER have shared before!

And so God's family grew and grew. They met together. They ate together. They loved each other. They prayed. They praised God often. They were living in the love of God, and living OUT the love of God! And every day, more people joined them! [416]

Talk About the Story: What things did Jesus' followers talk about? What did they do? How did people in Jerusalem feel about God's family? Why?

Scripture: "And they continued steadfastly in the apostles' teaching and fellowship, in the breaking of bread and in prayers." Acts 2:42

Family Time: What are some things we can do in the same way the believers in the early church did? How can we learn from the apostles teaching? How can we take part in fellowship with other believers? When can pray together with others?

Prayer: Jesus, we are excited to be part of Your church! We want to live like these people did. Help us to live in Your power and love all of the time. Help us to listen and to obey what You tell us. We want to shine with this kind of love. In Your mighty name, Amen.

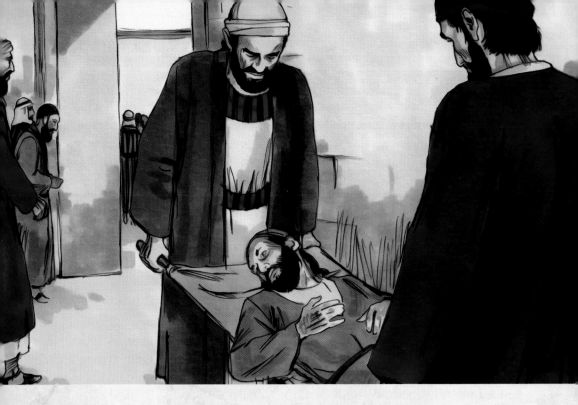

CRIPPLED MAN HEALED

Scripture: Acts 3:1–11
Place: Jerusalem
Time: May into June, 30 AD

Peter and John joined the crowds in their walk to the Temple. It was about three in the afternoon, a time when many people went there to pray.[252] On their way, they had to walk through the big gate called the Beautiful Gate. It was led toward the Temple area.

Now a gate in those days was not like the gate to your garden. The city had a thick, thick wall—as thick as a building. So a gate was more like a long hallway through this thick wall. It was shady and cool, out of the hot sun. And it was wide enough for people to pass through—and still have room for beggars to sit in the shade.

As Peter and John walked through the gate, they saw a man begging for money. This man's legs didn't work. He had never been able to walk in his entire life![435] So day after day, he sat on the ground, asking people for money, watching legs and feet walk, run, shuffle and pass him by. He called out to the feet and legs, "Please! A little money!" Sometimes the legs and feet would stop. Coins would drop into his bowl.

But on this day, something different would happen! "A little money, please!"

www.thefamilyprayerbible.com

he cried. Two sets of feet stopped right in front of him. He waited for the coins to drop. But instead, a man in front of him said, "Look at us."

For the first time, the lame man looked up. These legs had faces, too! He gazed into the faces of Peter and John. Surely, since they stopped they'd give him money. He must have smiled eager to be ready with his thanks.[20]

But Peter looked the lame man in the eye. He said, "I don't have any silver or gold."

OH! Then WHY did he stop? The lame man must have wondered.

Peter continued, "But I WILL give you what I DO have. In the name of Jesus Messiah from Nazareth, RISE UP AND WALK!"[214]

The man blinked, surprised. *What was this? What? WHAT?* Suddenly, Peter grabbed him by the arm. He could feel strength in his legs—and he STOOD! Unsteady at first, then he did a little happy dance. YES! His feet WORKED! His legs could HOLD him! He leaped straight up into the air! He could JUMP! He could twirl and dance with the best of them! He leaped and jumped and tiptoed and stomped, just for pure joy!

And then the no-longer-lame man began to shout his praise to God![484] "HALLELUJAH! YES! I am WHOLE! I am WALKING! Bless the Lord, O my soul!" And as the man shouted and praised God, he danced in little circles around Peter and John as they made their way into the Temple court! It must have been quite a sight, because soon people were running to see what this was all about![470]

The people in the Temple courts followed Peter, John and the dancing man to Solomon's Porch. Ah! Now they could all SEE this dancing man! They all knew him. They had all given him money. He was INDEED the man who had sat on the ground for YEARS outside the Temple courts. He could never come inside the Temple, because he was lame. But NOW! Now here he was, full of songs and shouts and dancing with joy to God!

Talk About the Story: Why was the man begging at the gate? What did Peter and John NOT have? What DID they have? What happened? How did the people around them react?

Scripture: "Then Peter said, 'Silver and gold I do not have, but what I do have I give you: In the name of Jesus Christ of Nazareth, rise up and walk'" (Acts 3:6).

Family Time: What are some amazing things God has done? What are some ways God has helped people you know?

Prayer: Lord Jesus, We are glad that in Your mighty name, anything can happen! Thank You that You are able to do more than we can ask or even imagine! We are glad to belong to You! Amen.

PSALM 107
GOD WORKING BEHIND THE SCENES

We don't know who wrote this song, nor do we know for certain when it was written. We do know it is one of the loftiest Psalms and should be sung by all believers when God does a special work for them.

Some Psalms describe the miracles God does for his people like the ten miraculous plagues delivering them from Egypt; also there is the miracle of God providing for them in the desert. But most of us don't see these types of actual miracles. We see how God works for us behind the scenes. This is the theme of Psalm 107, God working behind the scenes. Notice the five areas where God works behind the scenes.

The first area was that of delivering people from captivity. This probably refers to those who came back to Israel from the Babylonian captivity.

"Say thank you to God, for He is good,
Because of His love, you were released.
Let the redeemed of the Lord, tell others.
Because God has redeemed them from the enemy.
The Lord has gathered them from every direction
And brought them to their homeland."[394]

Next the song describes how God helps those lost in the desert. Some are lost in financial "deserts." Others are so lost they don't know where to turn.

"Some wandered in the wilderness, so hungry and thirsty
they almost died
The Lord redeemed them because they cried to Him.[112]
He led them to a city where they found life.
He satisfies the thirsty with living water,
He fills the hungry with spiritual food."[362]

The Psalmist remembers those in prison. They could be in an actual jail or they could be trapped in the prison of addiction to drugs, alcohol, or another sin.

"Some sat in a dark jail
Imprisoned by chains as miserable as iron.
They had rebelled against the Word of the Lord

And refused to listen to the Most High God.
That's why God had to break them with prison;
    They suffered alone with no one's help.[268]
Then they cried, 'Lord, Lord' in the trouble,
    And God snapped their chains and delivered them from their dis-
    tress."

The fourth area was those suffering from sickness or just physical pains. Sometimes when people rebel against God He allows illness or physical troubles to strike them.

"Some were sick because of their sins,
    Their bodies hurt because of disobedience.
They were so sick they couldn't eat
    And thought they would be better off dead;
When they called to God for deliverance[494]
    He spoke a healing word."

The last area described in the psalm was sailors lost at sea in a storm. This could also be a picture of people who are lost in a bad job, or in a bad crowd.

"Some went on ships to sea
    Trying to make their own way in the world.
God sent threatening winds to toss them about;
    The sailors were scared to death.
The waves were so deep, some thought they would never recover.
    'Lord,' they cried when they thought all was lost.[165]
As the Lord rescued them from drowning
    He calmed their storm with a whisper.
The threatening waves went away."

When we study the way God works in our lives, we see the hand of God in circumstances that accomplish His will for our lives.

Talk About the Psalm: What did you learn about the psalm writer in this story? What did you learn about God?

Psalm 107: Read this week's psalm in your Bible together. Choose a verse to read aloud as a prayer.

Prayer: Thank You, God, for the psalm prayers in the Bible. Thank You for teaching us about You and about how to pray. In Jesus' name, Amen.

PETER EXPLAINS

Scripture: Acts 3:12–26
Place: Jerusalem
Time: May into June, 30 AD

The crowd of people in Solomon's Porch stood in a tight knot. They craned their necks and bobbed around, trying to get a good look at the no-longer-crippled man. He was still dancing, full of shouts and leaps! GOD had done something—how ELSE could it have happened? And these men with the dancing man—who were they? How had they DONE this? Was it a trick? It couldn't be! They all knew this man had been lame all his life!

When Peter saw the crowd gather, it must have reminded him of the crowd that gathered when the Holy Spirit first came. It was time to tell people the good news about JESUS!

Peter stepped forward. He said to the crowd, "Why are you looking at us as if WE did this amazing thing?[470] We're not anybody special. THIS is the work of God—the God of Abraham, Isaac and Jacob! God the Father did it to honor Jesus, His Son! In Jesus' mighty name, this man was made completely well!"[147]

Peter went on quickly. He wanted them to understand about who Jesus is—and why He had to die and rise again. Some of these people had been part of the crowd who had cried out for Jesus to be killed. They had wanted to see Jesus crucified.[84]

"You killed Jesus, the Prince of life," Peter said. "But GOD raised Him from the dead.[405] We know it is true, because we SAW Him![478] And there is power in the name of Jesus the Messiah. You have just seen how Jesus has made this man strong! You've seen this man often. You know he has never walked! But Jesus has made him perfectly WELL, right here in front of you all, because Jesus gave this man faith to believe in Him."[466]

"People, I know that when you cried out for Jesus to be crucified, you did not know what you were doing. Your rulers didn't understand it either. But these things that happened? They were all part of God's plan! They had been foretold by God! His prophets said that the Messiah would suffer. Now Jesus, the Messiah, has done it. He has done JUST what God's Word said He would do!"

People looked at each other, amazed. WHAT? JESUS had fulfilled the words God had sent through the prophets? His death had been foretold? WOW! Peter was telling them the MOST important thing they'd ever heard!

"So all of you! Turn around!" Peter continued. "Go in the other direction, to follow Jesus! He will forgive your sins and will bring you the fresh joy of salvation from God!"[399]

Peter went on to tell them more about Jesus. He wanted them to know that God loved them and wanted them to join His family! God had made promises to these people long before. He wanted them to know that His promises never change!

Talk About the Story: Who healed the man? What did the people think? What did Peter tell the people about Jesus?

Scripture: "God, having raised up His Servant Jesus, sent Him to bless you, in turning away every one *of you* from your iniquities." Acts 3: 26

Family Time: Peter saw an opportunity to tell this crowd the truth about Jesus. When are some times we might have an opportunity to tell others about Jesus?

Prayer: Dear Father, help us to be aware of times we can tell others about Jesus. Thank You that you love and care for each person, and that You have the power to help and heal us. Amen.

ARRESTED!

Scripture: Acts 4:1–22
Place: Jerusalem
Time: May into June, 30 AD

More and more people crowded in to the Temple courts. The religious leaders grew more and more upset! The people were listening to those Jesus followers![358]

"It's all because of that beggar! The man who used to be crippled and begged at the gate is here! He is running and jumping and dancing!"

"Yes," another leader exclaimed. "We have to stop this! Everyone is going to want to become a Jesus follower!"

Peter, one of Jesus' closest disciples, was preaching to the crowd. And 5000 MORE people believed what they had seen with the no-longer-crippled" man, and believed what they had heard from Peter.[34] They all wanted to join God's family!

"STOP! Arrest those men!" one of the leaders shouted as he pointed toward Peter and John.

There was a crash of armor and a lot of shouting as the Temple guards dragged Peter and John to jail.[405] The leaders didn't know WHAT they were going to do, but they had to find some way to STOP these men—if they could!

The next morning, the whole council of Jewish leaders got together. They told the no-longer-crippled man to be there. Then they brought Peter and John from jail. They demanded, "Who gave you permission to tell people these things?"

The Bible says that Peter was filled with the Holy Spirit and began to answer them.[167]

"My leaders! Do you want to know how this man was healed? It's high time you began to realize that this notable miracle was done in the name of Jesus the Messiah, the One from Nazareth! He is the One you crucified, but God raised Him from the dead!"[405]

"By HIS power this man stands here before you, healed and well!" Peter pointed at the man, who dipped his head respectfully and did a little happy dance; just to be sure they knew he had full use of his feet!

Peter went on. "Jesus is the One you all rejected, just as the Scripture said you would. But now Jesus is the one who brings salvation! In fact, there is NO salvation in any other person. There is no other name under heaven by which we can be saved."[416]

Uh, oh! Peter and John didn't sound like they were going to be easy to scare after all! The leaders needed to talk. They sent Peter, John and the dancing man out of the room while they muttered to each other, pulled their beards, and walked around thinking. What could they SAY about this? The dancing man was standing there before them. He was PROOF that what Peter said was true. Everyone around knew this man. Everyone could SEE that he was healed. So whatever Peter said, they really could NOT say anything against it! They could NOT deny what God had done!

But they did NOT want to lose control. So they called the men back into the room.

"Listen!" they said. "We are COMMANDING you NOT to speak in the name of Jesus."[349]

Peter and John answered them, "We have to obey God, not human beings. We cannot stop telling what we have seen and heard!"[478]

The leaders were not happy, but they let Peter and John go. They couldn't deny that GOD HAD done this miracle, and EVERYONE knew it was true!

Talk About the Story: Why were the leaders upset? Why did they put Peter and John in jail? What did the leaders tell Peter and John? Do you think Peter and John obeyed them?

Scripture: "There is no other name under heaven given among men by which we must be saved" (Acts 4: 12).

Family Time: What did Jesus do that no one else could do? Why is believing in Him the only way to be saved? How does this make you feel?

Prayer: Father, we know that trusting in Jesus is the only way to be forgiven for the wrong things we do and to be made part of your family. Give us courage to tell others about Your love and salvation. We love You. Amen.

THE WHOLE TRUTH

Scripture: Acts 5:1–11
Place: Jerusalem
Time: May, 30 AD

Barnabas sold his field and then brought a large bag of money to share with everyone. People clapped and cheered and shouted praise to God! They were glad see such kindness and generosity. Of course, other people had land, too. One who owned a big piece of land was named Ananias.

Ananias and his wife, Sapphira, decided to sell THEIR land, too—maybe they hoped everyone would be JUST as excited to see THEM bring their money to the apostles! But they decided to keep back some of the money for themselves—and make it look as if they'd given it ALL.[310] *After all,* they reasoned, *you never can be sure what will happen. We're getting older. We might need that money some-day.*

So they sold the land without much problem, and Ananias brought the heavy bag of money into the place where Jesus' followers were meeting. He grunted a little because it weighed so much. It was even a BIGGER bag than what Barna-bas had brought! With a big, loud CHUNK he laid the bag on the table in front of Peter.

Ananias stood straight, smiling sweetly. "I'm giving all the money I got from selling my land!" His chest was tight, his heart was pounding, but he tried to breathe normally. After all, who could POSSIBLY know how much he got for the land? No one knew this was only PART of the money!

Peter looked Ananias in the eye. God's Spirit told Peter the truth about Ananias. Peter asked, "Why have you let Satan fill your heart? What makes you think you can cheat God's Holy Spirit?[101] You didn't have to sell that land. It was yours. Once you sold it, the money was also yours. You could have kept it all. So why did you decide to keep some and then pretend you had given it all? WHAT makes you think you can fool GOD? You have lied to HIM. You THINK you are tricking the church—but you've LIED TO GOD."[440]

Ananias's eyes opened wide, his face went pale, and he collapsed on to the floor, THUNK! He was DEAD.[99] A group of the younger men covered him with a sheet and took him out to bury him.

Three hours later, Sapphira, Mrs. Ananias, came to the place where Jesus' friends were gathered. She was looking for her husband—and she expected everyone to come around her and pat her on the back and thank her! But again, Peter looked her in the eye.

"Did you sell your land for this much?" he asked, holding up the bag of money.

"Oh, yes! That's all we got right there!" she smiled.[331]

"Why did you agree with Ananias to try to CHEAT the Holy Spirit?"[500] Peter thundered. He pointed. "See those men coming in the door? They've just BURIED your husband. He died three hours ago!"

Sapphira gasped. She opened her mouth to explain, but the words never came out. Her eyes got wide, and she collapsed onto the floor, DEAD.[268] The same young men took her body out and buried it next to her husband.

God's family was very serious after this. They could see that God's Spirit is JUST as real as Jesus is real—even though you can't see Him. NO one was going to even THINK about telling a lie or cheating—for any other reason! God's family needed to always be HONEST.[165]

Talk About the Story: What did Ananias and Sapphira do wrong? They still gave lots of money. Why wasn't that OK? What did God's family understand about God's Spirit after this?

Scripture: "Why have you conceived this thing in your heart? You have not lied to men but to God" (Acts 5:4).

Family Time: Having read this story, how important does GOD think it is for us to be honest? Is it OK to tell a little lie? What things happen when people lie to each other?

Prayer: Lord God, we know that we are all sinners. We thank You for forgiving the lies we all have told. We know that telling a lie is very serious. Please help us to tell the truth. In Jesus' name, Amen.

MANY MIGHTY MIRACLES

Scripture: Acts 5:12–16
Place: Jerusalem
Time: After Pentecost

The religious leaders were ANGRY. They had made what they thought was a good plan. First, they had killed Jesus, the One who said He was God's Anointed One, the Messiah. They thought THAT would put a stop to their problem. When Jesus was buried, they even put guards at the tomb—just in case. They thought THAT would stop their problem.

But then, Jesus came back to life, just as He said He would do! And over FIVE HUNDRED people had seen Him and talked with Him after He had risen! So it was no good to try to kill off everyone who had seen Jesus alive. What could they DO?[360]

When Jesus' followers said He'd gone back to heaven, the leaders said, "GOOD! Now they'll forget Jesus!"

But THEN Jesus sent the Holy Spirit! Now His followers had the POWER

www.thefamilyprayerbible.com

Jesus had promised them.[224] Even MORE people joined God's kingdom! The angry leaders' work had NOT put a stop to the followers of Jesus. Now, things got even WORSE for the leaders!

Every day, Peter and John and the rest of Jesus' disciples met at the Porch of Solomon, on the Temple grounds. There, they would tell people about Jesus. They would ask God to heal sick people and the people got well. They would pray for lame people and they could walk!

The disciples knew that God's Spirit was with them and was helping them. So they were not afraid of the religious leaders, even though the leaders TRIED to make them afraid—hoping that Jesus' friends would STOP telling people about Jesus and STOP preaching and STOP doing miracles! But God's family was not afraid of their threats and mean words![139]

So now, even more people were joining God's family. And more and more people believed that God would heal their sick friends and relatives. So they would bring out the sick people on mats, and lay them along the streets where Peter usually walked. That way, even if Peter's shadow fell on their sick friends, they would be healed. And they WERE!

God had given Jesus' friends power to do unusual miracles! These amazing things proved to everyone that Jesus IS who He says He is and that in God's kingdom, miracles happen! So now, after all their hard work to STOP God's family, the religious leaders were getting nowhere! They were finding that they could NOT do anything about God's power!

People even came from far away to Jerusalem. And they didn't come alone. They came bringing their sick friends and relatives, so that the sick ones could be healed. And they were![214]

Instead of the religious leaders' power STOPPING God's family, God's power was STOPPING the religious leaders! They had tried and tried, but they could NOT stop GOD![358]

Talk About the Story: Where did Jesus' followers meet in Jerusalem? What had the religious leaders done in order to stop God's family? Why couldn't they stop God's family from growing?

Scripture: "Say to God, 'How awesome are Your works! Through the greatness of Your power Your enemies shall submit themselves to You.'" Psalm 66:3

Family Time: What are some ways you have seen God's power? What is another time in the Bible when God's power stopped His enemies? What is a way you have seen God's power this week?

Prayer: Lord God, we are thankful that no one can stop Your power. Please help us to remember to ask Your help in everything! In Jesus' name, Amen.

THE COUNCIL LISTENS TO GAMALIEL

Scripture: Acts 5:17–42
Place: Jerusalem
Time: After Pentecost

The religious leaders had gotten more and more angry—and now, they had ARRESTED the disciples and put them in the jail, with locks locked, and guards standing at attention. They were SURE they could find a way to STOP Jesus' friends. And putting them in jail was one way![334]

But once again, the religious leaders did NOT remember that GOD'S power is far greater than their best idea or strongest jail! That night, an angel came and got the disciples from jail. They left the jail just as the sun was coming up.

The angel told them, "Go back into Solomon's Porch and keep on telling people about Jesus!"

So that's JUST what the men did! They went to the Temple as people were gathering for early morning prayer. They began to talk and tell people more about Jesus.

About that time, the religious leaders had all gotten together. They were ready to try scaring the disciples again, so they called for the guards to bring them from the jail.

The guards came back, breathless! "There is NO one inside the jail! The locks are locked. The guards are guarding. But the cell is EMPTY!"[109]

Oh, now the leaders were MORE angry. They were steaming! Furious!

Another guard ran in. "The men you're looking for are preaching in the Temple, right where they always are!"

So the leaders sent guards to bring the disciples—quietly. They didn't want people to start a riot! So The disciples soon entered the leaders' council. The leaders threatened them, "Don't talk about Jesus any more!" They had them beaten, but then let them go.[349]

The disciples and the rest praised God that they were worthy to suffer for Jesus' sake! But in the council, angry men were shouting!

Finally, a man named Gamaliel rose to his feet. He raised his hands for quiet. Everyone stopped and looked, then got quiet. They wanted to hear Gamaliel! He was wise and everyone trusted him.

Gamaliel said, "Friends, you remember Theudas? Many people followed him, but when he died, they all went home. Others have seemed to be starting something but when they died, it was over.

"We need to think carefully about what we are doing here. Because this Jesus has already died. They say He is alive again. And this is not stopping. If this is a human movement, it will stop soon. But if it is NOT, then we may be fighting against God Himself!"

The leaders knew it was true. Their work had NOT stopped what was going on. God's power was something they could not ignore![359]

So the leaders listened to Gamaliel. They'd wait to see what would happen.

Talk About the Story: Where were the disciples? How did they get out of jail? Where did they go? What did Gamaliel say about Jesus' followers?

Scripture: "Peter and the other apostles answered and said: 'We ought to obey God rather than men.'" Acts 5:29

Family Time: What is a time when people might have to choose between obeying God and obeying people in charge? What did the leaders want them to do? Why do you think the apostles said this?

Prayer: Lord, please help us to obey the people who are in charge of us, unless they ask us to do wrong. Then help us to obey You. Thank You. Amen.

ALMOST AN ARGUMENT

Scripture: Acts 6:1–7
Place: Jerusalem
Time: June–July, 30 AD

"It's not fair!" a Greek woman whispered. Her friend nodded.

"Yes. I THINK they are holding back some food from the Greek widows. It looks like they are giving the Hebrew widows more than we're getting!"

God's family was growing BIG very quickly! Everyone was sharing, and every day, people were being fed. When you have THOUSANDS of people, THAT is a big job! Everyone agreed that the women whose husbands had died—widows—should be taken care of. They were all being given food. But some widows were from Hebrew families—their families had always lived in Israel. The Greek widows' families had not always lived in Israel. Some people still thought of them as outsiders or immigrants. Other people simply didn't think about them when it was time to distribute food.

Matthew turned to James. "This is not good! No one should be left out or mistreated in God's family!"

"You are right! Jesus wants us to love and serve each person. We need to find a way to make sure each person is cared for." The apostles talked together and prayed. Then Peter called EVERYONE together.

He said, "Listen! It is not the best thing for we twelve to be in charge of giving out the food.[381] It takes a LOT of our time—and we need to spend more time studying God's Word and praying and preaching.[88] We could tell more people about Jesus if we didn't have this job, too."

"So here's what we believe God wants us to do: Look around. You all find seven men who are full of faith and full of the Holy Spirit.[167] They should be men who have skills to do this job. They will be in charge of all of the feeding and helping people that we've done until now."

Quickly all the people agreed on seven men who loved God, lived by faith and were known as people who did what was right because they were always listening to and obeying the Holy Spirit. All of them were from Greek or other "immigrant" families. With these men in charge of distributing food, the people who had felt neglected would know that they were being cared for in the very best way. They chose Stephen, a man full of faith and the Holy Spirit, and Philip, Prochorus, Nicanor, Timon, Parmenas, and Nicolas. The apostles prayed and laid hands on them, asking God to give them wisdom for this job.[536]

These men were willing to do this big job because they knew that they could ask God's Spirit for the wisdom and power to do it, just as He had given Jesus' disciples power to tell others about Him! A little hurt that could have become a BIG argument was solved when God's family relied on God for wisdom and help!

Talk About the Story: Who were the Hebrew widows? Who were the Greek widows? What did the apostles ask the people to do?

Scripture: "Seek out from among you seven men of *good* reputation, full of the Holy Spirit and wisdom, which we may appoint over this business; but we will give ourselves continually to prayer and to the ministry of the word." Acts 6:3–4

Family Time: Who are people that seem like outsiders in your neighborhood? In your church? What's a way your family can be like the seven deacons and help them feel included in God's family?

Prayer: Dear Jesus, Thank You that when we have little complaints or problems, we can ask You first for help. Please help us learn to get along with each other and to find ways to help others get along in Your family, too. In Your Name, Amen.

PSALM 108

A MORNING SONG TO GET YOU
READY FOR THE DAY

When Jeff left eating breakfast, his Dad asked, "Are you ready for your test in school?" It was an innocent question, but brought anguish to Jeff's face. He was thinking about the test, and had promised himself he wouldn't think about it till he walked into the room.

"Don't remind me Dad," Jeff rolled his eyes. "Thinking about it will ruin my morning."

The wise dad wanted Jeff to be ready for the test, but he also wanted him to have a happy morning. So the dad suggested, "Ignoring a problem won't make it go away." But Dad knew that suggestion wouldn't help, so he added, "If you face your problem, pray for God's help, and then study the best you can, you will do well."

Psalm 108 is a morning song, written by the warrior who is getting ready to go out to battle. He wanted God to help him in the battle and give him victory. This psalm is divided into two parts. In the first part, the psalmist thanked God for confidence to face the day. Second, the psalmist prayed for God to keep him in battle and give him victory.

Let's look at how Jeff can pray and get confidence. It is the same way a warrior gets ready for a battle, or a salesman gets ready to make a presentation.

"God, I've made up my mind to put You first;
        I will praise You to the best of my abilities.
I will get up early in the morning;
        I will tell You how great You are.[439]
I will tell all the people around me
        I have been singing praises to my God.
Your love reaches far above the clouds;
        It reaches everywhere.[364]

564   www.thefamilyprayerbible.com

Lord, lift Your glory above the clouds today;
Lift up Yourself in my life
So together we can see Your hand in my life.
Give me help for the problems of this day;
Give me victory and answer my prayers."

The second part of the psalm includes a prayer for victory in battle the warrior faced.[109] He reminded God that the enemies he faced were God's enemies. He then reminded God that victory is promised over surrounding nations that have rejected him.

The last section of the psalm is faith that depends on God. The psalmist prays for God's help and depends on it.

"Don't give up on me O Lord my God;
Be with me in my battle this day.
Please help me with this problem today;
If You don't help, I don't know who could.[219]
With Your help I will do my very best
And solve my problem today."

Talk About the Psalm: What did you learn about the psalm writer in this story? What did you learn about God?

Psalm 108: Read this week's psalm in your Bible together. Choose a verse to read aloud as a prayer.

Prayer: Thank You, God, for the psalm prayers in the Bible. Thank You for teaching us about You and about how to pray. In Jesus' name, Amen.

STEPHEN ANSWERS THE LIARS

Scripture: Acts 6:8—7:53
Place: Jerusalem
Time: June, 30 AD

66Are these charges TRUE?" the high priest asked Stephen. He and the other religious leaders were getting angrier by the minute. ANOTHER follower of the Way of Jesus stood before them. He needed to ANSWER these charges. His accusers said that he had spoken evil words about Moses and about God! This was serious! But this time, it wasn't Peter or John standing there. No, it was Stephen, one of the young men who had just been chosen as a deacon!

How did Stephen get into trouble with the religious leaders? First, he was full of the Holy Spirit and power![359] So besides doing the work of taking care of the hungry widows, he began to work miracles among the people on the streets of Jerusalem!

Of course, some people were GLAD to see God's power on display. They wanted to follow Jesus, too! But some people got MAD! They argued with Stephen about Jesus, but his answers were so wise and full of God's Spirit[451] that no one had anything more to say. This just made them MADDER. So they found some people who would tell lies about Stephen.[139]

The high priest stood glowering at him. The air was thick with tension and anger. Stephen knew that these "witnesses" had been paid to lie about him because they could not answer the things he said. They could not explain the miracles and signs God was doing through him. So he smiled back at the angry faces in front of him—and began to speak.

Stephen talked about Abraham and Isaac. He told about Joseph and Moses. He talked about the ways God had shown His power and how God had saved them and protected His people. He told how Moses had told God's people that a Prophet would come, a Leader that they would all listen to and obey—and Moses was talking about Jesus. Stephen talked about David and Solomon and how they built the Temple, even though God made everything and doesn't need a "place" to be. It all belongs to God!

But then, Stephen told about times closer to the present day. He told how God's people had killed prophets who God had sent with messages from Him.[349] They sat silent and angry—no one could deny this. Everything Stephen had said was true. And there was nothing bad said about Moses OR God.

But then, Stephen talked about how God had sent Jesus, the Prophet Moses had described, the person who did nothing wrong. He talked about how these very men had made sure that Jesus had been killed!

"You had God's law," Stephen said, "but you destroyed His law—on purpose. You did not want to obey God!"[327]

Stephen wasn't finished talking, but they were through LISTENING! They were FURIOUS!

Talk About the Story: Why did the people get angry with Stephen? Why do you think they did not want to see God's power? What did Stephen tell the council of leaders about what they did to Jesus?

Scripture: "This is that Moses who said to the children of Israel, 'The LORD YOUR GOD WILL RAISE UP FOR YOU A PROPHET LIKE ME FROM YOUR BRETHREN. HIM YOU SHALL HEAR.'" Acts 7:37

Family Time: Why do you think that people are not glad to see God's power or happy to hear God's Word to them? When is it hard for us to gladly listen to God's Word?

Prayer: Dear Lord, thank You that You love us even when we don't obey. Thank you for loving us when we don't like to hear what You have to say. Please forgive us. Please help us to listen and obey! In Jesus' name, Amen.

STEPHEN IS PROMOTED

Scripture: Acts 7:51—8:4
Place: Jerusalem
Time: June, 30 AD

The crowd of leaders was buzzing like an angry swarm of bees about to burst from their hive! But Stephen kept talking. He said, "You people are tough-skinned and hard-hearted. You resist God's Spirit![84] Your ancestors killed prophets God sent. And YOU killed Jesus, the One God sent![347] You broke God's law, even though you try to make everyone else obey God's law!"

The words were true. But this made the leaders SO ANGRY they couldn't stand it! Stephen's words cut like a knife in their hearts. They could have told God they were sorry. They could have turned around and believed Stephen's true words. But instead, they began to snarl and growl and shout, tearing their clothes to show how displeased they were!

Stephen ignored them—something else had his attention. He was so full of God's Spirit[167] that when he looked up, he could see something no one else could see! He said, "I see the glory of God. And I see JESUS standing at God's right hand!"[297]

THAT was more than these leaders could take. They put their HANDS over their ears so they couldn't hear ANY more! Yelling and screaming, they rushed together to GRAB Stephen. They dragged him OUT of the building, and then OUT of the city!

These angry men threw their coats in a pile at the feet of a young man named Saul, who was part of their group. He was glad to see that they were going to GET RID of Stephen! So he guarded the coats instead of throwing stones.

Once the crowd was outside the city gate, they threw Stephen to the ground in the middle of them. Then the angry men began to pelt him with stones.[374] The stones kept flying, and hitting with a THUNK. Stephen got weaker and weaker.

Stephen knelt in the middle of the flying stones and said, "Lord, don't hold this against them. Please forgive their sin."[130]

Finally, Stephen said, "Lord Jesus, receive my spirit!"[99] and then he fell down. His spirit had gone to be with Jesus, just as he had asked![197]

Stephen had been promoted to be with Jesus! Some friends buried his body.

God's family began to scatter out of Jerusalem, but as they went, they told everyone the good news about Jesus! So now God's family was growing more and more and MORE![199]

Talk About the Story: What did Stephen say that made the leaders cover their ears? Who watched the coats of the men who threw stones at Stephen? What did Stephen ask God to do, just before he died?

Scripture: "But he, being full of the Holy Spirit, gazed into heaven and saw the glory of God, and Jesus standing at the right hand of God, and said, 'Look! I see the heavens opened and the Son of Man standing at the right hand of God!'" Acts 7:55–56

Family Time: Stephen asked God to forgive the men who were hurting him. What have you said to people who are mean to you? When have you asked God to forgive people who've been mean to you? Why is it hard to forgive people who hurt us? Who can we ask to help us forgive? What are words you can say to show you forgive them?

Prayer: Dear Lord, thank You that You are powerful. We can trust You in scary situations. Thank You that You love us and that You are always at work. Please help us to forgive others. In Jesus' name, Amen.

PHILIP GOES TO SAMARIA

Scripture: Acts 8:1–8
Place: Samaria
Time: 30 AD

The people stood in a tight knot around Philip, amazed at what was happening right before their eyes! Philip spoke, and a horrible shriek came out of a child who had been sick and twisted in pain. The shriek seemed to carry into the sky! And this little girl, who had been so sick, fell to the ground. Was she dead? Suddenly, she sat up, shook her head and then LAUGHED! She leaped up, dancing around! "It's gone! It's GONE!" she sang. "I am FREE!"

She ran to Philip and hugged him. "Oh, thank you. THANK YOU!" Then she ran to her mother and hugged her with all her might. The two of them stood listening carefully to EVERYTHING Philip had to say. It was VERY clear that this man knew of a power greater than the horrible demon who had made this little girl so sick and twisted in pain! Philip had said a name—Jesus of Nazareth! And in that Name, he had told the unclean spirit to leave the girl—and it DID! This mother and daughter now wanted to know ALL about Jesus of Nazareth! Who was He? What did He do? How is it that His name has power over evil spirits?[27]

How did this happy ending begin? After Stephen was killed, people who followed Jesus were persecuted. That means they were threatened and chased away from Jerusalem. Now that might seem like a bad thing! After all, they were growing into a big happy family! But of course, God had a good plan in it! He always brings good out of bad!

Philip was one of the men who'd been chosen as a deacon, like Stephen. But when the persecution began, God told Philip to go to a city in Samaria. Philip went. And of course, he also began talking in public, telling people about Jesus the Messiah![145] But how did this stranger from Jerusalem gather groups of people who would not be likely to EVER listen to him? He was a Jew, and Jews did not like Samaritans, and Samaritans didn't like them either!

The Bible tells us that when the crowds saw the miracles Philip performed, they all paid close attention to what he said![359] So when they SAW what Philip did, they LISTENED! For with shrieks, impure spirits came out of many, like that little girl. And many who were paralyzed were healed.[214] So God even when things seem hard or strange to us, God always knows what is best. He had a plan in Philip leaving Jerusalem. He knew how to get the full attention of the people in that city. Many of them followed Jesus—and they had great joy!

Talk About the Story: Why did Philip go to Samaria? What happened to the demons, or impure spirits? Whose name is the strongest name ever? Why was there great joy in that city?

Scripture: "Those who were scattered went everywhere preaching the word." Acts 8:4

Family Time: What are some places you have gone? Philip might have felt like life was hard or confusing when he had to leave Jerusalem. But he obeyed God. What are ways your family can be like Philip, and even when you don't understand what God is doing? How can you share Jesus' love with people in the places you go?

Prayer: Jesus, we thank You that Your name is the most powerful name in the universe! Please help us to trust You when things happen to us that we don't like, or that make us feel confused. Remind us that You always have good plans! In Your name, Amen.

SIMON IS SILLY

Scripture: Acts 8:9–20
Place: Samaria
Time: 30 AD

Before Philip came to Samaria, the people who lived there had great respect for a man named Simon. They told each other, "Simon's got a power like God's power!" But the truth was, Simon's power was NOT from God. Many things Simon had done had amazed the people of that city! So, they had decided that Simon was someone VERY great! But it turned out that his "greatness" was fake.[113]

Here's what happened—first of all, Philip came! Philip left Jerusalem and came to Samaria. There, he began to tell people about Jesus. More than that, he SHOWED people about Jesus. Philip did many miracles, so people could SEE that Jesus' name is stronger than any name. Jesus can do anything! People were healed. They were freed from demons and sicknesses! And when they SAW and heard about who Jesus is, many people believed in Jesus.[30]

Simon watched what Philip was doing. Simon listened carefully to what Philip had to say, too! JESUS the Messiah has ALL POWER.[27] Simon knew that the power he'd been using was not like Jesus' power. Simon decided that Jesus IS God's Son.[470]

Later, Peter and John (remember them?) heard about the great things God was doing in this Samaritan town! So they went to visit Philip and these new members of God's family. These Samaritans had been baptized in Jesus' name, but they had not yet received the Holy Spirit. So Peter and John began praying with them, laying their hands on them to ask the Holy Spirit to come to them.[448] Now even MORE amazing things were happening!

All the time, Simon was watching. He knew THIS kind of power was not like anything he'd ever seen! So he went to Peter and John and said, "I'd like to buy some of this Holy Spirit power. I want to be able to lay my hands on someone and give them the Holy Spirit. How much shall I pay you?"[84]

Peter must have just shaken his head. WHAT was Simon thinking? God's power isn't something you can buy and use like water from a tap. God's power is GOD's. He GIVES it where He wants to. It can't be bought!

Peter said to Simon, "Quit this nonsense. You can't buy God's power! If that's how you think, you'll perish without God! Your heart is not right in God's sight. Turn around and change your mind about this. Ask God to forgive you. You are trapped by bitterness and sin."[231]

Simon asked Peter and John, "Pray to the Lord that none of the things which you've said may happen."[173] Simon knew that he didn't want Peter's words to come true!

Talk About the Story: What did Simon do before Philip came? What did he think he could buy? Why is that wrong? Who does God give His power to?

Scripture: "Be clothed with humility, for 'God resists the proud, but gives grace to the humble.'" 1 Peter 5:5

Family Time: When have you seen someone acting more important than they really are? When have you tried to act more important than you really are? Why do you think the Bible says, "God resists proud people but gives grace to humble people"? What's a way you can show you are humble? Pray together!

Prayer: Dear Lord, help us to always remember that You are the King! Help us not to try to show off or act important. Your power and gifts are good. Thank You that You will share them with us in Your time and Your way. In Jesus' name, Amen.

PHILIP AND THE ETHIOPIAN

Scripture: Acts 8:26–40
Place: The desert between Jerusalem and the Gaza
Time: 30 AD

Philip wondered what would happen next. He had been in Samaria when an angel came to him and said, "Go, head south on the road that leads to Gaza."[118] That was the ONLY thing the angel told Philip! But Philip obeyed. He began walking down that road through the dry, empty land.

It wasn't long before Philip saw a chariot ahead of him a little way. That's when the angel told him the NEXT part of his job! "Go and catch up with that chariot."[207] WELL! That was just as strange as walking down an empty road—but Philip obeyed!

He ran fast to catch up with the chariot. As he came along side the chariot, he suddenly understood JUST why God had sent him to this exact place. The man in the chariot was reading aloud from the book of Isaiah.

The words he was reading were probably not in his first language, so he read them aloud slowly, thinking about every word. And the words he was reading aloud from Isaiah were all about JESUS!

So Philip asked the man, "Do you understand what you are reading?"[456]

The man looked up and smiled, patting the seat beside him. "How could I understand this unless someone tells me about it? Please come and sit with me. Perhaps you can explain it to me." Of COURSE Philip could explain! He was delighted to explain!

Now this man was an important official, the treasurer of the country to south called Ethiopia. His queen, Candace, was very famous. And Mr. Treasurer had come to Jerusalem to worship God! He knew about the one, true God but he did not yet know about Jesus—but of course, THAT was going to change! The man read the words about Jesus, bit by bit. And bit by bit, Philip explained to him the good news about Jesus![444] He told Mr. Treasurer how God had sent Jesus to take the punishment for sin. He told how God was inviting EVERYONE into His family—all over the world!

Mr. Treasurer listened carefully. He could see how his time in Jerusalem, and his time reading this scroll of Isaiah, all fit together with the things Philip was telling him about Jesus. He noticed that the chariot was passing by some water. He said to Philip, "Look. There's water here! May I be baptized?"[30]

Philip must have laughed! Mr. Treasurer was VERY ready to follow Jesus! He said, "If you believe in Jesus with all your heart, of course you may be baptized!"[263]

Mr. Treasurer said, "I believe that Jesus is the Messiah, the Son of God!" Philip could see that it was true! So he took the man into the water there and baptized him! As Mr. Treasurer came up out of the water, the Holy Spirit took Philip away! Philip DISAPPEARED!

But Mr. Treasurer went on his way, full of joy, praising God for His love! Mr. Treasurer then took the good news of Jesus to Africa! Philip literally opened his eyes and boom! He was in Azotus, a little town on the coast. God had more important work for Philip. So Philip began to tell people about Jesus in Azotus. Then he went to the next town, and MORE people joined God's family![145]

Talk About the Story: Where did the angel tell Philip to go? Why did God send Philip there? What do you think Mr. Treasure did after Philip disappeared?

Scripture: "Philip opened his mouth, and beginning at this Scripture, preached Jesus to him." Acts 8:35

Family Time: Why do you think Philip had such cool adventures? When we obey God, He can do great things through us. When are times it's hard to obey God? What can we do when we don't want to obey?

Prayer: Dear Lord, we always want to obey You. Please help us to listen to Your Word and do what it says. In Jesus' name, Amen.

SAUL'S INTENTIONS

Scripture: Acts 8:1–4; 22:3; Galatians 1:11–24
Place: Jerusalem to Damascus
Time: 35 AD

Saul was a member of the Sanhedrin—one of the loudest and the angriest! He growled about these followers of the Way of Jesus of Nazareth. "They are EVERYWHERE!" he shouted, thumping the table to make his point. "They should ALL of them arrested and put in prison!"

And Saul was VERY sure that HE could stop them. The Sanhedrin was the religious council in Jerusalem who made the religious rules for everyone in Israel.[139] These leaders had their own soldiers and police. So they were quick to make people obey their rules, or be arrested![349]

Saul had been born in Tarsus, a city in modern-day Turkey. His parents were Roman citizens, so Saul was also a Roman citizen. (This would be important later on!) But his family likely moved to Jerusalem when he was a young boy. He grew up being taught by the famous rabbi Gamaliel. (You can read things

Gamaliel said in Acts 5. He was also in the Sanhedrin.)

Saul was SO angry. These followers of the Way of Jesus of Nazareth kept popping up EVERYWHERE. Now even some of the priests at the temple believed that Jesus is the Messiah. THEY were joyfully praising God for Jesus and worshiping with those other believers.[199] It made Saul FURIOUS.

He thumped the table again. In a commanding voice he said, "Authorize me. Give me soldiers and police. I'll arrest ANYONE who says Jesus is Messiah. I will SEE to it that NO one else follows this Jesus!"

You see, to Saul, there was only ONE God (which is true—Jesus also said that!). But Saul didn't understand how JESUS could be the one, true God come in a human body. As far as Saul was concerned, Jesus had declared that He was ANOTHER god! He thought Jesus was starting a new religion and was rebelling against God. So you can see why Saul REALLY wanted to stop followers of Jesus. He wanted this rebellion against God STOPPED. God's honor needed to be DEFENDED. Of course, God does not need to be protected—He's GOD! But Saul thought he needed to protect God's honor by STOPPING those followers of this Jesus!

So, the Sanhedrin gave Saul authority and soldiers and policemen, and Saul began to go from one house to the next in Jerusalem, knocking on every door, asking if people inside were followers of the Way. If they said yes, he would tell the soldiers to drag the people out of their houses and throw them into jail. Saul was feeling like he was doing a very GOOD thing.

I am PLEASING GOD! Saul thought to himself with great pride.

Talk About the Story: Who was angry about the growing number of people who followed Jesus? What group did this man belong to? What did the Sanhedrin to do help Saul stop the followers of the Way of Jesus? Why did Saul want to stop them? What did he do?

Scripture: "Therefore those who were scattered went everywhere preaching the word." Acts 8:4

Family Time: What might have happened differently if Saul had talked with Peter and understood more about Jesus? What is a question you need to ask to understand something better? Who can we always ask when we have questions?

Prayer: Dear Father, we thank You that You sent Jesus and that You promise it's OK to ask You for wisdom. We ask You to remind us to pray about everything, as You told us in the Bible. In Jesus' name, Amen.

PSALM 109

WHEN A BEST FRIEND TURNS AGAINST YOU

Jill had a best friend; at least Jill thought she was her best friend. They sat together in the same seat on class outings. They ate lunch together and both had been to each other's house for a play-date. Then Jill's best friend started telling lies to the other girls about Jill. She said Jill still drank milk out of bottle with a nipple and that Jill hated her mother and that Jill hated going to church. None of that was true. How should Jill pray?

King David had the same problem. Ahithophel had been David's friend and trusted counselor. They had taken trips together, ate together and at official palace events, they had stood around together to chat and meet friends.

When Absalom began gathering a crowd of followers to overthrow David's throne, Ahithophel was taken in by the propaganda of David's son. Ahithophel began criticizing David for doing a poor job, or for being sick; Ahithophel believed Absalom. Then Ahithophel began going places with Absalom. Finally, Ahithophel became the counsel to Absalom telling how the son could take over the throne from David. David had to flee Jerusalem.

> "O Lord, You are my Lord and my God,
>   Do not keep quiet when I need You;
>   Let me hear You speak to me.
> Do something when liars are betraying me;
>   My former friend is telling lies about me,
>   He has surrounded me with his hateful stories.[374]
> They are not true and they embarrass me;
>   He hates me without a cause.
>   I love him and did many things for him.
> I still pray for him
>   But he has accused me of things that are not true.
>   I do good things for him, but he pays me back with evil.[7]
>   I gave myself to him, but he hates me."

When someone tells lies about us, we should not get even by telling lies about them. When they steal from us, we shouldn't try to take away things from them. Listen to what Jesus says, "But to you who are willing to listen, I say, love your enemies! Do good to those who hate you. Bless those who curse you. Pray for those who hurt you" (Luke 6:27-28, *NLT*). Notice how David prayed,

> *"You are my Lord of my life and my Savior;*
> > *Your mercy is good, so be good to me.*
> > *I call on Your name to help me.*[109]
> *Save me because I am helpless and need Your help.*
> > *My heart is breaking with grief.*
> > *Am I just a shadow that is going to pass away?*
> *Am I an insect that the wind blows away?*
> > *My muscles are weak because I am not eating;*
> > *My body is thin and I am wasting away.*[161]
> *People are shocked when they see how thin I am,*
> > *They shake their heads in disbelief;*[349]
> > *Help me, O Lord, my God!*[219]
> *Be kind to me because You are kind;*
> > *Be merciful to me because You are mercy.*
> *Then will everyone know that You are the Lord*
> > *And You have saved me in spite of my former friend."*

As a result of David's retreat, his army was saved. He organized them into a fighting force. They went out and defeated Absalom and his army. Absalom was killed and David returned to Jerusalem. David prayed,

> *"I stood in front of a large crowd of people*
> > *To shout my great prayers to the Lord for victory.*
> *The Lord stood at the right hand of this poor man;*
> > *He has rescued me from an unjust situation."*

Talk About the Psalm: What did you learn about the psalm writer in this story? What did you learn about God?

Psalm 109: Read this week's psalm in your Bible together. Choose a verse to read aloud as a prayer.

Prayer: Thank You, God, for the psalm prayers in the Bible. Thank You for teaching us about You and about how to pray. In Jesus' name, Amen.

JESUS TURNS SAUL AROUND

Scripture: Acts 9:1–31; Galatians 1:11–24
Place: Jerusalem to Damascus, Syria
Time: 35 AD

Saul rode out of Jerusalem quickly, jaw set and his eyes ablaze. The letters and papers he carried said that HE had the authority to arrest people who followed Jesus.[349] With people along to help him; he had no time to waste. Paul was going to STOP these followers of the Way of Jesus!

When Saul had begun going from house to house to arrest the people in God's family, many of them had run to Damascus from Jerusalem. Saul felt sure that the Jews who lived in Damascus would help him. Saul was full of self-righteous determination. They were not going to get away from HIM!

As Paul got near Damascus, there was a flash of light, as if lightning had struck nearby.[377] Everyone was surprised. But something knocked Saul off his horse. The men with him didn't know WHAT had happened: They could hear a voice, but they didn't see anyone . . . except Saul on the ground!

The voice said, "Saul! SAUL! Why are you trying to hurt Me?[256]

Saul was still breathless from falling hard. "Who—who ARE You, Lord?" he gasped.[426]

www.thefamilyprayerbible.com

The Voice replied, "I AM JESUS—the One you're trying to hurt.[72] What you're trying to do will only hurt you. It's like trying to kick a pointed spear with your bare foot!"

Saul was shaking and astonished. ***WHAT was going on?!*** JESUS was talking to him. JESUS said his plan wasn't going to work.

"What do You want me to DO, Lord?" Saul asked.

"Get up and go into Damascus. Stay there until you find out what to do next.[207]

The men with Saul must have REALLY been confused. A Voice, but no person.[506] They picked up Saul from off the ground and tried to help him get back on his horse. That's when they noticed that Saul couldn't SEE! So they set him on his horse and led it to the house on Straight Street where they were staying.

For three days, Saul sat silent, thinking and praying. He didn't go to dinner or even drink any water. He had a LOT to think about.[41] If JESUS had talked to him, then Saul had NOT been pleasing God! This was a LOT for Saul to wrap his mind around! But God told Saul that a man named Ananias would pray for him. So Saul waited.

Meanwhile, God told Ananias[519] to go to Saul. "But LORD," he said, "this man has come here to ARREST people who love Jesus!" God reminded Ananias that He had a big plan for this Saul, and Ananias could trust Him for protection. So Ananias went to Saul and prayed for him—and suddenly, Saul was filled with God's Holy Spirit.[167] And he could SEE![214] He was SO EXCITED. He asked Ananias to baptize him in water. He ate and drank and then, he went OUT!

Saul went to the nearest marketplace in Damascus and began to PREACH to people, telling them how Jesus is God's Son and the Messiah! WOW! What a difference! Now the man who had wanted to STOP God's family was PART of God's family—and LOVED to tell everyone the story of how Jesus had turned him around!

Talk About the Story: What did Saul want to do to believers in Damascus? How did Jesus stop Saul? What did Saul do for three days? What did Ananias think about going to pray for Saul? What happened after Ananias prayed?

Scripture: "Praying always with all prayer and supplication in the Spirit, being watchful to this end with all perseverance and supplication for all the saints." Ephesians 6:18

Family Time: What are times when we feel confused? Angry? When we are surprised or confused, what is a good prayer to pray?

Prayer: Dear Lord, we are so glad that You tell us to pray in every circumstance. We want to know what YOU want us to do! In Jesus' name, Amen.

SAUL ESCAPES

Scripture: Acts 9:20–30
Place: Damascus to Jerusalem
Time: 35 AD

It was a Friday evening in Damascus. Nearly every Jew in the city was in the synagogue when a man named Saul rose to his feet and began to speak.[145]

Suddenly, the crowd began to whisper to each other. "Isn't this the same man who came here to arrest the followers of Jesus? WHAT is he SAYING? He is telling us that the MESSIAH has come—and that Jesus is the Messiah!" said one.[359]

"He says that the Romans crucified Jesus because the Jews in Jerusalem asked them to do it. Wow! And he says that now Jesus is ALIVE?! What kind of wild story IS this?" another said. Some were amazed and happy to hear what Saul said about Jesus. And others were ANGRY! They didn't want Saul saying that the leaders in Jerusalem killed Jesus!

Now that Saul was following Jesus, he did this over and over again in Damascus, and more and more people were listening![358] He told how Jesus had stopped him and changed him from the inside out. He told them about Jesus and how He had died to take the punishment for their sin, then came back to life to prove He

www.thefamilyprayerbible.com

is God's Son. More and more people believed in Jesus and joined God's family—so people who did NOT believe Jesus is God's Son were getting madder and MADDER! Over and over, Saul was proving that Jesus is the Messiah! They had nothing to say! And now they were FURIOUS! So finally, some men decided they would KILL Saul.

But of course, God knew all about this. And Saul's friends in Damascus, the other members of God's family, had a very interesting way to help him! The men who wanted to kill him stayed by the gate to the city all of the time.[139] That one, big gate was the only way in or out—or so they thought! But Saul's friends decided Saul could leave the city without going through the gate—with a little help!

His friends got a big basket and some rope. At night, they took Saul high up on the wall, where there was a window. Carefully, they tied the rope around the basket. Saul got inside, and then slowly, slowly, they let the basket down outside the city wall![516] Bump, bump, THUMP! And once again, Saul was on his way to the next big adventure God had for him! He was safe, and grateful at how God's family had helped him!

Talk About the Story: Where was Saul speaking? What did Saul say that made some people angry? What did the angry men decide to do? What did God's family do to help Saul?

Scripture: "A friend loves at all times, and a brother is born for adversity." Proverbs 17:17

Family Time: Who are your best friends? What makes them people you love? What are some ways your friends and relatives have helped you in adversity (during a hard time)?

Prayer: Dear Lord, thank You for your love. Thank You for giving us friends in Your family! We thank You for the people You have put into our lives. In Jesus' name, Amen.

TABITHA RAISED FROM THE DEAD

Scripture: Acts 9:36–42
Place: Joppa
Time: 35 AD

Peter could hear the wailing and crying that filled the air even before he got to the house. He'd been traveling toward the coast of the Great Sea (the Mediterranean), telling about Jesus and encouraging the new members of God's growing family! He'd just come from Lydda, which was on the road to the seacoast town of Joppa. There, a man who had been paralyzed for eight years was healed and everyone who lived near this man joined God's family!

But as Peter had been talking with people in Lydda, two men came up to him quickly. They said, "Please, come with us to Joppa!"

They explained that a woman named Tabitha (or Dorcas, in Greek) had died. She was a follower of Jesus and she had been very kind to people, especially poor people and widows. She was well known in Joppa and everyone in Joppa loved her very much![412] Her friends and family had gathered to mourn and prepare her

body for burial after she died. They had laid her body in a room upstairs—but then, someone came running with the news! They heard that Peter was not far away! Suddenly, the room buzzed with excitement. Tabitha's friends began to hope that maybe, MAYBE Peter could pray for Tabitha. Maybe, MAYBE she would LIVE again! So they had sent these two men to beg Peter to come with them RIGHT NOW to Tabitha's little house.

Peter came into the house and was led up into the room where Tabitha's body lay. Suddenly, Peter was surrounded. The room was full of widows,[474] women whose husbands had died. Each widow showed him clothes Tabitha had made for her. You see, widows usually were VERY poor. And clothing was VERY expensive. So a widow did not ever have new clothes. They wore clothes that were patched and worn some more, until they were rags! Tabitha cared about these widows. She made clothes and gave them to the widows! The widows knew they were loved and cared for!

Peter listened to the widows' stories. He could see that Tabitha had shown the love of Jesus to many people in her town. He sent the people out of the room, and then he knelt down and prayed.[443] He must have asked God, "What do YOU want to do here?"

Peter got his answer. So he turned to the body lying on the bed, and said, "Tabitha, stand up!"[423] Tabitha opened her eyes. SHE WAS ALIVE! She looked at Peter and sat up! (Maybe she had never met Peter before. She might have been very surprised to have a stranger in her room!)

And then, Peter took her by the hand and helped her walk out of the room, where he called everyone in and showed them their beloved Tabitha, alive and well![397] Now many MORE people could see God's power and they joined God's family![34] So Peter stayed there and taught them for quite a while!

Talk About the Story: What did Tabitha do that showed Jesus' love? What do you think Peter asked God when he knelt to pray?

Scripture: "Be anxious for nothing, but in everything by prayer and supplication, with thanksgiving, let your requests be made known to God." Philippians 4:6

Family Time: What do you think the widows worried about or were anxious about, when Tabitha had died? What are some things that make us worried or anxious? What can we thank God for in each of those situations?

Prayer: Dear Lord, thank You that even in hard times, we can pray to you. We are glad that we can trust You anytime we don't know what to do. Please help us remember to pray about everything and thank You for the answers You give! In Jesus' name, Amen.

PETER'S VISION

Scripture: Acts 10
Place: Joppa to Caesarea
Time: 35 AD

Peter stood on the rooftop of Simon the Tanner's house.[97] He could look out and see the sea. A fresh wind blew so that Peter could barely notice the smell of the tanning work Simon was doing in his workshop. Tanners always lived outside of town because their work could get pretty smelly!

Peter's stomach growled. It was almost lunchtime and he was hungry. As Peter waited for lunch to be prepared, he prayed. By now, Peter was pretty used to amazing things happening during prayer times! But Peter was NOT prepared for THIS—God was doing something completely new. And He used a VERY strange vision to show Peter what He wanted![520]

You see, until now, Peter and all of the other followers of Jesus had told other Jewish people about Jesus their Messiah. Until now, they didn't even think about Gentiles—people who were not Jews—because their laws had always said they had to stay away from Gentiles. But on THIS day, Peter was on the rooftop, praying while he waited for his lunch. Suddenly, God gave him a vision—a waking dream. What looked like a sheet was being let down by its four corners. In it were all kinds of animals: snakes and pigs, lizards and wild birds. But they all were animals that Jewish law said NOT to eat. Now, Peter was hungry. And God said, "Here, Peter. You can eat any of these animals you want."[327]

"NO WAY, Lord!" Peter shuddered. Those were UNCLEAN animals. He said, "I've NEVER eaten ANY of those animals in my LIFE! They are unclean—NOT OK to eat!"[504]

But God replied gently, "Don't call these unclean. God has said they ARE clean."

Peter sat, puzzled about this whole thing, with his stomach still rumbling! Just then, two men knocked at the gate of the house where Peter was. He looked down from the roof to see who it was—they were GENTILES. In fact, they were ROMANS—the people who were in control of the area. Jews did NOT like them much! But they asked for Peter. And God's Spirit said to Peter, "Go with them. I have sent them!"[207]

WELL! Peter was beginning to understand the vision. Like those animals God NOW said were clean, God was telling Peter that these people, who were always considered unclean, were declared clean by God. Peter could go to their houses. He could eat with them and tell them about Jesus![145] Jesus is the savior of EVERYONE—not just Jewish people!

Talk About the Story: Where was Peter? What was he doing? What did God show him? What did it mean?

Scripture: "The voice spoke again and said, 'Do not call anything impure that God has made clean.'" Acts 10:15

Family Time: Sometimes we think we are better than other people. Who are people that might make you afraid or uncomfortable? God loves all people. Who can we pray for today?

Prayer: Dear Lord Jesus, we are glad that You love us. We are thankful that You love everyone. Please help us to remember to pray even for people we don't like or are afraid of. In Jesus' name, Amen.

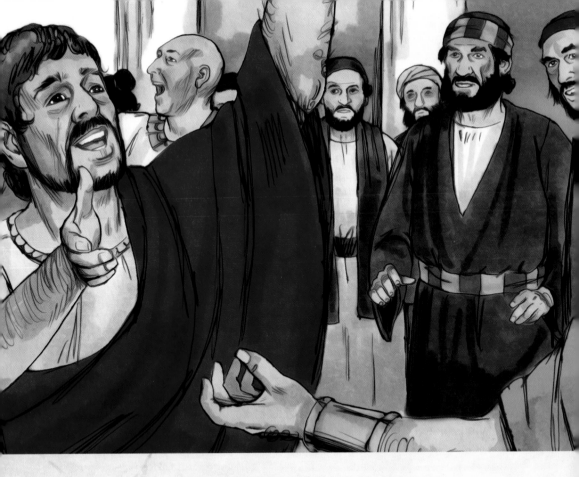

GENTILES JOIN GOD'S FAMILY

Scripture: Acts 10:1—11:18
Place: Joppa to Caesarea
Time: 35 AD

Peter's mind was whirling with new ideas! As he walked, he talked more to himself than to his six friends or to the two men who'd come to fetch him. He said, "So. If God says the Gentiles are NOT unclean, then He is inviting ALL people into His family. So. Jesus is not only OUR Savior and Messiah—He really IS Lord of All. He's the Savior and Messiah of the whole WORLD!"

The men who came to fetch Peter smiled. They didn't know much about this Peter, but they DID know God had told them to get him![70] They weren't sure he'd come to the home of Cornelius, their boss and master! Cornelius was an army officer over a large group of Roman soldiers at the fort in Caesarea, right on the edge of the Mediterranean Sea.

Cornelius had told his soldier and servant, "I have been trying to live to please God. While I was praying, an ANGEL came to me! The angel told me that God

had heard my prayers. I was amazed! He told me to send for Peter, who's staying in Joppa at the house of Simon the Tanner." They really didn't know much more than that. But an ANGEL said to do this! It was very important—and it mattered deeply to their master Cornelius!

When the men finally arrived at Cornelius' house, Cornelius came out to greet Peter. Cornelius knew that Jews did not come into Gentile homes. He bowed at Peter's feet to show how glad he was that Peter would come at all! Peter told him that God had shown him it was all right to enter Cornelius' house.[468] Soon, Cornelius had told Peter all about the angel's message and thanked him for coming so quickly.

Everyone in the household—family, soldiers, and servants—all gathered to listen to what Peter had to tell. They KNEW that God had sent Peter![207] Peter told them God's good news about Jesus! And while he was talking, God's Holy Spirit came! Peter could see that this was JUST as the Spirit had come to Peter and his friends at Pentecost! WOW! Peter and his friends realized, *GOD loves and accepts every kind of people! He has no favorites—He loves us all!*[199]

Peter baptized this household.[30] Then he stayed with them awhile, teaching them more about God's family! When he returned to Jerusalem, Peter told the other believers the whole story, from his strange vision to how God's Spirit had come to these Roman people! The six men who'd gone with Peter all agreed that they had seen it, too—God's Spirit had come to them. These Gentiles were now part of God's family! So now, the leaders of the Jerusalem church realized that YES! The good news of Jesus is for ALL people![188]

Talk About the Story: Who came to tell Cornelius to send for Peter? What did Peter learn from his dream and from watching God's Spirit at Cornelius' house? Do you think it was easy or hard for the believers in Jerusalem to accept the Gentiles? Why or why not?

Scripture: "They praised God. They said, 'So then, God has allowed even Gentiles to turn away from their sins. He did this so that they could live.'" Acts 11:18 *(NIV)*

Family Time: In what countries or cultures do missionaries you know live? What are some differences between the way their family lives and the way your family lives? What helps us remember that God loves every person?

Prayer: Dear Lord, thank You for loving EVERY person in the world. Thank You that because You love them, then we can love them and tell them God's good news about Jesus! In His name, Amen.

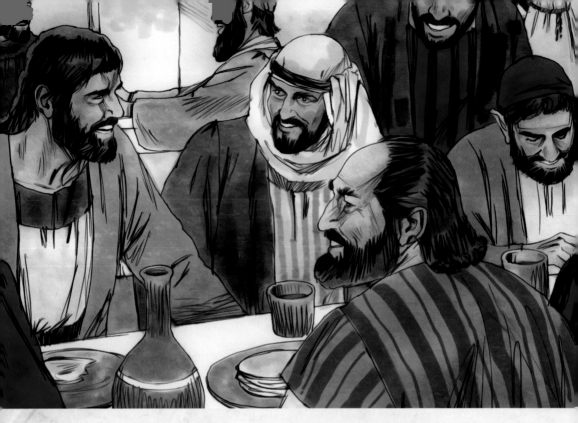

THE CHURCH AT ANTIOCH

Scripture: Acts 11:19–30
Place: Antioch
Time: 35 AD

A boy and girl sad wearily by the road, rubbing their tired legs. The boy said, "We're not even in Israel anymore, Papa. When we left Jerusalem, I never thought we'd travel this far!"

"Yes," their father replied. "We're in Syria now. We've traveled nearly 300 miles from where we started. And yes, this is far enough. I don't think anyone will come THIS far to persecute us for following Jesus![349] So let's look around to see where we can stay."

Like other families in Jerusalem, when Saul had begun to persecute Jesus' followers, this family began to move. But they didn't ONLY travel. They didn't ONLY settle. Wherever they went, they told the good news about Jesus!

Soon there were more and more followers of Jesus in Syria, in the city of Antioch, The believers began to tell EVERYONE about Jesus and how He had died on a Roman cross to take the punishment for the sins of everyone—not only Jews,[199] but for ALL people![145] So before long, God's family was growing and GROWING in Antioch.

www.thefamilyprayerbible.com

When word got back to the leaders of the church in Jerusalem, they wanted to find out what God was doing away up to the north! So they sent Barnabas, one of their friends who was full of God's Spirit. Barnabas traveled north that long way to see to see what was going on in Antioch!

When Barnabas arrived, he found that the believers from Jerusalem had indeed formed a community but it included Greek and Syrian and anyone else who had followed Jesus! He was very glad to see this! So he stayed for a while to preach and to teach—and more and MORE people joined God's family![327] These followers talked about Jesus Christ so much that others started calling them "Christians"—or little Christs.

After Barnabas had been there awhile, he went to get Saul who was nearby at his home in Tarsus! So now, Barnabas brought Saul, the SAME MAN whose persecution caused these families to LEAVE Jerusalem, to preach and teach these people about Jesus![126] God loves to bring good things out of what seem to be bad situations!

Then, when there was a need to send money to the church at Jerusalem, this new "church full of Christians"[58] all gave what they could and Saul and Barnabas took it back to Jerusalem with them. God's family was growing in numbers, in the kinds of people, and in generous hearts that showed their love for Him!

Talk About the Story: What happened to cause people in Antioch to hear the good news about Jesus? Who came to help this church? Who did he bring from Tarsus? How did the Christians show their love for Jesus?

Scripture: "And we know that all things work together for good to those who love God, to those who are the called according to His purpose." Romans 8:28

Family Time: When has your family moved from one place to another? What did you like about moving? What did you not like? Who are people you know who belong to God's family because someone else told them the good news about Jesus? Who are people you might tell this good news?

Prayer: Father God, we thank You that even when things seem hard, You are working out something good! Please help us share the good news of Jesus with everyone we meet, as the Christians did in Antioch. In Jesus' name, Amen.

PSALM 118

RETURN OF THE KING

The Psalm describes David's triumphant ride into Jerusalem as King. He was going to worship the Lord. He especially thanked God for protecting him safely when he was an exile chased by Saul's army to kill him.

David rode his white steed up the steep hill toward Jerusalem. The massive walls stood at the top of a steep hill. They kept out all the invading armies because they are so tall and thick. Today the walls were filled with people looking over the top—not soldiers defending the city—but with worshipers who would follow David to worship in the house of God.

Stretching out behind David was a long parade of officers, soldiers and supporters. They had fought with David on the battlefield, now they wanted to thank God with their king for victory.

David wrote a Psalm for the occasion as he approached the city. He remembered, "My enemy shut me in a prison, you answered and delivered me." Then David sang, "Lord, You are with me, I will not fear what anyone can do to me."

Saul who had been king sent his army to catch David and kill him. Heathen nations also chased David to kill him. For 13 years David had been in exile. Now he prayed, "Though hostile armies surrounded me, I defeated them in the Lord's name."

David remembered the hard days, but now he was victorious. He sang, "Lord, You are my strength in battle, I sing of You in my victory song."

As David approached the gates he cried, "Open the gates of the Temple for me, I will go in to thank the LORD" (Vs. 19). Then he added, "These are the gates of the Lord, only righteous people enter through them" (Vs. 20).[377] David wanted all who fought with him to now worship with him.

David was anointed king when he was 16 years old. That was 14 years before. Everyone had rejected David. So now as king, he sang, "The stone which the builders rejected has now become the cornerstone." He knew the cornerstone is the most important foundation in the wall. All the other stones rest on it and David knew the stability of the kingdom rested on him. And David realized his strength was in God.

David sang to God, "You have accomplished this great thing and it is marvelous to see."

Finally David prayed as he entered Jerusalem, "This is the day the Lord has made, I will rejoice in it and be very happy."[264]

Talk About the Psalm: What did you learn about the psalm writer in this story? What did you learn about God?

Psalm 118: Read this week's psalm in your Bible together. Choose a verse to read aloud as a prayer.

Prayer: Thank You, God, for the psalm prayers in the Bible. Thank You for teaching us about You and about how to pray. In Jesus' name, Amen.

HEROD ATTACKS

Scripture: Acts 12:1–5, 20–24
Place: Jerusalem
Time: 35 AD

❝This is terrible!" Peter said. "Just when things are getting peaceful, the evil one is at it again. This time it is coming through Herod. That false king! The Romans put him in power. Now he has KILLED James!"[349] Peter, James and John were best of friends. They grew up in the same town. Jesus called them (and Peter's brother Andrew) to follow Him. All of them had been with Jesus from the beginning! It was a painful blow to God's family!

Saul HAD been persecuting God's family, but now he was following Jesus! So after a short time of peace, Herod had started in on them. He was not really a king, but he called himself one. He lived in Caesarea during the summer, where Cornelius lived. Herod had Jesus killed—and now, he was trying to kill Jesus' followers! He could see that this made the religious leaders happy. And the more they liked him, the more power HE had.

www.thefamilyprayerbible.com

Now, it was about a year after Jesus had died and risen to life again. Herod had decided to arrest and kill James[197] to try to make everyone afraid of him. Then, he was going to arrest Peter. Herod wanted to put Peter on trial and kill him at Passover,[334] like Jesus had been killed! Herod was sure that would put an end to this great movement of people who followed Jesus. He thought that killing people would stop God—and that was just foolish!

Herod thought HE was in charge. Herod did not understand that God is in control and God always has the final say! Later that year, he was back in Caesarea when people from the northern part of his district were fighting with him about their food supply. So some of them came down to Caesarea to talk with Herod.

Herod appeared before this group of people in his "kingly" crown and his robes. The people, of course, wanted to flatter him. They needed Herod's help.

So after he spoke, they shouted, "This is the voice of a god, not the voice of a man!"[113]

Herod WAS very flattered. He thought it was right that they called him a god. BUT GOD did not think so. And so, while Herod stood there, basking in their praise, God struck him with a disease. Herod's insides were filled with worms and he DIED.[267]

Herod could have said, "Oh, I'm not a god. God is MUCH more important than I am." But he didn't. He accepted their worship[99] as if he were REALLY a god. God knew his heart and God said, "That's enough." And that was the end of Herod, the false king.

Talk About the Story: Who was killed by Herod? Why did Herod do this? What did people say about Herod just before he died? Why is it important to give God praise?

Scripture: "'Be still, and know that I *am* God; I will be exalted among the nations, I will be exalted in the earth!'" Psalm 46:10

Family Time: What does the word "exalted" mean? What are ways that we can praise God? Tell some reasons we can praise God. Then do it in prayer or song!

Prayer: Dear Lord, we agree that You are the King over all kings. We praise You and thank You for loving us and for always taking care of us! In Jesus' name, Amen.

A DREAMY WALK

Scripture: Acts 12:3–12
Place: Jerusalem
Time: 35 AD

Peter sat in the dungeon, chained to two strong soldiers. But he wasn't weeping or worrying—no, Peter was ASLEEP! He snored gently, relaxed and at peace in the hard, cold stone cell.

Peter had been arrested by Herod, and was going to be put on trial.[334] But Peter knew something that Herod didn't—he knew that God's family was praying for him with everything they had![87] So Peter didn't see any point in staying awake and worrying. Even chained to two soldiers, with two more outside the door to his cell, Peter saw no reason to worry. God had opened the doors of prisons before; He could do it again!

As Peter slept and the family of God prayed, something DID happen! God sent an angel. Suddenly, there was LIGHT in Peter's cell. But it didn't wake Peter— he slept on! So the angel shook him to wake him. Peter opened his eyes. He could see that an ANGEL was standing beside him![14]

"Get up," said the angel. WHAT? Peter was chained to TWO strong guards! How could he DO that? As soon as Peter began to move, the chains that held him fell off![109] And the CLANK didn't even bother the guards—they stayed soundly asleep!

"Get your clothes on," said the angel, "and don't forget your shoes."[207] Peter got up and did as the angel told him. He really thought that he was dreaming— after all, he HAD been asleep and it would be natural to dream about getting out of the jail! Peter pulled his cloak around him and slipped on his sandals.

The angel led Peter through the first door to the cell. Then they walked through the second door as it opened. They walked out of the building—but the huge iron gate stood between them and the street outside. Peter watched as the big iron gate swung open. Peter and the angel walked right through! He was still thinking this was a dream.

Peter began to walk down the street beside the angel when the angel disappeared.[466] Now Peter stood in the street outside the prison, in the middle of the night—alone! He shook his head hard. *Wait*, he thought. *I'm NOT dreaming. I'm NOT asleep! This is really HAPPENING! I am OUT OF THE JAIL! And there is NO one following me. WOW! Hallelujah! Thank You, Lord Jesus! Glory and praise to YOUR Name!*

Peter turned around and around to see where he was and whether anyone else was on the street. Everything was quiet. Once again, Herod thought he could STOP God's family, but God is greater than any man, no matter who he is. God is the One True King. And in His kingdom, ANYTHING is possible. He is stronger than anything or anyone![109]

Talk About the Story: Where was Peter? Who was beside him? Who had Peter arrested? What did Peter think was happening when the angel took him out of the prison?

Scripture: "Behold, I am the LORD, THE GOD OF ALL FLESH. IS THERE ANYTHING TOO HARD FOR ME?" Jeremiah 32:27

Family Time: What is the hardest thing you have ever had to do? What's something even harder than that? What is the biggest problem your family can think of? Tell what God says about hard things to do. Then pray. Invite Him to do what He wants to do in at least one impossible situation you thought of!

Prayer: Dear Lord, You are the King of all kings. We know that nothing is too hard for You. We are glad we can ask You to do things that seem impossible to us! In Jesus' name, Amen.

PRAYER MEETING SHOCKER

Scripture: Acts 12:11–19
Place: Jerusalem
Time: 35 AD

Rhoda's heart was heavy with sadness. People filled Mary's house wall to wall, but this was not a party. It was a prayer meeting! Some people stood praying with their hands upraised; others bowed down as they prayed. Some were kneeling. A few were face down on the floor. But no matter what, EVERYONE was praying! A few were weeping quietly. Peter had been arrested! And it seemed as if Herod, that false king, was going to KILL Peter just as he had killed James, their beloved leader.

Rhoda was a servant of Mary, the lady who owned the house. She was still a girl but she loved Jesus. And she knew that this prayer was serious business. These people who loved Peter KNEW that God could stop Herod's evil plan. They KNEW that nothing is too hard for God. So they prayed. They asked. They believed that God WOULD do something, and they began to thank Him for what He was going to do!

Just then, Rhoda heard a noise outside the gate. She walked out to see what was making that little *knock, knock* noise. Perhaps it was an animal. She got closer to the gate and heard the noise again—no, it was not an animal. Someone was knocking softly on the gate, in the middle of the night!

Rhoda slid back the little door in the gate to look out—and then, she gasped! It was PETER. He was standing outside the gate! Peter had somehow gotten out of the prison! Rhoda was so excited that she forgot to open the gate and let Peter inside![213]

Instead, Rhoda ran back into the house and clapped her hands. "Everyone! Listen," she said. "Peter is outside! He's at the gate!"[517]

The people in the house looked at Rhoda with their mouths open. PETER? How could that be? "You've lost your mind, girl!" said one.[504]

"No, no! It is true! Peter is outside the gate!" she insisted.

Someone else said, "Maybe they've already killed him and it's his spirit."

"NO!" said Rhoda. "PETER is outside!"

Meanwhile, Peter was still knocking—a little louder now! He was beginning to think that Rhoda was not going to come back and open the gate!

There was only one way to find out if Peter was really there—so Rhoda ran back out to the gate. She opened it and brought Peter inside! And even though they had been praying to God to get Peter out of jail, all of the people at the prayer meeting were shocked and amazed.[470] God HAD listened. He had freed Peter from the prison!

Peter told his friends the whole story of how the angel had come and walked him out of the prison cell and out into the street! Then he said, "Be sure to tell this to James, the brother of our Lord Jesus." Then Peter went back out into the night to stay in a secret place where Herod would not find him![142]

As dawn broke the next morning, the guards found empty chains. But they did not find Peter![105] Herod was furious! His plan was ruined—but God's plan was going along just the way God intended!

Talk About the Story: Who was at the gate of Mary's house? Why did Rhoda not open the gate at first? What did people say when she told them Peter was outside? What did God do when His people prayed?

Scripture: "Rejoicing in hope, patient in tribulation, continuing steadfastly in prayer." Romans 12:12

Family Time: When we have hope, it makes us glad. What are ways we can be more "steadfast" in our prayers? Try a new way to pray today!

Prayer: Dear Lord, thank You for loving us. We are glad to be part of Your family. Knowing You gives us hope and makes us glad! In Jesus' name, Amen.

CHAPTER 21

PAUL'S MINISTRY

The apostle Paul identifies himself as a slave of Christ Jesus (Romans 1:1), and twice refers to himself as an apostle to the Gentiles (Romans 11:13; 15:15–20). Paul's Hebrew name was Saul, and his Roman-Greek name was Paul. He probably had both names from childhood since he was born a Roman citizen (Acts 22:28) of Jewish parents (Acts 23:6; Phil 3:5). Paul was probably born about 10 years after the birth of Jesus, in the city of Tarsus in Cilicia (modern southeastern Turkey; Acts 22:3). He is called a "young man" about AD 34 (Acts 7:58), and he called himself an aged man about AD 61 (Phlm 9).

Paul's father was apparently a merchant and a native of Israel. He was a Roman citizen (Acts 22:28) and a strict Pharisee (Acts 23:6). Paul had at least one sister and a nephew, who lived in Jerusalem (Acts 23:16). He probably never got married since he urged unmarried men and widows to "remain [single] as I am" (1 Cor 7:7–9; 9:5).

Paul learned the trade of tent making as a youth. He may have attended university in Tarsus, but he stated in Acts 22:3 that he was brought up in Jerusalem. He studied under Gamaliel, one of the most famous Jewish rabbis at Jerusalem (Acts 22:3).

Paul became a leader in the persecution of the Christian church soon after its birth (Acts 8:3; Phil 3:6; 1 Tim 1:13). His conversion to Christ came at the height of his opposition to the church while he was on his way to Damascus to arrest Christian Jews (Acts 9:1–18). Afterwards, Paul immediately became an enthusiastic witness for Christ.

Paul's principal achievements were twofold: (1) he wrote 13 books of the New Testament, which are a primary source of theological information; and (2) he was the principal leader in extending the church into Asia Minor and Greece, becoming known as the premier apostle to the Gentiles.

Paul was a unique Christian leader, a fearless champion and exponent of Christianity, a genius of church planting and discipleship, and the most influential missionary, preacher, and teacher of the early church.

The book of Acts ends by describing Paul's first imprisonment in Rome. He was apparently released from this incarceration in about AD 62 and conducted a vigorous ministry in Crete, Asia (the province), Macedonia, and perhaps Spain. During Nero's persecution (c. AD 64–68), Paul was again arrested and put in a Roman prison. This time there was no hope of release (2 Tim 4:6). According to later church writers, he was beheaded (probably AD 66–67).

SAUL AND BARNABAS SENT

Scripture: Acts 13:1–5
Place: Antioch to Cyprus
Time: 47 AD

Saul's stomach rumbled and grumbled just a little. He stood and stretched, then took a drink of water and went for a short walk. Barnabas, too, was beside him and took a break before he settled back down to pray. The leadership team of the church at Antioch was doing something called fasting.[161] That means they didn't eat for a time. Instead, they spent that time praying. They did this from time to time, just to keep their hearts and minds sensitive to what God wanted them to do. Today, they were waiting for God to give them directions on what to do next. So they fasted, and prayed, and waited. It was far better than acting WITHOUT asking God what to do!

Saul and Barnabas had been in Antioch for at least a year, and there were now five teachers and prophets who led the church. One was Simeon Niger, from Africa. Lucius was Roman, from the island of Cyrene. Manaen had been raised with Herod. They had been boys together! Along with Saul, the well-educated Jew from nearby Tarsus, and Barnabas, a wealthy man from Cyprus, these five teachers were all very different! They came from different places and had different gifts. This was God's good plan, since Antioch was a crossroads for many different kinds of people. It was also one of the few places outside of Israel where Jewish settlers were treated well. It was an important Roman city, where officials and governors lived.

While these men fasted and prayed and waited, God's Holy Spirit spoke! He said to them, "Send Barnabas and Saul to a special job for which I am calling them."[199] So the men prayed and fasted and waited some more. They wanted to obey God fully and do whatever He asked of them. So they spent time asking God to tell them—and they listened and obeyed!

Then they laid their hands on Saul's and Barnabas' heads and prayed over them before they sent Saul and Barnabas to the seaport town of Seleucia.[224] Saul and Barnabas took John Mark with them—he could help take care of things that needed to be done.

Once they arrived in Seleucia, they must have fasted and prayed some more. Then the Holy Spirit told them to sail to the island of Cyprus, a fairly large island in the Mediterranean Sea. This was where Barnabas was from originally, although later he had lived in Israel.

When they landed, they were in a city that had a Jewish synagogue. They knew what God wanted them to do. So they went right to the synagogue. They began to preach about Jesus to the Jews who were gathered there![145] The first missionaries in history had been sent out, and they did not waste any time. They wanted to preach about Jesus to MORE people!

Talk About the Story: How many teachers were there in Antioch? What is fasting? Why is it something important to do? Who did Saul and Barnabas take with them? Where did they go when they landed on the island of Cyprus?

Scripture: "(Be) praying always with all prayer and supplication in the Spirit." Ephesians 6:18

Family Time: What makes a person a missionary? How is being a missionary different from just living in another country? What makes your family missionaries? How do you all fulfill that job God gave you?

Prayer: Dear Lord, thank You that You want us to pray to You and that You have important things to tell us. Please help us learn to listen for what You want us to do, as Saul and Barnabas did! In Jesus' name, Amen.

SAUL AND BARNABAS MEET A MAGICIAN

Scripture: Acts 13:4–12
Place: Cyprus
Time: 48 AD

Saul pointed at the man standing in front of him. "YOU!" he said. "You are opposing God,[84] you son of the devil! And now, God is going to stop you. You will be blind!"[467] The man stepped back, still proud—thinking that this little man could not do anything to him! But then, the man's face changed. He knew that what Saul (now called Paul) had spoken truth. Things were getting dark. He could NOT see! He began to reach out his hands, trying to find his way. He was BLIND!

Saul and Barnabas had been preaching on the island of Cyprus. Many people had heard the good news about Jesus and had joined God's family! God's church was growing and growing there! Now they were in the home of Sergius Paulus, the Roman governor. Sergius Paulus was a man who everyone thought was very smart and wise. He had actually invited Paul and Barnabas to his home to tell him about the good news they had been spreading! But as smart as people thought Sergius was, he had a magician named Elymas as one of his counselors or advisors. Elymas was around all of the time—and because Elymas really worked for the devil, he wanted to keep the governor from hearing the truth about Jesus. So when Sergius had invited Paul and Barnabas to come to his house and talk with him, Elymas made sure he was right there!

Elymas did everything he could think of to make it hard for Paul and Barnabas to have a conversation with the governor. It wasn't that they didn't know what to say. It was that Elymas was trying to keep them from telling the governor about Jesus! Elymas kept interrupting. He kept saying things to try to keep the governor from understanding. It was hard to tell Sergius anything! Elymas' actions were getting stranger and stranger! That's when Paul got serious and told Elymas that he would be blind. It was important that Governor Sergius understand who Jesus is and what He did so that every person, even a Roman governor, could be part of God's family and live with God forever!

As Elymas groped around the room, trying to find someone to lead him, Governor Sergius could see that Paul's words were true. He was absolutely amazed to see this happen right in front of him. There was no doubt in his mind that God Himself had stopped Elymas' interruptions! He realized that God's power is greater than anything the devil can do! And the governor chose to ask God's forgiveness for his sin. He chose to believe in Jesus—and became part of God's family![263] God can use even the things the devil tries to do for His glory and to show people that He is the one, true God—Father, Son and Holy Spirit!

Talk About the Story: What island were Paul and Barnabas on? Who invited them to his house to tell about Jesus? Who tried to stop them? What happened to Elymas? What did this show the governor?

Scripture: "The Son of God was manifested, that He might destroy the works of the devil." 1 John 3:8

Family Time: What is something that reminds you of how powerful God is? What is something that helps you to believe in Jesus? How did Jesus stop the devil's works?

Prayer: Dear Lord, we are glad that You love EVERY person. Please help us to listen to You, and then to be brave and obedient like Paul was. We want to help people become part of your family! In Jesus' name, Amen.

WORK FROM CYPRUS

Scripture: Acts 13:13–52
Place: Cyprus to Turkey
Time: 48 AD

S aul and Barnabas stood on the deck of the ship, watching as the coastland came closer and closer. They were a little excited. They were going to go a place they had never been! They about to travel inland to a place called Antioch of Pisidia. This city was FAR from Antioch on the coast of the Mediterranean. That's where they had preached and taught before God sent them to Cyprus. Antioch of Pisidia was in what is now Turkey. WHY were they going there? Because this is where God had told them to go—and they had learned that when God's Spirit speaks, the best thing to do is to obey!

Finally they arrived in the city where they were supposed to go. There was a synagogue in the city, so there were many Jews in that area. On the first Saturday, Paul and Barnabas joined in with the rest of the Jewish worshipers. Then the leader of the synagogue asked Paul, "Would you like to say something to encourage the congregation?"[145] OF COURSE Paul had something to say!

Paul began by telling the story of the Jewish people all through the Old Testament days. Then he began to tell about John the Baptist, and how Jesus showed everyone in Jerusalem that He is God's Son.[263] He told how Jesus died on the cross and then how He rose from the dead,[405] as King David had predicted. Paul finally said, "There is forgiveness of sin in Jesus. So pay good attention to what I'm telling you, because God is doing SUCH amazing things, you would not believe them if I told you!"

Paul and Barnabas then planned to leave, but many people wanted to hear more! Some of them believed already in Jesus! So they asked Paul and Barnabas to come back the next Saturday so that everyone could hear more![292]

The next Saturday, just about everyone in town showed up at the synagogue! But the Jewish leaders in town were getting nervous about all these people following Jesus.[334] It could upset their whole lives if they weren't in charge anymore! So they began to argue with Paul and Barnabas.

Paul said, "Listen. God has already said that He is showing His salvation to EVERYONE, not just to Jews." This made the non-Jews very happy! Many of them believed and were full of joy and the Holy Spirit. But the religious leaders got even MORE upset! So they got some people to have Paul and Barnabas thrown out of town![349]

Paul and Barnabas weren't worried. They shook off the dust of that city from their feet and were moving on to the next adventure. They had obeyed God's Spirit and many people had joyfully joined God's family![224] Paul and Barnabas had done what God had wanted them to do, and they could trust God to do the rest!

Talk About the Story: Where did Paul and Barnabas go? What kind of meeting did Paul speak at? Why do you think the leaders did not like for people to follow Jesus? For how many kinds of people did Jesus die?

Scripture: "I will also give You (Jesus) as a light to the Gentiles, that You should be My salvation to the ends of the earth." Isaiah 49:6

Family Time: See if you can go through the letters of the alphabet and name a people group, tribe or country that begins with each letter. Which ones does God love? What's a way your family can share God's good news with one of those people groups?

Prayer: Dear Lord, thank You for filling us with Your joy when we obey Your words. We want to do what pleases Jesus! In His name, Amen.

PSALM 121

A PSALM OF ASCENT

In Psalm 120, the obedient believer was getting ready to travel up to Jerusalem to worship God. In his home he faced danger, thieves, and neighbors who gossiped and slandered him.

Now in Psalm 121, the believer is leaving his home and climbing the mountain to the house of God in Jerusalem. It's on Mount Zion, the top of many mountains. He asked about looking for help to the mountains. So the travelers prays,

> *"I will lift up my eyes to the hills,*[183]
> *From where my help comes?"*

Some travelers may have thought they would receive help by just leaving the valley and hiding away in the mountains. But the Psalmist asked if his help came from the mountains. But he quickly realized that help doesn't come from a place, it comes from a person.

> *"My help comes from the Lord*
> *He made heaven and earth."*

Many warriors living in tents, facing an enemy have prayed this Psalm. Therefore it is sometimes called "Soldier's Psalm."

> *"He will not let your foot stumble,*
> *The One watching over Israel will not sleep.*
> *He will not get tired or slumber."*
> *The Lord, will watch over you.*
> *He will stand at your right hand to protect you."*

Help does not come from the mountains. Rather look to the Lord because He sees everything. He does not sleep. He comes to you in your hour of trouble. He can protect you when you sleep.

Many are afraid of the dark night. Maybe it's because they can't see what's hidden in dark places. People feel safe when they can see everything around them. God's children should realize God sees them when they sleep. He sees all dangers—possible and actual. The Psalmist prayed,

> *"The Lord Himself will watch over you,*[387]
> *He stands over you for protection*
> *The sun cannot hurt you in the day,*
> *Evil will not attack you when the moon is out."*

Help comes to God's children only from above. As travelers left home to travel to Jerusalem, they might be afraid of highway robbers, or wild animals, or any other danger. But they should not be afraid. Their protection is not hiding in the mountains, so don't lift your eyes to be safe in the hills. Your help comes from God.

> *"The Lord will protect me from all dangers.*
> *He will preserve me from evil.*[109]
> *The Lord will watch over me,*
> *As I go out and as I go in,*
> *Both now and forever more" (Vss. 7-8).*

Talk About the Psalm: What did you learn about the psalm writer in this story? What did you learn about God?

Psalm 121: Read this week's psalm in your Bible together. Choose a verse to read aloud as a prayer.

Prayer: Thank You, God, for the psalm prayers in the Bible. Thank You for teaching us about You and about how to pray. In Jesus' name, Amen.

PAUL BECOMES THE LEADER

Scripture: Acts 14:1–7
Place: Iconium
Time: 48 AD

Saul and Barnabas traveled all over, telling people about Jesus. But as they talked to more and more people who were not Jews, Saul stopped using his Jewish name, Saul. He became known by his Roman name, Paul. And Paul was becoming known as a leader in the Church.

Paul and Barnabas seemed to have reasons to be afraid wherever they went—and this time, they had a good reason to be afraid. People were out to stone them. That means these people wanted to throw rocks at them until they died! WHAT had they done in Iconium to cause people to be so mean? They were telling about God's love!

Paul and Barnabas had come to Iconium and gone right to the Jewish synagogue again. They preached, and told the good news of God's love in Jesus. And many people became followers of Jesus![145] In fact, there were so many that the

religious leaders who did NOT believe in Jesus got some of the Gentiles to make trouble for Paul and Barnabas![349] These leaders thought that maybe that would stop them.

But if we know anything about Paul and Barnabas, we know that they had learned how to obey God's Spirit. They had learned they could trust God and not to be afraid. So when these angry people began to argue with them and threaten them, they stayed right where they were. God was the One who would tell them when it was time to leave and not anyone else! They kept right on telling people the good news of God's love—and to make sure that the people noticed that what they said was true, God did many miracles and amazing things among these people![467] They could hear the truth. And they could see the truth,[173] too!

Pretty soon, everyone in Iconium had a very strong opinion about Paul and Barnabas. Some people thought they came from God and were telling the truth. Others were angry that God's love and power were making such a change in their city. They did not like that!

So, people in Iconium were either on the side of Paul and Barnabas, or on the side of the Jewish leaders.[349] And the people who were on the side of the religious leaders had an idea. They thought that if they could get rid of Paul and Barnabas once and for all, that would end the argument! (They forgot that many people had already decided to follow Jesus in their city, it seems!) So they were making plans to get Paul and Barnabas out to a safe place.

But of course, God made sure that His friends Paul and Barnabas heard about this plot.[142] They were not afraid, but they knew God had shown them this so they could be safe. They simply left town before anyone could hurt them, and moved on to Lystra and Derbe, which were pretty far away from Iconium. They were not afraid. God was with them, even when things seemed to be dangerous. God is always in charge!

Talk About the Story: Where did Paul and Barnabas go to tell about Jesus? What happened in the city of Iconium? Why do you think Paul and Barnabas were not afraid?

Scripture: "God is our refuge and strength, a very present help in trouble. Therefore we will not fear." Psalm 46:1–2

Family Time: What are some times we are afraid? Why can we trust God in those times? Take time today to make a list of reasons to thank God for His care in different situations.

Prayer: Dear Lord, thank You for giving Paul and Barnabas courage. Please help us to have courage and be brave too. We want to tell people about Jesus! In His name, Amen.

MAN AT LYSTRA

Scripture: Acts 14:8–15
Place: Lystra
Time: 48 AD
Time: Later in the day, Sunday, April 9

As Paul spoke, his eyes scanned the crowd. There were many people here at the city gate who were listening.[435] He could see that one man was listening very closely—he was a man who could not walk. Then God's Spirit told Paul that this man had the faith to be healed. Paul pointed at the man. "Stand up on your feet!"[466] he said in a loud, commanding voice.

The man looked back at Paul. He must have been startled that Paul was talking just to HIM. Suddenly, the man jumped to his feet! He COULD stand! He began to walk. He could walk! This man had never been able to walk, and of course everyone knew him as the man who sat and begged at the city gate because he couldn't walk. So everyone realized that they had just seen a miracle! The people

www.thefamilyprayerbible.com

all began shouting in their own language! But these people were NOT praising God—they were shouting, "The gods have come down to us, dressed like men!"

You see, these people had an old story in their minds that kept them from understanding! The story went like this: Long ago, Zeus and Hermes, two Greek gods, had come to Lystra. No one noticed them or paid them any honor except a poor elderly couple who invited them to eat. This made the gods angry, and they flooded the valley where Lystra was, but saved the old couple and made their shack into a temple.

Of course, this was just a story, but it was the reason these people were suddenly calling Barnabas Zeus and Paul Hermes! They thought the gods had come again! So these people wanted to be sure to show them great honor! They were running around yelling, and all very excited!

But since Paul and Barnabas did not speak the local language, they were not sure what was going on. Then the priest of Jupiter came with flowers for them, and bulls to be sacrificed to them![113]

Wait a minute! WHAT are these people doing? Paul and Barnabas wondered. But when they realized what these people wanted to do, they tore their clothes to show this made them very sad. They ran from the place where they'd been in the center of a big crowd, and instead ran into the crowd! They did NOT want people worshiping them!

They shouted as they ran, "Friends! Why are you doing this? We are men, humans just like you! We are here to tell you to stop worshiping false gods—the only One to worship is the God who made the heavens and the earth!"[444]

Talk About the Story: Who was healed? What was wrong with him? What did Paul say to him? What did the people of Lystra call Paul and Barnabas? Why did they want to worship Paul and Barnabas? How did this make Paul and Barnabas feel?

Scripture: "(We) preach to you that you should turn from these useless things to the living God, who made the heaven, the earth, the sea, and all things that are in them." Acts 14:8

Family Time: What are some things you know about God? About Jesus? If you had been with Paul and Barnabas hat would you have told the people of Lystra?

Prayer: Dear Lord, we are glad that You are the one, true God. We want to honor You because You are more important than anyone. Thank You for helping us to tell others true things about You!
Amen.

EXCITEMENT TO ANGER

Scripture: Acts 14:15–26
Place: Lystra to Antioch
Time: 48 AD

Paul and Barnabas were shouting as loud as they could, trying to get the attention of the people. The crowd was running in every direction, shouting. They were ALL very excited! But Paul and Barnabas realized that these people thought they were GODS! These people had it ALL WRONG! And here they Paul and Silas had come to tell these people about the One, true God, and the good news about Jesus![444]

Paul shouted, "Friends! We are people! Human beings! We are not gods! We have come to tell you that you do not have to worship false gods. The God who made everything wants you to know HIM!"

People began to stop their running around to listen. Since Paul was not speaking their first language, they had to listen carefully. Paul went on. "The God who

made the world—the sky and the sea, and everything and everyone who lives in it[93]—HE is the One we should worship! He has always sent us the rain and sun. He has always shown us His love and care. Until now, He has waited to send His Son. We have come to tell you the good news about Him!"

But just about the time that the people started to understand what Paul was saying and think about the God who made them, some of the people who had wanted to KILL Paul showed up at the edge of the crowd. They could see that this huge crowd was already excited and a little confused. So they began to yell and shout also![349]

"Don't listen to this man. He is evil. He has made trouble everywhere he goes. You should STONE him. He must die!" Those were the kinds of things these enemies of Paul began to yell, picking up stones to throw at Paul!

The people in the crowd forgot ALL ABOUT the miracle they had seen. They forgot completely that they had watched as God healed a lame man they all knew. He was standing right in front of them! Instead, they listened to the enemies of Paul. They began to scowl and reach for rocks, too. Soon, many people in the crowd who had been praising Paul and calling him a god were throwing ROCKS at him!

The people threw rocks at Paul until he fell to the ground. They thought he was dead. So they dragged him outside the gate to the city and left him there! But Barnabas and the other followers of Jesus went out to where Paul was. They gathered around him and prayed—and as they stood there, Paul got up and went back into town with them.[214] He stayed a while, then he and Barnabas traveled back through all of the places where they had preached and people had believed in Jesus. They finally traveled all the way back to Antioch, where they had started!

Talk About the Story: Why were these people excited? What had God done there? What did Paul tell them about the One, true God? When Paul's enemies came, what did they do? What did God do when Paul's friends prayed?

Scripture: "For You have delivered my soul from death, my eyes from tears, and my feet from falling. I will walk before the Lord in the land of the living." Psalm 116:8–9

Family Time: When it looked like Paul was dead, what happened? When people try to hurt us, what can we remember? What are some times we know God has saved our lives or protected us?

Prayer: Dear Lord, thank You that You are our protector. Thank You that we can trust You to take care of us in scary times. We love You. In Jesus' name, Amen.

NEW DIRECTIONS

Scripture: Acts 14:27—15:35
Place: Antioch to Jerusalem
Time: 48 AD

Paul and Barnabas had come "home" to Antioch. Now, they were telling their beloved family there all about the wild adventures God had taken them on! They told about all the miracles God had done and about all of the people who now believed in Jesus. Then they told how God had helped them know that He loves everyone and wants His good news to go to every person! God had shown them that they needed to tell all people, not just Jews, about Jesus.[478]

The church family at Antioch was excited and happy to hear about this! But then, some men came from Jerusalem. They told everyone at the Antioch church, "You can't be part of God's family unless you follow the rules Moses gave to the Jews."[277]

WELL! That was a shock! Here all of these people had been full of joy, growing in God's family, telling everyone in Antioch about God's good news . . . and

www.thefamilyprayerbible.com

now, these men said they were not part of God's family? Joy turned to doubt and sadness and worry!

But Paul and Barnabas stepped forward. They said, "You are wrong to tell people this. This is your own idea. It did NOT come from God! God has sent His Holy Spirit to ALL of us, even the Gentiles. We have seen this with our own eyes!"

The men from Israel argued and argued with Paul and Barnabas.[121] So Paul and Barnabas decided they would go to Jerusalem and tell what God had been doing in Antioch and in many other places they had gone![126] They would settle this once and for all!

When they arrived in Jerusalem, God's Jerusalem family welcomed them! That is, until Paul and Barnabas told how God was bringing Gentiles into His family![478] That's when those men began to argue again. They said that everyone had to live by Jewish law to be part of God's family![277] But Peter stood up. He reminded everyone about how God had sent him to Cornelius,[145] the Roman officer. He reminded them that NO ONE had been saved or put into God's family because of anything they had done. "God has forgiven us ALL by faith in Jesus,"[383] he said. "Why tell people to keep rules that we Jews never were able to keep before we joined God's family?"

James, the brother of Jesus, was in charge of the meeting of these leaders. So James gave some simple rules: Don't eat things offered to idols or false gods. Don't have sex outside of marriage. Don't eat meat from animals that are strangled, or eat blood."[430] Those simple things were enough to show that people in God's family were different from the people around them.[10] So the leaders sent letters and messengers to every church. Instead of trying to make everyone live like they were Jews, they wanted everyone who had followed Jesus to be full of the joy of God's Holy Spirit and grow in God's family!

Talk About the Story: Who came to the church at Antioch? What did the men from Israel say? How did people feel about this? Where did Paul and Barnabas go? What did the church's leaders decide?

Scripture: "God . . . made no distinction between us and them, purifying their hearts by faith." Acts 15:8–9

Family Time: If God loves everyone, then who are people we should love? When we trust Jesus as our Savior, what does God say about us? What are ways we can grow in God's family?

Prayer: Dear God, we are glad that You sent Jesus. Thank You that we don't have to become Jews to be part of Your family. Thank You for loving us! In Jesus' name, Amen.

JAMES WRITES A LETTER

Scripture: James 1:12
Place: Written from Jerusalem
Time: 60 AD

How would you like to be the younger brother of Jesus? We don't know how we might have acted around Jesus, but James never believed in Jesus, his older brother, when he was growing up. The Bible tells us that even Jesus' own brothers didn't believe He was the Messiah.[504]

But here we have a letter from Jesus' little brother. James probably became a believer when Jesus appeared to him after He had died and risen again. "He (Jesus) was seen by James" (1 Corinthians 15:7).[405] Many of the early church references call him "James the Just," meaning he was honest and fair. He had strong leadership qualities, and soon became one of the leaders of the church in

www.thefamilyprayerbible.com

Jerusalem, not only because of his connection to Jesus, but also because he was trusted. When Paul returned to Jerusalem from Damascus, one of the few he saw was "James, the Lord's brother."

An argument had broken out among Christians about whether they should make all Gentiles be circumcised to get saved. James who summarized the leaders' teaching that salvation is by grace. He wrote their conclusions down and sent out a letter that was read in all the churches. But this letter was not printed in our Bibles.

Later, when James heard that believers were being persecuted for their faith, he wrote the book that bears his name.

He began, "James a servant of God and of the Lord Jesus Christ, to the twelve tribes scattered abroad,"[431] which meant that this letter would also go from church to church to be read in many places.

This letter was among the first books written in the New Testament, perhaps as early as 45 A. D. James calls the people he writes to as "twelve tribes" and describes them as worshiping in synagogues. Only later did Christians stop meeting in Jewish synagogues.

It may also have been that those who received this letter were those who had come to Jerusalem as Jews for the feast of Passover or Pentecost. When they got converted they probably were influenced by James' teaching. It is only natural for them to write to him and for him to answer.

James wrote in short proverbs, such as: An indecisive man is unstable in all his ways[127;] man's anger does not accomplish God's righteousness; resist the devil, and he will flee from you;[549] friendship with the world is hostility toward God[537]; when we put bits into the mouths of horses to make them obey us, we also guide the whole animal.

James had good things to teach us about living the faith we say we have in Jesus!

Talk About the Story: Who was James' older brother? Why was James a leader? What did James write about?

Scripture: "For as the body without the spirit is dead, so faith without works is dead also." James 2:26

Family Time: What kinds of things does a dead person do? What are ways that we show we are alive in Jesus?

Prayer: Father, please help us to live the faith we say we have. We know that if we don't act, we can't say we have faith. In Jesus' name, Amen.

A LETTER TO THE GALATIANS

Scripture: Galatians 5:18–25
Place: Possibly Antioch in Syria
Time: 50 AD

On Paul and Barnabas' first missionary journey through Galatia (now in Turkey), they were followed by a group of Jews who argued with Paul. They lied about him, chased him from place to place, and finally got a mob to stone him until they thought he was dead. But God raised Paul up and he kept on spreading the good news that Jesus had died to pay for sin, and that people only needed Jesus to be saved—nothing else!

So when Paul heard that his dear friends in Galatia had decided they needed to add Jewish law to their belief in Christ, it made Paul angry! He wanted to see this lie STOPPED NOW![287]

These Jews who hated Paul's message of grace had taught the Galatians that they had to obey Jewish law in order to be saved. They tried to make people think that Paul was not telling the truth. So Paul writes with white hot zeal against the

www.thefamilyprayerbible.com

men he called "Judaizers," who wanted everyone to become a Jew in order to follow Jesus.

Paul's letter began, "From Paul, an apostle—not made an apostle by human decision, but an apostle through Jesus Christ and God the Father who raised Him from the dead."[405]

This letter is called the "Magna Carta of Christian liberty." It says we are saved by grace alone, through faith alone, in Christ alone. Nothing we can do—including obeying Jewish law—can save us.

This letter is divided into three parts. In the first part, Paul describes his first time in Jerusalem persecuting Christians, his second visit after he met Jesus, then how he had rebuked Peter for pretending to keep the law when it was not needed. Paul wrote, "My old self has been crucified with Christ. Now it is not me who lives, but Christ lives in me. So I live in this earthly body by trusting in Jesus, the Son of God. He loved me and gave himself for me."[96]

In the second part, Paul corrects the Galatians. He tells them how Abraham was saved by faith before there WAS a law. Then Paul compares Ishmael and Isaac, Abraham's two sons.

In the last part Paul says, "Stand firm in the freedom Christ gave us, to make us free."[177]

He points out if a person accepts keeping part of Jewish law in order to be saved, then that person must keep the whole law. People who trust Jewish law "have fallen from grace."[287] He tells them to walk in the Holy Spirit[441] and to show the fruits of the Spirit in their lives.[224] Then he tells them to love and serve one another.

Paul's simple formula for salvation is Christ's death, burial, and resurrection as payment for our sins. It is the only way to heaven. Salvation is by faith alone, in Christ alone, by grace alone.[416]

Talk About the Story: Who had chased Paul and lied about him? What had these people taught the church in Galatia? What does Paul say we need in order to be saved?

Scripture: "But if you are led by the Spirit, you are not under the law." Galatians 5:16

Family Time: Who is the Holy Spirit? What kinds of things does the Holy Spirit lead us to do? Why can we trust the Holy Spirit?

Prayer: Father, please help us to listen to Your Word and Your Spirit. Thank You that Jesus did everything to save us. We trust Him. Amen.

PSALM 122

TO BE SUNG WHILE GOING UP TO JERUSALEM

Abe and his wife were climbing up Mount Zion toward Jerusalem. It was spring and leaves filled the trees. Already some small green sprouts popped out of the ground. The farm fields were beginning to turn green.

They were climbing the road to Jerusalem to celebrate the feast of Passover. The couple walked over a small ridge and rejoiced to see the city of Jerusalem. Slowly they made their way to the walls of the city to enter the Temple courts. Abe began singing a Psalm.

"I was glad when they said to me,
Let us go into the House of the Lord.[183]
And now here we stand inside the gates of Jerusalem,
The eternal city where God dwells."

Just standing in God's city gave Abe great strength. It had been a tough winter on the farm. Some of his cattle died and there was a rumor of an invading tribe of nomads who would pillage their home. He repeated the next verse.

"Jerusalem is built to withstand dangers.
A strong city with walls that cannot be breached."

Abe felt safe in Jerusalem. No army could reach him there. He stood for a long while. It felt good to be in God's presence. There he was protected from all evil. When he looked around at the crowds surrounding him he sang,

"All God's people come here to worship,
And to give Him thanks for His protection.[541]
They came as God has told them come,
They do what the Lord tells them to do."

Abe felt deep gratitude for the peace he felt within its walls. He looked deep within his heart to thank God for the city and the house of God. Then he prayed,

> *"Pray for peace in Jerusalem,*
> *May all who love the Lord prosper.*[73]
> *May there be peace within these walls,*
> *May those who live here prosper.*
> *For my family and all who love God,*
> *I pray that Jerusalem will have peace."*

Abe realized it was one thing to enjoy physical protection that comes when the nation of Israel has peace. But it's another thing to have inward peace. That comes only when a person has lived for God, confessed their sins, and received forgiveness from God.

Abe rejoiced that Jerusalem was well protected by its walls. He looked toward the Temple sanctuary. It was there people find the real peace of God. He prayed,

> *"For the sake of ministry from your house O God,*[369]
> *I seek peace from you, and Jerusalem" (Vss. 8-9).*

Talk About the Psalm: What did you learn about the psalm writer in this story? What did you learn about God?

Psalm 122: Read this week's psalm in your Bible together. Choose a verse to read aloud as a prayer.

Prayer: Thank You, God, for the psalm prayers in the Bible. Thank You for teaching us about You and about how to pray. In Jesus' name, Amen.

PAUL CHOOSES SILAS

Scripture: Acts 15:22–41
Place: Antioch and beyond
Time: 50 AD

Paul and Barnabas were upset. They'd been the best of friends. They'd had hard times and good times and happy times and scary times together. But now, they were upset—and they were upset with EACH OTHER! They did NOT agree. And this disagreement was so sharp that they decided go two different ways![122] But God is with us even in hard times like this. God used this disagreement to send out twice as many missionaries as before!

This is what had happened. Paul and Barnabas had traveled back to Antioch with Silas and Judas,[145] two men from Jerusalem. The leaders had sent these two to help tell the church there about the meeting and the decisions the leaders had made. Everyone in Antioch was really glad to hear the good news of the simple things the leaders had decided. And they were glad when Silas decided to stay and teach there in their church![463]

But now Paul had said, "Let's go back and retrace our trip to the places where we preached. We can see how these churches are doing and can help them."[396] Barnabas thought this was a great idea! But Barnabas wanted to bring John Mark along. THAT was where the disagreement came. John Mark was Barnabas' relative. He may have come back with them from Jerusalem.

Paul said, "John Mark left us on our last trip. He went home halfway through.[287] I don't want to take him along!" But Barnabas believed in John Mark. He thought that John Mark would do well this time. Paul did not agree![122] He said, "If John Mark is going with you, then I won't go with you!"

So Barnabas and Paul went separate ways. Barnabas took John Mark with him, and they went back to Cyprus, the first place they'd gone on their first trip. They visited and took care of the churches. Then Paul chose Silas, the man from Jerusalem who had stayed in Antioch. They left together for Turkey and Syria—the places Paul and Barnabas had gone in the second part of their last trip. So really, twice as many people were now going back to help and encourage these churches![454]

And did Paul stay angry? Did he never talk to Barnabas again? Did everyone except Barnabas think John Mark was a problem? No. Later on, Paul was in prison. He wrote a letter to the church at Colosse and mentioned John Mark in the letter. It sounds as if John Mark was with Paul when he was writing. Then in his letter, Paul asks the Colossian church to welcome John Mark if he came to them.

Even when people in God's family disagree, they tell God their feelings. They forgive each other. And they look for ways God can bring good out of even the hard things like disagreements!

Talk About the Story: Who came to Antioch with Paul and Barnabas? Who stayed? Why did Barnabas and Paul disagree? What happened after they left with other helpers? How did God bring good out of this?

Scripture: "Be of the same mind toward one another. Do not set your mind on high things, but associate with the humble. Do not be wise in your own opinion." Romans 12:16

Family Time: Paul wrote the words of the verse above, later on. What do you think he learned about arguing? About forgiving? What are some things we can learn about getting along in our family from this verse?

Prayer: Dear Lord, thank You for bringing good things out of hard times. Please help us to keep unity and peace in our family. Help us to forgive each other because You forgave us in Jesus! In His name, Amen.

TIMOTHY JOINS PAUL

Scripture: Acts 16:1–4
Place: Derbe and Lystra
Time: 50 AD

Paul looked around, a little unsure of what might happen here! He was wondering if anyone recognized him. And he checked to be sure that no one was coming after him with a rock in their hand! You see, Paul and Silas were back in Lystra! This was the city where Paul had been stoned, dragged out of the city and left for dead!

But God had a gift for Paul and Silas. Even though things had been hard for Paul and Barnabas the first time they'd been there, God's family had grown there! There was a church in the city! And the people of this church wanted Paul and Silas to meet a young man named Timothy. The people in the church thought Timothy was a wonderful young man. Timothy was known and loved by the people of the church. He loved Jesus and wanted to learn all he could about Him. The church thought that Paul might want to mentor Timothy. Timothy's name means "precious" and over time, Timothy became very precious to Paul and Silas![478]

Paul and Silas also met Timothy's family. Timothy's mother was Jewish and she was a follower of Jesus, but his father was a Greek. Now in those days, Jewish people might look down on Timothy because he was half Jewish. But being half Jewish and half Greek—and ALL a follower of Jesus—made Timothy a perfect person to tell ANYONE the good news! He would be good at talking to both Jews and Gentiles, because he understood the cultures of both of his parents.

Timothy's mother and grandmother had taught him a lot about the Old Testament, and he was learning more and more about God's Holy Spirit and the work God was doing. God had already prepared Timothy through his family to do great things for Him!

Paul and Silas would be traveling a long way and through many adventures—and Paul invited Timothy to go along with them! Timothy was eager to join them, learn all he could from them about Jesus, and then become a teacher himself. Timothy traveled with Paul for a long time. He helped Paul in many situations, and was so close to Paul that he called Timothy "my son." He was even with Paul in prison, writing things down for him when Paul's eyesight got too bad to write on his own.

Timothy also was in charge of at least one church and often helped Paul as he preached, wrote and taught people.[204] Timothy became a precious gift to Paul over the years. So in this place where Paul had nearly been killed, God gave him a gift, a dear young friend who became like a son to him and carried on teaching and telling the good news of Jesus!

Talk About the Story: Where was Paul and Silas? What did the church in Lystra think of Timothy? What would Timothy do while he was with Paul and Silas? How did God prepare Timothy through his family?

Scripture: "They praised God. They said, 'So then, God has allowed even Gentiles to turn away from their sins. He did this so that they could live.'" Acts 11:18 (NIV)

Family Time: What are things about your family that people might think are surprising or different? How are these differences helping you to learn about Jesus? What things in your family are helping you grow and serve God? What are ways your family can help others know more about Jesus?

Prayer: Dear Lord, thank You for the way You work things out! Thank You for the things in our family that help us follow You better. Please help us to grow together in knowing and loving Jesus. In His name, Amen.

THE MACEDONIAN CALL

Scripture: Acts 16:6–12
Place: Troas to Macedonia
Time: 50 AD

Paul tossed and turned. Was he asleep? Was he awake? He couldn't tell! Suddenly, it didn't really matter, because a man was standing in front of him! Even if he was dreaming,[519] Paul could tell by his clothes that the man was from Macedonia. The man looked Paul in the eye and said, "Come over to Macedonia and help us!"[199] WOW! That was certainly strange. Now Paul was wide awake, thinking and praying about this strange vision. But other strange things had happened recently!

The first strange thing was that after Paul and Silas brought Timothy along with them to visit some of the churches, God's Holy Spirit told them not to go to some places they planned to go![58] This WAS strange, but it was also important for Paul and Silas and Timothy to obey God's plan. No matter how good their plans were, God's plan is best!

So instead of going east, Paul and his friends went west. Then came the next strange thing. The Holy Spirit would not let them go to the north or the south, either! So that left WEST—and they kept on going west, exactly the direction God wanted them to travel![207]

Heading west, they came to Troas. It was a port city on the Aegean Sea, near Greece. It was full of ships and sailors, cargo and merchants. They all were moving food and cloth and tools and other things from place to place by ship. This is where Paul and his friends got settled down for the night and went to sleep. But then, Paul had this amazing dream or vision of the man from Macedonia!

When Paul came to breakfast the next morning he said, "I believe God has called us to preach in Macedonia. I've had a vision. And I think we should leave as soon as we can."

Silas and Timothy looked at each other. They'd just gotten to Troas! And they didn't even know anyone in Macedonia. God's Spirit had made it clear that they were to travel west, but Macedonia was quite a BIT farther west!

But they all knew that they needed to obey God! So after breakfast, Paul went from ship to ship there in Troas' harbor. He was looking for the ship the God had already prepared for them—if God wanted them to go, then they'd find a ship going to Macedonia! Paul also went looking for Doctor Luke, who was nearby. He asked Luke to come along with them. So just as God had planned, Paul found a ship going to Philippi, a big port city in Macedonia. He paid for the tickets. Soon, Paul, Silas, Timothy and Luke were out on the water, heading west again, this time to a place they had never been—Macedonia![58]

Talk About the Story: What had Paul, Silas and Timothy been doing? What did God's Spirit tell them not to do? What country was the man in the dream from? Who else came with them? Whose plans are the best plans?

Scripture: "A man's heart plans his way, but the Lord directs his steps." Proverbs 16:9

Family Time: Where is a place you have never gone? Where is a place you've planned to go but did not go? What is a plan you've made that did not happen the way you expected? What can we learn about making plans from this story?

Prayer: Dear Lord, we thank You that we can ask You to show us where to go and what to do. Please help us to remember to ask You about everything! In Jesus' name, Amen.

LYDIA BELIEVES

Scripture: Acts 16:13–15
Place: Philippi
Time: 50 AD

"There is no end to God's surprises on this trip!" Paul laughed to himself. He had been looking for the man he'd seen in his dream who had asked for help. But Paul and his friends had seen no such man.

The next surprise was that there was not even a synagogue to go to here in Philippi. The synagogue was usually the first place Paul went in a new city! He would go and tell the people about Jesus, the Messiah! But there was no synagogue here. There were not even ten Jewish men in that city.

But the next surprise was that Paul and his friends heard that some WOMEN got together on Saturdays[373] to pray by the river outside of the city. So Paul and his friends went out to the river on Saturday morning to these women. So far, nothing was happening the way Paul expected! So he laughed at God's surprising ways as he looked up and down the river for the praying women!

They did find the women. And these women were eager to hear about Jesus! So Paul began to tell them all about Him. Paul told them how Jesus had loved and healed and taught. He told how Jesus had proven He is God's Son and the Messiah. He told how Jesus had died on the cross to take the punishment for our sins and had risen again after three days! All of the women listened carefully to everything Paul told them.

One woman was named Lydia. She was a businesswoman who sold purple dye. Making purple dye took a lot of work. But selling purple dye also made a lot of money. Only very wealthy people could afford purple clothes! So Lydia had a big house and plenty of servants who worked in her business and at her house.

But the best thing about Lydia wasn't her money or her business. It was that she BELIEVED in Jesus and joined God's family![541] So then she invited Paul to her house to tell everyone in the household about Jesus. Soon, everyone in the household was baptized[30] to show that they ALL believed in Jesus and wanted to follow Him![319]

Lydia said to Paul and his friends, "If you recognize that I really am a believer, then I ask you as your sister in God's family to come and be my guests." Lydia wanted them to have a good and safe place to stay, so that they could rest and preach and teach and tell more people in Philippi about Jesus! And that's just what Paul, Silas, Timothy and Luke did! They stayed at Lydia's for some time. Lydia was not the man in the dream. But she WAS the person God wanted them to meet so that many people of Macedonia could join God's family!

Talk About the Story: Where was the man Paul saw in his dream? Where did the women meet to pray? What job did Lydia have? What did she and her household do to show they loved and followed Jesus?

Scripture: Trust in the LORD WITH ALL YOUR HEART, and lean not on your own understanding; in all your ways acknowledge Him, And He shall direct your paths." Proverbs 3:5–6

Family Time: What is something that is hard to trust God about? Which is more important, things that make sense to us, or God's plan? Why? How does it make you feel to know that you can trust God to direct the way you go?

Prayer: Dear Lord, we are glad that we can always trust You because You always do what is best. That makes us feel loved and happy. We want to learn to rest in You. In Jesus' name, Amen.

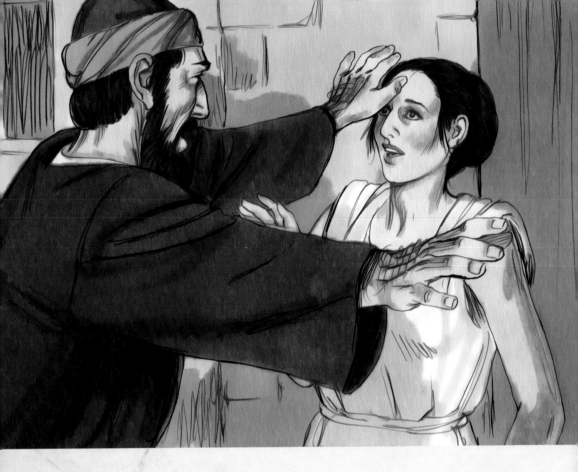

PAUL AND SILAS HELP A YOUNG GIRL

Scripture: Acts 16:16–22
Place: Philippi
Time: 50 AD

Soldiers were pulling the clothes off Paul's and Silas' backs—Paul and Silas were about to be flogged, or beaten with whips! And with all of the shouting and yelling around them, neither of them could get a word in to the rulers about their side of this story! What a confusing mess! And it all began with helping someone!

Paul and Silas now had many new friends in Philippi—even though none of them was the man Paul saw in his dream! Every day, they went to the place of prayer[97] to talk with people and to help them know Jesus. But one day—and for MANY days—a young girl met them on the way to the prayer place. But she didn't talk with them. She didn't walk with them. No, she did something VERY strange.

www.thefamilyprayerbible.com

The girl walked behind Paul and Silas. And she SHOUTED—all the time! She yelled, "These men are servants of the Most High God! They have come to tell us how to be saved!"

That might seem like a good advertisement—but there was a terrible problem. This girl was the slave of a demon![113] She knew the future and knew other things (like who Paul and Silas were) because an evil spirit controlled her and told her these things. She was also a slave to some men who did not care about HER at ALL—they only cared about the money she made for them by telling people's fortunes! So this girl was a double slave. It was time to stop this girl's suffering!

Paul stopped and turned around. He said to the demon, "I COMMAND you in the name of Jesus Christ to come OUT of her!" WOW! The name of Jesus is the strongest name in the world—and so, the demon left the girl, just like that![53]

The girl jumped up and down thanking Paul and Silas over and over—but then, her owners came! They could see that this girl was not controlled by the demon now! But this didn't make them glad. Their chance to make money was gone— and they were ANGRY!

So these men dragged Paul and Silas to the square where local rulers met with people who had a problem. They put Paul and Silas in front of the rulers and shouted, "These men are telling us to do things that Romans should not do!"[349] Of course, these men had not heard Paul and Silas say ANYTHING! But soon, a crowd gathered—and more people shouted bad things about Paul and Silas.[7]

Now, Paul was a Roman citizen. According to Roman law, Paul was supposed to be treated better than people who were not Roman citizens. No one was allowed to beat him! But Paul never even got to say a word! The rulers made their decision, and soon, the tearing blows of the whip tore at Paul and Silas's backs. Then they were put into prison without a trial—and the law was broken AGAIN![465] But the story was FAR from over. God had something GREAT and AMAZING coming!

Talk About the Story: What was wrong with the girl? What did Paul do? How do you think the girl felt? What did Paul and Silas not get to tell? Was this the end of the story?

Scripture: "I will call upon the LORD, WHO IS WORTHY TO BE PRAISED; so shall I be saved from my enemies." Psalm 18:3

Family Time: Tell about a time when your family or friends had difficulty. How did they feel? What good thing did God do that they didn't expect? What does it mean to call upon the Lord?

Prayer: Dear Lord, thank You that even when things are not fair, or hard things happen, that You love us. You are with us. We love You. In Jesus' name, Amen.

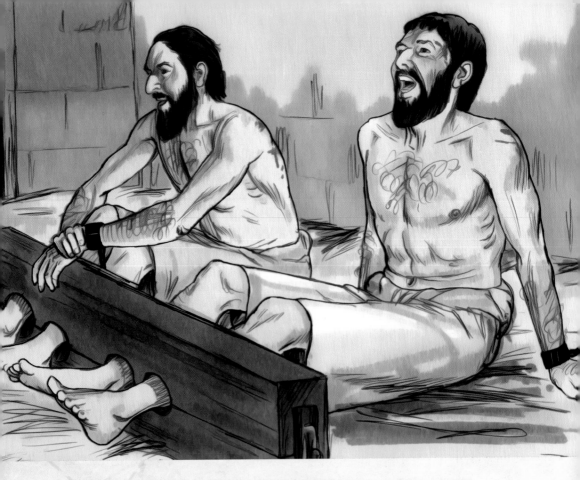

PAUL AND SILAS SHAKE UP PHILIPPI

Scripture: Acts 16:21–40
Place: Philippi
Time: 50 AD

It started with a little shake. Paul and Silas looked around. Their backs hurt and their legs were stiff, locked into stocks, big blocks of wood chained together with holes for feet to go through. But they had been SINGING and PRAYING and PRAISING GOD. And now, in the middle of the night, the shaking got STRONGER!

After Paul and Silas had been treated BADLY. They were unfairly beaten, and then put into the DEEPEST part of the jail.[341] The jailer put their feet in the stocks and locked the doors. They would NEVER get out—or so the jailer thought![465]

So Paul and Silas made a choice. They chose to think about God's goodness. They began singing to God and praying[254] to Him—and everyone else in the jail was listening!

About midnight, God sent an earthquake. The walls cracked! The chains fell

www.thefamilyprayerbible.com

off—and the DOORS opened![467] Of course, the jailer woke—he was terrified! If even ONE prisoner got out, he would be KILLED. So he ran to the jail with his sword in his hand. If anyone was missing, he'd kill himself instead of being killed.

But Paul called out, "DON'T HURT YOURSELF! We are ALL HERE!" The jailer grabbed a torch and ran into the jail.[164]

Once he could see that all the prisoners were really there, he knelt down before Paul and Silas. He knew that normal prisoners didn't SING to God. They didn't PRAISE God and PRAY. He asked, "Sirs, what must I do to be saved?"[318]

Paul smiled. HERE was the good thing God was bringing from this painful time! He said, "BELIEVE! Believe on the Lord Jesus Christ and you will be saved—you and all your household, too."[263]

The jailer took Paul and Silas to his house. He washed their wounded backs and their torn ankles as Paul told the whole household about Jesus![145] Everyone listened—after all, they'd just been awakened by an earthquake! They all BELIEVED. And everyone in the house was baptized to show they were followers of JESUS![30]

Not only that, but the jailer had the best breakfast EVER made, just to celebrate! Not only were Paul and Silas singing and praying and praising God—the whole household of the jailer joined in![213]

A little later, the rulers who'd had them put into jail sent a messenger, saying they could leave. But Paul said, "No. We are Roman citizens. What was done to us was ILLEGAL. They need to come here themselves and release us!"[196]

So the jailer sent for the rulers. The rulers were afraid when they realized what they had done to Roman citizens![164] They came to Paul and Silas and very politely begged Paul and Silas to leave! Paul and Silas went back to Lydia's—and what a story they had to tell! God brought the jailer's whole household into His family! He brought something wonderful out of the hard time.

Talk About the Story: What did Paul and Silas do while they were in the prison? Who heard them? What happened? What did the jailer ask? Who believed in Jesus?

Scripture: " You have also given me the shield of Your salvation; Your right hand has held me up, Your gentleness has made me great." Psalm 18:35

Family Time: What are some ways God protects your family? When have you see God help you in a hard time? Tell how God shows His gentleness to you.

Prayer: Dear Lord, we are amazed by Your kindness and gentleness, even when hard and scary things happen to us. Thank You that You are the King forever. What you decide, is! In Jesus' name, Amen.

PSALM 126
RESPONSE TO ANSWERED PRAYERS

Sennacherib, King of Assyria, surrounded the city of Jerusalem and tried to starve it to surrender. The inhabitants of the city were hungry and discouraged. They prayed for victory over Syria, but everything seemed to go wrong. Some of Israel's warriors were killed in scrimmages. People were terrified.

King Hezekiah received a letter from the Assyrians demanding their surrender and promised Jerusalem's hostages would be treated well. The king didn't believe the enemy. Hezekiah took the letter into the Temple, and spread it out to pray before God (Isaiah 37:14-20).

God heard the king's prayer, as well as the prayers of all the people in the city. In answer, "The angel of the Lord went out and killed in the camp of the Assyrians one hundred and eighty five thousand" (Isaiah 37:36). Then Israel sang,

"When the Lord brought back the captivity of Zion.
We were like those who dream.
Then our mouth was filled with laughter,
and our tongue with singing."[397]

They knew what the enemy was saying about its defeat and Israel's victory,

"The Lord has done great things for them."[404]

The people shouted in agreement, "Yes, the Lord has done amazing things for us" (Vs. 3). They rejoiced and could see their desert of suffering turn into streams of running water.

"The Lord has restored our fortunes[517]
As streams are renewed in the desert."

The Psalmist describes their victory like planting a farm. The people of Jerusalem had planted the seeds of prayer for deliverance. When their prayers were answered, they shouted for joy.

The people in Jerusalem had been scared to death. They prayed with tears and fears. God saw them trusting Him for deliverance. They sowed seeds of tears and God gave them victory.

"Those who sow seeds in tears,
Will bring forth a harvest in joy.
Those who weep in prayers they plant[444]
Will return with singing."

Talk About the Psalm: What did you learn about the psalm writer in this story? What did you learn about God?

Psalm 126: Read this week's psalm in your Bible together. Choose a verse to read aloud as a prayer.

Prayer: Thank You, God, for the psalm prayers in the Bible. Thank You for teaching us about You and about how to pray. In Jesus' name, Amen.

FROM PHILIPPI TO THESSALONICA

Scripture: Acts 17:1–10
Place: Thessalonica
Time: 50 AD

"Three weeks! I've only been here three weeks and already there is a RIOT! These men who follow us around—Lord, what can we do about them?" Paul threw up his hands in prayer and frustration! But this time, Paul was not in the middle of the trouble! Instead, some new members of God's family were in jail.

Paul, Silas, Timothy and Luke had left Philippi on a ship sailing for Thessalonica, in Greece. (You can still go there. It is now called Salonika.) Paul went to the synagogue there and began to tell the people how Jesus is the Messiah, how He died to take the punishment for their sins and how Jesus rose again! Many of the people believed in Jesus and joined God's family! Some were Jewish people, and some were Gentiles. Some of them were wealthy; some of them were poor. But they were all happy to be in the same family—God's family!

The happiness continued for three weeks.[194] And then, some of the men who did not believe in Jesus came into town. They could see that God's family was growing there. So they hired some men to start a RIOT. And not just any riot—they paid the men to STOP the followers of Jesus.[349] They were just like Paul before he met Jesus! Of course the men went looking for Paul and Silas—so they could get THEM put into jail. They heard that they were at the house of a man named Jason. But when they got there, they could not find Paul and Silas, so instead, they dragged Jason and another person to court!

"These men who have turned the world upside down have come here to our city," they shouted! "They defy Caesar. Instead of worshiping Caesar as a god, they say there is another King. His name is Jesus!"[374]

The officials were alarmed. A new king? Jesus? They had not heard about a new king! They were not sure what to do about this. So instead of keeping Jason and his friend in jail, the judge made Jason pay money to be sure he'd come back to court. Then they let him and his friend leave. But this trouble made God's growing family in Thessalonica worried about Paul and Silas! They wanted them to stay safe. So that night, they quietly said goodbye to Paul and Silas. They left for another city, where more adventures awaited!

Talk About the Story: What was the name of the city? What did the men trying to stop Paul and Silas pay men to do? Can anyone stop God? Who was put in jail?

Scripture: "Do not be overcome by evil, but overcome evil with good." Romans 12:21

Family Time: When people are mean to you, what does God's Word say to do about them? Read Romans 12:19–20 for the answer. Today, make a list of people don't like you. Make that your prayer list for this week!

Prayer: Dear Lord, we ask You to help us to care for and pray for people who don't like us. We know that Jesus' love is stronger than anything! In His name, Amen.

PAUL GOES TO BEREA

Scripture: Acts 17:10–15
Place: Berea
Time: 50 AD

Paul and Silas walked up the mountain road, watching the night sky as they went farther into the mountains. They had to stay one step ahead of the men who were trying to stop them! So leaving quietly at night was the best way to get time to tell people about Jesus before those men found out where they had gone, and followed them![142]

Paul and Silas were headed to Berea, a beautiful city with lots of mountains surrounding its valley. A big road went between Thessalonica and Berea, but Paul and Silas could move more quickly at night than in the day light.

"I wish these men who hate us so would simply listen to what we're saying," said Paul. "If they would HEAR, they might believe that Jesus is the Messiah and that He loves them. He could change their anger to joy!"[266]

"Yes," said Silas. "Leaving like this always makes me feel like I've done something wrong! Yet we have nothing to hide, and nothing but God's love and good news to share with people. When I hear the terrible lies those men tell about us, I wonder how many hear and believe their words instead of God's good news. It makes me sad."[334]

Finally, they could see the sun glistening off the tops of the mountains around Berea. They entered the city and asked someone where there was a synagogue— and went there. Since Paul and Silas were Jews, and most people in the synagogue were Jews, they would welcome Paul and Silas. Besides that, most Jews knew a lot about the first part of the Bible, the Old Testament. They already understood that Messiah was coming. So of course Paul and Silas wanted to tell them that Jesus is the Messiah! They wanted them to know that He came to live, die and rise again so that they all could join God's family![416]

Once Paul and Silas started telling about Jesus, the Jews in Berea listened carefully. They were different from other people Paul had preached to. They had copies of the Old Testament, or Tanach, in the synagogue. So when Paul told them about the messages God had given about the Messiah, they found those passages in the Scriptures. They read them for themselves! The people in Berea were eager to hear Paul and Silas talk every day! They listened, they looked at the Scriptures, and they believed! Jews and Greeks were joining God's family!

Soon, the men who were chasing them got to Berea.[494] So THIS time, Silas and Timothy stayed in Berea to continue teaching the people. But Paul headed down the river on another boat, which would take him to the next spot in his adventure with the Holy Spirit!

Talk About the Story: What was the name of this city? What was different about the people there? What is the name these people gave the Old Testament? What is your favorite part of the Old Testament?

Scripture: "Prophecy never came by the will of man, but holy men of God spoke as they were moved by the Holy Spirit." 2 Peter 1:21

Family Time: God gave messages to people so they would know about Jesus even before He came to Earth. What is something you know about God from the Old Testament? What do you know about Jesus from the Old Testament? What makes the Bible one big story of God's love?

Prayer: Father, we want to be like the Bereans. We want to learn Your Word to know more about Jesus. We love You! In Jesus' name, Amen.

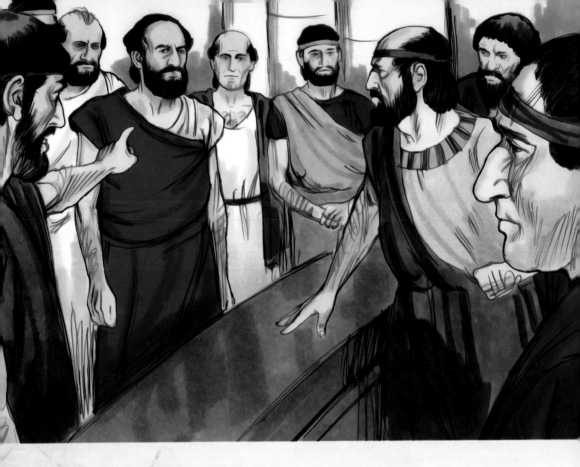

WRITING FIRST THESSALONIANS

Scripture: 1 Thessalonians 1:7
Place: Written from Corinth
Time: 51 AD

Paul had visited Thessalonica in the winter of A.D. 50-51. He preached three weeks in the Jewish synagogues. A number of Jews and Gentiles heard Paul's good news and believed in Jesus!

But the Jews who did NOT believe were upset! They said, "These who have turned the world upside down have come here, too!"[349]

These people started a riot! The mob attacked a believer named Jason and dragged him to court. Paul and Silas went on to Berea, but these angry Jews followed them! Paul escaped to Athens and then Corinth.

Paul sent word for Timothy and Silas to join him at Corinth. Paul was glad to see Timothy and Silas when they finally arrived. They embraced and soon Paul wanted to know, "What about the persecution from the Jews? Are the Thessalonians still living boldly for Jesus Christ?"[478]

Timothy and Silas told Paul, "The believers are strong and are telling God's good news to the surrounding cities."

But the two men told Paul about a problem. Some believers had died. The believers who were still alive had a question, "What happened to them?" They wanted to know will those believers who died still go to heaven when Jesus returns?" (Remember, at this time people were expecting Jesus to return any day!)

"I'll write immediately," Paul said.

He wrote, "Since Jesus died and rose again, God will bring those believers back with Him when He comes."[524]

Then Paul added, "The Lord will descend from heaven with a shout . . . the dead (bodies) in Christ will rise first. Then we who are alive will be caught up together with them in clouds to meet the Lord in the air."[405]

Paul wrote this letter to give his friends hope and understanding. The church was thriving in spite of persecution and unsaved people were still turning to Christ! God's family was growing in Thessalonica!

Finally Paul warned the Thessalonians, "Be watchful in these last days. Don't focus on yourselves, but wait for the Lord's return, build each other up. Help each other. Respect those in leadership and remain blameless before God and the world.[347, 477]

At the end, Paul gave them a series of short encouragements: "Don't pay back evil for evil. Do good to everyone. Rejoice in everything. Pray always, give thanks in everything. Pay attention to the Holy Spirit. Listen well to preaching. Test everything by the things you know about God. Hold onto the good things. Stay away from any kind of evil."[441]

Talk About the Story: What was the good news Silas and Timothy brought Paul about the Thessalonians? What confused the Thessalonians? Which of the short encouragements Paul wrote is your favorite? Why?

Scripture: "Rejoice always, pray without ceasing, in everything give thanks; for this is the will of God in Christ Jesus for you." 1 Thessalonians 5:16–18

Family Time: What does it sound like to give thanks in every situation? What will it not sound like? What does the Bible say that rejoicing, praying and being thankful is?

Prayer: Lord, we thank You for showing us Your will for us! In Jesus' name, Amen.

WRITING AGAIN TO THE THESSALONIANS

Scripture: 2 Thessalonians 1:10
Place: Written from Corinth
Time: 52 AD

Paul's second letter to the church at Thessalonica helped the believers think about the future in a different way from what was in the first letter.

The two letters were written only a few months apart. Timothy and Silas were with Paul when he wrote the first letter. One of them delivered the letter to the church. He then brought back good news! The church was growing, even though they were still being harassed by the Jews who didn't believe in Jesus.

The bad news was that persecution was getting more intense. Also, someone had come and preached to the church who said he had a letter from Paul. This man said that Paul's letter told that Jesus had already come back and that now, the church was in the terrible troubles that will happen at the end, called the Tribulation. SO of course, the believers in Thessalonica needed to know what was true and what was not!

Paul told his fellow workers, "I must write a letter to help them know what is true."

So Paul wrote to tell them that yes, there would be trouble, worse than they had ever seen. But, he told them that this very bad time will not come until after the antichrist, also called the "man of lawlessness" comes to power.[136] He will tell lies about God.[135]

He will be backed up by the power of the devil. And he will fool many people into thinking he is the Messiah.[422]

But the power of God's Spirit is still holding this evil one back. Later, after this time when the antichrist comes, the Lord Jesus Christ will come from heaven and will stop him.[18]

Paul didn't want them to be confused. He reminded them of God's love for them and the great hope that God's family has in Jesus.

Paul had also heard that some Christians in Thessalonica had stopped working. They were waiting for Jesus to come from heaven. So Paul wrote, "Don't hang around those who are lazy and disobedient. Follow my example. Work for your food and keep doing good.[103] If someone won't work, they shouldn't eat, either" (3:10).[275]

But Paul told the church to treat them like brothers and sisters, even when they were wrong, and warn them to do right.[327]

The church at Thessalonica was a joy and inspiration to Paul. In spite of their problems, they were growing in Christ. Paul's letter tells them and us, how to live in light of Christ's Second Coming. We shouldn't be afraid. We can look forward to the future with confidence, because we know the One who holds the future in His hands.

Talk About the Story: What had confused the church at Thessalonica? How do you think they could tell if a letter was from Paul? Who will stop the antichrist? Why can we be confident about the future?

Scripture: "But the Lord is faithful, who will establish you and guard you from the evil one." 2 Thessalonians 3:3

Family Time: What are reasons people fear the future? What can we be sure of? Who is the One who holds our future? Describe what you think "faithful" means.

Prayer: Lord God, You are faithful. Thank You that You protect and guard us from the evil one! In Jesus' name, Amen.

PAUL GOES TO ATHENS

Scripture: Acts 17:15–21
Place: Athens
Time: 52 AD

❝Thank You, Lord, that I don't get seasick," Paul said aloud. He sat swaying in a hammock below the deck of yet another small ship. Paul and Luke, along with some men from Berea, were sailing toward Athens, one of the oldest cities in the world. It is still a famous city, and it is the capital of Greece today.

Once Paul's group got to Athens, the men from Berea got ready to go back home. Paul asked them to send Silas and Timothy to Athens when they returned. (Remember, this was before phones or computers or a telegraph. To send a message, someone had to bring it to you!) So it would be a few weeks before Silas and Timothy arrived in Athens.

While Paul waited for his friends, he explored this large and very old city—the city named for the goddess Athena. The first thing Paul noticed about Athens was

that it was FULL of idols! LONG ago, God had given a command to the Jews to never make an idol or worship it. But here in Athens, most people had never heard of the one, true God. They believed in lots of gods. Nearly everywhere Paul looked, he saw a shrine with an idol or statue in it. Athenians prayed there and left food and gifts for the idol. And these shrines were all over town!

So Paul went to the synagogue where the Jews and Gentiles who knew about the one, true God met to pray. He told them the good news about Jesus! He also went into the big market square of Athens and told people about God, who made the world.[145] He told about Jesus, the One God had promised to send, and how He came to live on Earth, died and rose again!

Many different kinds of people were listening to Paul; some of them were called philosophers. The name means "lovers of wisdom," but they weren't exactly wise. They had their own ideas about how to live. Paul's ideas were different![444] So they said, "This man is saying we should worship a foreign god."

These philosophers took Paul to a place called the Forum, a place where a person could talk to many people at one time. They said, "We want to hear you tell more about this religion."[456]

But of course, this is NOT a religion. This is a relationship—when we follow Jesus, we're part of God's family! But these people did not know ANYTHING about God, so they asked Paul to speak. People in Athens loved to talk about new ideas—if it was new to them, then they wanted to hear all about it. Paul was glad that God's Spirit would help him tell them!

Talk About the Story: Who stayed at Berea? What city did Paul and Luke travel to? What did Paul notice about the city? What are philosophers? What did people in Athens like to talk about?

Scripture: "There is one God and one Mediator between God and men . . . Jesus, who gave Himself a ransom for all." 1 Timothy 2:5-6

Family Time: What does God say about worshiping anyone except Him? Who came to Earth to show us what God is like? A ransom is payment to free someone who's been kidnapped. How did Jesus give Himself as a ransom? Why did we need to be ransomed?

Prayer: Dear Lord, thank You that You care about everyone, even a person does not know You. Help us to tell people who don't know You all about Jesus and how to be part of Your family. In Jesus' name, Amen.

PAUL SPEAKS ON MARS HILL

Scripture: Acts 17:22–34
Place: Athens
Time: 52 AD

Paul stood to speak. It looked like he was in front of a SEA of people! It was possibly the biggest crowd he'd ever spoken to! The Forum on Mars Hill was HUGE. And on this day, it was full of people. People came here from all over the world, for Athens was the place to hear something new! If you wanted to hear about and talk about new ideas, this was the place to be!

"People of Athens!" Paul began. "I can see that you all are very religious.[113] As I walk through your city, I see shrines to every god imaginable. In fact, I even found a shrine marked, 'TO AN UNKNOWN GOD.' This is the reason I have come to Athens—to tell you all about this God you do not know. I know Him! He is the God who created the world and everything in it.[93]

"This God doesn't live in shrines made by human hands. And He does not need anything that we humans can do for Him! Instead, HE gives life to all of US!

www.thefamilyprayerbible.com

God made us all from one person. The human race came from that man. Humans scattered over all of the earth and God has determined how long each life will be and where that person will live.

"God wants all of us to search for Him, because He wants us to KNOW Him. He is not hard to find![426] He's right here, for we live and move and exist in Him. In fact, some of your Greek writers say that we all are His children. So if we are God's children, then we shouldn't think He is some sort of golden statue or carved idol.

"Until now, God has overlooked our wrong thinking. We humans didn't know any better. But now He tells us—each one, everywhere—to stop and pay attention![399] He has already set a day when He will expect each person to tell Him how he or she lived. To help us understand who He is and what He wants, God sent Someone He promised to send long ago. This Man showed us what God is like. He proved that He is the One God sent, when He was killed and God brought Him back to life!"[405]

When Paul said that God had brought Jesus back to life, some people laughed. They thought that was not possible! Maybe Paul was crazy! But other people said, "We want to hear more about this. Please come and talk to us again."

Paul then left the Forum, but he didn't leave alone. Some people followed him who wanted to know MORE. They had never heard about God, who made them and loved them and wanted them to know Him! So Paul talked more with these people. And they became believers in Jesus and joined God's family right there and then![319] Paul had spoken the truth. And God's Spirit was using the truth to change people's hearts and minds!

Talk About the Story: What city had a Forum on Mars Hill? What did Paul say about the "unknown God"? What caused some people to laugh? Why do you think they laughed? Why did God raise Jesus from the dead?

Scripture: "God, who . . . spoke in time past to the fathers by the prophets, has in these last days spoken to us by His Son." Hebrews 1:1–2

Family Time: When people don't know God, what do they worship? What is one of your favorite reasons to love and worship God? Together, sing a song that thanks God for sending Jesus to us!

Prayer: Dear Father, thank You for loving us. Thank You for Your patience with us. We are glad that You loved us first, even when we did not know You! In Jesus' name, Amen.

PSALM 127
THE BUILDER'S PSALM

David wanted to build a house for God where people could go to worship Him. But God told him no because he had fought many wars and in battle had killed his enemy. God said, "You are not the one to build a house for Me to live in" (1 Chronicles 17:4, *NLT*). God said, "Your son will build a Temple to house My name"(1 Chronicles 22:9-10, *NLT*). This son was Solomon who built the Temple.

So David spent the last years of his life gathering the material for the Temple. This included marble, granite, wood, and other valuable materials. Psalm 127 was written to instruct the workers to be diligent in building the house as they remembered that they were doing God's work and letting God work through them.

> *"Except the Lord build the house*[206]
> *They work in vain to build it."*

www.thefamilyprayerbible.com

We don't know if David wrote the Psalm to motivate his son Solomon to do an excellent job or if Solomon wrote the Psalm to motivate his workers.

> *"It is useless for you to work so hard,*[536]
> > *From early morning till late at night.*
> *Anxiously working for food to eat;*
> > *For God gives rest to his beloved one."*

The word "beloved" is *Jeddah* in the Hebrew language. It means "Beloved of the Lord" (2 Samuel 12:25). *Jeddah* is the name Solomon. So Solomon could have written this Psalm about himself, or David could have written it for his son.

The writer described God's blessing on those who serve Him, whether they are building houses, families, cities, fortresses or empires.

> *"Behold children are a gift to your life,*
> > *They are a reward from God.*[42]
> *Like arrows to defend yourself in life,*
> > *So are the children born to you.*
> *You will have a peaceful life with many children*[62]
> > *Because they will answer for you in the future."*

Therefore, whether building a business, a family, a church, or anything else, it is important to build it on God's principles, with God's help, for God's glory. "For every house has a builder, but the One who built everything is God" (Heb. 3:4, *NLT*).[93]

Talk About the Psalm: What did you learn about the psalm writer in this story? What did you learn about God?

Psalm 127: Read this week's psalm in your Bible together. Choose a verse to read aloud as a prayer.

Prayer: Thank You, God, for the psalm prayers in the Bible. Thank You for teaching us about You and about how to pray. In Jesus' name, Amen.

PAUL IN CORINTH

Scripture: Acts 18:1–15
Place: Corinth
Time: 52 AD

Paul was delighted to be working again! He loved to cut the pieces of rough cloth. He enjoyed seeing his tents come together, trying to make the edges perfect and the seams strong. His neck ached a little from sitting and sewing, but it felt good to be making tents again. He'd learned how to make tents when he was young, in Tarsus. Most every young man learned the skill his father had, so perhaps Paul's father was a tentmaker.

And now that he'd come to Corinth, Paul felt like he had a new tent-making family! He had met Aquila and Priscilla, a husband and wife. They had come from Turkey, but had lived in Rome. When the Roman emperor Claudius had decided that all Jews had to leave Rome, Priscilla and Aquila left with all the other Jews. Priscilla and Aquila came to Corinth where they met Paul—because they weren't only Jews; they also were followers of Jesus—and tentmakers!

So Paul worked with his new friends, making tents.[536] The other part of the time, he would go to the synagogue in Corinth. There, he'd talk to the Jews and anyone else around about Jesus. After Silas and Timothy arrived, he spent even more time in the synagogue and other places, trying to help people see that Jesus is the Messiah God promised to send and that He is the only way into God's kingdom![415]

Pretty soon, though, some Jewish men started getting mad at Paul. They didn't like what he was saying about Jesus, and they didn't like it that other people were following Jesus. So they threatened Paul and said they'd kill him if he didn't stop talking about Jesus.[334]

Paul looked hard at them as he removed his outer coat. Then he shook the coat hard. Dust flew off, lit by the sunshine. This was a way to say, "I'm done with you."

Paul said, "You will not listen. So I am going to preach to the Gentiles instead of the Jews."

Titius Justus lived next door to the synagogue, and he was a follower of Jesus.[54] So Paul moved the church meetings from the synagogue to Titius Justus' house! At first, he worried about this—he wasn't used to teaching in a house! But God told Paul that night, "Don't be afraid to leave the synagogue to worship in a house. Keep on preaching! I'll be with you and no one will harm you. I have many people in this city who are going to join My family!"

So Paul began to preach to Gentiles, people who were not Jews. And his friends all met at Titius Justus' house to worship Jesus. Soon Crispus, the man who had been in charge of the synagogue, came next door and joined God's family![319] The church there grew and grew, and for eighteen months, Paul stayed, making tents and teaching people more about Jesus!

Talk About the Story: What job did Paul know how to do? Where had Priscilla and Aquila lived? Why did Paul move the church to the house beside the synagogue? How long was Paul in Corinth?

Scripture: "The Gentiles should be fellow heirs, of the same body, and partakers of His promise in Christ through the gospel." Ephesians 3:6

Family Time: Who are some people you know who are from other countries? In which countries is it hard for people to learn about Jesus? Why? What are some things we can do as a family to help someone in one of these places?

Prayer: Dear Jesus, we are glad that You make everyone who believes in You a part of Your family! Please help people in (country) to learn about You. We are glad to be part of Your family around the world. In Your name, Amen.

APOLLOS TEACHES AND LEARNS

Scripture: Acts 18:24–28
Place: Ephesus
Time: 52 AD

Priscilla and Aquila sat up straight, surprised! They looked at each other, then at the man standing at the front. He was doing a good job of telling about the prophecies concerning Jesus. He knew a lot about God's Word! But he never mentioned Jesus. He didn't seem to know anything about Him—only what John the Baptist had said about the Messiah coming!

Priscilla and Aquila were now in Ephesus. Like their friend Paul, they had gone to the synagogue when they came to the city. Here at the synagogue, Apollos was speaking.[38] But even though Jesus had died, risen and gone back to heaven over ten years before, Apollos did not seem to know this very BEST PART of God's big story of the Messiah!

So after the meeting, Priscilla and Aquila invited Apollos home for dinner with

www.thefamilyprayerbible.com

them! They did not want to embarrass him or make him feel bad. He was telling everything he did know about God's promised Messiah! He just didn't know the whole story! As they ate, they talked with Apollos to find out how he had learned these things about John. As they got to know him, they could tell just what he needed to learn.[90]

Then they began to tell Apollos the wonderful story of what happened AFTER John the Baptist had told the people of Israel to get ready because the Messiah was about to come! There was SO MUCH to tell! First, they told Apollos about how John baptized Jesus—and how God had spoken from heaven, and His Spirit had come down like a dove! They told how Jesus had taught and healed and fed thousands of people. They described how Jesus had told the leaders when they were wrong, and how He was often away praying to His Father, God.

Priscilla and Aquila told Apollos how Jesus was arrested and killed on a cross, even though He had not done anything wrong. He had never sinned. They told how Jesus had taken the punishment for sin, as the prophets had said He would. And then, they told Apollos how Jesus rose to life again on the third day! They spent a lot of time with Apollos, helping him to learn all about Jesus and about the Holy Spirit and the amazing things God had done!

Finally, Apollos understood that Jesus the Messiah really had come, lived, died and risen again as the prophets had said He would! He could tell ALL of the story! And so, he went to Turkey (where Priscilla and Aquila had lived). They made sure that their friends in Turkey would invite Apollos into their homes and synagogues to listen to his whole story! When Apollos arrived there, he helped MANY people learn that Jesus is the Messiah, which made the church in Turkey grow strong![319]

Talk About the Story: What did Apollos know? What did he not know? Where did Priscilla and Aquila take Apollos to teach him? What country did Apollos go to next?

Scripture: "Let your speech always be with grace, seasoned with salt, that you may know how you ought to answer each one." Colossians 4:6

Family Time: What does salt do to our food? How is grace (God's kindness) like salt for our words? What are some things words you can say about who Jesus is?

Prayer: Dear Lord, thank You that You always love us and want what is best for us. Please help us to learn all we can about Jesus, so we can tell others about His love! In His name, Amen.

WRITING THE FIRST LETTER TO CORINTH

Scripture: 1 Corinthians 3:16
Place: Ephesus
Time: 54 AD

Paul was busy! The church was growing in Ephesus, the capital city of Asia Minor (now Turkey). Paul was preaching and many were turning to Christ!

But news arrived from Corinth: Some visitors from Chloe's home in Corinth told him that quarrels had been breaking out when the family of God was meeting. Instead worshiping God, people were arguing!

During Paul's second trip to tell the good news about Jesus, many people in Corinth had followed Jesus! Paul had been so grateful for this little group of believers! Now, he was heartbroken. The Christians in Corinth were being selfish and doing wrong things, instead of living a selfless life for Jesus.

Paul and his fellow workers quickly went to prayer. Soon after this, three more

people came from Corinth[195] to tell about other problems in the church there.

So Paul wrote a letter to them under the inspiration of the Holy Spirit. He wanted to help them straighten out their problems!

Paul began by reminding them that they were God's holy people: "To the church of God at Corinth to those who are sanctified (made holy) through Christ Jesus, called to be saints."[58] He encouraged them and told them to let the Holy Spirit produce in them "the mind of Christ,"[272] so that they would know the right things to do. God would make them wise if they would ask His help!

Then Paul went on to correct things they were thinking—and doing—that were wrong. Paul writes, "You have become arrogant"[92] or proud, thinking they had all the answers. People who follow Jesus should never be arrogant or proud. The Bible says that God resists proud people![228]

Paul went on to tell them to stop doing wrong in the way they treated each other. He wrote to them about how to have a good marriage.[429] He helped them understand that they needed to be wise about eating meat offered to idols, even though idols have no power.[451] He wanted them to help each other learn to follow Jesus!

Paul helped them understand more about why people remember Jesus' death by taking communion.[77] He taught them about ways people show they have spiritual gifts.[448] Right in the middle of this is a beautiful description of love. It is the kind of love God has for us and the kind of love we should show to each other.[293]

Last, Paul talked about the time when people who are part of God's family will live again.

Paul loved the Corinthians! Otherwise, he would not have taken time from his busy life to help them understand what is right. Paul wrote like a loving parent who teaches and corrects his child, then hugs and kisses the child. Paul wrote to correct their mistakes, and point them to a better way to live in God's family.[291]

Talk About the Story: Where was Corinth? What were some problems they had? How did Paul show his love for them?

Scripture: "Therefore, my beloved brethren, be steadfast, immovable, always abounding in the work of the Lord, knowing that your labor is not in vain in the Lord." 1 Corinthians 15:58

Family Time: What kinds of brothers (brethren) or family does Paul say the Corinthians are? What does "abounding" mean? Why can we keep working for the Lord?

Prayer: Lord, You helped Paul show Your better way to his friends at Corinth. Please help us to follow you in the very best way we can. Amen.

THE SECOND LETTER TO CORINTH

Scripture: 2 Corinthians 1:3–4
Place: Written from Macedonia
Time: 55 AD

Paul had written one letter to the people in the Corinthian church to correct all kinds of wrongs.[494] Corinth was a Roman city, famous for its big temple to Athena. It had the reputation of being a very wicked city!

Then, Titus came to see Paul. He had good news! Titus had visited the church in Corinth. They had repented, or changed their minds. They thought and acted differently now. They were following Jesus and growing as God's family![213]

Paul begins this letter by calling himself an apostle of Christ Jesus by God's will.[58] He had God's authority. So it was right for him to correct them and to show his care for them in this letter.

Paul wrote that God is the one who brings comfort out of hard times. He told them to comfort one another like he was comforting them in this letter.[494]

Now, false teachers had come to the church. They questioned Paul's authority. They were saying he should not be a leader. So in this letter Paul told his story. He told everyone how Jesus Himself sent him out to preach.

This letter is full of Paul's stories. The stories show his heart for doing what Jesus sent him to do. He told of the joys and struggles, the privileges and the sufferings, of serving Jesus.[465]

In the first letter, Paul had talked to certain people who were doing wrong. They had changed! So now Paul told the church to forgive these people and to accept and comfort them. Paul wanted them to stay unified, so they didn't leave any room for the devil to get a foothold! The devil often uses bitterness or hurt feelings to divide people and hurt God's family.[52]

In the first section of this letter, Paul explained his heart's passion. In the second section, he talked to those who still doubted Paul's calling as an apostle. The last part instructed them about what they needed to do to get ready for his visit. He encouraged them to show how much they had changed from being selfish and argumentative by giving an offering for God's family in Jerusalem, who didn't have much food.

Paul told them to not trust in themselves,[451] but in God. He described how following Jesus is like a triumphant Roman military parade. But then, he told how we are all like simple clay pots that hold treasure.

Paul wrote this letter under the Holy Spirit to help his friends to reject false apostles and do what is right, so that when he arrived for his visit, they would all be joyful together![213]

Talk About the Story: What was Corinth famous for? What did some false teachers say about Paul? Who made Paul an apostle? What did Paul say about unity in the church?

Scripture: "And God is able to make all grace abound toward you, that you, always having all sufficiency in all things, may have an abundance for every good work." 2 Corinthians 9:8

Family Time: When is it hard to give? When is it easy? What does God's grace give us? Who is someone your family can share with today?

Prayer: Father, we are glad that we can trust You to always give us enough and more than enough. Please teach us to freely give, as Paul taught the Corinthians. Amen.

JOHN'S DISCIPLES BECOME JESUS' DISCIPLES

Scripture: Acts 19:1–7
Place: Ephesus
Time: 55 AD

Paul was amazed. Here were a dozen men who'd been traveling around, preaching that people should get ready for Messiah to come, ever since they had learned about John's baptism! It was hard to believe that so many people STILL had not yet heard that Jesus, the Messiah, had come—but they had not!

Paul had never met Apollos. Priscilla and Aquila had been in Ephesus during the months when Paul had gone south to Jerusalem and Antioch. It was while Paul was gone that Apollos had come and preached so well about the coming Messiah. These men might have been disciples of Apollos, because they were preaching the same message he had preached until Aquila and Priscilla told him all about Jesus. These twelve men who were traveling from synagogue to synagogue, preaching John's message: "The Messiah is coming, so get ready! Repent! Be baptized if you believe Messiah is coming and you want to be part of His kingdom!"

www.thefamilyprayerbible.com

Just like Apollos, they had good news to tell! BUT they did not yet know the even BETTER news that Jesus the Messiah had come. He had lived and showed people what God is like. He had died to pay the price for sin. And He had risen to prove He is Lord over everything! So after these men had preached in the synagogue, Paul asked them, "Did you receive the Holy Spirit when you believed?"[224]

"We have never heard of the Holy Spirit. We don't know anything about it," they replied.[383]

So Paul asked, "When you were baptized, WHY were you baptized?"[30]

"To show that we believe the Messiah is coming and we want to be ready!" They said.

So Paul began to tell them about Jesus![263] Then it was THEIR turn to be amazed! REALLY? Jesus had come? He had fulfilled all of the prophecies? He had healed people and raised the dead? He had died to take the punishment for THEIR sin? And He rose to life again, then went to heaven? And Paul had MET this Jesus? WOW! Imagine how excited they were!

Once these twelve disciples had heard about Jesus and knew that He is just who John said He would be, they were baptized! This time, they were baptized in the name of Jesus![327] They wanted everyone to know that they now believed in the Messiah who had really, truly COME to Earth!

Then Paul laid his hands on each one of these new believers in Jesus. He prayed for each one and God's Holy Spirit came on them, just as He had come upon Paul when Ananias prayed for him.[383] Then the men spoke in languages they did not know,[167] just like people had done on the day when God's Spirit first came! The Holy Spirit was showing that these men were JUST as much a part of God's family as anyone who had known about Jesus from the beginning!

Talk About the Story: Who did Aquila and Priscilla help to know that Jesus had come? How many of these disciples of John were there? What did Paul ask them? Why do you think he asked that? What happened when Paul prayed for them?

Scripture: "But as many as received Him (Jesus), to them He gave the right to become children of God, to those who believe in His name." John 1:12

Family Time: What gives us the right to become part of God's family? How do we receive Jesus? Tell about the time you believed in Jesus and joined God's family.

Prayer: Father, we thank You for sending Jesus. Thank You for sending Your Spirit so that we can grow and show others that we belong to You! In Jesus' name, Amen.

MOVING OUT!

Scripture: Acts 19:8–11
Place: Ephesus
Time: 55 AD

Paul's jaw was set. His mind was made up. He loved his human family, the Jewish people. He really cared about them all. But they could be SO hardheaded! SO stubborn!

Paul had been speaking at the synagogue in Ephesus for three months.[52] He had so wanted the Jews there to see that Jesus is the Messiah God had promised![145] Paul had talked. He had argued. He had unrolled the scrolls of God's Word to point to the exact words of prophecy that Jesus had fulfilled. But not everyone believed.

Some of the Jewish people in Ephesus did hear Paul's words. They DID believe in Jesus and joined God's family! But then, other Jewish people in the synagogue didn't want to hear any more about Jesus. They didn't care if it was true. They

www.thefamilyprayerbible.com

just wanted it to STOP! So those people began to attack God's family with their words, telling lies about them to anyone in Ephesus who'd listen.[374]

That's what drew the line for Paul. God's family came before even his human family. He wanted very much for ALL of them to love and follow Jesus, but he knew that until some of their hearts were changed, they were going to be just like he had been before he met Jesus—stubborn and angry and hurtful to God's family!

He sighed deeply. Then Paul announced to the crowd in the synagogue, "Very well. Since some of you are so opposed to people learning about the MESSIAH here in the synagogue, then we will leave the synagogue. Anyone who wants to follow Jesus and learn more about Him, come with me. We'll meet at the school of Tyrannus every day from now on."[203]

The next day, quite a crowd waited for Paul! He smiled broadly and welcomed this new church family! Now they would not have to be lied about or harassed by the Jews who didn't want to hear about Jesus. They could still be God's own family, no matter where they met!

At that school, many people learned more about Jesus. They learned, and grew, and then they moved away. But they didn't move away because they were angry. They didn't move because they were afraid. No, they moved away because God's Spirit was telling them where to go! They moved away so that they could tell MORE people about Jesus, the Messiah God had promised! God's Spirit was directing them just as He had directed Paul.[199]

The church at Ephesus didn't just get bigger, it gave birth to MORE churches, more growing groups of God's family, all over the area! That's how God's family grows best!

Talk About the Story: Where did the Ephesian believers meet at first? Why did they leave? Where did they go? And what else did they do after they grew?

Scripture: "Grow in the grace and knowledge of our Lord and Savior Jesus Christ. To Him be the glory both now and forever. Amen." 2 Peter 3:18

Family Time: What other words would you use to describe "grace"? Why do you think Peter says to grow both in grace and knowledge of Jesus? What are some ways we can grow in grace.

Prayer: Dear Father, thank You that You give us what we need to grow in Your family. Please help us to be like the people of Ephesus who learned and grew, and then told others about Jesus! In His name, Amen.

PSALM 128

THE FAMILY PSALM

A Jewish father gathered his three teenage sons under the fig tree near his house. He began to challenge them about their future marriage. "Build more than a house; it is only a structure of stones and wood where you live. Build a home, which is made up of a father's love for his wife and children, and their love for the Lord." Then he observed, "The way a family loves each other is more important than the dwelling where they live."

The father challenged his sons to find a wife who "loves God with all her heart and loves you as she loves herself." He explained Psalm 128 to them

"Those who live in awe (fear) of God,[163]
   Will find a happy life.
You will be prosperous in your work
   And the fruit of your labor will make you happy."[397]

The father explained they will build a house for their wife when they get married. "You don't begin building stone on stone with mortar, then put wood in its place." He explained they must begin with a plan. Then he explained they also needed a spiritual plan to build a spiritual family. "Then build everyday according to the final goal." The plans begin with obedience to God.

"You will have a happy home for family
   When both you and your wife obey God,
Then your wife will be like a fruitful vine,
   Flourishing within your home.
Your children will be like vigorous young olive trees,
   As they sit around the table.[206]
They will have the Lord's blessing of happiness."

The father wanted his sons to teach their children the same way he instructed them. He mentioned they must go to worship God in the Temple in Jerusalem. So must their children.

"May the Lord continually bless you from Zion,
   And may you enjoy worshiping in Jerusalem.[183]
May I see my grandchildren worship there also,
   Then God will give peace to Jerusalem."[249]

The father finished by telling his sons, "The secret to living a long and enjoyable happy life is worshiping God, obeying His word, and teaching your children, just as I have taught you."

Talk About the Psalm: What did you learn about the psalm writer in this story? What did you learn about God?

Psalm 128: Read this week's psalm in your Bible together. Choose a verse to read aloud as a prayer.

Prayer: Thank You, God, for the psalm prayers in the Bible. Thank You for teaching us about You and about how to pray. In Jesus' name, Amen.

DATE ___/___

PAUL AND THE EXORCIST

Scripture: Acts 19:11–20
Place: Ephesus
Time: 55 AD

❝Did you HEAR?" said one man to his friend. "Those sons of the Jewish priest Sceva tried to cast out a DEMON. The evil spirit sneered at them. It said, 'I know JESUS. I know PAUL. But who are YOU?' And then, the demon beat up ALL SEVEN of them! The demon ripped off their clothes, and I hear that they ran home naked and screaming![141] It must have been quite a sight, I tell you! I have heard that Paul can tell demons to leave, though—and they LEAVE!"

What a wild story! But it was true! Paul had done many miracles in Ephesus.[466] In fact, God was using Paul to show these very superstitious Ephesians that there was a power FAR greater than the sorcery they practiced and the demons who seemed to be everywhere in Ephesus!

Paul prayed for sick people and they got well! Even if someone got hold of one of Paul's handkerchiefs, took it to a sick person, and prayed in faith, the sick person got well![53] The people of Ephesus were noticing—THIS power was something they had not seen before!

But Paul was not the only person in town doing amazing things. Another traveling preacher came through. He cast out demons by commanding them to go "in the name of Jesus, as Paul preaches!" So even though this man didn't fully understand who Jesus is, he DID know that Jesus' name is the strongest Name anywhere!

Besides this traveling preacher, there were Sceva's seven sons. They were from a Jewish priestly family, so maybe they thought that would give them power to cast out a demon.[159] But they were WRONG! The story of the demon beating them up became the talk of Ephesus.

Everyone heard about these men who tried to cast out a demon without having any power or authority—and it made everyone realize that Paul DID have that kind of power and authority. Paul always spoke in the name of Jesus! More and more people paid attention to Paul's message. And God's good news spread even FASTER!

Pretty soon, people who had been practicing sorcery and worshiping demons started following Jesus.[399] These new members of God's family brought their books of spells and their charms to the city square. And they BURNED them all! They wanted nothing to do with these old ways—they wanted to be rid of trusting in anything but Jesus![490]

Talk About the Story: Whose name is the strongest name anywhere? What did Sceva's sons try to do? What did they find out? What did the people do who had been sorcerers? Why?

Scripture: "God also has highly exalted Him (Jesus) and given Him the name which is above every name, that at the name of Jesus every knee should bow . . . and every tongue should confess that Jesus Christ is Lord, to the glory of God the Father." Philippians 2:9–11

Family Time: Who is Lord? What does it mean to "confess"? When we are part of God's family, what helps us to feel safe?

Prayer: Dear Jesus, we agree and say that You are Lord of all! We are glad that there is no one stronger than You. Please help us to remember to ask Your help, because You are Lord in every situation! In Your mighty name, Amen.

RIOT IN EPHESUS

Scripture: Acts 19:21–41
Place: Ephesus
Time: 55 AD

Gaius shouted to Aristarchus, "COME QUICKLY! There's a RIOT out in the streets!"

The two began to run toward the crowd. Gaius panted, "The silversmiths are angry! They're losing business . . . because so many people . . . are following Jesus. No one is buying their silver idols of Diana. And they are MAD!"

The two followers of Jesus tried to speak to the silversmiths to help calm things down—but instead, someone shouted, "LOOK! Gaius and Aristarchus! Followers of the Way of Jesus! GET THEM!" And suddenly, the two were being carried by the crowd to the big amphitheater in the middle of town!

It all began when Demetrius the silversmith called the other silver workers together. He said, "Paul has got people believing that our idols are not gods. We are losing our trade! Soon we won't have ANY business, if people keep believing in JESUS. And it's not just HERE. He's gone all over the country. The idol trade is going down EVERYWHERE!"

When Paul heard about this riot, he wanted to go to see if he could talk to the crowd. But his friends would not let him into the amphitheater—they didn't want Paul to be KILLED![141] Even the Roman officers in town told Paul to stay out and stay safe.

People were confused about why the crowd had gathered. But someone started a chant.[349] And soon everyone was shouting, "GREAT IS DIANA OF THE EPHESIANS!" They shouted this for TWO HOURS!

Well, by that time the town clerk got there and eventually quieted everyone down.

"Listen," he said. "Everyone knows Diana is the great goddess of our city. Everyone knows the story of how she fell from the sky. But if you have a problem with these followers of the Way of Jesus, then Demetrius and his friends should come and make a formal complaint.[382] We have a city council who can deal with this. Otherwise, we are going to end up in trouble with Rome for rioting. That means more Roman soldiers in our city. So go home!"

The people left. Suddenly, they were all tired of yelling! And Gaius and Aristarchus were safe! God's family was growing—and that always upset people, one way or another. But God was in charge. His plan was at work in all of it!

Talk About the Story: Why was Demetrius upset? What did he say about Paul? How do you think this story would have been different if Demetrius had believed in Jesus? What did the town clerk tell the people?

Scripture: "I will love You, O Lord, my strength. The Lord is my rock and my fortress and my deliverer." PSALM 18:1–2

Family Time: How would your life be different if you did not know Jesus? What are some ways God takes care of us every day? How has He shown His care in a scary time?

Prayer: Dear Jesus, You change everything when we belong to You. We ask You to help us follow You even when obeying You might feel scary. We love You! In Your name, Amen.

EUTYCHUS FALLS ASLEEP

Scripture: Acts 20:1–12
Place: Troas
Time: 55 AD

The room was crowded with people listening to Paul preach and teach. Paul had just arrived, and they couldn't wait to hear all that he had to say, even though it was late at night. They were so excited to hear of the amazing things God had been doing in the different places Paul had traveled! But suddenly there was a gasp, and then a crash and a thud. One person looked toward the window of the room. "Where's Eutychus?" he cried out. Eutychus, a young man, had been sitting there just a moment ago.[57]

People ran to the window, and then out the door and down to the street three stories below. "Oh, no! Eutychus has died!"[99] The people gathered around, feeling terrible. All the joy of listening to Paul's message was gone. As the men brought the body inside, women began to cry and people began to feel dreadful!

www.thefamilyprayerbible.com

Paul pushed his way through the crowd to where they had laid the boy's lifeless body. Paul knelt beside Eutychus' body. He hugged the boy to himself.

"Don't worry!" Paul said to the crowd around him. "There is life in him!"

Paul HAD preached a long time. He wasn't able to stay long here in Troas, so he needed to talk to these loved friends for as long as he could! It was very late by this time, and it was natural for a boy to fall asleep, especially when he was warm and cozy sitting in that windowsill. Since it was night, the lamps were burning, and their warmth made it even warmer up high! Eutychus probably sat in the window to catch the cool breeze that would help to keep him awake—but finally, sleep had overcome him. He relaxed, snored a little snore, and then—he was FALLING![112]

In those days, windows didn't have glass. Glass windows hadn't been invented! And there were not screens on them like we have now. So if a person fell out the window, they fell OUT! There was nothing to stop them. So when Eutychus fell, only the GROUND stopped him!

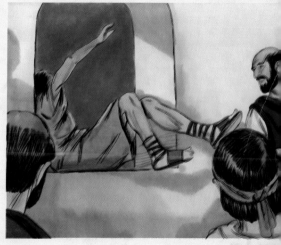

But of course, GOD knew what was going on. And Paul as he prayed over Eutychus, could then feel that God had brought life back to this young man! Everyone breathed a sigh of relief. Here they were expecting to have a FUNERAL tomorrow instead of seeing Paul off to his next destination![193] But now they could listen to Paul for as long as they could stay awake, and stay out of windows!

Talk About the Story: Were windows in Bible times like windows today? How were they different? Why did Paul preach so long? What did Paul say about Eutychus when he hugged him?

Scripture: "For You have delivered my soul from death, my eyes from tears, and my feet from falling. I will walk before the Lord in the land of the living." Psalm 116:8–9

Family Time: Tell about a time you got hurt. What happened? Who helped you? What helps you to remember that God cares about you?

Prayer: Dear Lord, we are glad that You care about us. Thank You for all of the ways You show us Your love! In Jesus' name, Amen.

DATE ___/___

THE HOLY SPIRIT WARNS PAUL

Scripture: Acts 20:13–38
Place: Ephesus, etc.
Time: 55 AD

Paul looked from one face to the next of his dear friends. They'd walked over 30 miles to meet with Paul—that's how much they loved him. Now they were all gathered on the deck of the ship to hear whatever he had to say.[344] Paul's throat tightened and his chest felt heavy. He loved these people very much. He'd first told many of them about Jesus. He had taught them for at least two years, and watched them grow into strong followers of Jesus.

And now, he knew that he would never see them again.

For a while now, in every city where Paul had gone, God's Holy Spirit had impressed the same message on him. Over and over, Paul heard three things: "Go to Jerusalem. Hardship and prison are waiting for you.[327] You will be in prison in Rome." Now Paul was about to tell his dear friends what he now knew.

Paul had been traveling from island to island, going a short way by boat or by land and then spending a day or two, maybe a week or so, in most places. He had spent three months in Greece; but otherwise, he was traveling most of the time! He was on his way to Jerusalem to celebrate Pentecost, and so he didn't stop in Ephesus. But while his ship was docked at Miletus, he sent for these dear Ephesian friends who'd walked down to the port to meet Paul.

Paul cleared his throat. He said, "God's Spirit has told me that I'm going to be persecuted and put into prison[494]—but this is all so that I can finish the important job Jesus gave to me long ago. It is all a part of telling the good news of God's grace for as long as I can![391] Now you need to know," he went on, "that I am sure we will never meet again until we meet in heaven. But I have given you everything I can. I have taught you all I know about God's grace."[358]

Paul went on to remind them of things he had taught them. He had never asked them for money or clothes. He had always worked to buy what he needed because he wanted to show them what they should do. He was generous with them, because he wanted them to become generous.[536] As Paul reminded them, "The Lord Jesus said it is better to give than it is to receive."[213]

The friends all knelt together and prayed for Paul and their own journey back to be faithful leaders in Ephesus. Then one by one, each of them hugged Paul tight, with tears running down their faces.[474] They would never see him again, yet they were glad to know that Paul was not afraid to obey God!

Talk About the Story: Where was Paul trying to get to by Pentecost? Who walked over 30 miles to see Paul? What things had Paul done that he reminded them about? Why did they cry?

Scripture: "For I am not ashamed of the gospel of Christ, for it is the power of God to salvation for everyone who believes, for the Jew first and also for the Greek." Romans 1:16

Family Time: Paul wrote these words. Why was he glad to tell the good news, or gospel, of Jesus Christ? (Christ means the same as Messiah, in Greek.) Who are people we could tell the powerful good news to?

Prayer: Lord Jesus, we are glad that the good news about You is powerful. We know it changes our lives. Please help us to gladly tell others the good news and boldly share God's love! In your name, Amen.

PAUL'S TRIP TO JERUSALEM

Scripture: Acts 21:1–16
Place: varied, to Jerusalem
Time: 55 AD

Paul sighed as he looked down at the man who had taken his belt. The man, Agabus, had tied his own hands and feet with it.[224] He said, "The owner of this belt will be bound hand and foot in Jerusalem, and then he will be handed over to the Gentiles."

Paul had been hearing God's Spirit telling him to GO to Jerusalem. But the closer he GOT to Jerusalem, the more people tried to tell him NOT to go! First friends in Tyre told Paul, "By the Holy Spirit, we say you ought NOT to go to Jerusalem."

But Paul knew the Holy Spirit had told him over and OVER to go to Jerusalem. He already knew that there was trouble waiting for him there.[99] But they ALSO knew that it was what God wanted him to do! These friends followed Paul to the

ship and prayed with him before he and his friends boarded the ship and sailed south toward Jerusalem.

They spent another day at Ptolemais, where the Christians kept telling Paul not to go to Jerusalem. Paul was getting VERY good at sighing by now! He sighed, bit his lip, and said nothing. There was NOTHING TO SAY. He knew that God wanted him to go and he was going!

Further south, they docked at Caesarea, where Philip lived—the same Philip who was one of the first deacons![145] His four unmarried daughters all spoke the Word of God. Paul and his friend stayed there for some time. It was while they were there at Philip's house that Agabus, the man who took Paul's belt, came to warn Paul that he'd be bound and turned over to the Romans. Then everyone who heard Agabus say this BEGGED Paul not to go to Jerusalem!

Paul sighed again as he looked around—at the prophet on the ground, tied up with Paul's belt, at the daughters, at Philip and all of his friends. He said to them, "Why are you trying to change my mind? I'm ready to be bound. In fact, I'm ready to DIE for the name of my Lord Jesus!"

Paul knew his friends loved him and he was glad that they all wanted him to stay out of trouble. But THIS time, Paul knew that into TROUBLE was just where God wanted him to go!

When his friends saw they couldn't change Paul's mind, they said, "God's will be done."[533] They quit pestering Paul, and Paul could quit sighing! When he left for Jerusalem, a lot of those same friends from Caesarea went with him and took Paul to the home of Mnason, one of the earliest followers of Jesus![154] He was an old man, but he welcomed Paul warmly. He had seen a lot. And he didn't try to persuade Paul to do anything except obey God!

Paul knew that he could rely on God to bring him to JUST the places he was supposed to go!

Talk About the Story: What did Paul's friends keep on telling him? What had God's Holy Spirit told him over and over? What did Agabus do to show Paul what was going to happen? Who could Paul trust to care for him, even in danger?

Scripture: "Commit your way to the LORD, trust also in Him, and He shall bring it to pass." Psalm 37:5

Family Time: Who is worthy of our trust? Why? What does it mean to commit your way to the Lord? How much of our lives does God care about? How much is He in charge of?

Prayer: Dear Lord, please help us to listen to You and to obey You, even when other people try to tell us not to obey You. We want to be strong in you and trust You to take care of us. In Jesus' name, Amen.

WRITING THE BOOK OF ROMANS

Scripture: Romans 1:16
Place: Corinth
Time: Winter, 56-57 AD

Paul was preaching and teaching in Corinth, Greece.[431] Corinth was an important city. All cargo ships going east or west passed through the Corinth canal Ahitophelthat linked the Aegean Sea to the Ionian Sea. By teaching in a place where so many people passed through, Paul could send the good news of Jesus to many more places! But now Paul wanted to go to Rome. It is in modern-day Italy. At the time, the city was the capital of the whole known world.

"I plan to go to Rome," Paul told his friends. "I'll write a letter to the church there, so that they'll know we are coming. We'll stop there on the way to Spain. After all, we haven't been to either of those places yet! And Jesus said to be witnesses to the ends of the earth, so that's where I'm going! I love to tell the Good News to people have never heard of Jesus."

"From Rome, we can tell the whole world."[199]

Paul did not know how important the church at Rome would become—but of course, God knew! So the Holy Spirit inspired Paul to write a unique letter.

This letter tells all about God's salvation both for Jews and for Gentiles (people who are not Jews). Then it tells how believers in Jesus can live through God's power. This letter would be copied and taken back to other churches to help them understand more about salvation and God's amazing grace to all people.

Paul told about God's grace to all people, especially since some Jews still wanted everyone who followed Jesus to obey Jewish laws and customs.

He started his letter by telling what sin is like. He told how we are guilty, we are all sinners. We are lost outside of Jesus Christ. Even though Jews knew the Law, Paul said they were just as guilty of sin as the Gentiles. And the Gentiles were guilty of sin even though they didn't have the Law.

Paul went on to show how it is only by faith[12] that people are saved and counted right with God, because Jesus took the punishment we deserve when He died on the cross.

Then Paul wrote about what Jesus did and how we can receive new life to live for God. He told how to live daily for Jesus Christ in the power of His Holy Spirit.[478]

Since there was still so much confusion between Jews and Gentiles, Paul also wrote about God's plan for the Jewish people. Even though Paul was a Jew, he said he was a debtor to both Jews and Gentiles. He told them, "I am ready to preach in Rome" and "I am not ashamed of the gospel because it is the power of God for salvation—for Jews and Gentiles alike."[250]

Talk About the Story: Why was Rome important? What did Paul say about all people, both Jews and non-Jews? What did Paul say about Jesus?

Scripture: "For I am not ashamed of the gospel of Christ, for it is the power of God to salvation for everyone who believes, for the Jew first and also for the Greek. For in it the righteousness of God is revealed from faith to faith; as it is written, "The just shall live by faith." Romans 1:16–17

Family Time: What is the gospel, or good news of Christ (Jesus)? Why was Paul excited about God's good news? How is God's righteousness shown? What's a way you can show your faith?

Prayer: Lord, we are thankful for Your good news! Please help us to be people who show our faith in You by our lives. Amen.

PSALM 133
A SONG OF HARMONY

The day was stressful; King David had sat on his throne all afternoon as a judge over disputes brought to him. When individuals or families argued, they wanted their king to hear their side of the problem. Everyone wanted their king to decide in their favor. David was glad to be away from arguing people. He asked, "Why can't an Israelite love the Lord his God with all his heart, and his neighbor as himself" (Deuteronomy 6:9; Leviticus 19:17).

When David returned home, his sons were arguing. David knew children fight, but as a parent he wanted them to love each other. Then it was time for the afternoon prayers in the Temple. David was happy to go into the presence of God because it was so peaceful. He began writing a Psalm.

"Behold, how peaceful and beautiful it is,
        When God's children live together in harmony.[166]
Because godly harmony is like anointing oil,
        Poured on the head of the High Priest
That ran down Aaron's beard,
        And dripped on to his priestly robes" (Vss. 1-2).

David smiled as he sang this new song as he entered the Temple. He wanted all Israel to see his harmony, so he began with the command, "Behold" which meant for them to come see this unity. It is found in God's presence in the Temple.

What was harmony? It was like oil, the symbol of God's spirit. When God brings people together in His presence for worship that is harmony. But not all Israelites could get into the Temple to see the anointing oil on the High Priest. So David asked himself, "Where can all of Israel see harmony?" He answered, "Everyone could see the fields and trees."

"The dew," David answered; God's dew on all trees bushes and grass. Dew is a picture of God's presence everywhere. So he sang,

"Harmony refreshes all things that grow
        Like the dew that falls on Mount Herman,
And falls on all growing life in Zion.
        Harmony is the way God blesses His people;
It is a picture of everlasting life after death."[47]

David was encouraged as he left the Temple. He had seen harmony in the oil on the priest, running down on the priestly robes. Then he looked out to see the hills surrounding Jerusalem. There would be dew on them tomorrow morning. So he had hope that harmony would come to all God's people.

Talk About the Psalm: What did you learn about the psalm writer in this story? What did you learn about God?

Psalm 133: Read this week's psalm in your Bible together. Choose a verse to read aloud as a prayer.

Prayer: Thank You, God, for the psalm prayers in the Bible. Thank You for teaching us about You and about how to pray. In Jesus' name, Amen.

QUESTIONS IN THE TEMPLE

Scripture: Acts 21:26–40
Place: Jerusalem
Time: 57 AD

Here comes the trouble I was told about, thought Paul. He had come to the Temple to worship God,[412] but suddenly the big, quiet Temple was ringing with shouts! Paul glanced around to see men running at him from all directions. Some were Temple guards, and some were men yelling things like, "STOP HIM! ARREST HIM!" and "THIS MAN DOESN'T KEEP THE LAW!" Another screamed, "He brought GENTILES into the TEMPLE! GET HIM!"[349]

Of course, the lies weren't true. He hadn't brought any Gentiles into the Temple. But that didn't matter. The angry men grabbed Paul and in a moment, Paul was being attacked by a mob! They dragged Paul out to the gate of the Temple. *THIS is the beginning of what God's Spirit told me so many times,* Paul thought. He was not afraid, but he was sad. These men were part of the same group of

www.thefamilyprayerbible.com

enemies who were determined to stop Paul, either by telling lies about him, or by killing him! But so far, NONE of that had worked well. And Paul knew that God was still in control!

The gate to the Temple shut behind him. The crowd was now in the street—and they wanted to kill Paul! But NOW he was in Roman territory. Roman soldiers showed up, shoving people aside and grabbing Paul from the middle of that crowd. When the Romans heard there was a riot, they came quickly! The Romans didn't like riots. And they didn't understand these Jews and their wild arguments about religion. But they did stop the crowd from beating Paul![217]

The Roman soldiers chained Paul's hands and feet—just as Agabus had said they would. The officer in charge was trying to find out who Paul was and why people were rioting, but there was so much shouting and yelling, he couldn't understand a thing anyone said! So he told the soldiers to carry Paul up the Temple steps to get him away from the angry crowd.

When the officer could hear Paul, he said to the officer, "Let me explain, please." Because he spoke to the officer in Greek,[478] the officer was surprised

He said to Paul, "Aren't you the Egyptian who is leading a rebellion?"

Paul smiled—this Roman officer didn't know the people of Jerusalem very well. He couldn't even tell an Egyptian from a Jew! "No," Paul said, in Greek. "I am a JEW. I am from Tarsus, a city in Turkey. And I am a Roman citizen. These people are rioting over a lie that was told in the Temple. Please, let me speak to these people. Perhaps I can help them to understand—and stop this riot."

Stopping the riot was what the Roman officer cared about. He would be in trouble himself if he couldn't stop the riot! So he said, "Very well. Speak to them.[494] We'll see if any of them can listen!"

Talk About the Story: Where was Paul when people began to shout at him? Who stopped to find out what was true? What did the Romans do that Agabus had said they would do? Paul spoke what language to the Roman officer?

Scripture: "In God I have put my trust; I will not be afraid. What can man do to me?" Psalm 56:11

Family Time: Why were the people angry? When have you encountered people who were angry because they believed a lie about you? What are some things we can do when people refuse to listen to us or believe lies about us? How can we show love in the midst of people being angry?

Prayer: Lord Jesus, we are glad that You are with us always. When people don't listen to us, please help us to trust You and stay calm. Help us to love people who are mean to us. In Your name, Amen.

PAUL PREACHING IN THE TEMPLE

Scripture: Acts 22:1–30
Place: Jerusalem
Time: 57 AD

Paul stood silently on the Temple step, looking out over this crowd of angry faces. He could see some faces he knew, for Paul had lived in Jerusalem since he was young, growing up with others who studied under Gamaliel, the famous rabbi. He sighed deeply and raised his hands to ask for their attention.[105]

Paul had talked with the Roman officer in Greek, but now he began to speak in Hebrew, the language of the Jewish people. Suddenly everyone calmed down and got quiet, for they ALL wanted to hear what Paul would say. Some of them didn't even know WHY they were rioting! They'd simply joined the howling crowd!

Paul began, "I'm a Jew, born in Tarsus.[478] But I grew up here, studying in Gamaliel's school! I knew every Jewish law and custom. I was determined to obey every rule.

"I used to persecute followers of the Way. Anyone in the Sanhedrin can tell you that I arrested and bound both men and women to jail and to death. In fact, I was on my way to Damascus to arrest MORE of Jesus' followers when a bright light from heaven blinded me! I fell to the ground and someone said, 'Paul, why do you persecute Me?'[25] It was JESUS HIMSELF who was speaking! Jesus told me to go into town and wait there.[256] I was blind and my friends had to lead me.

"But God sent a man named Ananias, a man who loved God and was respected by all Jews. He told me that God had chosen me to be a witness to all people of what I had seen and heard.[533] When he prayed, I could see again and was baptized to show God had forgiven my sins!

"Later, as I prayed in Jerusalem, God told me that He was sending me to the Gentiles."[199]

When Paul said the word "Gentiles," everyone went WILD, yelling and throwing dust into the air. They screamed, "He's not fit to live! Get rid of him!"

Of course the Roman soldiers were Gentiles! But because they didn't speak Hebrew, they still didn't understand what riot was about! So they took Paul to whip him—as they usually did, because people didn't normally tell the truth![349]

But Paul said to the officer, "Is it legal to whip a Roman citizen who hasn't even been charged with a crime?"[142] The officer stopped and sent for the commander.

The commander asked Paul, "You are really a Roman citizen?"

"Yes!" said Paul.

"I had to buy my citizenship," the commander said.

"Well, I was born a citizen!" said Paul.

Suddenly, everything had changed! The commander took off Paul's chains and ordered the Jewish leaders to meet with Paul.[165] Paul was going to have the chance to talk to many of his former friends in the Sanhedrin about Jesus! Paul was glad for this trouble, and trusting God to do some amazing things!

Talk About the Story: Where was Paul when he spoke? What language did he speak to the Jewish people? What word made them angry? What did Paul say about his citizenship?

Scripture: "For My thoughts are not your thoughts, nor are your ways My ways," says the Lord. "For as the heavens are higher than the earth, so are My ways higher than your ways, and My thoughts than your thoughts." Isaiah 55:8–9

Family Time: What is something about God or the things He does that amaze you? Surprise you? What things help you know that He is far wiser than we are?

Prayer: Dear Lord, we admit that we think we are pretty smart sometimes. But we know that You are far wiser than we are. Thank You for loving us and for doing things that amaze us every day! In Jesus' name, Amen.

CONFRONTATION IN THE SANHEDRIN

Scripture: Acts 23:1–11
Place: Jerusalem
Time: 57 AD

Paul rubbed his sore face. He'd just been SLAPPED in the face. He looked at the faces of the ruling religious leaders, the Sanhedrin. He knew many of them well. Here he was, in MORE of the "trouble" God had sent him into. It was the BEST way for his former friends in the Sanhedrin to hear about Jesus—even if these rulers slapped and insulted him!

Paul had begun speaking by saying, "My brothers, I have always lived with a clear conscience."[478]

That's when the head of the Sanhedrin told someone to slap Paul's mouth!

Paul shook his head and rubbed his jaw. "God will judge you, you hypocrite. How can you break the law by hitting me before I am found guilty?"[105] he said.

People near him said, "He's the high priest. You're insulting the high priest."

"I did not realize who he was," Paul apologized. "Scripture says, 'Don't speak evil about a ruler of the people.'"

As Paul looked around, God's Spirit gave Paul insight! He realized that there

www.thefamilyprayerbible.com

were two groups in the Sanhedrin—about half and half. The Sadducees were one half. They didn't believe in angels or that people can be raised from the dead. But the Pharisees DID believe in these things.

Paul declared, "I am a Pharisee and the son of a Pharisee.[478] And I am being judged here because I hope in the resurrection!"[405]

Suddenly, HALF of the Sanhedrin was on PAUL'S side! They began to shout, arguing with the Sadducees and getting louder and louder![142]

"We don't find ANYTHING wrong with this man," said some of the Pharisees. "What if an angel spoke to him? Maybe he was visited by a spirit!"

At this point, the commander ordered the Roman guards to move in. He could see that there would soon be ANOTHER riot! It was VERY likely that these men would begin beating Paul up again—and Paul was now in the protection of the Roman Empire! So the Roman soldiers pushed their way through and simply grabbed Paul out of the crowd of shouting men!

The soldiers took Paul to the Roman fortress in Jerusalem.[387] Now he was safe from being beaten. He was protected from his own people, the Jews, by the people the Jews disliked, the Gentile Romans! And of course, this was not the end of the story.

That night, the Lord spoke to Paul.[377] He said, "Take courage.[161] Cheer up! You have witnessed about Me in Jerusalem. Now, you will witness about Me in Rome."

WOW! Paul sat up straight. He would be going to ROME, the heart of the Gentile world! It would likely mean more trouble, but it was trouble he was glad to take—for God's good news about Jesus would be going a long, long way!

Talk About the Story: Who was Paul speaking to? What were the two groups of leaders? How were they different? Why did the Roman guard take Paul away? What did Jesus tell Paul he would be doing?

Scripture: "Now to Him who is able to do exceedingly abundantly above all that we ask or think, according to the power that works in us, to Him be glory in the church by Christ Jesus to all generations, forever and ever. Amen." Ephesians 3:20–21[1]

Family Time: How much more can God do than we can ask or think? What is the power that works in people who are part of God's family? What's something you can ask God's help with today?

Prayer: Dear Father, we are glad that You can do far more than we can ever ask! You are good and we know that You will help us when we ask You for help. Thank you for loving us. In Jesus' name, Amen.

A PLOT TO KILL PAUL

Scripture: Acts 23:12–15
Place: Jerusalem
Time: 57 AD

A group of angry men gathered in the street. "Paul has to be stopped!" one said.[99]

"Shh!" said another as he noticed a Roman soldier not too far away. "We need to talk about this in private!" The men nodded and then made plans to gather together behind locked doors to talk.

Soon more than forty men were crowded into the room. Each man had heard about the things Paul taught about Jesus—that He was the Messiah, God's Son, and that He came back to life after the Romans put Him to death on a cross. But instead of believing and being glad for God's love for people, they were furi-ous—furious that Paul thought that the good news of the Messiah could be for anyone other than them![334]

Some of these men had been following Paul as he traveled and preached about Jesus in one city after another. They had worked so hard to keep people from listening, to get Paul in trouble. But it never seemed to work out!

"Did you hear what Paul said about the Gentiles (non-Jews)?"

"Yes! He thinks that God sent the Messiah for them! That is not right at all!" On and on, they grumbled and complained.

"Stop!" said one of the men. "It is time to take care of this. I vow to not eat or drink until Paul is dead.[521] Who is with me?"

Shouts of agreement echoed around the room. Over forty men vowed to not eat or drink until Paul was dead!

So they talked and planned and talked and planned, and they realized that they would need to work quickly, or they would get pretty hungry and thirsty!

"I'll tell the leader of the Sanhedrin to ask the soldiers to bring Paul back for more questioning."

"And we'll hide and attack the soldiers on the way to the meeting."

"I have a sword at home!"

"Paul will be dead before morning!"

"And we'll have to act quickly before the soldiers have a chance to respond!"

Soon it was all arranged, and everyone ran off to prepare, some to talk with the high priest, others to gather weapons, and others to make sure they had a good escape route.[139]

But they didn't know that someone had overheard their plans!

Talk About the Story: Why were the men angry? What did they want to do? What do you think will happen next?

Scripture: "Yea, though I walk through the valley of the shadow of death, I will fear no evil; For You are with me; Your rod and Your staff, they comfort me." Psalm 23:4

Family Time: Who are some people facing persecution or danger because believe in or tell others about Jesus? Find out about present day missionaries or Christians in places with lots of persecution. Pray for them together.

Prayer: Father, thank You that You are always with us. Thank You that You are with people who are in danger because they tell others about You in dangerous places. Please help them and give them peace. Amen.

ESCAPE IN THE NIGHT!

Scripture: Acts 23:16–34
Place: Jerusalem
Time: 57 AD

Paul sat in the Roman fortress. He'd heard from a guard that the Sanhedrin, the Jewish rulers, were going to ask the commander for Paul to meet with them again—which seemed odd. After all, they hadn't listened to him before. They'd had a fight instead! But Paul didn't have to wonder for long. Just then, Paul's nephew came into Paul's room.

"Uncle Paul!" he said, sitting down next to Paul, "I have something to tell you. FORTY men have promised that they will not eat until they have KILLED you! They plan to kill you when you are taken to the Sanhedrin again."[521]

Paul smiled and shook his head. Once again, God had put the right person in the right place to save Paul's life! His nephew was young, but he certainly knew how to help his uncle! He gave his nephew a hug and said, "That's amazing good

www.thefamilyprayerbible.com

work, nephew! Now tell the commander of the fortress just what you told me."

He had the guard take the boy to the commander, who took him aside and said, "What do you have to tell me?"

Paul's nephew said, "The Jews are going to have the Sanhedrin ask for Paul to come back. But forty men will be waiting in the street to kill him! They are so serious about this that they have promised not to eat until they have killed my uncle. Please, can't you keep him safe?"

The commander started thinking! This Paul certainly was an interesting fellow; people either loved him or hated him! He said to the boy, "Be sure not to tell anyone that you've given me this information. I have an idea."

So the commander sent for two of his officers. He said to them, "Get soldiers ready to ride by nine o'clock tonight. Provide horses[387] for Paul to ride so he can get to Governor Felix in Caesarea, up north on the coast."[109]

Then the commander wrote a letter to Felix, the Roman governor. It said: The Jews seized this man and were about to kill him. I learned that he is a Roman citizen,[214] so I had my soldiers rescue him. I wanted to know what they were angry about, so I took him to their Council. He has not done anything for which he deserves to die or be in prison. They are upset about questions of Jewish law. When I discovered a plot against his life, I decided to send him to you at once.[480] I have told his accusers they will have to come before you."

So after dark, 70 soldiers saddled up, setting Paul on a horse in the middle of them. Then 200 spear-carrying soldiers made a human wall around the horses! Paul rode quietly out of Jerusalem, surrounded by Roman soldiers. The men who were waiting to kill him never saw him or even knew he left! God had worked every detail of this to protect Paul and get him on his way to Rome, as He had told Paul he would do!

Talk About the Story: Who heard about the plot made by the 40 men? What did he do about it? What did the commander do? How did God protect Paul?

Scripture: " He delivered me from my strong enemy, from those who hated me, for they were too strong for me." Psalm 118:17

Family Time: When God makes a promise, what does He do about that promise? Does God promise to help us when we ask? When we are afraid or in danger, what can we do?

Prayer: Dear Lord, thank You that You are the King over everything. Even when people are mean or we are afraid, You promise to be with us and help us. Thank you that You can do anything! In Jesus' name, Amen.

PAUL BEFORE FELIX

Scripture: Acts 24:1–27
Place: Caesarea
Time: 57 AD

Paul smiled. He was once again in front of a group of angry men—but this time, he had the Roman governor and the laws that protected a Roman citizen on his side! Some Jewish leaders had traveled from Jerusalem and brought a lawyer with them. Now this lawyer, named Tertullus, was laying out the Jewish leaders' complaint against Paul.[349]

Tertullus said, "Your Excellency, you have done great work in protecting the Jewish people.[196] We are grateful to you. To keep from taking up too much of your time, let me tell you what this Paul has done. He is a troublemaker! He has gone all over the known world stirring up trouble. He is a ringleader of the followers of the Way, believers in Jesus. He recently brought a non-Jew into our Temple, so we were about to arrest him and put him on trial among the Jews. But

www.thefamilyprayerbible.com

Claudius took him from us and ordered us all to be here."

Felix didn't reply. He had already heard Claudius' side of the story! He simply motioned to Paul to speak. Paul said, "Sir, I know you are a fair man. So I am confident you will hear me."[105]

"I went to Jerusalem only 12 days ago, not arguing with anyone![476] These men cannot prove a thing they have said about me. I am a Jew, I worship the God of my fathers and I believe the Law and the prophets.[541] I am part of the Way, which they call a sect. I do all I can to please God. I believe there will be a resurrection at the end of all things,[34] just as my accusers do. I came to Jerusalem to bring money for the poor. That is why I was in the Temple. There was no Gentile with me, and no disturbance. Then some Jews from Turkey saw me—they are the ones who should be here! They accused me of bringing a non-Jew into the Temple. I had no Gentile with me. Later, I spoke to the Sanhedrin, and they began to argue about the resurrection!"[405]

Felix said, "I'm calling the commander to testify. When he comes, I'll decide this case."

Then Felix gave Paul some freedom and allowed his friends to visit him.[177] It was becoming quite a pleasant seaside vacation! Felix and his wife Drusilla also invited Paul to tell them about Jesus.[145] As Paul spoke, the truth made Felix nervous! But he really wanted to hear more. So he told Paul, "You may go for now. I'll send for you again."[268]

Usually, people in jail paid a governor to let them go. So, Felix was hoping Paul would pay him and he would release him. But even though Paul often talked with Felix, he never offered him money. Paul stayed in the "prison" for two years, then Felix left the area and left Paul in jail to keep the Jews happy. But that was fine—God was still moving Paul to Rome, bit by bit. And he was telling more and more people in the army and the government about Jesus!

Talk About the Story: What did the Jews say Paul had done? What did Paul say about their complaint? Why do you think Felix got nervous when Paul told him about Jesus? Why did Felix leave Paul in jail?

Scripture: "Therefore, putting away lying, 'Let each one of you speak truth with his neighbor,' for we are members of one another." Ephesians 4:25

Family Time: Why is it important to tell the truth? What are some good things that come from telling the truth? What are some hard things that come from telling the truth?

Prayer: Dear Father, we are glad to see how Paul told the truth. Please help us to be truthful in our words and also kind in our words. We want to please You! In Jesus' name, Amen.

PSALM 134
A PSALM OF NIGHT WORSHIP

The Ark was brought into the house of Abinadab after it was returned from the Philistines. God had abundantly prospered Abinadab with a great harvest of grain and birth of livestock. David knew how God blessed Abinadab, so he brought the Ark of the Covenant to Jerusalem at the beginning of his reign. He knew the presence of God sitting on the Ark would bless the nation.

The Ark was set on Mount Zion, the hilltop next to David's palace. Every night the king went out to the back porch of his dwelling. There he could see multitudes gather around the Ark to pray. They were lifting their hands in worship. They were praying for God's blessing on them and their families. David directed them,

"Praise the Lord, all you serving the Lord with worship,[46]
You stand all night around the Ark and God's presence.
Lift your hands toward the sanctuary where God lives,
Shout your worship to the Lord."[183]

Did you notice the Psalms describe night worship? It describes people serving the Lord at night. Some serve God by teaching, others serve by singing for God in the choir and still others serve by giving money to the church or other worthy ministries. But David saw people all night long standing around the tent where the Ark of the Covenant was sitting. They served God by worshiping Him.

King David knew Israel would be a strong nation when its people sought the presence of God and they worshipped Him with all their inner being. David knew when the people sought the presence of God in the Temple; He in turn would pour His presence on their lives. Soldiers who are indwelt with God's presence are unbeatable.

"May the Lord who blesses heavens and earth,
Bless His people from Jerusalem where He lives."[540]

We can learn to pray before we go to sleep. Most of us will fold our hands in prayer. But the people in David's time lifted their hands in worship. We can do that, too. We can pray and worship in many different ways.

Talk About the Psalm: What did you learn about the psalm writer in this story? What did you learn about God?

Psalm 134: Read this week's psalm in your Bible together. Choose a verse to read aloud as a prayer.

Prayer: Thank You, God, for the psalm prayers in the Bible. Thank You for teaching us about You and about how to pray. In Jesus' name, Amen.

PAUL BEFORE FESTUS AND AGRIPPA

Scripture: Acts 25:1—26:32
Place: Caesarea
Time: 59 AD

Paul shook his head. This was like going back two years—the SAME men giving the SAME arguments, pointing and shouting the SAME lies! The only difference was the governor!

Two years had passed, and now Festus was the new governor—and the Jewish leaders wanted him on their side. So Festus told them to come to Caesarea again to make their complaint—and here they were AGAIN.

Paul said, "I have not committed any offense against the Temple. I have not done anything to offend Caesar."[109]

Festus wanted to please the Jewish leaders. So he asked, "Then will you go to Jerusalem and stand trial?" He knew the leaders wanted to take Paul back to Jerusalem.

But Paul said, "NO! I am here in the court of Caesar. I have done no wrong to the Jewish people. And I am not guilty of any crime under Roman law. They want

www.thefamilyprayerbible.com

to kill me. But their complaint cannot be proven. So you have no right to send me with them. I appeal to CAESAR!"[387]

Festus said, "You've appealed to Caesar. Then to Caesar you will go!"

King Agrippa and his wife Bernice soon arrived to visit. Festus told them about Paul. He told how Paul had been in jail for over two years, with NO charge against him! Agrippa and his wife wanted to hear Paul's story!

So Paul stood before King Agrippa. The king knew a lot about Jewish law, so Paul told about growing up in Jerusalem as a Pharisee,[478] part of a strict group of Jews. He told how the Jewish leaders were upset because Paul talked about God's promises being fulfilled by Jesus rising from the dead. He told how he'd hated Jesus' followers, and how Jesus had stopped him!

Paul said, "King Agrippa, Jesus told me what to do. I was not going to disobey! I began to preach, telling people to turn to God. The Jews tried to arrest me on a false charge, but God has protected me. I tell you, Jesus has fulfilled God's promises. He died and rose as the prophets said He would. I've come to tell you about this great salvation!"

Festus said, "Paul, your great learning has driven you crazy!"

Paul answered, "Your Excellency, I am sane. And I am speaking truth. These are well-known facts. King Agrippa, I know you believe the prophets!"[34]

King Agrippa smiled nervously. "Paul, you've almost persuaded me to follow Jesus!"[444]

Paul said, "I wish you would. I wish you were just like me, except for my chains!"

The king and his wife talked with the other officials. They said, "This man has not done anything worthy of death or prison. Festus, you could have released him. But he has appealed to Caesar—so to Rome he must go!"

Paul was on his way to Rome!

Talk About the Story: What was the new governor's name? Could the Jewish leaders prove their complaint? What did Festus say when Paul appealed to Caesar? What did King Agrippa say when Paul told him about Jesus?

Scripture: "But what things were gain to me, these I have counted loss for Christ. Yet indeed I also count all things loss for the excellence of the knowledge of Christ Jesus my Lord." Philippians 3:7–8

Family Time: What's something important your family does together? What is something you all like very much? What's a way to show that you think knowing Jesus is more important than anything?

Prayer: Dear Lord, Please help us to act and talk in ways that show that we think Jesus is more important than anyone. We love You! In His name, Amen.

ONWARD TO ROME

Scripture: Acts 27:1–26
Place: Mediterranean Sea
Time: 59 AD

Paul stood on the deck of ANOTHER ship, feeling the wind in his face. Luke and Aristarchus were with him and they were all excited. YES! They were finally on their way to Rome. God had said He would send Paul there, and now, they were sailing west!

Paul was still a prisoner, but Paul was a very kindly treated prisoner—in fact, he was often treated as an esteemed passenger! As the ship sailed west, the wind was strong against them, so they passed to the south of Crete and then struggled to sail to the harbor of Fair Havens.[207] It was at the southwestern end of the island. They stayed there several days because the wind was so dangerous.

Paul talked to the centurion and the commander of the ship. "Friends, this is going to be a dangerous voyage," he said. We'll possibly lose the cargo, the ship

www.thefamilyprayerbible.com

and also our lives."[507]

But the centurion listened more to the owner of the ship than he did to Paul—and the owner wanted to go on. Besides, Fair Havens wasn't a great place to stay for the winter. So the centurion decided to go on to Phoenix, where the harbor was safer.

For a while, it seemed that the centurion had made the right choice, but soon the gentle breeze got stronger. And STRONGER. A HUGE storm arose! And now the ship was not near any harbor at all. So all the crew could do was to take down the sails and let the ship go wherever the wind took it.[462] The waves grew higher—and so they threw the cargo overboard, hoping that would keep the ship from sinking. Then, they even threw out the lines and the parts of the ship the made the sails work—they were DESPERATE to save the ship, and their lives! But now they were giving up all hope.[130] The storm was NOT letting up!

For days, no one had eaten or slept.[161] Paul called everyone together. He said, "If you'd listened to me, we would not be in this trouble. But don't give up hope! Even though our ship will be lost, we will all live.

"Last night God, the One I serve, who made everything—He sent an angel to me. The angel told me, 'Don't be afraid. Remember, you are going to appear before Caesar. You'll do that. And everyone sailing with you will be safe.' So be strong, all of you. Take courage. Have something to eat. You'll need your strength, for it will happen just as God has said. We'll end up stranded on an island."[529]

The people on the ship were comforted by Paul's words. They took Paul's advice and ate! Even in the middle of a storm, God knew JUST where they were. He had not forgotten them. He was going to make sure they would live!

Talk About the Story: What did Paul tell the commander about sailing? Why didn't the ship stay in the harbor? What happened to the perfect breeze? Who told Paul he would get to Rome? How did the people feel before Paul talked to them? After he talked to them?

Scripture: "If I take the wings of the morning, and dwell in the uttermost parts of the sea, even there Your hand shall lead me, and Your right hand shall hold me." Psalm 139:9–10

Family Time: What is the farthest place you can think of? The tallest? The hottest? How do we know God is with us, even when we are in a scary or faraway place?

Prayer: Dear God, thank You that You always know where we are, even if we are lost! We are glad that You promise be with us wherever we go. Thank You for Your love. In Jesus' name, Amen.

DATE ___/___

SHIPWRECK!

Scripture: Acts 27:27—28:1
Place: Malta
Time: 60 AD

The storm raged on and on, tossing the boat around on the wide sea. The sailors and passengers had all but given up hope of surviving the storm, but Paul was not worried. God had told Paul they'd all come through this alive, and so they would—because God had said they would!

Finally, fourteen nights after the storm began, there the sailors saw something that gave them hope! "There is land ahead! I'm sure of it!" one sailor said. Quickly, they dropped a line to see how deep the water was. It was only 120 feet deep. Land really was near! A little later, it was 90 feet. They were definitely headed in the right direction!

But it was so dark—they wouldn't be able to see if they were going to run into rocks. The captain ordered the sailors to put out the anchors. "That should keep us safe until morning!"

But the sailors knew that there was still danger! They secretly planned to leave on the lifeboat. God knew what they were up to! Paul told the centurion, "Unless the sailors stay on board, we're all going to die." So the centurion had soldiers cut the ropes holding the lifeboat. The sailors had to stay!

As it got light, Paul urged everyone to eat. "God promised that not one of you will lose a hair of your head," he said. "You're going to be all right, so eat. Be ready!"[161]

Then Paul took bread and gave thanks[300] to God and passed the bread around. Everyone ate, and they felt better.[529]

As it got light, they could see a bay and a beach, but could not tell what was under the surface of the water. "Cut the anchors! We'll let the waves carry us to the shore!" the captain said.

Everyone watched and waited. Suddenly, the front of the boat struck a sandbar. The ship couldn't move—and now the waves were POUNDING the boat! It began to creak and groan. It would break into pieces soon!

The soldiers on board wanted to kill all of the prisoners so that none of them would escape. But the centurion was determined to get Paul to Rome! So he wouldn't let the soldiers hurt anyone!

The centurion ordered, "Everyone jump out and swim to shore if you can!" Then he got the people who could not swim to cling to boards or broken pieces of the ship and float to shore.

And soon, through the waves, EVERY PERSON on the ship got to the beach safely! They had made it! They were finally on land![142] There were no happier, wetter 276 people anywhere! Just as God had told Paul, the ship broke into pieces and it was lost. But not one person was lost. God's words were TRUE. No one was killed.

Everyone was SAFE—and Paul was still on his way to Rome![480]

Talk About the Story: How could the sailors tell they were near land? What did they plan to do? What did Paul say about them leaving the ship? Why didn't the soldiers kill Paul? How did people who couldn't swim get to the beach?

Scripture: "Because You have been my help, therefore in the shadow of Your wings I will rejoice." Psalm 63:7

Family Time: How does a mother bird protect her babies? What are ways God protects you? What are other words that mean the same as "rejoice"? Praise God together today in song!

Prayer: Dear Lord, we know that you have good plans for us. Please help us to show others that we trust in You when trouble comes. In Jesus' name, Amen.

SNAKE BITE

Scripture: Acts 28:1–7
Place: Malta
Time: 60 AD

Paul dropped a pile of sticks into the fire, then he froze. He stood looking down at his hand. A small snake was hanging on by its FANGS! The snake had been in the sticks Paul had gathered for the fire. It had bitten hard and deep.[99]

The people who lived on Malta had come running when they saw the shipwreck.[480] They were the ones who had built the fire and started to help care for all the people from the shipwreck. But now they just stopped and stared at Paul. They all knew how dangerous that snake was! Anyone bitten by that kind of snake would die in minutes!

"He is a prisoner who survived the shipwreck!" one of the survivors said.

An islander responded, "Oh! He must be a murderer. He escaped the shipwreck, but justice won't let him escape with his life! There is no way to help

www.thefamilyprayerbible.com

someone bitten by that kind of snake!"[268]

The crowd gathered closer around Paul, watching and waiting to see what would happen to him.

But Paul chuckled to himself as he shook the snake off. "Ouch! Be gone, little fellow!" he said. "GOD has told me that I will go to Rome. But I'm not taking you with me!"

The crowd watched Paul carefully. They waited for five minutes. Then five minutes more. They expected him to drop dead at any moment! But NOTHING HAPPENED. Paul's hand didn't swell from the snakebite. He didn't drop dead—or even get sick! The islanders kept watch for a very long time, but there was no sign that Paul suffered any harm from that snake.[467]

Pretty soon, the islanders started to change their minds about Paul. "This is amazing. This is IMPOSSIBLE. How can this be? He can't be a bad person who needs to be punished. Paul must be a GOD!"

News about Paul's miraculous escape from death spread around the island. It wasn't long before a message came from the leading citizen of the island! Publius was like a governor of the island, and he lived on a large estate. He invited Paul and his friends to stay with him. Publius fed them and entertained them for three days![363] This was going to be a great place to stay for the winter!

Talk About the Story: Who helped to take care of the people from the shipwreck? Why do you think they helped? What happened to Paul? What did the people think when they saw the snake? What did they think after they saw that Paul didn't die?

Scripture: "Preserve me, O God, for in You I put my trust." Psalm 16:1

Family Time: What do you think gave Paul confidence when he was bitten by a deadly snake? When are some times that you have been confident of God's help in a scary situation? What happened?

Prayer: Father, thank You for helping and protecting us in scary situations. We want to learn to trust You and follow You more. Amen.

DATE ___/___

MINISTRY ON MALTA

Scripture: Acts 28:7–10
Place: Malta
Time: 60 AD

The estate of Publius, the leading citizen of the island of Malta, was a great place to be! After a difficult ocean voyage, a shipwreck, and being bitten by a poisonous snake, Paul and his friends finally had a nice place to sleep, plenty of food to eat, and all the comforts of home. After three days of spending time with Publius and his family,[363] Paul head some distressing news. Publius' father was very sick.

Immediately, Paul asked to visit the man. When Paul arrived at his house, Paul walked in and laid his hands on him and prayed for him. Publius' father was well right away![214]

Now everyone on the island was talking about Paul. They knew who he was: He was the man who could be bitten by a poisonous snake—and not die! He was the man who could pray for a sick person—and God would heal the person!

Soon, the word went around on the island, "There's a man over at Publius' house who knows the God who can heal!" Most sick people came to where Paul was staying. They needed healing. Paul prayed for each of them—and they were all healed, too!

Because it was still winter, there were no ships traveling to and from the island. This gave Paul and his friends three months to spend on the island! So, what do you think they did? They grew God's family on the island of Malta! For the next three months, they prayed for the people there. They healed told them the good news about Jesus. They taught them about the one, true God who made everything and everyone!

For the people of Malta, this was new news and GOOD news! They had believed in false gods, but those false gods had never helped them when they were sick. They had never protected them from death and snakebite. The people could see that this Jesus, the Savior Paul told them about, had POWER over death and sickness. They were glad to hear the good news of Jesus!

Talk About the Story: When Paul prayed for Publius' father, what happened? How long did Paul and his friends stay on Malta? What did they do while they were there? Why do you think the people on Malta were ready to believe in Jesus?

Scripture: "And Jesus came and spoke to them, saying, 'All authority has been given to Me in heaven and on earth. Go therefore and make disciples of all the nations . . .'" Matthew 28:18–19

Family Time: Who has power over sickness and death? Over what else does Jesus have power? What did Jesus tell His friends to do? What does Jesus tell us to do? What is a way your family can do that this week?

Prayer: Dear Lord, we know that Jesus can do anything, and we are glad! We ask You to help us remember to ask for His help and power as we tell others the good news about Him! In His name, Amen.

MINISTRY IN ROME

Scripture: Acts 28:11–31
Place: Malta to Rome
Time: 60 AD

Paul took a deep breath, breathing in the fresh sea air. He looked around at the springtime sky, the gulls flying overhead, and said, "Father, You are good! When YOU say You're going to do a thing, it is DONE! There is nothing too hard for You!"

At last, Paul and his friends were on the last part of their journey to Rome. Paul was still a prisoner but a very loved, honored and esteemed prisoner! The ship moved from port to port, until they landed at the tip of what is now Italy. There, they found believers in Jesus, so they stayed with them for a week![166]

Meanwhile, the message was sent to the believers in Rome that Paul was on land and was coming their way! Paul and his friends, along with Paul's Roman guard, began to travel up the coast, and as they got near to the capital of the Roman Empire, the Roman believers all came out to meet them outside of the city. This made Paul's heart glad, as he heard about the great things God was already doing in Rome![484]

Paul was allowed to stay in his own rented house in Rome. Soldiers stayed there to guard him—which was more of a great protection than a problem![387] Paul invited the leaders of the Jews in Rome to meet with him. He told them his story and how he had appealed to Caesar because of what the Jerusalem Jews had said about him.

The Roman Jews said, "We haven't heard anything about this.[105] But we DO want to hear about what you believe. All we know about followers of Jesus is that they are hated everywhere!"

So a large number of the Jewish people of Rome crowded into Paul's house to hear Paul tell the WHOLE story of God's good news—from Moses and the prophets, to Jesus and His death and resurrection, to the coming of the Holy Spirit! They listened all day and into the evening.[145] Some of them were convinced,

and believed in Jesus! But others did not believe the good news Paul had shared.

He told these people, "Some of you Jews are spiritually blind. You will not see the truth or hear the truth because you refuse to believe this good news!"[50]

After the Jews left his house, Paul spent his time welcoming anyone who came to see him. He love to tell all who would listen about the kingdom of God, and taught them all he could about Jesus! For two years, even though Paul was a prisoner, he was allowed to preach and teach and pray and love people and help them. He was a prisoner with complete freedom—guarded not only by the Roman guards, but more than that, by the power of God![52]

Talk About the Story: How did Paul get to Rome? Who met him outside the city? Why did Paul talk to the Jews in Rome? Who did Paul talk to about Jesus after that? Who protected Paul?

Scripture: "For God has not given us a spirit of fear, but of power and of love and of a sound mind." 2 Timothy 1:7

Family Time: Who are people we might be afraid of? If God does not give us a spirit of fear, then where does it come from? What can happen when we show the love and power of Jesus?

Prayer: Dear Lord Jesus! You did amazing things in the stories of Paul's life. We want to live like this. Please help us to do what You tell us and to use the gifts You have given us. In Your great name, Amen.

PSALM 137

A PSALM OF REMEMBRANCE OF LOST HAPPINESS

Jerusalem was captured by Nebuchadnezzar in 586 B.C. and all Israelites were taken prisoner to Babylon. They were forced to work on government projects. These captives had seen their Temple burned and its worship objects put in heathen temples. Jerusalem was ruined. The Babylonians showed their slaves no mercy.

Then the Babylonians demanded entertainment with happy singing with accompaniment on their harps. The people of God replied,

> *"We sat beside the rivers of Babylon and wept,*
> *When we remembered our home in Jerusalem.*
> *We hung our harps on the branches of a poplar tree.*
> *But we couldn't sing because of our tears."*[303]

In life we must remember what makes us *laugh*, for our life is motivated by joy. Everyone likes to be happy sometimes, even when we have bad days. The Babylonians demanded a "happy" song.

> *"Our captors demanded we entertain them,*
> *Sing us a "happy" Zion song you enjoyed back home."*

The Jews just couldn't be *happy* in their pitiful slavery experience. They didn't want to put on a "happy" face and pretend they were having a good time. They remembered their peaceful days in the Promised Land. They answered,

> *"How could we ever sing a thankful song in the wilderness?*[439]
> *My fingers would fall off the strings,*
> *My tongue would swell up and choke me*
> *I remember Jerusalem and dream of its worship.*[183]
> *I can't forget God's presence gave me my greatest pleasure."*

God's people were captive in a heathen land. But three things kept them going. First, they knew what made them *cry*. When we know the source of things that make us sad, we not only control ourselves, we focus on getting over it.

Second, they knew what made them *laugh*. They would not fake a false smile. There was no pleasure in that. They knew that source of real joy. They knew happiness comes from God.

Third, they knew their *dreams*. They remembered their past happiness in the presence of God and wanted to return there.

Talk About the Psalm: What did you learn about the psalm writer in this story? What did you learn about God?

Psalm 137: Read this week's psalm in your Bible together. Choose a verse to read aloud as a prayer.

Prayer: Thank You, God, for the psalm prayers in the Bible. Thank You for teaching us about You and about how to pray. In Jesus' name, Amen.

CHAPTER 22

THE CHURCH CONTINUES

The book of Acts ends with a final "update" as Paul awaits his trial before Caesar. The gospel message continues spreading as the Church continues to grow. The book of Acts gives you a fascinating glimpse into the life of the early church.

The New Testament Epistles are personal letters written to churches and individuals. While they follow the typical form of first-century letters in the Roman world, they uniquely express Christian truth. Even Paul's greetings of "grace and peace" are unparalleled in the ancient world. Paul's letters are a primary source for his life, work, and knowledge of the beginnings of Christianity, for they are the earliest Christian documents, most having been written between ten and thirty years after the death of Christ.

The content of the New Testament Letters is doctrinal and personal. The apostolic authors wrote to express the great truths of the Christian life: love, forgiveness, grace, faith, salvation, and sanctification. They also wrote to answer

questions, solve problems, resolve conflicts, and give personal advice. The authors received God's grace through Jesus Christ and spent their lives spreading the message of that grace to the world.

The New Testament Letters written in common Greek range from rhetorical masterpieces designed for public dissemination (e.g., Romans, Hebrews) to short personal notes (e.g., Philemon, 2 and 3 John).

The Epistles are arranged in the New Testament as those written by the apostle Paul and signed by him (13 letters) and those written by James, Peter, John, and Jude (7 letters) with Hebrews recognized by some as Pauline and by others say Luke wrote it. It is positioned in the Bible between the Pauline and the General Epistles.

The General Epistles include Hebrews, James, 1 Peter, 2 Peter, 1 John, 2 John, 3 John, and Jude. The early church historian Eusebius (AD 265–340) designated the books from James through Jude as "catholic" (or universal) epistles because they are generally addressed to all the churches. The letter to the Hebrews has no greeting.

WRITING PHILIPPIANS

Scripture: Philippians 4:4
Place: Rome
Time: 61 AD

Paul sat in the sun on the balcony of his apartment in Rome. A Roman soldier was chained to him, but that didn't keep him from praying for all the churches he had planted. Some churches worried him, like the one in Colossae. They struggled with confusion. But as he prayed for the church in Philippi, a smile came over Paul's face. That was his first church plant in Europe. When he and Silas were imprisoned there, God sent an earthquake to release them from prison. It was also a church that kept sending money to support Paul's missionary outreach. The Philippians made his heart happy!

Paul called, "Luke? Would you bring paper and pen, please? I am going to write to our friends in the Philippian church." Luke came out from the apartment.

"Have they done something wrong?" Luke asked.

"No!" Paul answered. "I am going to write to thank them for their prayers, for their money, but most of all for continuing to be kind and loving."[484] Then Paul added, "I want to tell them how much joy (keyword in Philippines) they give me."[213]

The believers in Philippi were now a large group. But the church had begun with a small group of women.

Paul began to write. *My theme will be joy!* He chuckled to himself.

Paul told the Philippians, "I thank God every time I think of you! So I then pray for you often, and with lots of joy." [484]

He then told the reasons that they made him happy. Then Paul challenged them, "Rejoice in the Lord always—again I say it, rejoice! Let your gentleness be known by all. The Lord is coming soon!"[524]

Paul told them that he was full of joy, even with a soldier chained to him. He reminded them to be glad and thankful in happy times and sad times, in easy times and hard times.[213] He reminded them to be glad in the Lord, to have joy in Jesus, and to be glad about each other.[291]

In this letter Paul gave a beautiful word picture about Jesus. Jesus is God by nature, yet He became a humble servant. He died to take the punishment for our sins. But he took this punishment willingly. He wanted us to have salvation. Now Jesus is exalted to the highest place, given the highest name, and someday all everyone and everything in heaven and on earth will bow and say that Jesus Christ is Lord of all.[228]

Paul also talked about how we can rejoice even in hard times when we are suffering,[465] because we know Jesus is with us.

Paul said, "For me, living is all about Christ and dying is a good thing!"[256] To help his friends know that God would help them be strong, Paul also wrote, "I can do all things through Christ who strengthens me."[508]

Talk About the Story: Where was Paul when he wrote to the Philippians? What is the word that is the theme of his letter? What are some reasons we can be joyful in hard times?

Scripture: "Be anxious for nothing, but in everything by prayer and supplication, with thanksgiving, let your requests be made known to God; and the peace of God, which surpasses all understanding, will guard your hearts and minds through Christ Jesus." Philippians 4:6–8

Family Time: What's the best way to have a positive attitude? What does God's Word say to do for anxiety or worry? Why should we pray with thanksgiving? What is the promise God gives us here?

Prayer: Lord, we are thankful for giving us all we need to always be joyful! Please help us to remember that You will give Your peace when we pray to You! In Jesus' name, Amen.

DATE ___/___

711

WRITING TO THE EPHESIANS

Scripture: Ephesians 3:14–21
Place: From Rome
Time: 61–62 AD

Paul and his guard, Antonio, walked by the Tiber River that flowed through Rome. Paul was chained to his guard so he wouldn't run away, but Antonio couldn't get away, either! He listened to Paul's constant talk about Jesus Christ.

As they watched the royal barges on the river, Antonio asked, "Why do you follow this Jesus? Your countrymen have tried to kill you; Rome holds you prisoner."[43]

Paul smiled. This was a story he delighted to tell![415] "My sins were forgiven by the death of Jesus, and one day Jesus will take me to live with Him forever."[173]

Antonio told Paul, "There is no city more beautiful than Rome. I've been in the palace, I got an award from Caesar."

Paul answered. "Rome is a beautiful city. Yet we Christians will live in a city much more beautiful, in heaven. And we will be given awards beyond anything Caesar gives."

They walked past the Forum. They could see the giant Coliseum, and farther down, Caesar's palace.

Antonio pointed. "That is the greatest palace in the world," he said.

Paul answered, "It is great because some people there now follow Jesus. Life with Him is even better than life with Caesar."

Antonio answered, "But how can you say this life is good? You are in chains."

Paul answered, "On this earth, I'm a prisoner, but when I became a Christian I became a prisoner of Jesus Christ.[431]

"I just wrote a letter to the Ephesian Christians to tell how I am a prisoner here. But we who are in Christ are already in heavenly places!" Paul nodded, "These two phrases are the theme of my letter: 'In Christ' and 'in the heavenly places.'"[125]

"So it doesn't bother you to be in shackles?" Antonio asked.

"No," Paul replied, "Even when I'm in chains, I am free to serve Jesus." [431]

"The army of Rome is the most powerful force in the world; the church could never defeat her," Antonio reasoned.

"God's people fight a spiritual warfare," Paul answered. "I wrote to the Ephesians, 'We are not fighting against flesh-and-blood enemies, but against evil rulers and authorities of the unseen world, against mighty powers in this dark world, and against evil spirits in the heavenly places.[528] Therefore, put on every piece of God's armor so you will be able to resist the enemy in the time of evil.[114] Then after the battle you will still be standing firm.' (Ephesians 6:12, 13 *NLT*) [401]

"We do not fight with swords, but with truth. The power of God's good news captures people. We fight with prayer, love, and godly living. We do not capture to kill but to show people that God loves them and waits to give each one a new, wonderful life.'"[38]

The soldier thought Paul was chained to him. But really, Antonio was chained to Paul! Soon, the soldier gave his life to Jesus Christ. He was captured by the Savior!

Talk About the Story: What two things did Paul say are the themes of Ephesians? What kind of battle do God's people fight? What do we use to capture people for God's kingdom?

Scripture: "God . . . made us alive together with Christ (by grace you have been saved), and raised us up together, and made us sit together in the heavenly places in Christ Jesus." Ephesians 2:4–6

Family Time: Who made us alive? Was this by ourselves, or with someone? If we are in Christ, God sees us as already with Him in heavenly places! Talk about what it means to be in Christ.

Prayer: Lord God, we thank You for Your great love. Your grace is what saves us. You are good to us! Amen.

WRITING TO THE COLOSSIANS

Scripture: Colossians 4:7–18
Place: Written from Rome
Time: 62 AD

When Paul arrived in Rome, he was under house arrest. This meant he would be chained to a Roman guard until his trial. That could be as long as two years away!

No one wanted Paul stuck in a damp prison—so churches sent money to help pay for food and rent. Now Paul's friends could rent an apartment for Paul where he could stay with his team of fellow workers—and his new best friend, the Roman soldier assigned to guard him!

Epaphras (e PAF rus) arrived in Rome. He had come from the church in Colossae, carrying a gift for Paul's expenses.[166] He poured silver coins out on the table, sent with love from Colossae!

Paul said, "We have to write to the church in Colossae and thank them!"[69]

But Epaphras was not returning to Colossae. And it was a LONG time before there was a post office, or any other kind of delivery service. Any mail was brought by someone who came to visit! So Paul planned to send a letter with Tychicus (TIK ih kus) would bring it to the church at Colossae. Onesimus was also going and taking a letter to Philemon, a wealthy believer and his former owner.

(That's another story!)

Epaphras suggested, "Let me tell you about things we can pray with the Colossians about."

Epaphras told Paul and his friends that the Colossian church was having trouble because people were arguing about what they should or should not do.[90]

Paul and his followers prayed for the church and believers in Colossae. Paul wrote, "We always pray for you." He went on to tell them, "Don't let anyone judge you for what you eat, or drink, or what customs and holidays you celebrate."[277]

Epaphras also told Paul that some in the Colossian church were following a new teaching of worshiping angels.[331] So Paul wrote, "Don't let anyone make you feel less unless you act pious in showy self-denial or in worshiping angels. Their sinful minds have made them proud."

Next, Epaphras told Paul and the others that some in the church were showing off by using big words and quoting the Greek philosophers to impress everyone. Paul wrote, "Beware! Don't let anyone cheat you through philosophy and empty lies and traditions."[90]

Earlier, when the new church in Colossae was having trouble, Paul had sent Epaphras with some Ephesians to help with the church in Colossae, only 90 miles east of Ephesus.

So Epaphras sent greetings in the letter. "Epaphras, a member of your own fellowship, sends you greetings. He always prays earnestly for you."

Paul reminded his friends at Colossae of the great things Jesus had done for them and how they should grow in His good gifts.[517]

Talk About the Story: Who had come from Colossae? What did he bring? Who was going back to Colossae with the thank-you letter? Why didn't they just mail the letter? What two things did Paul tell the Colossians, "Don't let anyone . . ." do?

Scripture: "As you therefore have received Christ Jesus the Lord, so walk in Him, rooted and built up in Him and established in the faith, as you have been taught, abounding in it with thanksgiving." Colossians 2:6

Family Time: What do we do to help a plant be rooted? What are ways to root or establish ourselves in the faith? What can we abound or overflow with? What are some reasons we can abound with thanksgiving?

Prayer: Lord God, we love You and we thank You that we can be built up and made strong by Your word. Please help us to always be thankful! In Jesus' name, Amen.

WRITING THE BOOK OF PHILEMON

Scripture: Philemon v.10–11
Place: Rome
Time: 60-62 AD

Paul was under house arrest in Rome, chained to a soldier. Paul had an apartment, so visitors came and he preached often[145]—especially that soldier to whom he was chained![387]

Paul sat on the balcony one day, watching people in the street below. Suddenly, he saw a familiar face!

It was Onesimus, a slave from far-off Colossae! He was owned by a man named Philemon. Paul had led Philemon to Jesus! He now had a church in his house!

Paul stood and yelled, "Onesimus! Onesimus! Up here! It's Paul! I preached at your master's house!"

Onesimus froze. HOW could it be that PAUL was HERE? He wanted to run. But soldiers were on the street. A soldier stood beside Paul! He thought, *If I run, the soldiers will arrest me. They'll torture me. They'll KILL ME!*

Onesimus had tried to HIDE ever since he'd gotten to Rome. He was a runaway slave AND he had stolen money from his master. When he ran to Rome, he thought he'd be lost in the crowd.

But HERE was PAUL, waving and inviting him upstairs! Paul called, "Come on up! It's dinner time! Eat with us."

Well, Onesimus hadn't had much to eat in Rome. Hungry and scared, what else could he do? So Onesimus ate with Paul. He stayed with Paul. He felt safe there—except for that soldier. But soon, Oneismus (whose name means "useful") became a Christian because of Paul's kindness and teaching. He confessed that he had stolen from his master Philemon so he could run away.

Now Onesimus worked as Paul's servant. He shopped, cooked, and kept the apartment clean.[195]

One day at dinner, Paul and his friends were discussing Onesimus. Paul said, "We must send Onesimus back to Philemon."

The men around the table said, "No! Onesimus could be punished severely, even killed!"

"We must do what's right," Paul said thoughtfully. "I will write to Philemon. Now, the two of them are brothers in God's family! I'll tell him Onesimus has become a Christian and ask him to forgive Onesimus. After all, God forgave Philemon's sins just as God forgave Onesimus! Besides, I'm glad to pay back whatever Onesimus owes." [270]

Paul laughed, "I'll tell Philemon that Onesimus was useless before, but now, he's a Christian. He's 'useful' both to me and to Philemon. [512] I'd like to keep Onesimus with me, but I have to do the right thing and send him back to his master. [549] That way, I hope Philemon will send him back to me, gladly!"

Paul added, "I am also writing a letter to the church of Colossae. It meets in Philemon's home. I'm confident that Philemon will hear my plea and forgive Onesimus.[173] Tychicus, I'd like for you to take both letters at the same time—and take Onesimus, of course."

Onesimus listened silently. He was afraid, but he knew had to return to Philemon.

This short letter is a like a picture of us, too. Before we knew Jesus, we were useless and in trouble, like Onesimus! We sinned against God. He had the right to punish us. But like Paul, Jesus says, "Charge the sin to My account; I paid it all." Like Onesimus, we all can be thankful for pardon and forgiveness.[248]

Talk About the Story: Why was Onesimus in trouble? What did Paul say about his name? What did Paul say about what Onesimus owed Philemon?

Scripture: "That the sharing of your faith may become effective by the acknowledgment of every good thing which is in you in Christ Jesus.
Philemon 6

Family Time: What good things are in you because of Jesus? Telling what good things are in you because of Jesus is an effective way to share your faith. What are other ways to share your faith?

Prayer: Lord, we thank You for Your mercy. You are good to us. Jesus, thank You for paying our debt. We love You! Amen.

PAUL'S FIRST LETTER TO TIMOTHY

Scripture: 1 Timothy 3:15
Place: Rome
Time: 63 AD

Paul spent two years under house arrest in Rome. When his trial finally came up, the men who had him arrested didn't show up for the trial! So Paul was released in the fall of 62 A. D.

Paul began visiting the churches in northern Greece. Then he got word that Timothy was having a difficult time. Timothy was pastoring the church at Ephesus. Some thought Timothy was too young. On top of that, teachers had come in who told people that they had to obey Jewish laws to be saved.[245] Also other leaders were telling people wrong things, too! Timothy needed some encouragement.

Paul was glad to write to Timothy. He began, "To Timothy, a true child in the faith."[180]

Paul had known Timothy for a long time. He and Barnabas had stayed in Timothy's parents' home in Lystra when Timothy was about sixteen. His mother

Eunice and grandmother Lois were godly Jewish women,[206] but his father was a Gentile. Timothy had memorized large portions of the Bible.[41]

On Paul's second visit to Lystra, Timothy had joined Paul to help in the ministry. They had been like father and son in many ways. So Paul could write openly to Timothy.

Paul greeted Timothy and then wrote, "I urged you to stay in Ephesus to stop those who are teaching wrong doctrine."[121]

Then the old apostle added, "Timothy, my son, remember the prophetic words spoken to you at your ordination. Those words will give you confidence to fight the good fight of faith."[138]

In this short letter, Paul gave a clear description of the role of a pastor. He didn't talk about buildings or organization. Paul cared about teaching the truth. He wanted Timothy's inner character to grow as a pastor and spiritual leader.

Paul wrote about the power of prayer[17] and the role of women in the church meetings.[203] He explained the things that would help Timothy choose leaders for the church.[432] He warned about false teachers.[455] Paul reminded young Timothy how to act as he served Jesus.

Finally Paul told Timothy, "Fight the good fight of faith"[411] and "guard the ministry that has been entrusted to you."

Then Paul listed things to avoid: foolish talk, arguments with people who think they have so-called higher knowledge. Paul said that such people had missed the mark about the faith.[220]

Paul loved Timothy and reminded him that he was a man of God. He said, "Run from evil thoughts. Pursue a godly life with faith, love, gentleness, and solid belief in the truth."[418]

Paul wanted his "son in the faith" to grow strong in the Lord!

Talk About the Story: Why did Paul write to Timothy? How long had Paul known Timothy? Who had helped Timothy learn about God? What are some things Paul talked about in this letter? What did Paul call Timothy?

Scripture: "I write so that you may know how you ought to conduct yourself in the house of God, which is the church of the living God, the pillar and ground of the truth." 1 Timothy 3:15

Family Time: What are some things you know about your own church? Who is your pastor? Who teaches you about God? Thank God for these people!

Prayer: Father, we are glad that You have given us people who teach us about You. Please help us to learn all we can. In Jesus' name, Amen.

THE LETTER PAUL WROTE TO TITUS

Scripture: Titus 1:5
Place: Macedonia
Time: 64 AD

Titus was first seen in the New Testament at the Jerusalem council. Some were trying to make circumcision mandatory for salvation (Acts 15:1).[277] Paul and Barnabas attended the conference to argue that only God's grace was needed for salvation. No human good works were necessary. Paul took along Titus, a Greek who had been saved, but not circumcised according to Jewish law. Titus was a good example of salvation without following Jewish law.

Writing to Titus was a joy to Paul. He was another young man who was like a son. Paul had some important things to tell Titus, but he knew this letter would be read in many churches, many times. So how would he begin? He wanted to begin with a humble attitude, but be direct.

www.thefamilyprayerbible.com

Paul began, "Paul a slave of God, and messenger of Jesus Christ. I am commissioned to deliver faith to God's chosen people."[126]

Then Paul wanted everyone to know Titus was in Crete to help the churches in Paul's place. He wanted anyone who heard the letter to know the history of Titus' salvation. So he added, "To Titus my child in our common faith."[292]

Earlier, Paul had sent Titus to preach at the church in Corinth.[491] Titus told to Paul what was happening in the Corinthian church, and then delivered a follow-up letter (2 Corinthians) to the church.[337]

Paul probably founded the churches on the island of Crete on his first journey to Rome. Now Paul had been released from his imprisonment in Rome, and wanted to help those churches.

Titus was with Paul on this trip. Paul left Titus on the island of Crete so he could complete the work there and appoint elders in each town. This is what Paul had told him to do.[69]

Crete is a long, narrow island. The people mostly earned a living from fishing or shipping. The Cretans had a bad reputation. Paul quoted the poet Epimenides who said Cretans were "always liars, evil beasts, lazy gluttons."[374] To act like a Cretan was to be a liar. So the believers in Crete might have had a hard time with knowing and telling what is true! False teaching was threatening the churches there.[277, 90]

Paul's letter deals with church organization and Christian discipleship. Six times it refers to "good works" by believers.[272] Paul said that good teaching needed to help people change the way they spoke and acted.

Paul urged Titus to join him for the winter.[370] Titus was also with Paul for part of his last imprisonment. Church tradition claims Titus spent his later years on Crete. Paul told Titus and the whole church how important it is to preach the gospel, defend the faith, and live a life that shows we follow Jesus Christ.

Talk About the Story: When Titus was with Paul, where did they go? What island was Titus on? What things did Paul say are important ?

Scripture: "For this reason I left you in Crete, that you should set in order the things that are lacking, and appoint elders in every city as I commanded you." Titus 1:5

Family Time: What are some things your family sets in order every day? How does that help your family? What happens when some things are not set in order?

Prayer: Lord Jesus, You gave Paul and Titus great things to do. Please make us ready to do great things for You, too! In Your strong name, Amen.

PSALM 139

GOD KNOWS ME

David got up from his throne and walked out on to the balcony. He waved those in the throne room away. He wanted to be alone with God. He was troubled with a small sin he did yesterday. No sin is "small" to God, but David did something without giving it a second thought. We are like David, sometimes we fib, or stretch the truth, or take something that belongs to others, thinking they won't miss it.

David's little sin bothered him at breakfast so he couldn't eat. Then sitting on

the throne listening to his subjects, he couldn't think clearly.

David prayed, "God you know everything about me. You see every wrong thing I have ever done."[426] David confessed his "small" sin, but in his discouragement he admitted all the other sins he had ever done.

David looked out over Jerusalem from his balcony, and thought about all the sins of all the people. He asked himself, "How can God know all about all the people in the world? Then David asked, "How can God be everywhere at the same time to see everything done wrong by all the people?

First, David believed in the omnipresence of God, which means He is everywhere present at the same time. He prayed, "Lord You know every time I sit down, and stand up. You know everything I am thinking, even when I am far away."[81] Then surrendering to God he prayed, "You know what I am going to say, even before I say it." Then he confessed, "I can never escape from Your Spirit. I can never get away from Your presence."[377]

David realized there was no place he could run from God. "If I go to heaven, You are there. If I am buried in the grave, You are there. If I go to the other side of the ocean, You are there."[207] David knew he couldn't get away from God.

David thought more about God's knowledge of him. "You saw me being formed in my mother's womb, You saw me before I was born.[191] You have seen every deed I have done, and you know every thought of my mind. And You have recorded all these things in a book."

Then David thought about God's love for him, "Let me wake up every morning to live for You. Please God, do away with wickedness. I won't have anything to do with those who hate you." Finally David prayed,

> *"Search me O God, to know all my thoughts.*
> *Examine every part of my life and know me thoroughly.*[81]
> *Point out everything that I have ever done, and forgive me,*[174]
> *Then lead me to live the right way."*

Talk About the Psalm: What did you learn about the psalm writer in this story? What did you learn about God?

Psalm 139: Read this week's psalm in your Bible together. Choose a verse to read aloud as a prayer.

Prayer: Thank You, God, for the psalm prayers in the Bible. Thank You for teaching us about You and about how to pray. In Jesus' name, Amen.

PAUL'S SECOND LETTER TO TIMOTHY

Scripture: 2 Timothy 4:2
Place: Rome
Time: 64 AD

Paul sat in the cold Mamertine prison. It was a hole in the ground without sunshine or visitors or hope. He sat in this hole with over a dozen other prisoners. They all were condemned to die, and waited to be executed. Only Luke was allowed in, because he was Paul's doctor. And who did Paul want to see most of all? Timothy!

But Paul could write to Timothy. So he did! He probably had Luke do the writing, for by now Paul's eyesight was not good. He said, "Write, 'To Timothy my dear son.'"

As the jailer walked over to blow on a pile of coals, the red embers flickered. A small flame lit the cell.

Paul went on, "I want to remind you to fan into flame the spiritual gifts God has given you. I recognized God was calling you when I laid hands on your head at your ordination service."[499]

When Paul had sent his first letter to Timothy, he was living in his own rented apartment, chained to a Roman soldier. But now Paul was treated like a criminal.[138] At his trial, no one had stood with him.[1] Apparently Alexander the coppersmith testified against him. From his testimony, it was decided that Paul should be executed. Now Paul was waiting for the day he'd die. He told Timothy, "The time of my departure is coming soon."[99]

But before he died, Paul told Timothy that he longed to see him again. He went on, "I remember your tears when we parted. And I will be filled with joy when I see you again!"[166]

Paul also needed a few things, so he asked Timothy to bring Paul's coat he'd left at Troas, along with his papers and scrolls.[404]

Is seems that Paul was almost thrown to the lions in the Roman Coliseum, because he told Timothy, "The Lord . . . saved me from certain death."[109] But Paul knew that when he died, "The Lord will . . . bring me safely to his heavenly kingdom."[377]

Paul told Timothy, "Preach the Word." [90] "Endure hardship" and "do the work of an evangelist."[411]

Tradition says Paul died in Nero's persecution that began in A. D. 64. Paul died late in A. D. 65. He wrote what could have been put on his tombstone: "My life has already been poured out as an offering to God. The time of my death is near. I have fought the good fight, I have finished the race, and I have remained faithful. And now the prize awaits me—the crown of righteousness, which the Lord, the righteous Judge, will give me on the day of his return." (2 Timothy 4:6–8, *NLT*).[411, 94]

Talk About the Story: Where was Paul? Why could Luke visit him? Who did he want to have visit before he died? What did Paul say about his own life?

Scripture: "Preach the word! Be ready in season and out of season. Convince, rebuke, exhort, with all longsuffering and teaching." 2 Timothy 4:2

Family Time: Find the definitions of the words "rebuke," "exhort" and "longsuffering." Then tell why it is important to preach God's Word.

Prayer: Lord, we are grateful for Your Word. It is more powerful than any weapon. Help us learn it and understand it, so that we can tell others. In Jesus' name, Amen.

PETER'S FIRST LETTER

Scripture: 1 Peter 2:9–15
Place: Babylon
Time: 62 AD

Peter was at first a fisherman on Lake Galilee. He was brought to Jesus by his brother Andrew (John 1:41-42).[58] Jesus changed Peter's name to Cephas which means "rock" or "stone". He was the main spokesman for the 12 disciples, and preached on Pentecost where 3000 were saved (Acts 2:41-42).[30] Afterwards he preached in and around Jerusalem, and through Peter, the Holy Spirit did several significant miracles.

Even though God called Paul as a missionary to the Gentiles, Peter is the first sent specifically to a Gentile home. (Gentiles are people who are not Jews). God showed Peter, a Jew, that God wanted him to preach in the home of a Roman army officer who had been praying to God. The officer and his household followed Jesus![541]

www.thefamilyprayerbible.com

So, Peter traveled to preach in Antioch, Asia Minor (modern Turkey), and Babylon. Some claimed he preached in Rome where St. Peter's Basilica now stands, and even preached in Britain.

Most church leaders say Peter told Mark the stories which became the gospel of Mark. So it is the life of Jesus according to Peter. Both Peter and Mark liked action, so the gospel of Mark is an action-story of Jesus. The word "immediately" occurs over and over!

Peter writes to believers that they can expect suffering, "Dear friends, don't be surprised when the fiery ordeal comes among you to test you as if something unusual were happening to you."[465] Being a Christian does not mean life is easy or that we won't suffer. We should identify with Christ because we are partakers of His sufferings.[260] Peter probably remembered what Jesus said on the night before His death, "If the world hates you, understand that it hated Me before it hated you"[349] and "If they persecuted Me, they will also persecute you."

So, God's family must expect trials and sufferings, just as their Savior suffered and died for us.

But Peter also reminds his readers, "None of you, however, should suffer as a murderer, a thief, an evildoer, or a meddler." Believers can obey God no matter what, so that we look and act like Jesus in the world in which we live.[478]

Peter reminds his readers that they are "temporary residents on this earth."[101] Followers of Jesus are really citizens of another country—heaven! But while we live here, Peter says God's people must honor "every human authority" because of the Lord.[196] Even though we will one day go home to our true country, Christians must also be good citizens where we live now. It's another way to show we are like Jesus!

Talk About the Story: What are some of the exciting adventures Peter had? Whose gospel did Peter probably help to write? Why do you think Peter wrote this letter? What country do we really belong to?

Scripture: "But you are a chosen generation, a royal priesthood, a holy nation, His own special people, that you may proclaim the praises of Him who called you out of darkness into His marvelous light." 1 Peter 2:9

Family Time: What king chose us to be royal? What do you think it means to be a priest? Why does God honor us so well? What can we then do?

Prayer: Lord Jesus, we are glad You have called us out of darkness and into Your marvelous light! Please help us to live in ways that show we belong to You. Amen.

PETER'S SECOND LETTER

Scripture: 2 Peter 1:3–14
Place: Babylon or Rome
Time: 67 AD

Peter had written one letter to the persecuted Christians in what is now southern Turkey. But there were things he wanted them to remember. So he wrote a second letter to them.

He began, "Beloved, I now write this second epistle (in both I stir up your pure minds) to remember."[303] He wanted his readers to know he was going to die shortly, "Knowing this that shortly I must put off my tent, just our Lord Jesus Christ showed me."[99] Peter is referring to the time he and Jesus walked together after Jesus' resurrection. Jesus told Peter he would die a martyr's death.

Peter was executed in Rome by the emperor. Tradition tells us he asked to be crucified upside down because he was not worthy to die like Jesus, his Lord.

Peter introduces this letter with this magnificent statement: "Do you want more and more of God's kindness and peace? Then learn to know Him better and better. For as you know Him better, He will give you, through His great power, everything you need for living a truly good life . . . . learn to put aside your own desires so that you will become patient and godly, gladly letting God have his way with you.[271] This will make possible the next step, which is for you to enjoy other people and to like them, and finally you will grow to love them deeply. The more you go on in this way, the more you will grow strong spiritually and become fruitful and useful to our Lord Jesus Christ" (from 2 Peter 1:2-8, *LB*).[64]

Peter warns that in the last days, people will doubt that Jesus will return.[321] But Peter reminds them that the Lord will return unexpectedly. Unbelievers in the world will be surprised, as they were surprised in Noah's day when the flood came.[267] Knowing that this will happen, Peter reminds believers to look for "a new heavens and a new earth."[74]

Peter also told his friends that the Lord's coming might be delayed. Many other letters people were reading, from Paul and others, made people think that Jesus would come at any moment. Peter tells believers that they may have to suffer while they wait for Jesus' return.

But Peter is stern with those who say Jesus' return might not happen.[48] He reminds his loved friends that the Lord is not delaying what He promised: He is being patient, because He does not want anyone to perish. He wants everyone to come to repentance.[72] So the Lord delays His coming to give extra time for people to repent

Talk About the Story: Was Peter young or old when he wrote this letter? What are some ways we can live a life full of God's peace? Why has Jesus not come back to Earth yet?

Scripture: "His divine power has given to us all things that pertain to life and godliness, through the knowledge of Him who called us by glory and virtue, by which have been given to us exceedingly great and precious promises." 2 Peter 1:3

Family Time: What can God's power give us? How do we tap into this power? What are three ways you can know God better today? Do one of them!

Prayer: Lord, we are thankful that we can depend on You for everything we need. Help us to know You better and grow in Your family. In Jesus' name, Amen.

WRITING THE BOOK OF HEBREWS

Scripture: Hebrews 6:9
Place: Unknown
Time: Before 70 AD

No one knows who wrote the book of Hebrews. Many people think it was the apostle Paul. Others disagree. It may have been Barnabas, who became Paul's first friend in Jerusalem, and then his mission partner. Barnabas' family served in God's Temple, so he would have been very good at explaining things about the Temple. He also would have been respected by the Jewish believers (called "Hebrews" in the title of the book) because of his family.

But it's also possible that Luke wrote this book. He was with Paul for years and had learned a great deal from Paul. Luke was Paul's personal medical doctor. They traveled together over many miles!

When Paul was jailed in Caesarea for two years, Luke may have written the Gospel of Luke during that time. When Paul spent two years in house arrest in Rome, Luke had extra time again. It may be that this was when he wrote the Book of Acts.

We do know that Paul was concerned about the Christians in Jerusalem. Many of them were going back to the Jewish religion. They were making sacrifices in the Temple for their sins. They did not understand that Jesus had made one sacrifice—His own life![6] And that sacrifice was all anyone needed!

So it may be that Paul told Luke, "The believers in Jerusalem will not listen to me. Some of them had me arrested when I was in the Temple. But the blood of animals is not going to take away their sin. Jesus already did that!"[173]

Luke answered, "I'd be glad to write to them, but I am not a Jew. I'm a Gentile." Some Jews, even Jews in God's family, did not want to have much to do

www.thefamilyprayerbible.com

with any Gentiles, even Gentiles who loved Jesus!

Paul answered, "Christ is our peace.[205] He has made Jews and Gentiles one, and has broken down that wall of separation. Since God has made us all one, you could do it. He certainly will help you write to the Hebrews."

Then Paul added, "What you write will be read, if you don't put your name it. That will keep any Jews from missing the message because they're worried about you being a Gentile."

So even though Paul's and Luke's other books made it clear who wrote them, this one does not.

The theme of the book—whoever wrote it—is "Better."

- Christ is better than angels

- Christ is better than the Sabbath

- Christ is better than Moses

- Christ is better than the priesthood

- Christ is better than the sacrifices[36]

The theme of Hebrews shows how Jesus changed Old Testament worship forever. He is better than Temple worship. He is the Best Priest of all time. Believers now worship God without going through a priest or going to the Temple, or giving an animal sacrifice.[539]

The book went on to explain how all of those things were done to help us understand what Jesus would come to do. They were like pictures so we would recognize Jesus when He came. Now believers have direct access to the Father through Jesus Christ.[248]

Talk About the Story: Who might have written the letter to the Hebrews? What's another word for Hebrew? Why would Luke not have put his name on the letter? What is the theme of the book?

Scripture: "God, who at various times and in various ways spoke in time past to the fathers by the prophets, has in these last days spoken to us by His Son. . ." Hebrews 1:1–2

Family Time: What do prophets do? Why is Jesus better than a prophet? What are some things you know about Jesus?

Prayer: Jesus, You are better than any priest, any angel, any hero of the Bible. You are our King and we love You! Amen.

The illustration shows a bearded high priest wearing a turban with a plate reading "DEDICATED TO THE LORD."

HEBREWS: JESUS IS THE BEST PRIEST

Scripture: Hebrews 5—9:12
Place: Unknown
Time: Before 70 AD

Ever since Adam and Eve disobeyed God, people have done wrong things, or sinned— just like we do. The Bible says that everyone has sinned. We can confess our sin to God and know we are forgiven. (See 1 John 1:9.)[440] But in Old Testament times, here is what people had to do when they did wrong, or sinned: They had to bring an animal to the priest. The animal had to be perfect and healthy—a bird, if they were very poor, or a lamb, if they could afford it. The priest would sacrifice it—that means he would kill it. He did this to pay for the person's sin.[260] This may seem strange to us but this was a way to teach people that sin is serious. And when their best animal died to pay for their sin, it made people sad. It reminded them that God was sad about their sin. Every sin had to be paid for, and the payment was blood. Someone or something had to die to pay for sin.[173]

Then once a year, the High Priest, (the priest in charge), made a sacrifice for

EVERYONE in Israel. He went into the holiest place in the Temple. He went into a special room he could go only once a year. He offered the blood of a lamb to God. He did this to pay for ALL their sins for that year.[92] This is the way they could be forgiven by God and made right with Him.

These things were like pictures. They helped people understand what God was going to do when Jesus came to Earth. When Jesus came, He lived a perfect life. He was perfect, like that perfect animal to be sacrificed for sin. Jesus then sacrificed His life. He let people kill Him on a cross. His blood paid the price for ALL of our sin. It would not be only for a year, but forever! So Jesus is the LAST, BEST sacrifice—in fact, His friend John called Jesus "the Lamb of God, who takes away the sin of the world."

Here is another word picture: Jesus is also like the High Priest who went into the holiest place once a year. After Jesus died, Hebrews tells us that He went into the holiest place in heaven.[420] There, Jesus offered His OWN blood: "with His own blood He entered the Most Holy Place once for all, having obtained eternal redemption." (See Hebrews 9:12.)

"Eternal redemption" means that Jesus paid for our sins FOREVER. Now, we do not have to go to a priest. We do not have to bring an animal. Jesus has paid for all of our sins, once and for all! This is why Jesus is like the GREATEST High Priest ever. He paid for our sin, so that we can be forgiven, join God's family and belong to Him forever!

Talk About the Story: What did people have to sacrifice when they did wrong? What did John call Jesus? Where did Jesus offer His blood? Why can we say Jesus is better than the best priest?

Scripture: "Because He (Jesus) continues forever, has an unchangeable priest-hood, therefore He is also able to save to the uttermost those who come to God through Him, since He always lives to make intercession for them." Hebrews 7:24–25

Family Time: What do you like best about Jesus? How do we know Jesus lives forever? Sing a song together to thank Jesus for loving us forever!

Prayer: Dear Lord, we are glad that You were willing to obey God the Father and pay for all our sin. Please help us to remember to confess our sin to You right away. Thank You for Your great love! In Your name, Amen.

HEBREWS: THE STORY OF MELCHIZEDEK

Scripture: Genesis 14; Hebrews 7
Place: Unknown
Time: Before 70 AD

Many Jews now followed Jesus! They loved Jesus. But sometimes they were confused! Before Jesus came, they had gone to a priest and given an animal to sacrifice for their sins. They knew that priests all came from one family, the family of Levi.[42] But they learned through the letter to the Hebrews (or Jews) that Jesus is our priest FOREVER. And He is not from the family of Levi. Members of Levi's family all died. But Jesus is alive forever! So He must be from a different family—Hebrews says that Jesus IS a priest from the family of Melchizedek. Who is Melchizedek? This very, VERY old story is found in Genesis 14!

Abraham was the father of the Jewish family. He lived in the mountains in Hebron in the Promised Land. His nephew Lot lived in Sodom, near the Dead Sea. In those days, kings from the Euphrates River valley decided to attack

Sodom! These kings STOLE Lot, and his family, and everything Lot owned. They tied up the people and made them start walking—and walking and WALK-ING, because they were going to travel a long, long way.

Lot's family must have been VERY scared and sad. But someone escaped from Sodom found Abraham and said, "Lot and his family were stolen by the kings. They are headed north!"

Abraham loved his nephew and his family. He was NOT going to let them become slaves! So he called all the men in his household—318 men! They got weapons ready and rode after those kings. They caught up with them at Dan in the north Promised Land. Abraham divided his men and attacked those kings and SURPRISED them. They defeated the kings! And they took back Lot, his family, and everything that had been stolen.

Abraham was SO happy! He returned home with his family. As he got near to Jerusalem, two kings met him. One was the King of Sodom, where Lot lived. He wanted to make sure Abraham gave him everything that was stolen from him. Abraham said, "I don't want anyone to think that you have made me rich. You can have it all except what my men need."[185]

But the other king who met Abraham was the King of Salem. Salem means "peace."[102] This king of peace was named Melchizedek. No one knows about his parents or family line. Melchizedek brought out bread and wine. He spoke a blessing over Abraham in the name of God Most High. Then, the Bible says that Abraham gave a tenth of everything he had to Melchizedek.[297] Through his gifts and offerings, Abraham worshiped the Lord. The letter to the Hebrews says that by the help of Melchizedek, the priest, Abraham was really worshiping Jesus even before He ever came to Earth as a baby!

So Jesus is not only the BEST priest of all, He is also the ONLY priest like Melchizedek, the King of Peace, and He is the ONLY priest who lives forever!

Talk About the Story: Who was stolen by the kings? Who went to rescue him and his family? What did the King of Sodom want? What did the King of Salem do? What did Abraham give to Melchizedek?

Scripture: "For such a High Priest was fitting for us, who is holy, harmless, unde-filed, separate from sinners, and has become higher than the heavens." Hebrews 7:26

Family Time: What do you think the verse means when it says Jesus (our High Priest) is holy? What are some other words you would use to describe Jesus?

Prayer: Dear Lord Jesus, thank You that we can trust You, our High Priest. You are not like any other person ever! You are the One who saves us and helps us forever! Amen.

PSALM 140
ASKING GOD TO PUNISH THE WICKED

When Saul threatened to kill David not yet 20 years old, young David ran to hide in the wilderness. David needed many things, but most of all he needed a weapon.

David went to see Abimelech, the priest. It was then the priest of God gave David bread and wine. David asked, "Do you have a spear or sword?" The priest replied,

"I only have the sword of Goliath the Philistine, whom you killed."

David left with the sword, but there was a spy listening to the conversation. Doeg the Edomite told Saul what he had overheard. Soon Saul and his army showed up after David left.

Saul demanded, "Why did you give David food and a sword? Why have you consulted God for him?"[352] The king ordered his soldiers to kill the priest and

www.thefamilyprayerbible.com

his entire family. But they wouldn't do it because they feared God. Then Doeg "turned on them and killed them that day, eight-five priests in all, still wearing their priestly garments" (1 Samuel 22:18).[130]

Psalm 140 is a prayer for God to punish the wicked. When you read it, think of David's anger toward Doeg who killed 85 priests.

> *"O Lord, deliver me from evil people,*[109]
>> *And rescue me from those violent individuals.*[387]
> *They constantly think only of evil*
>> *And cause trouble everywhere they go.*
> *Their tongue drips with poison that kills,*
>> *Their lips will kill like a viper."*

But David doesn't just ask for protection against evil people. He pours out his righteous anger, he wants revenge on them. David wants them punished, he wanted retribution; he even told God how to get even with them.

> *"Lord, I want You to destroy my enemy,*[235]
>> *I want them to suffer the evil they planned for me.*
> *Pour fire and brimstone on their heads,*
>> *Throw them into the pit of hell,*
> *Or into a deep hole where they will drown.*
>> *Don't let liars get away with their lies,*
> *Torture them for their evil."*[267]

This seems to be too harsh for a man of God. God teaches in the New Testament, "Vengeance is Mine, I will repay" (Romans 12:19). David wants God to punish quickly, and thoroughly. But Jesus said, "Bless those who curse you. Pray for those who hurt you.[47] "If someone slaps you on one cheek, offer the other cheek also" (Luke 6:28–29).[330] What about those who crucified Jesus? He prayed for them, "Father, forgive them for they don't know what they are doing" (Luke 23:34).

Talk About the Psalm: What did you learn about the psalm writer in this story? What did you learn about God?

Psalm 140: Read this week's psalm in your Bible together. Choose a verse to read aloud as a prayer.

Prayer: Thank You, God, for the psalm prayers in the Bible. Thank You for teaching us about You and about how to pray. In Jesus' name, Amen.

HEBREWS: GOD'S COVENANTS

Scripture: Jeremiah 31:33; Hebrews 7:20-10:17
Place: Unknown
Time: Before 70 AD

There is one thing we know about God: He keeps His promises! Every promise in God's Word has been fulfilled, is being fulfilled, or will be fulfilled. God always does what He says He will do. Some promises in the Bible are called "covenants." These are agreements God made with people. To make a covenant, the people and God both agreed to keep their part of the covenant.

God made many of these covenant promises to people in Old Testament times. One was a promise God made after the flood. He said that He would never flood the whole world again. He put a rainbow in the sky to remind us of His covenant. There would be floods, but they would not cover the whole Earth.[497]

God made many promises and covenants with the people of Israel. But even though God always kept HIS promises, the people did NOT keep their part of these covenants. They decided to worship other gods and bow to idols and statues. This made God very sad, but He never stopped loving them.

So God sent a message to His people through a prophet named Jeremiah. He told the Israelites this: "Look! The time will come, says the LORD, WHEN I WILL MAKE A NEW COVENANT WITH THE HOUSE OF ISRAEL AND WITH THE HOUSE OF JUDAH."[92]

What was this new covenant? It would not be like the old covenants that the people had broken and forgotten. God went on to tell the people that there would not be more laws written, like the laws at Mt. Sinai. God said He would write His laws on the hearts of people, so that they would obey Him and be His.

How would God do this? Another promise God made was that He would send His Son, Jesus the Messiah. God did that at just the right time and Jesus did exactly what God said He would do. Jesus lived on Earth without ever doing one wrong thing. He always obeyed God His Father![327]

Just before Jesus died on the cross, Jesus and His friends were celebrating that old covenant. It was the promises God had given to the Israelites when He led them out of Egypt. But Jesus held up the first communion cup that reminded them of this old covenant. He said, "NOW this cup will remind you of the NEW covenant, which is in My blood." Jesus was announcing the NEW covenant that God His Father talked about way back in Jeremiah's day![385]

Jesus had made a covenant with His Father. Because Jesus died on the cross and then rose again, He started a whole NEW set of agreements with God. And we didn't have to DO anything except believe in HIM! The new agreement of covenant was that by believing in Him, we could be forgiven of our sin. By believing in Him, we could become part of God's family! God had promised this new covenant long ago. And now, Jesus had done everything that needed to be done—to bring us all into a whole new covenant![416]

Talk About the Story: When have you made a promise to someone else? Was it easy to keep? Hard to keep? What did Jesus do so we could join God's family? What is God's new covenant with us?

Scripture: "'This is the covenant that I will make with the house of Israel after those days,' says the Lord: 'I will put My law in their minds, and write it on their hearts; and I will be their God, and they shall be My people.'" Jeremiah 31:33

Family Time: What do we have to do to be forgiven of our sin? To belong to God's family and be His people? What could you tell someone about how Jesus made a new covenant for us?

Prayer: Dear Jesus, You always keep Your promises. Thank You! We want to learn to grow in God's family and understand more and more. We love You. In Your name, Amen.

HEBREWS: THE HALL OF FAITH

Scripture: Hebrews 11
Place: Unknown
Time: Before 70 AD

People talk a lot about faith. What is faith? Hebrews tells us that faith is proof that what we CAN'T see really is there! It's like electricity. You may not see it go rushing through the wires, but when your lamp comes on, you see PROOF that the electricity is there!

The book of Hebrews tells us that faith is what makes God glad. It also reminds us of many people who acted in faith. They believed and obeyed what God said and they were not afraid of what others would do.[151]

First came Abel, only the second person born on Earth. God told him how to worship, and he obeyed God. But his brother Cain got angry, and killed him—but Abel's faith is famous! Enoch also walked with God and trusted Him. Because Noah had faith, he built a big boat and saved all of the animals and his family.

www.thefamilyprayerbible.com

Abraham had faith, so he obeyed God and traveled to a new place to live that God gave to him. He took his family on the longest camping trip ever! He kept moving, looking for the place God had made ready for him.[155]

But it wasn't just men. Sarah believed God and even though she was VERY old, God gave her a son! Later, Abraham had faith to obey God when he was willing to offer his son as a lamb. He knew God could bring Isaac back to life. He trusted God![497]

Moses' family acted in faith that God would protect their baby boy, and God did! Then God made Moses a great leader of His people. He led them out of Egypt and was not afraid of the king, because he had faith in God. Because of faith, the people who followed Moses walked through the Red Sea on dry land!

Rahab was an outsider, and a prostitute, but she believed God. So she protected the two men who came to search out the land. She became part of God's heroes because of her faith.[34]

There are so many MORE people who acted in faith—Gideon, Barak, Joshua, David, and so many others—that there isn't room for all their stories! But they trusted God. They saw God do amazing things! God protected some from lions. He kept some from being killed. Some of them were brought back to life! Others did not have an easy time, but they kept on trusting God and acting in faith. God was pleased with all of them because of their faith![138]

Still, all these heroes died (except Enoch) before Jesus was born. They trusted that Jesus would come, but they never saw Him. God waited for just the right time to send Jesus. That way, they AND we could know Jesus and love Him! Now, these heroes are like the crowds in the stands. Up in heaven, they are watching and cheering us on to keep on having faith and trusting God![154]

Talk About the Story: Who are some of the people in God's hall of faith? What makes faith different than wishing? What helps us, when God asks us to do hard things?

Scripture: "But without faith it is impossible to please Him, for he who comes to God must believe that He is, and that He is a rewarder of those who diligently seek Him." Hebrews 11:6

Family Time: What does it look like when a person has faith? What do you think are the rewards of trusting God? What is a way you can "diligently seek Him" today?

Prayer: Dear Lord, You are trustworthy. Thank You that we can always trust in You, even when things look hard or scary. Please help us to have more faith. And help us to have faith in YOU more than anyone or anything! In Jesus' name, Amen.

WRITING THE FIRST LETTER OF JOHN

Scripture: 1 John 5:13
Place: Ephesus
Time: 85–90 AD

John was likely the youngest of Jesus' disciples. Now he's old, the last living disciple.

But John wasn't feeble, he was thinking about his beloved family—God's family.

Friends had told him how men had been coming to many churches trying to make themselves seem like the wisest men on Earth. They acted as if they knew things no one else knew. And they were not telling the truth about Jesus, John's best friend.

So a message was burning in John's heart. God's Spirit was urging him to write to the believers. They needed to know who Jesus is. They needed to understand that the fancy "knowledge" some people taught was not the truth.

After all, when John talked about Jesus, he KNEW who he was talking about![272] John's eyes had seen Him; his hands had touched Him. He had talked with Jesus, and heard His voice. He had stood at the cross while Jesus died—and Jesus had asked John to take care of Mary, His mother. John KNEW!

Soon God's Spirit gave John the words and ideas that brought together his love for his Savior, his love for God's people, and his love for the truth.[166]

John called his assistant, "Ansel! Would you bring the writing box, please?"

"What are you going to write, sir?" Ansel asked. He was a little in awe of John. He was always full of surprises!

"I'm going to write to the precious ones who love my Savior. I want them to KNOW who Jesus is (know is the key word in 1 John.) I want them to have fellowship with Jesus as I have. I want their joy to be full because they know Him![266]

"You see, Ansel, Jesus said that if we want to inherit His kingdom, we must all be like little children.[61] So, even though I am old, I am a little child. So are you. The sooner we understand that, the better we will love and please our Father, as Jesus did!"

Ansel nodded as he laid out the writing things. John dipped his pen, looked at the ceiling for a moment, then plunged into writing!

He had so much to tell the other little children! He told them not to sin, but that if they did, Jesus stood ready to help them. He said that if they confessed their sins, God would be faithful to His nature and would forgive them and cleanse them.[440] He told them true things they should know about Jesus and talked about ways they could grow in love for each other.

John had seen what happens when God's family loves one another.[296] That love shows everyone that God is at work in them. He still remembered when Jesus looked at them and said, "Love each other the way I have loved you. The world will know you are Mine if you love each other."[294]

John ended by telling them that they could know they had eternal life. They could be confident in God's love and power.[64] Finally, he said, "Little children, stay away from idols." Idols are any things or people we think are more important than Jesus.

John rolled the scroll and gave it to Ansel. It would be taken to be read in many places. Now God's little children could know they have eternal life in Jesus!

Talk About the Story: Who was the last disciple? What did he know about Jesus? What are some things he wanted the other little children to know?

Scripture: "God has given us eternal life, and this life is in His Son. He who has the Son has life; he who does not have the Son of God does not have life." 1 John 5:11–12

Family Time: What is something we can know from these verses? How do you know you have the Son of God?

Prayer: Father, help us to know what is true. Help us do what shows we love You first! In Jesus' name, Amen.

JOHN WRITING HIS SECOND LETTER

Scripture: 2 John 4–7
Place: Unknown
Time: 90 AD

John called out to his assistant, "Please bring my writing box." Young Ansel came running into the room with the box of inks, pens and scrolls. The ancient apostle sat ready, waiting at his table.

Even though John was over 90 years of age, his mind was keen and his eyes were sharp. He thanked his helper, then picked up his pen. Dipping it into the ink, he wrote, "The elder unto the elect lady . . . ."[291]

"Sir?" young Ansel, John's assistant interrupted. "Sir, why don't you write 'from the apostle'? That will remind them of how important you are!"

www.thefamilyprayerbible.com

John smiled, "Now our friend Paul used the title apostle to remind people of his authority. You see, Paul met Jesus AFTER Jesus had gone back to heaven! So it was unusual. But everyone knows I followed the Lord three and a half years, and I'm the only one left. They know I'm an apostle. And I'm the most elderly elder!"

"Why don't you use your name, sir?' asked the helper.

"People know who I am. I don't want to brag by using my name."

Young Ansel asked, "Who is the lady to whom you write?" John smiled up at his young helper who asked so many questions!

"The lady is the church! The church is like a bride who is waiting to be married to Jesus Christ!" Ansel nodded. "And elect means chosen by God. He loves us and chose us to be His!"[415]

John's letter wasn't long. And it was personal. He said, "I was very glad when I found my children walking in the truth." He was referring to Christians in the church.[218]

But John had heard about false teachings slipping into the church.[220] John wanted for everyone to worship Jesus Christ as Lord. He wanted every believer to know that Jesus is fully God and also fully human.

So John warned in the letter, "Many are trying to trick you. They say that Jesus did not come in a human body. Anyone who says this is fooled. And that person is fooling and tricking other people. That person is going against the truth about Jesus."

"If anyone comes to teach you, and he doesn't believe what Christ taught, do not even invite him to your home. Don't encourage him by giving him money. If you do, you will be partners with him in this wrong teaching."[430]

Then John finished, "Those who abide in the true teaching of Christ,[166] have the Father and the Son, Jesus the Messiah."[272]

Talk About the Story: Why did John call himself the elder? What was the problem John wrote about? What are some true things you know about Jesus?

Scripture: "This is love, that we walk according to His commandments. This is the commandment, that as you have heard from the beginning, you should walk in it." 2 John 6

Family Talk: When we love someone, is it easy or hard to do what that person asks? What does it show others when we obey Jesus? When we do what is right?

Prayer: Lord, thank You for sending Jesus as a baby in Bethlehem. Thank You that He is Lord of all. We want to obey Him in everything. Amen.

WRITING THE THIRD LETTER OF JOHN

Scripture: 3 John 1
Place: Ephesus
Time: 90s AD

The aged John's voice cracked as he called, "Ansel." His assistant came running to his side. "Diotrophes is up to his old tricks again." John the apostle of love didn't feel loving today. He snarled when he said, "Diotrophes is up to his old tricks again."

The church in Ephesus had sent preachers up to a sister church in the hills. This church had many wonderful people, but Diotrophes one of the leaders in the church had somehow seized control of the church.[67] No one could preach there without his permission. Diotrophes had gotten control of the money, and nothing was spent without his permission. Diotrophes had made himself boss of the church[440] but Jesus ought to be boss of the church.

www.thefamilyprayerbible.com

John told his young servant, Ansel, "Diotrophes loves to have first place." John told the church the problem, "I wrote to (you) the church, but Diotrephes, who loves to have the preeminence among them, does not receive us. Therefore, if I come, I will call to mind his deeds which he does, prating against us with malicious words. And not content with that, he himself does not receive the brethren, and forbids those who wish to, putting *them* out of the church. Beloved, do not imitate what is evil, but what is good. He who does good is of God, but he who does evil has not seen God" (3 John 9-11).

Then John added, "I like what my friend the apostle Paul said, 'That in all things, Christ shall have first place. And He is the head of the body, the church, who is the beginning, the firstborn from the dead, that in all things He may have the preeminence'" (Colossians 1:18).

Gaius was a good friend of John[42] and was one of the leaders in the church. John said, "I'll write a letter to Gaius asking him to correct this problem.[90] When Gaius reads this letter to the church, people will understand what's going on and do the right thing."[195]

"How about Demetrius?" Ansel asked about another leader in the church. "Demetrius is liked by everyone," the young Ansel added.

"Demetrius will support Gaius," John answered. Then added to his letter, "The two of them—Demetrius and Gaius—will stop Diotrophes' selfish actions."[374]

John told his young servant, "I shall write a letter to the church before I go there." When the people of the church stop following Diotrophes, he will lose his authority. John wanted the church to know why he was coming and what he would do when he got there.

Talk About the Story: Why did John write this letter? What do you think Gaius did when he received this letter?

Scripture: "Then He said to *them* all, 'If anyone desires to come after Me, let him deny himself, and take up his cross daily, and follow Me.'" Luke 9:23

Family Time: Who was John the apostle and how did he show his love to Jesus Christ?

Prayer: Father, I will put Jesus Christ first in my life. Help me learn more about Him so I can serve Him better. Amen.

WRITING THE BOOK OF JUDE

Scripture: Jude verse 3
Place: Among Roman Churches
Time: Late 60s AD

A craggy old apostle carefully chose his steps between rounded stones. He was climbing to a mountain village to preach to a small church.

His thick white beard bounced as he bobbed along slowly, finally reaching the house where this little group of believers met.

The old apostle was proud of his Hebrew name, Judah. It means "praise." Judah was the largest tribe in Israel, and Judah the son of Jacob was spokesman for his brothers. Jesus was also from the tribe of Judah.

Judah entered the home. It was the house of a wealthy man. His dining room was filled with Christians. They were already singing psalms. He didn't introduce himself with the Hebrew Judah, but with the Greek pronunciation, Judas.

"Grace and peace to you! My name is Judas; I am a disciple of Jesus Christ."

"NO," some men yelled out, "we won't hear you!" These men were confused. They thought this was Judas Iscariot, the one who betrayed Jesus Christ.[334]

Judas shook his head and plead for silence. He said, "No, no, no, I am not

www.thefamilyprayerbible.com

Judas Iscariot who betrayed Jesus Christ. He died long ago!"

He explained, "I'm the OTHER Judas. I am one of Jesus' disciples. I followed Jesus for three years!"

The following morning as he walked down the bumpy hill, Judas thought, *What am I going to do?*[207]

I'll change my name, he thought. *I'll no longer use the Greek Judas. I'll call myself Thaddeus. That's the Aramaic name for praise. Thaddeus will remind me of my Hebrew name Judah.*

Later Thaddeus added the name "Lebbaeaus" which is *white*. It's the word for white snow on the mountain tops. Everyone knew Thaddaeus by his snow white beard and hair.

For several years he was called Lebbaeaus Thaddeus. Matthew, Mark and Luke writing Acts listed him among the 12 disciples as Lebbaeaus Thaddeus, and by that name was accepted into churches.[69]

But those who had memorized the Jewish names of the 12 apostles didn't recognize that Gentile name, Lebbaeaus Thaddeus. So later on, Judah/Judas/Lebbaeus/Thaddeus thought to himself, *I'd like to go back to my original name! But, not the Hebrew name Judah. And not the Greek name, Judas. I know. I'll use the Latin name, Jude.*

Because he was always reminded of Judas Iscariot who betrayed Jesus, he wrote this letter using the name of Jude (the next to last book in the Bible).

Jude told the believers to stand against false teaching. "I urge you to defend the faith that was delivered to us by God." [84] He warned that "some men are creeping into the churches to teach that the Lord Jesus was not the Son of God.[277] They also teach people they don't have to be holy or keep themselves from sin."[504]

Jude wrote his letter to encourage Jesus' followers to be strong and defend their faith in Jesus Christ. He reminded them that God "is able to keep you from falling and will present you in His presence, innocent of sin." [460]

Talk About the Story: What was this apostle's name at first? Why did he change it? In his letter, what did he want to remind Christians to do?

Scripture: "But you, beloved, building yourselves up on your most holy faith, praying in the Holy Spirit, keep yourselves in the love of God, looking for the mercy of our Lord Jesus Christ unto eternal life." Jude 20–21

Family Time: What are ways to keep ourselves in God's love? List three ways you can build yourselves up in the faith. Do one today!

Prayer: Father, thank You for helping us to learn the truth about Jesus Christ. Help us to show our love to Him by serving others. Amen.

PSALM 142
A COMPLAINING PRAYER IN A CAVE

David was chased by jealous King Saul in the wilderness for 13 years. He was trying to kill David because God had anointed David to be the next king. David escaped each time Saul's army got close. One day near the cave Adullam, David turned left around a mountain. He didn't have a reason, it was an impulse. But God knew Saul's soldiers were around the mountain on the right, so He worked in David's mind to go left.

When his scouts reported to David that they just missed Saul's solders, David and his followers hid in Adullam. David went deep into the cave, leaving his men to guard its mouth. Caves made a good place to pray. They are quiet and separate from people, so they are also gloomy and lonely.

David prayed:

"I cry aloud to You Lord,
I prayed earnestly for Your help.[112]

I am complaining to You about all my troubles,
I have no one else to tell my problems.
I don't feel very brave but I am scared,[133]
You Lord know what I should do, You know the actual path I should
take."

David was trapped in the wilderness. He couldn't go home to see his mother, father or family. He couldn't go worship in the Temple. He couldn't even show his face in any town. Because he was so well known, someone might turn him into the authorities.

"I look to my right for help or friendship.[387]
No one is there to help me.
There is no safe place for me to go,
No one cares whether I live or die."

David turned to the only one who could help him. He turned to God. David prayed deep within the solitude of damp walls and scary shadows. His options were limited, so he yielded himself:

"Lord, I come to You in prayer.
You are the only One who gives me safety.[109]
You are all I need.
Listen to me as I pour out my heart,
Keep me safe from those who would kill me.
They are too powerful for me to protect myself.
Take me out of this prison wilderness,[367]
Give the right people help me
Then I will praise Your name for deliverance."

We can learn from David's troubles and loneliness. We can pray for God's help when there is no other help.

Talk About the Psalm: What did you learn about the psalm writer in this story? What did you learn about God?

Psalm 142: Read this week's psalm in your Bible together. Choose a verse to read aloud as a prayer.

Prayer: Thank You, God, for the psalm prayers in the Bible. Thank You for teaching us about You and about how to pray. In Jesus' name, Amen.

CHAPTER 23

JOHN WRITES ABOUT THE END TIMES

John was the human author of the last book and it was here that Jesus told him what to write. Jesus addressed the pastors of seven churches. He began by identifying some characteristics of Himself. In each case, Jesus confronted them with their failure. He is pictured as being in the midst of the churches (cf. Rev. 1:13). First, He made it clear their sin was offensive and would be judged severely if they did not repent. Second, He wanted to remind them He was as close to them as He had ever been and was within reach when they did repent.

THE SEVEN CHURCHES OF ASIA

Ephesus: The Church That Wandered in its Love
Smyrna: The Church That Remained Faithful in Trials
Pergamos: The Church That Compromised with the World
Thyatira: The Church That Was Entirely Corrupted
Sardis: The Church that Died and Kept Its Reputation
Philadelphia: The Church That Experienced Revival
Laodicea: The Church That Stopped Caring

There is a parallel between the condition of these seven churches and the general condition of the Christian church in the seven ages of church history. While every church has its own unique character often distinct from others, each church reflected different ages over the next 2,000 years. This interpretation of the seven churches is sometimes referred to as the seven church ages.

THE SEVEN CHURCH AGES OF REVELATION

Ephesus -The Apostolic Church (A.D. 30-100)
Smyrna - The Persecuted Church (A.D. 100-316)
Pergamos - The State Church (A.D. 316-500)
Thyatira - The Development of the Papacy (A.D. 500-1500)
Sardis - The Dead Church of the Reformation Era (A.D. 1400-1500)
Philadelphia - The Revived Church of the 17th to 19th Century
Laodicea - The Apathetic Church since the 1905 Revival

The rest of the book of Acts is a description of events and people during the end of the age. John ends the book of Revelation with the prayer, " Even so Jesus."

REVELATION: MESSAGE TO EPHESUS

Scripture: Revelation 2:1–7
Place: Patmos
Time: Around 90 AD

When Jesus told John, "Write!" that is exactly what John did![41] Jesus had messages He wanted sent to seven churches that were in the same part of the world. The first church was the church of Ephesus.

Ephesus was an important Roman city. Many people passed through Ephesus, because it was a port on a river that ran to the sea. It was located in the western part of what is now Turkey. It is one city where Paul the apostle lived for several years, teaching and helping the followers of Jesus in Ephesus to become a growing church.

The church in Ephesus was given a message from Jesus. Here is what Jesus told this church: First, Jesus said, "I know you and I know what you are doing." Jesus cared about these people and He knew how hard they had worked and how they had been patient when they had hard times.[430]

Jesus said other good things about them—that they did not put up with people doing wrong and that they did not listen to just anybody who came through. When a teacher came to their church, they made sure that the teacher was telling the truth and was teaching things that they already knew from God's Word.[477] That pleased Jesus!

Jesus also said He knew that they had not grown tired of working hard and had kept on being patient when things were hard. But then, Jesus said to them: "I have something against you, though. You have left your first love."[140]

What did that mean? They were working hard! They were patient! They wanted people to tell them the truth! But Jesus said that they'd forgotten something very important! What Jesus could see was that they did not love Him like they had loved Him when they first met Him. Now, Jesus told them that the thing they could do was to have the kind of love for HIM that they had when they first met Him.

Jesus said, "Turn around! Change. Go back to doing the things you did when you first loved Me!"[399]

Jesus did not want them to work harder. He did not want them to do more about having good teachers. He wanted to see them love Him like they once did—and then, do the things that showed they loved Him! Loving Jesus is more important than working hard or listening to good teaching.

Jesus went on to say, "I don't want to remove you from your place. So change your minds and love Me like you once did.[426] I'm glad that you don't tolerate those who do wrong, but listen to Me! I have a promise for you." Jesus went on to say that anyone who listened to Him and obeyed, would eat the fruit of the tree of life in God's paradise, heaven. People who loved and obeyed Jesus would live in heaven with Him forever![409]

Talk About the Story: What was the name of the city where this church was? What do you remember about the city? Why was Jesus pleased with this church? Why was He disappointed? Why do you think loving Jesus is more important than working hard?

Scripture: "We love Him (Jesus) because He first loved us." 1 John 4:19

Family Time: What are ways we know Jesus loves us? What do you think it means that He loved us first? What's the best way Jesus showed us love? How do we show we love Him?

Prayer: Dear Lord Jesus, we are glad that You know everything. Please help us to love You first and love other people, to show we love You! In Your name, Amen.

REVELATION: THE MESSAGE TO SMYRNA

Scripture: Revelation 2:8–11
Place: Patmos
Time: Around 90 AD

John was writing as fast as he could. He was writing down everything Jesus told him to write—and even though he did not understand it all, he knew it was important to obey Jesus!

Jesus said, "Write these words to the messenger of the church in Smyrna."[41]

Smyrna! Thought John. *That's not very far from Ephesus! It's a port town, with much trade. They are proud of what a beautiful city it is. Some people in Smyrna are very rich, but the believers in Jesus there are not rich.*

John wrote that, then dipped his pen in the ink again. He looked up, waiting to hear what Jesus would say next!

Jesus said, "I am the First. And I am the Last. I died, but now I am alive! Listen to what I tell you."[405]

Jesus went on to say some good things about the church. He said, "I know how much hardship you have had. You have suffered.[494] I also know that you are poor in money, but you are rich in other ways. I know what bad things people are saying about you—and these people say they are God's people! But they are not. They are from the devil's camp."[113]

I think I know the people Jesus is talking about, thought John. *There are some Jews in Smyrna who don't believe in Jesus. They have given the believers a lot of trouble, like Paul used to do before he met Jesus!*

"So, don't worry about the hard times to come,"[465] Jesus continued. 'The devil will throw some of you into jail, and you will have to suffer some bad times.[479] But it won't be for long"

John wrote faster. These were important things for his friends in Smyrna to know.

Jesus said, "I want you people to keep on trusting Me. Keep on believing in Me. Don't let anyone scare you or make you change your mind. Have faith in Me always. Keep trusting Me until you die. Then you will be crowned with a new life,[491] like the winner of a race gets a wreath of honor. And in heaven, you will be crowned with the life that God has promised to those who love Him. It will be a wonderful life."

"Listen if you have ears!" Jesus said in a commanding voice. "These are things that God's Spirit says to the churches.[285] A person who keeps trusting Me, will win this kind of victory. These people will not have to be hurt by the second death, spiritual death. Even though their bodies will die, they will be safe in heaven."[495]

Talk About the Story: What kind of city was Smyrna? Were the believers there rich or poor? What did Jesus tell the church there to do? What kind of crown would they get?

Scripture: "Blessed *is* the man who endures temptation (trouble, testing); for when he has been approved, he will receive the crown of life which the Lord has promised to those who love Him." James 1:12

Family Time: What kinds of things are temptations? How do trouble and hard times tempt us? What do you think the crown of life looks like? Draw a picture!

Prayer: Dear Lord Jesus, please help us to listen to You and then to keep on trusting You, like You told the people of Smyrna to do! We love you. Amen.

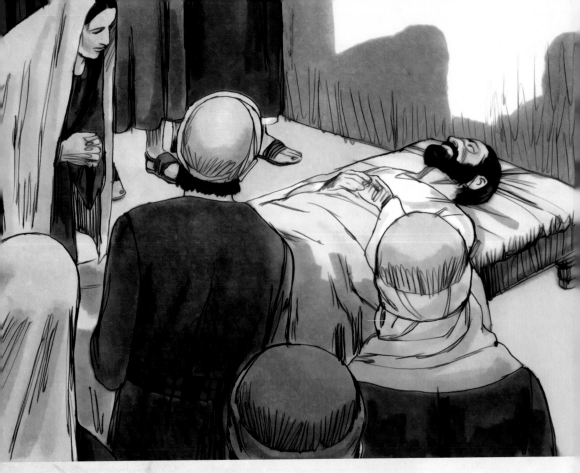

REVELATION: PERGAMUM

Scripture: Revelation 2:12–17
Place: Patmos
Time: Around 90 AD

John let out a big sigh. Writing was not hard work, but what Jesus was saying was SO important! There was a LOT to think about! John knew he needed to give Jesus his FULL attention! So he dipped his pen into the ink again. Jesus was ready to give him another message—seven messages for seven churches! This was church Number 3.

"This is what you must write to the church at Pergamum," said Jesus.[41]

John's eyes widened. Pergamum was well known. A man named Antipas had been killed there—because he followed Jesus! Antipas was what people call a "martyr." The word means "an accurate witness, one who tells the truth." Antipas must have told some people things they did not want to hear—like what Jesus had done for them. And so, like Jesus, he had been killed for saying what is true.

But opposition did not stop him from trusting Jesus and obeying Him.[197]

John began to write as fast as he could.

Jesus said, "I am the One who has the sharp sword. I will divide what is true from what is not true. I know that you live in the place where the devil has control. But I know that you are staying true to Me. Right there, where the devil has control, you keep on trusting Me. Even when you have had terrible trouble, you have not stopped trusting Me."[138]

Then Jesus said, "Right there where Antipas was taken and killed, you are staying true to Me. Even when he was killed, you didn't give up believing in Me." Jesus was glad for their strong trust in Him!

"But," Jesus went on, "I do have a few things against you. Some of you are following false teachers. These people are telling you to do things that are wrong! Now some of you are following their teachings." Jesus knew all about these teachers. He knew they were lying. He wanted His people to say and do what is true and right![90]

Jesus then said, "Turn around! Stop! If you do not turn around, and change, I will soon come and fight against these false teachers. And My words will cut like a sharp sword!"

John took another deep breath. John was glad that Jesus knows about every hard time we have and He is willing to help us, even when we have times as hard as Antipas did!

Jesus finished His message by saying, "If you have ears, then listen! God's Spirit is speaking to all of these churches.[285] I will give My precious food to everyone who wins the victory over what is not true.[40] I will give each of you a white stone that will have your new name written on it. No one else will know or understand that special name except the one I give it to.[402] "Jesus stopped speaking and John drew another deep breath. Jesus' words were amazing!

Talk About the Story: Who was a martyr? What did Jesus say about His sword? What did Jesus promise people who keep on trusting Him and saying what is true?

Scripture: "And now, little children, abide in Him, that when He appears, we may have confidence and not be ashamed before Him at His coming." 1 John 2:28

Family Time: What are ways we can abide in Jesus? Why would people be ashamed when Jesus returns? What will make us feel confident and strong when He returns?

Prayer: Dear Lord Jesus, we want to abide in You and keep trusting You. Please help us to think and say what is true, no matter what! In Your name, Amen.

REVELATION: THYATIRA

Scripture: Revelation 2:18–29
Place: Patmos
Time: Around 90 AD

John heard Jesus' voice again, strong and sure. It was loud, almost like thunder!
  "Write THIS to the church at Thyatira,"[41] said Jesus.
  John knew Thyatira. It was not far from Pergamum. Lydia, who followed Jesus in Macedonia, had come from Thyatira. It was a small place, but there was a growing church there. He dipped his pen into the ink.
  Jesus said, "I AM the Son of God! My eyes are like flaming fire, and my feet strong as heated bronze. Listen to what I tell you!"
  "I know everything about you. I know about your love and your faith. I know how you have served others and how strong you have been in hard times. I know that you're doing more than you've ever done before!"[121]
  John thought as he dipped his pen again, *Good. Jesus is pleased with the church at Thyatira!*

Then Jesus said, "But I have something against you!"

John paused. Jesus said, "You keep on letting that woman who says she is a prophetess lead you in wrong paths.[84] She is teaching you to do wrong things! She's leading some of you do to wrong things. She says wrong is all right. But it is not all right! I gave her a chance to stop doing these things. But she did not want to stop!"[441]

"So now," Jesus went on, "I am going to strike down this woman! And I will punish everyone who does these wrong things.[494] If they don't turn away from doing wrong, they will die. Then all of the churches will know that I know what is going on inside every person.[272] These people who are doing wrong will get the trouble they are asking for!"[409]

John swallowed hard. He had heard about this false prophetess. But he did not know how many people had listened to her lies! This was very SERIOUS!

The rest of the people at the church had not listened to these lies and had not done wrong. Then Jesus spoke to them and said, "Some of you don't know anything about the 'deep secrets' this woman talks about. But these secrets are from the devil!"[113]

Jesus went on, "I don't want to burden the rest of you with any of this. You are doing what is right. But hold firmly to the truth you know. Hold onto it until I return. I will give power over the nations to anyone who keeps on obeying Me until the end.[138] I will give each of them the same power that my Father gave Me. They will rule the nations with strength and will be strong to destroy what is not right.[27] And I'll give them the morning star. If anyone can hear, LISTEN to what the Spirit says to the churches!"[268]

John sat back and sighed. SO much to think about! He was amazed. Jesus KNEW everyone in Thyatira. He CARED for them. He wanted ALL of them to live in truth, not learning lies!

Talk About the Story: What did Jesus call Himself? What did He say about knowing the people at Thyatira? What good things did He know about them? What was the problem there? What did He promise to the people who were holding onto the truth?

Scripture: "Let love be without hypocrisy. Abhor what is evil. Cling to what is good." Romans 12:9

Family Time: What does "abhor" mean? If you hate what is wrong, then do you go away from it, or towards it? What are ways we can cling to what is good?

Prayer: Dear Lord Jesus, thank You that You are the way, the truth and the life. Please help us to listen to You, and not to anyone else! In Your name, Amen.

REVELATION: THE MESSAGE TO SARDIS

Scripture: Revelation 3: 1–6
Place: Patmos
Time: Around 90 AD

Jesus had another message for John to write. John dipped his pen and waited. Would Jesus have only good things to say about this church? Maybe Jesus would not have to warn them.

Jesus began, "Write this to the messenger of the church of Sardis."[41] Sardis was a smaller city, not far from Thyatira. It was a Roman city and probably a lot of Jews lived there, as well. John thought, *Well, I don't know of any problems over there in Sardis. Things are pretty quiet there. Maybe Jesus knows something I don't know!*

Jesus continued, "THIS message is from the One who holds the sevenfold Spirit of God and the seven stars." These words were coming from the VERY important King Jesus!

"I know what you've been doing," said Jesus. "People think you are alive. They think you are just fine, peaceful and quiet—but you're not peaceful, you are DEAD!"[463]

John dropped his pen. WOW. He had not thought much about Sardis. There were not any big problems there. No one was chasing them, no one was leading them to do wrong. BUT they had gotten so quiet about their love for Jesus that now Jesus said the church was DEAD! He did not see anything that showed Him they were alive!

Jesus thundered, "Wake up! Shake up what little is still alive in you! I find that you have not finished what you started in God's sight. So wake up! Remember what you have been taught.[303] Hold onto what you know, and turn around![399] If you choose to stay asleep, I will come like a thief.[529] You will not be ready for Me. You won't know when to expect Me."

John tapped his pen. Here it seemed like there was no trouble in Sardis—but their laziness was the trouble! They were not doing anything that looked like they even loved and followed Jesus! They were just going through the motions of "church."

Jesus had some good things to say, too. "Some of you have not gotten dirty with this sin of sleeping your lives away. You are worthy to walk with Me, dressed in white.[516] And anyone who overcomes will wear white too. My Father will keep the names of those people in His Book of Life. I will be glad to tell My Father that I know these people."[297]

"If anyone at Sardis can HEAR, then listen! This is what God's Spirit is saying to them—and to all the churches!"[286] Then Jesus stopped speaking.

The scratching of John's pen was the only sound in the room. He finished writing down what Jesus had said, set down his pen and blew out a long breath. What a message—people can be their own problem! If we don't keep growing, we die! John said to himself, "It's too easy to be like Sardis. We need to come out of our self-induced comas and live for Jesus!"

Talk About the Story: Was Sardis large or small? Who was causing their trouble? What did Jesus tell them to do? What did Jesus promise to the people who were not like the others?

Scripture: "Be sober, be vigilant; because your adversary the devil walks about like a roaring lion, seeking whom he may devour." 1 Peter 5:8

Family Time: Look up the words "vigilant," "adversary" and "devour." What will help you to be vigilant instead of sleeping? What can we do to resist the devil? What helps us to grow in God's family and show we love Jesus?

Prayer: Dear Lord Jesus, please help us to stay alert! Please help us to live for You, instead of acting like we are asleep! We want to serve You with our whole hearts! Amen.

PSALM 147

YOU BECOME WHAT YOU CELEBRATE

Do you realize the things that make you laugh reveal who you really are? Suppose someone tells a dirty story, but it makes you uncomfortable and you do not laugh. That's because you are clean inside and don't want to make fun of God or the things He has made. Notice the opposite. Suppose someone tells a story about good things like going to church or praying. You like the story. You smile. That reveals who you are on the inside.

When you enjoy praising the Lord, your joy reveals your love for God. Psalm 147 helps you celebrate the goodness of God. He cares for those who are hurt. Notice the "hurting" things that moved the Psalmist to gratitude,

> *"Praise the Lord, for His goodness;[211]*
> *It is good for us to sing praises to Him.*
> *The Lord is making Jerusalem grow again;[183]*
> *He is bringing back the exiles from captivity.*
> *The Lord is healing those who are broken hearted.*
> *He is putting bandages on the wounds of the hurting."[214]*

Next you should praise God because He is great. He can do anything He sets His mind to do. Again the Psalmist sang,

> *"Praise the Lord, He decided how many stars to create;*
> *He gave a name to every one of them.*
> *Praise God for His great wisdom;*
> *He understands everything in His universe."[364]*

Then you should praise the Lord because He supplies food for the needy. The Psalmist again praised God,

> *"Sing thanks to God for all He has done;[439]*
> *Make music to Him on your harp.*

The Lord places clouds in the heavens;
He sends rain for everything to grow.
The Lord provides food for all the animals;
There is food when the young ravens are hungry.
The Lord listens to the prayers of those who call to Him
for their food,[163]
Because they trust Him, He supplies their daily supply."

Then the Psalmist looked around at the things God has done for His people. He thanked God because He has supplied for their needs.

"All the children of God, praise the Lord;
All Jerusalem praises the Lord.[10]
He makes our country safe from attacks;[347]
He provides us with daily food.
He has told us how to live for Him
And what we must do to please Him.
He sometimes covers the hills with snow;
He sometimes sprinkles frost on the ground."
"He sometimes sends hail with the rain;
We all must learn to live in the elements."[362]

Finally the Psalmist was thankful for hearing the Word of God and for the privilege of obeying the Lord.

"The Lord shows His Word to His children;
He tells them how to worship and live for Him.[481]
The Lord has done good things for His children;
Unsaved people do not know and they do not obey God.
Hallelujah for all the things God does for us."[211]

Talk About the Psalm: What did you learn about the psalm writer in this story? What did you learn about God?

Psalm 147: Read this week's psalm in your Bible together. Choose a verse to read aloud as a prayer.

Prayer: Thank You, God, for the psalm prayers in the Bible. Thank You for teaching us about You and about how to pray. In Jesus' name, Amen.

DATE ___/___

REVELATION: THE MESSAGE TO PHILADELPHIA

Scripture: Revelation 3: 7–13
Place: Patmos
Time: Around 90 AD

John stretched his back and looked at the ceiling. He sighed. His head was spinning with the things Jesus was saying! So far, only Smyrna's church had been praised and not warned. It made John wonder about how many other churches needed to change!

But just then, Jesus began to speak again. John quickly took up his pen and dipped it into the ink. John didn't know it, but Jesus was nearly through with His messages to the seven churches of Asia—churches mostly in the area we now call the country of Turkey. This message was the sixth one. It is to the church in Philadelphia.

"Philadelphia" means brotherly love. It got this name because a king loved his brother. He promised his brother he'd rule the city when the king died. But by now, the city belonged to the Romans.

Jesus began, "This is to the messenger of the church in Philadelphia:[41] 'These words are from the Holy One, the True One. He is the one who has the key of David. What He opens, no one will shut. Whatever He shuts, no one opens.'"[364] This meant that Jesus is the One True Ruler of God's people—and He has all power, as He told His friends before He went back to heaven.

Jesus paused while John wrote. Then He said, "I know the things you have done. Now look. I have set an open door ahead of you! No one is able to shut that door. I know that you don't have much strength left, but you still have kept My word. You have not denied My name![327] Because you have kept on doing what is right, this is what I will do. There are people who are chasing and harassing you.[231] They call themselves Jews but they lie—they are not. Watch! I will make them come and bow down before you! They will see that I have loved you!"

John smiled as he wrote what was left of the first part. Jesus did not have anything against the little church in Philadelphia! That made John's heart happy!

Then Jesus continued. "You have obeyed Me patiently and you have stuck with what you know. So you can trust Me to keep you out of the troubled time that is coming on the whole world. This time of tribulation will show who follows Me. I am coming soon, so hold onto what you have. Don't let anyone take what you have, so that you win your crown. Be conquerors![413] I will make every conqueror a strong part of God's own temple forever![517] Each of those people will have God's name, and the name of the new Jerusalem written on them. I will write it Myself! Besides that, I will write My own new name for that person."[94]

John wrote fast! A part of God's temple! A new name chosen by Jesus! WOW!

Jesus ended, "Whoever has an ear, listen to what the Spirit says to the churches.[285]

"Yes, yes! Amen, Lord Jesus!" John murmured as he wrote the end. "I want to be a conqueror, too!"

Talk About the Story: What does "philadelphia" mean? What did Jesus say was wrong with this church? Who was bothering them? What did Jesus say He would do with the ones who were bothering them, if this church would hold onto what they knew is true?

Scripture: "Yet in all these things we are more than conquerors through Him who loved us." Romans 8:37

Family Time: Think of words we might use instead of "conqueror." We can win because of Jesus! What are ways we might obey God when others are doing wrong? How else can we show that we are conquerors?

Prayer: Dear Lord Jesus, we want to obey You and be conquerors. Help us to learn about You, and then do what is right. We love You! Amen.

REVELATION: THE MESSAGE TO LAODICEA

Scripture: Revelation 3:14–22
Place: Patmos
Time: Around 90 AD

John breathed in and then let out another sigh. What AMAZING things Jesus was saying. The best part was knowing that Jesus knew and CARED about all of these churches!

Suddenly, Jesus began to speak again. "Write this to the messenger of the church at Laodicea. This is from the AMEN—God's final Word. This is from the faithful and true Witness, the One who began God's creation. I know what things you have been doing. You are like a cold drink that isn't cold anymore, and like a hot drink that isn't hot anymore! Nobody wants that. You are neither cold nor hot. You are lukewarm.[440] So I will spit you out!"[275]

John thought, *Uh-oh. THIS isn't going to be a happy message to receive!*

Jesus went on in a very serious tone of voice. "You say, 'I am rich, I don't need anything!' But look at yourselves—you are a mess! You're poor and blind! You think you're dressed in fancy garments, but you have no spiritual clothes!"[101]

John wrote while Jesus waited. Then Jesus said, "This is what you need to do: Buy pure gold from Me, gold that has been refined in the fire. Then you'll be rich.[389] Buy My white garments so you won't have to be ashamed of being naked. Buy My medicine for your eyes so that you can really see again![450] I am telling you the truth because I love you! So don't delay. Turn around! Change your foolish thinking! Repent!"[399]

I certainly hope the Laodicean church listens to Jesus! John thought. *This is awful!*

Jesus went on, "Look! I am knocking at your door. If you'll hear My voice and open the door, I will come in and be with you, and you can be with Me."[145] John wrote as quickly as he could. He did not want to miss a word of this! He was so glad that Jesus loved these people so much. He told them the truth about how much trouble they were in. He wanted to help them change. And He wanted to be WITH them and show them His love!

That's my Jesus, thought John. *He is full of SUCH amazing love!*

Jesus ended with another promise. He said, "Here is My gift to the one who conquers: That one will sit with me on My throne, just as I conquered and sat with my Father on His throne![27] If you can listen, then listen! Hear what the Spirit says to the churches!"[286]

John finished, and then pushed back from his writing desk. What a promise. What love! What truth and kindness! He thought about how he had loved Jesus for a long, long time—since he was a young man, and now he was old. But today, writing these messages, he loved Jesus even MORE! What a Savior! What a Friend!

Talk About the Story: What did the Laodiceans say about themselves? What did Jesus say about them? What did Jesus tell them to do? What did Jesus promise to the conquerors?

Scripture: "Behold, I stand at the door and knock. If anyone hears My voice and opens the door, I will come in to him and dine with him, and he with Me." Revelation 3:20

Family Time: If Jesus were knocking at our door, why would we let Him in? Why might we not want to answer the door? Why do you think Jesus wants to spend time with us? How might spending time with Jesus change us?

Prayer: Dear Lord Jesus, please help us to hear what You are saying to the churches and to us. We want to hold onto what is true and do what shows we love You! Amen.

JOHN SEES HEAVEN

Scripture: Revelation 4:1–11
Place: Heaven
Time: Around 90 AD

John stopped his writing and looked up. He rubbed his eyes. He thought there was something wrong with his eyes. But he could still see it—an open door![136] It was above him—and the door opened into heaven! WOW! John's eyes got bigger.

The SAME voice that had spoken to him at first called, "Come up here! I will show you the things that must happen next."[274]

Suddenly, John was in heaven! He saw a throne, a king's seat—and Someone was sitting on it.[188] The One sitting on the throne was so BRIGHT and so BEAU-TIFUL that all John could think of was how He sparkled like jewels! GOD was on the throne! Around Him, above and below, there was an arch like a rainbow, but it was all green. It looked like an emerald![541]

Besides THAT, flashes of lightning and roars like thunder were coming out from this throne! It was astounding! And in front of the throne, seven torches blazed brightly. Their light was reflected in what looked like a huge lake, smooth as glass!

In front of the throne was a huge lake without waves or ripples. It was as still as a mirror and just as crystal clear as glass. It was reflecting the flashing lights from the throne, greater than any display of fireworks on earth.

John looked farther. There in a circle around that throne were 24 OTHER thrones! And on each of THOSE thrones, someone was sitting, too! Each person was wearing a white robe and a golden crown.

Around the throne were four amazing creatures who praised God all of the time! There were angels flying . . . singing . . . and shouting, "Holy . . . holy . . . holy . . . Lord God Almighty! You are the One Who was, Who is and Who is to come."[223] Because God lives forever, the angels sing praises to God all of the time.[46]

The twenty-four saints knelt with their faces to the ground before God, worshiping Him.[150] Each one took the crown that God had given, and laid those crowns before God's throne—you see, they knew that all the good they did on earth was because of God's power! Everything they accomplished was because of God Himself.[95]

As they gave God the crowns He first had given

them, now they called out, "Lord, You are worthy to receive honor, and worship for You have created everything, and everything was created for Your pleasure and glory."[93]

Talk About the Story: Why do you think God's throne is so bright? Who do you think the 24 elders might be? What did the elders do with their crowns? Why did they do this?

Scripture: "You are worthy, O Lord, to receive glory and honor and power; For You created all things, And by Your will they exist and were created." Revelation 4:11

Family Time: Why do we want to worship and honor God? What are ways we can show honor to God today? How do you think we will honor God in heaven?

Prayer: Dear Lord Jesus, we want to abide in You and keep trusting You. Please help us to think and say what is true, no matter what! In Your name, Amen.

WORTHY TO OPEN THE BOOK

Scripture: Revelation 5
Place: Heaven
Time: Around 90 AD

John had seen amazing things all around him. But as he looked closer at the throne of God, he could see something in God's hand; it was a scroll! This scroll is the book that proves who owns Earth. It is like a deed to the whole planet! But the book was sealed. No one could open it.[135]

A strong angel called, "Who is worthy to open this book?"

John waited. But no one was able to open the book and tell him what was inside. He began to cry!

Then one of the saints said, "Don't weep! There IS Someone who can open the book—Jesus! He is the Lion of the tribe of Judah. He won the victory over the devil! HE can open the book."[538]

Then John looked up past the twenty-four thrones that sat in front of God's throne. He could see that the elders from were gathered around what looked like a lamb—Jesus, the Lamb of God. He came up to God's throne. He took the book from His Father's hand.

Then the angels and the elders and everyone in heaven fell before the Lamb.[150] They began to sing a new song. Heaven filled with their voices! They sang,[15] "You are worthy to take the scroll and open its seals! For You died, and redeemed us to God by Your blood,[538] from every tribe and language, people and nation![12] And You made us kings and priests to God; and we shall reign on the earth."

John was amazed, caught up in the beautiful song to Jesus! He looked around again—the sound of voices singing was growing louder and LOUDER! Now, many MORE angels were joined by others in heaven. They ALL were singing—thousands and MILLIONS of voices! They sang, "Worthy is the Lamb who was slain to receive power and riches and wisdom, and strength and honor and glory and blessing!"[544]

And THEN, John could hear every creature in heaven and on the earth and under the earth and in the sea, all singing and shouting: "Blessing and honor and glory and power be to Him who sits on the throne, and to the Lamb, forever and ever!"[394]

Imagine such a sound! EVERYTHING in heaven and earth was praising God the Father and Jesus, who is worthy to open the scroll![290]

Then everyone in heaven fell down to worship Jesus Christ, the Lamb of God, who was alive, but died for us, was raised and now lives forever.[542]

Talk About the Story: Where was John? Why is Jesus worthy to open the scroll? How many voices do you think were singing to Jesus?

Scripture: "Blessing and honor and glory and power be to Him who sits on the throne, and to the Lamb, forever and ever!" Revelation 5:13

Family Time: Who sits on the throne? Why would you like to sing a song to Jesus? Sing a song together to praise Jesus. He is worthy!

Prayer: Lord Jesus, You are always worthy to be praised. We thank You for saving us. Amen.

THE PARADE OF MARTYRS

Scripture: Revelation 7:9-17
Place: Heaven
Time: The Future

John had seen amazing things since he had looked into heaven. Some of the things he had seen were wonderful. Some things were terrible. And he didn't understand a lot of what he saw! But he kept on writing down what he saw; it was what Jesus had told him to do. He wanted to obey Jesus!

As John kept looking, he saw a great crowd of people. It was bigger than a crowd—there were so many people that no one could begin to count them! Part of this crowd was people from every one of the families, or tribes of Israel. There were 144,000 of them! They were Jews who had faith in God and had lived faithfully for Him.[542]

Then John saw an even LARGER crowd! In this crowd were people from every ethnic group, people speaking every language known to man! These people were from all over the earth.

As different as these people were, there were two things about them that were the same. They all were holding palm branches and waving them. And all of them were dressed in white robes, sparkling and bright.

This crowd was not only HUGE, but the people were also singing and SHOUT-
ING! They all were shouting,

"Salvation comes from our God who sits on the throne,[188] and from the Lamb
who has purchased our salvation."[538]

The angels who surrounded the throne knelt with their faces to the ground[150] to
worship God saying, "Praise . . . glory . . . honor and power belong to our God,
forever and ever. Amen!"

One of the elders asked John, "Do you know who those people are who are
before the throne?"[197]

"I don't know," John answered.

"They are the ones who came through great time of suffering called the tribulation. Because they have faith in Jesus and His blood has washed them from their
sins,[173] they now stand close to God's throne.[377] They will worship Him day and
night.[488] They were willing to die for the sake of Jesus. So they have a special
place close to God's throne. They are ready to stand before God and worship Him
forever, because they are made clean from their sins. Their robes were washed in
the blood of the Lamb. They'll never suffer here—no hunger or thirst or trouble.
And God will wipe away every tear from their eyes."[452]

These people had all lived through the time of great trouble. Their lives had
been hard. But now, they had forgotten their troubles. They were close to God's
throne! So they were celebrating and praising Jesus and waving their palm
branches—it looked like a forest of palm trees, there were so many!

John was glad to know that even when we have to live through very hard times,
or even have to die because we follow Jesus, it is NOT the end! It is only the
beginning of life in heaven with Jesus—better than the best life anyone could
ever imagine!

Talk About the Story: What had happened to the people in white robes? Why do
you think they had palm branches? When did people in Bible times have palm
branches? What will Jesus do for these people? What will God wipe away?

Scripture: "The Lamb who is in the midst of the throne will shepherd them
and lead them to living fountains of waters. And God will wipe away every tear
from their eyes." Revelation 7:17

Family Time: Where else in the Bible is Jesus called our shepherd? What are
some reasons people might cry? Why do you think God will wipe away every
one of their tears?

Prayer: God, we thank You that in the middle of hard times, You love us. You
never leave us here, and You will take care of us forever. We love You! In Jesus'
name, Amen.

A BIG WEDDING SUPPER

Scripture: Revelation 19:1-10
Place: Heaven
Time: the Future

Many things had happened on Earth—wars and evil. God had allowed angels to release terrible troubles. But now, the ones who had rebelled against Jesus were in a place where they would be punished forever.

After this, John heard more voices in heaven shout, "Hallelujah! Praise the Lord! God has the glorious power to save!542 His judgments are true and right. The evil person who ruined the earth is gone."

Then the twenty-four elders and the creatures around God's throne knelt and worshiped God. They shouted, "Amen! Praise the Lord! Hallelujah!"

Another voice came from God's throne. It said, "Let all of God's servants who worship Him . . . no matter who they are . . . give praise to GOD!"366

Another HUGE shout began—SO many people were praising God that it sounded like a roaring waterfall!

"Hallelujah . . . hallelujah. . . God is forever the Strong King! We praise Him,

www.thefamilyprayerbible.com

because now it is time for the wedding day of the Lamb! His bride, His Church is ready. She will wear a wedding dress of pure white linen. This white linen stands for the kind and good things God's people did because they love Jesus."

This time is yet to come. It will be the final part of the wedding, like a wedding in Bible times. Then, a father of the husband made a wedding contract with the father of the bride. The father of the girl promised she would marry the other man's son. So God the Father has always planned for us to be Jesus' Bride.[195]

The second part of a Bible-times marriage happened when the son grew up. He would pay the bride price to his future bride's parents. Jesus paid the highest "bride price" ever—He laid down His life for us!

So now, John was seeing the future—the third and last part of the wedding: The actual wedding supper, the big celebration, something everyone who loves Jesus has always longed for and waited to see.

In Bible times, people came and stayed at this party for DAYS! But for us who belong to Jesus, this party is part of being with Jesus FOREVER!

Then the angel told John, "Put all of this in writing. Everyone invited to this wedding supper of Jesus the Lamb of God is blessed. These things God said would happen."[213]

John knelt before this angel. But the angel said, "Don't do that! I'm another servant, like you and everyone who serves Jesus and honors Him. Worship God. After all, anyone who serves Jesus and tells about Him will do it only because of the power of God's Spirit in his/her life."[544]

This is the MOST IMPORTANT wedding that has ever happened, or ever will. It is the biggest celebration of all time. And if we have invited Jesus to be our Lord, if we have asked Jesus to forgive our sin and have joined God's family, then WE WILL BE AT THIS FEAST—hallelujah!

Talk About the Story: When people got married in Bible times, how many parts were there to a marriage? How did Jesus pay our "bride price"? Which part of a marriage is John describing here? What do you think we will eat at this supper or feast?

Scripture: "Then a voice came from the throne, saying, 'Praise our God, all you His servants and those who fear Him, both small and great!'" Revelation 19:5

Family Time: What are some reasons you have today to praise God? What are some things you can praise God for that have not happened yet? Are great people more important to God than small people? Why?

Prayer: Lord Jesus, we are glad You have always loved us. We are thankful that You paid for us to be Yours. We are excited to think that one day, we will be with You forever! In Your strong name, Amen.

PSALM 150

WHY PRAISE GOD

A little guy was discussing prayer with his father. The little guy wanted to spend all his prayer asking for things. He wanted lots of candy and a new game one of his friends had.

"Wait," his father corrected him. "We must begin with praise, telling God how good He is. Then we can ask God for things we need."

"Why do we have to tell God He is good?" the son answered. "He already knows that."

The father read Psalm 150 to the son. But that didn't answer the son's questions. So the father said this Psalm will answer your questions if you will look at four questions closely. The father then pointed out the four: Where should we praise God? Why should we praise God? How shall we praise God? And who shall praise God?

Where should we praise God? In church and everywhere?

"Go to church and shout out loud, God you are the best of all;
Stand out in the open under the sky
Shout again, 'God You are the best of every person there is.'"[211]

Why should we praise God? Because of His great power and ability!

"Shout out loud, 'God You are very strong!'
God You are the strongest there has ever been!
God You are living everywhere in heaven and earth!
I praise You that You are the greatest person ever."[366]

How should we praise God? With singing, with music, and with words!

"God, I sing with music, You are the best!"
     I tell You the same while music and instruments play.
I praise You[541] with happy music,
     I move my hands, legs and body to show You my enthusiasm.
I tell God He is the best with lots of music,
     I tell Him with big and little musical instruments."[230]

The father wanted his son to not only love God and live for Him; the father wanted his son to praise God. So they came to the last verse in Psalm 150. It is the last exhortation in the whole book of Psalms.

"Everything that is alive and moving must shout,
     Lord You are the best, and You are mine."[10]
But more than someone to watch over me,
     Lord, You are the best and I love You!"[211]

So, we are to praise God with all our strength, with all our mind, and give Him our very best. God wants everyone to praise Him. Who does that include? Me!

Talk About the Psalm: What did you learn about the psalm writer in this story? What did you learn about God?

Psalm 150: Read this week's psalm in your Bible together. Choose a verse to read aloud as a prayer.

Prayer: Thank You, God, for the psalm prayers in the Bible. Thank You for teaching us about You and about how to pray. In Jesus' name, Amen.

JESUS COMES TO EARTH

Scripture: Revelation 19:11—20:3
Place: Earth
Time: The future

John finished writing down all of the wonderful things about the marriage supper of the Lamb of God, Jesus. He sat back and sighed happily. He was glad to know that one day, all of Jesus' followers will be together in heaven with Jesus at the biggest party in all eternity!

But now John looked up again. WOW! What did he see? It was Jesus—but like the time when Jesus came to John in the cave, Jesus looked DIFFERENT! This was still John's dearest Friend, Jesus—but now Jesus was dressed as a KING.

Jesus was wearing not just one crown, but many crowns on His head. That was because He is the King over all other Kings.[147] His eyes glowed like flames of fire! He was wearing a royal robe, but royal robes are usually purple. This one was red. It looked as if it had been dyed in blood.

John was hearing voices call Jesus "the Word of God." But on Jesus' royal

robe, John could see something written. It is ANOTHER name for Jesus: "KING OF KINGS AND LORD OF LORDS."

Jesus was now leaving heaven to finally stop the last of the rebellions on Earth. He was coming back to Earth as the King of everything and everyone!

Jesus was riding a beautiful, strong white horse that galloped from heaven. Jesus had armor, too, like He was ready for battle. But Jesus was not coming out of heaven by Himself. Beside Him and behind Him was an ARMY. The people in this army were all dressed in pure white linen and they were riding on white horses.[389] John's mouth hung open as he watched. What an amazing army. There is nothing said about their weapons, and they were wearing white. Perhaps they didn't plan to get dirty—and here's why!

Out of Jesus' mouth came a sharp sword. That means that when Jesus spoke, it was like a WEAPON, maybe like we would think of a laser beam that cuts everything it touches. So Jesus did not have to carry a sword and swing His sword. He simply had to SPEAK and His WORDS made it happen.[268]

Jesus and His army came to Earth. There, all of the kings of the earth and the evil beast who had started the rebellion came together to fight. They were ready to fight Jesus and His army, but Jesus stopped them all! He threw the evil beast into a burning lake along with the rest of the army that followed the kings and the beast died from the sword that came from His mouth.

Now an angel came down from heaven. This angel carried the key to a deep pit. The angel also carried and a big chain. The angel took the devil and tied him up with the chain. The angel threw the devil into that pit and locked it.

The devil would have to stay in that pit. It was locked and sealed. Now, no one living on the earth would be fooled by the devil for a thousand years!

But after that, God has decreed that the devil will be let out for a little while— just before God puts him away forever and ever![267]

Talk About the Story: What did Jesus look like when John saw Him? What was He riding? Who was with Jesus? Why did Jesus come back to Earth? Where did the devil have to stay? For how long?

Scripture: "Now to the King eternal, immortal, invisible, to God who alone is wise, be honor and glory forever and ever. Amen." 1 Timothy 1:17

Family Time: Use a dictionary to find these words: "immortal, invisible, eternal." Can we use these words about Jesus, as well? What is a way you can show honor and praise to Jesus? Do it!

Prayer: Lord, we praise and honor You today. You are the King of Kings. You deserve our praise every day! Amen.

THE NEW HEAVEN AND EARTH

Scripture: Revelation 21; 22
Place: Earth
Time: the Future

Old John shook his head to clear his vision. SO MUCH to think about! An old man could hardly keep up! But through all of these amazing things, one thing did not change: Jesus. He is the same now as He was yesterday—and He always will be!

Looking up, John saw the next—and the last—amazing thing that was yet to come! He could see that there was a new heaven and new earth![215] The first heaven and earth had been polluted by the devil and his evil. But now—NOW God was making something entirely NEW!

John looked around at fresh, new mountains and new trees. When he looked up, he saw a new CITY—it is called the New Jerusalem! It was coming down from heaven.

The city sparkled like diamonds and colorful gems! The city was higher than the highest mountain. John watched as an angel used a measuring stick to measure it. It was 1,500 square miles on each side. That's about as far as the distance between New York and Kansas City. And this city is as high as it is wide! So it is not like ANY city we have ever seen!

The streets in the city were paved with pure gold. But the gold is so pure, you could see through the streets like they are glass! It is surrounded by a high wall. The wall was laid on 12 foundation stones. Each foundation stone had the name of one of the 12 apostles engraved upon it. There were 12 gates. Each gate was a huge pearl, engraved with the name of one of the 12 tribes of Israel. An angel guarded each gate!

Then John heard a loud announcement from an angel, "Look! There is a brilliant light in the city. God has moved into its center. Now He lives there!"[377]

There was no more need for a sun or a moon or stars. God gave light to the city all of the time![517]

An angel explained, "God's dwelling now is with humans. God will now live with His people, and they will worship Him.[541]

"God will wipe away all tears from the eyes of His people. No one will cry again. No one will remember the sad things that happened on Earth. No one will die in this city, and no one will get sick. God has made everything new."

There was a sparkling river of fresh water flowing from the throne of God through the middle of the city and people in heaven will have fruit to eat from twelve trees growing on either side of the river.[377]

Jesus said, "I am making everything new, I will give pure water to thirsty people and they will be satisfied. I will be their God and they shall be My children."

Then John heard Jesus say, "Let everyone who wants to, come drink of the water of eternal life. Everyone may drink as much as they want. Yes! I am coming soon. Be ready."

Old John's eyes filled with tears. He said, "Even so, Lord Jesus, come."[524]

Talk About the Story: What do you think is the most amazing thing about the New Jerusalem? Why is there no sun? What good things will God's family enjoy?

Scripture: "There shall be no night there: They need no lamp nor light of the sun, for the Lord God gives them light. And they shall reign forever and ever." Revelation 22:5

Family Time: What do you think you will like to do in heaven? Will you have to sleep at night? What do you think it will be like to have God's light on all of the time? How would you describe "forever" to someone?

Prayer: Lord Jesus, You are the Creator, the One who saved us and the One who will bring us to heaven and then to the New Jerusalem. We are amazed at Your goodness. We love You! Amen.

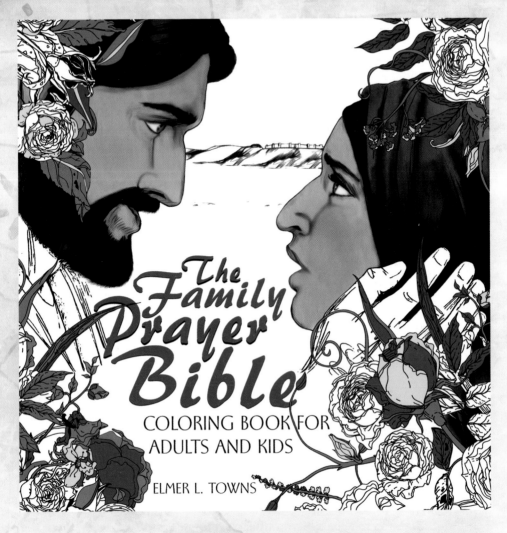

CREATE A COLOR KEEPSAKE THE WHOLE FAMILY CAN ENJOY

Coloring is not only relaxing, creative, and relieves stress, it is something the whole family can do together. In *The Family Prayer Bible Coloring Book for Adults and Kids*, you will find page after page of thought provoking drawings to enhance the family devotion time. Once a week the family can get together for a family fun night, creating original drawings just by coloring. Designed to be cherished for generations, these high quality pages will bring out the artist in every member of your family.

You can purchase your family copy at any fine bookstore near you.
Retail price is $16.95

www.thefamilyprayerbible.com